Designing and Implementing HR Management Systems in Family Businesses

Luca Gnan
University of Rome "Tor Vergata", Italy

Giulia Flamini
University of Rome "Tor Vergata", Italy

A volume in the Advances in Human Resources Management and Organizational Development (AHRMOD) Book Series

IGI Global
PUBLISHER of TIMELY KNOWLEDGE

Published in the United States of America by
IGI Global
Business Science Reference (an imprint of IGI Global)
701 E. Chocolate Avenue
Hershey PA, USA 17033
Tel: 717-533-8845
Fax: 717-533-8661
E-mail: cust@igi-global.com
Web site: http://www.igi-global.com

Library of Congress Cataloging-in-Publication Data

Names: Gnan, Luca, editor. | Flamini, Giulia, 1989- editor.
Title: Designing and implementing HR management systems in family businesses / Luca Gnan and Giulia Flamini, editors.
Description: Hershey : Business Science Reference, 2020. | Includes bibliographical references and index. | Summary: "This book explores how human resource management systems are similar and different in family business practices"-- Provided by publisher.
Identifiers: LCCN 2020012883 (print) | LCCN 2020012884 (ebook) | ISBN 9781799848141 (hardcover) | ISBN 9781799856801 (paperback) | ISBN 9781799848158 (ebook)
Subjects: LCSH: Family-owned business enterprises. | Personnel management.
Classification: LCC HD62.25 .D47 2020 (print) | LCC HD62.25 (ebook) | DDC 658.3--dc23
LC record available at https://lccn.loc.gov/2020012883
LC ebook record available at https://lccn.loc.gov/2020012884

This book is published in the IGI Global book series Advances in Human Resources Management and Organizational Development (AHRMOD) (ISSN: 2327-3372; eISSN: 2327-3380)

British Cataloguing in Publication Data
A Cataloguing in Publication record for this book is available from the British Library.

For electronic access to this publication, please contact: eresources@igi-global.com.

Advances in Human Resources Management and Organizational Development (AHRMOD) Book Series

Patricia Ordóñez de Pablos
Universidad de Oviedo, Spain

ISSN:2327-3372
EISSN:2327-3380

Mission

A solid foundation is essential to the development and success of any organization and can be accomplished through the effective and careful management of an organization's human capital. Research in human resources management and organizational development is necessary in providing business leaders with the tools and methodologies which will assist in the development and maintenance of their organizational structure.

The **Advances in Human Resources Management and Organizational Development (AHRMOD) Book Series** aims to publish the latest research on all aspects of human resources as well as the latest methodologies, tools, and theories regarding organizational development and sustainability. The **AHRMOD Book Series** intends to provide business professionals, managers, researchers, and students with the necessary resources to effectively develop and implement organizational strategies.

Coverage

- Skills Management
- Executive Compensation
- Performance Improvement
- Diversity in the Workplace
- Succession Planning
- Training and Development
- Coaching and Mentoring
- Job Enrichment
- Recruitment Process
- Corporate Governance

IGI Global is currently accepting manuscripts for publication within this series. To submit a proposal for a volume in this series, please contact our Acquisition Editors at Acquisitions@igi-global.com or visit: http://www.igi-global.com/publish/.

The Advances in Human Resources Management and Organizational Development (AHRMOD) Book Series (ISSN 2327-3372) is published by IGI Global, 701 E. Chocolate Avenue, Hershey, PA 17033-1240, USA, www.igi-global.com. This series is composed of titles available for purchase individually; each title is edited to be contextually exclusive from any other title within the series. For pricing and ordering information please visit http://www.igi-global.com/book-series/advances-human-resources-management-organizational/73670. Postmaster: Send all address changes to above address.

Titles in this Series

For a list of additional titles in this series, please visit: www.igi-global.com/book-series

Future of Work, Work-Family Satisfaction, and Employee Well-Being in the Fourth Industrial Revolution
Ethel Ndidiamaka Abe (University of KwaZulu-Natal, South Africa)
Business Science Reference • © 2021 • 382pp • H/C (ISBN: 9781799833475) • US $215.00

Handbook of Research on Cyberbullying and Online Harassment in the Workplace
Leslie Ramos Salazar (West Texas A&M University, USA)
Business Science Reference • © 2021 • 717pp • H/C (ISBN: 9781799849124) • US $265.00

Integration and Application of Business Graduate and Business Leader Competency-Models
Donta S. Harper (University of Washington, USA)
Business Science Reference • © 2021 • 275pp • H/C (ISBN: 9781799865377) • US $195.00

Human Resource Management Practices for Promoting Sustainability
Sulaiman Olusegun Atiku (Naimbia University of Science and Technology, Namibia) and Tinuke Fapohunda (Lagos State University, Nigeria)
Business Science Reference • © 2021 • 326pp • H/C (ISBN: 9781799845225) • US $195.00

Effective Strategies for Communicating Insights in Business
Ross Jackson (Wittenberg University, USA) and Amanda Reboulet (Air Force Civilian Service, USA)
Business Science Reference • © 2021 • 330pp • H/C (ISBN: 9781799839644) • US $195.00

Anywhere Working and the Future of Work
Yvette Blount (Macquarie University, Australia) and Marianne Gloet (University of Melbourne, Australia)
Business Science Reference • © 2021 • 287pp • H/C (ISBN: 9781799841593) • US $195.00

Implementation Strategies for Improving Diversity in Organizations
Claretha Hughes (University of Arkansas, USA)
Business Science Reference • © 2021 • 451pp • H/C (ISBN: 9781799847458) • US $195.00

Principles of Islamic Ethics for Contemporary Workplaces
Abdus Sattar Abbasi (COMSATS University Islamabad, Lahore Campus, Pakistan) and Razaq Raj (Leeds Beckett University, UK)
Business Science Reference • © 2021 • 275pp • H/C (ISBN: 9781799852957) • US $215.00

IGI Global
PUBLISHER of TIMELY KNOWLEDGE

701 East Chocolate Avenue, Hershey, PA 17033, USA
Tel: 717-533-8845 x100 • Fax: 717-533-8661
E-Mail: cust@igi-global.com • www.igi-global.com

Editorial Advisory Board

Table of Contents

Detailed Table of Contents

We have already entered into the so called VUCA World, a world of tumult, new technologies, and a new generation of employees. HR departments need to revise their mission, vision, strategies, and tools to answer to these new challenges. The main aim of this chapter is to evaluate, through an in-depth bibliographical analysis and an Italian case study, how HR departments can be supported in their strategic reflection by using a structured approach to becoming more effective in this VUCA World. Moreover, the chapter contributes to making HR managers and HR professionals aware of the HR Strategic Forum, a method that could help them to define in a shared way what the main pillars of the HR function are. These mainstays should never be forgotten, especially in times of constant change, such as the ones we are currently experiencing.

In this chapter, the authors propose to widen the perspective of human resource management within family businesses by considering the organization as not only one venture but a set of ventures. The authors select case studies to illustrate the process for maintaining trust between CEO of family businesses and partners. The cases showed that regardless of the family firms' ownership and size, the personal relationship was more important to keep the relationship than agreements sanctioned by formalized operation and contracts. The story of the three cases allows the authors to identify a human resource management process of trust maintenance between three inter-family firm relationships.

HR management departments are constantly evolving as a result of new technological advancements. For family HR firms, this technological evolution is vital in ensuring that they remain innovative and current with their competitors. Technology has impacted how companies recruit, retain, and evaluate employees. However, in order to ensure that technology is effectively and accurately adopted and integrated, companies need to understand how they can employ technology to enhance their daily operations and implement tools that provide an adequate return on investment for the technology they select. In family firms, a vast majority of employees are able to ensure that funds are invested in appropriate technology-enhanced projects and that they develop a family-like culture with their stakeholders. This chapter will seek to explore these emerging trends in order to present opportunity for family owned firms to function most efficiently and effectively in the modern, technology enhanced workplace.

The goal of the chapter is to provide an in-depth and comparative understanding of the instruments of organizational culture that exist and provide a review of academic research evidence on their performance in family firms. Furthermore, the chapter will provide an additional insight into a novel instrument for diagnosing organizational alignment – Vox Organizationis (the "voice" of the organization). The chapter will provide an introduction to family firms and the challenges and survival; comparative and critical review of existing relevant instruments of organizational culture and assessment of their implementation in measuring organizational culture in family firms and presentation of Vox Organizationis – an instrument based on a novel methodology for measuring organizational alignment, culture, and leadership values; and review of evidence and recommendations on its implementation in family firms. The chapter will provide the reader with an increased understanding of how and with which instruments to measure organizational culture and alignment in family firms.

Scholars have argued that business ethics is a crucial ingredient for the successful recipe of human resource management. However, little is known about the factors that trigger an organizational commitment towards the promotion of an ethical approach in crafting human resource management practices. This is especially true for family firms, whose ethical slant in devising human resource management practices has been under-researched. This chapter intends to push forward our knowledge in the field of business ethics investigating the role of familiness in determining ethically-rooted human resource management practices among small and medium-sized enterprises. More specifically, the authors investigated how awareness of business ethics issues and formalization of human resource management policies and practices affect the SMEs commitment to ethics. Family firms were found to be aware of the ethical challenges that characterize human resource management; however, no evidence was retrieved about the role of familiness in triggering an ethical commitment in managing human resources.

Issues associated with the fair distribution of resources for both current and future generations are gaining on more importance as a result of broad discussion worldwide relating to the ecological problems. One of the significant elements of these activities is embodied by family firms; hence, the aim of this chapter is an attempt to indicate what an important role in terms of building the future of family firms is played by the adoption of the principles of sustainable management with the participation of the employees and the owners on the basis of the appropriately designed functions of HRM. The chapter includes introductory elements to the significance and foundations of the concept of sustainable development in order for the subsequent sections to contain information on the subject of utilizing the concept of sustainable management in organizations and the departments of HR. The final section of the chapter constitutes indications referring to the creation of sustainable personnel in family firms as a challenge that is facing the departments of HR.

Today's markets require credibility, transparency, and sustainability. This demand obliges organisations to make ever greater advances in the field of management by values. Until recently, value-based management was considered just another management approach to be covered in day-to-day operations. Today, it is considered part of the strategic management of the firms. The paradigm shift began when pressure from the market and society as a whole began to insist that companies should behave like members of the ecosystem, taking full responsibility and employing their capacity to generate change. This implies that value-based management should be deployed throughout the entire organisation. This, in turn, requires companies to identify and commit to certain values that will become the cornerstone of their strategy and management style. The aim of this chapter is to claim that value-based management is a competitive advantage for family business in particular.

Family businesses have locomotive power in the economic life of countries. As a matter of fact, one of the main problems in family businesses is experienced in the management of human resources. In contrast to an institutional system in particular, favouritism on issues such as recruitment, promotion, etc. adversely affect the merit, fairness, and trust understandings of other professional internal stakeholders other than the favoured employee. The general perception of nepotism in family businesses and as stated in many studies in the literature is the favouritism of family members towards non-family professional workers. However, one issue that has not been emphasized in the literature is that the unqualified family member can also be favoured against another family member with expert knowledge. It is thought that the chapter will contribute to the literature in this regard. How a successful global family business was divided and destroyed as a result of nepotism practices has been dealt with as a case study.

HRM in family firm (FF) research has moved from its narrow focus on selection and succession planning towards studying the broader antecedents, content and outcomes of HRM. Today, HRM is acknowledged as a crucial factor for attracting new talent, improving employee attitude and behavior, enhancing performance, and fostering the long-term competitive advantages. The aim of this study is to identify which tools and practices FFs adopt with HR during succession planning. For example, do they use the replacement table with the aim of providing the firm and its management with a map that allows them to make the most appropriate decisions to replace a person who is no longer available to fill a certain position? Or is it possible to identify other tools? Similar questions help the authors to investigate around the importance regarding people in firms during generational succession.

This chapter examines some of the most relevant HRM problems in generational transition of family firms and proposes a number of legal instruments capable of resolving them. Use of corporations as vehicles to run the family business is examined, also with respect to consequences of this choice in business transition. Definition and "protection" of family roles within the firm are observed. Patrimonial issues are compared to personal issues and their interplay is explained by reference to five different scenarios. Last, the possibility to "select", so to say, the law applicable to one's succession under Regulation (EU) no 650/2012 of the European Parliament and of the Council of 4 July 2012 is explored. At the end, it is concluded that even if HRM in family business shows informality along with formality in designing business practices, generational transition of family firms requires structuring and needs be planned, appropriately and in detail, in advance.

Preface

AN OVERVIEW OF HR MANAGEMENT SYSTEMS IN FAMILY BUSINESSES

Human resources management (HRM) systems (Ulrich et al., 2013) manage people in organizations through a bundle of practices/policies, influencing their competencies, behaviors, and performances (Noe et al., 2010). Consequently, in designing HRM systems, the HR function reveals its strategic role (Zakaria, 2011; Karami et al., 2008; Ferris et al., 1999) to generate and maintain a sustainable competitive advantage. Nonetheless, only recently, literature recognized the HR function's strategic role, coping with growing pressure from both internal and external environmental dimensions.

The recognition of the HR strategic role asks for a significant shift from a deterministic and mechanical approach to organizations' study to a more psychological one. Revealing a positive relationship between HR practices' sophistication and the market value per employee, Huselid (1995) plays a critical role in this recognition process. Afterward, scholars developed a considerable bulk of studies on relationships between HRM systems and performance (e.g., Almajali et al., 2016; Alfes et al., 2013; Buller and McEvoy, 2012).

The literature considers the influence of different HRM practices, such as recruitment and selection, compensation, performance appraisal, training and development, workforce planning, career planning management, job design, and internal communication and a likewise varied collection of performance outcomes (Combs et al., 2006; Boselie et al., 2005). A firm configures its HRM system to warrant long-term survival. Family firms do not make any exception.

By the way, the family business literature on HRM mainly focuses on the formality and informality of specific practices, exploring the potential benefit of implementing different practices in family firms (Reid et al., 2002; Becker and Huselid, 1998; Delaney and Huselid, 1996).

For instance, family firms show less sophisticated HRM practices (HRMP) than their counterparts do (De Kok et al., 2006). Nevertheless, the literature reveals some gaps (e.g., Reid et al., 2002; Heneman et al., 2000; Upton and Heck, 1997) and the theory enrichment from time to time fails in agreeing the required settings for allowing validity to the supposed relationships between constructs/variables (Bacharach, 1989). Hence, it emerges a need for the structuring of the prevalent schemata adopted on designing HRM systems in family firms (Ferraro and Marrone, 2016; Gersick, 2015; Le Breton-Miller and Miller, 2014; Botero and Litchfield, 2013; Berrone et al., 2012; Stewart and Hitt, 2012).

Baird and Meshoulam (1988) argue that HRMP needs to fit environmental dimensions (Huselid, 1995). Saridakis et al. (2017) show that a bundle of integrated, mutually reinforcing HRMP has a more substantial influence on firm performance than HRMP individually. The already cited bulk of the research investigated relationships between HRM and performance (Batt, 2002; Guthrie, 2001; Wood,

1999; Ichniowski and Shaw, 1999; Becker and Gerhart, 1996; Huselid, 1995; MacDuffie, 1995; Arthur, 1992) and between HRM and a sustainable competitive advantage (Othman, 2009; Gooderham et al., 2006; Hiltrop, 2005; Wright et al., 2005; Collins and Clark, 2003; Guest et al., 2003; Panayotopoulou et al., 2003; Bjorkman and Fan, 2002; Huselid, 1995; Jackson and Schuler, 1995; Wright and McMahan, 1992; Ulrich, 1991; Schuler and MacMillan, 1984). Outcomes endorse considerable benefits from managing human resources, while many questions stay unanswered (Wright and Sherman, 1999; Delery, 1998; Wright and Snell, 1998).

Conversely, family business literature (Kidwell and Fish, 2007; Barnett and Kellermanns, 2006; Moshavi and Koch, 2005; Cascio, 1991) investigates HRMP insisting on their dissimilarities and quarreling how diverse practices (Jaskiewicz et al., 2018) present peculiar effects on managing people (Astrachan and Kolenko, 1994). Carlson et al. (2006) show that HRMP are crucial to growth in family firms. Tsao et al. (2009) reveal that HRMP affect the firm's performance significantly. A few studies show the potential benefit of implementing different combinations of practices in family firms (Reid and Adams, 2001; Reid et al., 2000; Becker and Huselid, 1998; Delaney and Huselid, 1996; Huselid, 1995) as suggested by Saridakis et al. (2017).

The book intends to offer advice and suggestions about possible future research lines in exploring how strategic and organizational choices affect decision-making processes on configuring bundles of HRM practices in family firms. Moreover, it aims to develop a consistent set of frameworks as a potential base for theoretic enhancements within the family business' literature and an interdisciplinary platform where scholars, coming from different backgrounds, can focus on family businesses.

The HRM Literature

To generate and maintain a sustainable competitive advantage, Porter (1985) advances HRM's strategic role as an organizational variable in supporting value creation (Mintzberg, 1979). Accordingly, HRM presents relationships with organizational performance (Zakaria, 2011; Panayotopoulou et al., 2003; Chang and Chen, 2002; Huselid et al., 1997; Youndt et al., 1996). For an increase on the environmental pressure, in the last twenty-five years, the HR function moved from a mere administrative role to a department with distinctive competencies in the achievement of a sustainable competitive advantage (Zakaria, 2011; Karami et al., 2008; Ferris et al., 1999). Consequently, organizations should adopt effective HRMs for organizational performance (Kehoe and Wright, 2013; Hitt et al., 2001; Grant, 1996).

A continuous accumulation of distinctive competencies in managing HR (Shaw et al., 2013; Coff and Kryscynski, 2011) invests in multiple relationships between performance and HRMP (Almajali et al., 2016; Alfes et al., 2013; Buller and McEvoy, 2012; Georgiadis and Pitelis, 2012; Sun et al., 2007; Combs et al., 2006; Wright et al., 2005; Datta et al., 2005; Boselie et al., 2005; Batt, 2002; Becker and Gerhart, 1996; Huselid, 1995; Arthur, 1994).

As a primary theoretical reference, RBV (Barney, 1991; Penrose, 1959) links HRM and performance (Buller and McEvoy, 2012; Boxall, 1996; Barney, 1991). Accordingly, distinctive competencies foster a competitive advantage if they are: a) value-producing, b) rare, c) imperfectly imitable, and d) without strategically equivalent substitutes (Barney, 1991). Human resources present these four characteristics (Marler and Fisher, 2013; Wright et al., 2001; Teece et al., 1997) becoming a strategic resource for performance (Naz et al., 2016; Karami et al., 2008; Stavrou and Brewster, 2005; Boxall and Purcell, 2003; Kaman et al., 2001;). Consequently, managing human resources supports systems and processes in implementing a successful firm strategy (Buller and McEvoy, 2012; Noe et al. 2010; Wright et al.,

2001; De Saa et al., 2002; Richard and Johnson, 2001; Hitt et al., 2001; Boxall, 1998; Barney and Wright, 1998; Delaney and Huselid, 1996; Wright and McMahan, 1992).

The Family Firms' HRM Literature

Recently, the literature on HRM in family firms became a quite popular and growing topic (Ferraro and Marrone, 2016; Botero and Litchfield, 2013; Cruz et al., 2011), evidencing four main streams of research with some relevant results and approaches adopted so far, and highlighting limitations too.

Firstly, family firms' scholars tend to support theories and conceptual models not strictly rooted in the HRM research, such as Agency Theory (Xianga et al., 2014; Schulze et al., 2003) and Stewardship Theory (Combs et al., 2010; Eddleston et al., 2008). Only some contributions referring to RBV (De Kok et al., 2006; Dyer, 2006; Poza et al., 2004) and Socio-Emotional Wealth (SEW) (Achleitner et al., 2014; Cruz et al., 2014, 2011; Berrone et al., 2012) present some relationships with traditional HRM streams of research.

Secondly, the family firms' HRM literature proposes a "patriarchal/paternalistic" family model (Cruz et al., 2011; Dale et al., 2008) to shape and consolidate relationships with employees. Succession planning and the nurturing of a successor are the most critical decisions taken by the patriarch (Cruz et al., 2011; Le Breton-Miller et al., 2004). The patriarchal/ paternalistic model involves job security in exchange for family loyalty, substituting the need for incentives. However, such a model assumes a unique, sole, decision-maker, e.g., the founder, reducing the probability to identify more complex situations where different family members share the decision-making power (Haberman and Danes, 2007). Moreover, under such an assumption of shared decision-making power, some HRM's theoretical approaches, such as utility theory and compensating wage theory, are too heavily adapted to the context of family firms, and this may alter their original goal (Levie and Lerner, 2009; De Kok et al., 2006; Schulze et al., 2003).

Thirdly, most contributions (Kidwell and Fish, 2007; Barnett and Kellermanns, 2006) investigate HR practices in family firms without considering this peculiar form of organizations' heterogeneity. Family firms are neither equal nor similar (Nordqvist et al., 2014), for example, about the size, i.e., large versus small and medium-sized family enterprises. Heterogeneity asks for adopting perspectives of theories and indications of the HRM practices in leading sense-making processes about how to interpret different internal and external environments.

Fourthly, a debate on the formality and informality of HRM practices (De Kok and Uhlaner, 2001) in family firms emerges. The family managers' resistance to formality exists (De Kok et al., 2006) since they search for a flexible approach to cope with higher levels of environmental uncertainty (Holten and Crouch, 2014). Informality helps develop a feeling of teamwork and strong social relationships and increase workers' motivation (Marlow and Patton, 2002). Employees may also feel that they can negotiate work responsibilities, hours and secure personal loans or other forms of aid within such informality (Marlow and Patton, 2002). Conversely, employees' perceptions of fairness are essential in developing their commitment (Reid et al., 2002). However, when grievance and discipline matters arise, people may perceive informal practices as arbitrary and unfair choices. Facing these tensions, balancing both formal and informal practices becomes one of the most significant challenges for family firms, despite the paucity of studies on this balance in adopting formal and informal practices (Reid et al., 2002; Becker and Huselid, 1998; Delaney and Huselid, 1996).

HRM And Performance: Four Approaches

HRM literature shows an exponential growth (Marler and Fisher, 2013; Kehoe and Wright 2013; Collins and Clark, 2003; Batt, 2002; Cappelli and Neumark, 2001) in investigating connections between HRM and performance.

Four different approaches explain the connections between HRM and performance: the universalistic, the contingency, the configurational, and the contextual one (Zakaria, 2011; Youndt et al., 1996).

Accordingly, with Human capital theory (Wiesner and Innes, 2010; Martín-Alcázar et al., 2005), the universal perspective focuses on a linear connection between progressively implementing all the possible HRMP and performance (Harney and Dundon, 2006; Youndt et al., 1996; Guest and Peccei, 1994). Firms with high-performance work practices, like recruitment and selection, extensive employees' involvement, training and development, and performance appraisal, present higher levels of employees' retention and financial performances (Chandler and McEvoy, 2000; Huselid and Becker, 1997; Delaney and Huselid, 1996; Delery and Doty, 1996; Huselid, 1995; MacDuffie, 1995) aligned with their strategy (Lepak et al., 2006; Pfeffer and Veiga, 1999; Delery, 1998; Huselid et al., 1997).

The contingency approach adopts a heuristic and an iterative model. Internal and external variables moderate how HRM relates to performance, neglecting a universal one best way of HR practices (Delery and Doty, 1996; Galbraith and Nathanson, 1978). Four different contingency dimensions appear (Martín-Alcázar et al., 2005): HR practices themselves (Martín-Alcázar et al., 2005; Begin, 1993; Begin, 1992; Cappelli and Singh, 1992; Butler et al., 1991; Miller, 1989; Kerr and Jackofky, 1989; Lengnick-Hall and Lengnick-Hall, 1988; Rhodes, 1988; Hax, 1985; Van de Ven and Drazin, 1985; Slocum et al. 1985; Kerr, 1985; Fombrun et al. 1984; Niniger, 1980), organizational variables (size, technology, or structure) (Jackson and Schuler, 1995; Jackson et al., 1989; Jones, 1984), international political relationships (Balkin and Bannister, 1993; Pfeffer and Langton, 1988; Pfeffer, 1987; Pfeffer and Davis-Blake, 1987; Jones, 1984; Pfeffer and Cohen, 1984), and external environmental factors (competitive, technological, macro-economic, and labor contextual dimensions) (Boxall, 1998; Becker and Gerhart, 1996; Jackson and Schuler, 1995; Schuler and Walker,1990; Kanter, 1989; Walker, 1988; Coates, 1987; Warner, 1984; Kanter, 1983).

The configurational approach describes HRM as a system of practices, differently combined to achieve consistent internal configurations with the environmental and organizational variables (Delery and Doty, 1996; Venkatraman and Prescott, 1990; Miller and Friesen, 1984). Configurational models present nonlinear relationships with organizational performances, since the interdependence multiply (or divide) the combined effect. HRM practices can be analyzed only as a complex and interactive system.

Finally, the contextual approach looks at social, environmental factors (Williamson and Cable, 2003). This perspective opens perspectives of practice and research toward a network of social and institutional stakeholders and political forces. HRM leads the managerial interplay with these forces (Ferligoj et al., 1997).

THE FOCUS OF THE BOOK

HRM Systems are an under-research area in family business studies, even though they arguably play an important role. To exploit their entrepreneurial orientation and achieve their goals, family firms adopt a specific configuration of the organizational variables. Accordingly, HRM, as a system of practices adopted to manage people, affects employees' competencies, behaviors, and family firms' performances. The design and the implementation of HRM systems reflect the relationships among cognition, action, and organizational performance, inspiring a decisional model as a sequence of consideration of contingent dimensions, their interpretation (sense-making), selection of actions, and performance evaluations. Contingent dimensions represent the antecedents and contextual factors in decision-making processes for allocating tasks, sharing information, and managing family firms' people. Contingent dimensions may relate to the following areas of interest (but not limited to): External Environment (competitive positioning perspective, country perspective, industry perspective), Firm Characteristics (Family ownership, Size, Actual Organizational variables, Professionalization, Firm life cycle, Past performances, Presence of knowledge and skills), and Family Characteristics (Family involvement, culture and family values, Family ties, Family embeddedness and resources, Family leadership styles, Family emotional attachment, Family entrepreneurial orientation, Family goals). Sense-making refers to the link between how family firms make sense of information and knowledge about contingent dimensions and how they act to influence their organizational outcomes. Specific family psychological and social dynamics are likely to affect both the process and the outcome of a family's decision to adopt specific HRM Systems. Sense-making refers to the cognitive and psychological processes that family firms adopt in framing their needs for making some HRM choices, on one hand, and, on the other, the behavioral processes that should be developed to foster these shared cognitive meanings, such as family norms, cognitive conflicts, and the family firm's use of its available knowledge and skills. Sense-making may be connected to different theories such as (but not limited to): Agency theory, Strategic intent, Socio-emotional Wealth, Stewardship Theory, Social Exchange Theory, and Justice Theory. The third domain characterizes organizational choices. Organizational choices relate to organizational structure and coordination mechanisms, HR practices, managerial succession, and governance systems and mechanisms, etc. Finally, the fourth domain represents the outcomes in terms of organizational performance.

TARGET AUDIENCE AND POTENTIAL USES

The target audience of the book is composed of professionals, scholars, family business instructors, and researchers working in the field of the family firm, HR, organizational behavior, and entrepreneurship in various disciplines, e.g., economics, business administration, administrative sciences, and management, education, sociology, among others. Moreover, the book provides insights and support executives, academics, advisors and consultants, policy-makers, and, in general, all those linked to family businesses concerned with HRM systems of the family business in different types of work communities and environments.

OUTLINE OF THE BOOK

The book presents 15 chapters.

Chapter 1, titled "Reflections of Human Resource Practices in Family Business: A Qualitative Research," written by Büşra Müceldili and Berivan Tatar, to better understand human resource management practices in the context of family firms, the chapter reports three interviews on experienced and successful family firm owners and human resource managers. The chapter findings reveal that family firms have a professionalized, formalized, and employee-oriented perspective in their human resource practices. Moreover, the chapter also shows that new generations in the family are more aware of human resources' importance and reflect this perspective to their human resource practices. Besides, through adhering to human resources practices, employees' organizational justice perception is strengthened, and, as a result, employees rely on their employer's equality behaviors.

Chapter 2, titled "Control and Commitment HRM Systems in SME Family Firms: A Qualitative Study of Hybrid Forms," written by Daniela Gauci Borda, Nina Katrin Hansen, and Julie Gore, focuses on the main characteristics of HRM systems adopted by family SMEs. The chapter's research question is whether these HRM systems resemble control, commitment, or hybrid HRM systems. The chapter provides several insights on the topic covered. It makes a valuable contribution to the literature by extending the knowledge available on HRM hybrid systems with the introduction of two new hybrid HRM systems: the "selective control" and the "informal commitment" HRM systems. The chapter reveals that the traditional control-commitment spectrum fails to consider hybrid forms implemented in practice. Organizations were also found to make up effective HRM systems by adopting HRM practices that best fit their unique context. Such results highlight the notion of "equifinality" of different HRM systems (Doty, Glick & Huber, 1993) and indicate many ways of effectively managing human resources within family SMEs. This implies that the context needs to be considered when implementing HRM systems.

Chapter 3, titled "Human Resources Management and the New Challenges in Family Firms: An Italian Case Study," written by Vittorio D'Amato and Elena Tosca, analyzes the impact of volatile, uncertain, complex, and ambiguous (VUCA) environment on HRM systems and practices in a family business and how they have to change to enable employees to work at their best and to be fully engaged. By using a structured approach called Strategic Forum, the chapter provides indications to define what HR managers must do to cope in this VUCA environment. The Strategic Forum helps create lasting group decisions by supporting participants' mental models to become more aligned. The chapter reveals how the Forum delivers a shared strategic map that contains all the strategic elements (mission, vision, distinctive competencies, golden rules) and challenges (strategic intents) that the HR department of an Italian family company, Angelini Group, will face in the next future, to be a valuable strategic business partner.

Chapter 4, titled "Process for Maintaining Trust Between CEO of Family Businesses and Partners: The Case of Long-Term Buyer-Supplier Relationships Among Family Businesses," written by Stephanie Lezama-Rogers and Séverine Le Loarne – Lemaire, analyzes how HRM can support trusting relationships between external stakeholders. This would help contribute to family businesses ' competitive advantage. The chapter reveals that family businesses would be at a competitive edge if their human resources have a more significant role in coordinating their relationships. The research was conducted in Trinidad, a small island developing state in the Caribbean Basin. The country prides itself as a proverbial 'melting pot' due to its diverse populace rooted in slavery, indentureship, and colonialism. The chapter applies case study research as a method of inquiry.

Chapter 5, titled "Utilizing Technology to Enhance Human Resource Practices," written by Kelly M. Torres and Aubrey Statti, reveals how HR management departments are continually evolving because of new technological advancements. And family firms are not an exception. This technological evolution is vital in ensuring that they remain innovative and current with their competitors. Technology has impacted how companies recruit, retain, and evaluate employees. However, to ensure that technology is effectively and accurately adopted and integrated, family firms need to understand how they can employ technology to enhance their daily operations and implement tools that provide an adequate return on investment for the technology they select. In family firms, a vast majority of employees can ensure that funds are invested in appropriate technology-enhanced projects and develop a family-like culture with their stakeholders.

Notwithstanding the academic literature contains an extensive discussion on the topic of organizational culture, Chapter 6, titled "Investigation of Organizational Culture in Family Firms: Review of Existing Evidence and Application of the New Vox Organizationis Model in Family Firms," written by Ana Tomovska Misoska, Miodraga Stefanovska-Petkovska, Marjan Bojadjiev, and Ivona Mileva, shows that there is a noticeable gap in the understanding of organizational culture in family businesses. The chapter provides an overview of some of the strengths and limitations of the available literature. However, the chapter reveals that there is still a gap in the application of specific organizational culture instruments in family businesses. The chapter also shows the benefits that family businesses may have when they assess and understand their culture, leadership, and alignment and their short- and long-term influence on performance.

Chapter 7, titled "Friends or Foe? Unravelling the Role of Familiness in Promoting Business Ethics in the Workplace," written by Manna Rosalba, Rocco Palumbo, and Massimiliano Pellegrini, explores two research streams, namely, shedding light on the ability of family firms to embrace an ethical slant in arranging human resource management practices, and disentangling the peculiar organizational approaches used by family firms to implement ethically reliable human resource management practices. Consequently, the chapter investigates how family firms acknowledge the topicality of ethical issues in managing human resources and the triggers of an ethical commitment to designing human resource management policies and practices among family and non-family SMEs. Through a quantitative research design, the chapter compares the ethical approach in managing human resources of family and non-family small and medium-sized organizations. The implications of the chapter are twofold. From a conceptual standpoint, it suggests that familiness – per se – is not relevant in triggering an ethical commitment to managing human resources. However, human resource management professionalization in family firms seems to create a fertile ground to allow business ethics to take root in family firms' human resource management practices. From a practical point of view, the chapter acknowledges that a gap exists between the family firms' awareness of ethical dilemmas in managing human resources and their ethical commitment to craft targeted human resource management policies and practices.

Merging the literature on family firms and the literature on sustainable development and sustainable HRM, Chapter 8, titled "Sustainable Human Resources as the Future of HRM Systems in Family Firms," written by Aneta Kuźniarska, appeals to the necessity of the conscious and gradual implementation of sustainable management in the sphere of HR in family firms. By perceiving HRM as a bundle of tools for the implementation of the strategic organizational aims, the chapter argues how an appropriately designed and implemented process of human resources management helps to guide the approach of the employees and actions on behalf of the execution of aims of the family firm as a whole. Moreover, the chapter reveals how clarified principles of sustainable management of human resources constitute the long-term physical, social and economic good of the employees, leading to an increased level of trust and participation of the employees in the process of the functioning of the family firm on a higher level than non-family firms.

Chapter 9, titled "Value-Based Management and Responsibility in the Management of People: A Competitive Advantage for Family Business," written by Alberto Trallero and Carmen Ruiz, shows how today's markets calls for credibility, transparency, and sustainability lead family firms to make even more significant advances in the field of management by values, considered as part of the Strategic Management of the family firms. The paradigm shift began when pressure from the market and society began to insist that family firms behave like members of the ecosystem, take full responsibility, and employ their capacity to generate change. This implies that value-based management should be deployed throughout the entire family firm. This, in turn, requires family firms to identify and commit to specific values that will become the cornerstone of their strategy and management.

Chapter 10, titled "Human Resources Management Understanding and Nepotism in Family Businesses," written by Meral Erdirençelebi and Mehmet Akif Cini, underlines family businesses' role as locomotive power in the economic life of different countries. By the way, family firms seem to experience some concerns in the management of their human resources. In contrast to an institutional system, family firms seem to suffer favoritism on recruitment, promotion, etc. This adversely affects the merit, fairness, and trust understandings of other professional internal stakeholders other than the favored employee. The general perception of nepotism in family businesses is the favoritism of family members towards non-family skilled workers. The chapter stresses that the unqualified family member can also favor another family member with expert knowledge.

Chapter 11, titled "Entrepreneurial Intention in Family Business," written by Ivona Mileva, Marjan Bojadjiev, Miodraga Stefanovska-Petkovska, Ana Tomovska Misoska, provides an understanding of the entrepreneurial intentions and succession intentions of potential entrepreneurs, namely graduated and undergraduate students in the Republic of North Macedonia. The chapter results are in line with the suggestions derived from literature and other empirical studies in which entrepreneurship is one the preferable career choice among the students, especially five years after graduation, regardless of whether their parents are self-employed or not. Concerning succession intentions, the students who perceive their parent's business to be a family business show higher succession intentions, a more positive attitude towards succession and social norm, and higher self-efficiency and commitment. In conclusion, the entrepreneurial intentions are linked to the parents' professional career, while the succession intentions are connected to the students' work experience within the family firms.

Chapter 12, titled "The Enhancement of the HRM Systems Through Entrepreneurial Succession in Family SMEs," written by Enrico Cori and Mariacristina Bonti, sheds light on the hidden relationship between the process of entrepreneurial succession within family SMEs and the development of the HR management system in such firms. Starting from a literature review, the chapter develops a reflection based on evidence from a sample of Italian family SMEs, collected through a longitudinal qualitative inquiry. The chapter challenges how the change at the top of the family firm may constitute an opportunity to develop or strengthen the HR management system. The chapter lays the foundation for building a conceptual model in which some possible relationships between the variables involved are outlined.

Having in mind the entrepreneurial role of the incumbent, the successor, and the family and the role played by other stakeholders in particular non-family managers and employees, Chapter 13, titled "Managing Generational Handover in Family Business: A Multi-Stakeholders Perspective," written by Barbara Barabaschi, Franca Cantoni, and Roberta Virtuani, provides an analysis of some case studies from the environmental, organizational, interpersonal and individual perspective. The chapter considers some critical points in paying attention to the results that family firms have achieved in managing the succession process, focusing on how HR practices have changed during the ongoing process.

Bearing in mind that succession, in terms of passing the business down to the next generation, has a strong influence on HR decisions, Chapter 14, titled "Organizing Human Resources in Family Firms During Generational Succession," written by Anna Maria Melina, Concetta Lucia Cristofaro, Marzia Ventura, and Rocco Reina, reveals how the adoption of a replacement table could open new avenues of research in such scope. The chapter helps identify the gaps still existing in the HR literature in family businesses and suggest some possible future research directions.

While there is much literature on HRM in family firms and inheritance law is widely studied as well, also regarding family firms, Chapter 15, titled "Law and HRM Challenges in Generational Transition of Family Firms," written by Emiliano Marchisio, puts these two areas together. The chapter provides a broader view of how the succession of family firms needs to take into consideration HRM features and, more in general, the interplay between business needs and strategies, on the one hand, and the law and the legal profession, on the other. Built on practical HRM problems emerging within family firms' succession, the chapter focuses on presenting legal techniques and strategies capable of facing and solving them. The chapter emphasizes legal precautions capable of meeting HRM issues, classifying the different HRM exigencies that may arise within family firms' succession into five different scenarios.

IMPACT AND VALUE OF THE BOOK

The book focuses on HRM in family businesses aiming at clarifying what HRM topics are relevant in family firms given their distinctive features, what the role of HR choices in family firms is, and how they differ in these forms of organizations. The book's goal was to bring together chapters that consider all three main areas of HRM: theories, practices, and competencies. The book contributes to management practice and research in family firms in different ways. First, replication studies within family businesses would enable the generalization and potential expansion of current knowledge and findings. Second, by emphasizing the family's importance, all the chapters contextualize the relationship between HRM systems and the organization. The aim was to improve our understanding of how and why some theories and practices would be more dominant than others in family firms' HRM systems.

In conclusion, the book summarizes and systematizes the relevant topics in the HRM systems of family businesses. It recognizes the main elements that affect the definition of HRM systems in Family Firms, analyzing the sources and consequences of family businesses' HR behavior. Consequently, it provides a consultation tool for those who manage and advise family businesses since it represents a practical tool for those who work (family and non-family) or are linked (i.e., family members, consultants, etc.) to family businesses. It is also an instrument of consultation and support for teaching about the family business from an academic perspective. Therefore, due to its characteristics, the book is attractive from a practical and academic perspective. Its quantitative and qualitative approach favors the scope and understanding of the HR issues about the family business.

REFERENCES

Achleitner, A., Gunther, N., Kaserer, C., & Siciliano, G. (2014). Real Earnings Management and Accrual-based Earnings Management in Family Firms. *European Accounting Review*, *23*(3), 431–461.

Alfes, K., Truss, C., Soane, E. C., Rees, C., & Gatenby, M. (2013). The relationship between line manager behaviour, perceived HRM practices, and individual performance: Examining the mediating role of engagement. *Human Resource Management*, *52*(6), 839–859.

Almajali, D., Mansour, K., & Maqableh, M. (2016). The Impact of Electronic Supply Chain Management Usage on Firm's Performance. *International Journal of Communications, Network and Systems Sciences*, *9*(06), 280–293.

Arthur, J. (1994). Effects of human resource systems on manufacturing performance and turnover. *Academy of Management Journal*, *37*(3), 670–687.

Arthur, J. B. (1992). The link between business strategy and industrial relations systems in American steel minimills. *Industrial & Labor Relations Review*, *45*(3), 488–506.

Astrachan, J. H., & Kolenko, T. A. (1994). A neglected factor explaining family business success: Human resource practices. *Family Business Review*, *7*(3), 251–262.

Baird, L., & Meshoulam, I. (1988). Managing two fits of strategic human resource management. *Academy of Management Review*, *13*(1), 116–128.

Balkin, D., & Bannister, B. (1993). Explaining pay forms for strategic employee groups in organizations: A resource dependence perspective. *Journal of Occupational and Organizational Psychology*, *66*(2), 139–151.

Barnett, T., & Kellermanns, F. W. (2006). Are we family and are we treated as family? Nonfamily employees' perceptions of justice in the family firm. *Entrepreneurship Theory and Practice*, *30*(6), 837–854.

Barney, J. B. (1991). Firm resources and sustained competitive advantage. *Journal of Management*, *17*(1), 99–120.

Barney, J. B., & Wright, P. M. (1998). On becoming a strategic partner: The role of human resources in gaining competitive advantage. *Human Resource Management, 37*(1), 31-46.

Batt, R. (2002). Managing customer services: Human resource practices, quit rates and sales growth. *Academy of Management Journal*, *45*(3), 587–597.

Becker, B. A., & Gerhart, B. (1996). The Impact of Human Resource Management on Organizational Performance: Progress and Prospects. *Academy of Management Journal*, *39*(4), 779–801.

Becker, B. E., & Huselid, M. A. (1998). High performance work systems and firm performance: A synthesis of research and managerial implications. *Research in Personnel and Human Resources Management*, *16*, 53–101.

Begin, J. (1992). Comparative human resource management (HRM): A systems perspective. *International Journal of Human Resource Management*, *3*(3), 379–408.

Begin, J. (1993). Identifying patterns in HRM systems: Lessons from organizational theory. *Research in Personnel and Human Resources Management*, *3*, 3–20.

Berrone, P., Cruz, C., & Gomez-Mejia, L. R. (2012). Socioemotional wealth in family firms: Theoretical dimensions, assessment approaches, and agenda for future research. *Family Business Review*, *25*(3), 258–279.

Bjorkman, I., & Fan, X. C. (2002). Human resource management and the performance of Western firms in China. *International Journal of Human Resource Management*, *13*(6), 853–864.

Boselie, P., Dietz, G., & Boon, C. (2005). Commonalities and contradictions in HRM and performance research. *Human Resource Management Journal*, *15*(3), 67–94.

Botero, I. C., & Litchfield, S. R. (2013). Exploring human resource management in family firms: a summary of what we know and ideas for future development. In K. X. Smymios, P. Z. Poutziouris, & S. Goel (Eds.), *Handbook of Research on Family Business* (2nd ed., pp. 371–405). Edward Elgar.

Boxall, P. (1996). The strategic HRM debate and the resource-based view of the firm. *Human Resource Management Journal*, *6*(3), 59–75.

Boxall, P. (1998). Achieving Competitive Advantage through Human Resource Strategy: Towards a Theory of Industry Dynamics. *Human Resource Management Review*, *8*(3), 265–288.

Boxall, P., & Purcell, J. (2003). Strategy and human resource management. *Industrial & Labor Relations Review*, *57*(1), 84.

Buller, P. F., & McEvoy, G. M. (2012). Strategy, human resource management and performance: Sharpening line of sight. *Human Resource Management Review*, *22*, 43–56.

Butler, J. E., Ferris, G. R., & Napier, N. K. (1991). *Strategy and human resources management*. South-Western.

Cappelli, P., & Neumark, D. (2001). Do "High Performance" Work Practices Improve Establishment-Level Outcomes? *Industrial & Labor Relations Review*, *54*(4), 737–775.

Cappelli, P., & Singh, H. (1992). Integrating strategic human resources and strategic management. In D. Lewin, O. S. Mitchell, & P. Sherer (Eds.), *Research frontiers in industrial relations and human resources: 165-192*. Industrial Relations Research Association.

Carlson, D. S., Upton, N., & Seaman, S. (2006). The Impact of Human Resource Practices and Compensation Design on Performance: An Analysis of Family-Owned SMEs. *Journal of Small Business Management*, *44*, 531–543.

Cascio, W. F. (1991). *Costing human resources: The financial impact of behavior in organizations*. PWS-Kent.

Chandler, G. N., & McEvoy, G. M. (2000). Human resource management, TQM, and firm performance in small and medium-size enterprises. *Entrepreneurship Theory and Practice*, *25*(1), 43–58.

Chang, P. L., & Chen, W. L. (2002). The effect of human resource management practices on firm performance: Empirical evidence from high-tech firms in Taiwan. *International Journal of Management*, *19*(4), 622–631.

Coates, J. F. (1987). An Environmental Scan: Projecting Future Human Resource Trends. *Human Resource Planning*, *10*(3), 219–235.

Coff, R., & Kryscynski, D. (2011). Invited editorial: Drilling for micro-foundations of human capital–based competitive advantages. *Journal of Management*, *37*(5), 1429–1443.

Collins, C. J., & Clark, K. D. (2003). Strategic human resource practices, top management team social networks, and firm performance: The role of human resource practices in creating organizational competitive advantage. *Academy of Management Journal*, *46*(6), 740–751.

Combs, J., Yongmei, L., Hall, A., & Ketchen, D. (2006). How much do high-performance work practices matter? A meta-analysis of their effects on organizational performance. *Personnel Psychology*, *59*, 501–528.

Combs, J. G., Penney, C. R., Crook, T. R., & Short, J. C. (2010). The impact of family representation on CEO compensation. *Entrepreneurship Theory and Practice*, *34*, 1043–1182.

Cruz, C., Firfiray, S., & Gomez-Mejia, L. R. (2011). Socioemotional wealth and human resource management (HRM) in family controlled firms. *Research in Personnel and Human Resources Management*, *30*, 159–217.

Cruz, C., Larraza-Kintana, M., Garcés-Galdeano, L., & Berrone, P. (2014). Are family firms really more socially responsible? *Entrepreneurship Theory and Practice*, *38*(6), 1–22.

Dale, M. C., Shepherd, D., & Woods, C. (2008). Family models as a framework for employment relations in entrepreneurial family businesses. *New Zealand Journal of Employment Relations*, *33*(1), 55–73.

Datta, D., Guthrie, J., & Wright, P. (2005). Human Resource Management and Labor Productivity: Does Industry Matter? *Academy of Management Journal*, *48*(1), 135–145.

De Kok, J. M. P., & Uhlaner, L. M. (2001). Organizational Context and Human Resource Management in the Small Firm. *Small Business Economics*, *17*(4), 273–291.

De Kok, J. M. P., Uhlaner, L. M., & Thurik, A. R. (2006). Professional HRM practices in family owned-managed enterprises. *Journal of Small Business Management*, *44*(3), 441–460.

De Saa-Peerez, P., & Garcia-Falcon, J. M. (2002). A resource-based view of human resource management and organizational capabilities development. *International Journal of Human Resource Management*, *13*(1), 123–140.

Delaney, J. T., & Huselid, M. A. (1996). The impact of human resource practices on perceptions of organizational performance. *Academy of Management Journal*, *39*, 949–969.

Delery, J. E. (1998). Issues of Fit in Strategic Human Resource Management: Implications for Research. *Human Resource Management Review*, *8*(3), 289–309.

Delery, J. E., & Doty, D. H. (1996). Modes of theorizing in strategic human resource management: Tests of universalistic, contingency, and configurational performance predictions. *Academy of Management Journal*, *39*(4), 802–835.

Dyer, W. G. Jr. (2006). Examining the 'Family Effect' on Firm Performance. *Family Business Review*, *19*(3), 253–273.

Eddleston, K., Kellermanns, F. W., & Sarathy, R. (2008). Resource configuration in family firms: Linking resources, strategic planning and technological opportunities to performance. *Journal of Management Studies*, *45*(1), 26–50.

Ferligoj, A., Prašnikar, J., & Jordan, V. (1997). Competitive advantage and human resource management in SMEs in a transitional economy. *Small Business Economics*, *9*(6), 503–514.

Ferraro, H., & Marrone, J. (2016). Examining employment relationship activities in family business research. *Journal of Family Business Management*, *6*(3), 210–224.

Ferris, G., Hochwarter, W., Buckley, M., Harrell-Cook, G., & Frink, D. (1999). Human resources management: Some new directions. *Journal of Management*, *25*(3), 385.

Fombrun, C., Tichy, N., & Devanna, M. (1984). *Strategic Human Resource Management*. Wiley.

Galbraith, J. R., & Nathanson, D. A. (1978). *Strategy implementation: The role of structure and process*. West Pub. Co.

Georgiadis, A., & Pitelis, C. N. (2012). Human resources and SME performance in services: Empirical evidence from the UK. *International Journal of Human Resource Management*, *23*(4), 808–825.

Gersick, K. E. (2015). Essay on practice: Advising family enterprise in the fourth decade. *Entrepreneurship Theory and Practice*, *39*, 1433–1450.

Gooderham, P., Nordhaug, O., & Ringdal, K. (2006). National embeddedness and calculative human resource management in US subsidiaries in Europe and Australia. *Human Relations*, *59*(11), 1491–1513.

Grant, R. M. (1996b). Prospering in dynamically-competitive environments: Organizational capability as knowledge integration. *Organization Science*, *7*(4), 375–387.

Guest, D. E., Michie, J., Conway, N., & Sheehan, M. (2003). Human resource management and corporate performance in the UK. *British Journal of Industrial Relations*, *41*(2), 291–314.

Guest, D. E., & Peccei, R. (1994). The nature and causes of effective human resource management. *British Journal of Industrial Relations*, *32*(2), 219–242.

Guthrie, J. P. (2001). High-Involvement Work Practices, Turnover, and Productivity: Evidence from New Zealand. *Academy of Management Journal*, *44*(1), 180–190.

Haberman, H., & Danes, S. M. (2007). Father-daughter and father-son family business management transfer comparison: Family FIRO model application. *Family Business Review*, *20*(2), 163–184.

Harney, B., & Dundon, T. (2006). Capturing complexity: Developing an integrated approach to analysing HRM in SMEs. *Human Resource Management Journal*, *16*(1), 48–73.

Hax, A. C. (1985). A New Competitive Weapon: The Human Resource Strategy. *Training and Development Journal*, *39*(5), 76–82.

Heneman, R. L., Tansky, J. W., & Camp, S. M. (2000). Human resource management practices in small and medium-sized enterprises: Unanswered questions and future research perspectives. *Entrepreneurship Theory and Practice*, *25*, 11–26.

Hiltrop, J. M. (2005). Creating HR capability in high performance organizations. *Strategic Change*, *14*(3), 121–131.

Hitt, M. A., Ireland, R. D., Camp, S. M., & Sexton, D. L. (2001). Strategic entrepreneurship: Entrepreneurial strategies for wealth creation. *Strategic Management Journal*, *22*, 479–491.

Holten, A. L., & Crouch, C. (2014). Unions in small and medium-sized enterprises: A family factor perspective. *European Journal of Industrial Relations*, *20*(3), 273–290.

Huselid, M. (1995). The Impact of Human Resource Management practices on turnover, productivity, and corporate financial performance. *Academy of Management Journal*, *38*(3), 635–672.

Huselid, M. A., Jackson, S. E., & Schuler, R. S. (1997). Technical and Strategic Human Resource Management Effectiveness as Determinants of Firm Performance. *Academy of Management Journal*, *40*(1), 171–188.

Ichniowski, C., & Shaw, K. (1999). The Effects of Human Resource Management Systems on Economic Performance: An International Comparison of US and Japanese Plants. *Management Science*, *45*(5), 704–721.

Jackson, S. E., & Schuler, R. S. (1995). Understanding human resource management in the context of organizations and their environment. *Annual Review of Psychology*, *46*(1), 237–264.

Jackson, S. E., & Schuler, R. S. (2000). *Managing human resource. A partnership perspective*. Southern-Western College Publishing.

Jackson, S. E., Schuler, R. S., & Rivcro, J. C. (1989). Organizational Characteristics as Predictors of Personnel Practices. *Personnel Psychology*, *42*(4), 727–786.

Jaskiewicz, P., Combs, J. G., Shanine, K. K., & Balkin, D. B. (2018). Making Sense of HR in Family Firms: Antecedents, Moderators, and Outcomes. *Human Resource Management Review*, *28*(1), 1–102.

Jones, G. (1984). Task Visibility, Free Riding, and Shirking: Explaining the Effect of Structure and Technology on Employee Behaviors. *Academy of Management Review*, *9*(4), 684–695.

Kaman, V., McCarthy, A. M., Gulbro, R. D., & Tucker, L. T. (2001). Bureaucratic and High Commitment Human Resource Practices in Small Service Firms. *HR Human Resource Planning*, *24*(1), 33–44.

Kanter, R. M. (1983). Frontiers for Strategic Human Resource Management. *Human Resource Management*, *22*(1/2), 85–92.

Kanter, R. M. (1989). The New Managerial Work. *Harvard Business Review*, *67*(6), 85.

Karami, A., Jones, B. M., & Kakabadse, N. (2008). Does strategic human resource management matter in high-tech sector? Some learning points for SME managers. Corporate Governance. *The International Journal of Business in Society*, *8*(1), 7–17.

Kehoe, R. R., & Wright, P. M. (2013). The impact of high-performance human resource practices on employees' attitudes and behaviors. *Journal of Management*, *39*(2), 366–391.

Kerr, J. L. (1985). Diversifications Strategies and Managerial Rewards: An Empirical Study. *Academy of Management Journal*, *28*(1), 155–179.

Kerr, J. L., & Jackofsky, E. F. (1989). Aligning Managers with Strategies: Management Development versus Selection. *Strategic Management Journal, 10*(S1), 157–170.

Kidwell, R. E., & Fish, A. J. (2007). High-performance human resource practices in Australian family businesses: Preliminary evidence from the wine industry. *The International Entrepreneurship and Management Journal, 3*(1), 1–14.

Le Breton-Miller, I., & Miller, D. (2014). Temporal considerations in the study of family firms: Reflections on "the study of organizational behaviour in family business". *European Journal of Work and Organizational Psychology, 23*(5), 669–673.

Le Breton-Miller, I., Miller, D., & Steier, L. P. (2004). Toward an integrative model of effective FOB succession. *Entrepreneurship Theory and Practice, 24*, 305–328.

Lengnick-Hall, C. A., & Lengnick-Hall, M. L. (1988). Strategic Human Resource Management: A Review of the Literature and a Proposed Typology. *Academy of Management Review, 13*(3), 454–470.

Lepak, D. P., Liao, H., Chung, Y., & Harden, E. E. (2006). A conceptual review of human resource management systems in strategic human resource management research. *Research in Personnel and Human Resources Management, 25*(1), 217–271.

Levie, J., & Lerner, M. (2009). Resource Mobilization and Performance in Family and Nonfamily Businesses in the United Kingdom. *Family Business Review, 22*(1), 25–38.

MacDuffie, J. P. (1995). Human Resource Bundles and Manufacturing Performance: Organizational Logic and Flexible Production Systems in the World Auto Industry. *Industrial & Labor Relations Review, 48*(2), 197–221.

Marler, J. H., & Fisher, S. L. (2013). An evidence-based review of e-HRM and strategic human resource management. *Human Resource Management Review, 23*(1), 18–36.

Marlow, S., & Patton, D. (2002). Minding the gap between employers and employees. The challenge for owner-managers of smaller manufacturing firms. *Employee Relations, 24*(5), 523–539.

Martín-Alcázar, F., Romero-Fernandez, P. M., & Sanchez-Gardey, G. (2005). Strategic human resource management: Integrating the universalistic, contingent, configurational and contextual perspectives. *International Journal of Human Resource Management, 16*(5), 633–659.

Miller, D., & Friesen, P. H. (1984). A longitudinal study of the corporate life cycle. *Management Science, 30*(10), 1161–1183.

Miller, P. (1989). Strategic HRM: What It Is and What It Isn't. *Personnel Management*, 46-52.

Mintzberg, H. (1979). *The structuring of organizations*. Prentice Hall.

Moshavi, D., & Koch, M. J. (2005). The adoption of family-friendly practices in family-owned firms. Paragon or paradox? *Community Work & Family, 8*(3), 237–249.

Naz, F., Aftab, J., & Awais, M. (2016). Impact of human resource management practices (HRM) on performance of SMEs in Multan, Pakistan. International Journal of Management. *Accounting and Economics, 3*(11), 699–708.

Niniger, J. R. (1980). Human Resources and Strategic Planning: A Vital Link. *Optimum (Paris)*, *11*(4), 33–46.

Noe, R. A., Hollenbeck, J. R., Gerhart, B., & Wright, P. M. (2010). *Human resource Management: Gaining a competitive Advantage* (7th ed.). McGraw-Hill/lrwin.

Nordqvist, M., Sharma, P., & Chirico, F. (2014). Family Firm Heterogeneity and Governance: A Configuration Approach. *Journal of Small Business Management*, *52*, 192–209.

Othman, A. E. A. (2009). Strategic HRM practices: Perspectives of Malaysian and Japanese owned companies in Malaysia. *Global Business and Management Research*, *1*(1), 1–22.

Panayotopoulou, L., Bourantas, D., & Papalexandris, N. (2003). Strategic human resource management and its effects on firm performance: An implementation of the competing values framework. *International Journal of Human Resource Management*, *14*(4), 680–699.

Penrose, E. T. (1959). *The Theory of the Growth of the Firm*. John Wiley.

Pfeffer, J. (1987). *Organizaciones y Teoria de la Organizacion*. El Ateneo.

Pfeffer, J., & Cohen, Y. (1984). Determinants of Internal Labor Markets in Organizations. *Administrative Science Quarterly*, •••, 550–572.

Pfeffer, J., & Davis-Blake, A. (1987). Understanding Organizational Wage Structure: A Resource Dependence Approach. *Academy of Management Journal*, *30*(3), 437–455.

Pfeffer, J., & Langton, N. (1988). Wage Inequality and the Organization of Work: The Case of Academic Departments. *Administrative Science Quarterly*, 588–606.

Pfeffer, J., & Veiga, J. F. (1999). Putting people first for organizational success. *The Academy of Management Perspectives*, *13*(2), 37–48.

Porter, M. E. (1985). *Competitive advantage*. Free Press.

Poza, E. J., Hanlon, S., & Kishida, R. (2004). Does the Family Business Interaction Factor Represent a Resource or a Cost? *Family Business Review*, *17*(2), 99–118.

Reid, R., Morrow, T., Kelly, B., Adams, J., & McCartan, P. (2000). Human resource management practices in SME's: A comparative analysis of family and non-family businesses. *IBAR-Journal of the Irish Academy of Management*, *21*(2), 157–181.

Reid, R. S., & Adams, J. S. (2001). Human resource management – a survey of practices within family and non-family firms. *Journal of European Industrial Training*, *25*(6), 310–320.

Reid, R. S., Morrow, T., Kelly, B., & McCartan, P. (2002). People Management in SMEs: An Analysis of Human Resource Strategies in Family and Non-Family Businesses. *Journal of Small Business and Enterprise Development*, *9*(3), 245–259.

Rhodes, D. W. (1988). Can HR Respond to Corporate Strategy? *The Journal of Business Strategy*, *9*(2), 57–59.

Richard, O. C., & Johnson, N. B. (2001). Strategic human resource management effectiveness and firm performance. *International Journal of Human Resource Management*, *12*, 299–310.

Saridakis, G., Lai, Y., & Cooper, C. L. (2017). Exploring the relationship between HRM and firm performance: A meta-analysis of longitudinal studies. *Human Resource Management Review*, *27*(1), 87–96.

Schuler, R. S., & MacMillan, I. (1984). Gaining competitive advantage through human resource practices. *Human Resource Management*, *23*(3), 241–255.

Schuler, R. S., & Walker, J. (1990). Human Resource Strategy: Focusing on Issues and Actions. *Organizational Dynamics*, *19*(1), 5–19.

Schulze, W. S., Lubatkin, M. H., & Dino, R. N. (2003). Toward a theory of agency and altruism in family firms. *Journal of Business Venturing*, *18*(4), 473–490.

Shaw, J. D., Park, T. Y., & Kim, E. (2013). A resource-based perspective on human capital losses, HRM investments, and organizational performance. *Strategic Management Journal*, *34*(5), 572–589.

Slocum, J. W., Cron, W. L., Hansen, R. W., & Rawlings, S. (1985). Business Strategy and the Management of Plateaued Employees. *Academy of Management Journal*, *28*(1), 133–154.

Stavrou, E. T., & Brewster, C. (2005). The configurational approach to linking strategic human resource management bundles with business performance: Myth or reality? *Management Review*, •••, 186–201.

Stewart, A., & Hitt, M. A. (2012). Why Can't a Family Business Be More Like a Nonfamily Business? Modes of Professionalization in Family Firms. *Family Business Review*, *25*(1), 58–86.

Sun, L., Aryee, S., & Law, K. S. (2007). High performance human resource practices, citizenship behavior, and organisational performance: A relational perspective. *Academy of Management Journal*, *50*(3), 558–577.

Teece, D. J., Pisano, G., & Shuen, A. (1997). Dynamic capabilities and strategic management. *Strategic Management Journal*, *18*(7), 509–533.

Tsao, C. W., Chen, S. J., Lin, C. S., & Hyde, W. (2009). Founding-family ownership and firm performance: The role of high-performance work systems. *Family Business Review*, *22*(4), 319–332.

Ulrich, D. (1991). Using human resources for competitive advantage. In R. Kilman, I. Kilman, & ... (Eds.), *Making organizations competitive* (pp. 129–155). Jossey-Bass.

Ulrich, D., Younger, J., Brockbank, W., & Ulrich, M. D. (2013). The state of the HR profession. *Human Resource Management*, *52*(3), 457–471.

Upton, N., & Heck, R. K. Z. (1997). The Family Business Dimension of Entrepreneurship. In Entrepreneurship 2000. Upstart Publishing.

Van de Ven, A. H., & Drazin, R. (1985). The Concept of Fit in Strategy Research. In L. Cummings & B. M. Staw (Eds.), *Research in Organizational Behavior* (Vol. 7). JAI Press.

Venkatraman, N., & Prescott, J. E. (1990). Environment-strategy coalignment: An empirical test of its performance implications. *Strategic Management Journal*, *11*(1), 1–23.

Walker, J. W. (1988). Managing Human Resources in Flat, Lean and Flexible Organizations: Trends for the 1990's. *Human Resource Planning*, *11*(2), 125–132.

Warner, M. (1984). New Technology, Work Organizations, and Industrial Relations. *Omega*, *12*(3), 203–210.

Wiesner, R., & Innes, P. (2010). Bleak house or bright prospect?: HRM in Australian SMEs over 1998-2008. *Asia Pacific Journal of Human Resources*, *48*(2), 151–184.

Williamson, I. O., & Cable, D. M. (2003). Organizational hiring patterns, interfirm network ties, and interorganizational imitation. *Academy of Management Journal*, *46*(3), 349–358.

Wood, S. (1999). Human Resource Management and Performance. *International Journal of Management Reviews*, *1*(4), 367–413.

Wright, P. M., Dunford, B. B., & Snell, S. A. (2001). Human resources and the resource based view of the firm. *Journal of Management*, *27*(6), 701–721.

Wright, P. M., Gardner, T. M., Moynihan, L. M., & Allen, M. R. (2005). The relationship between HR practices and firm performance: Examining causal order. *Personnel Psychology*, *58*(2), 409–446.

Wright, P. M., & McMahan, G. C. (1992). Theoretical perspectives for strategic human resource management. *Journal of Management*, *18*(2), 295–320.

Wright, P. M., & Sherman, S. (1999). Failing to Find Fit in Strategic Human Resource Management: Theoretical and Empirical Problems. In Research in Personnel and Human Resources Management. Greenwich, CT: JAI Press.

Wright, P. M., & Snell, S. A. (1998). Toward a Unifying Framework for Exploring Fit and Flexibility in Strategic Human Resource Management. *Academy of Management Review*, *23*(4), 756–772.

Xianga, D., Worthington, A. C., & Higgs, H. (2014). Family Ownership, Altruism and Agency Costs in Australian Small- and Medium-Sized Enterprises. *Applied Economics*, *46*(32), 3907–3921.

Youndt, M. A., Snell, S. A., Dean, J. W., & Lepak, D. P. (1996). Human resource management, manufacturing strategy, and performance. *Academy of Management Journal*, *39*(4), 836–866.

Zakaria, N. (2011). Investigating the role of human resource management practices on the performance of SME: A conceptual framework. *Journal of Global Management*, *3*(1), 74–92.

Chapter 1
Reflections of Human Resource Practices in Family Business:
A Qualitative Research

Büşra Müceldili
Yıldız Technical University, Turkey

Berivan Tatar
Gebze Technical University, Turkey

ABSTRACT

Although much has been discussed about human resource management practices in large organizations, studies in the family firms' context are nascent in the literature. To better understand human resource management practices in the context of family firms, this study performed interviews on three experienced and successful family firm owners and human resource managers. The research findings reveal that family firms have professionalized, formalized, and employee-oriented perspective in their human resource practices. This study also showed that the new generations in the family are more aware of the importance of human resources and reflect this perspective to their human resource practices. Besides, employees' organizational justice perception is strengthened by considering equality between family and non-family employees in human resources practices. Implications of these results for practice and further research are discussed.

INTRODUCTION

In today's business world, human resource management is crucial for attracting the best talents, retaining them within the organization, enhance their motivation and performance, developing desirable employee behaviors, and gaining short and long-term competitive advantages (Barney & Wright, 1998). Hence, over the past decades, effective management of human resources has also taken great attention from family firms scholarship (Chrisman et al., 2014). Nevertheless, family firms have difficulties in recruiting and hiring talented and qualified non-family employees mainly because of types of human resource

DOI: 10.4018/978-1-7998-4814-1.ch001

practices, perceptions of applicants about the professionalism of these practices (King et al., 2001), and the perception that family firms are small organizations (Botero, 2014).

Besides, non-family applicants and employees get the idea that family businesses will have privileges to family members, which harms their perceptions of organizational justice (Arijs et al., 2018). With this regard, these applicants and current employees tend to have negative stereotypes about that family firms have limited and few resources, lower level of salaries and compensations, lower professionalism, lower justice in organizational activities, and a higher degree of nepotism (Botero et al., 2018). In this vein, to change these negative thoughts and perceptions, human resources practices within the family firms should be defined clearly, determined broadly, and arranged to meet the expectations of non-family members. Therefore, effective human resource management in the family firm context requires deeper understanding (Hoon et al., 2019).

Additionally, past studies in the literature have addressed the difficulties faced by family companies in managing human resources, especially in terms of family members. Practicing human resources activities objectively is quite difficult for the CEO of the family firms because of their line of descent and role as a mother, father, or uncle with family members (Reid & Adams, 2001). In other respect, family members may also expect to have a favoured position in the organization's activities, rewarding, salary, and benefits because of their status (Kidwell et al., 2018). In a sense, hence, human resource practices need to be managed effectively through formal practices to prevent this conflict between family and business that harming the organization.

Furthermore, existing literature on family firms' scholarship has centred on the comparison of human resources practices in family and non-family firms. In a sense, family firms tend to use simple and informal human resource practices and unclear practices and criteria in the employment of family members (Blanco-Mazagatos et al., 2018). However, the past studies in the literature have compared family and non-family firms in terms of their human resources practices, the differences between these two organizations have not been revealed comprehensively and systematically (Reid & Adams, 2001). These practices, which will provide a competitive advantage, organizational success, and performance to family businesses, need to be addressed comprehensively (Blanco-Mazagatos et al., 2018).

On the other hand, from the family firms' perspective, existing studies mainly focus on specific human resource practices (Hoon et al., 2019). For example, in terms of compensation, past studies found that family firms pay less compensation by comparison with non-family firms (Michiels et al., 2013; Bassanini et al., 2013). Besides, in terms of recruitment and selection, past studies mainly accentuated the preferences of applicants for working in family firms and Botero (2014) found that job security, advancement, compensation, and prestige influence the employers' attractiveness of family firms. However, there is also a lack of studies examining the training and development of human resources within the context of family firms. Kotey and Folker (2007) concluded that family firms provide fewer opportunities for training activities contrary to non-family firms. Sánchez-Marín et al. (2019) also revealed that formalization of training and human resource development within the family firms enhance the firm performance.

In sum, turning to family firms' research, evidence suggests that human resource practices remain informal in the context of family firms. Concordantly, Pittino et al. (2016) found that formal high-performance work practices are mainly lower in family firms than non-family firms. Furthermore, these activities lead family firms "(a) to the adoption of unfair compensation and performance appraisal systems (b) to cases of managerial entrenchment, (c) to nepotism in-personnel recruiting and career decisions, (d) to scapegoating of non-family executives and employees, and, (e) to lower actions for the engagement and worker development of non-family employees" (Pittino et al., 2016: 75-76).

In this context, it is seen that researches on human resources in the field of family firms generally focus on the differences in human resources practices between family and non-family organizations. In fact, few studies are examining to what extent human resources practices are carried out professionally and formally in family organizations (Harris et al., 2004). Therefore, to fill this gap, we reviewed the existing literature extensively to understand how family firms use formal and informal human resource practices. In this regard, this research aims to contribute to family business literature via focusing on (1) human resources activities used in the family firms, (2) formality of human resource practices of family firms, and (3) the effectiveness of human resource practices of family firms.

The research is structured as follows: We review the existing family firms' literature on human resource practices and develop our research questions based on a resource-based view. Thereafter, we outline the research design and methods used in the present study. In the following section, we discuss the contributions, implications, and limitations of our study.

THEORETICAL BACKGROUND AND LITERATURE REVIEW

The Resource-Based View

According to the Resource-Based View, the abilities to gain competitive advantage largely derive from the resources of the organizations. These resources include assets, capabilities, organizational processes, firm attributes, information, and knowledge (Barney, 1991). In the same manner, firm resources are also classified as human, social, physical, organizational, and financial resources (Greene & Brown, 1997). In this vein, physical resources include tangible assets (machines, buildings, etc.) which are necessary for the operational activities of the organizations whereas financial resources consist of the monetary assets necessary for the establishment, operation, and continuity of the organizations. Organizational resources include organizational relationships, members, and information. Human resources refer to all people that organizations benefit from the talent, knowledge, and work experience (Greene & Brown, 1997). Finally, social resources consist of wealth, status, social ties, among the member of the organizations (Lin, Vaughn, & Ensel, 1981). Value, rareness, inimitability, and non-substitutability of the resources indicate the generation of sustainable competitive advantage for the organizations (Barney, 1991).

Moreover, the resource-based approach has also been the subject of many researches on family businesses. In this context, family firms also have several unique resources regarded as the "familiness" which is defined as "the unique bundle of resources created by the interaction of family and business" (Sirmon & Hitt, 2003: 339). These resources consist of social capital, and human capital, patient capital, and survivability capital (Sirmon & Hitt, 2003). However, these unique resources not only provide a variety of advantages to family businesses but also bring different difficulties in the effective management of these resources within the family organizations. The present study particularly focuses on challenges specific to human resources in the context of family firms due to the important role of human resources in increasing the productivity, providing a higher quality of work-life, and profitability (Cascio, 1992). Indeed, family firms have unique attributes as extraordinary commitment, warm, friendly, and intimate relationships, the potential for deep tacit knowledge in terms of the human capital of the organizations. Nevertheless, family firms mainly have difficulties in attracting and retaining highly qualified managers due to the negative perceptions such as exclusive succession, limited potential for professional growth, lack of perceived professionalism (Sirmon & Hitt, 2003), informal and less professional human resource management practices (Harris et al., 2004). On the other hand, the complexity arising from having relationships with family members both at home and work also creates challenges for family businesses (Kidwell et al., 2018).

In sum, although competitive advantage can be achieved with the financial, strategic, and technological resources, the most permanent source of competitive advantage is the human resources of the organizations and the ability to improve the organizational capability of the member of the organizations (Ulrich & Lake, 1990). Astrachan and Kolenko (1994) revealed that having limited organizational capability may be one key factor leading family firms to have a short lifespan in a highly competitive business market. Additionally, only having the best talented human resources is not enough for the firm to gain a competitive advantage. Besides, organizations should use, manage, and retain these resources effectively and efficiently (Collis & Montgomery, 1995). In this regard, based on the resource-based view, the current study focuses on the kinds of human resource activities, formality and effectiveness of human resources processes and practices, investment of family firms to their human capital, and based on the above discussion, following research questions were addressed: (1) Which human resource practices are implemented in family firms (for recruitment and selection, training and development, payment and compensations, promotion, etc.)?; (2) How do family firms invest in their human capital for sustained competitive advantage?; (3) Is there a difference between non-family firms in terms of human resource management and practices?; (4) How do human resource practices affect employees' behavior (motivation, performance, commitment, etc.)?; and (5) What kind of human resource activities are carried out to change the negative perceptions and stereotypes of non-family employees towards family firms?

In line with this research questions, this study aims to provide a comprehensive overview of human resources practices in family businesses, to identify existing human resource practices, the impact of these practices on the current employees' behavior, their way of investing their human capital, the difficulties faced by family businesses in human resources practices, and to identify what they do differently from non-family businesses.

Family Business

Family firms are a "*business governed and/or managed with the intention to shape and pursue the vision of the business held by a dominant coalition controlled by members of the same family or a small number of families in a manner that is potentially sustainable across generations of the family or families*" (Chua et al., 1999: 25). With this regard, it is revealed that family firms consist of two different social institutions as the family and the organizations. Hence, family firms exist for the family members whereas nonfamily firms aim to produce goods and services for gaining profit (Botero et al., 2018). Ferraro and Marrone (2016) also stated that family firms have three main goals: (1) transferring family firms to other generations, (2) managing firms by the family members, and (3) strategic management of firms in control of the family. Thus, family firms focus on the family rather than the organizational and strategic perspectives.

Besides, it is assumed that family firms give priority and importance to socioemotional wealth which includes organizational identification, emotional attachment, control, and impact of family members to the firm (Ferraro & Marrone, 2016). In addition, unlike other firms, family firms have family-oriented non-economic goals such as family harmony, family social status, and family identity linkage because of strong links among family members and desire for protecting the identity of the family (Chrisman et al., 2012).

Family firms, concerning their numbers, their contribution to employment, and the national income, have great importance for the world and country economies. According to statistics data, family companies generate 70-90% of the GNP and almost 75% of the companies in the world. Family firms also constitute 90% of all organizations in the United States, half of the U.S. GNP is provided by family companies, and 80% of the total employment in the U.S. is created by family companies. Additionally, one-third of Fortune 500 companies are family firms (Poza, 2013).

On the other hand, Turkey has hosted many family firms from the establishment of Hacı Bekir which is the first family business in 1777 to today. 95 percent of companies, 99 percent of SMEs, 75 percent of public companies are family firms. It is also an undeniable fact that family businesses contribute greatly to the national economy. In fact, the contribution of family businesses to the total national income is around 75 percent whereas approximately 90% of the gross national product is produced by family businesses in Turkey.

Despite their remarkable contributions to the economy, family businesses have a very short life span. Of all family-owned businesses, 30% is 2nd generation, 12% is 3rd generation, and 3% is 4th generation firms in Turkey and the average life of the family-owned firms is 25 years. In a sense, the sustainability of family businesses and factors contributing to their competitive advantage are an important issue in today's business world. It is undeniable that one of these factors is attracting highly-skilled human capital contributing to the longevity of family firms in Turkey. Besides, in terms of the resource-based view, talented human resources have a much greater significance in achieving competitive advantages for family-owned firms located in Turkey, where these firms have limited human resources in the business environment (Erdoğmuş et al., 2016).

Furthermore, Turkey has a collectivistic culture that relies on a mutually committed and family-like relationship (Yamagishi, et al., 1998). As a result of the national culture, family business in Turkey has some unique features as strong family ties, respect for ancestors and elder members of the family, helping each other and working together in the family (Özcan, 1995). Yalçınkaya and Durcan (2011) revealed that family firms in Turkey should be comprehensively reviewed in an organizational sense. In this vein, the present study has examined the current practices, formality, and professionalism of human resource activities to exhibit necessary strategies for the longevity of family firms in the context of Turkey.

Human Resources Management Practices in Family Business

The rise of uncertainty, competition, complexity, and challenges in the business environment heightens the needs of organizations to talented employees having diverse skills in recent years. With this regard, organizations make an effort to attract, hire, and retain the best talent via their human resource management practices. Family firms, as one of these organizations, also plan and carry out human resources activities in line with these purposes for gaining competitive advantages. The personnel selection, training, and compensations, which are among the basic human resources activities carried out in family companies, are mentioned within the scope of the current study.

In this context, family firms give preference to select candidates from the social networks in the recruitment and these candidates also consist of limited candidates sharing similar values with the family business (Dyer & Mortensen, 2005). These firms also use simple selection processes and selection criteria mainly in the meeting the requirements of the job (Sánchez-Marín et al., 2019). Botero and Litchfield (2013) parallel this view, stated that family firms use informal recruitment practices such as word of mouth and employee references for nonmanagerial positions whereas these firms use more formal practices such as Internet postings and use of agencies or head-hunters for managerial positions. Furthermore, family firms select the candidates who are reliable, long-term oriented, and make at least a problem in terms of trust and delegation in organizational activities (Lubatkin et al., 2007).

In terms of training, informal and short-term training is mainly preferred by family firms. Also, family firms focus on the development of specific talents of employees for their routine activities in the organization (Hill & Stewart, 2000). In this vein, these training activities are for their jobs in the short term, rather than the long-term development of the employees. However, applying informal training prevents family firms from gaining a competitive advantage through well-develop human capital. Besides, past studies revealed that family firms avoid from investing the management training on the ground that family members unwilling to lose their control (Loan Clarke et al., 1999). Training programs such as on-the-job training, job rotation, and apprenticeships are not included in the budget for training and not considered (Kotey & Folker, 2007).

On the other hand, Carrasco-Hernandez and Sánchez-Marín (2007) noted that there are differences between family-owned and managed firms and professionally managed family businesses in terms of payment and revealed that payment level in the family-owned and managed organizations is lower than the non-family firms. Additionally, incentives determine as a short-term oriented within the family-owned and managed firms. Family firms have also assigned promotions based on seniority and given importance to non-monetary incentives rather than performance-based compensations (Gomez-Mejia et al., 2003). Moreover, family firms have performed tenure-based compensation and considered the loyalty of employees for compensations rather than their achievements and performance (Davis & Harveston, 2001).

Based on the above discussion, it is concluded that family firms mainly use informal less professional human resource practices and family firms have less desire for professional human resource management practices than non-family businesses (Harris et al., 2004). On the other hand, human resource management is complex for family firms because of having relationships with family members both at home and work (Kidwell et al., 2018). In addition, non-family members' employees working in the firms heighten these complexities. In a sense, family business managers need to find a balance in the human resources policies that apply to family members and non-family members' employees.

RESEARCH METHOD

By virtue of providing detailed and rich data (Lune & Berg, 2017), a semi-structured interview method has been used in the current study. Firstly, we asked questions for getting demographic information about the family firms (firm's age, historical information, sector, family members in board, number of generations, generation managing the firms, and number of employees) and informants participating to interviews (age, gender, working position, and work experience). Table 1 represents the demographic profile of family firms and informants.

Interview guideline used for assessing the human resource practices was developed based on Resource-Based View and existing qualitative studies (e.g., Astrachan &Kolenko, 1994; Tokarczyk et al., 2007; Sieger et al., 2011) in the context family firms. Interview questions, in line with Resource-Based View and research questions of the current study, assessed human resources practices (recruitment and selection, training and development, salary and incentives, and promotions) in the family business; the way of selection, and the implication of these practices; investments in human resources to gain a competitive advantage; the human resource practices that make their family businesses unique; HR activities carried out to change the negative perceptions and prejudices of non-family workers towards family businesses; and effects of HR practices on the behavior of their employees.

Besides, purposeful sampling (Guba & Lincoln 1982) was used for sample selection to reach a rich seam of information. In the selection of organizations, serving in different sectors located in Turkey was used as the selection criteria for family firms. We aimed to reach more comprehensive information and to examine whether there is a difference among sectors by including family companies in different sectors. In this vein, family firms from the service, holding, and manufacturing sectors have been the subject of our research. All three firms were selected due to their positive reputation, recognized for their corporate activities and achievements in the regions where they operate, and being among the leading family businesses in their sectors. For example, Abalıoğlu and Seyran are located in Aegean Region which has a significant contribution to Turkey's national economy. Aegean Region has organized industrial sites and is the second most developed region in Turkey. Dosinia is located in the Mediterranean region which is the most important region in the Turkey tourism sector. Antalya is one of the most popular cities among foreign and domestic tourists (Kukulu & Öncel, 2009). In terms of interviewees, being a human resource manager or general manager in the family was determined as a sample selection criterion.

Table 1. Demographic profile of family firms and respondents

	Firm's age	Sector	Family Members in Board	# of Generations	# of Employees	Respondent's Position	Experience (Years)
Seyran Food	70	Food	2	3	112	General manager	20
Abalıoğlu Holding	76	Manufacturing, Copper	4/4	3	2100	Member of the board	15
Dosinia Luxury Resort Hotel	28	Hospitality	3/3	2	270	HR Manager	8

All interviews were transcripted verbatim by authors in the current study. Contrary to the validity and reliability criteria in quantitative research, qualitative studies focus on credibility, and four basic criteria have been determined to ensure credibility (Guba & Lincoln, 1982). Within the scope of this study, the researchers' triangulation method was used to meet the credibility criteria corresponding to the internal consistency, and we tried to reduce researchers' biases by ensuring that more than one researcher was involved in the transcription and evaluation of the data. In addition, the raw version of the data was retained for the referral adequacy materials and with the thought of contributing to future studies. In order to provide external validity, the transferability criterion, which expresses the power of the findings obtained to represent the population has been considered (Guba & Lincoln 1982). In addition to the human resource management literature, the findings are expected to be transferred to the studies in the family firm's literature. On the other hand, research methods and processes were tried to be explained in detail in the context of dependability. Finally, direct quotations were included in the research to ensure confirmability, which corresponds to the objectivity criterion in quantitative research. Besides, raw data and processed data were preserved and research findings were shared in detail.

RESULTS

Interview 1

Seyran Food is the manufacturer, exporter, and importer of nuts in Turkey providing service to a variety of markets in the world. Seyran Food has established in 1950 and has started exporting its products in 1976. We interviewed with Mr. Çaputçu, the general manager and shareholder of Seyran Food. He is 43 years old and he has been working in a company for about 20 years. Mr. Çaputçu describes his company as a company that is not overly corporate but tries to take the necessary steps towards institutionalization.

In terms of human resource practices within the firms, he stated that the company does not have an active human resources department, but they have a staff department. Human resource practices have been planned and determined by the personnel manager and operations manager. The recruitment process has been managed through online application sites (kariyer.net) and newspaper ads have also been used for recruiting white-collar employees. The organization has also internal and external training for the personal and professional development of the employees. Internal training has been generally given on the subject of food safety by food quality assurance managers. There is also an independent company from which firms receive training services regarding occupational health and safety. The firm also adjusts the salary scheme according to the firm's evaluation system. Mr. Çaputçu pointed out that they have a certain salary scale and set the salary of employees based on employees' seniority, position, works, and performance. Promotions are usually made within the organization. In the absence of a competent employee to fill the position within the company, candidates are sought from outside of the organization.

When we ask how being a family business and family dynamics affect HRM systems, Mr. Çaputçu notes that:

After all, this is a family business. I am the only one representing the family. As I said here, we don't have a very professional HR department, but our personnel department following all the jobs from payrolls to paying salaries.

Besides, Mr. Çaputçu shared that their firm does not concretely invest in human resources and added: *"As the most authoritative person at the company, I prefer to work with good people. We can be generous in point of money, as long as the performance of our employees and way of doing business suits us. I prefer to work with professionals. Therefore, many professionals work in our company. We also have professionals coming from outside the city."*

Mr. Çaputçu asserted that there are differences between the family company and other companies in terms of HR management and practices. *"There are also pros and cons of being family firms. The cons are, of course, because of not being more institutionalized. Sometimes, we do not have access to human resource as we want. Quick decision making and faster implementation constitute our advantages as a family firm".*

Additionally, Mr. Çaputçu expresses the differences between HR practices among generations as follows:

I am the third generation. Of course, there is a big difference between past habits and what is currently being practiced. If you ask what these differences are, I employ more professionals and we have a performance-based salary system. We have severance and performance-based salary system. Therefore, we now apply them more professionally compared to the past.

Interview 2

Abalıoğlu Holding is a Denizli-based holding company. It includes companies in the textile, copper, energy, service, technology, mining, agriculture, and papermaking sectors. It has over 10 companies. We interviewed with Beyza Abalıoğlu and Derya Kılıç. Mrs. Abalıoğlu is a board member of Abalıoğlu Holding and 38 years old. Mrs. Kılıç is working in the human resource department at Abalıoğlu Holding for about 15 years. She is 39 years old.

Abalıoğlu Holding manage their personnel selection and placement process to work with the most suitable candidates who adopt corporate values, have a high sense of responsibility, and open to continuous learning and change. When the position is opened, the relevant department manager defines the competencies of the person recruited in an open position. At this stage, the decision is based entirely on systems and processes. In other words, even if the family members are members of the board of directors and come with a reference, the person can start the business with the approval of the department manager at this point and if all inventory results are positive. While doing these, personality tests, English tests, competency-based interviews are conducted. Career planning is carried out in line with certain goals of the hired person. Of course, there is training to be received in this process and these training programs are also determined by HR and his manager.

In terms of training and development, activities have been planned towards the needs of employees as well as the organization, and the training schedule has started with orientation training and continued with training for personal development. Mrs. Kılıç stated that Abalıoğlu Holding is a group that has a mission firstly starting with "human". At this point, the most valuable resource is to value the development of human resources and summarized their training processes as:

For training, we first send a questionnaire to both our colleagues and managers. With this survey, we ask our colleagues: "What are your development goals for yourself? What is it for your department? What do you want for the whole company and what do you want to be in the future?" We take the expectations of employees in different segments. We talk with our department managers. It may be an education due to legal changes requested by the department manager. There can be training determined by each department in its own projection. We argue with them and then carry them to the directors. We say to the directors, "This is the work of your manager and your colleagues." After mutually saying "This is appropriate", we prepare all the works and send them to the higher institution, and the budgets are approved.

Payment and rewards have been determined according to the success and performance of the employees. Employees receive salaries based on the wage ranges of firms based on their work remunerate according to their performance. These human resources practices are selected and implemented by the decision of the director, manager, and HR manager.

Mrs. Abalıoğlu defined their firms exactly as a family company completed the institutionalization. She also stated that there are some difficulties in being a family business:

Being a family business is actually a very difficult thing. It looks beautiful from afar, but when sensualities become involved... For example, our cousins, my uncle, and my father have children. Let me call this the young generation. Of course, we have beauty, we all work together, but there are also disadvantages... These processes cannot be separated by sharp lines as it is done to so many people because of being a family member. For example, let me give an example from myself. I am currently a board member. For example, if someone from outside is a member of the board, perhaps he would not be a member of the board as fast. This is good for me, but in terms of organization, family businesses are actually an environment where it cannot be questioned whether the competencies be fully measured.

Mrs. Kılıç, arguing in what Mrs. Abalıoğlu said about this issue, has appended the following:

In fact, family members start on the factory floor, regardless of their position. Mrs. Abalıoğlu also started as an assistant specialist. Family members are employed in different departments to ensure rapid gains in competencies. Family members are coming to these positions by strengthening their different sides in different departments with the guidance of the HR managers to prepare for the management more rapidly. However, the point we are talking about institutionalization here is that the systems and processes depend on the process rather than the person.

On the other hand, Mrs. Abalıoğlu is the third generation in the family firms and stated the following in terms of HR practices differences between generations: "*They were focused on direct investment during my father's period. They never thought about wage or career issues. "I'm investing. Let me grow my business." They thought of it.*" At this point, Mrs. Kılıç stated that: "*Family businesses are a growing organism in which everyone develops itself. This organism is affected by environmental and living conditions. Unlike previous generations, more awareness has been raised in terms of human resources policy in this period. A completely different preparation will also continue in the next generation.*"

Additionally, for HR activities carried out to change the negative perceptions and biases of non-family employees towards family businesses Mrs. Abalıoğlu stated that: "In fact, system and process development and trust are the biggest deficiency or anxiety of people in family companies. So even if we are involved, if the general manager is defending something, with certain times, he will never say, 'It will be what I say. I'm the boss.' That's why people think that this firm is institutionalized".

Interview 3

Dosinia Luxury Resort Hotel, located in Antalya, Turkey, is a well-known organization in the hospitality industry. We interviewed with Funda ŞEN. She is 38 years old. She has been working in the hotel industry for about 8 years and she has working experience in the HR department in different sectors.

In terms of HR practices, firstly, department managers are hired, and after the department managers start to work, the sub-staff is hired. Then, compulsory and necessary training has been provided for the employees to be more efficient at work. Concerning payment, salaries have been determined by negotiating with the hotels in the region. In addition, promotions have been determined according to the individual's own performance and customer satisfaction. Promotions have been given according to the comments made by the guests about the staff and according to the observations of the department managers.

Mrs. Şen summarized the advantages of being a family business as follows:

Having a family business is always an advantage for us. It is managed like a family business. So, we can have a one-on-one conversation with our boss directly. In corporate places, you know, bosses are unknown and invisible. In other words, we cannot talk to them one-on-one, we cannot exchange ideas. However, since the general manager is always here because of being a family company, and the relationship between us is sincerer and we can do our job much better. That's why I prefer family businesses more.

Mrs. Şen also stated that HR practices in the organization have positive effects on employees: *"Commitment to the institution is very high. Because bilateral relations are much better, loyalty increases more. In 80% of our employees working in previous years, there is a desire to work with this company again. Therefore, we do not have any difficulties in finding personnel."*

Dosinia Luxury Resort Hotel has been managed by the second generation of the family. The family firm has a heterogeneous structure. Hence, the firms have family members only in the management position. She gave the following answer to our question regarding whether the firm has different practices for non-family workers and the perception of justice of non-family workers:

Absolutely nobody has a privilege here. When you go to our manager, he takes care of us even though we are not members of the family. No extra privilege is given to a family member for any extra salary or other social rights. As I said, this is a situation caused by our boss. So, our manager never gives any privilege to anyone.

DISCUSSION

With the changes and developments in the business world, the importance of human capital owned by organizations has increased in obtaining a competitive advantage. Today's businesses offer innovation and creativity-based products and services by taking advantage of employees' intellectual knowledge and experience, rather than standard and mass productions. Hence, it has become more important than ever to attract and retain talented employees in the organization. Nevertheless, whereas much is known about human resource management practices in large organizations, relatively little is known about family firms (Botero & Litchfield, 2013).

Here, the current study enhances our comprehension of human resource practices in the context of family firms. Firstly, we investigated the personnel selection and recruitment processes within the family firms and demonstrated that internet postings are used for personnel selection. Besides, candidates adopt corporate values, have a high sense of responsibility, and open to continuous learning and change. This finding extends past studies. For example, Botero and Litchfield (2013) suggested that family firms mainly use informal recruitment practices. Besides, Sánchez-Marín et al. (2019) revealed that family firms use simple selection processes and selection criteria. However, the current study demonstrated that family firms manage their personnel selection from the formal way as internet postings and use personality tests, language proficiency tests, competency-based interviews in the recruitment.

This study also showed the importance that family firms give to the training and development of employees. While past studies (e.g. Hill & Stewart, 2000) stated that informal, job-oriented, and short-term training is preferred by the family firms, we demonstrated that, contrary to popular belief, education activities in family companies are planned more comprehensively and based on the employee needs. In this context, family firms also organize internal and external training for not job-related development but the professional development of employees. Besides, family firms attach importance to the career development of their employees, and the training programs are planned in a way to contribute employees' career planning in three and five-year periods. Additionally, whereas past studies concluded that family firms determine promotions based on seniority compensations (Gomez-Mejia et al., 2003), we specifically found that employees' performance and customer satisfaction from the employees are the main criteria for the promotion decisions.

Next, this study showed that being a family business has both advantages and disadvantages for organizations. For example, quick decision making, accessibility of the managers, and faster implementation are the advantages of family firms while challenges in the process of institutionalization and conflicts in work-family relationships are disadvantages of the family business. This study further demonstrated the differences in human resource practices of family firms among generations. Results indicated that new generations have more professional perspectives on human resource practices and higher awareness of the importance of human capital. In addition, family firms mainly prevent the discrimination of family members with standard procedures and practices to create justice perceptions in terms of nonfamily employees.

PRACTICAL IMPLICATIONS

High competition and uncertainty in today's business world are a major obstacle for the survival and longevity of the organizations. In this case, the ability of organizations to manage their resources effectively is critical to cope with high competition and uncertainty. The human resources, which is the most important resource of family firms (Sirmon & Hitt, 2003), is also of great importance in gaining competitive advantage.

Based on the findings of the current study, we present practical implications for both practitioners, managers, and family firm owners. Firstly, managers should form human resource practices of the organizations based on professionalism, institutionalization, and formalization for gaining competitive advantage. Managers should also eliminate negative perceptions of employees about the organization. In this context, as we investigated from the cases of our study, managers should prevent differences in terms of human resource practices between family members and non-family members. Additionally, a sense of trust should be created in employees with competency-based career planning. For the longevity of the organizations, managers should plan the career of non-family employees as well as family employees, and provide necessary training and development opportunities and career-enhancing experience.

Managers should also be aware that the existence of family constitutions is critical to ensure transparency and openness within the organization. Besides, a constitution that includes all processes within the organization will enhance the positive perception regard of professionalism, institutionalization, and formalization of the organizations. Besides, managers should also consider employee satisfaction in this process where it is getting harder to retain employees. Managers should ensure that talented employees stay within the organization through producing solutions by the human resources department to issues that cause dissatisfaction. Managers, in this context, should also use external control mechanisms for the human resource practices of the organizations. External mechanisms that control human resources practices such as working conditions, working hours, job security, and salary payments will also create a sense of trust in employees. Finally, attracting, retaining, and motivating human resources through professionalized and formalized practices have a significant impact on gaining a competitive advantage.

LIMITATIONS AND CONCLUSION

There are some methodological limitations to this study. Specifically, we conducted in-depth interviews with human resource managers or general managers of three family firms operating in Turkey. The number of interviews should be increased in future studies to gather more in-depth and comprehensive information. Besides, data saturation should be adopted for the exact number of interviews for the generalizability of the results of the current study.

Furthermore, using a quantitative approach for the data gathering may also extend the current literature. On the other hand, the current study was performed by using Turkish family firms, future studies should be expanded to different cultural contexts. Additionally, the current study was conducted on family firms operating in the manufacturing and service sectors. The researcher may investigate family firms in other sectors to reveal a sectoral basis of similarities and differences in human resources practices.

On the other hand, the current study focused on the family member of the second and third generations. Interviews with members of the former and next generations will provide a broader view of understanding intergenerational differences in human resource practices. Besides, the findings of the research revealed that employees who are not family members have a high perception of justice in family companies. In future research, interviews with non-family employees will reveal more comprehensive findings on whether human resources practices are actually the same for family and non-family members.

To conclude, the current study addressed human resource practices in the context of family businesses. The results demonstrated that family businesses are taking firm steps towards achieving competitive advantage thanks to the professionalization, formalization, and employee-oriented perspective in their human resources practices. The change and evolution from the perspective of human resource management practices among generations have also lead to positive developments in human resources practices. The idea of planning the corporate lives of family members with family constitutions of family companies is also a step to prevent future conflicts. Besides, family firms planning their activities by considering non-family employees has heightened the perception of justice within the organization.

REFERENCES

Arijs, D., Botero, I. C., Michiels, A., & Molly, V. (2018). Family business employer brand: Understanding applicants' perceptions and their job pursuit intentions with samples from the US and Belgium. *Journal of Family Business Strategy*, *9*(3), 180–191. doi:10.1016/j.jfbs.2018.08.005

Astrachan, J. H., & Kolenko, T. A. (1994). A neglected factor explaining family business success: Human resource practices. *Family Business Review*, *7*(3), 251–262. doi:10.1111/j.1741-6248.1994.00251.x

Barney, J. (1991). Firm resources and sustained competitive advantage. *Journal of Management*, *17*(1), 99–120. doi:10.1177/014920639101700108

Barney, J. B., & Wright, P. M. (1998). On becoming a strategic partner: The role of human resources in gaining competitive advantage. *Human Resource Management*, *37*(1), 31–46. doi:10.1002/(SICI)1099-050X(199821)37:1<31::AID-HRM4>3.0.CO;2-W

Bassanini, A., Breda, T., Caroli, E., & Rebérioux, A. (2013). Working in family firms: Paid less but more secure? Evidence from French matched employer-employee data. *Industrial & Labor Relations Review*, *66*(2), 433–466. doi:10.1177/001979391306600206

Blanco-Mazagatos, V., de Quevedo-Puente, E., & Delgado-García, J. B. (2018). Human resource practices and organizational human capital in the family firm: The effect of generational stage. *Journal of Business Research, 84*(July), 337–348.

Botero, I. C. (2014). Effects of communicating family ownership and organisational size on an applicant's attraction to a firm: An empirical examination in the USA and China. *Journal of Family Business Strategy*, *5*(2), 184–196. doi:10.1016/j.jfbs.2014.01.004

Botero, I. C., Astrachan, C. B., & Calabrò, A. (2018). A receiver's approach to family business brands: Exploring individual associations with the term "family firm.". *Journal of Family Business Management*, *8*(2), 94–112. doi:10.1108/JFBM-03-2017-0010

Botero, I. C., & Litchfield, S. R. (2013). Exploring human resource management in family firms: a summary of what we know and ideas for future development. In *Handbook of Research on Family Business* (2nd ed.). Edward Elgar Publishing.

Carrasco-Hernandez, A., & Sánchez-Marín, G. (2007). The determinants of employee compensation in family firms: Empirical evidence. *Family Business Review*, *20*(3), 215–228. doi:10.1111/j.1741-6248.2007.00096.x

Cascio, F. F. (1992). *Managing Human Resources: Productivitiy of Life Profits*. Mc Grill-Hill Company.

Chrisman, J. J., Chua, J. H., Pearson, A. W., & Barnett, T. (2012). Family Involvement, Family Influence, and Family-Centered Non-Economic Goals in Small Firms. *Entrepreneurship Theory and Practice*, *36*(2), 267–293. doi:10.1111/j.1540-6520.2010.00407.x

Chrisman, J. J., Memili, E., & Misra, K. (2014). Nonfamily managers, family firms, and the winner's curse: The influence of noneconomic goals and bounded rationality. *Entrepreneurship Theory and Practice*, *38*(5), 1103–1127. doi:10.1111/etap.12014

Chua, J. H., Chrisman, J. J., & Sharma, P. (1999). Defining the Family Business by Behavior. *Entrepreneurship Theory and Practice*, *23*(4), 19–39. doi:10.1177/104225879902300402

Davis, P. S., & Harveston, P. D. (2001). *The Family Firm: A Cross-Generational Study*. Academic Press.

Dyer, W. G., & Mortensen, S. P. (2005). Entrepreneurship and family business in a hostile environment: The case of Lithuania. *Family Business Review*, *18*(3), 247–258. doi:10.1111/j.1741-6248.2005.00045.x

Erdoğmuş, N., Olcay, G. A., & Erdemir, E. (2017). Building Innovative Strategies for the Competitiveness of Family Firms in Emerging Markets. In Ü. Hacioğlu, H. Dinçer, & N. Alayoğlu (Eds.), *Global Business Strategies in Crisis. Contributions to Management Science*. Springer. doi:10.1007/978-3-319-44591-5_14

Ferraro, H., & Marrone, J. (2016). Examining employment relationship activities in family business research. *Journal of Family Business Management*, *6*(3), 210–224. doi:10.1108/JFBM-01-2016-0001

Gomez-Mejia, L. R., Larraza-Kintana, M., & Makri, M. (2003). The Determinants of Executive Compensation in Family-Controlled Public Corporations. *Academy of Management Journal*, *46*(2), 226–237.

Greene, P. G., & Brown, T. E. (1997). Resource needs and the dynamic capitalism typology. *Journal of Business Venturing*, *12*(3), 161–173. doi:10.1016/S0883-9026(96)00060-2

Guba, E. G., & Lincoln, Y. S. (1982). Epistemological and methodological bases of naturalistic inquiry. *Educational Communication and Technology*, *30*(4), 233–252.

Harris, R. I., Reid, R. S., & McAdam, R. (2004). Employee involvement in family and non-family-owned businesses in Great Britain. *International Journal of Entrepreneurial Behaviour & Research*, *10*(1/2), 49–58. doi:10.1108/13552550410521371

Hill, R., & Stewart, J. (2000). Human resource development in small organizations. *Journal of European Industrial Training*, *24*(January), 105–117. doi:10.1108/03090590010321070

Hoon, C., Hack, A., & Kellermanns, F. W. (2019). Advancing knowledge on human resource management in family firms: An introduction and integrative framework. *German Journal of Human Resource Management*, *33*(3), 147–166. doi:10.1177/2397002219847883

Kidwell, R. E., Eddleston, K. A., & Kellermanns, F. W. (2018). Learning bad habits across generations: How negative imprints affect human resource management in the family firm. *Human Resource Management Review*, *28*(1), 5–17. doi:10.1016/j.hrmr.2017.05.002

King, S. W., Solomon, G. T., & Fernald, L. W. Jr. (2001). Issues in growing a family business: A strategic human resource model. *Journal of Small Business Management*, *39*(1), 3–13. doi:10.1111/0447-2778.00002

Kotey, B., & Folker, C. (2007). Employee training in SMEs: Effect of size and firm type - Family and non-family. *Journal of Small Business Management*, *45*(2), 214–238. doi:10.1111/j.1540-627X.2007.00210.x

Kukulu, K., & Öncel, S. (2009). Factors influencing women's decision to have a home birth in rural Turkey. *Midwifery*, *25*(1), 32–38. doi:10.1016/j.midw.2006.12.009 PMID:17368665

Lin, N., Vaughn, J. C., & Ensel, W. M. (1981). Social resources and occupational status attainment'. *Social Forces*, *59*(4), 1163–1181. doi:10.2307/2577987

Loan Clarke, J., Boocock, G., Smith, A., & Whittaker, J. (1999). Investment in management training and development by small businesses. *Employee Relations*, *21*(3), 296–311. doi:10.1108/01425459910273134

Lubatkin, M. H., Durand, R., & Ling, Y. (2007). The missing lens in family firm governance theory: A self-other typology of parental altruism. *Journal of Business Research*, *60*(10), 1022–1029. doi:10.1016/j.jbusres.2006.12.019

Lune, H., & Berg, B. L. (2017). *Methods for the Social Sciences* (Global Edition).

Michiels, A., Voordeckers, W., Lybaert, N., & Steijvers, T. (2013). CEO compensation in private family firms: Pay-for-performance and the moderating role of ownership and management. *Family Business Review*, *26*(2), 140–160. doi:10.1177/0894486512454731

Özcan, G. B. (1995). *Small firms and local economic development: entrepreneurship in Southern Europe and Turkey.* Avebury.

Pittino, D., Visintin, F., Lenger, T., & Sternad, D. (2016). Are high performance work practices really necessary in family SMEs? An analysis of the impact on employee retention. *Journal of Family Business Strategy*, *7*(2), 75–89. doi:10.1016/j.jfbs.2016.04.002

Poza, E. J. (2013). *Family Business*. South-Western Cengage Learning.

Reid, R. S., & Adams, J. S. (2001). Human resource management-a survey of practices within family and non-family firms. *Journal of European Industrial Training*, *25*(6), 310–320. doi:10.1108/03090590110401782

Sánchez-Marín, G., Meroño-Cerdán, Á. L., & Carrasco-Hernández, A. J. (2019). Formalized HR practices and firm performance: An empirical comparison of family and non-family firms. *International Journal of Human Resource Management*, *30*(7), 1084–1110. doi:10.1080/09585192.2017.1289547

Sieger, P., Zellweger, T., Nason, R. S., & Clinton, E. (2011). Portfolio entrepreneurship in family firms: A resource-based perspective. *Strategic Entrepreneurship Journal*, *5*(4), 327–351. doi:10.1002ej.120

Sirmon, D. G., & Hitt, M. A. (2003). Managing Resources: Linking Unique Resources, Management, and Wealth Creation in Family Firms. *Entrepreneurship Theory and Practice*, *27*(4), 339–358. doi:10.1111/1540-8520.t01-1-00013

Tokarczyk, J., Hansen, E., Green, M., & Down, J. (2007). A resource-based view and market orientation theory examination of the role of "familiness" in family business success. *Family Business Review*, *20*(1), 17–31. doi:10.1111/j.1741-6248.2007.00081.x

Ulrich, D., & Lake, D. G. (1990). *Organizational capability: Competing from the inside out*. John Wiley & Sons.

Yalçınkaya, T., & Durcan, N. M. (2011). The Institutional Basis of the Socioeconomic Situation of Turkey in The Context Of Globalization. *Uludağ Üniversitesi İİBF Dergisi*, *30*(1), 95–112.

Yamagishi, T., Jin, N., & Miller, A. S. (1998). In-group bias and culture of collectivism. *Asian Journal of Social Psychology*, *1*(3), 315–328. doi:10.1111/1467-839X.00020

Chapter 2
Control and Commitment HRM Systems in SME Family Firms:
A Qualitative Study of Hybrid Forms

Daniela Gauci Borda
School of Management, University of Bath, UK

Nina Katrin Hansen
https://orcid.org/0000-0002-7913-1331
Chemnitz University of Technology, Germany

Julie Gore
https://orcid.org/0000-0003-1758-2871
School of Management, University of Bath, UK

ABSTRACT

Strategic HRM research in small and medium-sized enterprise (SME) family businesses still remains in its infancy. This chapter reports one of the first exploratory qualitative empirical studies in this field. Thirteen semi-structured interviews with managers and directors from SME family firms in Malta were completed. The empirical findings show that there is a variety in the implementation of different combinations of HRM practices on the spectrum between control and commitment HRM. Adapting a strategic HRM framework resulted in identify the potential of two new hybrid systems: the "selective" control and the "informal" commitment HRM systems. The findings shed light on the importance of context in implementing an effective HRM system. Furthermore, the authors derive relevant practical implications including the identification of key areas for potential improvement of HRM systems adopted by SME family businesses.

DOI: 10.4018/978-1-7998-4814-1.ch002

INTRODUCTION

In the field of strategic human resource management (HRM), research on HRM systems and firm performance has a long standing tradition (Lepak, Liao, Chung & Harden 2006; Jiang et al., 2012; Jackson et al., 2014). From a 'holistic' perspective on strategic HRM, 'best' HRM practices can be seen as the source of a firm's competitive advantage but rather specific bundles of internally aligned and synergetic HRM practices which are combined in a coherent HRM system (e. g. Arthur, 1992; e. g. Delery & Doty, 1996; Ichniowski, Shaw & Prennushi, 1997). Different types of HRM systems are, thereby, often depicted on a dyadic spectrum: With one side representing a control HRM systems and the other side representing a commitment HRM systems (e.g. Walton, 1985; Arthur 1994; Lepak & Shaw, 2008).

However, despite the extensive research on and the empirical evidence of the relevance of HRM systems, research on the specific characteristics of HRM systems and how they operate in specific empirical contexts remains underdeveloped (e.g. Jiang et al., 2012). Recent studies have questioned whether this spectrum of opposing HRM systems is "too narrowly defined" in that it fails to consider the many hybrid forms of HRM systems adopted in practice (Hauff, Alewell & Hansen, 2014, p.437). Especially empirical research that identifies these hybrid forms is very rare (e.g. Su & Wright, 2012; Hauff et. al., 2014): central examples that discuss hybrid forms are, Su and Wright (2012) who studied a hybrid HRM system between control and commitment in the Chinese context as well as Hauff, Alewell and Hansen (2014) who analyzed control and commitment HRM practice in the German context looking at four major industries (chemicals and pharmaceuticals, mechanical engineering, banking and insurance, and professional services).

Research has also opposed Walton's (1985) initial assumption that all firms will move towards commitment HRM systems, as findings still identify organizations that implement control HRM systems (Hauff et al., 2014). Additionally, studies call for more research on the internal and external factors that influence the effectiveness of HRM systems (Alewell & Hansen, 2012). Two central factors that are found to influence the HRM systems adopted by organizations are the size (Sels et al., 2006; Fabi, Raymond & Lacoursière, 2007) and owner structure of the firm (Hauff et al., 2014; Bello-Pintado & Garcés-Galdeano, 2017). Therefore, the context of SME family businesses could be a very interesting field of study viewed through a strategic HRM lens.

This chapter focuses upon the relevance *for* and specificity *of* strategic HRM in SME family businesses. The authors note that the HRM practices adopted in small and medium-sized enterprise (SME) family businesses are found to be different than those adopted in large organizations (Cassell et al., 2002) and non-family firms (Bacon & Hoque, 2005; Dekker et al., 2013). In fact, it is often assumed that practices adopted in large organizations can be applied within smaller organizations as smaller firms gain legitimacy by implementing larger firm HRM systems (Rauch & Hatak, 2016). However, this approach fails to value the uniqueness of small firms (Cassell et al., 2002; Hornsby & Kuratko, 2003). This study will contribute to the insight available on the HRM systems in SMEs by providing further clarity on the main characteristics of the HRM systems adopted in this context. SME family businesses are also unique in their abundant presence in economies and in the way they are run (Storey et al., 2010; Combs et al., 2018). In the European economy, SMEs are found to play a crucial role as 99% of businesses in the European Union fall under this category (European Commission, 2018). SMEs are seen as the foundation of a healthy economy (Matlay, 2002; Kachaner, Stalk & Bloch, 2012; Başkurt & Altindağ, 2017) and critical in generating employment (Duréndez, Madrid-Guijarro & García-Pérez-de-Lema, 2011; Neckebrouck, Schulze & Zellweger, 2018).

Notably, for readers interested in a highly focused perspective on family firms, Hoon, Hack and Kellermanns (2019) special issue sheds light on the importance of ownership of family firms, non-family employees and the role of human resource professionals. The authors suggest that our work complements this body of work and adds a potential different (strategic) lens to further scholarship in this area.

The empirical study reported in this chapter was conducted in the European member state of Malta where 98% of all businesses are SMEs and where this sector accounts for 80% of local employment (PwC Malta, 2016). A vast majority of SMEs are thereby family-owned (Matlay, 2002). This is also the case in Malta, which means that SME family businesses are considered a critical pillar and driver of the local economy (PwC Malta, 2016)

Against this theoretical backdrop, we examine and pose the following research question: *What are the main characteristics of HRM systems in SME family businesses and do these HRM practices resemble control, commitment or hybrid HRM systems?*

THEORETICAL CONTEXT

Control vs. Commitment HRM Systems as Central Concepts of Strategic HRM

A key attribute of the field of strategic HRM is the focus on the concept of HRM systems rather than individual HRM practices (Lepak et al., 2006; Jiang et al., 2012). The idea behind the systems perspective is that HRM practices are often not implemented in isolation, therefore, one must consider the impact of a set of HRM practices on organizational performance as complementary HRM practices may be more effective at achieving HRM and organizational objectives (Jiang et al., 2012). The distinction between control and commitment HRM systems can thereby be seen as the most prominent dichotomy in the early stages of strategic Human Resource Management research (Lepak, Liao, Chung & Harden 2006).

Control systems reward employees based on measured outputs and allow for compensation to be based on the idea of "a fair day's pay for a fair day's work" (Walton, 1985, p. 78). This HRM system is also characterized by simple, well-defined jobs which require minimum training, minimal experience and low skill demands (Lepak et al., 2006). Hauff et al. (2014) find that high control systems often implemented in firms with small HRM departments - that do not adopt a strategic role - and where the same HRM practices are used for all employees.

In comparison, the commitment HRM system aims to align employee objectives with organizational objectives (Arthur, 1994). In this way, trust is built between management and employees as autonomy is provided, through self-regulation, which motivates employees to work in line with organizational objectives (Walton, 1985; Lepak & Shaw, 2008). This shifts more responsibility into the hands of employees and encourages employee participation in decision-making with frequent communication between management and employees. Commitment HRM systems are built on the concept of "getting more from workers by giving more to them" (Baron & Kreps, 1999, p. 189). High-commitment systems include practices such as selective recruitment of skilled employees looking to remain with the firm in the long-term and extensive training programs that allow for opportunities to move up within the firm (Hansen & Alewell, 2013; Hauff et al., 2014). An emphasis on work-life balance has also recently been associated with commitment HRM systems models (Marchington et al., 2016).

Hauff et al. (2014) highlight that firms with high commitment systems often have strategic HRM departments with varying HRM practices for different employees. Baron and Kreps (1999) identify that it is not only the HRM system that varies between organizations, but also the HRM practices making up the system that also differ which gives rise to hybrid systems. These systems are often referred to as "hybrid" HRM systems (Lepak & Snell, 1999; Su &Wright, 2012). Hybrid systems can also be understood as the degree to which high commitment systems are implemented (Wood & de Menezes, 1998). The objective should be to find a balance between the two systems depending on the organization's context (Koopman, 1991). Studies also identify that HRM practices implemented under control and commitment HRM systems could even complement each other (Gustafson, 2013; Shaozhuang et al., 2016). There is an abundance of evidence in literature supporting the use of hybrids.

HRM in SME Family Firms

In this context SME's are identified as enterprises with "fewer than 250 persons and which have an annual turnover not exceeding EUR 50 million, and/or an annual balance sheet total not exceeding EUR 43 million" (European Commission, 2003, p.4). Although the definition of a family business varies in the literature, this business structure can be defined as "businesses in which families play a significant ownership or managerial role" (Gomez-Mejia et al., 2007, p. 107). Definitions also make reference to the family being involved in the firm's governance and owning over 50% of the firm's equity (Anderson & Reeb, 2003; Blanco-Mazagatos, de Quevedo-Puente & Delgado-García, 2018). So we can say that a SME family business has less than 250 employees and is owned and governed by the founding family members. Empirical evidence shows that *the size* of an organization influences the choice and kind of the implemented HRM system (Jackson & Schuler, 1995; de Kok & Uhlaner, 2001; Hornsby & Kuratko, 2003; Sels et al., 2006; Fabi et al., 2007). Therefore we assume that the smaller size of the SMEs will have a strong influence on whether a control or a commitment HRM systems or even a hybrid form will be implemented.

Overall, SMEs are often viewed as being at a disadvantage in comparison to larger firms (Cassell et al., 2002) and HRM systems in SMEs are found to be less developed and less formal than those in larger organizations (Cassell et al., 2002; Matlay, 2002; Hornsby & Kuratko, 2003; Bacon & Hoque, 2005; Storey et al., 2010). Yet the adoption of strategic HRM practices is found to result in more successful SMEs (Zheng, Morrison & O'Neill, 2006; Sels et al., 2006; Fabi et al., 2009; Samnani & Singh, 2013; Rauch & Hatak, 2016). In fact, Kim and Gao's (2010) study on family firms in China highlights firm size as a large determinant of formalised HRM systems within family firms.

Another factor that influences the type of HRM system implemented in an organisation is *owner structure* (Kopriva & Bernik, 2009; Kim & Gao, 2010; Hauff et al., 2014; Bello-Pintado & Garcés-Galdeano, 2017). Family ownership is often used to partly explain the variations in HRM systems adopted in SMEs (de Kok, Uhlaner & Thurik, 2006). Such businesses are found to implement informal and unprofessional HRM practices when compared to those adopted by non-family firms (Reid & Adams, 2001; Bacon & Hoque, 2005; de Kok et al., 2006; Storey et al., 2010). Family firms are said to adopt less professional HRM systems due to reduced organizational resources and capabilities (Reid & Adams, 2001) and the small size of the majority of family firms (de Kok et al., 2006). Additionally, owners of family businesses often have a lot of control of the firm (Bello-Pintado & Garcés-Galdeano, 2017), therefore, the adoption of structured HRM systems is restricted as this would mean less control over the business by the owners (Dekker et al., 2013). Previous research confirms the use of informal HRM systems in family firms despite studies confirming the importance of HRM in achieving organizational performance in family businesses (Carlson, Upton & Seaman, 2006; Kim & Gao, 2010; Stewart & Hitt, 2012; Başkurt

& Altindağ, 2017). Formal HRM systems are said to be important for family firms to achieve consistent and equal practices amongst employees (Kim & Gao, 2010). Mustafa et al. (2018) suggest that a balance needs to be found between formal and informal HRM practices in order to keep non-family employees motivated and committed to the firm.

The influence of a firm's age on the HRM system adopted is linked to owner structure (Rauch & Hatak, 2016). This is tied to the generational stage of a family business which is found to influence the objectives of the firm (Dekker et al., 2013; Blanco-Mazagatos, de Quevedo-Puente & Delgado-García, 2018). Studies show that firms with predefined HRM systems, such as those passed down from previous generations, are less likely to adopt commitment-based HRM systems (Baron & Kreps, 1999; Hauff et al., 2014). Having said this, previous studies highlight that new generations could bring in new approaches to HRM: Especially since new generations are more likely to have attained tertiary education (Reid & Adams, 2001).

Control and Commitment HRM Practices in SME Family Businesses

Previous studies on SMEs (e.g. Cassell et al. (2002) as well as Zheng, Morrison & O'Neill (2006)) show that SMEs often feature HRM practices of a commitment HRM system, such as decentralized decision making, training practices, selective recruitment and more responsibility in the hands of employees . On the contrary, the SME sector is also found to be characterized as having informal recruitment practices, underdeveloped training practices and employees that are not viewed as valuable assets but replaceable assets (Bacon & Hoque, 2005) which represent features of a control-oriented HRM system. Moreover, studies indicate that owners/managers of small businesses tend to retain the role of making final decisions with the majority resisting the delegation of responsibility and restricting access to information (Matlay, 2002). The previous literature highlights the various HRM practices adopted in SMEs, possibly implying a number of varying hybrids used within the sector, as SMEs are found to "pick and mix" HRM practices rather than employ a strategic HRM system (Cassell et al., 2002, p. 687). SMEs do not consider internal fit as the impact of new HRM practices on the overall system is not considered (Cassell et al., 2002). This is despite findings confirming that fit is equally important in SMEs (Sels et al., 2006; Samnani & Singh, 2013). However, Fabi, Raymond & Lacoursière (2007, 2009) in their studies on HRM bundles in SMEs identify that such firms are likely to have effective HRM systems even though this is not done with a strategic intention.

In analyzing the literature on HRM practices adopted in family firms, similarities to control and commitment HRM systems can also be found. Reid and Adams (2001) in their study on family businesses in Northern Ireland highlight that it is less likely for family firms to invest heavily in training, employ a human resource manager and provide compensation based on merit. Moreover, family firms are identified as adopting less training activities (Matlay, 2002), putting minimal emphasis on qualifications and experience (de Kok et al., 2006) and offering reduced wages and benefits (Neckebrouck, Schulze & Zellweger, 2018). Hauff et al. (2014) find that the majority of SME family businesses in their German sample adopt a high control HRM systems. This is supported by Başkurt and Altindağ (2017), who identify that the supervision approach in family businesses shows similarities to the control HRM system.

On the contrary, other studies find commitment features such as high trust between management and employees and an emphasis on long-term employees (Kachaner, Stalk & Bloch, 2012) in family firms. Previous studies also highlight that less monitoring is needed in family firms (de Kok et al., 2006), due to the participation of family employees in daily tasks (Bello-Pintado & Garcés-Galdeano, 2017). Additionally, family firms have also been found to give more responsibility to their employees, emphasize communication and encourage employee discretion (Chrisman, Chua & Litz, 2004). Despite these comparisons, Bello-Pintado & Garcés-Galdeano (2017) find that strategic HRM systems are less likely to be adopted in family firms than non-family firms. However, empirical studies confirm that organizational performance of family firms could be enhanced by giving importance to the fit of practices and the context of the family business (Bello-Pintado & Garcés-Galdeano, 2017; Hedberg & Luchak, 2018). Against this background, this qualitative empirical study aims to extend the literature on strategic HRM in family businesses by enhancing insight on HRM systems adopted by this context.

Table 1. Details of Sample

Interviewee	Company	Position	Employees	Generation	Years in Operation (Company)
Interviewee 1	Company A	Director	15	3rd	91
Interviewee 2	Company B	Director	24	2nd	34
Interviewee 3	Company C	Director	20	1st	34
Interviewee 4	Company D	Director	20	2nd	44
Interviewee 5	Company E	Director	20	4th	131
Interviewee 6	Company F	Marketing Executive	100	4th	153
Interviewee 7	Company G	Director	16	2nd	39
Interviewee 8	Company H	Co-Founder	30	1st	5
Interviewee 9	Company I	HR Manager	158	2nd	46
Interviewee 10	Company J	Director	148	2nd	35
Interviewee 11	Company K	Director	90	1st	30
Interviewee 12	Company L	Sales Manager	10	1st	8
Interviewee 13	Company M	Director	19	2nd	55

RESEARCH METHOD, DESIGN & PROCEDURE

Following Bacon and Hoque's (2005) guidance on research with SME's, we purposively selected thirteen organizations located in Malta. Organizations were all SME family businesses. SMEs are identified based on the number of employees, annual turnover and balance sheet total. Since the sample included private firms, access to financial statements was restricted. For this reason, sample members were defined as businesses with less than 250 employees. Participating firms also had to fit the criteria in order to be classified as a family business. These criteria were also adopted by other studies looking into HRM in family businesses (Reid & Adams, 2001; Carlson et al., 2006; Bello-Pintado & Garcés-Galdeano 2017; Mustafa et al., 2018; Blanco-Mazagatos, de Quevedo-Puente & Delgado-García, 2018).

Industries from which the sample was selected were limited to three sectors; wholesale and retail sector, industrial goods sector and the service sector. Variations in the sample members were limited to the generation and years in operation of the family business as seen in Table 1. The sample size was based on the suggestion that twelve interviews are said to be sufficient when the aim of a study is to gain insight on a common perception or experience (Guest, Bunce & Johnson, 2006). Thirteen one-to-one, face-to-face semi-structured interviews were conducted with managers or directors from SME family businesses to gain detailed insight on the HRM systems adopted in these firms. Interviews lasted approximately 45 minutes and often took place at the offices of the interviewee. Details of the study were sent to the participants prior to the interview so they could be prepared to discuss the subject area. A pilot study was also conducted prior to the collection of data to ensure the questions were clear and understandable. Participants were left to talk openly about the subject area in order to facilitate relevant insights (Alvesson, 2003).

DATA ANALYSIS

Once the data was collected via the semi-structured interviews, the process of thematic analysis was adopted to analyse it - by "encoding qualitative information" (Boyatzis, 1998, p.4). Our interpretist approach was non-linear, generating themes and codes using an inductive approach which included firstly understanding and becoming familiar with the data collected (Boyatzis, 1998). This was done by recording the interviews as they were conducted and transcribing the interviews manually soon after they were completed. Secondly, we coded the transcription data by highlighting potential themes and useful insights with Nvivo 10, as Boyatzis (1998) reports, to enhance the process of coding discussing with other individuals ensures clarity and consistency. Author coder inter-rater reliability was Kappa 0.70.

The next step in the process of analysis includes the identification of relationships within the coded data to form predominant themes (Braun & Clarke, 2006). Themes are the ideas and subjects that are found to be recurring in the data collected (Bryman & Bell, 2015). Transcript summaries and memos about potential themes and patterns in the data were recorded in a notebook to help with this process. The final step in the process of thematic analysis involves refining the themes and structuring the coded data under specific themes. This step includes identifying the final themes and analyzing the data within each theme.

FINDINGS

Inductive thematic analysis resulted in the identification of four main themes. The themes include:

- the varying forms of hybrid HRM systems,
- employee selection and development in SME family businesses,
- characteristics of a unique family culture and
- the role of SHRM in SME family businesses.

Theme 1: Varying Forms of Hybrid HRM Systems

When analyzing the specific HRM practices adopted by each SME family business it became evident that every firm adopted a unique form of HRM system. Table 2 highlights key characteristics of commitment HRM systems mentioned frequently in the literature and provides information on the practices adopted in SME family businesses.

Table 2. Characteristics of HRM Systems Adopted

Company	Broadly Defined Jobs	Selective Recruitment	Extensive Training	Decentralised Decisions	Above Average Wage	Long-term Perspective	Team Based Compensation
Company A	✓	✓	✗	✗	✗	✓	✗
Company B	✓	✓	✓	✓	✓	✓	✓
Company C	✓	✓	✗	✗	✓	✓	✓
Company D	✓	✓	✗	✗	✗	✓	✗
Company E	✓	✓	✗	✗	✗	✓	✗
Company F	✓	✓	✓	✓	✗	✓	✓
Company G	✓	✓	✓	✗	✗	✓	✗
Company H	✓	✓	✓	✗	✓	✗	✓
Company I	✗	✓	✓	✓	✗	✓	✓
Company J	✓	✓	✗	✗	✗	✓	✗
Company K	✓	✓	✗	✓	✓	✓	✓
Company L	✓	✓	✗	✗	✗	✓	✗
Company M	✓	✓	✗	✗	✗	✓	✗

It shows that that the majority of SME family businesses interviewed adopted a *hybrid* HRM system that include characteristics from both control and commitment HRM systems (Su & Wright, 2012). In fact, as supported by the quotations, participants often shared the view that it is difficult for them to categorize their HRM approach as either control or commitment HRM systems as they believed their HRM configuration fits somewhere in the middle which highlights the importance of hybrid HRM systems:

I.1: "I guess in certain aspects we do have a little bit of both."

I.4: "I think we take characteristics from both. I do not know if it should be like that."

I.9: "I say we are a bit of both, I cannot say we are black or white at all... it is never going to be so clear cut."

Despite the uniqueness of each HRM system adopted, control or commitment patterns were evident in the implemented hybrid HRM systems. Six out of the thirteen participants adopted a hybrid HRM system which was *control-oriented* with minimal training, centralized decision making, average wages and individual-based compensation. However, at the same time, the companies also adopted *commitment-oriented* HRM practices such as selective recruitment, broadly defined jobs and a long-term employment perspective for their employees. This hybrid was common in older generation firms who had been in operation for over thirty years. All companies interviewed adopted a long-term perspective with their employees, except the youngest company in the sample who said "we like fresh blood; the firm needs fresh blood" (I.8). Other participants made it clear that they searched for employees who will remain with them in the long-term and went on to identify employees who had been with them from the start.

I.1: "We have people who have joined the company at sixteen and retired with the company... We look for them to join us and stay with us forever."

I.7: "We take pride in the fact that we have employees who have been with us from the start... We have employees who have been with us for thirty-eight years. We want employees to stay for the long-term. It keeps the family vibe."

I.9: "The people we choose we choose because we believe they can grow within the company. I do not want someone coming in and leaving after two years."

Despite efforts to retain employees for the long-term, participants also realized that employees are no longer looking for a "job for life", therefore, finding long-term employees has become more of a challenge. Participants describe how employees today, "move on as soon as they find something better" (I.1). Another common characteristic of commitment HRM systems that the majority of participants related to are broadly defined jobs. Many stated that due to the small size of the firm, employees would often take on multiple roles rather than remain within the context of their job description. One respondent summarized the general view by stating: "everyone has to be willing to take on other jobs" (I.4).

The *commitment-oriented* approach was particularly common in the majority of family firms that are in their first generation. Having said that, the generation, years in operation and number of employees did not determine the HRM system adopted as the hybrids varied. In fact, two firms with over one hundred employees who were both in their second generation and had been over thirty years in operation were found to adopt differing HRM systems. The difference was that the firm with the low skilled employees was found to adopt more of a control-oriented approach while the company with highly skilled employees adopted more of a commitment-oriented approach. Despite participants limited knowledge of HRM systems each company was found to adopt a unique hybrid HRM system that fits well with their context.

However, while some showed wishful intentions to grow to be more commitment-oriented, others highlighted their doubts about the effectiveness of the commitment approach.

I.2: "I am not so convinced that it is the best but I would like to think that that is what works."

I.9: "I think it would work with some people and groups but it would not work with others."

I.10: "It would be ideal but economically it is difficult to implement."

Theme 2: Employee Selection and Development in SME Family Businesses

A common characteristic of SME family businesses' HRM systems is that the majority of participants identified employees as valuable assets. This is found to oppose the concept of the control HRM system in which employees are viewed as easily replaceable (Lepak et al., 2006). Participants frequently highlighted the idea that employees are the foundation of the business and its success.

I.6: "They are seen as very valuable assets. No one is easily replaceable. It is hard to find good people."

I.8: "Human resources are the most important thing for us. Without our people we are nothing."

I.9: "I think employees are the company, without employees the company would not have got to where we are today."

In line with this view, companies included in the sample unanimously agreed that their HRM system included selective recruitment, which is a feature of commitment HRM systems (Hansen & Alewell, 2013). Participants emphasized the importance of finding the right candidates that fit into the organization's culture:

I.1: "We are very careful who to choose because we want to make sure we have people who have our beliefs in terms of how to treat customers, what sort of service to give etc. They also need to fit in with the rest of the team otherwise the clashes, being so small, can sometimes cause problems."

I.9: "It is not about filling the gap but making sure the person has the right cultural fit."

Despite the efforts to be selective, a common challenge mentioned by all participants was the difficulty associated with finding talented people. One respondent went on to compare the difficulty in finding new recruits to "looking for free gold" (I.11). Although efforts to be selective are emphasized within the companies, they are sometimes limited to how selective they can be - given the limited pool of candidates. One respondent stated that in certain cases they "just have to close an eye and hope for the best" (I.2) when the choice of applicants is limited. Others mentioned that despite the limited pool they were still "picky" (I.9) with their recruits. Additionally, the level of investment in employees' training and development, as part of firms' HRM systems, varied considerably amongst the companies interviewed. Some participants realized the lack in formal training and the need to invest further:

I.1: "There isn't a very long term strategy of what training we need it is a little bit of management by crisis."

I.9: "We are not dedicating enough time to training and development within the company. It does not mean it is non-existent it just means it could be improved and developed so much more."

In fact, many interviewees responded to the questions on training by explaining that their training was limited to new employees shadowing another employee who had been with the firm for longer. As seen in Table 2, the level of training adopted by companies acted as a determining factor on whether the company adopted a more *control* or *commitment-oriented* HRM system. Although employees are valued within SME family businesses, which can be seen through the common implementation of selective recruitment, the development of employees is restricted: due to limited progression opportunities and lack of training seen in most companies in this sector.

Theme 3: Characteristics of a Unique Family Culture

Through the interviews conducted, it became clear that SME family businesses had a unique culture that portrays an evident family feeling. This resulted in a number of common characteristics that resemble features of the control and commitment HRM systems. Such characteristics were found not to have been implemented intentionally but occur as a result of being a SME family business. A unique feature that is shown through the data collected is that employees are often described as part of the "extended" family of the owners of the business. Interviewees also went on to state that their role in the business was more than just a job.

I.6: "I think that we are like a family here, everyone feels quite loyal to the company, especially when they have been here for quite a long period of time."

I.7: "The employees become part of our family… we will go the extra mile or ten miles to help them."

I.10: "It is like a duty more than a job… it is a responsibility."

This family culture results in limited supervision, high trust and a workforce that goes beyond their contract duties willingly, which are all characteristics of the *commitment-based* HRM system (Walton, 1985). Participants stated that they often did not use strict supervision, as adopted under a control HRM system, as it is a common occurrence that directors would be working alongside employees given the size and structure of the firms: "we are with them on the shop floor so to say on a daily basis" (I.1). One respondent argued that this approach would not be found in larger organizations. Strict supervision is also not required as employees are loyal to the firm and are trusted to "make decisions in line with company objectives" (I.2). The following quote sums up the general feel of the majority of SME family firms interviewed:

I.6: "We are like a family here. Everyone pulls the same rope. So we help each other out even if it is not in our job description, all hands on deck sort of thing… They are not expected to go beyond their job description but they do it out of their own free will."

This family culture also shows a critical characteristic from the control HRM system as due to the family structure the majority of participants identified their HRM approach with centralized decision-making. In fact, in the majority of cases employees were not involved in strategic decisions: "decision making is more in the hands of the family members… the final decision is always ours" (I.5). Additionally, as a result of this family culture, the companies included in the sample all adopted an informal HRM approach in which HRM decisions are taken on a "case by case basis" (I.1). Due to their small size, limited resources and specific management style, the informal approach was identified as a key feature influencing the HRM systems adopted by SME family businesses.

I.2: "It is informal cause of the size, limited resources, and apart from that because we are so small it is more like a family so you cannot really be that formal you know… People are not just numbers, they become friends. It becomes more difficult to use procedures with people that you have known for a very long time… It is not because we resist formal approaches it is just very difficult to implement."

I.3: "I think it is underdeveloped because it is our approach more than anything… Even the staff feel much more comfortable with an informal approach… and happier staff means a better environment at work."

Participants agreed that employees preferred an informal approach and becoming more formal in their HRM would alter the culture and employer reputation of the firm. One respondent went on to say a "balance" (I.11) had to be found between formal and informal HRM systems. While some participants were "happy and comfortable" (I.7) with the informal approach adopted, stating it was "good enough" (I.11), others recognized the need to be "more formal in the future" (I.5). The only company that adopted a more formalized approach was found to have the largest number of employees in the sample and the only company to have an HR manager employed.

In discussing future HRM systems, responses shed light on the different perspectives to change each company had. Some companies said change was difficult in family firms because HRM approaches were passed on from past generations. These participants described family businesses as being "stuck in our way" (I.7); with one director summing up a common perception that it was difficult to "let go of the way I know" (I.13). Change was found to be especially challenging with employees who have been with the firm for a long time as it was difficult to change the way they are treated after many years. One respondent expressed their frustration at trying to change their method of performance appraisal stating that "everyone wants to stick to the same one" (I.6). On the contrary, other interviewees acknowledged the developments achieved with each new generation.

I.1: "I am pretty sure it has changed from past generations. I mean till a couple of years back we would have never done something like performance appraisal. Even just a simple interview, in the early days, one would just get someone who would recommend his son or something and you just employ without actually doing a formal selection and recruitment procedure. Today that has changed."

I.9: "It has changed a lot, HR has only formally existed as a department for five years, since I joined. Before it was there on a needs basis."

In fact, the majority of participants agreed that younger generations coming into the firm brought in new ideas on HRM with some linking these changes to younger generations attaining more education.

I.1: "With the family members being more educated and knowing more about certain HRM practices I am pretty sure they would try and implement them in the business."

I.3: "Yes, we are always open to new ideas… I do not have any formal education while younger generations are all going into tertiary education."

I.13: "I think a lot of change comes from education as my son has a lot of knowledge which we do not have".

Theme 4: The Role of SHRM in SME Family Businesses

On the whole, participants had a very basic understanding of SHRM. In fact, twelve out of the thirteen interviewees stated that they did not have an HR manager which often meant that the role was taken on by the directors or managers within the firm who did not have any HRM expertise. Some participants highlighted the challenges that this approach brings with it, stating that the ideal situation would be to "have a person who is handling HR who is separate from the family" (I.2). In fact, the same respondent went on to say it was very difficult to become more formalized in their HRM approach as a director could not go from being informal with an employee on one day to being formal the next day. Another interviewee highlighted that with managers handling HRM, employees had no one to turn to if they had a problem with their manager. On the contrary, some of the participants did not see the need for an HR manager given their size and limited resources.

I.4: "Being small, we do not feel we need an HR manager."

I.5: "I know HR is important, but indirectly there is a cost to employ someone for HR. For our company, 20 people, I do not think it is worth the cost. It is better to pass on the cost to increase the wages of the employees."

On the subject of SHRM, participants lacked knowledge on internal fit, which refers to the alignment of HRM practices (Jiang et al., 2012). Interviewees stated that HRM functions were often seen separately rather than as part of an integrated HRM system. In fact, many had not given much thought to whether HRM functions were aligned.

I.6: "I do not think we look at HR functions all together. I do not think we are that structured... That is why we would need an HR manager to fit everything together."

I.13: "We see them as very separate functions. Again I am not saying it is right. Do not forget we do not have any HR expertise in here, I do not have anyone who studied on HR. Very often we do things the way we know."

Additionally, it was recognized that certain companies distinguished between the HRM systems adopted for certain groups of employees (as suggested by Lepak & Snell (1999; 2001) in their HR architecture concept). However, this was not done with a strategic intention. Participants stated that they naturally have a different approach with different employees depending on how long they have been with the firm, the nature of their job, whether employees are skilled or unskilled and how critical employees are to the company. In fact, one respondent stated that control-oriented HRM systems were adopted with junior staff while commitment-oriented HRM systems were implemented for more senior positions. Participants also sometimes distinguished between family and non-family employees stating that:

I.7: "There will be preference to family members as our aim is to keep the company within the family."

I.10: "Family members like me, my father and my sister are treated differently because we are part of the ownership."

I.12: "Family members are not treated the same they are on a higher level. The company will become theirs eventually."

In other companies it was found that no distinction was made between family and non-family employees as this would cause conflicts. One respondent summed up this perspective by stating that "just because your name is on the door means nothing here" (I.9). In fact, participants highlighted that family employees were sometimes treated worse than non-family employees as they were expected to set an example.

I.1: "There is no HR relation within family. We only look after HR when it is in relation to employees. You never try to see if family is happy or not."

I.3: "Family is treated the same if not worse. They do not get better treatment, on the contrary, it is a point that when they come to work here they are not family. It has to be done."

I.6: "Family and non-family are treated exactly the same. They are very strict on that actually... family, if anything, may be treated worse because we are an example so we need to set standards."

Despite participants' limited understanding of SHRM, the majority of interviewees emphasized that human resources were considered a strategic factor within the firm. In fact, HRM was described as "one of the main pillars" of the business. They also agreed that perhaps a more formalized approach could positively impact their organizational performance. Others contradicted this view stating that they believed their informal approach worked well for their current needs. This view is also supported by the significant number of years the majority of the sample have been in operation as seen in Table1. The years in operation indicate that the organizations survived despite having an informal HRM approach. Having said this, many participants admitted that their HRM systems could be further improved. Interviewees also considered that such improvements could result in an enhanced overall organizational performance. In fact, many were open to try new HRM approaches but also emphasized that they would need to consider the cost and resources needed to implement these approaches.

I.1: "We have realized more and more how important HR is to the company so we are trying to give it a bit more of a formal approach... Yes, I am keen to try new HR approaches depending on how much they cost."

I.6: "I definitely consider HR at one of the highest levels. I think that people, your human resources, are the most important resource that we have. I definitely think that it needs to be given more importance in here."

I.9: "There is always room to improve and develop in... It is not perfect so yes I would try other approaches."

I.12: "It is informal perhaps it needs to be better as we said, there are areas to improve on but you have to have the time and you have to have the resources as well."

Discussion

Despite the abundance of HRM systems identified in the literature (Guest, 2011), the distinction between control and commitment HRM systems remains most relevant in understanding HRM systems adopted by organizations (Lepak et al., 2006). Thereby, previous authors have often posed the idea that commitment-based HRM systems are going to replace traditional, more control-focused HRM systems over time (Walton, 1985). This argument is based on studies that have provided empirical evidence that commitment-based HRM systems positively impact organizational performance (Arthur, 1994; Delery & Doty, 1996). Early studies have also questioned whether control-oriented systems are effective in today's dynamic business environment (Walton, 1985). Contrary to these ideas, Hauff, Alewell & Hansen (2014) in their recent study on HRM systems identify many organizations in the German context that still adopt a high-control system. In fact, the universal view of high-commitment HRM systems has been criticized for the high related costs and the possibility of the commitment system to fail within certain contexts (Baron & Kreps, 1999; Guest, 2011). Against this theoretical background, this empirical study contributes to the literature on strategic HRM by acknowledging whether this evident shift in HRM systems has occurred amongst SME family businesses.

Our study contributes to the literature in three central ways: *First*, against the background of only a few studies on hybrid HRM systems we contribute to the current HRM literature by identifying two new hybrid forms: the *selective* control HRM system and the *informal* commitment HRM system. The first hybrid HRM system is characterized by control features identified in the previous literature such as lack of training, average wages, individual compensation and centralized decision-making (Arthur, 1994; Walton, 1985). These features are seen to be adopted alongside commitment characteristics of selective recruitment, long-term employment relationships and broadly defined jobs (Hansen & Alewell, 2013; Verburg et al., 2007). This hybrid system, labeled *the selective control HRM system*, shows similarities to Hauff et al.'s (2014) long-term-oriented control system in that it aims to achieve long-term relationships with employees despite adopting a control-oriented system. Having said this, the selective control system differs from the long-term-oriented control system in that it does not include substantial investments in continuous training. On the contrary, training efforts were described as underdeveloped and not extensive. The second HRM hybrid system evident in our sample is labeled *the informal commitment HRM system*. This HRM system is a result of the unique family culture evident in a significant proportion of the SME family businesses included in the sample. The family culture means employees are treated as part of the family with directors often working alongside employees. This results in employees being seen as "valuable assets" and, therefore, priority is given to selective recruitment and long-term employment. The family culture shows similarities to findings on family firms in the literature in that results depict high trust and limited supervision of employees (de Kok et al., 2006; Kachaner, Stalk & Bloch, 2012). This is the result of loyal employees who work together towards organizational objectives. Besides employee commitment, this also results in the willingness of staff members to go beyond their contract duties. These are all features of the commitment-oriented HRM system (Walton, 1985). However, results show that despite the commitment-oriented approach, decisions are still held in the hands of the family, therefore, this HRM system incorporates centralized decision making which is a feature of the control HRM system (Walton, 1985). A distinct aspect of this hybrid HRM system is that it encompasses an informal approach to HRM with limited formal HRM structures implemented.

Previous empirical studies highlight the role of context in this regard: Su and Wright (2012), for example highlight the use of hybrid systems in Chinese- firms as being more effective than commitment-oriented HRM systems. Additionally, Gustafson (2013) identifies varying degrees to which control and commitment HRM systems are applied in organizations in the travel industry in Sweden. Indeed, Hauff et al. (2014) go on to identify two HRM hybrid systems - long-term-oriented control system and regulated commitment system, - along with the high control and the high commitment HRM systems within a large sample of German firms from different industries. The variety of responses from interviewees in our study resulted in evident similarities to hybrid HRM systems that feature characteristics from the control and commitment HRM systems (Lepak & Snell, 1999; Su & Wright, 2012). Findings support the idea that organizations adopt their own version of HRM systems to fit their unique context (Hauff et al., 2014). In fact, many participants agreed with Koopman's (1991) argument that it is not easy to relate specifically to control or commitment since their HRM system adopted features from both. Amongst the variety of hybrid HRM systems implemented by the SME family businesses in the sample, distinct commonalities were also recognized. The two new hybrids identified within the context of SME family businesses substantiate the argument that the control-commitment spectrum fails to acknowledge the many varying forms of hybrid HRM systems implemented in practice (Hauff et al., 2014).

Second, we add to the previous HRM literature by analyzing specific bundles of HRM practices in the field of SME and family business thereby taking into account the specific internal and external factors of this type of firms such as their size and ownership structure. Although family businesses are significantly discussed in the literature due to their critical role in economies globally (Carney et al., 2015), only a few studies focus on the HRM approach of family firms (Astrachan, 2010; Dekker et al., 2013; Combs et al., 2018). Although the sector acts as a pillar for many economies, the current literature on this topic remains sparse and fails to provide sufficient insights on HRM within this business sector to assist managers in this field (Matlay, 2002; Carlson et al., 2006; Hedberg & Luchak, 2018).

Pioneering studies on HRM systems have thereby focused on large organizations (Arthur, 1994; MacDuffie, 1995; Delery & Doty, 1996; Huselid, 1995) with little emphasis on SMEs (Carlson et al., 2006). Additionally, research in the field of SME family businesses has focused on individual HRM practices rather than the HRM systems adopted by this sector (Fabi et al., 2007). Despite the evidence that the adoption of HRM practices is found to be critical to the survival and competitiveness of SME family businesses, the HRM practices adopted remain underdeveloped when compared to non-family enterprises (Bacon & Hoque, 2005; Dekker et al., 2013). In fact, the SME family business sector remains challenged by HRM issues, such as attracting and retaining employees (Carlson et al., 2006). Many authors have called for increased studies in this sector due to the lack of current research (Hornsby & Kuratko, 2003; Astrachan, 2010). This study, therefore, responds to the many calls for further research in the area of HRM systems in SME family businesses (Astrachan, 2010; Daspit et al., 2018).

The main characteristics common in the majority of SME family businesses included in the sample both contradict and support previous studies conducted in this field: SME family businesses interviewed support the idea that rather than adopting a strategic HRM system, SMEs "pick and mix" HRM practices to make up an HRM system (Cassell et al., 2002, p. 687). The majority of findings contradict Zheng, Morrison & O'Neill's (2006) conclusions that SMEs are often characterized by decentralized decision making and extensive training practices. On the contrary, findings support results depicting underdeveloped training practices (Reid & Adams, 2001; Bacon & Hoque, 2005; Kopriva & Bernik, 2009) and centralized decision-making (Matlay, 2002) in SME family businesses. This study opposes the belief that family businesses adopt comprehensive control HRM systems (Hauff et al., 2014) as the majority of participants in the sample identified with hybrid HRM systems. Results also contradict Walton's (1985) vision that all firms will adopt commitment HRM systems. A significant number of participants related with Carlson, Upton and Seaman (2006) as well as Kachaner, Stalk and Bloch (2012) in that selective recruitment and long-term employment relationships are given priority within family firms. To summarize, our study sheds light on the varying combinations of HRM practices along the control-commitment spectrum in SME family businesses. In fact, the many years in operation of the firms included in the study indicate that characteristics from the control and commitment HRM systems can successfully complement each other (Gustafson, 2013; Shaozhuang et al., 2016).

Third, we offer one of the first qualitative empirical studies on the topic of HRM system hybrids. All previous studies on hybrid HRM systems are quantitative in nature. With our study we respond to calls for more qualitative research, both in strategic HRM in general (Samnani & Singh, 2013) as well as in research on SME and family firms in specific (e.g. Reid et al., 2002). Whilst we recognize that any generalizability is not possible from our study we suggest that it provides qualitative insights showing how hybrid HMR systems are evident in SME family businesses in Malta. It would be interesting to replicate the study in similar European countries to look for more detailed comparative data.

Notably, the sample of the study is also made up of private SME family businesses. Future research could explore whether findings such as loyal employees and a family culture are also evident in large family firms and public family firms. Such studies will contribute to the literature by gaining insight into the whole population of family firms. Moreover, insight into family firms can be further extended by conducting a longitudinal study, rather than a cross-sectional study. This perspective could shed light on the evolution of HRM systems adopted in family firms over different generations.

An area that would also benefit from further exploration is the effect of other contextual factors, besides size and owner structure, such as technology, culture and life-cycle phase on the HRM systems adopted by businesses (Jiang et al., 2012).

REFERENCES

Alewell, D., & Hansen, N. K. (2012). Human Resource Management Systems – A Structured Review of Research Contributions and Open Questions. *The German Journal of Industrial Relations*, *19*, 90–123.

Alvesson, M. (2003). Beyond Neopositivists, Romantics, and Localists: A Reflexive Approach to Interviews in Organisational Research. *Academy of Management Review*, *28*(1), 13–33. doi:10.5465/amr.2003.8925191

Anderson, R. C., & Reeb, D. M. (2003). Founding-Family Ownership and Firm Performance: Evidence from the S&P 500. *The Journal of Finance*, *58*(3), 1301–1328. doi:10.1111/1540-6261.00567

Astrachan, J. H. (2010). Strategy in Family Business: Toward a Multidimensional Research Agenda. *Journal of Family Business Strategy*, *1*(1), 6–14. doi:10.1016/j.jfbs.2010.02.001

Bacon, N., Ackers, P., Storey, J., & Coates, D. (1996). It's a Small World: Managing Human Resources in Small Businesses. *International Journal of Human Resource Management*, *7*(1), 82–100. doi:10.1080/09585199600000119

Bacon, N., & Hoque, K. (2005). HRM in the SME Sector: Valuable Employees and Coercive Networks. *International Journal of Human Resource Management*, *16*(11), 1976–1999. doi:10.1080/09585190500314706

Başkurt, G., & Altindağ, E. (2017). The Impact of Institutionalization of Family Business on Strategic Human Resources Management and Company Performance. *Business Management Dynamics*, *7*, 10–25.

Bello-Pintado, A., & Garcés-Galdeano, L. (2017). Bundles of HRM Practices in Family and Non- Family Firms: The Impact on Enhancing Performance. *International Journal of Human Resource Management*, 1–22.

Boyatzis, R. E. (1998). *Transforming Qualitative Information: Thematic Analysis and Code Development*. SAGE Publications.

Braun, V., & Clarke, V. (2006). Using Thematic Analysis in Psychology. *Qualitative Research in Psychology*, *3*(2), 77–101. doi:10.1191/1478088706qp063oa

Bryman, A., & Bell, E. (2015). *Business Research Methods* (4th ed.). Oxford University Press.

Carlson, D. S., Upton, N., & Seaman, S. (2006). The Impact of Human Resource Practices and Compensation Design on Performance: An Analysis of Family Owned SMEs. *Journal of Small Business Management*, *44*(4), 531–543. doi:10.1111/j.1540-627X.2006.00188.x

Carney, M., Van Essen, M., Gedajlovic, E. R., & Heugens, P. P. M. A. R. (2015). What Do We Know About Private Family Firms? A Meta-Analytical Review. *Entrepreneurship Theory and Practice*, *39*(3), 513–544. doi:10.1111/etap.12054

Cassell, C., Nadin, S., Gray, M., & Clegg, C. (2002). Exploring Human Resource Management Practices in Small and Medium Sized Enterprises. *Personnel Review*, *31*(6), 671–692. doi:10.1108/00483480210445962

Chua, J. H., Chrisman, J. J., & Bergiel, E. B. (2009). An Agency Theoretic Analysis of the Professionalized Family Firm. *Entrepreneurship Theory and Practice*, *33*(2), 355–372. doi:10.1111/j.1540-6520.2009.00294.x

Combs, J. G., Jaskiewicz, P., Shanine, K. K., & Balkin, D. B. (2018). Making Sense of HR in Family Firms: Antecedents, Moderators, and Outcomes. *Human Resource Management Review*, *28*(1), 1–4. doi:10.1016/j.hrmr.2017.05.001

Corbin, J., & Strauss, A. (2015). *Basics of Qualitative Research: Techniques and Procedures for Developing Grounded Theory* (4th ed.). SAGE Publications, Inc.

Daspit, J. J., Madison, K., Barnett, T., & Long, R. G. (2018). The Emergence of Bifurcation Bias from Unbalanced Families: Examining HR Practices in the Family Firm Using Circumplex Theory. *Human Resource Management Review*, *28*(1), 18–32. doi:10.1016/j.hrmr.2017.05.003

de Kok, J. M. P., Uhlaner, L. M., & Thurik, A. R. (2006). Professional HRM Practices in Family Owned Managed Enterprises. *Journal of Small Business Management*, *44*(3), 441–460. doi:10.1111/j.1540-627X.2006.00181.x

Delery, J. E. (1998). Issues of Fit in Strategic Human Resource Management: Implications for Research. *Human Resource Management Review*, *8*(3), 289–309. doi:10.1016/S1053-4822(98)90006-7

Delery, J. E., & Doty, D. H. (1996). Modes of Theorizing in Strategic Human Resource Management: Tests of Universalistic, Contingency, and Configurational Performance Predictions. *Academy of Management Journal*, *39*(4), 802–835. doi:10.5465/256713

European Commission. (2018). *What is an SME?* Retrieved June 23, 2018, from https://ec.europa.eu/growth/smes/business-friendly-environment/sme-definition_en

Fabi, B., Raymond, L., & Lacoursière, R. (2007). HRM Practice Clusters in Relation to Size and Performance: An Empirical Investigation in Canadian Manufacturing SMEs. *Journal of Small Business and Entrepreneurship*, *20*(1), 25–40. doi:10.1080/08276331.2007.10593384

Fabi, B., Raymond, L., & Lacoursière, R. (2009). Strategic Alignment of HRM Practices in Manufacturing SMEs: A Gestalts Perspective. *Journal of Small Business and Enterprise Development, 16*(1), 7–25. doi:10.1108/14626000910932854

Gomez-Mejia, L. R., Takacs Haynes, K., Nunez-Nickel, M., Jocobson, K. J. L., & Moyano-Fuentes, J. (2007). Socioemotional Wealth and Business Risks in Family- Controlled Firms Evidence from Spanish Olive Oil Mills. *Administrative Science Quarterly, 52*(1), 106–137. doi:10.2189/asqu.52.1.106

Guest, D. (2011). Human Resource Management and Performance: Still Searching for Some Answers. *Human Resource Management Journal, 21*(1), 3–13. doi:10.1111/j.1748-8583.2010.00164.x

Guest, G., Bunce, A., & Johnson, L. (2006). How Many Interviews Are Enough? An Experiment with Data Saturation and Variability. *Field Methods, 18*(1), 59–82. doi:10.1177/1525822X05279903

Gustafson, P. (2013). Control and Commitment in Corporate Travel Management. *Research in Transportation Business & Management, 9*, 21–28. doi:10.1016/j.rtbm.2013.03.002

Hansen, N. K., & Alewell, D. (2013). Employment Systems as Governance Mechanisms of Human Capital and Capability Development. *International Journal of Human Resource Management, 24*(11), 2131–2153. doi:10.1080/09585192.2012.725071

Hauff, S., Alewell, D., & Hansen, N. K. (2014). HRM Systems Between Control and Commitment: Occurrence, Characteristics and Effects on HRM Outcomes and Firm Performance. *Human Resource Management Journal, 24*(4), 424–441. doi:10.1111/1748-8583.12054

Hedberg, L. M., & Luchak, A. A. (2018). Founder Attachment Style and its Effects on Socioemotional Wealth Objectives and HR System Design. *Human Resource Management Review, 28*(1), 33–45. doi:10.1016/j.hrmr.2017.05.004

Hoon, C., Hack, A., & Kellermanns, F. W. (2019). Advancing Knowledge on Human Resource Management in Family Firms: An Introduction and Integrative Framework. *German Journal of Human Resource Management, 33*(3), 147–166. doi:10.1177/2397002219847883

Hornsby, J., & Kuratko, D. (2003). Human Resource Management in U.S. Small Businesses: A Replication and Extension. *Journal of Developmental Entrepreneurship, 8*, 73–92.

Huselid, M. A. (1995). The Impact of Human Resource Management Practices on Turnover, Productivity, and Corporate Financial Performance. *Academy of Management Journal, 38*, 635–672.

Jackson, S. E., & Schuler, R. S. (1995). Understanding Human Resource Management in the Context of Organizations and Their Environments. *Annual Review of Psychology, 46*(1), 237–264. doi:10.1146/annurev.ps.46.020195.001321 PMID:19245335

Jackson, S. E., Schuler, R. S., & Jiang, K. (2014). An Aspirational Framework for Strategic Human Resource Management. *The Academy of Management Annals, 8*(1), 1–56. doi:10.5465/19416520.2014.872335

Jiang, K., Lepak, D. P., Han, K., Hong, Y., Kim, A., & Winkler, A. L. (2012). Clarifying the Construct of Human Resource Systems: Relating Human Resource Management to Employee Performance. *Human Resource Management Review, 22*(2), 73–85. doi:10.1016/j.hrmr.2011.11.005

Kachaner, N., Stalk, G., & Bloch, A. (2012). What You Can Learn from Family Business. *Harvard Business Review*, *90*, 102–106.

Kim, Y., & Gao, F. Y. (2010). An Empirical Study of Human Resource Management Practices in Family Firms in China. *International Journal of Human Resource Management*, *21*(12), 2095–2119. doi:10.1080/09585192.2010.509619

Koopman, P. L. (1991). Between Control and Commitment: Management and Change as the Art of Balancing. *Leadership and Organization Development Journal*, *12*(5), 3–7. doi:10.1108/01437739110004947

Lepak, D. P., Liao, H., Chung, Y., & Harden, E. E. (2006). A Conceptual Review Of Human Resource Management Systems In Strategic Human Resource Management Research. *Research in Personnel and Human Resources Management*, *25*, 217–271. doi:10.1016/S0742-7301(06)25006-0

Lepak, D. P., Liao, H., Chung, Y., & Harden, E. E. (2006). A Conceptual Review of Human Resource Management Systems in Strategic Human Resource Management Research. *Research in Personnel and Human Resources Management*, *25*, 217–271. doi:10.1016/S0742-7301(06)25006-0

Lepak, D. P., & Shaw, J. D. (2008). Strategic HRM in North America: Looking to the Future. *International Journal of Human Resource Management*, *19*(8), 1486–1499. doi:10.1080/09585190802200272

Lepak, D. P., & Snell, S. A. (1999). The Human Resource Architecture: Toward a Theory of Human Capital Allocation and Development. *Academy of Management Review*, *24*(1), 31–48. doi:10.5465/amr.1999.1580439

MacDuffie, J. P. (1995). Human Resource Bundles and Manufacturing Performance: Organizational Logic and Flexible Production Systems in the World Auto Industry. *Industrial & Labor Relations Review*, *48*(2), 197–221. doi:10.1177/001979399504800201

Marchington, M., Wilkinson, A., Donnelly, P., & Kynighou, A. (2016). *Human Resource Management at Work* (6th ed.). Chartered Institute of Personnel and Development.

Matlay, H. (2002). Training and HRD strategies in Family and Non- Family Owned Small Businesses: A Comparative Approach. *Education + Training*, *44*(8/9), 357–369. doi:10.1108/00400910210449196

Mustafa, M. J., Caspersz, D., Ramos, H. M. L., & Siew, C. M. M. (2018). The Satisfaction of Non-Family Employees with High Involvement HR Practices: Evidence from Family SMEs. *Human Resource Development International*, *21*(3), 163–185. doi:10.1080/13678868.2017.1410005

Neckebrouck, J., Schulze, W., & Zellweger, T. (2018). Are Family Firms Good Employers? *Academy of Management Journal*, *61*(2), 553–585. doi:10.5465/amj.2016.0765

Rauch, A., & Hatak, I. (2016). A Meta- Analysis of Different HR- Enhancing Practices and Performance of Small and Medium Sized Firms. *Journal of Business Venturing*, *31*(5), 485–504. doi:10.1016/j.jbusvent.2016.05.005

Reid, R., Morrow, T., Kelly, B., & McCartan, P. (2002). People Management in SMEs: An Analysis of Human Resource Strategies in Family and Non-Family Businesses. *Journal of Small Business and Enterprise Development*, *9*(3), 245–259. doi:10.1108/14626000210438571

Reid, R. S., & Adams, J. S. (2001). Human Resource Management - A Survey of Practices Within Family and Non- Family Firms. *Journal of European Industrial Training*, *25*(6), 310–320. doi:10.1108/03090590110401782

Sadun, R., Bloom, N., & Van Reenen, J. (2017). Why Do We Undervalue Competent Management? *Harvard Business Review*.

Samnani, A. K., & Singh, P. (2013). Exploring the Fit Perspective: An Ethnographic Approach. *Human Resource Management*, *52*(1), 123–144. doi:10.1002/hrm.21516

Saunders, M. N. K., & Bezzina, F. (2015). Reflections on Conceptions of Research Methodology Among Management Academics. *European Management Journal*, *33*(5), 297–304. doi:10.1016/j.emj.2015.06.002

Sels, L., Winne, S., Delmotte, J., Maes, J., Faems, D., & Forrier, A. (2006). Linking HRM and Small Business Performance: An Examination of the Impact of HRM Intensity on the Productivity and Financial Performance of Small Businesses. *Small Business Economics*, *26*(1), 83–101. doi:10.100711187-004-6488-6

Shaozhuang, M., Silva, M. G., Callan, V. J., & Trigo, V. (2016). Control and Commitment HR Practices, Job Satisfaction and Turnover Intentions: A Comparison Between Local and Multinational Firms in China. *International Journal of Human Resource Management*, *27*(9), 974–990. doi:10.1080/09585192.2015.1052535

Stewart, A., & Hitt, M. A. (2012). Why Can't a Family Business Be More Like a Nonfamily Business? *Family Business Review*, *25*(1), 58–86. doi:10.1177/0894486511421665

Storey, D. J., Saridakis, G., Sen-Gupta, S., Edwards, P. K., & Blackburn, R. A. (2010). Linking HR Formality with Employee Job Quality: The Role of Firm and Workplace Size. *Human Resource Management*, *49*(2), 305–329. doi:10.1002/hrm.20347

Su, Z. X., & Wright, P. M. (2012). The Effective Human Resource Management System in Transitional China: A Hybrid of Commitment and Control Practices. *International Journal of Human Resource Management*, *23*(10), 2065–2086. doi:10.1080/09585192.2011.610335

Wood, S., & de Menezes, L. (1998). High Commitment Management in the U.K.: Evidence from the Workplace Industrial Relations Survey, and Employers' Manpower and Skills Practices Survey. *Human Relations*, *51*(4), 485–515. doi:10.1177/001872679805100403

Zheng, C., Morrison, M., & O'Neill, G. (2006). An Empirical Study of High Performance HRM Practices in Chinese SMEs. *International Journal of Human Resource Management*, *17*, 1772–1803. doi:10.1080/09585190600965282

KEY TERMS AND DEFINITIONS

Commitment System: A human resource management system that encourages autonomy, participation in decision-making, selective recruitment, long-term employment and investments in training and development.

Control System: A human resource management system that emphasizes measured outputs, low skill demands and defined jobs with minimal investment in training.

Family Business: A business structure in which families play an influential role, through ownership or managerial positions.

Human Resource Management System: A combination of human resource practices implemented alongside each other having a collective impact on the achievement of organizational and human resource management objectives.

Hybrid System: A human resource management system that aims to include characteristics from control and commitment systems to find a balance that fits a specific organization.

Small and Medium-Sized Enterprise: An enterprise where staff headcount and turnover or balance sheet total do not exceed certain limits.

Strategic Human Resource Management: An area within human resource management aimed at adapting human resource practices to the internal and external context of an organization.

APPENDIX 1: INTERVIEW QUESTIONS

Introduction

1. What is your position in the firm?
2. How many employees does the firm employ?
3. Are the majority of shares held within the family?
4. Is the family involved in the management of the firm?
5. What generation currently manages the firm?
6. How many years has the firm been in operation?

HRM Approach

7. How would you describe the HRM approach adopted in your firm?
8. Which HRM system do you relate to most – are you more inclined towards control or commitment HRM systems?
9. Do you apply the same HRM practices for all employees?
10. Has your HRM approach been adopted from past generations or has it changed with time?

HRM Practices

11. Do you put a lot of effort into selecting your staff?
12. Can you tell me about your training procedures?
13. How do you compensate your employees?
14. Is performance management based on team or individual performance?

Employee Relationships

15. How would you describe the relationship between employees and managers?
16. Are jobs well-defined and standardised or are employees expected to go beyond their contract duties?

Strategic HRM

17. How do you think being an SME family business effects your HRM approach?
18. Do you have an HRM department or manager?
19. Do you think a more formalised HRM system can improve your organisational performance?
20. Will you consider HRM systems more after this interview?

APPENDIX 2: EMERGENT THEMES FROM TRANSCRIPTS

Table 3.

Interviewee	*Emergent Themes*
Interviewee 1	1. Benefits/disadvantages of SME family businesses 2. Commitment characteristics due to family culture 3. Realizing the importance of HRM 4. Long-term and not defined jobs 5. Informal HRM
Interviewee 2	1. Challenges of SMEs in attracting employees 2. Informal HRM due to family vibe 3. Doubts on commitment HRM system 4. Realizing the importance of HRM 5. Long-term and not defined jobs 6. Realizing the importance of SHRM
Interviewee 3	1. Unique approach to have underdeveloped HRM not because of size or cost 2. Age affects the HRM approach, older staff not used to commitment 3. Family treated worse 4. Family vibe 5. Long term and not defined jobs 6. Training resembles mentoring 7. Disadvantages of family firm, limited career progression 8. More importance given to HRM as the firm grows
Interviewee 4	1. Employees as valuable assets 2. Little knowledge on SHRM and HRM systems 3. Treat employees differently but not done strategically 4. No need for supervision as directors always there 5. Informal HRM works well
Interviewee 5	1. Informal HRM due to size 2. Flexibility in job design is important 3. Challenge to attract people 4. No need for supervision as directors always there 5. Training resembles mentoring 6. Treat employees differently but not done strategically 7. Family vibe
Interviewee 6	1. Problems due to not having an HR manager 2. Realizing need for an HR manager 3. Challenge of attracting employees 4. Family vibe results in commitment 5. Treat employees differently but not done strategically 6. Realizing the need for improving HRM
Interviewee 7	1. Long-term 2. Family vibe and basic approach 3. Difficult to change but new generation bring in new ideas 4. Benefits of a family business 5. Limited career with family business 6. Commitment characteristics due to family culture 7. Centralized decisions 8. No internal fit 9. HR role taken on by directors
Interviewee 8	1. Employer branding 2. Family culture 3. Use of technology in HRM 4. Short term approach

continues on following page

Table 3. Continued

Interviewee	Emergent Themes
Interviewee 9	1. Developed approach and have an HR manager 2. Room to improve 3. Different HRM systems depending on level 4. Associate with hybrid 5. Family treated worse 6. People treated differently cause of the nature of the job
Interviewee 10	1. Doubts on commitment HRM system 2. Challenge to attract people 3. Realising need for improvement 4. Family culture results in commitment in that it is more of a duty than a job 5. Difficult to change
Interviewee 11	1. Benefits of a family business 2. Informal approach is good enough 3. Valuable employees 4. Majority commitment 5. Everyone treated the same 6. HR changes with time 7. Challenge to attract people 8. High trust in employees
Interviewee 12	1. Family treated differently 2. Family vibe 3. Changes brought on by younger generations 4. There can be problems in family businesses 5. Realizing the need for improvement but need resources
Interviewee 13	1. Difficult to change 2. Realizing the need for improvement 3. Family business makes job more of a duty 4. Personal approach to HRM 5. Broadly defined jobs 6. Difficult to attract people

Chapter 3
Human Resources Management and the New Challenges in Family Firms:
An Italian Case Study

Vittorio D'Amato
LIUC-Università Cattaneo, Italy

Elena Tosca
LIUC-Università Cattaneo, Italy

ABSTRACT

We have already entered into the so called VUCA World, a world of tumult, new technologies, and a new generation of employees. HR departments need to revise their mission, vision, strategies, and tools to answer to these new challenges. The main aim of this chapter is to evaluate, through an in-depth bibliographical analysis and an Italian case study, how HR departments can be supported in their strategic reflection by using a structured approach to becoming more effective in this VUCA World. Moreover, the chapter contributes to making HR managers and HR professionals aware of the HR Strategic Forum, a method that could help them to define in a shared way what the main pillars of the HR function are. These mainstays should never be forgotten, especially in times of constant change, such as the ones we are currently experiencing.

INTRODUCTION

The last twenty years have experienced drastic changes in the business environment. New technologies and a new generation of employees are all factors that contribute to what is often called a VUCA world (volatile, uncertain, complex and ambiguous) (Bennet & Lemoine, 2014; Millar, Groth, & Mahon, 2018).

The "V" in the VUCA acronym stands for volatility, indicating the nature, speed, volume, and magnitude of change occurring in an unpredictable pattern.

DOI: 10.4018/978-1-7998-4814-1.ch003

The "U" in the VUCA acronym stands for uncertainty, or the lack of predictability in events. These volatile times make it difficult for managers to use past issues and events as predictors of future outcomes. (As a current example, just think of COVID 19). The only certainty is that future will be different from the past (Birkinshaw, 2010).

The "C" in VUCA stands for complexity. There are often numerous and difficult to understand causes and mitigating factors involved in a problem. This layer of complexity, added to the turbulence of change and the absence of past predictors, adds to the difficulty of decision making.

Finally the A stay for Ambiguity, the lack of clarity about the meaning of an event. Col. Eric G. Kail (2011) defines ambiguity in the VUCA model as the inability to accurately conceptualize threats and opportunities before they become lethal.

These new characteristics of volatility, complexity, uncertainty and ambiguity that are added to the existing competitive dynamics, combined with the typical characteristics of family firms (risk averse, resistance to change, governed by traditions, family first behavior over business), make it increasingly difficult the role of HR department in this kind of company (Schuman, Sage-Hayward, & Ransburg, 2016). Having said that, our research question can be formalized in the following way: How the HR department of a family firm must get transformed in order to become a strategic business partner and contribute in a significant way to the business and the family needs in this new VUCA world? In such a VUCA world, in which for managers and family, strategic decisions are becoming more and more difficult to take, HR department has to redefine its role. It has to change, transforming itself from a mere staff support to an unavoidable partner in building the company future and an architect of the family company where people is fully engaged (Birkinshaw, 2010; De Kok, Uhlaner, & Thurik, 2006).

The HR departments of family companies has to help the entire organization to become more and more adaptable, resilient and innovative in order to maintain a sustainable competitive advantage (Amar, Hentrich, & Hlupic, 2009).

Functional silos have no place in the VUCA world. Managers need to model participative and collaborative behaviour with the strategic partnership of the HR department (Birkinshaw, 2010). As Vlatka Hlupic 2014 says on p. 3 of her book *The Management Shift*: "In traditional managed organizations, structures distribute power and processes distribute tasks. Structures and process are about creating stability, repeatability and predictability, and this is happening in an unstable, chaotic world, which demands innovation. So, we ask people to innovate in a system that is designed to produce the reverse. We cannot then be surprised that many organizations are not utilizing their potential for innovation". Hamel (2012), says that we need now more than ever organizations that allow human begins to do just that. He claims that an organization will never be fully capable unless it's fully human.

Most of the old rules and management models no longer fit in with the new context, where people engagement matter at least as much as, or even more, than solid structures. (Arregle, Hitt, Sirmon, & Very, 2007; Hamel, 2009).

Family firms face an added complexity regarding human resource management in this new VUCA world. In contrast to nonfamily firms, family businesses have many overlapping dimensions and layers of complexity to navigate due to the integration of family, business and ownership systems also for the following reasons (De Kok, Uhlaner, & Thurik, 2006):

- Family businesses often treat employees – whether family or nonfamily – as family, thus putting more attention and pressure on the need to handle HR issues with great care and respect.

- Family dynamics complicate the emotional environment of a family business, and this could add ambiguity over ambiguity.
- The livelihoods and fortunes of business families are often tied up in the enterprises they run, so they need to maximize the value of the business.

The new challenges imposed by the current VUCA world require a rethinking of the HR function of family businesses, which must completely rethink its mission and vision by transforming itself from executors into strategic business and family partners. (Birkinshaw, 2013; Gratton, 2011).

Although very few HR scholars and practitioners have analysed the impact of such a VUCA world on HRM of the family business systems and have studied how the latter have to change to enable employees to work at their best and to be fully engaged, no conclusions on the topic have yet been reached. (Gupta & Sharma, 2016; DeNisi & Murphy, 2017).

All the considered studies are extremely useful to get a complete theoretical overview of the topic, but none of them outlines a concrete action plan, listing the steps which have to be put into practice (Basco & Rodriguez, 2011).

Therefore, the authors will try to contribute to this research debate providing guidance using, with the HR department of an italian family company, a structured approach called Strategic Forum. The Strategic Forum is a method based on an open guided and participative discussion that support the alignment of the various mental models of the people involved and create commitment on strategic decisions (Richmond, 1997).

A gap therefore exists in the managerial literature on this topic. The main aim of this chapter is to help to close this gap, evaluate, through an in-depth bibliographical analysis and an italian case study of a family company (Angelini Group), how the HR department can be supported in its strategic reflection by using a structured approach and become more effective in order to be a real strategic business partner in this VUCA world.

The chapter will be organised as follows. After a brief introduction underlining the main goals of the work, section 2 will conduct a thorough bibliographical analysis in order to collect and review all the most recent, robust and relevant literature contributions on the subject. Section 3 will both describe the adopted methodology and method and give reasons for its use. The findings will be reported in section 4, while the last section contains conclusions and managerial implications.

LITERATURE REVIEW

This new VUCA world has changed the very nature of how HR managers have to work in a strategic partnership with functional managers in order to enable people to do their best and to be fully engaged (Mintzberg, 2013).

The main problem is that the classic Human Resources Management systems, models and practices that have been adopted today by the majority of the organizations are no longer an effective option for coping with this new world. HR managers are struggling with how to properly lead their work in a VUCA world. (Hamel, 2012).

The sad news is that very few organizations are prepared to operate on this higher level of complexity.

Vieira and Dixit (2019), give some general guidelines that organizations and HR department can use to start the transition to a VUCA world:

- Move from a hierarchy to self-organization: Push decisions down to the edge of the organization, where information is the freshest and most salient.
- Move from protecting information to the democratization of information: To empower employees to make decisions, make communication frictionless.
- Speed up interactions: Accelerate the speed of interaction as much as possible. In the VUCA age, speed matters more than perfection.
- Use simple rules to make quick decisions, rather than perfect analysis.

The described socio-economic environment impacts on how the different organizational functions operate. HR departments, in particular in family companies, where the relationships between the management of the firm and the family increase the complexity of organizational and management issues, should revise practices, instruments and tools to face the new challenges and, especially, their mission and vision (Daniels & Whitener, 2000).

While in the last 10 years, many HR scholars and practitioners have demonstrated that HR management practices in family companies are different for a lot of reasons, reported below, there few exist on how HRM of family companies has to change in order to face the new challenges of this VUCA world.

First, family businesses are ubiquitous and so also the challenges they encounter in order to face this VUCA world. While human resources (HR) and talent management are of utmost importance to all firms, the unique interplay of *'family'* and *'business'* systems means family businesses experience multiple, complex, and interrelated issues. Much of the existing scholarly and practitioner literature in the area of family business has focused on topics of succession planning, family relationships and wealth transfer. However, any family business, of any significant size, is reliant on the quality and effectiveness of family and non-family talent to ensure continued success and growth. Despite notable exceptions there is a dearth of knowledge surrounding HR practices and policies in the context of family businesses (Carlson, Upton, & Seaman, 2006; Steier, 2001).

Second, in family companies, ownership and continuity are key features. Conventionally, either an individual founder or the family owns and controls the business because of the lack of boundaries between work and family. The commitment of family employees to the business is shaped by how these members were first introduced to the enterprise and how work responsibilities had been characterized by the previous generation (Kelly, Athanassiou, & Crittenden, 2000). This imprinting which occurs both at the workplace and at home often leads family employees to accept, and not question, the structures and rules established in the family firm (Chami, 1999).

Third, parental altruism is another important phenomenon that can be imprinted within the family and then enter the family firm as a learned behaviour, becoming an element of the firm's culture. Instances of parents being overly generous toward their children can later encourage the children to remain dependent on their parents and shirk their responsibilities within the family firm (Schulze, Lubatkin, & Dino, 2003). Parental altruism can also cause parents to use excessive enticements to retain family members and prevent them from leaving the family firm. Therefore, it appears that parental altruism encourages family firm leaders to manipulate HRM practices to benefit their children who are working in the firm and of course this increase the complexity of managing people (Astrachan & Shanker, 2003).

Fourth, the process by which values and behaviours are transmitted from the parent company to the spinoff can be similar to the way values and behaviours are passed down from parents to their children (Jaskiewicz, Combs, Shanine, & Balkin, 2018). The founding generation imprints key family values on the family and the firm, which may have been beneficial to the success of the family business. The next generation of owners is then faced with keeping those cultural elements that represent positive attitudes, values and behaviours and unlearning those that stand in the way of firm performance.

Trust within the firm enables managers to communicate and collaborate more effectively and facilitates stewardship (Schuman, Sage-Hayward, & Ransburg, 2016).

Furthermore, it may be easier for family firms to establish trusting relationships outside the firm (Miller & Le Breton-Miller, 2016). This is due, in part, to evidence that family firms have higher standards and expectations of maintaining a favourable reputation and are less inclined to act in ways that would violate a business partner's trust. Because the family firm's reputation is closely tied to family members' identities, family firms are less likely to engage in activities that would damage the firm's reputation. As a result, family firms are more attentive toward their business partners and work harder to align their goals with them (Berrone, Cruz, & Gomez-Mejia, 2012).

In addition, family firms show greater interdependence, and a stronger sense of organizational identity than nonfamily firms. A strong organizational identity, coupled with knowledge sharing and open communication within the family, may translate into a sense of confidence in the firm's ability to achieve its goals (De Kok, Uhlaner, & Thurik, 2006).

The specificities analyzed and the competitive forces family firms face today in the new VUCA world, and will continue to face in the future, demand organizational excellence through which HR departments could make a real contribution to the business through their value-added. Unfortunately, many family firms still follow a transactional and administrative role for their HR practices, and eventually their HR departments are viewed as necessary, but not of great value. Due to radical changes occurred in the last decade, HR departments have to redefine first of all their mission and their vision in order to be really an effective strategic partner (Bart, Bontis, & Taggar, 2001).

The main aim of the next section will be to present a rigorous and practical method called Strategic Forum that could of significant help in order to redefine or to analyse how to better structure, share and implement the strategic reflections of the HR people in family companies in order to become really a strategic business and family partners.

This method is particularly suitable for family companies since it helps to promote a long-term view, facilitate the creation of a strong organizational identity and contribute to increasing engagement and knowledge sharing, all elements that characterise a family company.

THE METHODOLOGY AND METHOD

As previously mentioned, the authors used the Strategic Forum, that is a method based on open guided discussions that support the alignment of the various mental models of the people involved. This method has been applied to the HR department of an italian family company, Angelini Group, because the top management of this family company believes in the valuable contribution of all their employees and therefore they asked to the HR department to rethink about its strategic role.

HR department'Angelini Group is an Italian family company, founded 100 years ago. Having a long pharmaceutical tradition, over the years the Group has diversified and extended its business activities into other sectors, including personal care, machinery, perfumery, skincare, and wine.

Angelini Group has been founded by Francesco Angelini in the 1919 with the name ANFERA. It made its mark with the development of a network for delivering medicinal products directly to pharmacies in central-southern Italy, becoming the first Italian distributor in the sector in 1939.

In 1941, the company was dissolved and Francesco Angelini founded ACRAF – Aziende Chimiche Riunite Angelini Francesco. The 1950s brought about hallmark moments to the company's expansion: the decision to move the administrative offices to Rome; the start of marketing for Tachipirina, which still today remains one of the highest-selling drugs in Italy; and the acquisition of FATER, a company engaged in the production of mass-market goods. Angelini invested in pharmaceutical research and began producing its first original and patented molecules. During the same decade, Fater made its way into the homes of Italian families with the Lines brand, revolutionising the country's hygienic-sanitary market with the first disposable baby diapers and feminine hygiene products. In 1972, benzydamine-based Tantum Verde and trazodone-based Trittico arrived on the market. Fameccanica was founded in 1975 in Abruzzo and specialized in the production of machinery for the absorbent hygiene product market. During this period, Angelini expanded beyond its domestic borders: in 1979, Barcelona-based pharmaceutical group Lepori was acquired, marking the beginnings of an international expansion process that began with Spain and Portugal. In 1985, Angelini understood the potential of the analgesic ibuprofen for the Italian market and launched Moment®, an over-the-counter analgesic product specifically for headaches and a prime example, in Italy, of marketing applied to pharmaceutical products. In 1992, Angelini further consolidated its position in the hygienic-sanitary sector through a joint venture with Procter & Gamble for the management of Fater and Fameccanica. In 1994, the group entered the wine sector with the acquisition of three Tuscan wineries: Trerose, Val di Suga and San Leonino; as well as the fragrances market, with the acquisition of the Spanish company Idesa Parfums. In 2000, Angelini acquired Amuchina, a company known for its disinfectant and sanitisers. Fameccanica expanded into China and North America. In the wine sector, the Puiatti and Bertani wineries were acquired.

Today Angelini's turnover is approximately € 1.6 bn. The company has 6,000 employees and a direct presence in 17 countries and runs 11 production sites. Though projected towards the future, it is always proud of the values at the basis of its family business philosophy. Professional skills, competitiveness, involvement, ethics and cooperation at every level are the fundamental values of the corporate spirit that allow the company to respond to internal and external challenges quickly and effectively. It is a clear example of a family business that is conducted very well by its owners and its group of managers; together, they face future challenges with a vision that respects the family values that shaped the organization and which its members still share. Since its origins, the Angelini Group has always believed in people and in building a collaborative and meritocratic environment. Angelini values, ethics and responsibility, performance, innovation, engagement have always guided the strategies of the HR department in its various functions (recruitment & section, training & development, compensation, industrial relations).

These reasons are part of why the group has been listed in the "Great Places to Work" rankings and why it won the "Welfare Award" in 2018. Moreover, Statista, an independent German research institute, ranked Angelini second in its listing of chemical-pharmaceutical companies where employees work best. In addition, Angelini was among the top 20 companies listed in the "Best Employer of Choice" ranking for 2015. The survey was conducted on a sample of 2,500 new graduates by Cesop Communication, an Italian leader in the field of corporate communication services for the recruitment of graduates and young professionals.

Getting back to the methodology, the Strategic Forum, formerly developed by Barry Richmond (Richmond, 1997), works well for a variety of strategic reasons. Due to its structured approach, it is especially suited for situations where the future is full of uncertainty and where multiple scenarios are likely to occur (Vermeulen, 2010). Furthermore, it is convenient to use in organizations where there are different debates occurring about multiple strategies, and where different mental models have to be shared in order to create lasting group decisions; in these cases, the Strategic Forum supports the alignment of the various mental models of the persons involved (Scott, 2019).

It is possible to identify four connected phases at the heart of the Strategic Forum approach:

Phase One: Analysing strategic issues. In order to identify and develop new strategies, the focus at the beginning is on gaining an in-depth understanding of the current and future big issues and challenges that the organization must face, as well as the key elements that will strongly impact overall performance.

Phase Two: Engaging employees and other stakeholders. The success of new strategy implementation is related to how much all the stakeholders are mobilized and committed. For this reason, it is important to involve them in the process, avoiding a top-down approach.

Phase Three: Developing different strategic options and choosing a strategy. With the continuous feedback that characterizes the methodology of the Strategic Forum, all the issues are analysed without fear of judgement in an atmosphere of openness, trust and dialogue.

Phase Four: Implementing and executing the chosen strategy. The commitment built during the previous phases is crucial to the implementation phase. Concrete and clear action plans are made involving all the key players of the processes and/or activities affected.

In the Angelini Group case, the Strategic Forum engaged the entire HR team in a rigorous process designed to align strategy and business processes with stated objectives. It was a chance to better understand how their business functions and to ensure ongoing, internal consistency regarding objectives, strategy, and business processes (Richmond, 1997).

The HR Strategic Forum was a moment of deep reflection: for two days in a residential workshop, all the issues related to the methods and strategies of Angelini's HRM were reconsidered, with all those involved in the process, trying to find innovative solutions to successfully compete in the new VUCA world.

In a family business, there is a special and sensitive relationship between the family and the HR department (Jaskiewicz, Combs, Shanine, & Balkin, 2018). That is why the HR department of the Angelini Group has for several years paid special attention to the definition of its mission, vision and strategic intents, so as to align them, not only with business challenges, but also with the family culture. The result of this strategic discussion is a document summarizing five elements: the mission, the distinctive competencies, the golden rules, the vision and the strategic intents of the HR department. It is important that all the HR managers involved deeply understand the meaning of what has been written and are thoroughly aligned so that they can share the same message throughout all of the Angelini Group's companies. The answer to the need for a more effective and productive process that is able to ensure strategy feasibility is the result of the rigorous Strategic Forum method, which followed specific steps (adapted from Barry Richmond's original method):

Step 1: Choice of the participants

In the first part of the process, about 10 people consisting of all the HR senior managers of the Angelini Group's main member companies were involved. The choice was made so as to integrate the different perspectives and opinions of people working in the HR departments.

Step 2: Individual interviews

With the selected group of people, the authors conducted structured and open-ended interviews.

As the literature suggests (Turner, 2010), an open-ended interview is a methodology used for gathering information while interacting with people. It is considered open-ended because it is based on some defined open questions and the contents of the response may vary from person to person. Open-ended interviews are classified into three groups based on the level of structuring: informal, semi-structured and structured. The authors decided to use the structured type so that the interviewers could only use the same exact questions for each interview. The questions are designed to avoid ambiguity. In addition to meeting the main objective of the interviews, this type of questioning can open up new directions. In this way, interviewers may be able to capture perspectives and opportunities they did not have in mind at the beginning. Participants can also clarify the meaning of their answers and the underlying assumptions. The limitation of this kind of interview is related to the fact that it is quite difficult to have quantifiable data.

The main points of the open-ended interviews that the authors have conducted can be summarized in the following characteristics:

a. **Defined open-ended questions.**
   Questions were sent to the interviewees ahead of the face-to-face interview to allow them to reflect on the issues beforehand. Questions were worded so that respondents could spell out their points usefully. Most of the questions begin with "How," "What" or "Why", giving respondents the freedom to express their answers in their own words, and were designed to find out how people were feeling, as well as what they were thinking.
b. **Semi-structured format.**
   The authors had to pre-plan the key questions in order to clearly understand the phases that these companies had put in place in order to cope in a VUCA world.
c. **Seek understanding and interpretation.**
   During all the interviews, all conducted by two interviewers, the authors used active listening skills to reflect upon what the speaker was saying. The interviewers would then try to interpret what was being said and sought out clarity and understanding throughout the sessions. In conducting this kind of activity, it is also important to hear what is not being said and by whom, as all of this information is useful. Another objective of the interviews is to gain team members' confidence and create the prerequisite for an open and transparent environment, which is a pillar for the success of the Strategic Forum session.
d. **Recording responses.**
   All the interviews lasted between 60 and 90 minutes and were taped and later transcribed.
   The interviewers accompanied the interviewees' responses with written notes, which included real time observations of verbal and non-verbal behaviours, as well as the interviewers' immediate personal reflections about the interview.

Step 3: Strategic Forum planning

Once the interviews had taken place, an analysis of the answers was necessary in order to see if any alignment or differences occurred in considering and interpreting the role and the challenges of the HR department of the Angelini Group.

At this stage, it was possible to create a general Strategic Map of the department; even if it was not used during the Strategic Forum itself, it did function as a reference map for the researchers.

This phase also typically includes the development of a set of exercises that participants will work on (in small groups) during the Forum session.

Step 4: Strategic Forum execution

According to the methodology, and in order to be effective, it is recommended that the Forum takes place off-site so that participants are completely free of distraction to focus on and discuss the issues. The HR Strategic Forum with Angelini's HR managers and their direct reports involved around 40 people; with them, the authors defined the mission, vision, golden rules, distinctive competencies and Strategic Intents of the HR department itself - the key elements of the Strategic Map (D'Amato, 2015).

Mission: a mission statement can be defined as a formal written document aimed at identifying and explaining the unique and enduring purpose of an organization (Bart, Bontis, & Taggar, 2001). Thus, the authors can state that the role of the mission is mainly to explain the purpose and the reason for the existence of the organization or department. Through its mission statement, the department clarifies and describes its identity, the kind of services (at times products) offered, the internal (or even external) customers and the particular methodology or technology that makes it unique. Mullane (2014) argues that in order to be effective, a mission statement should identify the main stakeholders and state the department's dedication to meeting the stakeholder's needs.

Golden Rules: golden rules are the principles that are fundamental to us and inherently desirable, what allows us to state that a certain behaviour or way of being is personally or socially preferable to another. Golden rules are heartfelt, the fundamental concepts at the base of the ideal behaviour. A golden rule is a certainty which comes from within ourselves, a lifestyle, it is a way of being that we would like to transfer to our employees.

Distinctive competencies: the term distinctive competence was first coined by Selznick (1957). It is defined as a capability that is visible to the customer, seen as superior to other firms' competencies, and difficult to imitate. Distinctive competencies help a firm stand out in its markets and are marked by three key attributes: they must be a skill or capability; they must be distinctive, meaning that it must be clear to customers or clients that they offer a superior level of performance; and, last but not least, the competencies must be difficult to imitate (Boyatzis, 2008).

Vision: vision is an idealistic projection of the company or a department in an undefined future. Vision is not a dream; in fact, it is very concrete. It is an idealistic projection of what the company or the team might be and might achieve. The roots of this projected image should be well-defined in the company's current business dynamics (Brătianu & Bălănescu, 2008). Vision is a very strong integrator, for people sharing the same future image will strive to find the best solutions to transform that vision into reality (Levin, 2000).

Strategic intents: strategic intents represent a proactive mode in strategizing. They are a symbol of the organization's determination about the future, and energize all organizational levels for a collective purpose. Strategic intents direct the accumulation of necessary competencies, giving the intra-organizational evolution processes a common target, "something to 'aim' for" (Lovas & Ghoshal, 2000). To achieve the final result of the HR Strategic Forum, it is important that all participants know that they will be challenged and that there is no 'right' or 'wrong' approach. On the contrary, the methodology that will be considered is dialogue, functioning as the pillar of conversation for all members. The first aim is to create the right conditions for exploratory discussions (Bang, Fuglesang, Ovesen, & Eilertsen, 2010) so that dialogue can be used as the type of communication that is able to increase the effectiveness of the teamwork. It should also be kept in mind that business people are not usually accustomed to thinking in the kind of intensely disciplined manner that characterizes most Forum experiences. That is why the role of the facilitator is so important, not only to guide the discussion, but also to observe the dynamics and catch any sign of fatigue, suggesting breaks when needed. Participants should expect that this will be done, and they will be asked to assist in ensuring that it is done effectively.

Four intertwined processes stand at the heart of the approach:

- **Exploring strategic issues:** Before leaders can develop a new strategy, they need to thoroughly understand the big issues that substantially and structurally affect their firm's overarching performance. This process gives them and their stakeholders superior insights into what the real strategic issues are and avoids 'boiling the ocean' with exhaustive and irrelevant analyses.
- **Engaging employees**: The purpose is to mobilise these stakeholders in order to get their commitment and support, and to avoid the weaknesses of a top-down approach and the problems of stakeholder politics.
- **Developing strategic options and choosing a strategy**: The purpose here is to create winning strategies and avoid the black box of strategy development by outlining clear routes to strategic options. Again, business leaders will need to engage stakeholders, including the most critical ones.
- **Executing the chosen strategy:** With this process, leaders want to anticipate and prevent the roadblocks to strategy execution. The authors outline how to deconstruct strategic choices in a set of concrete actions to successfully execute a new strategy, and also how to learn from execution to improve the strategy when needed.

All the elements of the Strategic Map are built by switching between theoretical background, small team activity, plenary presentation and plenary discussion. Working on a small team allows participants to be more likely to open up and overcome some of the risks that come from exposing their ideas to a bigger audience (Men, 2017). In that way, they can present and test their own opinions and points of view with other members of the small group before exposing them to the full team.

At the end of each plenary discussion, a draft of the items analysed is formulated and submitted for team approval. In the discussions, the objective is to make surface the participants' deepest mental models and beliefs. All the flipchart sheets with mission, vision, distinctive competencies, golden rules and strategic intents are taped up and remain visible over the course of the Strategic Forum. This is useful in order to focus and re-focus the discussion, but also to make the process visible.

Step 5: Communication of the results

After the Forum, the authors meet the team for a wrap-up discussion. The aim of this follow-up is to revisit the final output of the HR Strategic Forum: mission, golden rules, distinctive competencies, vision and strategic intents of the HR department. In most cases, there are no significant changes, though there occurs what is generally referred to as "fine tuning". Wording is important, and the researchers have to check that what is written is suited to the intention and organizational language. A final document is drawn up and distributed to the overall population of the HR departments. The booklet contains and summarizes the pillars of the HR department Strategy that were developed

Figure 1. Strategic Map

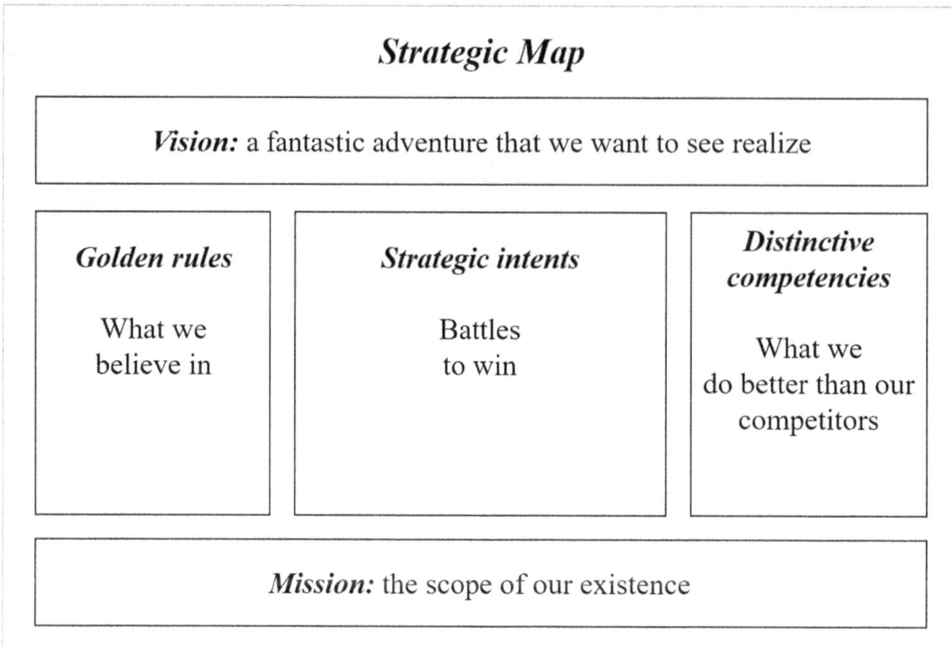

during the Forum. All the statements are explained, in order to ensure a common understanding, and key terms are illustrated so that the meanings are clear and interpreted the same way by all. The authors call this "meaning beyond the words". In literature, much has been said about the importance of language commonality (Schomaker & Zaheer, 2014).

It is shown that language commonality influences the quality of discussions and dialogue: it helps to facilitate sense-making, develop mutual understanding, and reinforce knowledge sharing because it develops shared vision and mutual understanding between people coming from different cultural backgrounds.

Step 6: Implementation of the decisions

Once the Strategic HR Map has been approved and shared, the last phase of the process can begin.

This means that the authors need to transform the strategic intents into operative actions. Thus, strategic intents are translated into strategy objectives with Key Performance Indicators and measurement criteria, and concrete action plans are then developed. According to recent research, companies are increasingly using project management to attain company goals. Effective strategy implementation addresses the fundamental importance of project management. Work through projects facilitates continuous dialogue, communication and coordination during the implementation process, thus increasing the effectiveness of the process itself. Now, more than ever, changes in the environment require a fast response and the ability to adapt quickly (Patanakul & Shenhar, 2012). In addition, strategy implementation with a project management approach increases the possibilities to expand active participation and engagement within the organization. Project leaders and team members are identified, creating the opportunity to broaden the number of parties included in the initiative, while adopting alternative forms of involvement. Internal sponsors – the top managers of the HR department - are defined in order to support the teams and guarantee proper project management (Bryde, 2008). The internal project sponsor role is generally accepted to be held by a person in senior management, in our case from HR, given the level of authority needed to ensure the appropriate and ongoing commitment of resources and to overcome any internal obstacles and resistance. Once the projects and teams have been established, a schedule of follow up meetings is set up. About every month, all the project leaders and sponsors meet to present the progress of their projects. In this way, communication and the exchange of information is guaranteed, and all involved are aligned with the most current status of the situation.

RESULTS

This research differs from previous types due to the fact that, through the analysis of a concrete case study of an italian family company, it provides a practical method to follow, this approach was previously missing from the works of both academia and management.

Our research has identified the pillar elements of the Strategic Map of the HR department of the Angelini Group: mission, vision, golden rules, distinctive competencies and strategic intents using the Strategic Forum Methodology.

Each element answers a fundamental strategic question for the HR department:

- Why do we exist?
- What are our guiding principles?
- What do we do very well that our clients/colleagues appreciate?
- What is our dream?
- What are the battles to win?

Below is an explanation of each element.

Mission

In the final document used to communicate the HR Strategic Map, the mission is defined as the HR department's ultimate aim. It focuses on the present and must clearly define who we are, what we do and why we do it (Bartkus, Glassman, & McAfee, 2006).

The mission of the HR department of the Angelini Group states: "We are business partners in attracting, developing and enhancing people. We are key players in the creation of a unique culture and in organisation development, through integrated tools and systems, in order to support competitiveness and the value growth of our businesses in the world."

In the mission statement, the focus is on the fact that the HR department aims to seek out those people who best meet the needs of the business. It is also committed to defining growth and development paths that enable people to express their full potential.

In addition, it plays a leading role in supporting the Angelini Group to define and spread common behaviour inspired by company values. At the same time, it designs and implements organisational models, procedures and operational mechanisms that are consistent with the changes of the market and the company complexity, contributing to creating a competitive, sustainable advantage.

All members of the HR department are also focused on creating management and development systems and tools that are simple, practical, consistent, innovative and able to communicate with each other.

Figure 2. Strategic Map of the HR department of Angelini Group

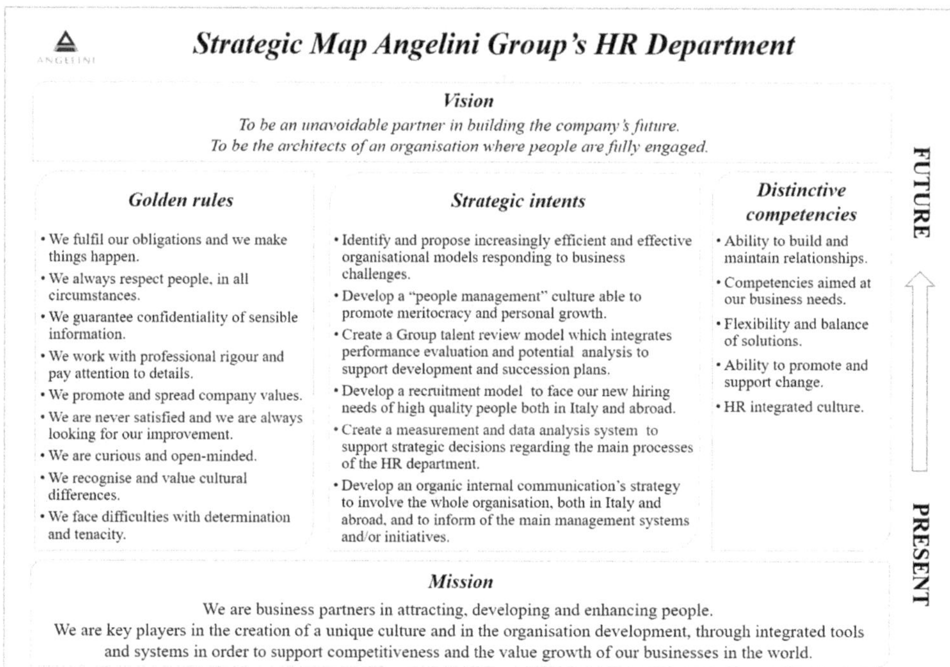

Distinctive Competencies

As said before, the distinctive competencies are the set of knowledge and skills that the HR department possesses in a unique and exclusive way. They allow for distinguishing it from others and to be recognised and appreciated by the entire organization (Boyatzis, 2008).

They answer the question: What do we do very well that our clients/colleagues appreciate? The distinctive competencies of HR department of Angelini Group are:

- Ability to build and maintain relationships.
- Competencies aimed at our business needs.
- Flexibility and balance of solutions.
- Ability to promote and support change.
- HR integrated culture.

The HR department is recognized as formed by genuine and transparent people who inspire trust and are able to build and maintain high quality and long-lasting relationships.

HR people also have in-depth knowledge of the various businesses and are able to satisfy real needs in a proactive way. Colleagues also appreciate the capacity to propose ideas and solutions that can be adapted to various needs but that are consistent with the Angelini Group's policies.

The HR department is seen as being able to support, sustain and encourage people at all company levels and adopt new models and behaviour that are in line with the needs of the business.

On a deeper level, the HR department is valued for its ability to promote a common company culture focused on people, creating a common identity and a sense of HR community.

Golden Rules

The golden rules are defined as the most important types of behaviour that people in the HR department are committed to keeping and respecting, and which align with company ideals and culture, also in order to cope with the new VUCA world.

They lead our actions, both inside our department and in the relationships with other stakeholders, and they allow us to work in an effective, consistent and distinctive way.

They answer the question: what are the "home's rules"?

The golden rules of the HR department are the following:

- We fulfil our obligations and we make things happen.
- We always respect people, in all circumstances.
- We guarantee confidentiality of sensitive information.
- We work with professional rigour and pay attention to details.
- We promote and spread company values.
- We are never satisfied and we are always seeking self-improvement.
- We are curious and open- minded.
- We recognize and value cultural differences.
- We face difficulties with determination and tenacity.

Vision

The vision is defined as the image of the future the HR department wants to build. It is the guiding star that shows the way and steers not only decisions that will have an impact on the future, but also the choices made on a daily basis (Blanchard & Stoner, 2004).

The vision of the HR department of the Angelini Group is: "To be an unavoidable partner in building the company's future. To be the architects of an organization where people are fully engaged."

The vision contains the desire to reach such a rate of expertise and deep knowledge of the environment and its players that it will always enable the HR department to add value.

In their image of the future, the HR people see themselves as the creators and proponents of the best methods and conditions that can respond to the needs of their business and people.

All these things can be achieved with people who are intellectually, emotionally and physically committed to their work and are in a strong relationship with their company.

Strategic Intents

The strategic intents are the macro-objectives that lead the HR department's projects and resources in the near future. They represent the challenges that will channel the energy and commitment.

They answer the question: Which projects/actions will be launched to close the gap between the mission and vision?

The strategic intents of the HR department are to:

- Identify and propose increasingly efficient and effective organizational models that responds to business challenges.
- Develop a people management culture able to promote meritocracy and personal growth.
- Create a group talent review model which integrates performance evaluation and potential analysis to support development and succession plans.
- Develop a recruitment model to face our new hiring needs of high quality people both in Italy and abroad.
- Create a measurement and data analysis system to support strategic decisions regarding the main processes of the HR department.
- Develop an organic internal communication's strategy to involve the whole organization, both in Italy and abroad, and to inform all concerned of the main management systems and/or initiatives.

Several important implications for practitioners might derive from the results of our study. First,

the involvement of the managers and front lines of the HR department from the very beginning to construct the HR Strategic Map contributed significantly to increasing a sense of engagement and responsibility for the project. In fact, to succeed in the implementation of a Strategic Map, it is essential that the key stakeholders participate in its creation. Through the Strategic Forum, employees also look for bosses who care about what employees think and have to say. When their managers listen to them, employees feel important and recognized as being a part of the company, which has a great impact on their level of engagement and, consequently, on performance (Gruman & Saks, 2011). Second, people who take part in the construction of the Strategic Map are more likely to share the results with the whole organization, creating word-of-mouth diffusion. A Strategic Map should be thought of as the path to follow while pursuing the mission, in order to aim at the target represented by the vision. In a few words, a Map helps to reduce the gap between the mission and the vision. Third, an organization, and so its departments, will certainly be subject to continuous change along its journey and may be required to take an alternative route. In this case, a strategic map can be instrumental in selecting, focusing and communicating about which direction to take.

A final mention is due to the learning and growth processes that occur when people are involved in the construction of the Strategic Map, for this action helps its participants to reflect on both the present and the future. In addition, it not only contributes to the development of a short-term vision, but also creates a fundamental perspective to be competitive in a VUCA world.

CONCLUSIONS AND FUTURE IMPLICATIONS

The major bibliographical findings of the study revealed that HR managers in family companies are struggling with how best to be a real business partner in a VUCA world. Most of the old rules and management models, typical of family companies, no longer fit in with the new context (Hamel, 2009). In fact, today numerous companies still use structures, processes, hierarchies and control systems that were invented more than 100 years ago by pioneers of management, such as Frederick Taylor. These systems and structures were fundamentally oriented towards efficiency, reducing production costs and product standardisation. This model of industrial management has been incredibly successful and has contributed to the success of many family companies during the nineteenth and twentieth centuries. However, it is no longer able to function in a dynamic and hypercompetitive business world (Birkinshaw, 2010). Leading and managing this VUCA world requires a different HR management approach in order to be capable of quickly sensing and responding to changes in the business environment and that can enable employees to develop to their full potential and to be fully engaged. Many HR scholars and practitioners have analysed the impact of such a VUCA world on HRM systems and practices of family business and how they have to change in order to enable employees to work at their best and to be fully engaged. However, no practical conclusion had been reached. Therefore, by using a structured approach called Strategic Forum, the authors have tried to contribute to this research debate providing guidance to define what HR managers must actually do in order to cope in this VUCA environment. Due to its structured and engaging method, the Strategic Forum is especially suited to issues where the future is full of uncertainty, where multiple scenarios are likely to occur and where different mental models have to be shared.

The Strategic Forum helps create lasting group decisions by supporting the mental models of participants to become more aligned. As the authors have described in this chapter, the final result of the Forum is a shared strategic map that contains all the strategic elements (mission, vision, distinctive competencies, golden rules) and challenges (strategic intents) that the HR department of an Italian family company, Angelini Group, will face in the next future, in order to be a valuable strategic business partner.

Finally, this work contributes to a broader research agenda that recognises, in family businesses, the importance of applying, not only to the HR department but also to the others, the Strategic Forum as a method able to contribute to a deep strategic reflection in order to become a real partner of the business and of the family.

ACKNOWLEDGMENT

The authors thank the Angelini Group and in particular the HR department for allowing the use of the results of the HR Strategic Forum.

REFERENCES

Amar, A. D., Hentrich, C., & Hlupic, V. (2009). To Be a Better Leader, Give up Authority. *Harvard Business Review*, *87*(12), 22–24. PMID:19968054

Arregle, J. L., Hitt, M. A., Sirmon, D. S., & Very, P. (2007). The Development of Organizational Social Capital: Attributes of Family Firms. *Journal of Management Studies*, *44*(1), 73–95. doi:10.1111/j.1467-6486.2007.00665.x

Astrachan, J. H., & Shanker, M. C. S. (2003). Family Businesses' Contribution to the U.S. Economy: A Closer Look. *Family Business Review*, *16*(3), 211–219. doi:10.1177/08944865030160030601

Bang, H., Fuglesang, S. L., Ovesen, M. R., & Eilertsen, D. E. (2010). Effectiveness in top management group meetings: The role of goal clarity, focused communication, and learning behavior. *Scandinavian Journal of Psychology*, *51*(3), 253–261. doi:10.1111/j.1467-9450.2009.00769.x PMID:20132458

Bart, C. K., Bontis, N., & Taggar, S. (2001). A model of the impact of mission statements on firm performance. *Management Decision*, *39*(1), 19–35. doi:10.1108/EUM0000000005404

Bartkus, B., Glassman, M., & McAfee, R. B. (2006). Mission statement quality and financial performance. *European Management Journal*, *24*(1), 86–94. doi:10.1016/j.emj.2005.12.010

Basco, R., & Rodriguez, M. J. P. (2011). The Cognitive Legitimacy of the Family Business Field. *Family Business Review*, *24*(4), 322–342. doi:10.1177/0894486511416356

Bennet, N., & Lemoine, G. J. (2014). What VUCA Really Means for You. *Harvard Business Review*, *92*(1-2), 27.

Berrone, P., Cruz, C., & Gomez-Mejia, L. R. (2012). Socioemotional Wealth in Family Firms: Theoretical Dimensions, Assessment Approaches, and Agenda for Future Research. *Family Business Review*, *25*(3), 258–279. doi:10.1177/0894486511435355

Birkinshaw, J. (2010). The critical need to reinvent management. *Business Strategy Review*, *21*(1), 4–11. doi:10.1111/j.1467-8616.2010.00636.x

Birkinshaw, J. (2013). *Becoming a better boss*. Jossey-Bass.

Blanchard, K., & Stoner, J. (2004). The Vision Thing: Without It You'll Never Be a World-Class Organization. *Leader to Leader*, *31*(31), 1–8. doi:10.1002/ltl.59

Boyatzis, R. (2008). Competencies in the 21st century. *Journal of Management Development*, *27*(1), 5–12. doi:10.1108/02621710810840730

Brătianu, C., & Bălănescu, G. V. (2008). Vision, mission and corporate values. A comparative analysis of the top 50 U.S. companies. *Management & Marketing*, *3*(3), 19–39.

Bryde, D. (2008). Perceptions of the impact of project sponsorship practices on project success. *International Journal of Project Management*, *26*(8), 800–809. doi:10.1016/j.ijproman.2007.12.001

Carlson, D. S., Upton, N., & Seaman, S. (2006). The impact of human resource practices and compensation design on performance: An analysis of family-owned SMEs'. *Journal of Small Business Management*, *44*(4), 531–543. doi:10.1111/j.1540-627X.2006.00188.x

Chami, R. (1999). *What's different about family businesses?* University of Notre Dame Working Paper. University of Notre Dame.

D'Amato, V. (2015). Management Innovation Road Map. Milano: Egea.

Daniels, A. C., & Whitener, B. (2000). *Bringing out the best in people: How to apply the astonishing power of positive reinforcement*. McGraw-Hill.

De Kok, J. M., Uhlaner, L. M., & Thurik, A. R. (2006). Professional HRM practices in family owned-managed enterprises. *Journal of Small Business Management*, *44*(3), 441–460. doi:10.1111/j.1540-627X.2006.00181.x

DeNisi, A. S., & Murphy, K. R. (2017). Performance Appraisal and Performance Management: 100 Years of Progress. *The Journal of Applied Psychology*, *102*(3), 421–433. doi:10.1037/apl0000085 PMID:28125265

Gratton, L. (2011). Workplace 2025: What will it look like? *Organizational Dynamics*, *40*(4), 246–254. doi:10.1016/j.orgdyn.2011.07.002

Gruman, J. A., & Saks, A. M. (2011). Performance management and employee engagement. *Human Resource Management Review*, *21*(2), 123–136. doi:10.1016/j.hrmr.2010.09.004

Gupta, N., & Sharma, V. (2016). Exploring Employee Engagement – A Way to Better Business Performance. *Global Business Review*, *17*(3), 45–63. doi:10.1177/0972150916631082

Hamel, G. (2009). Moon Shots for Management. *Harvard Business Review*, *87*(2), 91–98. PMID:19266704

Hamel, G. (2012). *What Matters Now. How to Win in a World of Reletless Change. Ferocious Competition, and Unstoppable Innovation*. Jossey-Bass.

Jaskiewicz, P., Combs, J. G., Shanine, K. K., & Balkin, D. B. (2018). Making Sense of HR in Family Firms: Antecedents, Moderators, and Outcomes. *Human Resource Management Review*, *28*(1), 1–4. doi:10.1016/j.hrmr.2017.05.001

Kail, E. G. (2011). *Leading Effectively in a VUCA Environment: A is for Ambiguity*. Retrieved from https://hbr.org/2011/01/leading-effectively-in-a-vuca-1

Kelly, L., Athanassiou, N., & Crittenden, W. F. (2000). Founder Centrality and Strategic Behavior in the Family Owned Firm. *Entrepreneurship Theory and Practice*, *25*(2), 27–42. doi:10.1177/104225870002500202

Levin, I. M. (2000). Vision revisited. *The Journal of Applied Behavioral Science*, *36*(1), 91–107. doi:10.1177/0021886300361005

Lovas, B., & Ghoshal, S. (2000). Strategy as guided evolution. *Strategic Management Journal*, *21*(9), 875–896. doi:10.1002/1097-0266(200009)21:9<875::AID-SMJ126>3.0.CO;2-P

Men, L. R. (2017). Strategic Internal Communication: Transformational Leadership, Communication Channels, and Employee Satisfaction. *Management Communication Quarterly*, *28*(2), 264–284. doi:10.1177/0893318914524536

Millar, C. C. J. M., Groth, O., & Mahon, J. F. (2018). Management Innovation in a VUCA World: Challenges and Recommendations. *California Management Review*, *61*(1), 5–14. doi:10.1177/0008125618805111

Miller, D., & Le Breton-Miller, I. (2016). *Managing for the Long Run: Lessons in Competitive Advantage from Great Family Businesses*. Harvard Business School Press.

Mintzberg, H. (2013). Simply Managing: What Managers Do – and Can Do Better. Oakland, CA: Berrett-Kloehler.

Mullane, J. V. (2014). Reinvigorating the mission statement through top management commitment. *Management Decision*, *52*(3), 446–459. doi:10.1108/MD-10-2012-0736

Patanakul, P., & Shenhar, A. J. (2012). What Project Strategy Really Is: The Fundamental Building Block in Strategic Project Management. *Project Management Journal*, *43*(1), 4–20. doi:10.1002/pmj.20282

Richmond, B. (1997). The Strategic Forum: Aligning objectives, strategy and process. *System Dynamics Review*, *13*(2), 131–148. doi:10.1002/(SICI)1099-1727(199722)13:2<131::AID-SDR121>3.0.CO;2-J

Schomaker, M. S., & Zaheer, S. (2014). The role of language in knowledge transfer to geographically dispersed manufacturing operations. *Journal of International Management*, *20*(1), 55–72. doi:10.1016/j.intman.2013.10.004

Schulze, W. S., Lubatkin, M. H., & Dino, R. N. (2003). Toward a Theory of Altruism in Family Firms. *Journal of Business Venturing*, *18*(4), 473–490. doi:10.1016/S0883-9026(03)00054-5

Schuman, A. M., Sage-Hayward, W., & Ransburg, D. (2016). *Human resources in the family business: maximizing the power of your people*. Palgrave Macmillan.

Scott, R. (2019). Explaining how group model building supports enduring agreement. *Journal of Management & Organization*, *25*(6), 783–806. doi:10.1017/jmo.2017.12

Steier, L. (2001). Family firms, plural forms of governance and the evolving role of trust. *Family Business Review*, *14*(4), 353–367. doi:10.1111/j.1741-6248.2001.00353.x

Taylor, F. W. T. (1997). *Principles of Scientific Management*. Dover Publications Inc.

Turner, D. W. (2010). Qualitative Interview Design: A Practical Guide for Novice Investigators. *Qualitative Report*, *15*(3), 754–760.

Vermeulen, F. (2010). *Business exposed: The naked truth about what really goes on in the world of business*. Prentice Hall.

Vieira, W., & Dixit, M. (2019). *The 5 Gs of Family Business*. SAGE.

Vlatka, H. (2014). *The Management Shift. How to Harness the Power of People and Trasform Your Organization for Sustainable Success*. Palgrave Macmillan.

ADDITIONAL READING

Goffee, S. R., & Jones, G. (2006). Extraordinary leadership. *London Business School Review*, *17*(2), 30–33.

Gratton, L., & Ghoshal, S. (2005). Beyond Best Practice. *Sloan Management Review*, *46*(3), 49–57.

Sinek, S. (2009). *Start with Why. How Great Leader Inspire Everyone to Take Action.* Penguin Portfolio.

Sutton, R. (2010). Good Boss, Bad Boss. How to Be the Best...and Learn from the Worst. Grand Central Publishing.

KEY TERMS AND DEFINITIONS

Engagement: The ability to involve mentally and emotionally people in an activity.

Management Model: A management Model is the choices by executives of a firm regarding how they define objectives, motive effort, coordinate activities, and allocate resources, in other words, how they define how work of management gets done.

Management Shift: Managerial cultural change required to face the new challenges imposed by the market.

Organizational Identity: Strong value bond existing between a group of people.

Strategic Forum: Structured activity that allows a group of people to confront each other effectively on strategic issues.

Strategic Map: Map that contains the definition of the mission, distinctive competencies, golden rules, values and vision of a company or department.

VUCA World: The belief that the world is becoming more and more volatile, uncertain, complex, and ambiguous. The notion of VUCA was first introduced by the U.S. Army War College to describe the new multilateral world which resulted from the end of the Cold War.

Chapter 4
Process for Maintaining Trust Between CEO of Family Businesses and Partners:
The Case of Long-Term Buyer-Supplier Relationships Among Family Businesses

Stephanie Clothilda Lezama-Rogers
Grenoble Ecole de Management, France

Severine Sophie Le Loarne-Lemaire
Grenoble Ecole de Management, France

ABSTRACT

In this chapter, the authors propose to widen the perspective of human resource management within family businesses by considering the organization as not only one venture but a set of ventures. The authors select case studies to illustrate the process for maintaining trust between CEO of family businesses and partners. The cases showed that regardless of the family firms' ownership and size, the personal relationship was more important to keep the relationship than agreements sanctioned by formalized operation and contracts. The story of the three cases allows the authors to identify a human resource management process of trust maintenance between three inter-family firm relationships.

BACKGROUND

During the last two decades, companies split their value chain and mostly outsourced some parts of their competencies and competitive advantage to suppliers or partners (Contractor et al., 2010). Meanwhile, there is a growing consensus in International Marketing and Purchasing (IMP) literature that the retention of suitable buyers provides a competitive edge for suppliers (Nyaga & Whipple, 2011). This is because suppliers can increase profits by 95% by retaining existing buyers than acquiring new ones (Gallo 2014). More so, and just like any other stakeholders, they must ascertain the most appropriate approach to build

DOI: 10.4018/978-1-7998-4814-1.ch004

and maintain relationships with buyers that are family businesses and vice versa. Quite recent literature review about human resources management (HRM) considers that human resource management goes beyond the boundaries of one organization. Therefore, it should be extended to business partners of the organization (Acquah et al., 2020; Kang et al., 2007; Ulrich & Beatty, 2001). Such a claim is based on the statement according to which organizations position their value proposition beyond their boundaries (Lengnick-Hall et al. 2003). Consequently, they could benefit from greater partner allegiance, continuous manufacturing, or service planning (Anderson & Narus 1991), cost reduction, and service delivery (Trevelen 1987). However, in such a trend, family businesses do not remain an exception.

Family businesses desire to develop and maintain serious and long-term stakeholder relationships with their stakeholder groups (Pieper, 2019; Lude & Prügl, 2019; Rose, 2017). However, they are not often strategic in building and maintaining these business ties. Consequently, relative to non-family businesses, they cooperate less and rarely partake in inter-firm cooperative arrangements (Kontinen & Ojala, 2011; Roessl 2005). These family businesses' attributes would also make it challenging to build trust with their exchange partners (Roessl 2005). Their culture and belief form this distinction. It could conflict in how they communicate with their counterpart's non-family business.

Family businesses are a pervasive group, and the problems they faced daily are even more pervasive. Human resource practices hold extreme significance for all organizations. However, family businesses' inimitability, the interaction between the family and the business suggests these entities endure complex, intricate, and interconnected problems. Sherer, Adams, Carley & Wiebe (1989) posits that the lack of growth of family businesses makes it a deterrence for the proceeding generation to be involved in the firm's entrepreneurial undertakings. Thus, when family businesses are relationship orientated, it increases their survival (Kontinen & Ojala, 2011; Swinth & Vinton, 1993) and effectiveness within the supply chain (Panayides and So 2005). Consequently, practitioners and scholars have a growing interest in discovering novel practices in cultivating stronger sufficient business ties with family firms (Pieper, 2019; Lude & Prügl, 2019; Neubaum 2018; Rose 2017).

One key aspect of human resource management (HRM) is maintaining trusting relationships between external stakeholders. This would help contribute to family businesses ' competitive advantage. Trusting relationships that combine a firm's human capital with external business partners could develop more formidable abilities (DeNisi, Hitt, & Jackson 2003). The human resource capabilities, such as having the right fit of employees and employers, are critical to building and maintaining trusting relationships with suppliers or buyers (Wu et al., 2013; Lengnik-Hall et al., 2013). These capabilities could also enhance a family business knowledge capacity, fuel innovation (Sirmon and Hitt 2003), and reduce transaction costs (Das & Teng 1996). HRM could also preserve those human abilities rooted in relationship networks that could pose as a threat for family businesses rivals to monitor, recognize, or replicate (Lengnick-Hall et al. 2003). Human resource work practices that are oriented towards relationship-type processes could increase efficiency, reduce cycle times and turnover, and deepen ties between business partners (Becker, & Huselid, 1998).

This chapter reveals that family businesses would be at a competitive edge if their human resources have a more significant role in coordinating their relationships. The research was conducted in Trinidad, a small island developing state in the Caribbean Basin. The country prides itself as a proverbial 'melting pot' due to its diverse populace rooted in slavery, indentureship, and colonialism. The study applies case study research as a method of inquiry. In essence, this chapter's critical objective is to answer the following research question: Which processes; *eventually, practices*, allow the duration of a trust relationship between buyers and suppliers within the specific context of family businesses?

LITERATURE REVIEW

Human Resource Management as a Relationship Builder for Family Businesses

Family businesses' growth and sustainability, irrespective of firm type, also significantly rely on effective HRM practices and processes, particularly in their interaction with relational partners/ stakeholders. In that respect, the literature purports that HRM can be a source of competitive advantage for the family business (Habbershon, Williams, and Kaye 1999). Also, relative to a non-family business counterpart, family business HRM is undertaken differently (Reid and Adams, 2001). According to Ward (1988), family business peculiar behavior may develop a more family-centric workplace atmosphere, which would result in a more loyal workforce. More studies found positive correlations between a family business and their HRM on revenue and employee job satisfaction (Leon-Guerrero, JcCann, and Haley 1998). Unlike other business functions, HRM is in a unique place to enable, harmonize, and scrutinize a company's body of relationships that is of importance to them (Lengnick-Hall et al. 2003). As a result of the interlinked between family members within the organization's various tiers, HRM, which speaks about people and relationships, becomes even more pervasive in the family business milieu. Traditionally, the philosophy of HRM design has been one that focused on internal administrative business functions such as selection, training, promotion of people within an organization. According to Lengnick-Hall and Lengnick-Hall (1999), HRM needs to deviate from its narrow focus (single employer-employee relationship). It should also expand its organizational boundaries to include their external partners (Marchington, Lee Cooke & Hebson 2010; Snell, Shadur, & Wright, 2000).

To date, more research on human resource roles within inter-firm relationships has begun to increase (Rubery et al., 2004). Family businesses that desire to develop strong relationships with external stakeholders (based on knowledge exchange, cooperation, and trust) can incorporate HRM in their processes. According to McAfee et al. (2002), this would involve treating internal staff and outside employers, e.g., customers and suppliers, as long-term investments. A multi-employer study by Marchington et al. (2005) revealed that employers could utilize several approaches to strengthen their firm's brand or image by using their suppliers' employees. The intent is to increase an employee's emotional commitment to the buyer rather than to their employer. Reputable airlines might instruct their subcontracted handling agents to change uniforms several times a day when they provide check-in and boarding passes for different airlines (Marchington et al., 2005). In return, these airlines would aim to increase' relationship bonding' with their subcontracted handling agents by providing incentives such as free flights and team-building activities (Rubery et al., 2003). Ulrich and Lake (1990) stated that organizations must acclimatize to external stakeholders' shifting expectations to decrease the response period. Most firms desire to establish close longstanding inter-firm relationships; however, the expectation required by these arrangements are rarely managed accordingly.

HRM could step in as a relationship instigator and builder to improve working relationships between the employers in these inter-firm relationship dyads. According to Lengnick-Hall & Lengnick-Hall (1999), customers and suppliers could be quasi workforce participants. Firms could use HRM to guide customers' behavior and create customer inclusivity in the development of products. They could also utilize customers as assessors to provide feedback on the practices to initiate, grow, or maintain the firm. In a study, Dyer and Nobeoka (2000) showed that trust and strong relational bonds were established between Toyota, their suppliers, and core management groups. Customers can also take a quasi-role in managing certain aspects of human resource function by tailoring how they should treat them. Berry (1995) illustrates this point by using the Ritz-Carlton Hotel policy as an example. The organization developed a conflict resolution policy that allows employees to fix issues quickly when they do arise and prevent it from happening in the future.

Forming these fruitful relationships with external stakeholders is significant for family businesses than ever before. Family members also influence how internal and external stakeholders view and identify with the organization. (Laplume et al., 2008). For instance, when it comes to family business customers, they can effectively utilize HR practices to attend to their needs. A study conducted by Saffieddine and Rabbath (2008) showed that the customer services provided by family businesses were based on their ability to adapt and be flexible. As a result, it gave employees more independence when dealing with customer complaints. Ultimately, there would also be a period when the business would be transferred to a potential successor in the family business life cycle. During this process, a critical HRM decision needs to be made, such as where these outside relationships to family businesses stand? How should these relationships be maintained for the long term? According to (Gaumer et al. 2018), a successor in a family business is forged with the responsibility to cultivate and maintain the present customer or supplier relationship, mainly if it is a longstanding one. The proceeding section would introduce the anatomy of a family business and stakeholder relationships, followed by the antecedents of trust.

The Anatomy of Family Business Stakeholder Relationships

Stakeholders play a pivotal role in an organization (Di Maddaloni, Davis 2017). Family businesses hold their salient or primary stakeholders (e.g., customers, employees, competitors, and suppliers) dearly. For instance, the exchanges amongst family businesses salient internal stakeholders or individual family members give rise to social relationships. Kotler and De Massis (2013) categorized this form of transaction as being familial since they happen in informal, casual gatherings amongst family members. More so, according to Hoffman et al. (2006), when family members engage in the informal interchange, the beliefs of the individual family members are transmitted into a shared understanding. These traits could positively or adversely influence how they interact with external stakeholders and how outside stakeholders perceive them. The diverse strengths and weaknesses characterizing family businesses (Kets de Vries, 1996) can be both a source of competitive advantage or challenge for family businesses entering and maintaining relationships with external stakeholders. Family businesses have been characterized as more flexible and make faster decisions, which would make them better relationship partners. Their long-term orientation and transgenerational outlook have been associated with reliability, stability, and a commitment to the firm. These attributes make them ideal ultimate entities to build long-term relationships (Kets de Vries, 1996). Despite this, other characteristics of these firms associated with their unwillingness to share information, risk-averse behavior could adversely affect their relationship with external stakeholders (Arino, 2005). According to Clarkson (1995), one such stakeholder important to family business competitiveness is their suppliers. In a revised editorial piece in the Family Business Review, Neubaum (2018) highlighted the need to expand the research domain to include underrepresented topics like supplier relationships in family business research. Suppliers for family firms are not just cost centers; they are creative partners contributing directly to family businesses' performance.

The Antecedent of Trust in Family Business

Trust is a crucial element for family business relationships. However, scholars are not privy to a comprehensive inquiry of what makes family business relationships truly work with stakeholders, particularly under diverse exchange arrangements. Through a scan of the literature, family businesses, as trustees or trustors, may give or take trust differently depending on the exchange partners. Some scholars assert that trust could be thin or thick. Trust is thick when the relationship exchange is particularistic, while thin trust is governed by universalism. Thus, it may be likely that some organizations may trust some stakeholders over others and vice versa (Dinç & Gastman, 2012). Below are some of the underlying research that indicates a family business role as trustors versus trustees.

The Perceived Context of Family Businesses as Trustees

In the literature, fulfilled customers are relatively least apt to look for new suppliers (Flint et al., 2011). Relative to non-family businesses, family businesses are widely perceived positively among customers (e.g., Orth and Green 2009). Family business relationships with their customers (Lyman, 1991) reveals that they are principally cognizant of offering exceptional services to their customers (Ward, 1997). More so, from the perspective of the customers, research indicated that customers view a family business more positively than non-family businesses (Orth & Green 2009). Nonetheless, current research has unanimously revealed that a family business's behavior and performance are distinct from a non-family business. Research shows that this is evident in their long-term orientation, governing structures, competencies, and corporate practices (Benavides-Velasco et al., 2013; Chrisman et al., 2010).

Through a scan of family business companies over the internet, it was found that the first generation or the founder were prominent companies worldwide. Companies like Forbes, Ford Motors, Walmart, S.C Johnson, to name a few, chose to endorse their dynasty to the world using the family's name. Craig quotes: "family brand identity is a rare, valuable, imperfectly imitable and nonsubstitutable resource." (Craig, Dibrell, & Davis 2008). For Miller and Le Breton-Miller (2003), these attributes associated with the family business are their commitment, trust, and, most of all, customer-oriented nature. Craig, Dibrell, & Davis (2008) posits family businesses used their family brand identity to inspire customers buying choices. More so, this is further in agreement with Orth and Green (2009) that have empirical confirmation that family businesses can build and sustain more solid relationships with customers. Family businesses achieve this by responding to customers' needs promptly, a passion for offering a superior product or service, displaying the family's name, and a sincere yearning to deliver an exceptional product or service to their customers Orth and Green (2009). Orth and Green (2009) collected 138 responses from students to understand how they perceive grocery retail stores' services. The authors came back with an exciting finding that compared to non-family businesses, family businesses were evaluated more positively. Particularly as it relates to trust, the benevolence of their employees, and services. Thus, the way relationships are fashioned and maintained can influence trust among the buyer (Nguyen and Mutum, 2012)

Dyer (2006) contends that building and guarding the family identity brand holds great significance for the family business. The family element could be used to cultivate social capital between these firms and their stakeholders. Explicitly, Dyer (2006) further argues that these firms' unique characteristics can positively impact their relationships with external stakeholders. Miller and Le Breton Miller (2003) also note that this relies on the degree to which the family can personify the firm. In another study, Miller and Le Breton-Miller (2005) revealed in the eyes of the customer's family businesses are more trusting.

The Perceived Context of Family Businesses as Trustors

There have been inconsistent findings of the conditions governing and prohibiting the development of strategic partnerships. Some scholars also asserted that family businesses were least likely strategic and unwilling to develop their networking connections in a business-to-business context (e.g., Roessl 2005). Scholars posit this could be associated with their risk-averse behavior (Meroño-Cerdán et al. 2018) resistance to change. It could also be related to their unwillingness to partake in inter-firm cooperative arrangements with outside entities due to their fear of losing their independence (Roessl 2005;). Posso (2003) posits that these entities operate like a locked system with specific cultures and beliefs that form this distinction. This could conflict in how they communicate with their counterpart's non-family business. Tushman (1977) posits that dissimilarity intensifies the challenges to interact, and this could be a recipe for conflict. It was also found that family businesses have difficulties employing strategic organizational practices (Astrachan and Kolenko, 1994). These entities tend to be more informal and conservative in their business operations (McConaughy et al., 2001). Due to this, family business unique attributes may make them rarely strategic in building and maintaining inter-firm relationships.

Memili et al. (2011) further support these arguments. They postulated that family business is also less likely to depend on subcontractors relative to their non-family counterparts. They recognize the more significant amount of proficiencies by directing certain undertakings internally. When specific tasks hold great significance or importance, the family business prefers to complete the activities internally and avoid subcontracting the actions to sustain their competitive advantage. Memili et al. (2011) applied the transaction cost theory, defined by Arrow, 1969: 48, the "the costs of running the economic system" to understand the subcontracting relationship between a family business and external entities. The challenges with the transaction cost theory are that it tends to focus on the contract. Since transaction cost tends to focus on contractual arrangements, the argument falls short in explaining the non-contractual or informal agreements among family businesses.

Pittino & Visintin (2011) supports work by Memili et al. (2011). Pittino & Visintin (2011) were among the few scholars that empirically tested some of these findings. Their study focused on family business influence and their decisions towards establishing a strategic partnership. Their research draws from a sample of 272 SMEs in Italy. For Pittino & Visintin (2011), the decision to subcontract is significantly influenced by kinship ties. Thus, when in-group trust among the family is high, trust in other entities is lower. Because of this, the transaction cost with other entities is augmented with outside entities. The researchers' work also supports some of Roessl (2005) theoretical predictions that family business was least likely to cooperate with external entities.

Research conducted by Roessl (2005) examines the family business 'fundamental belief system'. These beliefs specific to family business included their lack of immunity to change, a philosophy based on thrift, risk-averse. Family businesses were also perceived as having difficulty in building trust. Myths as reference figures ("a warning from the entrepreneur widow to the 3rd generation entering the FB "This company has achieved everything from savings") also impacted family business relationships. For Roessl (2005), these attributes are the cornerstone affecting the family business decision-making process to engage with an external entity versus working in silos. These findings were consistent with some of the scholars mentioned above. The research fails to account for the number of cooperative arrangements established and the scope and the type of arrangements that family business prefers. Also, the kind of partners or entities family business may be more inclined to have a cooperated agreement with (for instance, is family business more apt or willing to work with the family business or non-family business). Conversely, other scholars have presented different arguments in how family business relationships work.

Similarly, researchers have further put forward evidence that family businesses could cultivate relationships that are more resilient through social capital (Zahra 2010). As previously mentioned, family businesses are generally more long-term oriented in preserving the firm's continuity and legacy (Zellweger, 2007). These firms also value solidity compared to taking a risk (Daily and Dollinger, 1993). They aim to maintain ownership and control of the business. Therefore, they would most likely engage with groups with similar identities. This value system shared similar characters to the family. Based on past research, these groups were also felt to be more trusting than different groups (Hadjielias & Poutziouris 2015; Lester & Cannella 2006; Roessl 2005; Swinth & Vinton 1993). Swinth & Vinton (1993) conceptualize that family businesses in international joint ventures may have tremendous success when the exchange partner is also a family business. Swinton & Vinton (1993) family businesses would have similar values, such as their long-term orientation, trust, commitment. However, non-family businesses in these types of alliances seek short-term goals to capitalize on shareholders' dividends.

RESEARCH DESIGN

The authors focus their analysis on Trinidad, where family businesses contribute most of the GDP. There is 200,000 Micro, Small, and Medium Enterprises (Trinidad and Tobago Chamber of Industry and Commerce). Approximately 70% of these firms could be classified as a family business (Nicholson and Lashley 2016).

The authors selected 3 cases (table 1) for cross-case comparison (Eisenhardt, 1989). In total, ten in-depth interviews were undertaken with key participants. A maximum of 3 to 4 interviews was held per case. This entailed family members from the buying family business side and one representative from the supplier side. The interviews ranged in length from 30 minutes to 90 minutes. Each case was theoretically framed based on Mayer's (1995) trust model: Ability, Benevolence, and Integrity. The proceeding three cases provide a sequence of procedures and practices that demarcates the approach in which these human relationships are organized.

Table 1. Summary of the cases

Cases	Buyer/Supplier	Sector	Staff	Years in Business relationship	% family owned	Family involvement during interview time	Total Family involvement in the business	Interviewees
Case 1	Buyer	Personal Care	200	28	100	1st 2nd	5	3
	Supplier	Chemical	20		100	1st 2nd	4	1
Case 2	Buyer	Food and Beverage	100	25	100	1st 2nd	6	2
	Supplier	Labeling	8		100	1st 2nd	4	1
Case 3	Buyer	Logistics	6	7	100	1st 2nd	6	2
	Supplier	Brokerage	2		100	1st	2	1

Case Study: Long-term Buyer-supplier Relationships Among Family Businesses

The authors focus on the story of the close relationship between actors in buyer-supplier relationships. The results are transcribed following the "time bracketing events" strategy defined by Van de Ven (Langley, 1999; Langley et al., 2013). Such a process might reduce the capacity to generalize results and provide a more reliable and accurate analysis (Langley, 1999). In the authors' account, attention would be placed on the similarities and differences between the three cases.

Description of Case one

Firm A1 is a private manufacturer in the personal care business (Firm and its principal supplier in chemicals (Firm A2). The family business that purchases are situated in Trinidad and the providing family business in Miami. The two businesses likewise have a stable family center with various generations actively involved in their daily operations. Both family businesses are developing along similar paths as they have recently appointed their sons as their business's successors. The larger family business in this inter-firm relationship (over 200 employees) is the buyer. The smaller family business is the supplier (20 employees). Firm A1 is also Firm A2 second-largest buyer in the Caribbean. Together they share a long business history (30 years), and over time the relationship has moved towards a closer relationship.

Description of Case two

Firm B1 is a family-owned and operated Food and Beverage Company, and its principal supplier is in the packaging industry (Firm B2). The Managing Director is the founder's son, and his responsibility is to spearhead overall operations. There is also the Managing Director's daughter, who holds the position of General Manager for production and inventory. Additionally, working in the firm is also the Managing Director's wife (financial manager and his son, who is now taking up a management role. In Firm B1, there have been instability and incongruence in values among family members in this firm. According to the granddaughter, "Trend of thoughts. Too many generations. This generation gap significantly affected proper succession planning and how they work as a private firm. However, in Firm B2, there was more harmony and value congruency across generations. Despite this, the two firms likewise have a stable family center with various generations actively involved in their daily operations. The larger family business in this inter-firm relationship (over 75 employees) is the buyer. The smaller family business is the supplier (20 employees). Together they share a long business history (25 years), and over time the relationship has also moved towards a closer relationship.

Description of Case three

Firm C1 is a private service provider in the Logistics business, and its principal supplier is in the Brokerage's area (Firm C2). The two firms likewise have a stable family center. The buying family business has various generations actively involved in the daily operations of the business. At the same time, their major suppliers are husband and wife duos in the business. Together they share a long business history (10 years), and over time the relationship has moved towards a closer one.

The Pre Relationship Stage: The Search for Familiarity (Shared History and Culture)

In cases 1 and 3, signs of trust are seen from the outset. Greater emphasis on the part of the supplier was placed on actively searching for buyers based on familiarity (e.g., shared history and culture). However, this was not the same for case 2, as trust was not the determining factor in entering the business relationship. The prior interactions in cases 1 and 3 created the first opportunity to develop trustworthiness. In case 1 started in 1987, the supplying family was looking for potential partners in the Caribbean. The supplying family business utilized the support of their export manager (boundary spanner), a Trinidadian working in Miami. Because the export manager was familiar with the country's cultural environment, it became its starting point. The Firm A2, with advice from their export manager, began their initial research in Trinidad, where they came across the Firm A1 the buying family business products on the supermarket shelf. Firm A2 further probed through word of mouth from several supermarket owners referred to the Firm A2 to Firm A1. The relationship in Case 3 also shares a similar experience as case 1. Both partners also believed in forging close relationships with people they knew. The founder's son on the Firm C1 states, *"Its possible dad even worked with him before, which is why he reached out to him. The founder's son knew him technically as well"*. However, for case 2, signs of trust were more challenging to determine. Firm B2, the supplying family business, recruited a competent sales representative to pitch their service offering. The relationship between both firms started based on the sales representative explaining the supply family business competency.

- Human Resource Role at the Pre-relationship Stage
    - Selective Hiring and Recruitment

For most of the cases presented (e.g., cases 1 and 2), it was more critical at the pre-relationship stage to recruit key personnel with diverse skills and cultural attributes. For instance, the supplying family business founder case 1 indicated that they hired and recruited diverse employees and managers based on the market they planned to tap in. The founder of the buying family business corroborated these findings by stating, *" their marketing manager was a Trinidadian. " "I guess he went on the supermarket shelf and looked at our products*." In this case, selective allocation meant that employees were selected to work with specific clients based on their cultural background, followed by their competency. As a result, the appropriate boundary spanner's recruitment and selection to support the relationship process needs to be carefully chosen. In case 2, however, the supplying family business stresses more on the employee's competency in discussing their product offering. The third case, the buying family business, recruited a supplier that they shared a common history.

The Initial Interaction Stages: Communication at the Interpersonal and Organizational Level

At this stage, there is a series of organized interpersonal and professional meetings in all 3 cases. Communication was associated with developing relational bonds across the cases. The competency of the supplier was also tested.

Interpersonal relationships were imperative in inter-family business buyer-supplier relationship exchange. In case 1, the Firm A2, the key export manager in Miami, frequently visited Trinidad and conducted face to face meetings with the Firm A1 founder. The meetings aimed to assist their new start-up client with their personal care line related to product formulation and market access. By introducing the key export manager, Firm A1 in Trinidad became acquainted with all the family members in Firm A2 from Miami. Initially, the Firm A1 founder and family members (wife and kids) were invited to Firm A2 for dinner and other social gatherings. The Firm A2 also used this stage as an opportunity to leverage their "familiness." Familiness created a positive, friendly atmosphere.

In case 2, however, the supplier's (Firm B2) ability to provide excellent service was problematic as they were new to the market. The supplying family business in case 2 had to demonstrate benevolence and responsiveness immediately. Unlike cases 1 and 3, the supplying family business (Firm B2) was more vulnerable than the Firm B1. The Firm B1 could change the supplier at any time and be less dependent on the Firm B1. As a result, the Firm B2 had to prove themselves by being very responsive to Firm B1. Firm B2 undertook this by involving Firm B1 at each stage of the value chain operation, such as technology and product upgrade. Firm B2 openly admitted to not always have the solution but would seek answers to Firm B1 needs. In case 3, the supplier (Firm C2) was incrementally given a small task (Firm C1). Once the founder in Firm C1 was happy with Firm C2, the task increased.

- Human Resource Role at the Initial Interaction Stage
    - Training and Development

In the initial interaction stage, the personnel representing the supplying family business must engage in training and development. This was an HRM investment requirement for the family business suppliers, particularly in cases 1 and 2, when fostering relationships with family business buyers. Thus, supplying family business employees and family members needed to be trained with unique skills when representing the organization. Training and development at this stage entailed a clear understanding of the supplying family business product offering and communication skills to transact effectively with family members or other employees from the buying family business side.

The Relationship Growth Stage: Family Ownership as Drivers of Competency and Professional Benevolence

The personal relationship, supplier's competency, and benevolence particularly predominated in all three cases. In case 1, capacity was based on the supplier's ability to develop chemical formulations for Firm A1, the buying family business personal care, and janitorial product line. Furthermore, in case 1, the supplier (Firm A2) capacity to deliver on the best chemical formulations was also reliant on their chemical firms' network affiliations. These affiliations created a positive outlook on Firm A2 as the place to source the best chemical. However, in case 2, service quality relied on the Firm B2 to keep abreast of new ways to provide better services to their partner. However, in case 3, the supplier's ability was based on efficiency when completing the task. The founder son from Firm C1, the buying family business, states: *"Yeah, just as much as everything else, the efficiency, the level of service we get from him it has been fantastic over the years. I have no complaints at all"*.

The 3 cases also showed signs of professional benevolence. Family business buyers were hesitant to conduct business with suppliers that are inaccessible, aloof, or may not be familiar with on a personal basis. As a result, the supplier's availability, responsiveness, the communication needed to be high, as seen in the three cases. Across the cases, family members on the buying family business management team felt general flexibility among the family business suppliers. They were usually accessible to the family business buyers 24/7. The reason for this assertion was that the founders of the business were more connected to the outcomes, and the family ownership appeared to explain this as well. The buying family business organization and private lives were significantly tied to the business. They anticipated that their family business suppliers did the same. It was also found that communication rarely got lost, as the firms in each case were in constant contact with each other.

- Human Resource Role at the Relationship Growth Stage

In the relationship growth stage, HRM had a much larger role. For instance, coordination, job design, continuous training and development, and knowledge and skills were most significantly mentioned as essential HRM functions. The key personnel's job design representing the supplying family business and other family members was also authorized to be decision-makers. This helped to increase the responsiveness of the supplying family business. As the workload increased at this stage, there were also more **coordination efforts** on the HRM team's part on the supplying family business side. For instance, in all three cases, inspection visits were undertaken by the supplying family business to ensure that their employees were undertaking proper floor management practices at the buying family business organization. **Diverse knowledge and skill** set were significantly required at the relationship growth stage. Some of the required skills family business suppliers must possess communication skills that could be used at multi-levels. Other skills needed were good interpersonal skills, an understanding and appreciation of culture, and an ability to show cultural compassion.

The Maintenance Stage: Long- term Horizon Across Multiple Generations

At the maintenance stage, integrity, interpersonal relationships, personal benevolence, and familiarity predominate in all three cases. In case 1, integrity entailed honesty and reliability. According to case 1 buyer (Firm A1), *"they are very reliable if we say that we want something by a certain time unless it is really beyond their control, we usually get it by that period."* More so, for case 1, the relationship would not have reached this stage if the supplying family business (Firm A2) did not show moral character. Firm A1 states, *"So we tend to work with this supplier because they are very honorable people, but in-between you get some suppliers who are not so good. Those are the ones that you tend not to go the distance with".*

Similarly, in case 2, integrity was defined as faith, moral character, and mutual respect. Both family businesses in case 2 are strong in their religious beliefs and believe that faith helped maintained the relationship. Furthermore, integrity for case 2 was extended to the moral character of the leaders as well. Case 2 buyer quotes, *"The character of the leader in that company is what shapes the business, and you know what their mentality and standard of quality are like."*. Similarly, in case 3, integrity also prevailed at it, mainly entailed predictability. The buyer in Firm C1 quotes, *"you could follow up if you need to, but the trust is that you do not need to follow up."*

There was also a positive relationship between the years of interaction across multiple generations and trust. All partners were in harmony with each other and confident that the relationship shared helped them work at comfort. The 2nd generation in case 1 felt this harmoniousness derives from him knowing the now CEO also the 2nd gen founder son since they were kids. These years of familiarity created trust and synergy between the family businesses. The presence of this familiarity was a contributory factor to both entities' capability to work effortlessly with each other in accomplishing their business goals at this stage of the relationship.

Familiarity also created mutual respect among multiple generations. Mutual respect also emanated due to the alignment in values between each family business. There are a legacy and reputation to uphold once you're a family business. Regardless of size, each family business buyer mirrored the values they had as congruent with their family business suppliers. Words such as family-oriented, ethics, West Indian orientation, religion, and development along similar paths describe this congruency or alignment. All buying family businesses had a long-term horizon for their organization's continuity. The family business buyers also perceived that this was the case for their family business suppliers. This shared relational value created a sense of confidence and certainty in the succeeding generations' relationship and respect. In case 2, the 3rd generations state, *"as generations pass, you will find us not having a direct relationship, the same way that dad and the owner, they would have. So, let us say it's two dads. So, dad and dad from two companies. Son and daughter from either company may not get along as closely as the dads would, but mutual respect still holds"*. The proceeding generations felt that the precedent set by the founder makes it possible to resolve conflicts.

- Human Resource Role at the Maintenance Stage

In the maintenance stage, compensation and pay, coordination efforts, and succession planning were most significantly mentioned as essential HRM functions that supported the maintenance of trust between the family business buyers and their suppliers.

- Compensation and Pay

In cases 1 and 2, as it pertains to compensation and pays, key personnel in the supplying family business were given incentives to avoid employee turnover as it may disrupt the relational ties between family businesses and external personnel. Personnel's length of service and ability to maintain relational ties with the buying family business was considered a yardstick when allocating compensation and pay. Therefore, employees and employers were rewarded for their ability to secure family business buyers' allegiance to their organization and vice versa. Compensation and pay were not discussed in case 3.

- Coordination Efforts

As part of HRM coordination efforts, the same key personnel who usually interacted with the buying family business were not moved around as much. As a result, the buying family business could not lose track of who they were.

- Succession Planning

The founder's duty was perceived as creating familiarity among the 2nd or 3rd generation family members in the early stages of the supplier relationships in this study. Thus, having other family members, key personnel's and potential successors involved in the relationship phase increased familiarity and mutual respect between potential successors and suppliers. The family founders were also more optimistic about the business relationships' continuity as the succeeding generations were quite familiar with the relationships previously developed. This familiarity helped created mutual respect among multiple generations, as seen in Cases 1, 2, and 3. Thus, HRM involving multiple generations (e.g., the 2nd. 3rd, etc.) in the early stages of the buyer-supplier relationship seems to increase cultural imprint and the chances of the next relationship continuity of generation successors

Table 2. Results summary of the Inter-family firms Trust relationship Lifecycle

Stages	Dimension	Case 1	Case 2	Case 3
Pre relationship Stage	Antecedents of trust	**High Trust:** • Familiarity (Shared Culture)	**Low Trust:** • Supplier Competency	**High Trust** Familiarity (Shared History/Experience)
	HR role	• Selective Hiring and Recruitment (cultural background) • Skills and education	• Selective Hiring and Recruitment (competency) • Skills and education	• Selective Hiring and Recruitment (familiarity)
Initial Interaction Stage	Antecedents of trust	**High Trust:** • Professional Benevolence: Communication • Ability	**Moderate Trust** • Professional Benevolence: Communication, Availability, and responsiveness • Ability • Vulnerability and uncertainty	**Moderate Trust** • Professional Benevolence: Communication • Ability
	HR role	• Training and Development (communication and product usage)	• Training and Development (communication and product usage)	No HRM practices are discussed at this stage.
Relationship Growth Stage	Antecedents of trust	**High Trust** • Professional benevolence: Communication availability and responsiveness • Ability	**High Trust** • Professional benevolence: Communication availability and responsiveness • Ability	**High Trust** • Professional benevolence: Communication availability and responsiveness • Ability
	HR role	• Knowledge and skills: • Coordination efforts • Job Design	• Training and Development: • Coordination efforts • Job Design	• No HRM practices are discussed at this stage. • Coordination efforts
Maintenance Stage	Antecedents of trust	**High Trust** • Integrity: Reliability, moral character • Personal benevolence: Acts of generosity • Organizational similarity	**High Trust** • Integrity: Reliability, faith, moral character • Mutual Respect • Organizational similarity	**High Trust** • Organizational similarity
	HR role	• Compensation and Pay • Succession Planning	• Compensation and Pay • Succession Planning	• Compensation and Pay • Succession Planning

DISCUSSION

The buyer-supplier relationship should be of utmost importance for HRM (Sweeney 2013). However, these relationships in family businesses have only grown in recent times (Pieper, 2019; Lude & Prügl, 2018; Rose 2018). The authors' inquiry is the first attempt in family business research to intertwined buyer-supplier trust research and HRM. By elucidating the factors that motivate the trust process between two family businesses, this chapter provides fresh insights into Mayer et al. (1995) Ability, Benevolence, and Integrity (ABI) Trust Model from the family business perspective. The study has discovered the significance of family values as a crucial part of the family business capacity to trust other families. The relational content of trust did not vary between two family businesses as they identified with each other. Lewicki and Bunker (1995) referred to this type of trust as identification-based trust.

The study found that family business buyer CEOs are willing to be loyal and engage in long term relationships with other family businesses. This is the case, especially when their key personnel (e.g., non-family employees, family employees, or employers) have the following skillset: communication, technical, interpersonal, and intercultural skills. These skills were needed throughout the relational development process. This was the key to binding two family firms together. Apart from skillset, job design was also an important HRM function to influence this trust process. For instance, staff job design empowered them to contribute to the decision-making process, which promoted this benevolence (e.g., responsiveness and availability). This finding is consistent with the work of Saffieddine and Rabbath (2008). They showed that family businesses' customer services were based on their ability to adapt and be flexible. As a result, it gave employees more independence when dealing with customer complaints. The study also indicated that key personnel was rarely job rotated. Consequently, family business buyers did not have to be concerned about building trust with new personnel. The findings support Ring and Van de Ven (1994) claim that introducing new personnel into existing stakeholder ties could result in a loss of flexibility and efficiency.

Finally, this study's findings further add to the discussion of family members' involvement in businesses, especially multiple generations. Steijvers and Niskanen (2013) posit that the agency cost between the family members, mainly the second and third generations, and outside stakeholders is deepened during the transgenerational phase. Steier (2001) posits that when the incumbent leaves the family business, its social capital becomes a threat. According to Pan et al. (2018), the succeeding generation is generally perceived as rookies with lower reputational assets. This research confirms that trust can be maintained between CEOs or founders of firms and across generations, especially when someone quits, dies, or becomes the successor. This study is the first to show the HRM implication that transition incidents and the involvement of other family members in the supplier relationship, especially potential successors, could significantly influence whether a buyer-supplier relationship continues across succeeding generations. This is because prior family members involved in the relationship could influence potential successors' and suppliers' outlook on the founder and the supplier's relational ties and vice versa. The founder could embed other family members in the buyer-supplier relationship life cycle, thus increasing the chances of these relationships continuing post-succession period. Thus, this study found that the role of the buying family business founder is pivotal in fostering relational ties at the initial stages of the relationship development process with suppliers.

CONCLUSION: CONTRIBUTION, LIMITATIONS, AND FURTHER RESEARCH

The authors argue that this chapter provides an interesting twist to the way to perceive HRM among family businesses but focusing on the family business as a network of businesses that gathers several families. By proposing a trust management model based on the three components of trust – ability, benevolence, and integrity- the authors show how HRM could help manage the process. Thus, the three cases come from a specific location and culture, Trinidad. Our results might differ across locations and cultures. However, despite this limitation, the study provides unique practical insights into how family business suppliers could use this research to better articulate how to organize their HRM functions. Case in point, training and development, job design, coordination, compensation, and pay to enhance family trust allegiance. The study also has theoretical implications: Firstly, this study offered a significant contribution to theory by providing unique insights into how family businesses operate in relational exchanges. Secondly, the academic contributions of buyer-supplier relationships from the family business context are scant. Very few scholars have researched family businesses in supplier relationships (Pieper, 2019; Lude & Prügl, 2019; Rose 2017). Thirdly, most HRM research usually focuses on stakeholder relationships within the firm's parameters, ignoring its impact on outside stakeholders (Janssen & Steyaert, 2009). Thirdly, HRM has begun to set its precedence in buyer-supplier research (Sweeney 2013). However, no studies to date have discussed this topic from the family business context. In this research, scholars are now privy to a comprehensive inquiry of what makes family business relationships truly work with stakeholders, particularly under diverse human resource exchange arrangements. As further research, the authors would call for an analysis of the management of the psychological contract between these family businesses, as theorized by Rousseau (1991). Future research could also examine how family businesses use their HRM processes to manage these external relational ties, particularly under crisis conditions such as COVID 19 (Gustafsson et al., 2020).

REFERENCES

Acquah, I.S.K., Agyabeng-Mensah, Y. & Afum, E. (2020). Examining the link among green human resource management practices, green supply chain management practices and performance. *Benchmarking: An International Journal*, ahead-of-print.

Arino, A., De LaTorre, J., & Smith Ring, P. (2005). Relational quality and inter-personal trust in strategic alliances. *European Management Review*, *2*(1), 15–27. doi:10.1057/palgrave.emr.1500026

Arrow, K. J. (1969). *The organization of economic activity: Issues pertinent to the choice of the market versus non-market allocations*. Joint Economic Committee of Congress.

Astrachan, J. H., & Kolenko, T. A. (1994). A neglected factor explaining family business success: Human resource practices. *Family Business Review*, *7*(3), 251–262. doi:10.1111/j.1741-6248.1994.00251.x

Becker, B. E., & Huselid, M. A. (1998). High performance work systems and firm performance: A synthesis of research and managerial implications. In G. E. Ferris (Ed.), *Research in Personnel and Human Resources Management* (Vol. 16, pp. 53–102). JAI Press, Inc.

Benavides-Velasco, C. A., Quintana-García, C., & Guzmán-Parra, V. F. (2013). Trends in family business research. *Small Business Economics*, *40*(1), 41–57. doi:10.100711187-011-9362-3

Berry, L. L. (1995). Relationship marketing of services growing interest, emerging perspectives. *Journal of the Academy of Marketing Science*, *23*(4), 236–245. doi:10.1177/009207039502300402

Chirico, F., Ireland, R. D., & Sirmon, D. G. (2011). Franchising and the family firm: Creating unique sources of advantage through familiness. *Entrepreneurship Theory and Practice*, *35*(3), 483–501. doi:10.1111/j.1540-6520.2011.00441.x

Chrisman, J. J., Kellermanns, F. W., Chan, K. C., & Liano, K. (2010). Intellectual foundations of current research in family business: An identification and review of 25 influential articles. *Family Business Review*, *23*(1), 9–26. doi:10.1177/0894486509357920

Craig, J. B., Dibrell, C., & Davis, P. S. (2008). Leveraging family-based brand identity to enhance firm competitiveness and performance in family businesses. *Journal of Small Business Management*, *46*(3), 351–371. doi:10.1111/j.1540-627X.2008.00248.x

Daily, CM & Dollinger, M.J. (1993). Alternative methodologies for identifying family vs. non- family managed businesses. *Journal of Small Business Management, 31*(2).

Das, T. K., & Teng, B. (1996). Risk types and inter-firm alliance structures. *Journal of Management Studies*, *33*(6), 827–843. doi:10.1111/j.1467-6486.1996.tb00174.x

DeNisi, A., Hitt, M. A., & Jackson, S. E. (2003). The knowledge-based approach to sustained competitive advantage. In Managing knowledge for sustained competitive advantage: Designing strategies for effective human resource management. San Francisco: Jossey Bass.

Di Maddaloni, F., & Davis, K. (2017). The influence of local community stakeholders in megaprojects: Rethinking their inclusiveness to improve project performance. *International Journal of Project Management*, *35*(8), 1537–1556. doi:10.1016/j.ijproman.2017.08.011

Dinc, L., & Gastmans, C. (2011). Trust and trustworthiness in nursing: An argument-based literature review. *Nursing Inquiry*, *19*(3), 223–237. doi:10.1111/j.1440-1800.2011.00582.x PMID:22050646

Dyer, J., & Nobeoka, K. (2000). Creating and managing a high-performance knowledge-sharing network: The Toyota case. *Strategic Management Journal*, *21*(3), 345–367. doi:10.1002/(SICI)1097-0266(200003)21:3<345::AID-SMJ96>3.0.CO;2-N

Dyer, W. G. Jr. (2006). Examining the "family effect" on firm performance. *Family Business Review*, *19*(4), 253–273. doi:10.1111/j.1741-6248.2006.00074.x

Eisenhardt, K. M. (1989). Building theories from case study research. *Academy of Management Review*, *14*(4), 532–550. doi:10.5465/amr.1989.4308385

Flint, D. J., Blocker, C. P., & Boutin, P. J. Jr. (2011). Customer value anticipation, customer satisfaction, and loyalty: An empirical examination. *Industrial Marketing Management*, *40*(2), 2019–2230. doi:10.1016/j.indmarman.2010.06.034

Gallo, A. (2014). The value of keeping the right customers. *Harvard Business Review*.

Gaumer, C. J., & Shaffer, K. J. (2018). Family business succession: Impact on supplier relations and customer management. *Human Resource Management International Digest*, *26*(6), 1–4. doi:10.1108/HRMID-05-2018-0104

Gustafsson, S., Gillespie, N., Hope Hailey, V., Ros, S., & Dietz, G. (2020). Preserving organizational trust during disruption. *Organization Studies*. Advance online publication. doi:10.1177/0170840620912705

Habbershon, T., Williams, M., & Kaye, K. (1999). A resource-based framework for assessing the strategic advantages of family firms. *Family Business Review*, *12*(1), 2. doi:10.1111/j.1741-6248.1999.00001.x

Hoffman, L., Marquis, J., Poston, D., Summers, J. A., & Turnbull, A. (2006). Assessing family outcomes: Psychometric evaluation of beach center family quality of life scale. *Journal of Marriage and the Family*, *68*(4), 1069–1083. doi:10.1111/j.1741-3737.2006.00314.x

Jamali, D., Safieddine, A., & Rabbath, M. (2008). Corporate governance and corporate social responsibility: Synergies and inter-relationships. *Corporate Governance*, *16*(5), 443–459. doi:10.1111/j.1467-8683.2008.00702.x

Kahneman, D., & Tversky, A. (1979). Prospect theory an analysis of decisions under risk. *Journal of the Econometric Society*, *47*(2), 263–291. doi:10.2307/1914185

Kang, S. C., Morris, S. S., & Snell, S. A. (2007). Relational archetypes, organizational learning, and value creation: Extending the human resource architecture. *Academy of Management Review*, *32*(1), 236–256. doi:10.5465/amr.2007.23464060

Kets de Vries, M. F. R. (1996). The anatomy of the entrepreneur: Clinical observations. *Human Relations*, *49*(7), 853–883. doi:10.1177/001872679604900701

Kontinen, T., & Ojala, A. (2011). *Network ties in the international opportunity recognition of family SMEs. In International Business Review* (Vol. 20). Elsevier.

Kotlar, J., & De Massis, A. (2013). Goal setting in family firms: Goal diversity, social interactions, and collective commitment to family-centered goals. *Entrepreneurship Theory and Practice*, *37*(6), 1263–1288. doi:10.1111/etap.12065

Langley, A. (1999). Strategies for theorizing from process data. *Academy of Management Review*, *24*(4), 691–710. doi:10.5465/amr.1999.2553248

Langley, A. N. N., Smallman, C., Tsoukas, H., & Van de Ven, A. H. (2013). Process studies of change in organization and management: Unveiling temporality, activity, and flow. *Academy of Management Journal*, *56*(1), 1–13. doi:10.5465/amj.2013.4001

Laplume, A. O., Sonpar, K., & Litz, R. (2008). Stakeholder theory: Reviewing a theory that moves us. *Journal of Management*, *34*(6), 1152–1189. doi:10.1177/0149206308324322

Lawler, E. E., & Mohrman, S. A. (2003). HR, as a strategic partner, what does it take to make it happen. *Human Resource Planning*, *26*, 15–29.

Lengnick-Hall, M. L., & Lengnick-Hall, C. A. (1999). Expanding customer orientation in the HR function. *Human Resource Management Journal*, *38*(3), 201–214. doi:10.1002/(SICI)1099-050X(199923)38:3<201::AID-HRM3>3.0.CO;2-B

Lengnick-Hall, M. L., & Lengnick-Hall, C. A. (2003). *Human resource management in the knowledge economy: New challenges, new roles, new capabilities*. Berrett- Koehler.

Leon-Guerrero, A. Y., McCann, J. E. III, & Haley, J. D. Jr. (1998). A study of practice utilization in family businesses. *Family Business Review*, *11*(2), 107–120. doi:10.1111/j.1741-6248.1998.00107.x

Lester, R. H., & Cannella, A. A. (2006). Interorganizational familiness: How family firms use interlocking directorates to build community-level social capital. *Entrepreneurship Theory and Practice*, *30*(6), 755–775. doi:10.1111/j.1540-6520.2006.00149.x

Lyman, A. R. (1991). Customer service: Does family ownership make a difference? *Family Business Review*, *4*(3), 303–324. doi:10.1111/j.1741-6248.1991.00303.x

Marchington, M., Cooke, F. L., & Hebson, G. (2010). Human resource management across organizational boundaries. In The SAGE Handbook of Human Resource Management (pp. 460-474). SAGE Publication. doi:10.4135/9780857021496.n27

Marchington, M., Grimshaw, D., Rubery, J., & Willmott, H. (Eds.). (2005). *Fragmenting Work: Blurring Organisational Boundaries and Disordering Hierarchies*. Oxford University Press.

Mayer, R. C., Davis, J. H., & Schoorman, F. D. (1995). An integrative model of organizational trust. *Academy of Management Review*, *20*(3), 709–734. doi:10.5465/amr.1995.9508080335

McAfee, R. B., Glassman, M., & Honeycutt, E. D. Jr. (2002). The effects of culture and human resource management policies on supply chain management strategy. *Journal of Business Logistics*, *23*(1), 1–18. doi:10.1002/j.2158-1592.2002.tb00013.x

McConaughy, D. L., Matthews, C. H., & Fialko, A. S. (2001). Founding family-controlled firms: Efficiency, risk, and value. *Journal of Small Business Management*, *39*(1), 31–49. doi:10.1111/0447-2778.00004

Memili, E., Chrisman, J. J., Chua, J. A., Chang, E. P., & Kellermanns, K. W. (2011). The determinants of family firms' subcontracting: A transaction cost perspective. *Journal of Family Business Strategy*, *2*(1), 26–33. doi:10.1016/j.jfbs.2011.01.003

Meroño-Cerdán, A. L., López-Nicolás, C., & Molina-Castillo, F. J. (2018). Risk aversion, innovation and performance in family firms. *Economics of Innovation and New Technology*, *27*(2), 189–203. doi:10.1080/10438599.2017.1325569

Miller, D., & Le Breton-Miller, I. (2003). Challenge versus advantage in the family business. *Strategic Organization*, *1*(1), 127–134. doi:10.1177/1476127003001001222

Miotti, L., & Sachwald, F. (2003). Cooperative R&D: Why and with whom? An integrated framework of analysis. *Research Policy*, *32*, 1481–1499. doi:10.1016/S0048-7333(02)00159-2

Neubaum, D. O. (2018). Family business research: Roads traveled and the search for unworn paths. *Family Business Review*, *31*(3), 259–270. doi:10.1177/0894486518792948

Nguyen, B., & Mutum, D. S. (2012). A review of customer relationship management: Successes, advances, pitfalls, and futures. *Business Process Management Journal*, *18*(3), 400–419. doi:10.1108/14637151211232614

Nicholson, L. A., & Lashley, J. (2016). *Understanding the Caribbean Enterprise Insights from MSMEs and Family-Owned Businesses*. Palgrave Macmillan. doi:10.1057/978-1-349-94879-6

Orth, U. R., & Green, M. T. (2009). Consumer loyalty to family versus non-family business: The roles of store image, trust, and satisfaction. *Journal of Retailing and Consumer Services*, *16*(4), 248–259. doi:10.1016/j.jretconser.2008.12.002

Osterwalder, A., & Pigneur, Y. (2010). *Business Model Generation, A Handbook for Visionaries, Game Changers, and Challengers*. John Wiley & Sons, Inc.

Pan, Y., Weng, R., Xu, N., & Chan, K. C. (2018). The role of corporate philanthropy in family firm succession: A social outreach perspective. *Journal of Banking & Finance*, *88*, 423–441. doi:10.1016/j.jbankfin.2018.01.011

Panayides, P. M., & So, M. (2005). Logistics service providers-client relationships, relationships. *Transportation Research Part E, Logistics and Transportation Review*, *41*(3), 79–200. doi:10.1016/j.tre.2004.05.001

Pieper, T. M. (2019). Editor's note. *Journal of Family Business Strategy*, *10*(1), 1–2. doi:10.1016/j.jfbs.2019.04.001

Pittino, D., & Visintin, F. (2011). The propensity toward inter-organizational cooperation in small- and medium-sized family businesses. *Journal of Family Business Strategy*, *2*(2), 57–68. doi:10.1016/j.jfbs.2011.03.005

Posso, M.L. (2003). *A expansão das empresas familiares através de alianças est*. Academic Press.

Reid, R., & Adams, J. (2001). Human resource management—A survey of practices within family and non-family firms. *Journal of European Industrial Training*, *25*(6/7), 310–320. doi:10.1108/03090590110401782

Roessl, D. (2005). Family businesses and interfirm cooperation. *Family Business Review*, *18*(3), 203–214. doi:10.1111/j.1741-6248.2005.00042.x

Rubery, J., Carroll, M., Cooke, F. L., Grugulis, I., & Earnshaw, J. (2004). Human resource management and the permeable organization: The case of the multi-client call-centre. *Journal of Management Studies*, *41*(7), 22–2380. doi:10.1111/j.1467-6486.2004.00472.x

Rubery, J., Cooke, F. L., Earnshaw, J., & Marchington, M. (2003). Inter-Organizational Relations and Employment in a Multi-employer Environment. *British Journal of Industrial Relations*, *41*(2), 265–289. doi:10.1111/1467-8543.00272

Scherer, R. F., Adams, J. S., Carley, S. F., & Wiebe, F. A. (1989). Role model performance effects on the development of entrepreneurial career preferences. *Entrepreneurship Theory and Practice*, *13*(3), 53–71. doi:10.1177/104225878901300306

Sirmon, D., & Hitt, M. (2003). Managing resources: Linking unique resources, management, and wealth creation in family firms. *Entrepreneurship Theory and Practice*, *27*(4), 339–358. doi:10.1111/1540-8520.t01-1-00013

Snell, S. A., Shadur, M. A., & Wright, P. M. (2000). *Human resources strategy: The era of our ways* (CAHRS Working Paper #00-17). Ithaca, NY: Cornell University, School of Industrial and Labor Relations, Center for Advanced Human Resource Studies.

Steier, L. (2001). Next-generation entrepreneurs and succession: An exploratory study of modes and means of managing social capital. *Family Business Review, 14*(3), 259–276. doi:10.1111/j.1741-6248.2001.00259.x

Steijvers, T., & Niskanen, M. (2013). The determinants of cash holdings in private family firms. *Accounting and Finance, 53*(2), 537–560. doi:10.1111/j.1467-629X.2012.00467.x

Sweeney, E. (2013). The people dimension in logistics and supply chain management – its role and importance. In R. Passaro & A. Thomas (Eds.), *Supply Chain Management: Perspectives, Issues, and Cases* (pp. 73–82). McGraw-Hill.

Swinth, R., & Vinton, K. (1993). Do family-owned businesses have a strategic advantage in international joint ventures? *Family Business Review, 6*(1), 19–30. doi:10.1111/j.1741-6248.1993.00019.x

Tushman, M. (1977). Special Boundary Roles in the Innovation Process. *Administrative Science Quarterly, 22*(4), 587–605. doi:10.2307/2392402

Uhlaner, L. M., Goor-Balk, H. J. M. V., & Masurel, E. (2004). Family business and corporate social responsibility in a sample of Dutch firms. *Journal of Small Business and Enterprise Development, 11*(2), 186–194. doi:10.1108/14626000410537128

Ulrich, D., & Beatty, D. (2001). From partners to players: Extending the HR playing field. *Human Resource Management, 40*(4), 293-307.

Urlich, D., & Lake, D. (1990). *Organizational Capability*. John Wiley & Sons.

Ward, J. (1997). Growing the family business: Special challenges and best practices. *Family Business Review, 10*(4), 323–337. doi:10.1111/j.1741-6248.1997.00323.x

Zahra, S. A. (2010). Harvesting family firm's organizational social capital: A relational perspective. *Journal of Management Studies, 47*(2), 345–366.

Zellweger, T. (2007). Time horizon, costs of equity capital, and generic investment strategies of ðrms. *Family Business Review, 20*(1), 1–15. doi:10.1111/j.1741-6248.2007.00080.x

KEY TERMS AND DEFINITIONS

Ability, Benevolence, and Integrity Model: Ability reflects the knowledge, capacity. Benevolence and integrity are aspects of the leader's character. They require more time and attention on the part of followers before they can be reliably judged.

Buyer-Supplier Relationships: Two or more related organizations that partner and cooperate in order to provide expanded products and services.

Customer Relationship Management: Customer relationship management is a method used to manage organization communication with existing and potential customers.

Familiness: This refers to family business unique abilities and capital that influence their interaction in the family institutional system.

Relationship Stages: Relationship develop through five overall stages acknowledged as the pre-relationship, initial interaction, growth, maintenance, and dissolution. Each phase represents a significant transition in how parties regard one another.

Stakeholder: A person or organization with a stake in something, especially a business.

Trustee: The trustee provides trust. Typically, the trustor is a consumer.

Trustor: The trustor holds trust, and this trust relates to expectations of future behaviors based on perceived motivations and actions of the trustee's past behavior. Typically, the trustor is a consumer.

Chapter 5
Utilizing Technology to Enhance Human Resource Practices

Kelly M. Torres
The Chicago School of Professional Psychology, USA

Aubrey Statti
The Chicago School of Professional Psychology, USA

ABSTRACT

HR management departments are constantly evolving as a result of new technological advancements. For family HR firms, this technological evolution is vital in ensuring that they remain innovative and current with their competitors. Technology has impacted how companies recruit, retain, and evaluate employees. However, in order to ensure that technology is effectively and accurately adopted and integrated, companies need to understand how they can employ technology to enhance their daily operations and implement tools that provide an adequate return on investment for the technology they select. In family firms, a vast majority of employees are able to ensure that funds are invested in appropriate technology-enhanced projects and that they develop a family-like culture with their stakeholders. This chapter will seek to explore these emerging trends in order to present opportunity for family owned firms to function most efficiently and effectively in the modern, technology enhanced workplace.

INTRODUCTION

There are many ways that technology has impacted professional practices. One particular field that has been revolutionized by technology is human resource (HR) management. When technology is used effectively, HR staff are able to refine their practices and procedures to be more efficient, to provide clearer communication to employees, to track employee progress and needs, and to recruit the best candidates in the workplace. Essentially, advances in technology have fundamentally reshaped how individuals work and organizations function and provide services. Indeed, Stone et al. (2015) proclaimed that technology has had a profound impact on HR processes and practices and that diverse technological tools can be utilized to attract, motivate, and retain employees. Also, Turulja and Bajgorić (2016) shared that the

DOI: 10.4018/978-1-7998-4814-1.ch005

adoption of technology positively influences an organization's performance. For example, technological resources have been found to monitor employee turnover, improve employee experiences, and increase employees' levels of satisfaction and commitment (Carlson et al., 2017).

By integrating technological tools, employees may also become more productive thus increasing the company's success. Further, providing employees opportunities to become more productive is an essential component in developing a workforce that is more satisfied and motivated (Stewart & Brown, 2020; Suyono et al., 2019). The use of technology may be particularly essential in family HR management firms since they may operate similar to extended family units. Particularly, Sharma (2012) proposed that family owned firms may face unique challenges since emotions can interfere with business processes and decisions. The inclusion of technology-enhanced HR processes may be vital in helping family owned firms engage in objective and practical practices. Particularly, ensuring effective HR practices in family owned firms is a requisite for continual strategic gains (Clinton, 2016). However, based on their work through the lens of imprinting theory, Kidwell et. al (2018) noted the potential for bad habits in HR practices to continue through generations of family HR management firms. The inclusion of innovative technologies has the potential to disrupt these bad habits and creative new, effective management processes and communication styles in HR. Further, these technologies are vital in family owned firms since there is a notion that these types of organizations are slow to embrace new technologies into their companies.

BACKGROUND

The Impact of Technology on Human Resources Professional Practice

Technology has transformed how HR management and organizations recruitment candidates, interact with individuals, and target their talent pool. Even in family owned businesses and HR firms, hiring non-family members is key to the company's success. Indeed, Clinton (2016) proclaimed that the effectiveness and quality of a family business is reliant on family and non-family talent. The advent of platforms such as LinkedIn, Twitter, and Facebook provide companies the opportunity to post jobs and attract and recruit a wider and more diverse range of applicants (Collmus et al., 2016; Koch, et al., 2018; Melanthiou et al., 2015; Tufts, et al., 2014; Zide et al., 2014). Moreover, many companies now communicate with job seekers in cyberspace and use mobile technologies to evaluate potential candidates (Holm & Haahr, 2018). We live in a society where we are seeing a greater emphasis on the importance of engagement with community, whether that be a specific location, a group of family or friends, or a workplace community. Further, we often see that individuals who feel a part of something and connected with those around them are more confident, successful, and are generally more productive in the workplace. Therefore, family firm organizations are also able to benefit from HR policies that actively foster this type of connectivity and engagement in the workplace for their employees.

Wilton (2016) postulated that positive psychological contact in organizations results in increased motivation, lower turnover rates, enhanced job satisfaction, and organizational commitment. The inclusion of technology can also be impactful in providing HR staff the necessary tools needed to make more informed and effective decisions. In family owned firms, HR informed decisions may be more likely to be focused on subjective rather than objective input. Specifically, decisions made regarding family members may be driven by emotional factors in comparison to business ones that are derived by rationales (Clinton, 2016). By utilizing technology to determine how to handle particular situations, emotions can be separated out of the decision-making process when making determinations about employees.

The inclusion of virtual work options allows employees to become time and place independent (Hecklau et al., 2016), meaning employees can now work full time remotely outside of their company's physical structure, time zone, and even country or continent of residence. In fact, it has become ever more common for employees to successfully contribute to their company's mission and success, without actually ever stepping foot in their company's building or meeting their co-workers or clients face to face. This significant change in opening up the workplace is made possible through several technological advances and practices that companies have bought into. Further, the use of virtual meeting platforms helps to further provide family owned firms access to a vast array of training resources that may be vital in helping them better structure their companies. This type of training can be particular crucial for family HR management firms that experience challenges in training employees. Başkurt and Altindağ (2017) proposed that training within family firms may be particularly problematic with the second generation. Through the inclusion of technology, family owned firms are able to hire outside trainers who may be more successful in preparing younger family generations in their company roles.

Primarily, the adoption of virtual teams has become more widespread among organizations and is considered a primary way to structure work environments (Dulebohn & Hoch, 2017). As a result, companies can utilize virtual meeting platforms, such as GoToMeeting and Zoom, to provide flexibility for employee workplace preferences. Employees no longer need to spend travel time commuting to and from their office in order to meet with colleagues or work teams. Instead, employees can save time and commuting costs in meeting from their home offices and in turn, companies can save financial costs in funding office space for every employee on staff. These virtual meeting spaces can be seen as a way to strengthen employee connectivity. Staff members participating in a team think session can utilize web cameras to interact visually with one another as well as their clients or customers, increasing engagement, trust, and oftentimes more likeability than an email or other form of written communication. Additionally, computer sharing tools, allow staff to visually share the content of their computer screens with others in a meeting in order to provide timely communication, productive discussion, and effective problem solving in a team environment.

However, Serrat (2017) cautioned that managing virtual teams involves possessing an in-depth understanding of individuals, processes, and technology and that trust may be more limiting in comparison to face-to-face interactions. Hence, HR staff need to understand the technological necessity of certain tools and be able to verify if employees possess the skill sets needed to use these tools (DeCenzo et al., 2016). Companies are also now incorporating a wider range of technologies that promote and support employee's abilities to perform their jobs and promote awareness of their organization. There is a plethora of technological platforms and tools that can help support HR professionals in their daily professional responsibilities. The following sections will provide an overview of diverse forms of technology that can be utilized to help family owned firms more effectively oversee their businesses and better support customers, staff, and potential employees. Throughout this chapter, these ideas will be explored in detail. Further, we discuss specific recommendations for technology integration into HR professional practice as well as provide useful resources for these practices.

MAIN FOCUS OF THE CHAPTER

Overview of Innovative Technologies

Family owned firms are innovative in how they adopt technology to enhance organizational practices and HR policies. For example, companies with effective HR practices utilize technology to ensure that employees readily have access to professional development opportunities (Stewart & Brown, 2020). Further, companies are exploring the benefits of using social network sites to attract applicants and to further share information about their organizations (Melanthiou, et al., 2015). As a result of the advances in technology, corporations are able to have further outreach to applicants and clients and continuously modify their business practices. The inclusion of appropriate technological tools is vital in family owned firms and HR departments since their staff are responsible for the development, implementation, and oversight of company policies. Notably, Stewart and Brown (2020) proposed that "companies with effective human resource practices make use of technology to ensure that employees have access to a variety of developmental opportunities" (p. 378). Essentially, technological changes have resulted in providing family owned firms many advantages and opportunities for developing and expanding their businesses. Employee engagement with technology may differ across generations in family owned firms with younger relatives implementing more advanced forms of technology to meet their business goals and visions.

Social media. Statistica (2019) reported that in 2018 there were approximately 2.65 billion active users of social media worldwide with this estimate increasing to 3.1 billion by the year 2021. Moreover, consumers of social media in the United States are projected to engage with these types of platforms for almost two hours per day (Statistica, 2019). The popularity of social media platforms has resulted in more organizations strategically determining how to integrate this technology into their day-to-day operations. The inclusion of social media into organizational functions has been found to serve several purposes including knowledge management and sharing (El Ouirdi et al., 2015), organizational communication (Ngai et al., 2015), and assisting in applicant selection processes (Tufts et al. 2014, Wolf, et al., 2014). Additionally, an increasing number of companies are utilizing social media as a tool to be more competitive and to extend their recruitment practices (Aguado, 2016). For example, job tools like Indeed, ZipRecruiter, and Glassdoor, allow potential employees to search listings and apply in a short period of time, thus providing HR recruiters an opportunity to review potential candidates quickly and with a clearer picture of the candidates' qualifications and skills.

When using social media platforms as part of the selection process for hiring candidates, organizations should implement assessments that are well-conducted and provide well-documented evidence that predict the candidate's job performance (Davison et al., 2016). Organizations are also searching social media sites to gather information about potential employees as an effort to make more informed hiring decisions (Acikgoz & Bergman, 2016; Roth, et al., 2013). While still a somewhat controversial practice, organizations often use social media to ensure that their employees and a potential candidate's personal life aligns with the professional mission of the company. This approach can be helpful for family firms who are interested in hiring employee who have similar values, beliefs, and morals. Further, family firms are able to monitor the social media accounts of their hired family members as well as non-family employees in order to ensure their posts are reflective of the mission of the company.

Social media has had a particular impact on HR practices in regards to recruitment (Landers & Shcmidt, 2016). For example, organizations are now using social media sites like LinkedIn, Twitter, and Instagram to tell their organization's success story through photos, blogs, and other types of social media posts. Social media allows individuals to feel connected to organizations or companies they may support, frequent, or apply to and in turn strengthen the overall global community of a business. Through social media postings, family owned firms are able to share their company's evolution and approaches to providing their customers a *family like* experience. Further, Agbim (2018) suggested that social media platforms provide a wider range of interactions for all stakeholders. Additionally, Dhaenens et. al (2018) noted that mentorship is a key component in the success of a family owned HR management firm. Therefore, social media provides a multitude of platforms and connection avenues that allow for family members to receive outside mentorship and support in order to further develop the goals and outcomes of their family's firm.

Cloud technology. Another emerging HR technology trend is the use of cloud technology. This trend has become more popular due to the benefits it provides in document sharing and collaboration. Also, cloud technologies are gaining more popularity due to their ease of use, access to network resources, and minimal management effort that is required for their usage (Birje et al. 2017). Furthermore, the inclusion of cloud technologies are also considered to be cost effective storage options (Yang et al., 2018). Gupta et al. (2018) reported that in 2017 approximately 73% of companies used at least one HR cloud process. Essentially, cloud technologies have had a fundamental and transformational impact on organizational behaviors. Because family owned firms have been described as innovative (Rondi et al., 2019), the inclusion of cloud technology can help them to remain cutting edge in their business practices.

There are many benefits of cloud technology including it being considered safe, economical, user friendly, and global (Kumar, 2017). Moreover, cloud sharing platforms provide HR staff the opportunity to improve system securities, increase efficacy and resource utilization, and reduce costs and physical spaces (Navimipour et al., 2015). Likewise, cloud platforms provide business agility that allows for the ability to scale up faster. Cloud-based applications are also useful for data collection and storage (Bedell, et al, 2018). To alleviate concerns regarding the security challenges associated with cloud platforms (e.g., viewing private documents), organizational leaders are able to only assign privileges to employees who need access to the application or specific files (Odun-Ayo et al., 2017).

Bring your own technology. Advancements in mobile technologies have provided opportunities for employees to work from anywhere (Gokce & Dogerlioglu, 2019; Taperesu & Van Belle, 2017). As a result, Bring Your Own Device (BYOD) is also another popular movement that companies are starting to embrace. This trend has also been referred to as Bring Your Own Technology (BYOT), Bring Your Own Computer (BYOC), Bring Your Own Laptop (BYOL), and Bring Your Own PC (BYOPC). This concept has been described as the use of personal devices to access data and assets that are business owned (Scarfo, 2012). Deloitte (2013) further defined BYOD as the use of employee owned devices to access company content and networks.

Zayed (2016) suggested that the inclusion of BYOD has significantly changed the corporate workplace landscape. BYOD policies have become more popular since employees have been found to be able to better balance their personal and professional lives when they use their own devices for completing work tasks. Likewise, many employees prefer to use their own devices for work (Johnson & Kavanagh, 2018) and BYOD programs have positively impacted employee productivity when they are offered in organizations (Hayes & Kotwica, 2013). Through BYOD initiatives, employees have been found to be more productive and companies have experienced a reduction in information technology expenses (Lee et al., 2016), have observed increases in staff morale (Ward et al., 2017), and discovered areas of improved efficiency (Garba et al., 2015). Taperesu and Van Belle (2017) discovered that factors that influence companies to adopt this trend include security, mobile device management, change management, and connectivity. However, BYOD has become more commonplace due to the technologies such as smartphones providing employees the opportunity to respond to emails and access work applications from outside of the office and beyond the standard workday.

Employees may also be more likely to be cautious with technology in BYOD programs since they own it as well as are more comfortable using the technology due to it being their personal tool of choice. When using this type of company policy, organizations need to be mindful that employees may share devices with their family members and that private, confidential work information may be kept on the technology. Therefore, to avoid conflict among relatives in a family owned firm, employees may need to be mindful of sharing devices within their homes. Particularly, sharing devices within an employee's home may create unforeseen situations since the family members will be familiar with all employees at the organization and they may become privy to information that should not be shared outside the context of the company HR department.

Wearable technologies. Top companies such as Google, Apple, and Microsoft are providing wearable technology in a variety of formats ranging from smartwatches to glasses. Examples of wearable devices include smart clothes, helmets, and eyeglasses. The use of wearable devices are becoming more widespread since they can be used to help employees stay connected and improve their time management skills. Further, the use of wearable technologies has been found to enhance employee engagement and increase productivity (Hao & Helo, 2017). Additionally, the use of wearable devices has been found to increase employee satisfaction rates (Nayak et al., 2019). Particularly, when employees are provided with more resources to be better and more efficient at their jobs, their satisfaction rates tend to increase.

Jacobs et al. (2019) found that employee's positive past experiences impacted their selection of wearable devices and that they are more likely to adequately inform the organization about data use when they perceive the technology more favorably. They further discovered that company incentives for wearable technology use can affect employees willing to use the technology. These types of technological resources can help bridge differences in technological perceptions across generations of family members. For example, younger generations of family members within the firm can provide their relatives an overview of the importance of the technology and how it can promote organizational practices. Through this approach, family members who are more hesitant to utilize innovative technologies can more effectively understand the affordances provided by the tools and receive mentorship in their integration of it. Wearable technology has grown more acceptance (Nascimento et al., 2018) and may as a result become more commonplace in HR practices. Because HR is dedicated to providing organization and structure for the company's daily operations, the inclusion of wearable technologies can help to further engage employees, increase productivity, and enhance safety.

Artificial intelligence. Industry leaders have started to implement innovative technologies such as artificial intelligence (AI) to improve client and employee experiences. AI enables machines to *think like humans* and perform tasks such as learning, problem-solving, reasoning, and language processing. McKinsey (2017) described the use of AI as including assisted, augmented, and autonomous intelligence. The use of smart technologies such as AI are now enabling HR teams to solve critical business challenges, drive exponential performance improvements, and even impact larger business outcomes and profitability. Moreover, organizations are utilizing AI chatbots in order to provide consumers answers to their queries via platforms such as Facebook messenger and webchats (Nawaz & Gomes, 2019). Family owned firms should consider how AI can impact their organizational practices and their workforce. In essence, AI is often used for tasks that are perceived as low-value and repetitive since it can help to place more employee focus on strategic workplace activities. As a result, family owned firms need to consider what tasks may be most suitable to replace with AI without losing the core values that they consider to be essential to providing their clients a family like business approach and atmosphere.

AI cognitive engagement technologies have been utilized to answer frequently common questions (Davenport & Ronanki, 2018). Further, the use of AI is being utilized by HR departments in areas such as employee recruitment. In addition to improving efficiency, AI is also helping HR leaders overcome human bias in decision making and has focused on areas such as candidate searches, employee turnover predictions, staff rostering, and genetic algorithms (Strohmeier & Piazza, 2015). In essence, the inclusion of AI can be a powerful tool to transform work and optimize automated work practices. Through this tool, HR staff are able to implement procedures that will allow them to learn more about their employees and shape their company culture. This technology tool can be helpful for family owned firms since they are able to utilize AI to better understand their customers, maximize time of their employee workforce, and provide them a competitive edge.

Virtual reality. Companies are also focusing on approaches to more effectively recruitment, promote, and retain their employees. The inclusion of technologies such as virtual reality (VR) provide businesses the opportunity to promote their organizations, recruitment potential employees, and train current employees through interactive and creative means. VR technology provides individuals the opportunity to inhabit an entirely virtual environment. In this type of environment, subjects and objects can be perceived as real-life scenarios. When individuals enter a virtual world, they are immersed in an interactive experience that provides a life-like quality (Sherman & Craig, 2019). For example, researchers have discovered that VR can be used to provide individuals the opportunity to enhance their public speaking skills (Harris et al., 2004; Lindner et al., 2019) and improve training effectiveness (Feng et al., 2018; Matass & Vosniakos, 2017).

The inclusion of VR technology in HR departments has been valuable in providing recruits and current employees value-added experiences and training opportunities (Khadelwal & Upadhyay, 2019). Li (2016) contended that training design is a fundamental skill of HR professionals. As such, HR departments need to be conscious of how to design trainings that are inclusive of technologies such as VR in order to provide employees effective opportunities to improve their performance and track their progress. VR technology can also be used to evaluate candidates' abilities and aid employees in their acquisition of the skills and knowledge needed to perform their jobs successfully.

VR is being used in companies to help employees gain skills and knowledge that they are able to transfer to improve their job performance (Farrell, 2018). Further, some companies perceive the inclusion of VR technology as providing a positive employee impact through training and in providing information reduction and navigation (Koh, 2017). Similar to other business, the use of VR in family owned HR firms can help to eliminate inefficiencies and entice clients and customers. This technology can be particularly powerful in providing family owned firms the opportunity to expand their services beyond their geographical location and they can use VR for fundraising and marketing purposes. Further, family owned firms are also able to use VR for friendly employee competitions and to engage younger generations in their acquisition and acceptance of organizational processes that may be perceived as "drier" or more "boring" to them.

Analytical tools. Turner et al. (2014) predicted that digital data that is generated worldwide will continue to increase by 40% over the next decade. This influx in data makes it imperative to include technology such as analytics to help companies conduct analyses and better understand the massive volumes of generated data that they produce each year. Analytics has been described as being a *must have* tool for HR departments since it provides them an opportunity to strengthen their strategic influence (CIPD,

2013). These technological tools can help to examine employee data and provide actionable insight. For example, analytics can be performed in order to determine the effectiveness of current practices and therefore provide potential changes in policy or practice to recruitment strategies, employee engagement, or performance management. Specifically, HR analytics provide evidence-based approaches for decision-making and consists of numerous tools ranging from metrics to predictive modeling (Bassi, 2011; Marler & Boudreau, 2017). These predictive analytical tools can be particularly vital for family owned HR firms by providing them diagnostic data that illustrates possible outcomes for new processes or projects. Further, this type of data, can guide family owned firms in their consideration of factors that impact their daily work practices (e.g., what they are doing well, their communication trends, areas of improvement, etc.).

In addition to utilizing analytics to examine and develop organizational change, analytical tools and other technology platforms can be used to identify potential areas of growth for individual employees. Further, analytical tools can enhance data that guides HR staff in determining which employees possess skill sets directly aligned with specific organizational goals (Leonardi & Contractor, 2018). Data captured through analytical tools can also provide valuable insight into how to best train and coach employees (Dearborn & Swanson, 2018). However, Urban et al. (2017) cautioned that analytical tools are only beneficial if companies utilize these resources extensively and frequently. Therefore, companies who purchase analytical tools should also invest in the research to select the appropriate and needed tools as well as the training required to most effectively utilize the data.

Gamification. Gamification refers to incorporating gaming elements into non-game contexts (e.g., education, businesses). When used optimally, gamification can help to encourage employees to apply learning directly to their workplace role since they are provided real workplace situations in a controlled environment. Gamification is also utilized to capture job seekers' interest in employment openings and for self-analysis and intelligent screening. Specifically, gamification is being used in HR in order to assess, select, and recruit employees (Korn et al., 2017). The use of gamification can help recruiters to capture information on applicants' levels of creativity, innovation, aptitude, and problem-solving capabilities. Using gamification for family owned firms can be beneficial in developing a more creative, diverse workforce within the organization.

Armstrong et al. (2016) described gamification as having the potential to provide assessment methods that provide applicants game-like experiences in which they are able to react to tasks. Analytical tools also help in increasing predictions related to employee job performance. Further, the inclusion of gamification elements promotes employee behavioral changes and motivates individuals to develop skills and they can be incorporated to drive innovation (Burke, 2014). The inclusion of gaming elements leads to behavioral changes in employees by evoking emotional responses (McCathy et al., 2019). For instance, through the use of digital badges and leaderboards, game mechanics can be motivators for staff to improve their levels of productivity, develop positive organization changes, and foster collaborative team efforts (Metzger et al., 2016). Gamification has been found to provide employees meaningful user engagement experiences (Suh, 2017). Particularly, gamification can provide employees training and employment experiences that are engaging, interactive, and memorable. For example, Damian et al. (2015) found that individuals who completed a training program with gamification elements displayed improvements in their interview social skills in comparison to people who were provided more traditional training methods. Since family HR firms may spend a considerable amount of time on skill development and building, the inclusion of gamification can help to create engaging and motivating learning environments that could become tense between family members. The inclusion of games can also help to solidify relationships among relatives within the organization and bridge generational differences. Additionally, these types of technological tools can positively impact collaboration and engagement within the family owned firm.

Mobile learning. The rise of mobile phone use has resulted in an increase in apps that are designed to make communication, transactions, and a variety of other tasks easier, which has resulted in transforming the way we function and communicate. This technological trend results in workforces being more mobile and easily accessible (Alawani & Singh, 2017; Bedell et al., 2018). Attributes of mobile learning include key elements of customizability, portability, connectivity, accessibility, and immediacy (Korucu & Alkan, 2011; Traxler, 2009). Mobile learning allows for information-sharing and is time-optimized and cost-effective. This type of learning format allows for training to be learner-focused, allowing participants to control how and when they learn. As a result, the learning experience is customized for the employee's unique requirements, which can help to empower employees and boost engagement. As a result, training experiences in family owned HR firms can be adapted to individualized needs and technology skill levels.

Mobile phones have also increased employees access to HR data and relevant work apps needed to perform diverse tasks (e.g., Workday and SuccessFactors) (Kavanagh & Johnson, 2018); record work completed, engage in location management, complete employee check-ins (Maditheti, 2017); and result in increased levels of organizational effectiveness (Bhargava, 2018). Further, mobile learning can be tailored to provide personalized learning experiences (Chiang et al., 2015; Crompton et al., 2016; Elkhair & Mutalib, 2019; Fakomogbon & Bolaji, 2017; Khaddage et al., 2016). Individuals may perceive mobile learning more positively when they possess a more favorably attitude toward this type of technology. Particularly, younger generations in family owned firms may be more receptive to mobile learning and the benefits it affords. For example, Briz-Ponce et al. (2017) found that learners' attitudes and experiences were correlated and impacted their willingness to recommend mobile learning technology. By implementing this type of technology in family owned firms, employees across generations are able to encourage one another to embrace this innovative learning approach. As a result of this educational model, families are able to embrace the value of acquiring new knowledge through advanced technologies and begin working collaboratively together as an organizational model as a *learning family*. Through the inclusion of mobile learning, individuals are able to engage in experiences that are untethered from formal learning and conceptualize information in various ways (Shuck et al., 2017).

CONSIDERATIONS AND SOLUTIONS

Although the advent of technology has resulted in more advanced and efficient forms of workplace procedures and policies, companies may have reservations about its implementation. Indeed, Morris and Revels (2012) proclaimed that HR professionals need to be aware of potential technology challenges since they are continuously being introduced to new technological trends and technology-based strategies. Particularly, in light of recent trends, such as BYOD, more companies are integrating precautions to ensure there are not security and privacy risks associated with employees using their own technology for company purposes. Particularly, Veljkovic and Budree (2019) proclaimed that BYOD is creating concern for information technology professionals in how they can adequately ensure the safe and appropriate use of this trend. The most problematic issues with these programs are "end-user non-compliance with security policies and lack of awareness" (Zayed, 2016, p. 277). Nevertheless, companies must determine how best to secure organizational data while balancing concerns related to employee privacy.

In comparison, the adoption of other forms of technology such as analytical tools can be impacted by financial and technical variables, personal values, and support provided by senior managers (Torres et al., 2015). For example, family owned HR firms can require that employees do not share devices within their homes, and they are able to create a technology and security plan to ensure the safe use of devices. Further, family owned firms can monitor employee's internet usage and conduct periodic risk assessments to determine potential security threats.

Employers and employees may also have security concerns regarding document sharing via the cloud. In fact, security concerns are the most noted reason for a company objecting to the adoption of cloud technology (Ghudayyer et al., 2017; Ho et al., 2017; Nakayama et al., 2017; Oliveira et al., 2014). However, integrating innovative technologies can be particularly valuable for family owned firms who need to effectively manage costs while remaining innovative. The inclusion of cloud technologies can be valuable in reducing family owned firms' overhead costs (e.g., printing and mailing documents). Marler and Fisher (2017) proposed that the potential risks associated with using cloud platforms is no greater than other internal storage methods. Birje et al. (2017) recommended having countermeasures in place that outline rules and regulations and performing security assessments in order to reduce possible company breaches.

As with other organizations, many family owned firms are expanding and are in need of more laborers. Indeed, the United States Bureau of Labor Statistics (2019) reported a significant increase in the number of professional and business service jobs available. As a result of increased employment opportunities, companies in these business sectors may experience an influx of applicants. The use of AI chatbots can help to decrease the time required to complete certain tasks such as screening numerous job applications (Nawaz & Gomes, 2019; Mohan, 2019; Rusydan et al., 2019). To determine if new cutting-edge technologies are appropriate for family owned firms, they are able to use free online platforms to determine if these tools would be appropriate to include in their organizations. Further, family members who are more technology savvy could be charged with exploring new technological tools and providing an overview of the benefits and disadvantages for using the technology within their company.

The acceptance of new technology may also be dependent on employee perceptions of its usefulness. For example, Jacobs et. al. (2019) shared that employees should be involved in the selection of wearable technologies and that organizations should inform employees about who, how, and why data will be used and protected. However, Yildirim and Ali-Eldin (2019) found in their research that privacy was not a significant concern for employees using wearable devices due to them being less conservative with privacy when at work. Companies can utilize VR technology to provide safety assurances for their assets and employees (Higgins, 2017). To create positive and equitable work environments, family owned firms can also use these types of tools for training, marketing, and recruiting purposes.

CONCLUSION

Navimipour et al. (2015) proposed that HR is one of the most vital aspects of an organization and that this department significantly impacts the company's overall success. Technological change has influenced all aspects of HR management (Stewart & Brown, 2020) impacting the way that staff recruit, interact, and train employees. Thus, importance needs to be placed on how HR policies and practices can be enhanced to better promote a company's values and vision and provide employees positive work experiences. Li (2016) asserted that "there is no doubt that technology advancement has been credited for creating performance improvement opportunities through achieving greater effectiveness and efficiencies for individuals and organizations" (p. 189). Within family HR management firms, employees often very quickly respond to rapidly changing events allowing them to extend their resources across a range of technological innovations. They should also consider how the inclusive of technology-enhanced organizational practices will impact younger generations and what really *matters* in the longevity of their companies.

The role of HR departments in family firms are integral in ensuring company practices encompass values-driven goals and practical tools that allow for creating a culture of success in the organization. HR departments should not simply embrace technological trends but perceive technology as enabling them to conduct their processes differently (Kavanagh & Johnson, 2018) and to engage in the global workplace most effectively. The adoption of technology provides companies powerful tools that assist them in becoming more efficient and effective in their processes, policies, and procedures. Indeed, Alami et al. (2016) proclaimed that "in today's world, IT is the key factor of human development in organizations" (p. 189). Moreover, Turulja and Bajgorić (2016) found that technology impacts a business's performance but is more important in enhancing the capabilities of HR. This finding is particularly important in family owned firms since their constant evolution contributes to their continual success. Essentially, the inclusion of technology into the family owned firms provides them the opportunity to work more effectively while attracting and retaining a talented and supportive workforce that optimizes and enhances organizational practices.

REFERENCES

Acikgoz, Y., & Bergman, S. (2016). Social media and employee recruitment: Chasing the run away bandwagon. In R. Landers & G. Schmidt (Eds.), *Social media in employee selection and recruitment* (pp. 175–195). Springer. doi:10.1007/978-3-319-29989-1_9

Agbim, K. C. (2018). *Social networking and the family business performance: A conceptual consideration. Journal of Entrepreneurship, Management, and Innovation.* doi:10.7341/20191514

Aguado, D., Rico, R., Rubio, V., & Fernández, L. (2016). Applicant reasons to social network web use in personnel section and assessment. *Revista de Psicología del Trabajo y de las Organizaciones*, *32*(3), 183–190. doi:10.1016/j.rpto.2016.09.001

Alami, R., Gorji, O. H., Asrami, M. S., Saravi, H. R., Soteh, M. J., & Ahangari, F. R. (2016). The role of information technology (IT) in development and increase of the efficiency of human resources. *Journal of Social Science Studies*, *3*(2), 188–197. doi:10.5296/jsss.v3i2.8602

Alawani, A. S., & Singh, A. D. (2017). A smart mobile learning conceptual framework for professional development of UAE in-service teachers. *International Journal of Management and Applied Research*, *4*(3), 146–165. doi:10.18646/2056.43.17-012

Armstrong, M. B., Ferrell, J., Collmus, A., & Landers, R. (2016a). Correcting misconceptions about gamification of assessment: More than SJTs and badges. *Industrial and Organizational Psychology: Perspectives on Science and Practice*, *9*(3), 671–677. doi:10.1017/iop.2016.69

Başkurt, G., & Altindağ, E. (2017). The impact of institutionalization of family business on strategic human resources management and company performance. *Business Management Dynamics*, *7*(3), 10–25.

Bassi, L. (2011). Raging debates in HR analytics. *People & Strategy*, *34*, 14–18.

Bedell, M., Canniff, M., & Wyrick, C. (2018). Systems considerations in the design of an HRIS: Planning for implementations. *Human resource information systems: Basics, applications, and future directions*. In M. J. Kavanagh & R. D. Johnson (Eds.), *Human resource information systems: Basics, applications, and future directions* (pp. 45–66). Sage.

Bhargava, A. (2018). A study of the role of mobile technology on organizational effectiveness. *International Journal of Pure and Applied Mathematics*, *118*(15), 97–102.

Birje, M. N., Challagidad, P. S., Goudar, R. H., & Tapale, M. T. (2017). Cloud computing Review: Concepts, technology, challenges, and security. *International Journal of Cloud Computing*, *6*(1), 32–57. doi:10.1504/IJCC.2017.083905

Briz-Ponce, L., Pereira, A., Carvallho, L., Juanes-Méndez, J. A., & García-Peñalvo, F. J. (2017). Learning with mobile technologies – Students' behavior. *Computers in Human Behavior*, *72*, 612–620. doi:10.1016/j.chb.2016.05.027

Burke, B. (2014). *Gamify: How gamification motivates people to do extraordinary things*. Bibliomotion, Inc.

Carlson, J. R., Carlson, D. S., Zivnuska, S., Harris, R. B., & Harris, K. J. (2017). Applying the job demands resources model to understand technology as a predictor of turnover intentions. *Computers in Human Behavior*, *77*, 317–325. doi:10.1016/j.chb.2017.09.009

Chiang, F. K., Zhu, G., Wang, Q., Cui, Z., Cai, S., & Yu, S. (2015). Research and trends in mobile learning from 1976 to 2013: A content analysis of patents in selected databases. *British Journal of Educational Technology*, *47*(6), 1006–1019. doi:10.1111/bjet.12311

CIPD. (2013). Talent analytics and big data: The challenge for HR. *Chartered Institute for Personnel and Development*. https://www.cipd.co.uk/Images/talent-analytics-and-big-data_2013-challenge-for-hr_tcm18-9289.pdf

Clinton, E. (2016). Human resources in the family business-maximsing the power of your people. *Irish Journal of Management*, *35*(2), 176–178. Advance online publication. doi:10.1515/ijm-2016-0014

Collmus, A. B., Armstrong, M. B., & Landers, R. N. (2016). Game thinking within social media to recruit and select job candidates. In R. Landers & G. Schmidt (Eds.), *Social media in employee selection and recruitment* (pp. 103–124). Springer. doi:10.1007/978-3-319-29989-1_6

Crompton, H., Burke, D., Gregory, K., & Cräbe, C. (2016). The use of mobile learning in science: A systematic review. *Journal of Science Education and Technology*, *25*(2), 149–160. doi:10.100710956-015-9597-x

Damian, I., Baur, T., Lugrin, B., Gebhard, P., Mehlmann, G., & André, E. (2015). Games are better than books: In-situ comparison of an interactive job interview game with conventional training. In N C. Conati, N. Heffernan, A. Mitrovic, & F. M. Vergejo (Eds.), Artificial intelligence in education (pp. 84-94). Springer.

Davenport, T., & Ronanki, R. (2018). Artificial intelligence for the real world. *Harvard Business Review.* https://www.kungfu.ai/wp-content/uploads/2019/01/R1801H-PDF-ENG.pdf

Dearborn, J., & Swanson, D. (2018). *The data driven leader: A powerful approach to delivering measurable business impact through people analytics*. Wiley.

DeCenzo, D., Robbins, S. P., & Verhulst, S. L. (2016). *Fundamentals of human resource management*. Wiley.

Deloitte. (2013). *Understanding the bring-your-own device landscape.* https://www2.deloitte.com/content/dam/Deloitte/uk/Documents/about-deloitte/deloitte-uk-understanding-the-bring-your-own-device%20 landscape.pdf

Dhaenens, A., Marler, L., Vardaman, J., & Chrisman, J. (2018). Mentoring in family businesses: Toward an understanding of commitment outcomes. *Human Resource Management Review*, *28*(1), 46–55. doi:10.1016/j.hrmr.2017.05.005

Dulebohn, J. H., & Hoch, J. E. (2017). Virtual teams in organizations. *Human Resource Management Review*, *27*(4), 569–574. doi:10.1016/j.hrmr.2016.12.004

El Ouird, A., El Quird, M., Segers, J., & Henderickx, E. (2015). Employees' use of social media technologies: A methodological and thematic Review. *Behaviour & Information Technology*, *34*(5), 454–464. doi:10.1080/0144929X.2015.1004647

Elkhair, Z., & Mutalib, A. A. (2019). Mobile learning applications: Characteristics, perspectives, and future trends. *International Journal of Interactive Digital Media*, *5*(1), 18–21.

Fakomogbon, M. A., & Bolaji, H. O. (2017). Effects of collaborative Learning styles on performance of students in a ubiquitous collaborative mobile Learning environment. *Contemporary Educational Technology*, *8*(3), 268–279.

Farrell, W. A. (2018). Learning becomes doing: Applying augmented and virtual reality to improve performance. *Performance Improvement*, *57*(4), 19–28. doi:10.1002/pfi.21775

Feng, Z., Gonzálex, V. A., Amor, R., Lovreglio, R., & Cabrera-Guerrero, G. (2018). Immersive virtual reality serious games for evacuation training and Research: A systemic literature review. *Computers & Education*, *127*, 252–266. doi:10.1016/j.compedu.2018.09.002

Garba, A. B., Armarego, J., Murray, D., & Kenworthy, W. (2015). Review of the information security and privacy challenges in bring your own device (BYOD) environments. *Journal of Information Privacy and Security*, *11*(1), 38–54. doi:10.1080/15536548.2015.1010985

Ghudayyer, M. B., Javed, Y., & Alenezi, M. (2017). A security perspective on adoption and migration to mobile cloud technology. *International Journal of Informatics Visualization*, *1*(4), 143–149. doi:10.30630/joiv.1.4.54

Gokce, K. G., & Dogerlioglu, O. (2019). "Bring your own device" policies: Perspectives of both employees and organizations. *Knowledge Management & E-Learning*, *11*(2), 233–246.

Gupta, P., Fernandes, S., & Manish, J. (2018). Automation in recruitment: A new frontier. *Journal of Information Teaching Cases*, *8*(2), 118–125. doi:10.105741266-018-0042-x

Hao, Y., & Helo, P. (2017). The role of wearable devices in meeting the needs of cloud manufacturing: A case study. *Robotics and Computer-integrated Manufacturing*, *45*, 168–179. doi:10.1016/j.rcim.2015.10.001

Harris, S. R., Kemmerling, R. L., & North, M. N. (2004). Brief virtual reality therapy for public speaking anxiety. *Cyberpsychology & Behavior*, *5*(6), 543–550. doi:10.1089/109493102321018187 PMID:12556117

Hayes, B., & Kotwica, K. (2013). *Bring your own device (BYOD) to work*. Elsevier.

Hecklau, F., Galeitzke, M., Flachs, S., & Kohl, H. (2016). Holistic approach for human resource management in industry 4.0. *Procedia CIRP*, *54*, 1–6. doi:10.1016/j.procir.2016.05.102

Higgins, V. (2017). Augmented & virtual reality: The future of work, not just play. *Vantage Point*, *62*(6), 86–87.

Ho, S. M., Ocasio-Valázquez, M., & Booth, C. (2017). Trust or consequences? Causal effects of perceived risk and subjective norms on cloud technology adoption. *Computers & Security*, *70*, 581–595. doi:10.1016/j.cose.2017.08.004

Holm, A., & Haahr, L. (2018). e-Recruitment and selection. In M. Thite (Ed.), e-HRM digital approaches, directions, & applications (pp. 374-398). Routledge.

Jacobs, J. V., Hettinger, L., Huang, Y. H., Jeffries, S., Lesch, M. F., Simmons, L. A., Verma, S. K., & Willetts, J. (2019). Employee acceptance of wearable technology in the workplace. *Applied Ergonomics*, *78*, 148–156. doi:10.1016/j.apergo.2019.03.003 PMID:31046946

Kavanagh, M. J., & Johnson, R. D. (2018). A brief history and overview of technology in HR. In M. J. Kavanagh & R. D. Johnson (Eds.), *Human resource information systems: Basics, applications, and future directions* (pp. 2–23). Sage.

Khaddage, F., Müller, W., & Flintoff, K. (2016). Advancing mobile learning in formal and informal settings via mobile app technology: Where to from here, and how? *Journal of Educational Technology & Society*, *19*(3), 16–26.

Khadelwal, K., & Upadhyay, A. K. (2019). Virtual reality interventions in developing and managing *human resources. Human Resource Development International*, 1–15. doi:10.1080/13678868.2019.1569920

Kidwell, R., Eddleston, K., & Kellermanns, F. (2020). Learning bad habits across generations: How negative imprints affect human resource management in the family firm. *Human Resource Management Review*, *28*(1), 5–17. doi:10.1016/j.hrmr.2017.05.002

Koch, T., Gerber, C., & de Klerk, J. J. (2018). The impact of social media on recruitment: Are you LinkedIn? *SA Journal of Human Resource Management*, *16*(1), 1–14. doi:10.4102ajhrm.v16i0.861

Koh, D. (2017). *The future of VR/AR tech in the public safety domain*. www.opengovasia.com/blogs/5-opengov-expert-opinion/post/7321-the-future-of-vrar-tech-in-the-public-safety-domain

Korn, O., Brenner, F., Börsig, J., Lalli, F., Mattmüller, M., & Müller, A. (2017). Defining recruitment: A model and a survey on the gamification of recruiting and human resources. In L. E. Freund & W. Cellary (Eds.), *Human side of service engineering* (pp. 37–49). Springer.

Korucu, T., & Alkan, A. (2011). Differences between m-learning (mobile learning) and e-learning, basic terminology and usage of m-learning in education. *Social and Behavioral Science*, *15*, 1925–193. doi:10.1016/j.sbspro.2011.04.029

Kumar, R. (2017). Cloud technology and human resource management. *Research Journal of SCMS*, *5*, 82–91.

Landers, R. N., & Schmidt, G. B. (2016). Social media in employee selection and recruitment: An overview. In R. N. Landers & G. B. Schmidt (Eds.), *Social media employee selection and recruitment* (pp. 3–14). Springer. doi:10.1007/978-3-319-29989-1_1

Lee, J., Warkentin, M., Crossler, R., & Ontondo, R. F. (2016). Implications of monitoring mechanisms of bring your own device adoption. *Journal of Computer Information Systems*, *57*(4), 309–318. doi:10.1080/08874417.2016.1184032

Leonardi, P., & Contractor, N. (2018). Analytics: Better people analytics. *Harvard Business Review*. https://empowerment.ee/wp-content/uploads/2018/11/Better-People-Analytics-Measure-Who-They-Know-Not-Just-Who-They-Are.pdf

Li, J. (2016). Technology advancement and the future of HRD research. *Human Resource Development Journal*, *19*(3), 189–191. doi:10.1080/13678868.2016.1181846

Lindner, P., Miloff, A., Fagernas, S., Anderson, J., Sigeman, M., Andersson, G., Furmark, T., & Carlbring, P. (2019). Therapist-led and self-led one session virtual reality exposure therapy for public speaking anxiety with consumer hardware and software: A randomized controlled trail. *Journal of Anxiety Disorders*, *61*, 45–54. doi:10.1016/j.janxdis.2018.07.003 PMID:30054173

Maditheti, N. N. (2017). A comprehensive literature review of the digital HR research field. *Information and Knowledge Management*, *7*(4), 15–20.

Marler, J. H., & Boudreau, J. W. (2017). An evidence-based review of HR analytics. *International Journal of Human Resource Management*, *28*(1), 3–26. doi:10.1080/09585192.2016.1244699

Marler, J. H., & Fisher, S. L. (2017). *Making HR technology decisions: A strategic perspective*. Business Expert Press.

Matass, E., & Vosniakos, G. C. (2017). Design of a virtual reality training System for human-robot collaboration in manufacturing tasks. *International Journal of Interactive Design and Manufacturing*, *11*(2), 139–153. doi:10.100712008-015-0259-2

McCathy, I., Plangger, K., Robson, K., Kietzmann, J., & Pitt, L. (2019). Dynamic game plans: Using gamification to entrain strategic renewal with environmental velocity. In A. Tunchdogan, A. Lindgreen, van den Bocsh, & Volberda, H. (Eds), Handbook of strategic renewal (pp. 391-405). Elsevier.

McKinsey & Company. (2017). *Smartening up with artificial intelligence*. https://www.mckinsey.com/industries/semiconductors/ourinsights/smartening-up-with-artificial-intelligence

Melanthiou, Y., Pavlou, F., & Constantinou, E. (2015). The use of social network sites as an e-recruitment tool. *Journal of Transnational Management*, *20*(1), 31–49. doi:10.1080/15475778.2015.998141

Metzger, E. C., Lubin, L., Patten, R. T., & Whyte, J. (2016). Applied gamification: Creating reward systems for organizational professional development. In D. Ifenthaler, N. Bellin-Mularski, & D. K. Mah (Eds.), *Foundation of digital badges and micro-credentials*. Springer. doi:10.1007/978-3-319-15425-1_25

Mohan, R. (2019). The chatbot revolution and the Indian HR professional. *International Journal of Information and Computing Science*, *6*(3), 489–499.

Morris, M., & Revels, M. A. (2012). Technology impacts in organizational recruitment and retention. *Franklin Business & Law Journal*, *1*, 61–69.

Nakayama, M., Chen, C., & Taylor, C. W. (2017). The effects of perceived functionality and usability on privacy and security concerns about cloud application adoptions. *Journal of Information Systems Applied Research*, *10*(2), 4–11.

Nascimento, B., Oliveira, T., & Tam, C. (2018). Wearable technology: What explains continuance intention in smartwatches? *Journal of Retailing and Consumer Services*, *43*, 157–169. doi:10.1016/j.jretconser.2018.03.017

Navimipour, N. J., Rahmani, A. M., Navin, A. H., & Hosseinzadeh, M. (2015). Expert cloud: A cloud-based framework to share the knowledge and skills of human resources. *Computers in Human Behavior*, *46*, 57–74. doi:10.1016/j.chb.2015.01.001

Nawaz, N., & Gomes, A. M. (2019). Artificial intelligence chatbots are new recruiters. *International Journal of Advanced Computer Science and Applications*, *10*(9), 1–5. doi:10.14569/IJACSA.2019.0100901

Nayak, B., Bhattacharyya, S. S., & Krishnamoorthy, B. (2019). Integrating wearable technology products and big data analytics in business strategy: A study of health insurance firms. *Journal of Systems and Information Technology*, *21*(2), 255–275. doi:10.1108/JSIT-08-2018-0109

Ngai, E. W., Moon, K. K., Lam, S. S., Chin, E. S., & Tao, S. S. (2015). Social media models, technologies, and applications: An academic review and case study. *Industrial Management & Data Systems*, *115*(5), 769–802. doi:10.1108/IMDS-03-2015-0075

Odun-Ayo, I., Misra, S., Omoregbe, N., Onibere, E., Bulama, Y., & Damasevicius, R. (2017). Cloud-based security driven human resource management system. In J. Mizera-Pietraszko, R. Rodriguez, & A. Pérez (Eds.), *Advances in digital technology* (pp. 96–106). IOS Press.

Oliveira, T., Thomas, M., & Espadanal, M. (2014). Assessing the determinants of cloud computing adoption: An analysis of the manufacturing and service sectors. *Information & Management*, *51*(5), 497–510. doi:10.1016/j.im.2014.03.006

Rondi, E., De Massis, A., & Kotlar, J. (2019). Unlocking innovation potential: A typology of family business innovation postures and the critical role of the family system. *Journal of Family Business Strategy*, *10*(4), 100236. Advance online publication. doi:10.1016/j.jfbs.2017.12.001

Roth, P. L., Bobko, P., Van Iddekinge, C. H., & Thatcher, J. B. (2013). Social media in employee-selection-related decisions: A research agenda for uncharted territory. *Journal of Management*, *42*(1), 269–298. doi:10.1177/0149206313503018

Rusydan, W. M., Ibrahim, W., & Hassan, R. (2019). Recruitment trends in the era of industry 4.0 using artificial intelligence: Pro and cons. *Asian Journal of Research in Business and Management*, *1*(1), 16–21.

Scarfo, A. (2012). New security perspectives around BYOD. *Seventh International Conference on Broadband, Wireless Computing, Communication and Applications.*

Serrat, O. (2017). *Tools, methods, and approaches to drive organizational performance*. Springer.

Sharma, E. (2012). HR issues and intervention model for family business. *International Journal of Business Economics & Management Research*, *2*(12), 288–297.

Sherman, W., & Craig, A. (2019). *Understanding virtual reality: Interface, application, and design.* Morgan Kaufman Publishers.

Shuck, S., Kearney, M., & Burden, K. (2017). Exploring mobile learning in the third space. *Technology, Pedagogy and Education*, *26*(2), 121–137. doi:10.1080/1475939X.2016.1230555

Statistica. (2019). *Number of social network users worldwide from 2010 to 2021.* https://www.statista.com/statistics/278414/number-of-worldwide-social-network-users/

Stewart, G. L., & Brown, K. G. (2020). *Human resource management.* Wiley.

Stone, D. L., Deadrick, D. L., Lukaszewski, K. M., & Johnson, R. (2015). The influence on technology on the future of human resource management. *Human Resource Management Review*, *25*(2), 216–231. doi:10.1016/j.hrmr.2015.01.002

Strohmeier, S., & Piazza, F. (2015). Artificial intelligence techniques in human resources management: A conceptual exploration. In C. Kahraman & O. S. Çevik (Eds.), *Intelligent techniques in engineering management: Intelligent systems reference library* (pp. 149–172). Springer. doi:10.1007/978-3-319-17906-3_7

Suh, A., Cheung, C. M., Ahuja, M., & Wagner, C. (2017). Gamification in the workplace: The central role of the aesthetic experience. *Journal of Management Information Systems*, *34*(1), 268–305. doi:10.1080/07421222.2017.1297642

Suyono, A. A., Radianto, D. O., & Elisabeth, D. R. (2019). Antecedents of job satisfaction of production employees: Leadership, compensation and organizational culture. *International Journal of Entrepreneurship and Business Development*, *3*(1), 96–110. doi:10.29138/ijebd.v3i1.955

Taperesu, B. A., & Van Belle, J. P. (2017). Organisational capabilities required for embracing Employee mobility through bring-your-own-device concept. *Business Systems Research*, *8*(1), 17–29. doi:10.1515/bsrj-2017-0002

Torres, I. B., Riba, A., & Freeman, J. (2015). Influence of personal values and the adoption of analytical tools using laddering methodology. *International Journal of Information Management*, *5*(1), 37–56.

Traxler, J. (2009). Defining, discussing, and evaluating mobile learning: The moving finger writes and having writ…. *The International Review in Open and Distance Learning*, *8*, 1–13.

Tufts, S. H., Jacobson, W. S., & Stevens, M. S. (2014). Status update: Social media and local government human resource practices. *Review of Public Personnel Administration*, *35*(2), 193–207. doi:10.1177/0734371X14558066

Tufts, S. H., Jacobson, W. S., & Stevens, M. S. (2014). Status update: Social media and local government human resource practices. *Review of Public Personnel Administration*, 1–15.

Turner, V., Gantz, J. F., Reinsel, D., & Minton, S. (2014). The digital universe of opportunities: Rich data and the increasing value of the internet of things. *IDC Corporate.* http://www.idcdocserv.com/expired.asp?1678

Turulja, L., & Bajgorić, N. (2016). Human resources or information technology: What is more important for companies in the digital era? *The Journal of Society for Advancing Innovation and Research in Economy*, *7*(1), 35–45. doi:10.1515/bsrj-2016-0003

Urban, S., Bobek, S., & Tomin, P. (2017). TAM based research of CRM analytical tools acceptance. *SIES Journal of Management*, *17*(13), 3–17.

U.S. Bureau of Labor Statistics. (2019). *Current employment statistics highlights.* https://www.bls.gov/web/empsit/ceshighlights.pdf

Veljkovic, I., & Budree, A. (2019). Development of bring-your-own device risk management model: Case study from a South African organization. *The Electric Journal of Information Systems Evaluation*, *22*(1), 1–14.

Ward, J., Dogan, H., Apeh, E., Mylonas, A., & Kators, V. (2017). Using human factor approaches to an organisation's bring your own device scheme. In T. Tryfonas (Ed.), *Human aspects of information security, privacy and trust* (pp. 396–413). Springer.

Wilton, N. (2016). An introduction to human management. *Sage (Atlanta, Ga.).*

Wolf, M. V., Sims, J., & Yang, H. (2014). Social media utilization in human resource management. In Web based communities and social media 2014 conference, Lisbon, Portugal.

Yang, Y., Hu, T., Ye, Y., Gao, W., & Zhang, C. (2018). A knowledge generation mechanism of machining process planning using cloud technology. *Journal of Ambient Intelligence and Humanized Computing*, 1–12.

Yildirim, H., & Ali-Eldin, A. (2019). A model for predicting user intention to use wearable IoT devices at the workplace. *Journal of King Saud University – Computer and Information Sciences, 31*(4), 497-505.

Zayed, K. (2016). Information security awareness: Managing web, mobile, and endpoint security; overcoming the challenges of bring your own device. *International Journal of Teaching and Case Studies*, *7*(3-4), 271–288.

Zide, J., Elman, B., & Shahani-Denning, C. (2014). LinkedIn and recruitment: How profiles differ across occupations. *Employee Relations*, *36*(5), 583–604.

Chapter 6
Investigation of Organizational Culture in Family Firms:
Review of Existing Evidence and Application of the New Vox Organizations Model in Family Firms

Ana Tomovska Misoska
https://orcid.org/0000-0003-2018-1606
University American College, Skopje, Macedonia

Miodraga Stefanovska-Petkovska
University American College, Skopje, Macedonia

Marjan Bojadjiev
University American College, Skopje, Macedonia

Ivona Mileva
University American College, Skopje, Macedonia

ABSTRACT

The goal of the chapter is to provide an in-depth and comparative understanding of the instruments of organizational culture that exist and provide a review of academic research evidence on their performance in family firms. Furthermore, the chapter will provide an additional insight into a novel instrument for diagnosing organizational alignment – Vox Organizationis (the "voice" of the organization). The chapter will provide an introduction to family firms and the challenges and survival; comparative and critical review of existing relevant instruments of organizational culture and assessment of their implementation in measuring organizational culture in family firms and presentation of Vox Organizationis – an instrument based on a novel methodology for measuring organizational alignment, culture, and leadership values; and review of evidence and recommendations on its implementation in family firms. The chapter will provide the reader with an increased understanding of how and with which instruments to measure organizational culture and alignment in family firms.

DOI: 10.4018/978-1-7998-4814-1.ch006

INTRODUCTION

Culture influences how people think, thus making it an important tool in understanding and managing an organization (Hofstede, 1997). Organizational culture is a topic of considerable interest to organizational researchers, management consultants, and corporate executives alike. The concept of organizational culture is one of the most popular concepts in the field of management and organizational behavior and it has been demonstrated that employees, both individually and in groups, can be equally influenced by the unwritten norms and values, as much as the written rules of the organization (Dyer, 1988; Hofstede et al, 1990; Schein, 2004). This influence, according to Hofstede et al (19990), was exhibited trough symbols, heroes, rituals, and values, while Schein (2004) and Dyer (1988) claimed that is was exerted trough artifacts, perspectives, values and assumptions. The research is in the field of organizational culture is quite important as findings point to certain organizational cultured being tied to superior organizational financial performance (Ogbonna and Harris, 2000). Previous research has demonstrated the link between organizational culture and performance (Cameron and Quinn, 2011). More specifically, studies have suggested that the strength of culture is related to the measures of corporate performance including ROA, ROI, sales growth, and market share (Denison, Lief and Ward, 2004). It should be noted that although the performance of an organization is dependent on the degree to which the values of the culture are widely shared, as well as their strength, successful organizations are distinguished by their ability to promote cultural values which are consistent with their chosen strategies (Ouchi, 1981; Pascale and Athos, 1981; Peters and Waterman, 1982). Research that followed through the years extended this claims to propose culture is associated with superior performance only if the organizational culture is adaptive to the changes in the environment. In addition, an organizational culture of a sustainable and well-performing organization would have traits and characteristics that are rare and difficult to be imitated (Denison, 1990).

The issue of achieving competitive advantage and financial stability is quite important in companies operating in transition economies where the environment is unstable and changing (Sorasalmi and Tuovinen, 2016) and culture might play a role in helping the companies grow and thrive. This is especially important for SME's and family firms which are center of economic activity in developing and transition economies (Aga, Francis, and Rodríguez-Meza, 2015) and the interest in family firms has been growing in North Macedonia in recent years (Debarliev and Janeska-Iliev,2015). However the investigations of organizational culture has been mainly tied to the developed countries and to large companies (Cummings and Worley, 2009) and a number of authors point to adapting the instruments and approach to the broader cultural context (Dastmalchian et.al., 2000) such research has been sparse in the Republic of North Macedonia especially in the family firms (Tomovska-Misoska et al., 2011). Therefore the aim of this paper is to provide evidence of application of an instrument and approach to measuring organizational culture in the context of family firms and SME's originating from the Republic of North Macedonia.

Organizational culture provides a background for human resource management practices (Dubkevics and Barnars, 2010). Studying organizational culture in family firms is a complex matter and one that has not been much examined within the current Human Resource Management literature. Within this scope of work it has to be noted that the dynamics of the family firms and the human resource management practices are intertwined with the issues of control and compliance. As such, the organizational culture is also part of the overall dynamics of the family member employees and the employees that are not part of the family in the same way that other human resource management practices are also used

(Ainsworth and Cox, 2003). Imposing strong family values as part of the organizational culture and not disassociating the human resource management practices from the family values might make the family firms quite vulnerable from decision making and practices that are not optimal to the business (Bertrand and Schoar, 2006). Some studies have found that the type of organizational culture of the family firms impacts on their innovativeness and performance and the entrepreneurial orientated culture might be most conducive if also supported by appropriate human resource management practices (Cherchem, 2017; Laforet, 2016). Family businesses might be driven by different ideologies (values imposed hat are part of the culture) of the founders that impact how the firms is structured, controlled, governed and what type of human resource management practices are undertaken as part of the everyday functioning and this is also related to the macro environment within which the firms operate (Gupta and Levenburg, 2012). As such the leadership values conveyed through the human resource management practices and implied by the managers and the founders as well as family members are quite important when looking at the organizational culture in the family firms (Aisnworth and Cox, 2003; Gupta and Levenburg, 2012).

In order to present the evidence of the research done in family firms context in the republic of North Macedonia this paper will first outline the understanding of organizational culture and leadership values. It will then outline the Vox Organziationis model that that has been developed in the context of the Republic of North Macedonia. The paper will then illustrate one example of using the model in companies from the textile industry in the country and provide discussion of the results and conclusion outlining the applicability of such approach for understanding the organizational culture in family firms that can then be used to inform the human resource management practice in the companies in the country.

ORGANIZATIONAL CULTURE AND LEADERSHIP

The topics of leadership and organizational culture have attracted considerable interest from both academics and practitioners. One way of detection the relationship between organizational culture and leadership is to investigate how leadership has been conceptualized in organizational culture theory. However, there have been differing opinions in the academic community on the direction of the relationship between leadership and culture. Although the existence of the link itself, is rarely disputed, the discussion is centered on how the relationship is conceptualized.

1. Culture can be manipulated

One way to view organizational culture is to see it as something that can be manipulated. In other words this would mean that the leader is able to mold and adjust the organizational culture in the company based on the need and circumstances of the environment, as well as the personal power, abilities and preferences of the leader. This is often found in the literature on transformational leadership.

2. Culture is an fundamental part of the organization

This viewpoint is opposite to the one presented above, since it advocates that the culture is a unique and unalterable segment of the organization. It is independent of the influence of the personal (leaders and members) and environmental trends and preferences. More specifically, it suggests that exerted influence is from the culture to the leader and members – meaning the the culture itself has the power to mold the leader.

3. There is a dynamic link between culture and leadership

This is one of the most widely accepted viewpoints on the relationship between culture and leadership. It suggests that the relationship is not a one-way street, but is a dynamic expression of influence between the leader and the organization resulting in the formation of a unique organizational culture. More specifically, the view advocates that in the process of forming the organization the leader also forms the organizational culture by integrating a set of values and beliefs. However, as time passes, the culture takes on a life of its own. It develops its own personality and builds the capacity to influence the leader and his/her leadership style (Schein, 1992).

However, despite the established connection of organizational culture, leadership and performance, the review of the relevant academic literature reveals that little critical research attention has been devoted to exploring the alignment between the two concepts and the formal part within family businesses.

ORGANIZATIONAL CULTURE AND FAMILY BUSINESSES

In the early 1900s, a young immigrant hotel worker named Guccio Gucci became impressed with the luxurious luggage guests brought with them at the upscale Savoy Hotel. In 1921 in Florence, Tuscany, Guccio Gucci founded the House of Gucci which became a prominent player in the fashion industry, starting with luggage and later on becoming famous for fashionable handbags. The company was led by Gucci and his three sons Aldo, Vasco and Rodolpho, and after his death in 1953 the company is inherited by his son Aldo who internationalized it. While the company significantly prospered through the 1970s, it started facing internal family disputes. In an attempt to save the company from failure, Rodolpho's son Maurico and Aldo's son Paolo took over the company and dismissed Aldo who served prison for tax evasion. However, although they shared control over the company, they had different visions and aspirations. A disastrous fashion line which was launched under the leadership of Paolo caused a massive loss of money, and forced him into exile. Afterwards the company was left to Mauricio who led it into a negative net worth US$17.3 million and US$40 million in personal debt. The company was sold to Investcorp in 1988, while Murizio's remaining stocks were sold in 1993.

The prediction of the three generation curse of family business is present in many cultures across the globe - "Shirtsleeves to shirtsleeves in three generations" in America, "Rice paddies to rice paddies in three generations" in Japan, "Wealth never survives the third generation" in China or "The father buys, the son builds, the grandchild sells, and his son begs" in Scotland. The available data supports this warning on the danger of the declining family wealth across generations. In example, a study from Leenders and Waarts (Leenders and Waarts, 2001) found that only 30% of the first generation of family businesses successfully passes down to the second generation. According to Harvard Business Review, 70% of family-owned businesses fail or are sold before they are passed down to the second generation and solely 10% remain to be passed down to the third generation. In addition, the extended CEO tenure in family businesses (20 to 25 years on average) can increase the difficulties of coping with shifts in technology, business models, and consumer behavior (Stalk Jr. and Foley, 2012)

In 2018 PwC conducted the Global Family Business Survey among 2953 senior executive across 53 territories. The results suggested that family businesses - built around strong values and with an aspirational purpose - have a competitive advantage in disruptive times. More specifically, 75% of survey participants felt that having a clear set of values created a competitive advantage for their business (PwC, 2018). This points to an often overlooked solution to the challenges that firms businesses face and what makes family businesses different from the rest – their organizational character or their organizational culture. This is considered the greatest strength of family businesses recognized for its role to determine organizational success beyond the first generation, although it has often been ignored (Dyer, 1989).

With this argument in mind, the Vox Organizationis model was constructed to provide the first comprehensive measure of organizational culture, leadership and alignment. It was inspired by four relevant models/frameworks of organizational culture: Competing Values Framework (Cameron and Quinn, 2006), Hofstede model of organizational culture and Denison Model. In line with the relevant models from this field, Vox Organizationis represents a departure from the traditional qualitative approach in studying organizational culture, and argues that organizations can be studied according to cultural traits or dimensions common to all human organizations (Denison and Spreitzer, 1991). The instrument was designed to assess organizational alignment trough the investigation of organizational culture, leadership and the formal part of the organization. However, it has the power to assess each of these segments individually (Figure 1).

Figure 1.VOX Organizational Culutre

The VOX Organizational Culture – "4CT"

The instrument proposes a typology of "4 Culture Types" or "4CT" (Figure 2). Those are:

- Entrepreneurial Autocracy;
- Entrepreneurial Democracy;
- Conservative or Managerial Autocracy and
- Conservative or Managerial Democracy.

Figure 2. 4 Culture Types

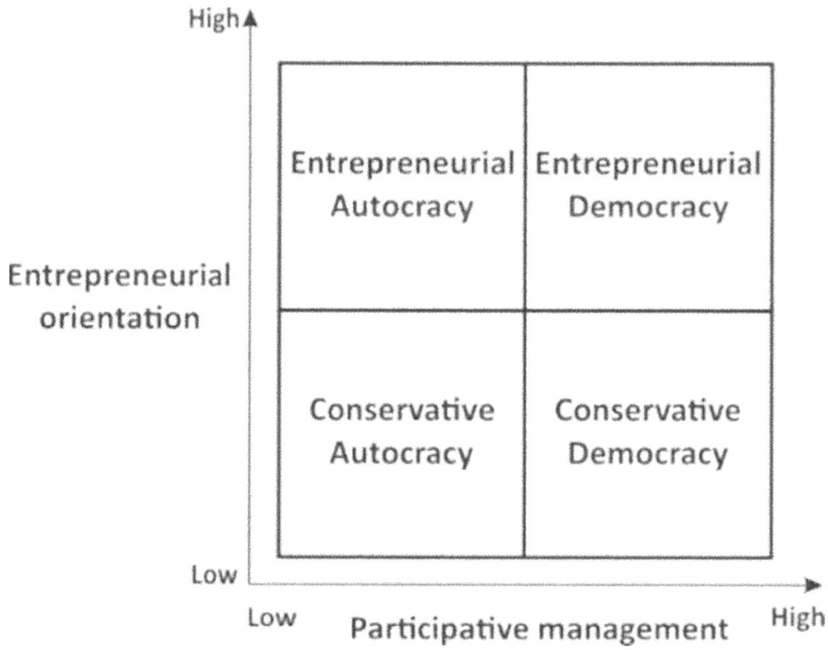

The VOX Leadership Styles – "4LT"

Furthermore, leadership styles typology model "4LT" is based on two dimensions:

- Decision Making styles (Democratic and Autocratic), and
- Entrepreneurship an Innovativeness (Entrepreneurial or Risk Averse) style

For the purposes of a wider acceptance of our theory, Vox Organizationis links leadership styles with famous individuals, positions or types of businesses. Thus, we define Entrepreneurial autocracy as being "Steve Jobs like Leadership style" (Agrawal, 2016) and Entrepreneurial Democracy as being "Jack Welch Like" leadership style (Chris, 2015). Welch, on the other hand, being one of the "rock stars" in the business, is known for his participatory management style (Bartlett and Wozny, 1999).

Figure 3. 4 Leadership Types

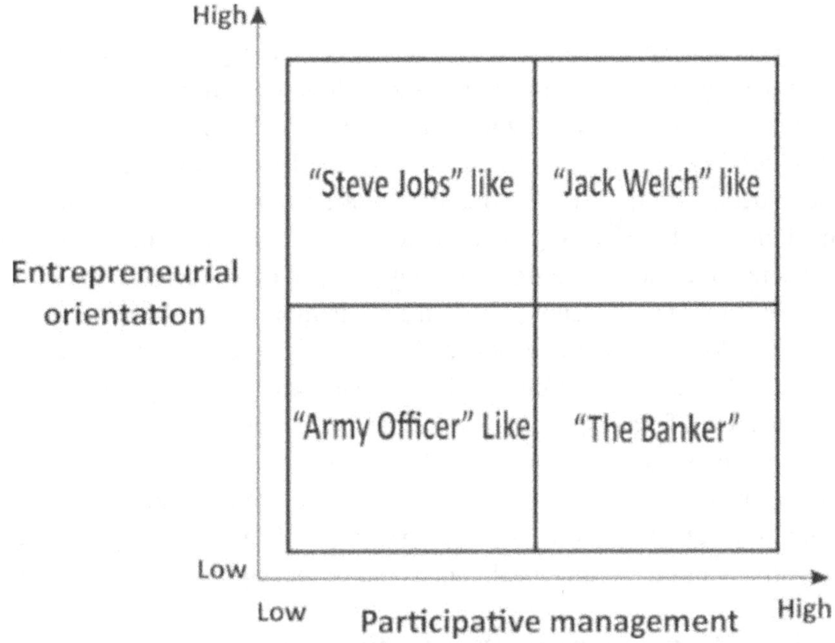

The Formal Part of the Organization

Finally, the model assesses the formal part of the organization as well. The formal part of the organization is any formal document, including but not limited to policies, procedures, strategic plans and the like that might influence the behavior. It might include documents like: remuneration policy, office hours, decision making process and any other policies and procedures that might be deemed relevant for the evaluation of organization's character.

The model developing and testing of the model is recorded through numerous scientific papers (Bojadjiev, Tomovska Misoska, Mirocevic and Stefanovska-Petkovska, 2018; Bojadjiev,Kostovski, Handjiski Krliu and Shindilovski, 2017; Naumovski, Bojadziev,Tomovska Misoska and Stefanovska Petkovska, 2016; Bojadziev, Tomovska Misoska, Pesev and Stefanovska Petkovska, 2016; Limani, Tomovska-Misoska and Bojadziev, 2015) and master thesis. All these provided the opportunity to test the performance of the model, and hence improve it, in specific industries (such as IT, construction, engineering etc.). Furthermore, it allowed for experimenting in the combination of different segments of the instrument such as with the alignment between culture and leader's values only (Naumovski, et.al, 2016), or alignment between all three elements (Bojadziev, et.al., 2016).

Item Description

The instrument has 21 items and uses a 5 point Likert-type scale to measure 4 dimensions. The first core dimension is titled Participative Management that distinguishes between Democratic versus Autocratic Organization. This dimension actually has question along three sub dimensions: Decision Making and Behavior is measured with 6 items designed to measure the flow of information and the decision making processes within the company and an example of such question is the following: Subordinates are consulted by managers during the decision-making process. Two of the items in this dimension are reverse coded. The dimension People versus task orientation is designed to grasp the attention paid to the needs of the employees in the organization and is comprised of 5 items with one reverse coded. An example of an item in this dimension is: The organization takes care of work-life balance. The third dimension titled Open versus Closed system is trying to understand whether the organization fosters collaboration with various stakeholders, sectors and other organizations as well as the environment. This dimension is measured with 3 items, such as: The organization fosters collaboration among employees in the same sector. The second core dimensions is Entrepreneurial Orientation and tries to measure the openness of the organization towards taking risks and overcoming challenges ties to the process of innovation. This dimension has 6 items, two of which are reverse coded. A sample item is: Employees are encouraged to develop new and original ideas and/or products. For each dimension an aggregate variable is computed and to diagnose the position of the respondents along the dimensions of the Vox Organizationis a cut-off point positioned on the theoretical mean is used (3). As such the results give an approximation of the culture type of the organization along the two core dimensions: Democratic vs Autocratic Organization and Entrepreneurial Orientation thus giving an opportunity to determine the positioning of the perceptions of the organizational culture in one of the four culture types proposed by Vox Organizationis.

Comparison of Vox Organizationis With Other Instruments

As presented in Table 1, while the majority of existing instruments measure solely organizational culture types and provide a diagnosis of the organization, Vox Organizationis assesses both leadership values and organizational culture types to determine organizational alignment. More specifically, the instrument is built around the philosophy "of listening to the voice of the organization". A well trained piano tuner will have a fork: with resonance of 440 Hz (tune A) and upon which can tune the whole 8 octaves on the piano. Similarly, good car mechanic can identify the cause of trouble shouting, purely by listening to the sound of the engine. Vox Organizationis diagnoses organizational alignment by providing the capability to listen to the sound of the organizations; tune the tones which are not tuned, and provide the opportunity to create efficiency and harmony (Bojadjiev, 2019).

Table 1. VOX Organizational culture types and leader's types (Bojadjiev,2019)

Culture Types	Leader's Type
Entrepreneurial Autocracy	"Steve Jobs like: Leader type
Entrepreneurial Democracy	"Jack Welch like" Leader type
Conservative or Managerial Autocracy	"Army officer like: Leader type
Conservative or Managerial Democracy	"Banker like" Leader type

As discussed throughout this chapter, the research on organizational culture of family enterprises has been scarce and mostly theoretical. Therefore, in order to bridge this gap and gain a better understanding of family firms, we are administering Vox Organizationis to explore the organizational culture and alignment of these companies.

Table 2. Comparison of organizational culture instruments

	Organizational Culture Assessment Instrument (OCAI)	**Hofstede model of organizational culture**	**Denison model**	**Vox Organizationis**
Understanding of culture	The way we do things around here	Collective programming of the mind, which distinguishes the members of one category of people from another	Based on OCAI understanding of culture	Organizational culture is an unwritten system of values and norms that determines interactions, behaviors, decision making and processes within the organizations. It is the voice of the organization
Dimension characteristics	Unipolar dimensions	Bipolar dimensions	Unipolar dimensions	Bipolar dimensions
No. of culture types	4	6	4	4 Culture types (4CT) and 4 Leadership types (4LT)
Dimensions	1) Clan culture 2) Adhocracy culture 3) Market culture 4) Hierarchy culture	1) Process oriented vs. Result oriented 2) Employee oriented vs. Job oriented 3) Parochial vs. Professional 4) Open system vs. Closed system 5) Loose vs. Tight control 6) Normative vs. Pragmatic culture	1) Adaptability 2) Mission 3) Involvement 4) Consistency	**4CT** 1) Entrepreneurial Autocracy 2) Entrepreneurial Democracy 3) Conservative or Managerial Autocracy 4) Conservative or Managerial Democracy **4LT** 1) Democratic 2) Autocratic 3) Entrepreneurial 4) Risk Averse style

APPLYING VOX ORGANIZATIONIS IN FAMILY FIRMS

For the purpose of this chapter, we have tested the instrument in practice. The research was conducted in January 2020 in a textile sector in a town in North Macedonia that is considered as a hub for textile factories. The sample consisted of 19 participants from 6 factories that are family owned businesses. All the respondents came from administrative sectors of the companies. Thirteen of the respondents were employees and 6 had lesdership positions within the factories. Most of the respondents were females (57.9% or 11) and the rest were males. When it comes to age distribution, the majority of the respondents were between 35 and 40 years (36.8% or 7), followed by those aged over 50 (31.6% or 6), then those aged 30 to 35 (26.3% or 5) and one person was between 40 and 50 years.

To get an initial idea of the perceptions of the employees about the four dimensions, a mean and standard deviation for each dimension was calculated which are given in Table 1 where the scores for the core dimensions are given in bold. This calculation was based on the answers of all respondents together. As it can be seen respondents have a tendency to perceive the organizational culture of the companies as democratic (M=3.4). This means that the respondents perceive that the companies stimulate openness in decision making, consultations with employees, free flow of information and there is a shared awareness of the appropriate behaviors. The respondents also perceive the culture of the company where they work to be people oriented (M=3.64) and that means that there is respect for the employees, opportunities for work-life balance, timely feedback and care for the physical conditions of work places. In addition the respondents also deem the organizational cultures as being open (M=3.56) and fostering collaboration between employees, sectors as well as the external environment. However taken as a whole along the core dimensions Democratic versus Autocratic organization the participants deem the overall culture of the company to be Democratic (M=3.51). The only dimension where the respondents are undecided is the Entrepreneurial Orientation (M=2.9) which is very close to the cut-off point. This means that the respondents are undecided whether the organizational culture is stimulating experimentation, development of new product and ideas or is more oriented towards stability. The respondents actually perceive the organizational culture of their companies as being on the border of Entrepreneurial Democracy and Conservative Democracy.

Table 3. Mean and standard deviation for the dimensions of Vox Organizations

Dimension	Mean	SD
Decision Making and Behavior	3.4	.39
People versus Task	3.64	.48
Open versus Closed	3.56	.48
Democratic vs Autocratic Organization	3.51	.34
Entrepreneurial Orientation	2.99	.39

To provide deeper understanding of the perceptions and views of the organizational culture a series of comparisons have been made for different demographic groups. Table 2 presents the results of the t-test for perception of organizational culture for gender for the four dimensions. As it can be seen both genders have very similar perceptions regarding the dimensions of the organizational culture with an exception of the dimension Decision Making and Behavior. As can be seen in Table 2 there is statistically significant difference between males and females on a level $p<0.05$. The males perceive the organizational culture as more democratic than females, although both genders show tendency to perceive the culture as more democratic than bureaucratic. Again when it comes to the core dimension Democratic versus Autocratic organization both gender perceive the company to be more Democratic than Autocratic, although there is statistically significant difference between the gender and males perceive the organizational culture as more Democratic than females. All in all both genders consider the organizational culture to be placed on the border of Entrepreneurial Democracy and Conservative Democracy.

Another t-test was done for difference in the perceptions between respondent on leadership positions and those that do not have such positions. The results presented in Table 3 show that there are no statistically significant differences in the opinions about the organizational culture between the two groups. This means that both the leaders and the employees think that the organizational culture of the companies is Democratic and they are undecided on the dimension Entrepreneurial Orientation. Therefore it can be concluded that both the leaders and the employees place the organizational culture on the border of Entrepreneurial Democracy and Conservative Democracy.

To test the differences in perceptions of organizational culture between different age group an ANOVA test was used and the results are shown in Table 4. As it can be seen there are no statistically significant differences between different age groups. This means that all age groups perceive the company culture as Democratic and are undecided on the Entrepreneurial orientation. To summarize all age group place the organizational culture on the border of Entrepreneurial Democracy and Conservative Democracy.

Table 4. T-test results for gender

Dimension	Gender	Mean	SD	Mean difference	Sig (2-tailed)
Decision Making and Behavior	female	3.23	.34	.41	.02
	male	3.64	.33		
People vs Task	female	3.55	.38	.23	.32
	male	3.78	.6		
Open vs Closed	female	3.42	.45	.33	.15
	male	3.75	.49		
Democratic vs Autocratic Organization	female	3.37	.08	.34	.03
	male	3.71	.12		
Entrepreneurial Orientation	female	2.94	.4	.08	.65
	male	3.02	.38		

Table 5. T-test for leaders versus employees

Dimension	Position	Mean	SD	Mean difference	Sig (2-tailed)
Decision Making and Behavior	Employee	3.43	0.4	0.08	0.68
	Leader	3.34	0.41		
People vs Task	Employee	3.63	0.54	0.05	0.85
	Leader	3.67	0.37		
Open vs Closed	Employee	3.54	0.57	0.07	0.77
	Leader	3.61	0.25		
Democratic vs Autocratic Organization	Employee	3.51	0.11	0.01	0.97
	Leader	3.51	0.1		
Entrepreneurial Orientation	Employee	2.97	0.4	0	0.99
	Leader	2.97	0.39		

DISCUSSION AND CONCLUSION

The main aim of the research was to explore the organizational culture in family businesses. For this purpose, the component of Vox Organizationis for investigating organizational culture was implemented in 6 textile companies.

Organizational Culture in Family Businesses

Regarding organizational culture, family business is defined as one in which the family and the organization willingly share part or all of its culture and tradition. The following segment of the discussion will focus on the nexus between organizational culture and family firms. As it was presented in the Results section, the findings from the research suggested that the participants in the survey perceive that their company is people oriented. More specifically, the results indicated that the employees feel that compa-

Table 6. ANOVA results for age

Dimension	Age group	Mean	SD	F	Sig (2-tailed)
Decision Making and Behavior	30-35	3.46	0.48	0.55	0.66
	35-40	3.33	0.34		
	40-50	3.86	0		
	50	3.37	0.42		
	Total	3.4	0.39		
People vs Task	30-35	3.4	0.28	2.26	0.12
	35-40	3.74	0.5		
	40-50	4.6	.		
	50	3.6	0.46		
	Total	3.6	0.48		
Open vs Closed	30-35	3.53	0.18	2.21	0.13
	35-40	3.47	0.6		
	40-50	4.67	.		
	50	3.5	0.35		
	Total	3.56	0.48		
Democratic vs Autocratic Organization	30-35	3.45	0.08	2.02	0.16
	35-40	3.49	0.16		
	40-50	4.27	0		
	50	3.46	0.11		
	Total	3.51	0.08		
Entrepreneurial Orientation	30-35	2.87	0.59	0.9	0.46
	35-40	3.04	0.27		
	40-50	3.5	.		
	50	2;9	0.29		
	Total	2.97	0.39		

nies stimulate openness in decision making, consultations with employees, free flow of information and there is a shared awareness of the appropriate behaviors, with respect for the employees, opportunities for work-life balance, timely feedback and care for the physical conditions of work places. The organizational culture was described as open and initiating collaboration within and outside the company. The overall culture was described as Democratic and bordering between Entrepreneurial Democracy and Conservative Democracy.

Several studies have analyzed the culture of family business using OCAI (Cameron and Quinn, 2011). According to the proposed methodological and theoretical framework of this instrument, the majority of the studies agreed that family firms are highly influenced by clan culture (Dyer, 1988; Merino, Monreal-Pérez and Sánchez-Marín, 2015; Sánchez Marín et al., 2016). This means that the culture is deeply rooted in the family values and traditions. In many cases it is the first generation of founders that creates the basis of the culture and the values. With this culture, the company is less open to the outside environment and innovations, making it very risk-averse, traditional and introvert. Some of the stated reasons why clan culture exists include flat organizational structure, higher degree of team orientation, adaptability to external environment and low level of bureaucracy (Tipu, 2018). This characteristic highly differs from the one that is indicated by Vox. In fact, one explanation of this difference is that within the process of professionalization of the company and the integration of new-non family employees. In fact, he later have the power to remodel the culture and integrate new values and norms within the company. According to previous research (Gómez-Mejía et al., 2007; Kalm and Gomez-Mejia, 2016) the non-family employees tend to transform the company into more prone to risk taking, less traditional and more entrepreneurial. A similar situation is observed in family businesses where the family is not directly involved in the management of the company, and the company is characterized with increased change orientation compared to family owned businesses where the management is derived from the family itself. Therefore, the non-family businesses demonstrated higher tendency towards the market and hierarchical culture in accordance to the OCAI model.

Some opposing arguments suggest that family businesses are characterized by authoritarian leadership (Barnett and Kellermanns, 2006) in which one dominants family members will dictate all the decisions and coordinate the processes with the company. In addition to these arguments, a recent research used the psychodynamic theory approach to investigate the relationship between the dynamics of the leadership in a family and certain dimensions of organizational culture in the family business. The results indicated that family businesses demonstrated a strong tendency to autocratic leadership (occasionally situational). In summary, the research identified an organizational culture with inflexible dynamic, centralized and bureaucratic following the values and the norms set by the founder (Coury and Pecanha, 2016). Vallejo (2008) suggests that family businesses have a stronger culture in comparison to non-family businesses. Some of the reasons include that they experience greater employee commitment, improved working environment, long-term orientation, and more organizational harmony. In addition to the previous arguments, it is considered that the family business employees have a higher level of identification in the company, trust, loyalty and participation.

Demographic Differences in Perception of Organizational Culture

A review of the relevant academic literature revealed that the masculine-gendered organizations were characterized with bureaucracy, rationality, rule-following, competitiveness and self-assertion, and feminist-gendered organizations stressed their interdependence, cooperativeness, emotionalism, intuition and creation (Chen, Fosh and Foster, 2007).

The results of the research indicate that both genders have very similar perceptions regarding the dimensions of the organizational culture with an exception of the dimension Decision Making and Behavior. There is statistically significant difference between males and females in the perception of organizational culture with males perceiving the organizational culture as more democratic than females, although both genders show tendency to perceive the culture as more democratic than bureaucratic. Regarding the core dimension Democratic versus Autocratic organization both gender perceive the company to be more Democratic than Autocratic, although there is statistically significant difference between the gender and males perceive the organizational culture as more Democratic than females. Similar to previous findings, both genders consider the organizational culture to be placed on the border of Entrepreneurial Democracy and Conservative Democracy.

The review of the academic literature reveals that there are gender differences in perceiving culture. More specifically, different approaches may be employed by male and other by females in leading and organizing the dealings with the company (Tipu, 2018). Other research has found significant differences in succession planning processes across male and female-owned family businesses (Harveston, Davis and Lyden, 1997). Another interesting study examined differences in perceptions of organizational cultures of male and female bank managers. They found that each bank type was characterized by a distinct pattern of gender differences that was related to the ownership, history and type of business of that bank type. The differences in perceptions of organizational cultures can be explained with the extent of organizational socialization and the adoption of various human resource practices, including team-working and targeted recruitment and selection, and the respondents' age and education (Chen, Fosh and Foster, 2007).

However the nexus of gender and organizational culture can be analyzed in another direction. More specifically, examine how values comprising organizational culture impact on employees' job satisfaction, taking also into account their gender and age. The study found that employee gender and age influence the way that the organizational culture affects their self-reported level of job satisfaction. In this study, an ANOVA test was conducted to test the differences in perceptions of organizational culture between different age groups. However, no statistically significant differences between different age groups we found. All age group place the organizational culture on the border of Entrepreneurial Democracy and Conservative Democracy.

Considering all the above mentioned discussion on the nexus of organizational culture, we may consider that gender differences may contribute to our further understanding of different cultural orientations in family firms.

Perception of Organizational Culture and Position in the Company

Finally, the analyses of the difference in the perceptions between respondent on leadership positions and those that do not have such positions, suggested that there are no statistically significant differences in the opinions about the organizational culture between the two groups. This means that both the leaders and the employees think that the organizational culture of the companies is Democratic and they are undecided on the dimension Entrepreneurial Orientation. Therefore it can be concluded that both the leaders and the employees place the organizational culture on the border of Entrepreneurial Democracy and Conservative Democracy. The academic literature does not contain many studies on positional differences and the perception of organizational culture. The dearth of empirical research linking leader characteristics and organizational phenomena, particularly organizational culture, may be due in part to the difficulties in obtaining measures of psychological characteristics such as personality traits from upper echelon leaders (Giberson et al., 2009). However, there is one particular interesting study that was conducted on a sample of 40,000 executives, mid-level managers and non-managerial employees from business organizations in six countries: Brazil, China, Germany, India, the UK and the US. The study results indicated that executives had the most positive assessment of ethical business culture within their respective organizations. Employees' assessments were less positive, and mid-level managers' assessments fell in the middle (Ardichvili, Jondle and Kowske, 2012). No specific studies were identified regarding family businesses. On the other hand, a study empirically examined organizational culture theorists' assertions about the linkages between leadership and the cultures that emerge in the organizations they lead. A sample of 32 CEOs completed measures of the Big-Five personality traits and personal values and a total of 467 employees across the 32 organizations completed a competing values measure of organizational culture. The findngs of the study indicated support for several hypothesized relationships between CEO personality and cultural values. Exploratory analyses indicated that several CEO personal values were related to culture values. A very important implication of the research for practice was that organizations need to seriously consider the ''fit'' between the current or desired organizational culture and CEO characteristics.

LIMITATIONS OF THE RESEARCH

The limitation of this study are not exempt. The first limitation is the risk of social desirability bias. Although the undertaken research was completely anonymous, voluntary and employees could do it on their own schedule, there is still a risk that respondents may not have been completely honest about their company and provided an honest answer. The second risk is the self-selection bias, since it is not known whether the respondents in the survey are representative of the total population of textile workers. The third limitation is the demographic location of the respondents. This research only investigated the textile companies that are located in Stip. Although this is the center is the textile production, these further studies should provide a more comprehensible analysis of such variables

RECOMMENDATIONS FOR FUTURE RESEARCH

These limitations may provide interesting lines of future research. First, although our classification of family firm and measurement of organizational culture is validated, the future research should take into consideration the national difference that exists in the definitions. This is still an open question and future research should take it into consideration in the attempt to provide in international comparisons of the family business characteristics and performance. Second, other intermediate variables, should be integrated in the model as, for example, characteristics of managers, human resource management strategies and practices, and structure and characteristics of the job and industry in general etc. All of these would probably demonstrate significant effects into the relationships between family firm and organizational culture. Furthermore, future research may include variables such as environmental factors as moderators of organizational culture in family businesses. Finally, although we theoretically assume organizational culture as a unique intangible resource that is critical for performance, further investigation is needed into the influence of the cultural type (with regards to the methodology of the instrument that is used for its identification) in terms of firm performance and success.

IMPLICATIONS FOR PRACTICE

This study also has important implications for practitioners. Primarily, managers in family businesses should be able to adequately identify, understand and use the culture of their company, so that it can be used towards achieving the strategic objectives of the company. Furthermore, managers should be aware on the importance of assessing organizational alignment. Although no similar studies exist within the family business literature, the analysis of these aspects will enable the family to ascertain their influence in the firm and to determine whether that influence compares favorably or not with other resources in the organization. Finally, in case the ruling family desires to change the culture type f the company (in example from less entrepreneurial and risk averse to a business with higher entrepreneurial intentions and risk prone), family owners and managers may encourage a professionalized and dynamic culture that is more open, and likely sustain family wealth and prevent the loss of family control and the three generation curse.

CONCLUSION

Although. The academic literature contains an extensive discussion on the topic of organizational culture, yet there is an observable gap in the understanding of organizational culture in family businesses. At the same time, the provided discussion in this chapter provides an overview of some of the strengths and the limitations of the available literature. However, there remains the requirement for the application of selected organizational culture instruments in the context of family business. With regard to the identified type of organizational culture in family businesses, there are diverging opinions on which culture characterizes and prevails in family businesses. In addition, there is also lack of research with regard to different experiences of organizational culture in family firms such as hierarchy, risk taking, openness etc. The discussion that is provided also reveals the benefits that family businesses may have when they asses and understand their culture, leadership and alignment, as well as their short and long term influence on performance of the family business

The research findings suggest that both genders consider the organizational culture to be placed on the border of Entrepreneurial Democracy and Conservative Democracy. The organizational culture was described as open and initiating collaboration within and outside the company. The overall culture was described as Democratic and bordering between Entrepreneurial Democracy and Conservative Democracy. The findings of this study have confirmed that family businesses should recognize the benefits from organizational culture, leadership and organizational alignment in the workplace and use them as a toll for producing a more satisfied and productive workforce.

REFERENCES

Aga, G. A., Francis. D. and Rodríguez-Meza. J. (2015). *SMEs, age, and jobs: A review of the literature, metrics, and evidence*. World Bank policy research working paper. https://openknowledge.worldbank.org/handle/10986/23455

Ainsworth, S., & Cox, J. W. (2003). Families divided: Culture and control in family business. Organization Studies, 24, 1463-1485. http://dx/doi.org/ doi:10.1177/0170840603249004

Andrews, R., & Beynon, M. J. (2011). Organizational form and strategic alignment in a local authority: A preliminary exploration using fuzzy clustering. *Public Organization Review*, *11*(3), 201–218. doi:10.100711115-010-0117-4

Ardichvili, A., Jondle, D., & Kowske, B. (2012). Minding the gap: Exploring differences in perceptions of ethical business cultures among executives, mid-level managers and non-managers. *Human Resource Development International. Routledge*, *15*(3), 337–352. doi:10.1080/13678868.2012.687625

Barnett, T., & Kellermanns, F. W. (2006). 'Are We Family and Are We Treated as Family? Nonfamily Employees' Perceptions of Justice in the Family Firm', Entrepreneurship Theory and Practice. *SAGE PublicationsSage CA: Los Angeles, CA*, *30*(6), 837–854. doi:10.1111/j.1540-6520.2006.00155.x

Bertrand, M., & Schoar, A. (2006). The role of family in family firms. *The Journal of Economic Perspectives*, *2*, 73–96.

Biggs, A., Brough, P., & Barbour, J. P. (2014). Strategic alignment with organizational priorities and work engagement: A multi-wave analysis. *Journal of Organizational Behavior*, *35*(3), 301–317. doi:10.1002/job.1866

Bojadjiev, M. (2019). Development of Instrument for Measurement of the Organizational Alignment - from Vox Organizationis to "Four Organizational Culture Types and Four Leadership Styles". *Universal Journal of Management.*, *7*(5), 186–199. doi:10.13189/ujm.2019.070504

Bojadjiev, M., Tomovska Misoska, A., Mirocevic, B., & Stefanovska-Petkovska, M. (2018). Organizational culture and the "voice" of Small Entreprises in the electrical engineering service sector in the Republic of Macedonia, Universal. *Journal of Management*, *6*(8), 263–272. doi:10.13189/ujm.2018.060801

Bojadziev, M., Tomovska Misoska, A., Pesev, A., & Stefanoska Petkovska, M. (2016). Organizational alignment in the ICT company in the Republic of Macedonia. *Business and Economic Review*, *6*(2), 424–438. doi:10.5296/ber.v6i2.10258

Cameron, K. S., & Quinn, R. E. (2011). *Diagnosing and Changing Organizational Culture: Based on the Competing Values Framework*. John Wiley & Sons Ltd. Available at: https://books.google.co.uk/bookshl=en&lr=&id=EgADAwAAQBAJ&oi=fnd&pg=PR9&ots=o_tE2JRg-R&sig=_igxZgoJ8ik-Z4TNLeUSzUlp9Sg&redir_esc=y#v=onepage&q&f=false

Chen, C. C., Fosh, P., & Foster, D. J. (2007). Gender Differences in Perceptions of Organizational Cultures in the Banking Industry in Taiwan. *The Journal of Industrial Relations*, *50*(1), 139–156. doi:10.1177/0022185607085698

Choi, Y. S., Seo, M., Scott, D., & Martin, J. (2010). Validation of the OrganizationalCultureAssessment Instrument: An application of the Korean version. *Journal of Sport Management*, *24*(2), 169–189. http://digitalcommons.wayne.edu/cgi/viewcontent.cgi?article=1002&context=coe_khs. doi:10.1123/jsm.24.2.169

Coury, C., & Pecanha, D. L. (2016). Leadership and organizational culture in family businesses: Systemic and psychodynamic case study. *Boletim Academia Paulista de Psicologia*, *36*(91), 465–488. Retrieved March 6, 2020, from http://pepsic.bvsalud.org/scielo.php?pid=S1415-711X2016000200014&script=sci_abstract&tlng=en

Crots, J. C., & Ford, R. C. (2008). Achieving service excellence by design: The organizational alignment audit. *Business Communication Quarterly*, *71*(2), 233–240. doi:10.1177/1080569908317319

Cummings, T. G., & Worley, C. G. (2009). *Organizational development and change* (9th ed.). Cengage.

Dastmalchian, A., Lee, S., & Ng, I. (2000). The interplay between organizational and national cultures: A comparison of organizational practices in Canada and South Korea using the Competing Values Framework. *International Journal of Human Resource Management, 11*(2), 388–412.

Debarliev, S., & Janeska-Iliev, A. (2015).Challenges for the family business in transition economics: with an emphasis on the Republic of Macedonia economic recovery in the post-crisis period. *Proceedings from the International Conference held at the Faculty of Economics*, Skopje, Macedonia.

Denison, D. R., & Mishra, A. K. (1989). Organizational culture and organizational effectiveness:A theory and some preliminary empirical evidence. *Academy of Management Proceedings, 1*(1), 168–172. doi:10.5465/ambpp.1989.4980714

Denison, D. R., & Spreitzer, G. M. (1991). Organizational Culture and Organizational Development: A Competing Values Approach. *Research in Organizational Change and Development, 5*, 1–21.

Dickson, M. W., Aditya, R. N., & Chhokar, J. S. (2000). Definition and interpretation in crosscultural organizational culture research. In N. M. Ashkanasy, C. P. M. Wilderom, & M. F. Peterson (Eds.), *Handbook of organizational culture and climate* (pp. 447–464). Sage.

Dubkevics, L. and Barbars, A. (2010). The role of organizational culture in human resource management. *Human Resource Management and ergonomics*, 4 (1), 1-10.

Dull, M. (2010). Leadership and organizational culture: Sustaining dialogue between practitioners and scholars. *Public Administration Review, 17*(6), 857–866. doi:10.1111/j.1540-6210.2010.02217.x

Dyer, W. G. (1988). Culture and Continuity in Family Firms. *Family Business Review, 1*(1), 37–50. doi:10.1111/j.1741-6248.1988.00037.x

Freiling, J., & Fichtner, H. (2010). Organizational culture as the glue between people and organization: A competence-based view on learning and competence building. *German Journal of Research in Human Resource Management, 24*(2), 152–172. doi:10.1177/239700221002400204

Giberson, T. R., Resick, C. J., Dickson, M. W., Mitchelson, J. K., Randall, K. R., & Clark, M. A. (2009). Leadership and Organizational Culture: Linking CEO Characteristics to Cultural Values. *Journal of Business and Psychology, 24*(2), 123–137. doi:10.100710869-009-9109-1

Gómez-Mejía, L. R., Haynes, K. T., Núñez-Nickel, M., Jacobson, K. J. L., & Moyano-Fuentes, J. (2007). 'Socioemotional wealth and business risks in family-controlled firms: Evidence from Spanish olive oil mills', Administrative Science Quarterly. *Cornell University, 52*(1), 106–137. doi:10.2189/asqu.52.1.106

Gupta, V., & Levenburg, N. (2012). Cultures, ideologies and family business. *Journal of Family Business Management, 2*(1), 57–75. doi:10.1108/20436231211216420

Harveston, P. D., Davis, P. S., & Lyden, J. A. (1997). 'Succession planning in family business: The impact of owner gender', Family Business Review. John Wiley & Sons. *Ltd, 10*(4), 373–396. doi:10.1111/j.1741-6248.1997.00373.x

Hofstede, G. (1997). *Cultures and Organizations: Software of the mind*. McGraw-Hill.

Hofstede, G., Neuijen, B., Ohayv, D. D., & Sanders, G. (1990). Measuring organizational cultures: A qualitative and quantitative study across twenty cases. *Administrative Science Quarterly*, *35*(2), 286–318. doi:10.2307/2393392

Kalm, M., & Gomez-Mejia, L. R. (2016). Socioemotional wealth preservation in family firms. *Revista de Administração, 51*(4), 409–411. . doi:10.1016/j.rausp.2016.08.002

Labovitz, G.H. (2004). The power of alignment: How the right tools enhance organizational focus. *Business Performance Management*, 30-34.

Lafforet, S. (2016). Effects of organizational culture on organizational innovation performance in family firms. *Journal of Small Business and Enterprise Development*, *23*(2), 379–407. doi:10.1108/JSBED-02-2015-0020

Limani, A., Tomovska-Misoska, A., & Bojadjiev, M. (2015). Organizational alignment as a model of sustainable development in the public sector in the Republic of Macedonia. *Journal of Sustainable Development*, *5*(12), 51–68.

Merino, F., Monreal-Pérez, J., & Sánchez-Marín, G. (2015). 'Family SMEs' Internationalization: Disentangling the Influence of Familiness on Spanish Firms' Export Activity', Journal of Small Business Management. *Blackwell Publishing Ltd*, *53*(4), 1164–1184. doi:10.1111/jsbm.12111

Merron, K. A. (1994). Creating TQM organizations. *Quality Progress*, *27*(1), 51–54.

Mozaffari, F. A. (2008). A study of relationship between organizational culture and leadership. *International Conference on Applied Economics*, 679-688. Retrieved from: https://faculty.mu.edu.sa/public/uploads/1360858719.3627organizational%20cult180.pdf

Naumovski, S., Bojadjiev, M., Tomovska-Misoska, A., & Stefanovska-Petkovska, M. (2017). Organizational alignment in the food industry: Case study of a company in the Republic of Macedonia. *Economic Development*, *18*(3), 267–280.

Powell, T. C. (1992). Organizational alignment as competitive advantage. *Strategic Management Journal*, *13*(2), 119–134. doi:10.1002mj.4250130204

Sánchez Marín, G., Carrasco Hernández, A. J., Danvila del Valle, I., & Sastre Castillo, M. Á. (2016). 'Organizational culture and family business: A configurational approach', European Journal of Family Business. *Malaga University*, *6*(2), 99–107. doi:10.1016/j.ejfb.2017.05.002

Schein, E. H. (1992). *Organizational culture and leadership* (2nd ed.). Jossey-Bass.

Schein, E. H. (2004). *Organizational culture and leadership*. Jossey Bass.

Semler, S. W. (1997). Systematic agreement: A theory of organizational alignment. *Human Resource Development Quarterly*, *8*(1), 23–40. doi:10.1002/hrdq.3920080105

Sorasalmi, T., & Tuovinen, J. (2016). Entering emerging markets: A dynamic frame-work dynamics in logistics. 675–683.Berlin: Springer

Stalk, G. Jr, & Foley, H. (2012, January-February). Avoiding Traps That Can Destroy Family Businesses. *Harvard Business Review*, •••, 25–27.

Tipu, S. A. A. (2018). *What have we learned? Themes from the literature on organizational culture in family firms. European Business Review* . doi:10.1108/EBR-02-2017-0042

Tomovska-Misoska, A., Bojadizev, M., Stefanoska, M., & Nikolovska, Z. (2011). *Vox-Organizationis – theoretical basis and methodological considerations in the development of an instrument for organizational culture*. MPRA Paper No. 42571. http://mpra.ub.uni-muenchen.de/42571/

Tosti, D. T. (2007). Aligning the culture and strategy for success. *Performance Improvement*, *46*(1), 21–25. doi:10.1002/pfi.035

Waterman, R. H. Jr, Peters, T., & Phillips, J. R. (1980). Structure is not organization. *Business Horizons*, *23*(3), 14–26. doi:10.1016/0007-6813(80)90027-0

Chapter 7
Friends or Foe?
Unravelling the Role of Familiness in Promoting Business Ethics in the Workplace

Rosalba Manna
National Institute for Documentation, Innovation, and Educational Research, Italy

Rocco Palumbo
University of Rome "Tor Vergata", Italy

Massimiliano Pellegrini
https://orcid.org/0000-0002-5722-2988
University of Rome "Tor Vergata", Italy

ABSTRACT

Scholars have argued that business ethics is a crucial ingredient for the successful recipe of human resource management. However, little is known about the factors that trigger an organizational commitment towards the promotion of an ethical approach in crafting human resource management practices. This is especially true for family firms, whose ethical slant in devising human resource management practices has been under-researched. This chapter intends to push forward our knowledge in the field of business ethics investigating the role of familiness in determining ethically-rooted human resource management practices among small and medium-sized enterprises. More specifically, the authors investigated how awareness of business ethics issues and formalization of human resource management policies and practices affect the SMEs commitment to ethics. Family firms were found to be aware of the ethical challenges that characterize human resource management; however, no evidence was retrieved about the role of familiness in triggering an ethical commitment in managing human resources.

DOI: 10.4018/978-1-7998-4814-1.ch007

INTRODUCTION

Business ethics is a relevant, yet under-researched topic in the family business realm (see, among others: Vazquez, 2018; García-Sánchez, Martínez-Ferrero, Cuadrado-Ballesteros, & Rodríguez-Ariza, 2015; Payne, Brigham, Broberg, Moss, & Short, 2011). Contributing to the construction of a positive firm image and enhancing the organizational climate, business ethics advances family firms' success (Zellweger, Kellermanns, Eddleston, & Memili, 2012). Attention to ethics in making managerial decisions ensures a positive overlapping between family-related values and business-related concerns (Sharma, 2004), setting the conditions for enhancing the family business longevity (Goto, 2013). Nevertheless, family firms are not used to design formal policies and/or implement structured practices to promote ethical behaviors in their organizational environment (Adams, Taschian, & Shore, 1996; Long & Mathews, 2011). This could be related to the fact that family firms often prefer a lean and informal approach to tackle organizational and managerial issues (Chrisman et al., 2009). Such an informal approach is usually inherited from past habits and behaviors, which create a path dependency amongst family firms (Kidwell, Eddleston & Kellermanns, 2018). Moreover, family firms' owners have been argued to be unaware of the specific challenges that affect the promotion of business ethics in daily organizational dynamics (Fassin, Van Rossem, & Buelens, 2011). This situation is prompted by the propensity of family firms to confound business ethics with issues that are related to corporate social responsibility (Tabor, Madison, Daspit, & Holt, 2019).

Diverging insights into the ethics of family firms have been proposed in scientific and professional literatures. On the one hand, family firms have been argued to outperform non-family firms in terms of organizational virtue orientation, showing higher levels of moral integrity and conscientiousness (Payne, Brigham, Broberg, Moss, & Short, 2011) and being able to pragmatically handle the managerial challenges related to business ethics (Ding & Wu, 2014). On the other hand, ethics violations – such as the buying of loyalties and the mismanagement of organizational power – have been found to negatively affect the ethical standing of family firms (Gallo, 1998; Greve, Palmer, & Pozner, 2010; Cormier & Magnan, 2017).

Failures in business ethics are especially dangerous when they concern human resource management practices (Atrachan & Kolenko, 1994; Reid & Adams, 2001). Ethical violations in human resource management compromise the establishment of a positive organizational climate and impair the achievement of organizational citizenship (Ciasullo, Cosimato & Palumbo, 2017), leading to impoverished organizational behaviors and performance (Bernhard & O'Driscoll, 2011; Crane, Matten, Glozer, & Spence, 2016). In spite of these considerations, the interplay between business ethics and human resource management practices in the family business context has been largely overlooked by scholars and practitioners (Greenwood, 2002).

Without claims of exhaustiveness, human resource management practices can be conceived of as "*...a group of organizational functions which are used to manage and improve human resources and assuring that* [they] *are utilized efficiently in order to attain goals of organization*" (Mathew & Kannan, 2019: p. 16). From this standpoint, human resource management practices involve both micro (*i.e.*, functional aspects) and macro factors (*i.e.*, strategic issues) that are instrumental for enhancing individual and collective performances (Wright & Boswell, 2002). Whilst studies intended to investigate the role played by human resource management practices in underpinning organizational excellence are well established (Ciasullo, Cosimato, Gaeta & Palumbo, 2017), identifying them as preconditions to the achievement of increased organizational effectiveness (Delery & Gupta, 2016) and stronger competitive advantage

(Schuler & MacMillan, 1984), relatively limited attention has been paid to the distinguishing characteristics of such practices and on their implications on business ethics (Guerci, Radaelli, Siletti, Cirella, & Rami Shani, 2015). This is surprising, since previous research emphasized that the organizational ethical climate is strictly dependent on the ability of organizations to foster employees' compliance and commitment to ethical values (Weaver & Trevino, 2001). From this point of view, further developments are needed in order to: 1) shed lights on the ability of family firms to embrace an ethical slant in arranging human resource management practices, and 2) disentangle the peculiar organizational approaches used by family firms to implement ethically reliable human resource management practices (Bertrand & Schoar, 2006; Vallejo, 2008; Firfiray, Cruz, Neacsu, & Gomez-Mejiad, 2018). This chapter intends to contribute in these two research streams, trying to answer to the following research questions:

RQ. 1: Do family firms acknowledge the topicality of ethical issues in managing human resources?
RQ. 2: What are the triggers of an ethical commitment in designing human resource management policies and practices among family and non-family small and medium-sized enterprises?

A quantitative research design has been designed to answer these research questions. More specifically, a comparison of the behaviors of family and non-family small and medium-sized organizations allowed us to shed some lights into the factors that affect their ethical approach in managing human resources. This chapter is organized as follows. Section 2 presents the conceptual background which inspired the study. Section 3 articulates the conceptual framework against which our research was conceived. Section 4 describes the study methods and presents the sample of family and non-family firms that participated in this study. Section 5 reports the research findings, which are critically discussed in Section 6. Section 7 identifies some areas for further developments, whilst Section 8 ends up the paper, synthesizing its main conceptual and practical implications.

BACKGROUND

Even though there is no agreement about what is meant by ethics in the managerial context (Maclagan, 1998; Brewis & Way-Bliss, 2008), organizations have been found to have both "...*ethics problems and problems with ethics*" (Donaldson, 2008: p. 299). Business ethics is a complex and multifaceted concept (Drucker, 1981; Jones, Parker, & Bos, 2005), which ranges from the organizational ability to maintain a viable interplay with the external environment (Muskin, 2000; Oliveira & Lumineau, 2019) to the fair management of intra-organizational dynamics and behaviours (Sternberg, 2000; Kidwell, Eddleston, Cater III, & Kellermanns, 2013). Whilst defining business ethics is "...*like nailing jello to a wall*" (Lewis, 1985, p. 377), several attempts have been made to pinpoint the contours of this concept and to define the most fitting methods and approaches to deal with it (see, among others: Randall & Gibson, 1990; Velasquez, 2002; Jones, Parker, & ten Bos, 2005; Palanski, et al., 2019; Freeman & Greenwood, 2020).

Generally speaking, business ethics involve "...*the study of how personal moral norms apply to the activities and goals of the organization...* [and] *of how individuals, at all levels of an organization, try to make decisions and live their lives according to a standard of or right or wrong behavior*" (Heller & Heller, 2011: p. 30). This definition emphasizes that business ethics is related to human resource management (Winstanley, Woodall, & Heery, 1996). Actually, the ethical dimension of human resource management has been largely stressed from both a conceptual and an empirical point of view (Winstanley

& Woodall, 2000; Deckop, 2006). Furthermore, the relevance of ethics in crafting successful and viable human resource management practices has been emphasized both in the scientific and the professional literatures (Buckley, et al., 2001; Schumann, 2001).

Although organizations attempt to establish human resource management strategies and practices on ethical considerations (Dachler & Enderle, 1989), still little is known about the role and the implications of ethics in shaping the firms' approaches in managing and organizing human resources (Vickers, 2005). This is especially true as far as family firms are taken into consideration. In fact, the interplay between human resource management and business ethics has been rarely investigated in the family firms setting (Botero & Litchfield, 2013). Whilst most of the scholarly attention has been paid to the framing of business ethics as a macro and inter-organizational issue (Campopiano & De Massis, 2015; LeBreton-Miller & Miller, 2016; Labelle, Hafsi, Francoeur, & Amar, 2018), a paucity of studies tries to contextualize the challenges met by family firms to achieve fairness in the management of human resources at the micro, inter-personal level (Broccardo, Truant, & Zicari, 2019).

In sum, in spite of its momentous implications on the effectiveness and viability of family firms the attainment of organizational justice in the workplace has been relatively understudied (Samara & Paul, 2019). Previous studies emphasized that the influence of the family might have negative effects on the perception of justice in the workplace (Barnett & Kellermanns, 2006). In fact, family and non-family employees are likely to have distinguishing – and potentially conflicting – needs in terms of human resource management practices (Sanchez-Bueno, Muñoz-Bullón, & Galan, 2020). The inability to create a bridge between these different expectations of family and non-family members of the organization may pave the way for perceptions of unfairness and injustice (Krishnan & Peytcheva, 2019), that imply organizational conflicts and imperil organizational performances (Samara & Arenas, 2017). This circumstance is further complicated by the propensity of family firms to use informal – rather than formal – approaches in designing and implementing human resource management practices. Lack of formalization leads to the emergence of rule of thumbs, that do not permit to have landmarks or clear reference points to deal with conflicts or organizational struggles (Poza, Alfred, & Maheshwari, 1997; Aldrich & Langton, 1998; Kotey & Sheridan, 2004; Nguyen & Bryant, 2004; der Heyden, Blondel, & Carlock, 2005).

CONCEPTUAL FRAMEWORK AND RESEARCH HYPOTHESES

Family firms are characterized by a strong awareness of issues and challenges that are related to business ethics (Ding & Wu, 2014). The overlapping of ownership and managing responsibilities urges family firms to adopt an extended horizon in framing the strategies and the organizational orientations that inspire individual and collective behaviors (James, 1999). Literature has stressed that "*...vision, intentions, and behavior are what should be used to distinguish family business from all others*" (Chua, Chrisman, & Sharma, 1999: p. 35). Moreover, family firms have been recognized as schools in values, due to their unity, commitment, and focus on industriousness (Gallo, 2004). From this standpoint, the family firms' awareness of ethical issues and challenges derive from the deeply-rooted organizational social capital that characterizes this type of companies (Sorenson, 2011). In fact, the contamination between the family social capital and the organizational social capital in family firms is likely to involve greater appreciation of relevant ethical issues (Arregle, Hitt, Sirmon, & Very, 2007). The concept of "familiness" has been proposed to emphasize such a peculiarity of family firms (Habbershon & Williams, 1999; Habbershon, Williams, & MacMillan, 2003). It broadly refers to "*...the idiosyncratic firm-level* *bundle of resources and capabilities a particular firm has because of the systemic interaction between the family, its individual members and the business*" (Irava & Moores, 2010: p. 131). In light of these considerations, it is assumed that:

Hp. 1: Family firms report a greater awareness of ethical issues in managing human resources as compared with non-family firms;
Hp. 2: Family firms state a greater awareness of ethical failures that may determine unfairness and discrimination in managing human resources.

Family firms have been generally found to prefer informal – rather than formal – tools and procedures to handle both business ethics (Adams, Taschian, & Shore, 1996) and human resource management practices (Sánchez-Marín, Meroño-Cerdán, & Carrasco-Hernández, 2019). This especially applies to small-sized organizations, which are more prone to adopt an informal way of managing human resources (Kim & Gao, 2010). Informality relies on the virtue orientation of managers (Del Baldo, 2013). Besides, it is related to the need of achieving plasticity and flexibility in dealing with the ethical issues faced by organizations (Palumbo, 2016). On the one hand, the use of informal methods to deal with issues related to business ethics and human resource management allows family firms to build and maintain binding ties within the organization (Gomez-Mejia, Cruz, Berrone, & De Castro, 2001). On the other hand, lack of formalization paves the way for conflicts and ambiguities at the meso-organizational level, which are thought to damage organizational behaviors and performances (Steijvers, Lybaert, & Dekker, 2017; Memili, Chang, Kellermanns, & Welsh, 2015). Hence, it is hypothesized that:

Hp. 3: Family firms are less likely to formalize the tools and methods they use to deal with issues and challenges related to ethics in managing human resources.

Even though family firms have been considered to suffer from an inherent unethical slant in managing human resources, favouring family members over non-family ones (Perry, Ring, Matherne, & Markova, 2013) and, consequently, being unable to make "*...the plurality of HRM visible*" (Janssens & Steyaert, 2009), it should be noted that non-structured approaches and tools can be used to guarantee and promote ethically consistent behaviors in human resource management (Cater, James, Kidwell, Camp, & Young, 2019). The use of informal tools to handle the ethical challenges of human resource management can be triggered by the desire of family firms to minimize the occurrence of organizational injustice (Madison, Daspit, Turner, & Kellermanns, 2018) and to protect the integrity of organizational reputation (Deephouse & Jaskiewicz, 2013). From this point of view, it can be assumed that:

Hp. 4: Family firms are more likely to develop tailored policies and strategies to promote organizational justice and ethical behavior in managing human resources.
Hp. 5: Family firms are more likely to use targeted strategies and interventions in order to promote organizational justice and ethical behavior in managing human resources.

A variety of factors influences the organizational propensity to embrace an ethically reliable approach in managing human resources. Whilst formalization of strategies and management approaches seem to be more effective for non-family firms, family firms tend to exploit informal methods and tools to establish a sound ethical climate within the organization, even when they undertake a professionalization path (Falkenberg & Herremans, 1995; Perrini & Minoja, 2008; Camfield & Franco, 2019). Drawing on these considerations, it is hypothesized that:

Hp. 6: Ethical commitment in managing human resources is related to the family firms' awareness of ethical issues and to the arrangement of informal strategies inspiring ethically consistent human resource management practices.

METHODS

Research Strategy

An empirical approach was taken to test the hypotheses and to provide an answer to the research questions that inspired this study. Secondary data were collected from the survey about "*Fairness, dignity and respect in SME* (Small and Medium-sized Enterprises) *workplaces*" which was commissioned by the UK Equality and Human Rights Commission[1] to Industrial Facts and Forecasting (IFF) Research. Detailed information about this survey can be retrieved in a report published by the Equality and Human Rights Commission in 2015 (Winterbotham, Oldfield, Stewart, Rossiter, & IFF Research, 2015). The survey had two concurrent purposes: 1) to understand the knowledge, attitudes and practices of SME employers in managing issues related to human rights in the workplace; and 2) to investigate the ability of SME employers to ensure free treatment in recruitment, promotion and employment practices.

The use of a secondary source of information allowed us to expeditiously collect relevant data about our research topic. However, secondary data did not permit us to tailor the process of data collection to the specific aims of this research. Our research strategy was articulated in three stages. Firstly, we went through the dataset, in order to identify data which matched the scope of our study. Secondly, we aggregated individual variables in macro-variables, as reported below. Thirdly, we performed a twofold statistical analysis. On the one hand, some descriptive statistics were used to shed light into the use of ethical practices among the units of analysis. On the other hand, we implemented some regression analysis to illuminate the factors which influence the willingness of SMEs to inspire their human resource management approaches to ethical principles. In line with the specific aims of this research, an effort was made to elicit differences in behaviors between family and non-family firms.

Study Design, Data, and Measures

The survey involved 1,002 SMEs operating in UK at the moment of data collection. Firms with a minimum of 5 employees and a maximum of 249 employees were approached for participation. A variety of sectors were contemplated, including: agriculture, mining, utilities, manufacturing, construction, retail and wholesale, accommodation, food services, finance, transport, leisure, education, and health services. Data collection was performed between January, 2015 and February, 2015. A cross-sectional one-time study approach was designed. The units of analysis were recruited using a multi-stage stratified random sample. The initial sample – which was purchased from Dun and Bradstreet's UK Trading File – consisted of 6,044 firms. Telephone interviews were used to collect data. Interviews were conducted by a team of 26 expert interviewers and they lasted from a minimum of 20 minutes to a maximum of

28 minutes. The response rate was about 16%. Secondary data were made available to the public for research purposes at the end of 2015.

Table 1 summarizes the main data and measures which were used in this study. The measures were obtained by summing the set of variables included in the dataset that referred to the same macro-item. Firstly, our attention was focused on the SMEs' awareness of ethical issue in managing human resources. In particular, we were interested in assessing the degree of respondents' consciousness of the relevance of fair and empowering working conditions as a basic human right of employees. Secondly, we paid attention to a specific form of awareness of ethical-related challenges in managing human resources, that is to say discrimination in the workplace. In fact, workplace discrimination was acknowledged as a failure in the adoption of an ethical approach in managing human resources, leading to a deterioration of the organizational climate and to the de-humanization of working conditions. Thirdly, we tried to elicit the respondents' willingness to formalize their efforts to ensure fairness and dignity in managing their business. Fourthly, we attempted to shed light on the SMEs' propensity to inspire their human resource management policies to ethics. Similarly, we wanted to acknowledge the willingness of the units of analysis to inspire their arrangement of human resource management practices to ethical reasoning. Lastly, yet importantly, we focused on the respondents' self-reported commitment toward ethics in managing human resources. These variables were gathered in an electronic worksheet and they were statistically analyzed using IBM's Statistical Package for the Social Sciences, version 24.

Sample

As previously anticipated, the study sample consisted of 1,002 SMEs. In most of the cases, the interviewee was either the managing director (14.4%) or the Human Resource Manager (15.8%). In several circumstances, a senior manager (12.5%) or a middle-line manager (11%) was entrusted to participate in the survey. Only in few circumstances the owner (8.9%) or the company director (7.9%) were directly involved in the survey. People working for the Human Resource department (5.1%), the administration staff (4.8%), and general management (4.5%) followed. Most of the units of analysis had either a single owner or an individual with a majority shareholding (51.4%). About a third had a managing director (34.5%) who coordinated the entire business. In general, single owners and managing directors were predominantly male (86.6%) and white (91.1%). Only a sixth of them were aged 44 years or below (15%). More than a third (36.6) had a university diploma or a doctoral degree, whilst less than a third had primary education or no specific educational attainment (29.2%).

Table 2 shows an overview of the characteristics of the units of analysis. The majority of the sample was represented by organizations operating in the fields of finance or business services (26.4%). A fourth consisted of firms operating in the primary sector (24.8%). Retail and wholesale (20.1%) and food and accommodation services (13.8%) followed. England accounted for 7 in 10 units of analysis (69.9%). Scotland (16.4%) and Wales (13.7%) covered little more than a tenth of the sample, respectively. The majority of the firms involved in this study had less than 10 employees (30.9%). Nevertheless, more than a sixth of the units of analysis had a number of employees ranging between 100 and 249 (17.9%). The sample was evenly balanced among firms which were owner managed (40.2%) and firms which were team managed (56.3%). Lastly, yet importantly, most of the firms had an organizational age of 10 years and above (85.9%). More than a third of respondents (37.5%) did not report to have a designated HR department or person.

Table 1. Data and measures used in the study

Variable (ID)	Description	Scale	Observations	μ	σ
Awareness of Ethical Issues in HRM (AE)	Awareness of the importance of fair, value-based, and empowering working conditions as a human right of employees	Discrete 10-points scale (1 = unaware; 10 = strongly aware)	1,002	9.16	1.58
Awareness of Discrimination in HRM (AD)	Awareness of the occurrence of failures in managing human resources that may lead to unfair and/or discriminatory Human Resource Management Practices	Discrete 10-points scale (1 = unaware; 10 = strongly aware)	1,002	8.55	0.99
Formalization of ethically-rooted HRMP (FH)	Formalization of Human Resource Management Practices that promote fair, non-discriminating, and empowering working conditions	Discrete 10-points scale (1 = low formalization; 10 = high formalization)	1,002	7.11	2.92
Promotion of ethics in designing HRM policies (PH)	Adoption of tailored strategies to promote ethics in devising Human Resource Management policies	Discrete 5-points scale (1 = absent or low adoption; 5 = strong adoption)	1,002	2.13	1.37
Promotion of ethics in crafting HRMP (PP)	Adoption of targeted organizational models and strategies to promote ethics in arranging Human Resource Management Practices	Discrete 10-points scale (1 = absent or low adoption; 10 = strong adoption)	1,002	5.15	1.95
Ethical Commitment to HRM (EC)	Degree of ethical commitment in managing human resources and in crafting Human Resource Management Practices	Continuous scale ranging from: 1 = lowest commitment 5 = highest commitment	984	2.70	0.30

Source: Authors' re-elaboration from IFF Research, 2015

FINDINGS

Table 3 shows some descriptive statistics concerning the firms' awareness of ethical issues in managing human resources and the approach they adopted to ensure an ethically consistent way of crafting human resource management practices. Even though family and non-family firms showed more or less analogous behaviors, it is interesting to note that they presented some peculiarities. Firstly, whilst both the type of firms reported a strong awareness for ethical issues, family firms scored – on average – better than non-family firms. This was especially true as far as awareness of the importance of fair, value-based, and empowering working conditions was concerned. Alternatively, non-family firms were found to be more prone to use formal tools and tailored organizational arrangements to ensure ethics in the workplace. In sum, commitment to ethics was equal in the two sub-sample involved in the analysis, although non-family firms disclosed greater formal commitment to ethics than family ones.

Table 2. The study sample (n = 1,002)

Variable	Total	
	No.	**%**
Type of interviewee		
Owner	89	8.9
Company director	79	7.9
Managing director	144	14.4
HR manager	158	15.8
Senior Manager	125	12.5
Middle Manager	110	11
Staff of the HR department	51	5
Member of the administration staff	48	4.8
Staff of the general management	45	4.5
Other	153	15.2
Type of sector		
Primary sector	247	24.7
Retail and wholesale	201	20.1
Food and accommodation services	138	13.8
Finance and business services	265	26.4
Other	151	15
Geographical location		
England	700	69.9
Scotland	164	16.4
Wales	138	13.7
Organizational dimension		
9 employees and below	309	30.9
Between 10 and 19 employees	215	21.5
Between 20 and 49 employees	147	14.7
Between 50 and 99 employees	151	15
100 employees and above	180	17.9
Type of business		
Owner managed	402	40.2
Team managed	563	56.3
Both owner and team managed	12	1.1
Family managed	5	0.4
Other/Do not know/do not answer	20	2

Source: Authors' elaboration

Table 3. Descriptive statistics depicting the awareness of ethical issues and the approach used to promote ethics in managing human resources

		AE	AD	FH	PH	PP	EC
Non-family firms	Mean	9.07	8.54	7.15	2.12	5.19	2.72
	N	515	515	515	515	515	505
	Std. Deviation	1.681	1.07	2.82	1.35	1.94	0.31
Family firms	Mean	9.30	8.56	7.03	2.14	5.09	2.67
	N	466	466	466	466	466	458
	Std. Deviation	1.442	0.89	3.05	1.39	1.95	0.29
Total	Mean	9.18	8.55	7.10	2.13	5.14	2.70
	N	981	981	981	981	981	963
	Std. Deviation	1.575	0.99	2.93	1.37	1.95	0.31

Source: Authors' elaboration

An independent samples *t* test was run to obtain some statistical evidence about differences in the means of the measures that assessed the awareness of ethical issues and the approaches used to ensure ethics in managing human resources among family and non-family SMES. Table 4 summarizes the results of this statistical analysis. We found evidence of a positive and statistically significant difference of means related to the firms' awareness of ethical issues in managing human resources. More specifically, family firms showed a greater awareness of the ethical challenges that affect the management of human resources. A negative and statistically significant difference of means was retrieved with reference to the formalization of human resource management practices inspired to business ethics. That is to say, non-family firms were more likely to formalize their efforts intended to ensure ethics in the management of human resources. Conversely, we did not notice significant differences of means for the other variables contemplated in this study. In sum, whilst we found support for *Hp. 1* and *Hp. 3*, *Hp. 2*, *Hp. 4*, and *Hp. 5* were not supported.

Next, an Ordinary Least Square (OLS) regression analysis was performed. The firms' awareness of ethical issues in managing human resources and the approaches used to ensure ethics in crafting human resource management practices were used as independent variables. The commitment toward ethics in managing human resources was run as the dependent variable. In order to avoid biases in the elaboration of data, the independent variables were transformed in dichotomous variables, with "1" indicating the occurrence of the related item and "0" indicating that it did not occur. Two different regression models were elaborated. On the one hand, attention was exclusively focused on the relationship between the independent and the dependent variables (Model '1'). On the other hand, some control variables were included in the analysis, such as the organizational age of the firm, the economic sector of activity, the organizational dimension, and the professionalization of the company (Model '2').

Model '1', which is reported in Table 5, suggested that the promotion of ethics in crafting human resource management policies and the promotion of ethics in designing human resource management practices were positively and statistically significantly related ($p < 0.001$) to the firms' commitment to achieving business ethics in human resources management. This was true for both family and non-family firms.

Table 4. The result of the independent samples t test

Independent Samples Test										
		Levene's Test for Equality of Variances		t-test for Equality of Means						
		F	*p*- value	T	df	*p*-value (2-tailed)	Mean Difference	Std. Error Difference	95% Confidence Interval of the Difference	
									Lower	Upper
AE	Equal variances assumed	6.683**	0.010	2.212*	979	0.027	0.222	0.101	0.025	0.420
	Equal variances not assumed			2.229	976.242	0.026	0.222	0.100	0.027	0.418
AD	Equal variances assumed	0.856	0.355	0.352	979	0.725	0.022	0.064	-0.103	0.147
	Equal variances not assumed			0.356	971.896	0.722	0.022	0.063	-0.101	0.146
FH	Equal variances assumed	4.823*	0.028	-0.646	979	0.518	-0.121	0.188	-0.489	0.247
	Equal variances not assumed			-0.644	948.895	0.520	-0.121	0.188	-0.491	0.248
PH	Equal variances assumed	1.890	0.169	0.286	979	0.775	0.025	0.088	-0.147	0.197
	Equal variances not assumed			0.286	962.625	0.775	0.025	0.088	-0.147	0.198
PP	Equal variances assumed	0.098	0.754	-0.835	979	0.404	-0.104	0.125	-0.349	0.140
	Equal variances not assumed			-0.835	968.563	0.404	-0.104	0.125	-0.349	0.140

* Significant at the 0.05 level
** Significant at the 0.01 level
Source: Authors' elaboration

Table 5. The OLS model investigating the triggers of firms' commitment to ethics – Model '1'

Model Summary						
Model '1'	R	R^2	Adjusted R^2	Std. Error of the Estimate		
Non-family firms	0.467	0.218	0.210	0.279		
Family firms	0.316	0.100	0.090	0.279		

ANOVA							
		Sum of Squares	df	Mean Square	F	*p*-value
Non-family firms	Regression	10.863	5	2.173	27.859	0.000
	Residual	38.914	499	0.078		
	Total	49.777	504			
Family firms	Regression	3.887	5	0.777	10.020	0.000v
	Residual	35.068	452	0.078		
	Total	38.954	457			

Coefficients						
		Unstandardized Coefficients		Standardized Coefficients	t	*p*-value
		B	Std. Error	Beta		
Non-family firms	(Constant)	2.525	0.030		83.188	0.000
	AE	0.026	0.026	0.041	1.019	0.309
	AD	0.042	0.030	0.058	1.417	0.157
	FH	0.031	0.029	0.049	1.090	0.276
	PH	0.147***	0.028	0.219	5.180	0.000
	PP	0.195***	0.028	0.308	6.949	0.000
Family firms	(Constant)	2.555	0.031		81.345	0.000
	AE	0.037	0.029	0.058	1.281	0.201
	AD	0.001	0.031	0.001	0.022	0.983
	FH	0.033	0.030	0.056	1.102	0.271
	PH	0.103***	0.030	0.165	3.398	0.001
	PP	0.103***	0.030	0.173	3.470	0.001

*** Significant at the 0.001 level
Source: Authors' elaboration

Model '2', which is summarized in Table 6, yielded analogous results. In fact, the SMES' propensity to promote ethics at the policy and the organizational levels continued to be positively related to their commitment to ethics in managing human resources. However, whilst small organizational dimensions were found to be negatively and significantly ($p > 0.01$) related to ethical commitment among non-family firms, the professionalization of family firms positively and significantly ($p > 0.01$) affected their commitment to ethics. From this standpoint, we did not find support for Hp. 6.

Table 6. The OLS model investigating the triggers of firms' commitment to ethics – Model '2'

Model Summary						
Model '2'	R	R^2	Adjusted R^2	Std. Error of the Estimate		
Non-family firms	0,481	0.232	0.218	0.277		
Family firms	0,349	0.122	0.104	0.277		
ANOVA						
		Sum of Squares	df	Mean Square	F	*p*-value
Non-family firms	Regression	11.328	9	1.259	16.429	0.000
	Residual	37.539	490	0.077		
	Total	48.867	499			
Family firms	Regression	4.741	9	0.527	6.852	0.000
	Residual	34.140	444	0.077		
	Total	38.881	453			
Coefficients						
		Unstandardized Coefficients		Standardized Coefficients	t	*p*-value
		B	Std. Error	Beta		
Non-family firms	(Constant)	2.547	0.051		49.584	0.000
	AE	0.021	0.026	0.033	0.830	0.407
	AD	0.031	0.030	0.042	1.024	0.306
	FH	0.028	0.029	0.045	0.982	0.327
	PH	0.149***	0.028	0.223	5.244	0.000
	PP	0.171***	0.028	0.272	6.016	0.000
	Sector (1 = Service)	0.014	0.025	0.021	0.531	0.596
	Dimensions (1 = < 10 employees)	-0.084**	0.028	-0.122	-2.980	0.003
	Organizational age (1 = < 5 years)	-0.006	0.037	-0.006	-0.150	0.881
	Professionalization	0.031	0.027	0.047	1.154	0.249
Family firms	(Constant)	2.518	0.055		45.938	0.000
	AE	0.037	0.028	0.059	1.304	0.193
	AD	0.003	0.031	0.005	0.099	0.922
	FH	0.033	0.030	0.056	1.104	0.270
	PH	0.098***	0.030	0.157	3.240	0.001
	PP	0.091***	0.030	0.152	2.974	0.003
	Sector (1 = Service)	0.030	0.027	0.050	1.104	0.270
	Dimensions (1 = < 10 employees)	-0.017	0.029	-0.028	-0.596	0.551
	Organizational age (1 = < 5 years)	-0.011	0.038	-0.014	-0.304	0.761
	Professionalization	0.079**	0.027	0.135	2.965	0.003

*** Significant at the 0.001 level

** Significant at the 0.01 level

Source: Authors' elaboration

DISCUSSION

Table 7 synthesizes the outputs of research hypotheses' testing. Whilst the findings of the independent samples t test provided support for hypothesis 1, suggesting that family firms expressed a greater awareness of ethical issues in handling human resource management-related challenges, hypothesis 2 was not supported, with familiness being not relevant in increasing the SMES' acknowledgement of the ethical failures which may engender unfairness and discrimination in managing people. It is worth noting that family firms were found to be less likely to formalize policies, strategies, approaches, and tools to tackle the triggers of unethical behaviors in managing human resources, thus upholding hypothesis 3. Nevertheless, no significant differences between family and non-family SMES were noticed in the firms' willingness to design tailored strategies to ensure ethics in human resource management policies and to implement targeted organizational interventions to promote ethically-rooted human resource management practices: therefore, both hypothesis 4 and hypothesis 5 were rejected. Lastly, yet importantly, ethical commitment turned out to positively affect the promotion of ethics in designing human resource management policies and in crafting human resource management practices. This was especially true for family firms, whose ethical orientation is strictly related to the virtue orientation of the organizational apex. Hence, hypothesis 6 was supported.

Table 7. An overview of research hypotheses' testing

Hypothesis number	Description	Outcome	Discussion
Hp. 1	Family firms report a greater awareness of ethical issues in managing human resources as compared with non-family firms	Supported	Even though both family and non-family firms are aware of the importance of ethics in managing human resources, non-family firms report a greater consciousness of ethical-related issues than non-family firms
Hp. 2	Family firms state a greater awareness of ethical failures that may determine unfairness and discrimination in managing human resources	Rejected	Familiness seemed to be not relevant in affecting the firms' ability to acknowledge ethical failures and to gauge their implications on unfair human resource management practices
Hp. 3	Family firms are less likely to formalize the tools and methods they use to deal with issues and challenges related to ethics in managing human resources	Supported	Family firms were less willing than non-family ones to formalize and institutionalize tools and approaches aimed at tackling unethical human resource management policies and practices
Hp. 4	Family firms are more likely to develop tailored policies and strategies to promote organizational justice and ethical behavior in managing human resources	Rejected	Family firms and non-family firms showed analogous behaviors in designing tailored policies and strategies to ensure fairness in managing human resources
Hp. 5	Family firms are more likely to use targeted strategies and interventions in order to promote organizational justice and ethical behavior in managing human resources	Rejected	Both family and non-family firms fell short in crafting targeted strategies to promote organizational justice in human resource management
Hp. 6	Ethical commitment in managing human resources is related to the family firms' awareness of ethical issues and to the arrangement of informal strategies inspiring ethically consistent human resource management practices	Supported	Ethical commitment was found to trigger a greater propensity of SMES to design tailored policies and strategies to ensure fairness and justice in managing human resources

Source: Authors' elaboration

The research findings should be contextualized to the limitations which affected this research. As previously anticipated, the use of secondary data did not allow us to tailor the research strategy and design to the specific purposes of our study. Nevertheless, the secondary data of information provided by the IFF Research turned out to be a reliable and fitting source of information to shed lights on the topics addressed by this work. Besides, the study results are not generalizable at the international level. In fact, only firms established in the UK were involved in this research. Lastly, the cross-sectional approach constrained the breadth of this research, providing a snapshot of SMEs' orientation towards ethics in the management of human resources.

In spite of these shortcomings, the study results provided some intriguing insights about the factors that affect the ethical commitments of SMEs in managing human resources, Also, they contribute in advancing our knowledge about the role of familiness in influencing the implementation of ethically-rooted human resource management practices. As expected, family firms were characterized by a lower formalization of ethically consistent human resource management practices (Borda, Hansen, & Gore, 2019). Nevertheless, they had a greater awareness of the importance of business ethics in managing human resources as compared with non-family firms: this may pave the way for a higher consideration of the employees' needs and expectations at the management level (Kim, Haider, Wu, & Dou, 2019). These findings seem to be at odds with the arguments of the scientific literature arguing that family firms are more likely to show unethical behaviors, "*...consistent with entrenchment theory, according to which family members may behave opportunistically to extract rents and potentially expropriate the firm's resources*" (Krishnan & Peytcheva, 2019). In fact, family firms have been claimed to be biased towards insiders (Navarro & Ansón, 2009), which may lead to ethical dilemma in tackling managerial challenges (Litz & Turner, 2013).

Whilst family firms were more prone to adopt tailored strategies intended to promote ethics in designing and implementing human resource management policies, non-family firms were more willing to use targeted organizational models and strategies to ensure ethics in arranging human resource management practices (Ramírez-Solís & Baños-Monroy, 2019). This situation further confirms that, even though "*... family firms engage very well with internal stakeholders such as employees*" (Sanchez-Bueno, Muñoz-Bullón, & Galan, 2020: p. 48), they tend to embrace an informal slant in conceiving and implementing their ethical focus (Adams, Taschian, & Shore, 1996; O'Boyle Jr, Rutherford, & Pollack, 2010).

In sum, familiness was not found to influence the SMEs' propensity to embrace an ethical approach in handling human resource management policies and practices. On the one hand, non-family firms disclosed a greater commitment to ethics in managing human resources. On the other hand, the promotion of ethics in designing human resource management policies and human resource management practices turned out to be relevant determinants of SMEs' ethical commitment. These results should be read in light of the family firms' greater propensity to use conventionality rather than strategic and organizational alignment in dealing with business ethics-related issues (Richards & Schembera, 2019). In turn, the prevalence of conventionality over alignment may impair the firms' formal commitment to ethics in managing human resources, with negative drawbacks on their ethical performances (López-Cózar, Priede, & Hilliard, 2014; López-Pérez, Melero-Polo, Vázquez-Carrasco, & Cambra-Fierro, 2018).

FUTURE RESEARCH DIRECTIONS

Further research is required to unravel the influence of familiness on the firms' willingness and ability to adopt an ethical conduct in managing human resources. Firstly, scholars are proposing several concepts which may help in bridging the gap between business ethics and human resource management, such as organizational resilience (Santoro, Messeni-Petruzzelli, & Del Giudice, 2020; Palumbo & Manna, 2019), humane entrepreneurship (Kim, Eltarabishy, & Bae, 2018; Parente, Eltarabishy, Vesci, & Botti, 2018), and emotional capital (Elicegui-Reyes, Barrena-Martínez, & Romero-Fernández, 2017). Conceptual and empirical developments are needed to better understand how these – and similar – constructs may contribute in the achievement of ethics in the design and the implementation of human resource management practices. Secondly, the research findings suggested that professionalization may have an effect in pushing an ethical commitment in managing human resources. This is in line with previous research, that has emphasized the role of professionalization in ascribing a "*…regenerative function*" to human resource management (Jayakumar, 2020: p. 25). Thirdly, an expansion of this research is required to check the consistency of the study findings. On the one hand, evidence from other geographical contexts are needed to generalize the results discussed above. On the other hand, a longitudinal analysis would be beneficial to assess the evolution of human resource management practices and to obtain more reliable insights into the SMEs' propensity to undertake a human resource management approach rooted in business ethics.

CONCLUSIONS

The implications of this research are twofold. From a conceptual standpoint, the study suggests that familiness – *per se* – is not relevant in triggering an ethical commitment to managing human resources. However, the professionalization of human resource management in family firms seems to create a fertile ground to allow business ethics to take root in family firms' human resource management practices. It can be argued that the contamination of the family firms' propensity to adopt a conventionality-based approach in ensuring fairness in the workplace with a strategic alignment model boosted by the professionalization of human resource management may pave the way for the enhancement of business ethics in managing people. Embracing a practical point of view, the chapter acknowledges that a gap exists between the family firms' awareness of ethical dilemmas in managing human resources and their ethical commitment to craft targeted human resource management policies and practices. Tailored actions are needed in an attempt to turn the family firms' awareness in purposive actions intended to ensure ethics in managing human resources. Obviously, such actions should include both hard interventions, such as the establishment of an organizational unit assigned with the management of issues related to business ethics, and soft initiatives, such as the promotion of an open and empowering organizational climate.

REFERENCES

Adams, J. S., Taschian, A., & Shore, T. H. (1996). Ethics in Family and Non-Family Owned Firms: An Exploratory Study. *Family Business Review*, *9*(2), 157–170. doi:10.1111/j.1741-6248.1996.00157.x

Aldrich, H. E., & Langton, N. (1998). Human resource management and organizational life cycles. In P. D. Reynolds, W. Bygrave, N. M. Carter, P. Davidsson, W. B. Gartner, C. M. Mason, & P. P. McDougall (Eds.), *Frontiers of Entrepreneurship Research* (pp. 349–357). Babson College, Center for Entrepreneurial Studies.

Arregle, J. L., Hitt, M. A., Sirmon, D. G., & Very, P. (2007). The development of organizational social capital: Attributes of family firms. *Journal of Management Studies*, *44*(1), 72–95. doi:10.1111/j.1467-6486.2007.00665.x

Atrachan, J. H., & Kolenko, T. A. (1994). A Neglected Factor Explaining Family Business Success: Human Resource Practices. *Family Business Review*, *7*(3), 251–262. doi:10.1111/j.1741-6248.1994.00251.x

Barnett, T., & Kellermanns, F. W. (2006). Are We Family and Are We Treated as Family? Nonfamily Employees' Perceptions of Justice in the Family Firm. *Entrepreneurship Theory and Practice*, *30*(6), 837–854. doi:10.1111/j.1540-6520.2006.00155.x

Bernhard, F., & O'Driscoll, M. P. (2011). Psychological Ownership in Small Family-Owned Businesses: Leadership Style and Nonfamily-Employees' Work Attitudes and Behaviors. *Group & Organization Management*, *36*(3), 643–665. doi:10.1177/1059601111402684

Bertrand, M., & Schoar, A. (2006). The Role of Family in Family Firms. *The Journal of Economic Perspectives*, *20*(2), 73–96. doi:10.1257/jep.20.2.73

Borda, D. G., Hansen, N., & Gore, J. (2019). *Control and Commitment HRM Systems in SME Family Firms: A Qualitative Study of Hybrid Forms. In Understanding the inclusive organisation.* Academy of Management Conference.

Botero, I. C., & Litchfield, S. R. (2013). Exploring human resource management in family firms: a summary of what we know and ideas for future development. In K. X. Smyrnios, P. Z. Poutziouris, & S. Goel (Eds.), *Handbook of Research on Family Business* (pp. 371–405). Edward Elgar.

Brewis, J., & Way-Bliss, E. (2008). Re-searching Ethics: Towards a More Reflexive Critical Management Studies. *Organization Studies*, *29*(12), 1521–1540. doi:10.1177/0170840607096385

Broccardo, L., Truant, E., & Zicari, A. (2019). Internal corporate sustainability drivers: What evidence from family firms? A literature review and research agenda. *Corporate Social Responsibility and Environmental Management*, *26*(1), 1–18. doi:10.1002/csr.1672

Buckley, M. R., Beu, D. S., Frink, D. D., Howard, J. L., Berkson, H., Mobbs, T. A., & Ferris, G. R. (2001). Ethical issues in human resources systems. *Human Resource Management Review*, *11*(1/2), 11–29. doi:10.1016/S1053-4822(00)00038-3

Camfield, C., & Franco, M. (2019). Theoretical framework for family firm management: Relationship between personal values and professionalization and succession. *Journal of Family Business Management*, *9*(2), 201–227. doi:10.1108/JFBM-06-2018-0020

Campopiano, G., De Massis, A., & Kotlar, J. (2019). Environmental Jolts, Family-Centered Non-Economic Goals, and Innovation: A Framework of Family Firm Resilience. In E. Memili & C. Dibrell (Eds.), *The Palgrave Handbook of Heterogeneity among Family Firms* (pp. 773–789). Palgrave-Macmillan. doi:10.1007/978-3-319-77676-7_28

Cater, J., James, K., Kidwell, R., Camp, K., & Young, M. (2019). HRM practices and effectiveness: A comparison of US Hispanic and non-Hispanic family firms. *Journal of Small Business and Enterprise Development*, *26*(5), 726–746. doi:10.1108/JSBED-12-2018-0364

Chrisman, J. J., Chua, J. H., & Kellermanns, F. (2009). Priorities, Resource Stocks, and Performance in Family and Nonfamily Firms. *Entrepreneurship Theory and Practice*, *33*(3), 739–760. doi:10.1111/j.1540-6520.2009.00324.x

Chua, J. H., Chrisman, J. J., & Sharma, P. (1999). Defining the family business by behaviour. *Entrepreneurship Theory and Practice*, *23*(4), 19–39. doi:10.1177/104225879902300402

Ciasullo, M., Cosimato, S., Gaeta, M., & Palumbo, R. (2017). Comparing two approaches to team building: A performance measurement evaluation. *Team Performance Management*, *23*(7/8), 333–351. doi:10.1108/TPM-01-2017-0002

Ciasullo, M., Cosimato, S., & Palumbo, R. (2017). Improving health care quality: The implementation of whistleblowing. *The TQM Journal*, *29*(1), 167–183. doi:10.1108/TQM-06-2016-0051

Cormier, D., & Magnan, M. (2017). Does a firm's exposure to ethical failures matter to financial markets? A governance perspective. *The Journal of Management and Governance*, *21*(2), 267–289. doi:10.100710997-016-9341-9

Crane, A., Matten, D., Glozer, S., & Spence, L. J. (2016). *Business Ethics: Managing Corporate Citizenship and Sustainability in the Age of Globalization*. Oxford University Press.

Dachler, H. P., & Enderle, G. (1989). Epistemological and ethical considerations in conceptualizing and implementing human resource management. *Journal of Business Ethics*, *8*(8), 597–606. doi:10.1007/BF00383028

Deckop, J. R. (2006). *Human Resource Management Ethics*. Information Age Publishing.

Deephouse, D. L., & Jaskiewicz, P. (2013). Do Family Firms Have Better Reputations Than Non-Family Firms? An Integration of Socioemotional Wealth and Social Identity Theories. *Journal of Management Studies*, *50*(3), 337–360. doi:10.1111/joms.12015

Del Baldo, M. (2013). CSR-Oriented SMEs: A Question of Entrepreneurial Virtues in Action? Reflections in Theory and Practice. In J. Okpara & S. Idowu (Eds.), *Corporate Social Responsibility. CSR, Sustainability, Ethics & Governance* (pp. 145–170). Springer. doi:10.1007/978-3-642-40975-2_9

Delery, J., & Gupta, N. (2016). Human resource management practices and organizational effectiveness: Internal fit matters. *Journal of Organizational Effectiveness: People and Performance*, *3*(2), 139–163. doi:10.1108/JOEPP-03-2016-0028

Ding, S., & Wu, Z. (2014). Family Ownership and Corporate Misconduct in U.S. Small Firms. *Journal of Business Ethics*, *123*(2), 183–195. doi:10.100710551-013-1812-1

Donaldson, L. (2008). Ethics Problems and Problems with Ethics: Toward a Pro-Management Theory. *Journal of Business Ethics, 78*(3), 299–311. doi:10.100710551-006-9336-6

Drucker, P. F. (1981). What is Business Ethics? *The Public Interest, 63,* 19–36.

Elicegui-Reyes, J. I., Barrena-Martínez, J., & Romero-Fernández, P. M. (2017). Emotional Capital and Sustainability in Family Businesses: Human Resource Management Perspective and Sustainability. In M. A. Camilleri (Ed.), *CSR 2.0 and the New Era of Corporate Citizenship* (pp. 231–250). IGI Global. doi:10.4018/978-1-5225-1842-6.ch012

Falkenberg, L., & Herremans, I. (1995). Ethical Behaviours in Organizations: Directed by the Formal or Informal Systems? *Journal of Business Ethics, 14*(2), 133–144. doi:10.1007/BF00872018

Fassin, Y., Van Rossem, A., & Buelens, M. (2011). Small-Business Owner-Managers' Perceptions of Business Ethics and CSR-Related Concepts. *Journal of Business Ethics, 98*(3), 425–453. doi:10.100710551-010-0586-y

Firfiray, S., Cruz, C., Neacsu, I., & Gomez-Mejiad, L. R. (2018). Is nepotism so bad for family firms? A socioemotional wealth approach. *Human Resource Management Review, 28*(1), 83–97. doi:10.1016/j.hrmr.2017.05.008

Freeman, R. E., & Greenwood, M. (2020). Deepening Methods in Business Ethics. *Journal of Business Ethics, 161*(1), 1–3. doi:10.100710551-019-04374-7

Gallo, M. A. (1998). Ethics in Personal Behavior in Family Business. *Family Business Review, 11*(4), 325–335. doi:10.1111/j.1741-6248.1998.00325.x

Gallo, M. A. (2004). The family business and its social responsibilities. *Family Business Review, 17*(2), 135–149. doi:10.1111/j.1741-6248.2004.00009.x

García-Sánchez, I. M., Martínez-Ferrero, J., Cuadrado-Ballesteros, B., & Rodríguez-Ariza, L. (2015). Ethics and corporate performance in family firms. In K. Nelson (Ed.), *Business Intelligence, Strategies and Ethics* (pp. 127–148). Nova Science Publishers.

Gomez-Mejia, L. R., Cruz, C., Berrone, P., & De Castro, J. (2001). The Bind that Ties: Socioemotional Wealth Preservation in Family Firms. *The Academy of Management Annals, 5*(1), 653–707. doi:10.5465/19416520.2011.593320

Goto, T. (2013). Secrets of family business longevity in Japan from the social capital perspective. In K. X. Smyrnios, P. Z. Poutziouris, & S. Goel (Eds.), *Handbook of Research on Family Business* (2nd ed., pp. 554–587). Edward Elgar Publishing.

Greenwood, M. R. (2002). Ethics and HRM: A Review and Conceptual Analysis. *Journal of Business Ethics, 36*(3), 261–278. doi:10.1023/A:1014090411946

Greve, H. R., Palmer, D., & Pozner, J. E. (2010). Organizations gone wild: The causes, processes, and consequences of organizational misconduct. *The Academy of Management Annals, 4*(1), 53–107. doi:10.5465/19416521003654186

Guerci, M., Radaelli, G., Siletti, E., Cirella, S., & Rami Shani, A. B. (2015). The Impact of Human Resource Management Practices and Corporate Sustainability on Organizational Ethical Climates: An Employee Perspective. *Journal of Business Ethics*, *126*(2), 325–342. doi:10.100710551-013-1946-1

Habbershon, T. G., & Williams, M. L. (1999). A Resource-Based Framework for Assessing the Strategic Advantages of Family Firms. *Family Business Review*, *12*(1), 1–25. doi:10.1111/j.1741-6248.1999.00001.x

Habbershon, T. G., Williams, M. L., & MacMillan, I. C. (2003). A unified systems perspective of family firm performance. *Journal of Business Venturing*, *18*(4), 451–465. doi:10.1016/S0883-9026(03)00053-3

Heller, N. A., & Heller, V. L. (2011). Business Ethics Education: Are Business Schools Teaching to the AACSB Ethics Education Task Force Recommendations? *International Journal of Business and Social Science*, *2*(20), 30–38.

Heyden, L. V. D., Blondel, C., & Carlock, R. S. (2005). Fair process: Striving for justice in family businesses. *Family Business Review*, *18*(1), 1–21. doi:10.1111/j.1741-6248.2005.00027.x

Irava, W. J., & Moores, K. (2010). Clarifying the strategic advantage of familiness: Unbundling its dimensions and highlighting its paradoxes. *Journal of Family Business Strategy*, *1*(3), 131–144. doi:10.1016/j.jfbs.2010.08.002

James, H. (1999). Owner as manager, extended horizons and the family firm. *International Journal of the Economics of Business*, *6*(1), 41–56. doi:10.1080/13571519984304

Janssens, M., & Steyaert, C. (2009). HRM and performance: A plea for reflexivity in HRM studies. *Journal of Management Studies*, *46*(1), 143–155. doi:10.1111/j.1467-6486.2008.00812.x

Jayakumar, T. (2020). Professionalising Indian Family Firms: An Analysis of the Role of HR—Current Reality and Future Perspectives. *NHRD Network Journal*, 25-37.

Jones, C., Parker, M., & ten Bos, R. (2005). *For Business Ethics. A critical approach.* Routledge.

Kidwell, R. E., Eddleston, K. A., Cater, J. J. III, & Kellermanns, F. W. (2013). Harmony, Justice, Confusion, and Conflict in Family Firms: Implications for Ethical Climate and the "Fredo Effect". *Business Horizons*, *56*(1), 5–12. doi:10.1016/j.bushor.2012.08.004

Kidwell, R. E., Eddleston, K. A., & Kellermanns, F. W. (2018). Learning bad habits across generations: How negative imprints affect human resource management in the family firm. *Human Resource Management Review*, *28*(1), 5–17. doi:10.1016/j.hrmr.2017.05.002

Kim, K., Eltarabishy, A., & Bae, Z. (2018). Humane Entrepreneurship: How Focusing on People Can Drive a New Era of Wealth and Quality Job Creation in a Sustainable World. *Journal of Small Business Management*, *56*(1), 10–29. doi:10.1111/jsbm.12431

Kim, K., Haider, Z. A., Wu, Z., & Dou, J. (2019). Corporate Social Performance of Family Firms: A Place-Based Perspective in the Context of Layoffs. *Journal of Business Ethics*, ahead of print. Doi:10.100710551-019-04152-5

Kim, Y., & Gao, F. Y. (2010). An empirical study of human resource management practices in family firms in China. *International Journal of Human Resource Management*, *21*(12), 2095–2119. doi:10.1080/09585192.2010.509619

Kotey, B., & Sheridan, A. (2004). Changing HRM Practices with Firm Growth. *Journal of Small Business and Enterprise Development*, *11*(4), 474–485. doi:10.1108/14626000410567125

Krishnan, G., & Peytcheva, M. (2019). The Risk of Fraud in Family Firms: Assessments of External Auditors. *Journal of Business Ethics*, *157*(1), 261–278. doi:10.100710551-017-3687-z

Labelle, R., Hafsi, T., Francoeur, C., & Amar, W. B. (2018). Family Firms' Corporate Social Performance: A Calculated Quest for Socioemotional Wealth. *Journal of Business Ethics*, *148*(3), 511–525. doi:10.100710551-015-2982-9

LeBreton-Miller, I., & Miller, D. (2016). Family firms and practices of sustainability: A contingency view. *Journal of Family Business Strategy*, *7*(1), 26–33. doi:10.1016/j.jfbs.2015.09.001

Lewis, P. W. (1985). Defining 'business ethics': Like nailing jello to a wall. *Journal of Business Ethics*, *4*(5), 377–383. doi:10.1007/BF02388590

Litz, R. A., & Turner, N. (2013). Sins of the Father's Firm: Exploring Responses to Inherited Ethical Dilemmas in Family Business. *Journal of Business Ethics*, *113*(2), 297–315. doi:10.100710551-012-1305-7

Long, R. G., & Mathews, K. M. (2011). Ethics in the Family Firm: Cohesion through Reciprocity and Exchange. *Business Ethics Quarterly*, *21*(2), 287–308. doi:10.5840/beq201121217

López-Cózar, C., Priede, T., & Hilliard, I. (2014). Family and Non-Family Business Differences in Corporate Social Responsibility Approaches. *Asean Journal of Management & Innovation*, *1*(2), 74–85.

López-Pérez, M. E., Melero-Polo, I., Vázquez-Carrasco, R., & Cambra-Fierro, J. (2018). Sustainability and Business Outcomes in the Context of SMEs: Comparing Family Firms vs. Non-Family Firms. *Sustainability*, *10*(11), 4080. doi:10.3390u10114080

Maclagan, P. (1998). *Management and Morality: A Developmental Perspective*. Sage Publication.

Madison, K., Daspit, J. J., Turner, K., & Kellermanns, F. W. (2018). Family firm human resource practices: Investigating the effects of professionalization and bifurcation bias on performance. *Journal of Business Research*, *84*(3), 327–336. doi:10.1016/j.jbusres.2017.06.021

Mathew, T. P., & Kannan, R. (2019). Effect of Human Resource Management Practice on Jov Performance of Employees in Luxury Hotels in Cochin. *Global Journal for Research Analysis*, *8*(3), 16–19.

Memili, E., Chang, E. P., Kellermanns, F. W., & Welsh, D. H. (2015). Role conflicts of family members in family firms. *European Journal of Work and Organizational Psychology*, *24*(1), 143–151. doi:10.1080/1359432X.2013.839549

Muskin, J. B. (2000). Interorganizational Ethics: Standards of Behavior. *Journal of Business Ethics*, *24*(4), 283–297. doi:10.1023/A:1006008506543

Navarro, M. S., & Ansón, S. G. (2009). Do families shape corporate governance structures? *Journal of Management & Organization*, *15*(3), 327–345. doi:10.5172/jmo.2009.15.3.327

Nguyen, T. V., & Bryant, S. E. (2004). A Study of the Formality of Human Resource Management Practices in Small and Medium-Size Enterprises in Vietnam. *International Small Business Journal, 22*(6), 595–618. doi:10.1177/0266242604047412

O'Boyle, E. H. Jr, Rutherford, M. W., & Pollack, J. M. (2010). Examining the Relation Between Ethical Focus and Financial Performance in Family Firms: An Exploratory Study. *Family Business Review, 23*(4), 310–326. doi:10.1177/0894486510375412

Oliveira, N., & Lumineau, F. (2019). The Dark Side of Interorganizational Relationships: An Integrative Review and Research Agenda. *Journal of Management, 45*(1), 231–261. doi:10.1177/0149206318804027

Palanski, M., Newman, A., Leroy, H., Moore, C., Hannah, S., & Den Hartog, D. (2019). Quantitative Research on Leadership and Business Ethics: Examining the State of the Field and an Agenda for Future Research. *Journal of Business Ethics*, ahead of print. doi:10.100710551-019-04267-9

Palumbo, R. (2016). Challenging Servant Leadership In The Nonprofit Sector: The Side Effects Of Servant Leadership. *Journal of Nonprofit Education and Leadership, 6*(2), 81–98. doi:10.18666/JNEL-2016-V6-I2-6824

Palumbo, R., & Manna, R. (2019). Una ricetta per rendere un'organizzazione. *Impresa progetto – Electronic Journal of Management, 2019*(2), 1–22.

Parente, R., Eltarabishy, A., Vesci, M., & Botti, A. (2018). The Epistemology of Humane Entrepreneurship: Theory and Proposal for Future Research Agenda. *Journal of Small Business Management, 56*(1), 30–52. doi:10.1111/jsbm.12432

Payne, G. T., Brigham, K. H., Broberg, J. C., Moss, T. W., & Short, J. C. (2011). Organizational Virtue Orientation and Family Firms. *Business Ethics Quarterly, 21*(2), 257–285. doi:10.5840/beq201121216

Perrini, F., & Minoja, M. (2008). Strategizing corporate social responsibility: Evidence from an Italian medium-sized, family-owned company. *Business Ethics (Oxford, England), 17*(1), 47–63. doi:10.1111/j.1467-8608.2008.00519.x

Perry, J., Ring, J. K., Matherne, C. F., & Markova, G. (2013). Ethical Human Resource Practices from the Perspective of Family Ownership. *Academy of Management Proceedings, 2013*(1). . doi:10.5465/ambpp.2013.172

Poza, E. J., Alfred, T., & Maheshwari, A. (1997). Stakeholder perceptions of culture and management practices in family and family firms - A preliminary report. *Family Business Review, 10*(2), 135–155. doi:10.1111/j.1741-6248.1997.00135.x

Ramírez-Solís, E., & Baños-Monroy, V. I. (2019). Dangerous Liaisons? Ethical Challenges on Entrepreneurship in Family Business. In S. R. Nair & J. M. Saiz-Álvarez (Eds.), *Handbook of Research on Ethics, Entrepreneurship, and Governance in Higher Education* (pp. 263–282). IGI Global. doi:10.4018/978-1-5225-5837-8.ch012

Randall, D. M., & Gibson, A. M. (1990). Methodology in business ethics research: A review and critical assessment. *Journal of Business Ethics, 9*(6), 457–471. doi:10.1007/BF00382838

Reid, R., & Adams, J. (2001). Human resource management – a survey of practices within family and non-family firms. *Journal of European Industrial Training*, *25*(6), 310–320. doi:10.1108/03090590110401782

Research, I. F. F. (2015). *Fairness, Dignity and Respect in Small- and Medium-Sized Enterprise Workplaces*. UK Data Archive.

Richards, M., & Schembera, S. (2019). Managing Legitimacy Through Conventionality Rather Than Alignment: Anti-Corruption at Family Versus Non-Family Firms. ahead of print. doi:10.2139srn.3484973

Samara, G., & Arenas, D. (2017). Practicing fairness in the family business workplace. *Business Horizons*, *60*(5), 647–655. doi:10.1016/j.bushor.2017.05.008

Samara, G., & Paul, K. (2019). Justice versus fairness in the family business workplace: A socioemotional wealth approach. *Business Ethics (Oxford, England)*, *28*(2), 175–184. doi:10.1111/beer.12209

Sanchez-Bueno, M. J., Muñoz-Bullón, F., & Galan, J. I. (2020). Socially responsible downsizing: Comparing family and non-family firms. *Business Ethics (Oxford, England)*, *29*(1), 35–55. doi:10.1111/beer.12244

Sánchez-Marín, G., Meroño-Cerdán, Á. L., & Carrasco-Hernández, A. J. (2019). Formalized HR practices and firm performance: An empirical comparison of family and non-family firms. *International Journal of Human Resource Management*, *30*(7), 1084–1110. doi:10.1080/09585192.2017.1289547

Santoro, G., Messeni-Petruzzelli, A., & Del Giudice, M. (2020). Searching for resilience: the impact of employee-level and entrepreneur-level resilience on firm performance in small family firms. *Small Business Economics*, ahead of print. . doi:10.100711187-020-00319-x

Schuler, R. S., & MacMillan, I. C. (1984). Gaining competitive advantage through human resource management practices. *Human Resource Management*, *23*(3), 241–255. doi:10.1002/hrm.3930230304

Schumann, P. L. (2001). A moral principles framework for human resource management ethics. *Human Resource Management Review*, *11*(1/2), 93–111. doi:10.1016/S1053-4822(00)00042-5

Sharma, P. (2004). An Overview of the Field of Family Business Studies: Current Status and Directions for the Future. *Family Business Review*, *17*(1), 1–34. doi:10.1111/j.1741-6248.2004.00001.x

Sorenson, R. L. (2011). *Family business and social capital*. Edward Elgar Publishing. doi:10.4337/9781849807388

Steijvers, T., Lybaert, N., & Dekker, J. (2017). Formal human resource practices in family firms. *Journal of Family Business Management*, *7*(2), 151–165. doi:10.1108/JFBM-07-2016-0016

Sternberg, E. (2000). *Just Business: Business Ethics in Action*. Oxford University Press.

Tabor, W., Madison, K., Daspit, J. J., & Holt, D. T. (2019). The Heterogeneity of Family Firm Ethical Cultures: Current Insights and Future Directions. In *The Palgrave Handbook of Heterogeneity among Family Firms* (pp. 615–642). Palgrave MacMillan. doi:10.1007/978-3-319-77676-7_23

Vallejo, M. C. (2008). Is the Culture of Family Firms Really Different? A Value-based Model for Its Survival through Generations. *Journal of Business Ethics*, *81*(2), 261–279. doi:10.100710551-007-9493-2

Vazquez, P. (2018). Family Business Ethics: At the Crossroads of Business Ethics and Family Business. *Journal of Business Ethics*, *150*(3), 691–709. doi:10.100710551-016-3171-1

Velasquez, M. G. (2002). *Business Ethics: Concepts and Cases*. Prentice Hall.

Vickers, M. R. (2005). Business ethics and the HR role: Past, present, and future. *Human Resource Planning*, *28*(1), 26–32.

Weaver, G. R., & Trevino, L. K. (2001). The role of human resources in ethics/compliance management: A fairness perspective. *Human Resource Management Review*, *11*(1/2), 113–134. doi:10.1016/S1053-4822(00)00043-7

Winstanley, D., & Woodall, J. (2000). The ethical dimension of human resource management. *Human Resource Management Journal*, *10*(2), 5–20. doi:10.1111/j.1748-8583.2000.tb00017.x

Winstanley, D., Woodall, J., & Heery, E. (1996). Business ethics and human resource management: Themes and issues. *Personnel Review*, *25*(6), 5–12. doi:10.1108/00483489610148491

Winterbotham, M., Oldfield, K., Stewart, G., Rossiter, H., & Research, I. F. F. (2015). *Fairness, dignity and respect in SME workplaces*. Equality and Human Rights Commission.

Wright, P. M., & Boswell, W. R. (2002). Desegregating HRM: A Review and Synthesis of Micro and Macro Human Resource Management Research. *Journal of Management*, *28*(3), 247–276. doi:10.1177/014920630202800302

Zellweger, T. M., Kellermanns, F. W., Eddleston, K. A., & Memili, E. (2012). Building a family firm image: How family firms capitalize on their family ties. *Journal of Family Business Strategy*, *3*(4), 239–250. doi:10.1016/j.jfbs.2012.10.001

ENDNOTE

1 As reported in its institutional website (https://equalityhumanrights.com/en/about-us/who-we-are: last accessed on March, 9th 2020): "...*The Equality and Human Rights Commission is Great Britain's national equality body and has been awarded an 'A' status as a National Human Rights Institution (NHRI) by the United Nations.*" It was established under the Equality Act 2006 to work towards the elimination of unlawful discrimination, to promote equality of opportunity and to protect and promote human rights. The Commission operates independently and "...*aim*(s) *to be an expert and authoritative organisation that is a centre of excellence for evidence, analysis and equality and human rights law*."

Chapter 8
Sustainable Human Resources as the Future of HRM Systems in Family Firms

Aneta Kuźniarska
https://orcid.org/0000-0002-2786-2781
Jagiellonian University, Poland

ABSTRACT

Issues associated with the fair distribution of resources for both current and future generations are gaining on more importance as a result of broad discussion worldwide relating to the ecological problems. One of the significant elements of these activities is embodied by family firms; hence, the aim of this chapter is an attempt to indicate what an important role in terms of building the future of family firms is played by the adoption of the principles of sustainable management with the participation of the employees and the owners on the basis of the appropriately designed functions of HRM. The chapter includes introductory elements to the significance and foundations of the concept of sustainable development in order for the subsequent sections to contain information on the subject of utilizing the concept of sustainable management in organizations and the departments of HR. The final section of the chapter constitutes indications referring to the creation of sustainable personnel in family firms as a challenge that is facing the departments of HR.

INTRODUCTION

The word "sustainable" is increasingly integral to various areas of the activities of enterprises. Its beginnings that were associated with restricted access to natural resources and the prevalent ecological trend developed with the passing of time to the concept of sustainable development that functions in three dimensions as follows: economic, social and environmental aspects.

In the current market conditions, responsibility for all the composite elements of the concept are transferred to the area of activities of enterprises, which in turn, forces the organizations to take account of them in the processes of management. The obligation of their implementation first and foremost lies

DOI: 10.4018/978-1-7998-4814-1.ch008

with the managerial staff, which in the case of family firms means the owners, while subsequently the departments of HR, and the consequence of their effectiveness is dependent on the personnel employed in the organization at hand. One of the main successes of the effective functioning of the assumptions of sustainable development is embodied by the departments of HR, while the key element of this area of management is indicated by the employees, managers and other managerial staff, while in the case of family firms this mainly relates to the owners. It is important that the people employed in the organization are guided by the principles of sustainable development and create sustainable personnel.

By means of listing the literature on the subject matter of family firms, while also literature associated with sustainable development and sustainable HRM, this paper is to appeal to the necessity of the conscious and gradual implementation of sustainable management in the sphere of HR in family firms.

BACKGROUND

The first definition of sustainable development was presented in the report entitled "Our Common Future" (known as the Brundtland Report), according to which, *sustainable development is the development that meets the needs of the present without compromising the ability of future generations to meet their own needs* (WCED, 1987). Nevertheless, environmental problems were noticed prior to this – at the first International Conference on the Human Environment in Stockholm, Sweden in 1972, at which environmental issues were touched on. Its consequence was to create the United Nations Environmental Program (UNEP), whose task became activity on behalf of the environment mainly by means of information activity. This was to enable the improvement of the quality of life of communities without depriving the future generations.

Together with the passing of time, a change has occurred in the political debate referring to the notion of "sustainable". In Rio de Janeiro in 1992 during the Earth Summit, a move from the main emphasis on environmental issues in the direction of issues formulating the common focus on environmental, social and economic development, to be followed by further summits at Millennium in 2000 and the world summit in Johannesburg in 2002, at which the main emphasis was placed on reducing poverty worldwide. The processes aimed at protecting the environment in terms of serving the development of mankind was commenced, while simultaneously calling for the improvement of the well-being of the poorest at present and in the future (Bac, 2008). Since the UN World Summit on Sustainable Development in 2002 in Johannesburg, the following definition of sustainable development has been adopted: *a collective responsibility for the progress and strengthening of mutually dependent and mutually reinforcing pillars of sustainable development - economic development, social development and environmental protection - at local, national, regional and global level* (UN, 2002).

The development of the concept naturally has its continuation and is played out with the significant participation of the European Union. Within the framework of the strategies conducted by the EU that are associated with the implementation of sustainable development in EU member states - "Europe 2020. Strategy for smart, sustainable and inclusive growth", apart from the aspects of environmental protection, issues associated with the social factor (human resources) became important, while also within their framework, among others, the rate of employment of people aged 20-64, or the restriction of people living in Europe below the level of poverty (COM, 2010).

One of the multitude of definitions indicates that sustainable development encompasses the models of economic and social development, which should simultaneously protect the environment and lead to building social justice (Dunphy, Benveniste, Griffiths, & Sutton, 2000; Guerci & Carollo, 2016). Simultaneously, each decision undertaken should take account of all the three listed dimensions of sustainable management (Kassenberg, 2007). Only after maintaining the relational nature of the environmental, social and economic dimensions, while also their mutual codependencies, does it become a real way to achieve sustainable development (Borim-de-Souza, Balbinoto, Travis, Munck, & Takahashi, 2015).

1. Origins and Definitions of Sustainable Management

Both in theory and in practice, management encounters differentiated terminology associated with sustainable development, such as the following: Green Management, Pro-ecological Management and Environmental Management (Ahmad, 2015). As a consequence, they refer to the activities in the same scope. The definition of sustainable management encompasses a long-term concept with the simultaneous optimization of the aims of the enterprise in the economic, ecological and social areas aimed at generating long-lasting and excellent financial performance of the firm at hand (Elkington, 1997).

The entities that are interested in sustainable management may be external stakeholders, namely clients, owners, suppliers, investors, while also internal stakeholders, in particular employees (Kaufman, 2015). The latter exert influence on the organization by means of various mechanisms of activity and behaviour that support the environmental value and social responsibility (Freeman, 1984).

As regards sustainable HRM, which would provide a better reflection of the way in which organizations are currently changing and developing in the direction of a more multi-faceted perspective, this subject matter started to be undertaken approximately 20 years ago, yet this notion has still not been defined in its entirety (Aust, Matthews and Muller-Camen, 2020). Likewise, there is still no singular set of features established that is characteristic of the sustainable practices of HRM, which would help in the operationalization of the corporate business strategies in the sphere of sustainable development (Mariappanadar, 2020). An attempt to classify the notion was undertaken by Dyllick and Muff (2016), while subsequently by, among others, Aust, Matthews and Muller-Camen (2020) in distinguishing 4 types of socially responsible HRM as follows:

1. Type 1 leads to economic and social values (while placing emphasis on the economic values),
2. Type 2 - green HRM, which leads to economic and ecological values (while placing emphasis on the economic values).
3. Type 3 - Triple Bottom Line, which leads to the triple financial performance (while placing emphasis on the economic values),
4. Type 4 - Common Good HRM, which leads to the increase in the value of the common good while placing emphasis on finding solutions to the great challenges in the sphere of sustainable development).

The lack of an unequivocal definition of sustainable HRM on the one hand, facilitates great flexibility in terms of defining and executing the tasks within this sphere, while on the other hand, constitutes great challenges for the organizations that are only contemplating the implementation of this concept.

The afore-mentioned corporate social responsibility (CSR) is one of the key elements of sustainable management and constitutes an important element of management and image, both in large corporations, as well as in small firms. Its essence consists of the assumption that business and society are inter-connected (Wood, 1991), while activities of social responsibility are ones that are totally voluntary and which take account of business interests both in social terms, as well as those connected with the external and internal environments of the enterprise (Schuler & Jackson, 2014). The obligation to conduct such activities lies with the entrepreneurs (Bowen, 1953) due to their responsibility to society (European Commission, 2011) and according to the expectations of the society (Caroll, 1979). They are the result of the conviction of the righteousness of this behaviour rather than the necessity to apply it owing to legislative regulations, albeit adherence to the law constitutes one of the elements of CSR (Hopkins, 2003). It is strategically profitable for an organization to be socially responsible as this provides the possibility to transform the social obligations into business opportunities, thanks to which the firm may be more effective and competitive (Drucker, 1984).

In the case of family firms whose owners are guided by the existential needs during the course of decision-making that encompass the need to survive on the market (Grudzewski & Hejduk, 2000), the realization of the concept is mainly based on the realization of social aims on behalf of the local community (Piasecki, 1998), whereas it is more seldom to relate to the employees themselves directly. The attitudes of the members of the family firms, their level of involvement, loyalty and sincerity, while also the values expressed by them (the sense of belonging to the enterprise on the part of the family members, assiduity, perseverance in the pursuit of the established aims and allegiance to the sector) all lie at the basis of the notion of CSR (Jeżak, Popczyk, & Winnicka-Popczyk, 2004).

As noted by Brzeziński (2016), the area in which the concept of CSR should be particularly executed is the area of human resources management (Morgeson, Aguinis, Waldman, & Siegel, 2013; while also Jamali, Dirani, & Harwood, 2015). These authors suggest that HRM may constitute an area of management by supporting the organizational effort in translating the strategies of CSR prepared into practical actions and consequently into the results of management at the level of the entire organization.

When referring to HRM and the concept of CSR, it is necessary to take account of firstly, the activities focused on the need for the systematization of the employer - employee relations, secondly, activities geared towards the accomplishment of the aims of the organization while taking into consideration the possibilities of fulfilling the needs of the employees. Fulfilling these needs may have a positive impact on the work efficiency of the employees, which is the result of four principal aspects as follows: attitude, knowledge, skills and experience. Each of these aspects may be appropriately strengthened in accordance with the notions of CSR, while also the principles of sustainable development.

With regard to the basis, namely building the level of involvement and working under the "ethical leadership" of the boss, the employees adopt his way of behaviour and designate similar ethical principles of action (Wilkinson, Hill, & Gollan, 2001). Such actions in family firms have the chance to be implemented and developed due to the relatively easy access of employees to the managerial staff. It is worth drawing attention to the fact that standards of excellence appeal more to employees than discipline imposed on them by their superiors (Edersheim, 2007).

In the case of knowledge perceived in the concept of sustainable development as attention to the development of human resources and counteracting social exclusion, the creation of programs of development for the employees in the organization should guarantee equal opportunities for each of them in terms of the access and participation in all the forms of education and development, while also taking account of the needs of all the employees in this sphere. Langwell & Heaton (2016) discovered that training is of fundamental importance for the perception of the significance of sustainable development. A significant role is played in terms of this issue by the person in management, or the owner himself, who decides on the process of learning in the organization (Sadler-Smith, Gardiner, Badger, & Chaston, 2000), who is frequently under the influence of personal factors, personal experiences, motivation, while also the approach to the role of the training courses themselves (Hill & Stewart, 2000; Sadler-Smith & Lean, 2004).

Building the so-called "green competences" of employees should be based on planning the recruitment process by taking account of the appropriate analysis of work in varying positions, while subsequently describing the necessary skills for the particular positions. Only in the subsequent stages should the appropriate training be envisaged (Hart & Sharma, 2004).

The development of the necessary skills for the implementation of the sustainable principles in an organization should primarily encompass the skill of restricting the creation of waste and emissions of pollution, while also save power and water (Cohen, Taylor, & Muller-Camen, 2012).

The effect of management by the owner in terms of the employees in a responsible way may become a team that strongly identifies with the organization. Thanks to the appropriately built systems of ethical values, while also role models conveyed by the employers (the owners in family firms), which are accepted and professed by the employees, the organization may create its own culture that will be the basis of ethical behaviour and build the appropriate relations, both within and outside of the organization (Almada & Borges, 2018).

2. Determinants of Sustainable HRM in Family Firms

The determinants forming the circumstances of the development of the family firms are of both an internal and external nature. The external factors are the result of the socio-economic macro and micro-environment, whereas internal factors are primarily conditioned by the system of values and behaviour of their owners. As indicated by Jeżak (2004), the latter type of factors determines the future development of the family firms by forcing the owners to track the changes in the environment and pursue the current trends in such a manner that the decisions undertaken, including those in the area of HRM, had favourable consequences for the management of the entire organization. From this perspective, monitoring the progress of other organizations in the development of sustainable management may become an important element for family firms from the viewpoint of surviving on the market and the growth of their level of competitiveness (Singh & Srivastav, 2012). This may also have an impact on the systems of HRM that support organizations in terms of the achievement of their aims in the sphere of sustainable development (Ehnert, Harry and Zink, 2014). From another perspective, the implementation of the sustainable approach to HRM may be motivated by pressure on the part of the stakeholders (Crifo, Durand and Gond, 2019).

Analysis of family firms reveals that the family nature of business has a significant impact on the way of conducting business activities and illustrates the following features that may have an impact on their competitive position (Stradomski, 2010):

- they are capable of making fast decisions,
- they are more prone to undertaking daring and risky ventures,
- they are featured by a more rapid and more effective form of communication between the members of the management,
- they can change better and faster into responses to the new market needs.

This is particularly important when we take the research results into account, in which the attitude of the members of family firms with regard to change is presented as adaptive (Safin, 2007). This attitude is associated with the strategy of adjusting to the environment in order to maintain balance in this sphere. On the other hand, greater adaptiveness to change in the environment is the result of the flexible approach of the owners to, among other things, the organization of work itself, or the skilful adjustment to the changing needs of the stakeholders. In this context, conducting a sustainable family business signifies the preparation for all types of potential threats and crises (Mikušová, Friedrich, & Horváthová, 2020).

The implementation of the principles of sustainable development in a family firm requires the owner to adopt such an attitude which is adaptive, thanks to which faster changes in response to new market requirements are possible and such a need is currently being set by sustainable development. All the features indicated that have an impact on the competitive position of a firm in this case constitute an undoubtable attribute: both fast decision making leading to more effective implementation of sustainable principles, as well as faster and more effective communication enabling the allocation of tasks by the owners, or feedback from the employees.

With the aim of achieving sustainable HRM in family firms, it is necessary to first and foremost do the following (Docherty, Forslin, & Shani, 2002; Ehnert, 2008; Hirsig, Rogovski, & Elkin, 2014):

- promote social dialogue,
- support cooperation at the workplace,
- develop the skills and competences of employees,
- ensure equality and respect for human rights,
- eliminate discrimination,
- create a safe working place,
- pay attention to the constant enhancement of the general working conditions,
- pay attention to the balance between the performance of the organization and the quality of the professional life of employees.

At this point, it is worth answering the following question: Why do employees constitute such a significant element of the organization?

The resource theory indicates that human resources, together with physical and organizational resources constitute the source of a long-lasting competitive advantage. Their value, rarity, difficulty in terms of imitation and impossibility of replacement are the result of heterogeneity, intricacy and the conditions in which they prevail (Barney 1991; Barney & Wright 1998; Wright, McMahan, & McWilliams, 1994). Its aim is cooperation that on the one hand facilitates the neutralization of weakness, while on the other hand optimizes the use of both talents and the strong sides of the hired employees (Drucker, 1976). As a result of building the specified competences of the employees (Walls, Phan, & Berrone, 2011), the changes to their attitudes and behaviour and favouring innovations (Parkes & Borland, 2012), the impact on their efficiency has become visible (Barney & Wright, 1998; Walls, Phan, & Berrone, 2011). The consequence of the aforesaid aspects is the strategic management of human resources, which with the co-participation of management of the highest level leads to the achievement of a long-lasting competitive advantage (Rothenberg, Hull, & Tang, 2017).

3. The Role of the Personnel Function in Building a Sustainable Organization

Actions undertaken in the sphere of the personnel function should be characterized by a high level of effectiveness, as well as being responsible for the local needs of the community, having perfect adaptive abilities, while also facilitating the adjustment to the new conditions in the environment over a short time period and enabling the enterprise to gain a competitive advantage (Stor, 2010; Rothenberg, Hull, & Tang, 2017). With reference to such challenges as: enhancing the level of competitiveness, gaining new and increasingly ecologically conscious clients, as well as gaining new trading partners and retaining the hitherto trading partners that pay great attention to the fulfilment of environmental requirements, it would seem to be increasingly difficult without taking responsibility for the natural environment on the part of family firms (Mazur-Wierzbicka, 2016). In the context of these challenges, such a method of managing human resources in family firms is becoming important, which by means of implementing the concept of sustainable management of human resources leads to the building of sustainable personnel in the organization.

A significant role in the function of human resources management in the creation of organizational change based on sustainable development is emphasized by Guerci and Pedrini (2014) by acknowledging that it has a significant impact on the designing and implementation of sustainable practices in the organization as a whole. As early as in 1998, Ulrich acknowledged that the transformation of the systems of human resources management was essential with the aim of executing sustainable strategies and the aims of the organization.

Sustainable HRM is deemed to be an area which currently integrates corporate sustainable practices and strategies (Clarke, 2011; Ehnert, 2009; Ehnert, Harry, & Zink, 2014; Ehnert, Parsa, Roper, Wagner, & Muller-Camen, 2016). Its role is the concentration on the optimal use and respect for human resources in the organization, which build a clear relation between the strategic policies of the organization and its environs. A key aspect in this constitutes a long-term vision and integration with the strategy of the organization and policy of CSR (De Prins, 2011). As noted by Kramar (2014), sustainable HRM consists of a set of strategies and practices of HR which are to lead to the achievement of economic aims, as well as social and environmental aims, while simultaneously increasing the level of human capital over a long-term perspective. The principal composite elements of the concept of SHRM encompass a long-term orientation, care for employees and their development, care for the environment, external partnership, flexibility, conformance with the regulations of labour law, management of safety and hygiene of work, cooperation of employees, justice and equality (Stankevičiūtė & Savanevičienė, 2018).

The notion of the sustainable management of human resources constitutes the effect of the ties between the concept of sustainable development and management in the area of personnel (Renwick, Redman, & Maguire, 2013). This obliges organizations to not only take account of the economic aims in the process of executing personnel functions, but also social and ecological aspects. Making changes in the philosophy of managing human resources is becoming a necessary prerequisite for the execution of this aim by means of including ecological and social aims in all the functions relating to this area of management, ranging from the planning of employment levels, recruitment, selection, development, motivation, evaluation of employees to shaping the working conditions (Pabian, 2015; Pocztowski, 2016). The implementation of sustainable human resources management in an organization should be based on far-reaching, long-term activities that are not only associated with the afore-mentioned processes that exist in the area of HR, but also in terms of the allocation of employees, or the development of effective leadership in social and economic terms (Pellegrini, Rizzi, & Frey, 2018; Thom & Zaugg, 2004; Zaugg, Blum, & Thom, 2001). A significant role in these processes is played by the managers of the area of HRM, who frequently have a direct impact on their course and effect (Harvey, Williams, & Probert, 2013; Jabbour & Santos, 2008). In family firms, the owners of these organizations have a direct impact on the aforesaid processes.

The effect of implementing the philosophy of sustainable management in the area of HR should be the minimization of the negative impact of the activities of an enterprise on the natural environment and people, including the local community (Kramar, 2014; Kennedy, 2017; Weissenrieder & Kosel, 2010). Some authors note that a lower orientation of global family firms translates in a positive sense to the level of involvement in the strategies that are environmentally friendly (Safin, 2007), while others note that family firms often conduct business interests that take account of the benefits to their own regional environment, while bypassing the pursuit of rational and economic aims associated with the maximization of profit and its replacement with aims that help to accumulate the "social and emotional" wealth, or build the reputation and image of the firm at hand (Sharma P. & Sharma S., 2011).

Borges and Michalisin (2009) indicate that the implementation of green practices in an organization commences from the strategic management of human resources. With this aim in mind, it is necessary to reformulate the hitherto practices of management in such a manner that they take the environmental problems into consideration. Environmental strategies become effective when a firm acquires green skills (Walls et al, 2011) and taking the role of employees into consideration in terms of the strategies of environmental protection is essential in this area (Chan, 2005). Attentiveness to the environmental issues should be embedded in the organizational culture of the firm which is geared towards the aims and activities of the employees (Dubois C. & Dubois D., 2012). These activities may be based on, among others, the encouragement of the employees to develop the appropriate competences by offering environmental training for both the employees and the managers, including ecological criteria in the periodical evaluation system, sharing knowledge in the sphere of environmental programs, while also rewarding them for their execution, encouraging ecological behaviour at the workplace or restricting the negative impact on the natural environment by means of improving quality (Ahmad, 2015; Bangwal & Tiwari, 2015; Mandip, 2012).

However, acting on behalf of the environment and the local community are not the only areas of interest in terms of sustainable development. The strategies conducted by the EU in the preliminary section of this chapter also relate to aspects associated with employees. In terms of this issue, the subject-related literature illustrates several barriers as regards the functioning of family firms. One of them, relating to the personnel function is that of the lack of competences, or experience of the members of the family responsible for the positions occupied (Banasiak, 2012; Wach, 2008; Więcek-Janka, 2013), whereby incompetent members of the family hold high positions in the organization, while also a high staff turnover outside of the family (Sułkowski, 2003). Another barrier is that of the program of action that exists in family firms in the process of recruitment, which involves the fact that employees are first and foremost searched for within the family itself and subsequently among acquaintances and finally among strangers (Marjański & Sułkowski 2009). Economic logic and the principles of sustainable management suggest that the competences of the candidates should be taken into consideration as a priority and only later should there be any family connections (Grześ, 2012). Due to counteracting discrimination at the workplace, while also ensuring equality for the employees who come from outside of the family, it is significant to implement clear principles of cooperation in the family firms, including a departure from nepotism and favouring members of the family, or even discrimination of the employees who are not family members. These elements constitute one of the fundamental aspects of implementing the sustainable principles in the area of HRM. Such an approach to management first of all leads to the building of sustainable HRM in accordance with the principles of the strategy of EUROPA 2020, while secondly, it leads to the elimination of some barriers associated with the functioning of family firms defined in subject-related literature (Gupta, Levenburg, Moore, Motani, & Schwarz, 2008).

Likewise, it is also worth drawing attention to the fact that firms that do not belong to the group of family firms prefer to hire employees with a pro-ecological approach and perception of the necessity of environmental protection as this is of significance for the development of the business processes and support for the sustainable efficiency of the whole organization (Ehnert, 2009). Hence, this also gives rise to an important message for family firms on the subject of implementing the principles of sustainable development.

4. Charakteristics of Areas of Building Sustainable Personnel in an Organization

The definition of sustainable personnel is based on the assumption that the foundation of sustainable management in an organization is shaped by the employees who know and understand, while first and foremost apply the principles of sustainable development in their work, namely, in the organization that hired them. These employees should not only be sensitive to any economic, ecological or social problems that emerge in the global economy, but also work in accordance with these principles. With regard to the constantly growing interest in the subject of implementing sustainable activities in organizations, the search for ways to ensure human resources (employees) that fulfil the sustainable criteria would seem to be the necessary prerequisite (Kuźniarska, 2018b). The role of employees in terms of creating a sustainable enterprise is significant, while an important impact in terms of transforming the employees into sustainable employees is exerted by the decisions taken by managers of high level, or the owners themselves (Trojanowski, 2017).

Building sustainable personnel in an organization should be based on effective communication, a system of planning employment levels, a system of recruitment and selection, a system of training and enhancement of the hired employees, their motivation and remuneration, or the previously hired sustainable employees (Kuźniarska, 2018b). Consideration of the features (competences, skills, or experience) which sustainable employees should have would seem to be the first priority, while also the definition of the areas of activity that should characterize such employees, preparation of the strategies associated with the acquisition of personnel of the required features and areas of activity, or strategies enabling the transformation of the previously hired employees into sustainable personnel (Pabian, 2017). In each of these areas it is significant to select the activities that directly translate to the sustainable behaviour of the future and present employees. This is all the more important at the micro-level of the practices of HRM, as indicated in the research conducted by Flamini and Gnan (2019), whereby a common vision and total perception among all the line employees and HR departments must be prepared and implemented.

Some of the activities within the framework of the functions of HR, together with the justification of the need for their implementation are presented in Table 1. The process of creating a personnel in the organization that displays sustainable features requires both time and consistency in activities, as well as in financial outlays.

The implementation of the concept of the sustainable HRM and the creation of the sustainable human resources in family firms is possible thanks to undertaking actions aimed at increasing the awareness of all the employees of the need to act in accordance with the principles of sustainable development. Owners, managers of high level and their deputies, line managers and executive employees should all participate in the process of educating the employees on issues relating to the ecology and the social policies of the firm. In the process of recruiting and selecting new employees, particular attention should be paid to the approach of candidates to environmental and social issues. A verification of the aforesaid aspects should take place during the job interview by taking account of these areas in the questions asked (Dubois C. & Dubois D., 2012; Parkes & Borland, 2012). Parkes and Borland (2012) suggest that the systems of HR may have an impact on the behaviour of employees in terms of the sustainability of the firm by means of evaluation, rewards and training.

Table 1. Characteristics of areas of sustainable personnel in an organization

Process	Justification of implementation	Characteristics of activities
Planning employment	In the context of implementation in the organization of sustainable human resources, it is essential to prepare plans for gaining and training employees, while also motivational activities. Likewise, it is necessary to optimize plans while taking account of, among others, the time necessary to conduct recruitment, allocation, or retraining personnel.	1) preparation of the vision of the sustainable development of personnel, 2) preparation of strategic programs in the sphere of creating sustainable personnel, 3) choice of one of the strategies to ensure the appropriate number and type of employees of a sustainable orientation: – total transformation, – gradual transformation, 4) securing the means for developing resources in the direction of sustainable management, 5) creating the systems of information flow, 6) analysis and description of work positions from the viewpoint of conformance with the principles of sustainable development, 7) preparation of the appropriate competence profiles
Recruitment and selection of employees	With relation to the progressing changes in the concept of sustainable management of human resources, it is becoming necessary in organizations to shape the new competences and talent and knowledge management among the hired employees. This brings with it necessary changes in the systems of training and improvement in the direction of a team learning process that is geared towards shaping the attitudes and involvement in the organization.	1) preparation of description of work position and profile of personal requirements of candidates by taking account of competences that are in conformance with the notion of sustainable development 2) preparation of job offer that includes the required aspects of green competences 3) preparation of the appropriate set of questions for conducting interviews in order to verify the attitudes of candidates, 4) distinguishing candidates during the process of selection that have a pro-ecological and pro-social approach, 5) conducting preliminary interviews by taking account of questions relating to the principles of sustainable development, 6) accepting employees that have a high development potential at their disposal, 7) hiring employees that are initially prepared (with certain experience) for executing sustainable strategies,
Onboarding	Newly hired employees must be retrained within the framework of a necessary program of green research and development in order to attain a higher level of involvement in sustainable activities	1) choice of account manager who works in accordance with the principles of sustainable development 2) making an employee familiar with the firm and the principles of its operations within the framework of sustainable activities 3) initiating an employee into a new position
Training and improving employees	Training courses constitute the basis for executing the strategies adopted by an enterprise, including the implementation of sustainable development. They constitute an alternative to acquiring sustainable personnel, particularly in situations where the wholesale replacement of personnel is not possible due to practical and financial aspects. Simultaneously, training courses have an impact on ecological activities by increasing the level of involvement of the employees applying green practices with the aim of competing on the market in a manner that is environmentally friendly.	1) establishing the training needs, 2) guiding employees towards post-graduate studies and in-house and external training, 3) allocating trainers or moderators to employees of an orientation towards sustainable development,

continues on following page

Table 1. Continued

Process	Justification of implementation	Characteristics of activities
Motivating	Effective motivation may lead to the widespread and long-lasting involvement of employees in socio-ecological activities.	1) an example of behaviour from the managerial staff, company heads, 2) implementation of system of incentives for employees with the aim of spreading socio-ecological initiatives, 3) preparation of instruments that have an impact on the sustainable behaviour of employees, particularly in the following relations: – employee - enterprise, – employee – superior, – employee – work position
Remuneration	Responsible remuneration should be based on processes, procedures and tools of remuneration, which create the conditions for an employee to lead to the sustainable development of the organization	1) taking account of binding legislative norms, 2) taking account of moral and ethical norms 3) subjective treatment of employee
Organization of work of sustainable employees	Benefits of sustainable personnel in organization: – decrease in costs of business activities of enterprise, – reduction of harmful impact of man on the environment, – elimination of waste of the factors of production. – increasing awareness of employees of ecological activities, – growth in labour efficiency.	Sustainable personnel is characterized by the following: 1) knowledge of issue of the state of socio-ecological danger, while also the ways of counteracting them, 2) sensitivity and reaction towards the problems of this sphere, 3) innovativeness in rational ways in terms of resource management, 4) openness to new technologies and propositions of rational production and consumption, 5) activeness and reaction to the existing ecological and social problems, 6) initiation of change in terms of the equipment and environment of the work position, or the way of executing work itself.

Source: Self-analysis on the basis of the following: (Aktar & Islam, 2019; Beck-Krala, 2017; Hilarowicz, 2015; Klimkiewicz & Beck-Krala,2015; Oczkowska, 2014; Pabian, 201; Pabian, 2016)

5. Gauges of Personnel Controlling Associated with Sustainable Personnel

With the aim of the appropriate execution of the process of transforming the firm in the direction of a sustainable organization that has a personnel of sustainable features at its disposal, it is necessary to answer a range of questions that are adequate to the personnel functions executed in the organization. These may be expressed by means of qualitative and quantitative gauges applied in personnel controlling, which is presented in Table 2.

Personnel controlling takes on the form of a separate organizational cell, depending on the magnitude of the organization, while in small and medium-sized firms, which family firms are most frequently classified as, this function is taken over by a managerial person, while this is most frequently the owner in family firms. Familiarity with the criteria taken into consideration in the creation of a sustainable personnel significantly facilitates not only the implementation processes themselves, but also the retention of the appropriate level of knowledge among the employees who are familiar with the sustainable principles.

The gauges of personnel controlling presented in Table 2 have been divided up in accordance with the personnel functions that facilitate the evaluation of the degree of the execution of tasks set out by the system of HRM in the organization. Such an evaluation should be conducted on the basis of the analysis and observations carried out, whose effect over a long-term perspective should be more effective and efficient, both in the area of human resources, as well as the organization as a whole.

Table 2. Gauges of personnel controlling associated with sustainable personnel

HRM area	Qualitative gauges for building sustainable personnel in an organization
Planning employment	1. Has a vision of sustainable personnel been developed in the organization? 2. Are there plans to acquire sustainable employees? 3. What is the necessary time period for conducting recruitment of sustainable employees? 4. What is the necessary time period for conducting selection? 5. What is the necessary time period for conducting requalification of the personnel? 6. Does the organization have the necessary means at its disposal for securing the development of human resources in the direction of sustainable management? 7. Do the appropriate systems of the flow of information exist? 8. Who, when and in what sphere should the analysis and new description of work positions that take account of sustainable principles be conducted? 9. Who will be responsible for the preparation of competence profiles?
Recruitment and selection of employees	1. What will be the form of attracting candidates of a sustainable profile? 2. Who will be responsible for the preparation of questions for conducting interviews in order to verify the approaches of candidates to work? 3. According to which criteria shall the new employees be recruited? 4. Will the experience of candidates in terms of the execution of sustainable strategies be the principal criteria in choosing an employee during the course of recruitment? 5. Will research be conducted in the field of accuracy in terms of the selection of candidates?
Training and enhancement of employees	1. What are the training needs in the sphere of sustainable aspects? 2. Do plans for such training exist? 3. Are the aims of these training courses clearly defined? 4. Is there a sufficient number of employees of competences that would facilitate the execution of such training courses? 5. What would the cost of this training be? 6. Would the training be conducted independently, or by external firms? 7. Will we be allocating employees trainers, mentors of an orientation towards sustainable development? 8. In what way will the evaluation of the training in terms of sustainable aspects be conducted?
Evaluation	1. Who will conduct the evaluation of employees from the viewpoint of sustainable development? 2. What methods, techniques and criteria shall be applied in the evaluation? 3. In what way will the results of the evaluation be utilized? 4. At what frequency shall the evaluation be conducted? 5. What will the cost of conducting such an evaluation be?
Motivation	1. What motivators may we propose to employees with the aim of encouraging them to spread sustainable initiatives? 2. What will the cost of implementing motivators be? 3. When should the system of motivators be? 4. Who and according to which criteria shall allocate the motivators?
Information	1. What channels may communicate information to employees with regard to information on the sustainable practices implemented in the organization? 2. Who will be responsible for the preparation and transfer of information relating to sustainable activities? 3. How detailed will the information transferred be? 4. At what frequency shall the information transferred be? 5. Who will verify the extent of which the information transferred is understandable?
Hired sustainable employees	1. How to verify the state of knowledge of employees on the subject of sustainable development? 2. What is the reaction of employees to the problems of sustainable management? 3. Are there employees that are characterized by innovativeness in the rational management of resources? 4. How do the employees refer to the new technologies? 5. What is the reaction of employees to the propositions of rational production? 6. What is the reaction of employees to the propositions of rational consumption? 7. What is the relation of employees to the ecological problems? 8. What is the relation of employees to the social problems? 9. Do the employees initiate changes themselves in the equipment of the work positions? 10. Do the employees initiate changes themselves in the environment of the work positions? 11. Do the employees initiate changes themselves in the way of executing work?

Source: (Kuźniarska, 2018a)

It is essential to draw attention to the necessity of a cyclical and regular execution of the evaluation process, which would facilitate the ongoing control and elimination of mistakes.

SOLUTIONS AND RECOMMENDATIONS

The principal arguments in favour of the implementation of the sustainable management of human resources in family firms are as follows:

1) due to the fact that family enterprises often operate on the local market, their sustainable activities undertaken in the area of HRM have the chance of spreading rapidly, building a positive image as an employer, while the implementation itself may also lead to savings (reduction of costs) (Final Report for EC, 2011),
2) the transition to a sustainable economy brings far-reaching effects for the labour market and as a consequence it is indispensable for employers in terms of effective management, whose task is to predict the structural changes in the firm (including family firms) (OECD, 2012),
3) sustainable management leads to transformation as a result of which, new workplaces are created, some of them are eliminated, while others try to redefine themselves, which for family firms constitutes a challenge from an organizational viewpoint,
4) the market is gradually forcing firms to support "green employment", but first and foremost the elimination of gaps in terms of qualifications in this area and equally important – predicting changes in the demand for the appropriate human capital,
5) the possibility of taking fast decisions relating to the implementation, thanks to its uncomplicated organizational structure (Petruškevičius, 2016),
6) SHRM enhances the efficiency of an organization as it is possible to acknowledge it as a new model of organizational development, in which the most important determinant is that of human capital; while it also leads to development and the wellbeing of employees, which has an impact on the progress of the organization at hand (Cleveland, Byrne, & Cavanagh, 2015).

FUTURE RESEARCH DIRECTIONS

It is worth drawing attention to the problem of the environment and ecology, or actions taken on behalf of counteracting social exclusion and putting it forward as a subject matter of debate on the global, regional and local economies. It is certain that the escalation of the afore-mentioned issues will in time force all organizations to implement progress and actions in the fight against the aforesaid problems. Thus, family firms should not hesitate to implement the principles of sustainable development within the framework of their business activities. Furthermore, it is necessary to assume that the area of HR which constitutes the subject matter of the herein chapter, will more than once face the challenges of the necessity to change behaviour, habits, competences and skills of the employees when taking account of the principles of sustainable development. The area of interest for researchers may constitute the issue of the impact of the principles of sustainable management implemented in family firms in terms of efficiency, effectiveness, the level of involvement, skills, competences, or staff turnover. Likewise, it may also be important to search for the cause-effect ties among the variables.

From another perspective, a significant research area may become the search for balance between the needs and expectations of stakeholders and business aims, while also environmental and employee aims.

CONCLUSION

By perceiving HRM as a means and aim of the execution of the strategic organizational aims, it is possible to argue about the importance of the sustainable development of HRM in family firms with regard to the fact that the appropriately designed and implemented process of human resources management helps to guide the approach of the employees and actions on behalf of the execution of aims of the enterprise as a whole (Taylor, Osland, & Egri, 2012; Mishra & Sarkar, 2020). Moreover, clearly clarified principles of the sustainable management of human resources constitutes the long-term physical, social and economic good of the employees (Stankeviciute & Savaneviciene, 2013), leading to the increased level of trust and participation of the employees in the process of the functioning of the organization on a higher level than non-family firms as indicated by research results on family firms (Vallejo-Martos, Antequera-Solis, & Ruiz-Jiménez, 2013). This directly translates to favourable working conditions for the employees and professional satisfaction, which in turn may have an impact on the financial and non-financial performance of the enterprise, in spite of the unfavourable and changeable external environment (Lemańska-Majdzik & Sipa, 2015).

Likewise, it is essential to remember that the employees who are operating in accordance with the principles of *sustainable activities* in an organization and bringing their knowledge to a private sphere have an impact on pro-ecological and pro-social activities in a broader sense thanks to this behaviour.

With regard to the arguments presented, as well as the rapid development of the concept of sustainable management in connection with its execution in the area of the personnel function, the subject matter proposed in this chapter is deemed to be important for the development of HRM in family firms.

REFERENCES

Ahmad, S. (2015). Green Human Resource Management: Policies and Practices. *Cogent Business & Management*, (2), 1–13. Retrieved from https://www.cogentoa.com/article/10.1080/23311975.2015.1030817

Aktar, A., & Islam, Y. (2019). *Green Human Resource Management Practices and Employee Engagement: Empirical Evidence from RMG sector in Bangladesh*. Academic Press.

Almada, L., & Borges, R. (2018). Sustainable Competitive Advantage Needs Green Human Resource Practices: A Framework for Environmental Management. *Revista de Administração Contemporânea, 22*(3), 424–442. doi:10.1590/1982-7849rac2018170345

Aust, I., Matthews, B. & Muller-Camen, M. (2020). Common Good HRM: A paradigm shift in Sustainable HRM?', *Human Resource Management Review, 30*(3), 1-11. doi:10.1016/j.hrmr.2019.100705

Bac, D. P. (2008). A history of the concept of sustainable development: Literaturt review. *The Annals of the University of Oradea, Economic Sciences Series, 17*(2), 576–580. Retrieved from http://steconomice.uoradea.ro/anale/volume/2008/v2-economy-and-business-administration/101.pdf

Banasiak, A. (2012). Bariera finansowa w rozwoju firm rodzinnych sektora MSP. *Przedsiębiorczość i Zarządzanie*, *13*(8), 137–155.

Bangwal, D., & Tiwari, P. (2015). Green HRM –A way to greening the environment. *Journal of Business and Management*, *17*(12), 45–53. doi:10.9790/487X-171214553

Barney, J. (1991). Firm resources and sustained competitive advantage. *Journal of Management*, *17*(1), 99–120. doi:10.1177/014920639101700108

Barney, J., & Wright, P. (1998). On becoming a strategic partner: The role of human resources in gaining competitive advantage. *Human Resource Management*, *37*(1), 31–46. doi:10.1002/(SICI)1099-050X(199821)37:1<31::AID-HRM4>3.0.CO;2-W

Beck-Krala, E. (2017). *Badanie efektywności wynagrodzeń: od kontroli kosztów do aktywizowania pracowników*. Wydawnictwo AGH.

Beck-Krala, E., & Klimkiewicz, K. (2016). Occupational Safety and Health as an Element of a Complex Compensation System Evaluation within an Organization. *International Journal of Occupational Safety and Ergonomics*, *22*(4), 523–531. doi:10.1080/10803548.2016.1183338 PMID:27191788

Borim-de-Souza, R., Balbinot, Z., Travis, E. F., Munck, L., & Takahashi, A. R. W. (2015). Sustainable development and sustainability as study objects for comparative management theory. *Cross Cultural Management*, *22*(2), 201–235. doi:10.1108/CCM-02-2013-0027

Bowen, H. R. (1953). Social Responsibilities of the Businessman. Academic Press.

Brzeziński, A. (2016). Społeczna odpowiedzialność firm rodzinnych. *Przedsiębiorczość i Zarządzanie*, *17*(6), 147–158.

Carroll, A. B. (1979). A Three-Dimensional Conceptual Model of Corporate Performance. *Academy of Management Review*, *4*(4), 497–505. doi:10.5465/amr.1979.4498296

Chan, R. Y. K. (2005). Does the Natural-Resource-Based View of the Firm Apply in an Emerging Economy? A Survey of Foreign Invested Enterprises in China. *Journal of Management Studies*, *42*(3), 625–672. doi:10.1111/j.1467-6486.2005.00511.x

Clarke, M. (2011). Sustainable HRM: A new approach to people management. In M. Clarke (Ed.), *Readings in HRM and sustainability* (pp. 1–7). Tilde University Press.

Cleveland, J. N., Byrne, Z. S., & Cavanagh, T. M. (2015). The future of HR is RH: Respect for humanity at work. *Human Resource Management Review*, *25*(2), 146–161. doi:10.1016/j.hrmr.2015.01.005

Cohen, E., Taylor, S., & Muller-Camen, M. (2012). *HR's role in corporate social responsibility and sustainability*. SHRM Foundation Executive Briefing. Retrieved from https://www.shrm.org/foundation/ourwork/initiatives/building-an-inclusive-culture/Documents/HR%27s%20Role%20in%20Corporate%20Social%20Responsibility.pdf

COM. (2010). *Europe 2020: A strategy for smart, sustainable and inclusive growth*. Retrieved from https://ec.europa.eu/eu2020/pdf/COMPLET%20EN%20BARROSO%20%20%20007%20-%20Europe%202020%20-%20EN%20version.pdf

Crifo, P., Durand, R., & Gond, J. P. (2019). Encouraging Investors to Enable Corporate Sustainability Transitions: The Case of Responsible Investment in France. *Organization & Environment*, *32*(2), 125–144. doi:10.1177/1086026619848145

De Prins, P. (2011), Duurzaam HRM: Synthetische academische introductie. In I. Rompa (Ed.), *Explorative research on Sustainable Human Resource Management*. Retrieved from https://www.innovatiefinwerk.nl/sites/innovatiefinwerk.nl/files/field/bijlage/sustainable_hrm.pdf

Docherty, P., Forslin, J., & Shani, A. B. (2002). *Creating Sustainable Work Systems: Emerging Perspectives and Practice*. Psychology Press.

Drucker, P. F. (1984). The new meaning of corporate social responsibility. *California Management Review*, *26*(2), 53–63. doi:10.2307/41165066

Dubois, C. L. Z., & Dubois, D. A. (2012). Strategic HRM as social design for environmental sustainability in organization. *Human Resource Management*, *51*(6), 799–826. doi:10.1002/hrm.21504

Dunphy, D., Benveniste, J., Griffiths, A., & Sutton, P. (2000). *Sustainability; the Corporate Challenge of the 21st Century*. Allen & Unwin.

Dyllick, T., & Muff, K. (2016). Clarifying the Meaning of Sustainable Business. *Organization & Environment*, *29*(2), 156–174. doi:10.1177/1086026615575176

Edersheim, E. H. (2007). *Przesłanie Druckera. Zarządzanie oparte na wiedzy*. Warszawa: MTBiznes.

Ehnert, I. (2009). *Sustainable Human Resource Management. A conceptual and exploratory analysis from a paradox perspective*. Physica-Verlag.

Ehnert, I., Harry, W., & Zink, K. J. (2014). Sustainability and HRM. In I. Ehnert, W. Harry, & K. J. Zink (Eds.), *Sustainability and human resource management developing sustainable business organizations* (pp. 3–32). Springer.

Ehnert, I., Parsa, S., Roper, I., Wagner, M., & Muller-Camen, M. (2016). Reporting on sustainability and HRM: A comparative study of sustainability reporting practices by the world's largest companies. *International Journal of Human Resource Management*, *27*(1), 88–108. doi:10.1080/09585192.2015.1024157

Elkington, J. (1997). *Cannibals with forks: the triple bottom line of 21st century business*. Captone.

European Commission. (2011), *Communication from the Commission to the European Parliament, the Council, the European Economic and Social Committee and the Committee of the Regions, A Renewed EU Strategy for Corporate Social Responsibility*. Retrieved from https://op.europa.eu/en/publication-detail/-/publication/ae5ada03-0dc3- 48f8-9a32-0460e65ba7ed/language-en

Flamini, G., & Gnan, L. (2019). Family Firms' HrM Practices Configurations: an empirical analysis. In L. Gnan & M. Stefanovska–Petkovska (Eds.), *Innovating Europe* (pp. 29–84). University American College Skopje. doi:10.5281/zenodo.3533762

Freeman, R. E. (1984). Strategic management: A stakeholder approach. Academic Press.

Grudzewski, W., & Hejduk, I. (2000). Kierowanie mała firmą – wyzwania przyszłości. *Ekonomika i Organizacja Przedsiębiorstw*, *1*, 3–5.

Grześ, A. (2012). Specyfika pozyskiwania zasobów ludzkich w firmach rodzinnych. *Przedsiębiorczość i Zarządzanie*, *13*(7), 157–176.

Guerci, M., & Carollo, L. (2016). A paradox view on green human resource management: Insights from the Italian context. *International Journal of Human Resource Management*, *27*(2), 212–238. doi:10.1080/09585192.2015.1033641

Guerci, M., & Pedrini, M. (2014). The consensus between Italian HR and sustainability managers on HR management for sustainability-driven change – towards a 'strong' HR management system. *International Journal of Human Resource Management*, *25*(13), 1787–1814. doi:10.1080/09585192.2013.860388

Gupta, V., Levenburg, N., Moore, L., Motani, J., & Schwarz, T. (2008). Exploring the Construct of Family Business in the Emerging Markets. *International Journal of Business and Emerging Markets*, *1*(2), 189–208. doi:10.1504/IJBEM.2008.020869

Hart, S. L., & Sharma, S. (2004). Engaging fringe stakeholders for competitive imagination. *The Academy of Management Perspectives*, *18*(1), 7–18. doi:10.5465/ame.2004.12691227

Harvey, G., Williams, K., & Probert, J. (2013). Greening the airline pilot: HRM and the green performance of airlines in the UK. *International Journal of Human Resource Management*, *24*(1), 152–166. doi:10.1080/09585192.2012.669783

Hilarowicz, A. (2015). Koncepcja pracownika we współczesnych modelach zarządzania zasobami ludzkimi. *Zeszyty Naukowe Politechniki Śląskiej. Seria Organizacja i Zarządzanie*, *79*, 77–85.

Hill, R., & Stewart, J. (2000). Human Resource Development in Small Organizations. *Journal of European Industrial Training, 24*(2/3/4), 105-117.

Hirsig, N., Rogovski, N., & Elkin, M. (2014). Enterprise sustainability and HRM in Small and Medium-Sized Enterprises, a Decent Work Perspectives. In K. J. Z. Ehnert & W. Harry (Eds.), *Sustainability and Human Resource Management: Developing sustainable business organizations*. Springer. doi:10.1007/978-3-642-37524-8_6

Jabbour, C. J. C., & Santos, F. C. A. (2008). The central role of human resource management in the search for sustainable organizations. *International Journal of Human Resource Management*, *19*(12), 2133–2154. doi:10.1080/09585190802479389

Jamali, D., El Dirani, A., & Harwood, I. A. (2015). Exploring human resource management roles in corporate social responsibility: The CSR–HRM co-creation model. *Business Ethics (Oxford, England)*, *2*(2), 125–143. doi:10.1111/beer.12085

Jeżak, J., Popczyk, W., & Winnicka-Popczyk, A. (2004). *Przedsiębiorstwo rodzinne: funkcjonowanie i rozwój*. Difin.

Kaczmarska-Krawczak, J. (2012). Specyfika działalności firm rodzinnych. *Przedsiębiorczość i Zarzadzanie*, *13*(7), 177–190.

Kassenberg, A. (2007). Zrównoważony rozwój a koncepcja przestrzennego zagospodarowania kraju. In G. Gorzelak & A. Tucholska (Eds.), *Rozwój, region, przestrzeń* (pp. 53–90). MRR, Euroreg.

Kaufman, B. E. (2015). Evolution of Strategic HRM as Seen Through Two Founding Books: A 30th Anniversary Perspective on Development of the Field. *Human Resource Management*, *54*(3), 389–407. doi:10.1002/hrm.21720

Kennedy, H., & Lakshmi, V. R. (2017). The role of business sustainability in Human Resource Management: A study on Indian manufacturing companies. *The South East Asian Journal of Management*, *11*(1), 70–85.

Kramar, R. (2014). Beyond Strategic Human Resource Management: Is Sustainable Human Resource Management the Next Approach? *International Journal of Human Resource Management*, *25*(8), 1069–1089. doi:10.1080/09585192.2013.816863

Kuźniarska, A. (2018a). Controlling personalny jako narzędzie wspomagające tworzenie zrównoważonego personelu w organizacji. *Humanizacja Pracy*, *4*(294), 31–45.

Kuźniarska, A. (2018b). Pillars of Creating Sustainable Personnel in an Organization. *Entrepreneurship and Management*, *19*(6), 159–172.

Lemańska-Majdzik, A., & Sipa, M. (2015). *Selected Aspects of Family Company Management in Employees View in Poland, Aktualne problemy podnikovej sfery 2015. Zbornik vedeckych prac*. Vydavatel'stvo EKONOM.

Mandip, G. (2012). Green HRM: People Management Commitment to Environmental Sustainability. *Research Journal of Recent Sciences*, *1*, 244–252.

Mariappanadar, S. (2020). Characteristics of Sustainable HRM System and Practices for Implementing Corporate Sustainability. In *Sustainable Human Resource Management* (pp. 9–35). Springer Singapore., doi:10.1007/978-981-15-5656-2_2

Mazur–Wierzbicka, E. (2016). Odpowiedzialność wobec środowiska naturalnego w biznesie rodzinnym. *Przedsiębiorczość i Zarzadzanie*, *17*(6), 229–238.

Mikušová, M., Friedrich, V., & Horváthová, P. (2020). Who is More Sustainable? Family Business or Non-Family Business? Czech Evidence. *Sustainability*, *12*(14), 5540. doi:10.3390u12145540

Mishra, R. K., & Sarkar, S. (2020). Sustainable HRM Practices - A Drive Towards Sustainability (The case of NLCIL). In Sustainable Human Resource Management. Singapore: Springer Singapore. doi:10.1007/978-981-15-5656-2_11

Morgeson, F. P., Aguinis, H., Waldman, D. A., & Siegel, D. S. (2013). Extending corporate social responsibility research to the human resource management and organizational behavior domains: A look to the future. *Personnel Psychology*, *66*(4), 805–824. doi:10.1111/peps.12055

Oczkowska, R. (2014). *Rozwój zasobów ludzkich organizacji*. Difin.

Pabian, A. (2011). Sustainable personnel – pracownicy przedsiębiorstwa przyszłości. *Zarządzanie Zasobami Ludzkimi*, *5*, 9–27.

Pabian, A. (2015). Zrównoważone zarządzania zasobami ludzkimi – zarys problematyki. *Zeszyty Naukowe Politechniki Częstochowskiej*, *17*, 7–16.

Pabian, A. (2016). Pozyskiwanie pracowników w koncepcji zrównoważonego zarządzania zasobami ludzkimi. *Marketing i Rynek*, (3), 671–680.

Pabian, A. (2017). Planowanie strategiczne z perspektywy sustainability. *Handel Wewnętrzny*, *3*(368), 341–350.

Parkes, C., & Borland, H. (2012). Strategic HRM: Transforming Its Responsibilities Toward Ecological Sustainability-The Greatest Global Challenge Facing Organizations. *Thunderbird International Business Review*, *54*(6), 811–824. doi:10.1002/tie.21505

Pellegrini, C., Rizzi, F., & Frey, M. (2018). The role of sustainable human resource practices in influencing employee behavior for corporate sustainability. *Business Strategy and the Environment*, *27*(8), 1221–1232. doi:10.1002/bse.2064

Petruškevičius, D. (2016). A consideration of sustainable HR management implementation in a SME context: The T optimus case. *Humanities and Social Sciences:Latvia*, *24*(2), 84–109.

Pocztowski, A. (2016). Zrównoważone zarządzania zasobami ludzkimi w teorii i praktyce. *Journal of Management and Finance*, *14*(2), 303–314.

Renwick, D. W. S., Redman, T., & Maguire, S. (2013). Green Human Resource Management: A Review and Research Agenda. *International Journal of Management Reviews*, *15*(1), 1–14. doi:10.1111/j.1468-2370.2011.00328.x

Report, F., & the European Commission. DG Employment. (2011). *Studies on sustainability issues — Green jobs; trade and labour*, Cambridge Econometrics. Retrieved from https://www.google.com/url?sa=t&rct=j&q=&esrc=s&source=web&cd=1&ved=2ahU

Report, F., & the European Commission. DG Employment. (2012). *The jobs potential of a shift towards a low carbon economy*; *OECD Employment Outlook 2012*. Retrieved from https://www.oecd.org/els/emp/50503551.pdf

Report of the World Commission on Environment and Development. (1987). *Our Common Future*. Retrieved from http://www.un-documents.net/ocf-02.htm#I

Rothenberg, S., Hull, C. E., & Tang, Z. (2017). The Impact of Human Resource Management on Corporate Social Performance Strengths and Concerns. *Business & Society*, *56*(3), 391–418. doi:10.1177/0007650315586594

Sadler-Smith, E., Gardiner, P., Badger, B., Chaston, I., & Stubberfield, J. (2000). Using Collaborative Learning to Develop Small Firms. *Human Resource Development International*, *3*(3), 285–306. doi:10.1080/13678860050128483

Sadler-Smith, E., & Lean, J. (2004). The Practice of HRD in Smaller Firms. In J. Stewart & G. Beaver (Eds.), *HRD in Small Organizations. Research and Practice* (pp. 124–148). Routlege.

Safin, K. (2007). *Przedsiębiorstwa rodzinne, istota i zachowania strategiczne*. Wydawnictwo Akademii Ekonomicznej.

Schuler, R., & Jackson, S. (2014). Human resource management and organizational effectiveness: Yesterday and today. *Journal of Organizational Effectiveness: People and Performance*, *1*(1), 35–55. doi:10.1108/JOEPP-01-2014-0003

Sharma, P., & Sharma, S. (2011). Drivers of Proactive Environmental Strategy in Family Firms. *Business Ethics Quarterly*, *21*(2), 309–334. doi:10.5840/beq201121218

Singh, T., & Srivastav, S. K. (2012). QWL and Organization efficiency: A proposed framework. *Journal of Strategic Human Resource Management*, *1*(1), 1–13.

Stankeviciute, Z., & Savaneviciene, A. (2013). Sustainability as a concept for human resource management. *Economics and Management*, *18*(4), 837-846. doi:10.5755/j01.em.18.4.5631

Stankevičiūtė, Ž., & Savanevičienė, A. (2018). Designing Sustainable HRM: The Core Characteristics of Emerging Field. *Sustainability*, *10*(12), 4798. doi:10.3390u10124798

Stor, M. (2010). Międzynarodowe zarządzanie kadrami. In T. Listwan (Ed.), *Zarządzanie kadrami*. C.H. Beck.

Stradomski, M. (2010). *Finansowanie obce firm rodzinnych na rynku niedoskonałym*. PWE.

Sułkowski, Ł. (2003). Bariery rozwoju przedsiębiorstw rodzinnych. In H. Bieniok (Ed.), *Przedsiębiorczość, konkurencyjność oraz kondycja małych i średnich przedsiębiorstw w obliczu integracji z Unią Europejską* (pp. 444–445). Wydawnictwo Akademii Ekonomicznej.

Sułkowski, Ł., & Marjański, A. (2009). *Firmy rodzinne. Jak osiągnąć sukces w sztafecie*. Poltext.

Taylor, S., Osland, J., & Egri, C. P. (2012). Guest Editors' Introduction: Introduction to HRM's Role in Sustainability: Systems, Strategies, and Practices. *Human Resource Management*, *51*(6), 789–798. doi:10.1002/hrm.21509

Thom, N., & Zaugg, R. (2004). Das prinzip nachhaltigkeit im personal management. *Personal Führung*, *7*, 52–55.

Towards a sustainable Europe by 2030, COM. (2019). Retrieved from https://ec.europa.eu/commission/sites/beta-political/files/rp_sustainable_europe_30-01_en_web.pdf

Trojanowski, T. (2017). Innovations in Human Resource Management through the Creation of Sustainable Staff Members. *Handel Wewnętrzny*, *1*(366), 119–128.

Ulrich, D. (1998). Os campeões de recursos humanos (7th ed.). São Paulo: Futura.

United Nations. (2002). *World Summit on Sustainable Development*. Retrieved from https://www.un.org/ga/search/view_doc.asp?symbol=A/CONF.199/20&Lang=E

Vallejo-Martos, M. C., Antequera-Solis, J. M., & Ruiz-Jiménez, M. C. (2013). *Are Family Firms More Harmonious Organisations? An Analysis of the Effects of Organisational Harmony on Their Performance*. International Conference on Business Strategy and Organizational Behaviour (BizStrategy), Global Science and Technology Forum, Singapore.

Wach, K. (2008). *Regionalne otoczenie małych i średnich przedsiębiorstw*. Wydawnictwo Uniwersytetu Ekonomicznego.

Walls, J. L., Phan, P. H., & Berrone, P. (2011). Measuring Environmental Strategy: Construct Development, Reliability, and Validity. *Business & Society*, *50*(1), 71–115. doi:10.1177/0007650310394427

Weissenrieder, J., & Kosel, M. (2010). *Nachhaltiges Personalmanagement in der Praxis: mit Erfolgsbeispielen mittelstandischer Unternehmen*. Gabler Verlag. doi:10.1007/978-3-8349-8588-0

Więcek-Janka, E. (2013). *Wiodące wartości w zarządzaniu przedsiębiorstwami rodzinnymi*. Wydawnictwo Politechniki Poznańskiej.

Wilkinson, A., Hill, M., & Gollan, P. (2001). The sustainability debate. *International Journal of Operations & Production Management*, *21*(12), 1492–1502. doi:10.1108/01443570110410865

Wood, D. J. (1991). Corporate Social Performance Revisited. *Academy of Management Review*, *16*(4), 691–718. doi:10.5465/amr.1991.4279616

Wright, P., McMahan, G., & McWilliams, A. (1994). Human resources and sustained competitive advantage: A resource based perspective. *International Journal of Human Resource Management*, *5*(2), 301–326. doi:10.1080/09585199400000020

Zaugg, R., Blum, A., & Thom, N. (2001). *Sustainability in Human Resource Management. Evaluation Report*. Retrieved from https://www.researchgate.net/publication/276906300_Sustainability_in_Human_Resource_Management

KEY TERMS AND DEFINITIONS

CSR: The voluntary implementation of a concept by organizations that constitutes one of the tools of the sustainable development of enterprises.

Personnel Controlling: The concept of management in the personnel area that takes account of the achievement of aims in the sphere of personnel policies with the use of the appropriate tools.

Sustainable Development: The principles of development that respect the ecological, economic, and social equality.

Sustainable HRM: Taking account of elements in the processes of human resource management that enable employees to execute the ecological, economic, and social aims in accordance with the sustainable assumptions.

Sustainable Management: The management of an organization in a manner that takes account of the ecological, economic, and social dimensions.

Sustainable Organization: An organization that respects the principles of sustainable development in its activities.

Sustainable Personnel: the employees of an organization that operate in accordance with the principles of sustainable development.

Chapter 9
Value-Based Management and Responsibility in the Management of People:
A Competitive Advantage for Family Business

Carmen Ruiz-Viñals
Universidad Abad Oliba, Spain

Alberto Trallero-Fort
Universidad Abad Oliba, Spain

ABSTRACT

Today's markets require credibility, transparency, and sustainability. This demand obliges organisations to make ever greater advances in the field of management by values. Until recently, value-based management was considered just another management approach to be covered in day-to-day operations. Today, it is considered part of the strategic management of the firms. The paradigm shift began when pressure from the market and society as a whole began to insist that companies should behave like members of the ecosystem, taking full responsibility and employing their capacity to generate change. This implies that value-based management should be deployed throughout the entire organisation. This, in turn, requires companies to identify and commit to certain values that will become the cornerstone of their strategy and management style. The aim of this chapter is to claim that value-based management is a competitive advantage for family business in particular.

DOI: 10.4018/978-1-7998-4814-1.ch009

INTRODUCTION

Markets evolve at great speed. This means that company strategies must be continuously reviewed, management models continuously adapted to new situations and goals must be set in terms of increasingly shorter times (Harmon, P., 2019). The first consequence when talking about ways of managing is that over the years it has evolved from a traditional model of management by instructions (MBI) to one of management by objectives (MBO). The model that is implemented these days is, however, management by values (MBV, or Value-driven Management) because any company that wants to be competitive must be a company focused on the management of people, which is based on the strengthening of its values, since these will form the backbone of its company policies (Lepak, D. & Gowan, M., 2019). The fundamental difference between these three models lies in the role that people play in defining business strategies, since under the new paradigm people management comes to the foreground.

Let us specify the differences between the three models in relation to the role of people management in each of them.

Management by Instructions, which emerged after the Industrial Revolution of 1920, consists of a passive relationship between the employee and the company. The command gives some orders or instructions, which the employee is limited to execute. It is therefore a unidirectional relationship, based on authority and it is specially given in situations of low training and low qualification that involve repetitive and mechanical tasks. It can also be given in emergency situations in which very precise and quick instructions must be given in order to focus on the resolution of a problem (Fernandez Aguado, 2002).

Management by Objectives, it already implies a greater interaction of the person and therefore it already becomes a bidirectional relationship, in which those objectives that allow to maximize the profitability of the company, taking advantage of the resources to the maximum, prevail. This model was implemented in the 60s and is already an important step in the consideration of the person in the organizations.

Its limitation is given by the scarce participation of the employee in the setting of objectives. Employee's opinion, in general, is not taken into account, which often generates frustration and the feeling that the organization's objectives do not respond to a specific strategy. As the companies evolved, the system was bettered and the participation of people in the definition of the firm objectives was greater, but it was necessary to give sense to all this (Norlin, 2020).

The sense was given by Value-driven Management, that is implemented in late 90s. It is a complement to MBO. It does not cancel it out, but gives it meaning. What is sought is a systematization of the firm and employees' values, and place them as part of the strategy, so, everything that is decided in the company, has a common bond (Barret, 2017).

Values are the non-visible part of corporate culture, which in turn is the way to internalize corporate social responsibility (CSR) in an organization (Fink, L., 2018).

More than two decades ago, CSR became more of a market requirement in this changing environment rather than reflecting the full conviction of many businesses in terms of company development (Alexander, P., 2015). Thus, in many organizations, CSR became an aesthetic operation that, whilst not without intrinsic value, reflection or results, was more as a result of actions that undoubtedly impacted on the best corporate reputation rather than reflecting a strategic definition based on conviction and deep internal reflection. Corporate culture is the way to internalize CSR within an organization and values form part of that culture; they are the non-visible part (Schein, E., 1998) and are part of the reputation of an organization in a broader sense. That is why MBV goes beyond mere external CSR.

Economic cycles, social tendencies and the macro environment change continuously and challenge organizations to constantly adapt, to continuously analyse threats and opportunities, and demand of them the ability to change direction in order to maintain their competitiveness. Added to an environment dominated by VUCA (Volatility, Uncertainty, Complexity and Ambiguity), this means that companies have to have an agility and elasticity that allows them to adapt to changes. A company cannot possibly have such an ability if it does not include in its strategy the need for people to feel important in the organization, to be able to promote initiatives and to have the right environment to create such initiatives and to feel committed to the organization (Ruiz, C. & Parra, C., 2013). All company changes go through people and therefore we have to create the conditions so that they have the best possible environment to accompany and manage these changes, with alignment through values being a powerful tool to achieve this.

Another current aspect to consider is that talent is a scarce commodity. Talent is increasingly understood as having the ability to adapt to changes and make decisions in this kind of environment, rather than simply having knowledge and functional experience, i.e. talent in terms of emotional abilities and empathic connection rather than rational intelligence. In other words, Howard Gardner's twelve intelligences (1983) gain extraordinary importance in this environment because beyond global intelligence, which used to be analysed through tests such as the IQ test, these are the skills a person must have in order to be talented, among which we would highlight emotional, collaborative, verbal, interpersonal and intrapersonal intelligence. It is therefore extremely necessary to retain scarce talent and foster its loyalty and to achieve this. From the point of view of the enterprises, attention should be paid to taking care of their people and putting them at the centre of their operations. Defining a set of key values within the company's strategy that both define the character and the corporate culture of the company, as is usually the case with family businesses, would be the basis of this way of understanding business management.

In short, in this chapter we want to demonstrate that Value-driven Management, places the Person at the center of its actions, being a necessary model for the long-term firm's survival and continued growth of the companies, especially in the case of family businesses. Therefore, it is necessary to define company values as a fundamental part of the strategy of cultural change, as an integrating axis of the human team, of people and as a way of internalizing CSR within the organization. Here, we focus on family businesses, where CSR is a key differentiating competitive element for their survival and sustained growth.

BACKGROUND: FROM CSR TO MANAGEMENT BY VALUES

CSR is a concept that was coined in the United States around the time of the late 1950s and early 1960s as a result of significant social issues such as the Vietnam War. It arrived in Europe at the end of the 1990s and was promoted among other stakeholders through associations that defended, for example, the common interests of customers in the event of possible positions of strength and unfair competition by companies. The concept appealed to the social responsibility of corporations to produce not only goods and services but to return to society part of what it had provided them. The aim was therefore for companies to commit themselves responsibly to the environment and to society, since they form a fundamental part of the ecosystem (Fawad Latif, K. *et alli*, 2020).

Indeed, CSR emerged as a trend that forced companies to reflect on identifying where they caused greater impact in order to give an active responsible answer to this impact and to incorporate CSR into the organization's structure. In deciding who was going to implement it, in most cases CSR departments were created, whilst in others it was Human Resources itself that was responsible for implementing it;

in other cases, organizations created foundations in which to cement these policies, seeking tax benefits in doing so and separating it from the core business (Chiavenato, I., 2011).

CSR in this case responded to a trend and to a response that was necessary in order to adapt to the new times and market demands. The concept is evolving due to the market's demand for transparency and commitment to society and care for the environment, culminating in a commitment of the 2030 European Agenda for Sustainable Development and its SDGs (Sustainable Development Goals), which will help organizations choose where to focus their social impact in line with their activity. Each country contributes its peculiarities and its way of understanding and applying corporate responsibility (Miniaoui, Z. *et alli*., 2020). Moreover, there is also a very important effect that shifts the whole concept, such as new forms of communication, the globalization, social networks, …, among others that have an impact on firms' reputation.

Since the publication of the United Nations' Principles of Responsible Investment (PRI-2005), the concept Environment, Social and Governance (ESG) is used to define corporate responsibility. These factors correspond to the pillars on which any company that wants to be considered socially responsible has to operate. Firstly, it has to develop an activity that respects the environment. Secondly, it must be respectful of society and the company's stakeholders. Finally, corporate governance policies must be developed that comply with legal requirements and that foster the development of the people in the organization.

These factors raise awareness in companies of the need to incorporate policies that no longer simply respond to a trend or to a behavioural aesthetic but also truly emerge through a conviction that people are the most important asset of the organization and that the way to structure their alignment with the organization is through values.

It is extremely important to incorporate people and make them participants in socially responsible policies as this is what enables the actions to be internalized and ensures that they are not just seen as an action carried out as a gesture to the outside world.

The triple verbalization of a company's management strategy, which involves defining the mission, vision and values and which has always been built exactly in this order to respond to the questions What do we do? (mission), Why do we do it? (vision) and How do we do it? (values), evolves towards a verbalization in which "values" (the non-visible part) and behaviours (the visible part) must be prioritized and therefore respond firstly to how we are going to manage things and what will identify our behaviour and attitudes.

The idea is to value the concept of corporate culture (Dolan et alli, 2014), which is enjoying a boom in strategic definition. Edgar Schein (1999) divides corporate culture into artefacts: the visible part (leadership style, behaviours, design, spaces, infrastructure, etc); assumptions (a non-visible part representing the fundamental beliefs of the organization); and values (also a non-visible part that represents a way of specifying the organization's assumptions and that gives rise to specific, discrete behaviours and management styles).

As a consequence, management by values emerged This does not refer to changing the company's mission and vision but to subjecting them to the behaviours with which we want the company to be identified (Dolan, S., 2016). It is another step in the formulation of CSR because it involves integrating it into our DNA, making employees the main actors and stakeholders of these policies.

As Fisher, C.D. (2010) says, values are a belief, a standard, a mission or a principle loaded with meaning and utility. Values are ingrained beliefs about what is right and proper. Values help both individuals and organizations to shape the way they act if they are to be valuable and useful to society. Values are many. Each company gives importance to a specific list of values. These values will define the corporate culture of the companies. When values are defined, MBV must proceed to develop strategies to implement these values both in the company policies and in the day-to-day management. This strategic way of proceeding is innate to family businesses due to the influence of the role of the founder who transmits his/her personal values to the company. Also, the influence of the values of the different generations of the family stablish the base for a MBV that is very specific of family firms.

As will be explained further on, this is the great opportunity of family businesses, since those that have survived over time and have been able to generate sustainable competitive advantages have a common denominator of intergenerational values, perhaps without being aware of it themselves.

VALUES AS THE BACKBONE OF THE STRATEGY

The profound and rapid changes generated by society today lead us to a very significant situation that is already a reality in all organizations, namely intergenerational diversity. Whereas previously three types of employees could coexist in generational terms, which we could generalize as the newly incorporated, those with an established professional life and senior professionals in the latter stages of their career, today at least four generations coexist as a result of the shortening of the stages that define people through new ways of understanding life, technology, the relationship with the community and new forms of communication (Corona, J. F., 2017). Today, baby boomers, those of generation X, millennials (or generation Y) and centennials (or generation Z) coexist in an organization. Even within these large groups, there are smaller sub-groups or communities that identify themselves according to certain social parameters and especially on the short or long treasured work experience.

In short, people management has become much more complex and requires new skills to be able to align teams towards the same common goal. The identification of a company's values and their declaration has become an extraordinary method of alignment in the pursuit of goals (Bondarouk, T. *et alli*, 2016).

Whilst it is true that the values that each of these groups prioritize are different, the important thing is that we get them to identify with those the company wants to enhance through its defined culture. It is necessary to be able to combine the different visions because where for example long-term vision prevailed before, immediacy now prevails; where stability and consolidation of success factors prevailed before, freedom and the feeling of not being tied to anything now prevail.

Is it possible for all of this to coexist with a basic concept of companies, namely the primary sense of continuity, of generating sustainable wealth, of strengthening models and generating sustainable competitive advantages? Are these basic concepts associated with the company's sense of continuity compatible with the primary values of today's generations in which everything is volatile, fast and short-lived?

Here is the real challenge of organizations and managers today and it is perfectly compatible to align a company's goals with those of each group of people working in it (Boonstra, J., 2017). The key lies in a correct identification and declaration of the values and in a powerful and firm internal communication of them. This is what we call corporate culture, which, in order to be changed, must not be left in the visible part alone —the deepest values and beliefs must be worked on.

It is true that today strategic cycles in organizations are much shorter and that this requires highly elastic, flexible and adaptable organizations (Vázquez, A., 2001). However, this is precisely the reason why companies have to have values that are strong, identified with, aligned, and communicated to all employees. This strengthens us in this process of cultural change, of the transmission of beliefs and these become the backbone of managerial success and business succession in family organizations. Values are a fundamental tool to manage today's complexities in terms of human resources and therefore depend clearly on the management of people, which becomes a key element in the strategy of organizations, unlike years and cycles where financial management prevailed, which being important and also key, is something that is still operative. People management is cross-cutting and concerns all managers and company areas (Dessler, G. 2010). Hence, the alignment and commitment of senior management is essential for the success of a strategy of values and people.

NEW VALUE-BASED LEADERSHIP

Leadership through the MBV model represents an important competitive advantage for modern organizations. As part of the community and as in any area of society, a company needs exemplars, people who mark the way, transformational leaders (Bass, B., 1985). Until recently, these people were more associated with success understood in economic terms, in financial terms. These days, the people who mark the destinations and who are established as exemplars of organizations are more associated with the values they exemplify. In other words, business leaders are identified with their behaviours and their way of managing, which lead them to success (Antonakis, J. *et alli,* 2003). And it is here that the implicit values that accompany the way a manager manages clearly emerge with full force.

It matters therefore how management is carried out. The coherence between what is said and what is done matters. Normally what is said and what is done is forgotten more often than how something is done. This is what truly impacts and therefore the current business market demands leaders capable of aligning by example. Any manager who has to manage and direct people must commit to the organization's values. There must be an alignment of interests and goals so that the manager fully identifies with the company's values. A leader cannot be an example if s/he is antagonistic to what the organization wants. Therefore, today, in the recruitment and selection processes, especially for managerial positions, both the "values" and the various "intelligences" mentioned above must be taken into account (Cheong, M. *et alli*, 2019).

As Albert Einstein said, setting an example is not the best way to influence others, it is the only way. Leadership that is exercised through the manner of directing is the strongest leadership because it leaves a mark on people without being noticed. The way this leadership is exercised is through values. The key to value-based management is the values-based behaviour adopted as a guide for action in management.

VALUES AS A COMPETITIVE ADVANTAGE IN THE FAMILY BUSINESS

When we talk about values being in the DNA of a family business, we are referring to just this —that no family business exists without values because by definition it would not be viable. For a family business, this building of the deepest sense of the organization is the surest way to stay in the market and to give meaning to what the family business does (Ruiz, C. & Álvarez, F., 2018).

When we think of family businesses, for a long time those chosen as successors were determined either by purely generational factors, the so-called firstborn, or by having accompanied previous generations in the company. In other words, that their added value was determined by the length of time they had spent within the company, that knowledge and experience of the business, which was undoubtedly a value, formed the basis of leadership in the family business. From the perspective of transformational leadership, it is not considered a sufficient basis to engender the credibility that leadership requires (Bass. B., 1985). It is the opposite of the transactional leadership that normally prevailed.

Transformational leadership starts from a culture, beliefs and values and bases its way of managing teams on charism and individualized influence, the individualized consideration of the person, the fostering of intellectual creativity and inspiration as a basic way of relating.

With the knowledge society, where knowledge is globalized and society enjoys greater access to it, fierce competition in the market exists in all sectors of activity. This obliges family businesses to include in their selection process for a successor to the company's management board the gaining of higher education and, if possible, international experience. Therefore, training is added to the business's generational or knowledge criteria.

Nowadays, what can make a family business distinct and, above all, strengthen its future continuity, is to have inspiring leaders, exemplars, who exercise their leadership through the values that identify them. These values are shared both at the family level and at the family business level (Corona, 2017), resulting in the professionalization of family business management in which managers who are part of the family coexist alongside managers who are hired based on their professionalism and the fact that they share the family business's values (Miller, D. et allí., 2013).

There are, therefore, three known family dimensions that determine business succession: power (which would be something similar to the economically strongest), experience (which is related to the person who has experienced the business and has had more contact with it), and culture (which is related to tradition and values). Thus, from here, the structure of the process of succession in the family business should focus mainly on who best embodies the spirit and values of the company (Tapies, J. 2018). It is necessary to prepare the successor in terms of the marks of company identity such as trust and ethical conduct, aspects that are key for the continuity of the organization over time.

It is necessary at this point to refer to the study conducted by Miguel Angel Gallo and Kristin Cappuyns (2004) in relation to the family business and the converging values in all family businesses that enjoy continuity and success, namely Excellence, Labour ethics, Initiative, Simplicity and Austerity.

In many organizations, and especially in family organizations, a particularly successful management model is one in which the organization's management is carried out by two people who complement each other perfectly, which could be represented by the typical structure of President + CEO, or CEO + Managing Director. On analysing best practices, it is observed that in many cases this tandem structure works because one plays the role of visionary (strategy) and the other plays the role of manager (executor). Therefore, the first focuses more on the vision and the second, on the mission; however, what provides the backbone to the management is complementarity. The sum of forces whose axis is values is the driver of the value-based management that is implemented these days in strategic management. It is impossible for this union to work if there is no common thread to the behaviour that guides these people. And that would be perfectly applicable, travelling a little further down the organization's structure, to the entire Board of Directors. Being aligned by values should be something non-negotiable, although it is still far from being achieved in current management models (Cortés. C. & Carreras, I., 2019). The influence of CSR in the management of people as a competitive advantage for family business lies in the way values shape the company's CSR.

Returning to the example of the tandem management structure and again thinking about family businesses, there are many examples in which this has been the case over the years and generations, in which there has been a natural leadership based on values, and that this has been a factor in continuity and stability (Sloof, R. & Von Siemens, F., 2019; Tapies, J., 2018). By looking back and analysing the reason for that success, we find values to be the common denominator in many of the examples of success. However, when analysing large family businesses that have maintained themselves for generations but have finally collapsed, it is usually due to two fundamental factors: either because the company did not know how to re-orientate the business in the face of market and competition threats or because the organization fell into the hands of a leader who abandoned the company's historical roots and values. The guide to the values may not have been written down on paper but it was in the company's DNA.

To exemplify this idea, we could mention the case of two renowned Spanish family businesses. The first is Inditex, a textile design company in which the entrepreneur-manager tandem has led the company to the highest positions in the business rankings. Amancio Ortega (the visionary) and Pablo Isla (the manager), who has recently been awarded the prize for best CEO of the decade by Forbes Magazine and also appears as one of the best executives in the world according to the Harvard Business Review, are the architects of the company's success. The statements made by the manager when he heard about the award were, "*the most important asset of companies are people. The key to what has been and what will come to be in the future is still people. Therefore, promoting and motivating people preserves the most valuable thing in an organization and makes it sustainable when thinking in the long term*". Moreover, he emphasized that Inditex is a "unique company" thanks to the effort and commitment of its employees. Such commitment is achieved thanks to the shared values and CSR is a way of reinforcing and building these values.

The second case is that of the insurance company Catalana Occidente, a family business that recently celebrated its 150th anniversary. Asked about the reasons for the success of his company, its President José María Serra declared that the "*character*" of the company is what has preserved its success and stability, adding that the following generations "*must be responsible shareholders*".

In short, in both cases, we are presented with statements of survival based on values that must always accompany a good market and financial business strategy. Today more than ever, family businesses enjoy continuity through the values that define them (Ruiz, C.& Álvarez, F., 2018).

This is the great competitive advantage of the family business, namely that there is an unwritten, inner current, that passes from generation to generation, that has shaped a character, a personality, a way of doing things naturally. There is no need to invent anything; it is simply a case of being able to identify, by looking inwards, what has made the company survive over the years beyond having a good product or service or good financial management (Tapies, J. & Ward, J. L., 2008).

Identifying it, declaring it, putting a value to it and communicating it is a necessary task in any strategic business management. This is the competitive challenge of family businesses. And although at a given time a company must, for market reasons, hire a director who is not from the family, this should not be a problem as long as they are clear about the company's values and incorporate managers who identify with and preserve these values.

In conclusion, values in a family business are always a facilitating factor and never a barrier, since there is a natural current of affinity among its members. This scheme of shared values in a non-family business must be built and generated. Hence the competitive advantage that the family business has when organizing its management based on values.

HOW TO BUILD A MANAGEMENT MODEL FROM VALUES

In this management process -in which we said that a governance based on values is an indispensable factor for the success and continuity of the company-, we must be able to align teams through a certain form of behaviour that should mark our entire daily operation. It is no point in doing things any old way; indeed, it is not acceptable. There are, however, certain behaviours based on ethics whose responsibility and execution is entrusted to the Compliance departments, where everything related to standards and good practices would be dealt with. This way of proceeding is more related to complying with ethical precepts that safeguard the company from any type of claim and complaint by its stakeholders. Compliance only has a mitigating test objective to alleviate potential damages resulting from any employee malpractice (Caron, F. *et alli* 2013). Ethics goes beyond, it does not reside in regulation; legally, it goes further, because it entails decisions and behaviours that will be based on the company's principles and values, which are not limited to the implementation of legislation, but which constitute voluntary decisions executed through ethical convictions associated with the principles and values of the organization (Camacho, I. *et alli*, 2013).

However, behaviours based on values go beyond what is simply required by regulation. They are associated with the will and conviction of the company to want to manage things in a certain way towards employees, suppliers, customers and stakeholders in general. In short, they concern the orientation of the company's action towards the entire universe of actors that have any type of interaction with the organization. This was reiterated by Tom Peters and Robert H. Waterman Jr. (1982) said in their best seller "In Search of Excellence" when they analysed the success of the leading U.S. companies of the time and identified "management by values" as one of the 10 success factors of companies. Therefore, we are not facing anything new. What is new and innovative is the role that values acquire in the modern, strategic management of a company.

The value model is built from a previous determination of the need for cultural change in the organization. In other words, the first step is to become aware that cultural transformation must be worked on and that this cultural change is designed by declaring the most profound principles of the organization, which are then manifested in certain values and will be translated into certain behaviours (Avolio, B. J.& Walumbwa, F.O, 2014).

Indeed, the process of building a values model must start from a premise that is no less important, namely the company's firm conviction regarding changing its way of managing and presenting itself to the market. It should never be dictated by trends nor should it be a consequence of an external project carried out by a consultant who has praised how good the business model is. None of this would make sense. Management by values refers to something that has to permeate deep into the organization and therefore implies being aware that the model needs to be changed, with values and transformational leadership placed at the centre (Schein, E., 1999).

Once a company is determined and convinced that it wants to implement this model, it must declare the values the company wants to identify with. As with goals, which should be clear, concise and measurable, with values a thorough overview exercise needs to be carried out and those values that will define the company and through which stakeholders will identify the company should be stated.

An interesting process is to carry out a historical analysis to identify a particular value that forms part of the DNA of the family business, to identify a value for which the company was founded and for which it has endured over time. On this, the family business enjoys a significant advantage because it only needs to examine the deep roots of past generations. Next, a certain value must be added that is related to the company's present form, with what the company is today. And finally, a value must be added that will project the company into the future, to how we want the company to be identified.

Bernard Bass (1985) speaks of a construction of values based on three categories: ethical-social values; emotional or personal development values; and economic-pragmatic values.

This method for building a company value framework is not unique. Those mentioned are given by way of example. However, each company is unique and therefore must build its own identifying model with certain values. The company should not, however, start from scratch. There is a past and a present that should be respected and be seen in the values that identify the company.

It is true that in declaring these values there are currents that speak of the democratization of the process, that is, that the greater the number of people involved in the process of value selection, the richer this process will be (Dolan, S. *et alli*, 2014). Undoubtedly, the diversity of opinions gives richness to the concept, but it is also true that on this point there is a significant difference between family businesses and traditional businesses. Family businesses can rely on their various generations and it makes sense to do so. Traditional companies must assign this process to senior management and always to the Board of Shareholders. It is a very important, very serious process and will mark the future of the organization and therefore it must be given its due relevance.

As when building a SWOT (Strengths, Weaknesses, Opportunities and Threats) or CAME (Correct, Adapt, Maintain, Explore) matrix, it should also be noted that in the process of defining values, it is necessary to consider how the company wants to relate to the business environment, i.e. with the competition, fostering good practices and respectful treatment; with customers, who demand from companies an honest, rigorous, transparent, cordial, close treatment and that services and products truly meet their needs; with employees, who wish to be treated with respect, dignity and to be taken into consideration; with suppliers, who want their treatment to be more similar to a cooperation; and with society, understood as an ecosystem that relates to the company in aspects such as the environment, sustainability and good practices.

An interesting diagnosis to be made, once we have defined the corporate culture, principles and values, is to carefully observe what the true situation is and what the desired situation is and detect the gap through focus groups and internal surveys. This will allow us to define a global action plan and choose the exemplary leaders, which were discussed above, who will be responsible for translating what the company wants (Galpin, T. J, 2018).

We have to analyse whether all those who hold managerial posts or positions of responsibility, especially in relation to the management of teams, represent the values that we want to transmit or at least are not antagonistic to them. If so, we need to make decisions, even if they are drastic. However, what we cannot do is keep managers who create contradiction between what we convey and what we do.

Within the Action Plan, once the values that are to be incorporated into the company's strategy have been defined, as something essential that should mark all its actions, the fundamental stage is internal communication. This is an extremely important process that must be given its due importance and be dedicated the human and time resources necessary for the message to reach all levels of the organization clearly (Velilla, R. & Valduérteles, J. 2016).

The first key link in this communication is the Board of Directors itself. From here, communication must gradually percolate down through the entire organization, ensuring that it is the managers themselves who transmit the concept, since this gives great credibility to the process.

Finally, once the values have been defined and have been incorporated into the company's strategy, and, therefore, into the company's values-mission-vision matrix, the next step is internal communication. Once the values have been communicated, the next step is a highly important phase that should allow the company to ensure that its goals are being met and that the organization is going in the desired direction guided by the values.

It is necessary to define a KPI (Key Performance Indicator) that allows us to ensure compliance with the company's values. For example, if "Quality" has been defined as a critical value, any measure that goes in this direction will make it possible to determine whether the company is on the right path or whether corrective actions must be implemented. In the management of people, if one of the guiding values is "Confidence", work environment surveys, 360-degree feedback, or a key indicator such as staff turnover can give clues as to whether the company's goal is being achieved or not (Parry E. & Tyson S., 2013).

In the monitoring phase, we must also include the management of resistance to change, which is natural in organizations, especially small and medium sized ones. Resistance to change is managed by identifying it, working on it and supporting the transmission of values with institutional events that give an image of determination and coherence and that help understanding. This aspect is especially relevant in family businesses (Muñoz-Bullon, F. *et alli*, 2018).

Today, in an environment where teleworking is becoming particularly relevant and we are moving towards a completely different model of working relationship between employer and employee, the communication of values and the sense of what we do becomes even more important. It is precisely this corporate culture that becomes the basic link for all kind of companies (Razaq *et alli*, 2019).

SOLUTIONS AND RECOMMENDATIONS: COMPETITIVE ADVANTAGES OF THE MANAGEMENT OF PEOPLE BY VALUES

Throughout this chapter we have seen the importance of management by values and of the need for organizations to incorporate it as a necessary strategic management model, given the changing market situation and the need for companies to constantly adapt to the environment. Such an adaptation can only be carried out through people.

Management by values strengthens companies, especially family businesses, and makes them more competitive. Let us now look at what specific aspects in relation to people management it generates an added benefit.

At the level of work team performance, it has been shown that management by values is a very powerful tool in terms of attracting and earning the loyalty of talent. What is referred to as the "emotional salary" has an incremental value for the employee who works in an organization that adopts the management by values model. Talent retention is a consequence of the employee feeling that s/he is at the centre of the organization, that s/he is taken into consideration and that s/he is being taken care of, and this brings with it a very strong sense of belonging (Avolio, B. J. & Gardner, W.L., 2019). The terms "engagement" and "commitment" refer to this concept, which can also be related to employee motivation. An employee who believes in what s/he does is more involved with the organization.

In addition to being an element in positive talent retention, it is also an element in talent acquisition, not only because the company's reputation in the market is increased, thereby attracting good professionals, but also because existing employees become the best brand ambassadors. With management by values, a very positive current is generated to attract good professionals to the company (Barrett, R., 2016). Many of the vacancies that are generated in companies are filled through direct references and in this regard there is no better publicity than the one company employees carry out. We also need to consider the importance of today's immediate communication channels as social media, which can be a great opportunity to promote the business brand among certain groups.

Productivity is another aspect that increases considerably with management by values. In this regard it can be said that management by values is profitable (Galpin, T., 2018). The company stops seeing people as a cost centre and starts seeing them as an investment centre. If an employee feels valued and committed to the organization, it is obvious that his/her level of performance increases. However, there is also a multiplier effect on the positive attitude. When in a team, everyone enjoys feeling important and this connection generates a significant multiplier effect.

Nowadays, working using collaborative methods is encouraged and involves professionals from different areas coming together to find solutions to certain problems (Bradford, M. & Leberman, S., 2017). The exponential capacity that can be generated by a team connected by values, by attitudes, in addition to their talent, is immense (Carrington, D. J., 2018).

The alignment of the entire company through values also generates a very beneficial effect for the company's relationship with all the company's stakeholders, especially with customers, who are the key to commercial and economic growth, and also with suppliers, whose relationship becomes a relationship of partners, with shareholders and with all social agents and people who have a relationship with the company.

We have seen the competitive advantages that a Value-driven Management generates, but we also have to pay attention to the critical voices to the model. We will try to refute these limitations with arguments we have already exposed in the chapter.

One of the criticisms is about the inability of some managers to implement such a model. It is true that this is an important change and that not all managers are capable of carrying it out, but as we said before, it must be a strategic decision of the company. It is necessary to have the appropriate and convinced managers to carry it out.

Another criticism of the model is that the personality of the individual can be annulled by the personality of the company, being this one imposed. We consider that it is not incompatible that an individual in his micro management can work with his own values, and that the company modulates its own. What is clear is that these values cannot be in contradiction with those of the company and the individual must adapt to them. This is especially relevant for family businesses. The right people must be found to lead the process according to their identification with the company's DNA. It does not seek the annulment of the individual but the alignment of interests of all members of the organization with the interests of the company. In fact it is a subject for future research.

One more criticism is that putting the focus on values can divert us from the first objective of any organization, which is profitability. We believe that profitability, in terms of financial results and reputation, will be increased with a solid Value-driven Management. It is not something dissociated from the business, as it was in some cases with the CSR, it is a strategic decision that will improve the firm position in the market, as it has been mentioned in the competitive advantages of Value-driven Management application.

Finally, there may be a lack of congruence between the values of some managers and the organization. In this case we have already commented that the company must be forceful and must have the managers to ensure the implementation of the company's model.

Consequently, the criticisms and limitations of the Value-driven Management model are true, but we think that the model must prevail over the resistances since it is demonstrated that the long-term results are better for the companies.

FUTURE RESEARCH DIRECTIONS

In relation to all of the above, one of the topics that generates the most debate among Value-based Management scholars is whether, or not, an organization can have its own values and how to align the values of people with those of the organization. Further research is needed since there are as many definitions of values as there are people.

There are those who argue that values can only be held by people and not by organizations. It is evident that, after all that has been exposed in this chapter, the organizations have them and must be able to transmit them. However, it is necessary to continue working on the formulation of these values and on how to incorporate them in the firm's strategic management.

Another trend is that the business model that we know, is evolving towards an organization by projects. In this new model, the autonomy of people is increasingly critical, in which trends such as teleworking and conciliation are imposed. This autonomy in the work organization given to the people will depend on how they are aligned with the values of the organization. The reason is that the values are manifested in the concrete empoyees' behaviours.

CONCLUSION

In conclusion, companies can internalize corporate responsibility, expressed by CSR through a cultural transformation that has its greatest exponent in management by values. MBV is a great opportunity and is a path of no return for companies, both family and non-family. The demands of the market and the uncertainty in the face of the continuous changes that shape our globalized society and economy force companies to put their focus on "people" and place them at the centre of their operations. Values are a powerful alignment tool for the goals of companies and organizations. Moreover, correct management by values increases the profitability of companies and the commitment of employees. In the case of family businesses, regardless of their size and sector, it is a necessary path for responsible succession, since values form part of the company from its foundation. Executing a transition to the next generation based on management by values entails giving the company an added value and a competitive advantage that will be demonstrated through its capacity for sustainability over time.

The process is strategic. It is based on the firm organization's determination to undertake a profound cultural transformation that will mark a change in the way every area of the enterprise is managed internally. Therefore, it is necessary to focus on a critical part of the process, which is strategic planning to face the organizational change. Resources must be dedicated to this initial stage of the integral, strategic process. MBV is a competitive advantage both for family and non-family firms. However, management by values constitutes a competitive advantage for family business due to the definition of the vision, mission and values of the company by the founder or the re-definition by successive family generations.

REFERENCES

Aguado, J. (2002). *Dirigir y motivar equipos, claves para un buen gobierno*. Madrid: Ariel.

Alexander, P. (2015). *Corporate Social Irresponsibility*. Routledge. doi:10.4324/9781315863108

Antonakis, J., Avolio, B., & Sivasubramaniam, N. (2003). Context and leadership: An examination of the nine-factor full-range leadership theory using the Multifactor leadership Questionnaire. *The Leadership Quarterly, 14*(3), 261–295. doi:10.1016/S1048-9843(03)00030-4

Avolio, B. J., & Gardner, W. L. (2005, June). Authentic leadership development: Getting to the root of positive forms of leadership. *The Leadership Quarterly, 16*(3), 315–338. doi:10.1016/j.leaqua.2005.03.001

Avolio, B. J., & Walumbwa, F. O. (2014). Authentic leadership theory, research and practice: Steps taken and steps that remain. In D. V. Day (Ed.), *Oxford library of psychology. The Oxford handbook of leadership and organizations* (pp. 331–356). Oxford University Press.

Barret, R. (2017). *The Values-Driven Organization. Cultural health and Employee Well-Being as a Pathway to Sustainable Performance*. Routledge. doi:10.9774/gleaf.9781315558530

Barrett, R. (2016). *La Organización impulsada por valores: Liderando el potencial humano para maximizar rendimiento y beneficios*. Editorial Lulucom.

Bass, B. (1985). *Transformational Leadership*. Taylor & Francis.

Bondarouk, T., Trullén, J., & Valverde, M. (2016). Conceptual and empirical discoveries in successful HRM implementation. *International Journal of Human Resource Management, 27*(8), 906-909.

Boonstra, J. (2017). Aptitudes para aconseguir un impacto en el cambio estratégico y cultural. *Harvard Deusto Business Review, 6*(267), 78–83.

Bradford, M. & Leberman, S. (2017). *Bewedo: a dynamic approach to leadership development for co-creation.* Sage.

Camacho, I., Fernández, J. L., González, R., & Miralles, J. (2013). *Ética y Responsabilidad Empresarial.* Desclée De Brouwer.

Caron, F., Vanthienen, J., & Baesens, B. (2013, February). Comprehensive rule-based compliance checking and risk management with process mining. *Decision Support Systems, 54*(3), 1357–1369. doi:10.1016/j.dss.2012.12.012

Carrington, D. J., Combe, I.A., & Mumford, M.D. (2018). Cognitive shifts within leader and follower teams: Where consensus develops in mental models during an organizational crisis. *The Leadership Quarterly, 30*(3), 335-350.

Casillas, J. C., Díaz, C., Rus, S., & Vázquez, A. (2014). *La gestión de la empresa familiar. Conceptos, casos y soluciones*. Paraninfo.

Cheong, M., Yammarino, F. J., Dionne, S. D., Spain, S. M., & Chou-Yu, T. (2019, February). A review of the effectiveness of empowering leadership. *The Leadership Quarterly, 30*(1), 34–58. doi:10.1016/j.leaqua.2018.08.005

Chiavenato, I. (2011). *Administración de recursos humanos: el capital humano de las organizaciones.* McGraw Hill.

Corona, J. F. (Coord.). (2017). Empresa familiar: análisis estratégico. Barcelona: Ed. Deusto.

Cortés, C., & Carreras, I. (2019). *La influencia de la RSE en la gestión de personas: buenas prácticas*. ESADE.

Dessler, G. (2010). *Human Resources Management*. Prentice Hall-Pearson.

Dolan, S. (2012). *Coaching por valores*. Madrid: LID Editorial empresarial, colección Acción Empresarial.

Dolan, S. (2014). *Gestión de personas y del talento*. McGraw Hill.

Dolan, S. (2016). Reflections on leadership, coaching and values: a framework for understanding the consequences of value congruence and incongruence in organizations and a call to enhance value alignment. *The Study of Organizations and Human Resource Management Quarterly*, *1*(2), 56-74.

Fawad Latif, K. (2020). Revisiting the relationship between corporate social responsibility and organizational performance: The mediating role of team outcomes. *Corporate Social Responsibility and Environmental Management*, *27*(1).

Fink, L. (2018). *BlackRock CEO Annual Letter to CEOS 2018*. Academic Press.

Fisher, C.D. (2010). Happiness at work. *International Journal of Management Reviews, 12*, 384-412.

GalloM. A.CappuynsK. (2004). *Effort, Loyalty and Idealism.* IESE Business School Working Paper No. 571. https://ssrn.com/abstract=619321 doi:10.2139srn.619321

Galpin, T. J. (2018). Realizing your strategy's potential: A seven-step model for its effective execution. *Strategy and Leadership*, *46*(6), 35–43. doi:10.1108/SL-09-2018-0088

Harmon, P. (2019). *Business Process Change*. Morgan Kaufmann Publ. Imprint Elsevier. doi:10.1016/B978-0-12-815847-0.00001-7

Lepak, D., & Gowan, M. (2019). *Human resources management*. Pearson Prentice Hall.

Miller, D., Minichilly, A., & Corbetta, G. (2013). Is Family Leadership always benefitial? *Strategic Management Journal*, *34*(5), 553–571. doi:10.1002mj.2024

Miniaoui, Z. (2020). The impact of country-level institutional differences on corporate social responsibility disclosure engagement. *Corporate Social Responsibility and Environmental Management*, *26*(6), 1307-1320.

Muñoz-Bullon, F., Maria, J., Sanchez-Bueno, M. J., & Suárez-González, I. (2018). Diversification decisions among family firms: The role of family involvement and generational stage. *Business Research Quarterly*, *2018*(21), 39–52. doi:10.1016/j.brq.2017.11.001

Norlin, L-M. (2020). *The Courage to Lead through Values: How Management by Values Supports Transformational Leadership, Culture and Success*. London: Routledge.

Parry, E., & Tyson, S. (2013). *Managing people in a contemporary context*. Routledge. doi:10.4324/9781315885872

Peters, T. & Waterman R.H. Jr (1982). *En busca de la excelencia*. Madrid: Harper bolsillo.

Razaq, R., Beck, V., & Soliman, A. (2017). Utilization of Value-based Management in the Strategic Management of German Automotive Industry. *Global Business Review*, *20*(4), 871–886.

Ruiz, C. (2016). Responsabilidad empresarial y Recursos Humanos: gestión responsable de las personas. In C. Ruiz & F. Álvarez (Eds.), *Empresa Familiar Responsable*. Huygens.

Ruiz, C., & Parra, C. (Eds.). (2013). *New Forms of Organisation in Knowledge-Based Societies*. Routledge. doi:10.4324/9780203082874

Ruiz-Viñals, C., & Álvarez-Gómez, F. (2018, August). Ownership and the Desire for Continuity Over Time, the Principal "Drivers" of the Family Business Culture en China-USA. *Business Review*, *17*(8), 419–437.

Rus, S., & Trevinyo-Rodríguez, R. N. (2011). *Redefiniendo la empresa familiar. In Empresa familiar: aspectos jurídicos y económicos*. Centro Libros PAPF.

Schein, E. (1999). *The Corporate Culture: Survival Guide*. Jossey Bass Publishers.

Sloof, R. & Von Siemens. (2019). Effective leadership and the allocation and exercise of power in organizations. *The Leadership Quarterl, 29*. Available at doi:10.1016/j.leaqua.2018.12.001

Tapies, J. (2018). *Empresa Familiar: 30 años de preguntas con respuesta*. Editorial Cátedra de Empresa Familiar.

Tàpies, J., & Ward, J. L. (Eds.). (2008). *Family Values and Value Creation: The Fostering of Enduring Values Within Family-Owned Businesses*. Palgrave Macmillan. doi:10.1057/9780230594227

United Nations. (2005). *Principles of Responsible Investment (PRI- 2005)*. Author.

Vázquez, A. (2001). *Retando al Futuro*. Editorial Díaz de Santos.

Velilla, R., & Valduérteles, J. (2016). *Claves para la comunicación interna de las empresas*. Madrid: Almon.

KEY TERMS AND DEFINITIONS

Corporate Social Responsibility: It is the set of policies that a company develops to have a responsible impact on society. Society is understood as the set of stakeholders that interact with the company: customers, employees, shareholders, suppliers, competitors, public administration, and society in general.

Culture: It is the set of rules of action that identify an organization. It is the way of showing itself internally and externally. These rules are defined to align the behaviors of its members. It is shown through tangible elements (infrastructure, spaces, behaviors) and not tangible (values and principles).

Family Firms: According to the Institute for Family Business (IEFam) a family firm is an Enterprise where the majority of the property belongs to the family and at least one member of the family participates in the business' governance.

Governance: It is the way in which the Senior Management is organized and relates to the rest of the company and to each other. Governance is one of the ways in which the Culture of the company is manifested.

Management Tool: All the resources that the organization has to achieve its objectives.

Strategy: It is the definition of a plan for a given period of time and the actions aimed at achieving it.

Value-Based Management: Management by Values is a management style based on focusing on People and placing them at the centre of our decisions. It is about aligning the behaviour of all members of the organisation: based on the principles that identify us, which brings added value and differentiation to the company.

Chapter 10
Human Resources Management Understanding and Nepotism in Family Businesses

Meral Erdirencelebi
https://orcid.org/0000-0002-7705-6067
Necmettin Erbakan University, Turkey

Mehmet Akif Cini
https://orcid.org/0000-0001-7619-978X
Selcuk University, Turkey

ABSTRACT

Family businesses have locomotive power in the economic life of countries. As a matter of fact, one of the main problems in family businesses is experienced in the management of human resources. In contrast to an institutional system in particular, favouritism on issues such as recruitment, promotion, etc. adversely affect the merit, fairness, and trust understandings of other professional internal stakeholders other than the favoured employee. The general perception of nepotism in family businesses and as stated in many studies in the literature is the favouritism of family members towards non-family professional workers. However, one issue that has not been emphasized in the literature is that the unqualified family member can also be favoured against another family member with expert knowledge. It is thought that the chapter will contribute to the literature in this regard. How a successful global family business was divided and destroyed as a result of nepotism practices has been dealt with as a case study.

INTRODUCTION

In today's intense competition environment, all functions of enterprises should serve a common purpose in order to ensure their sustainability. Elements such as speed, flexibility, innovation, low cost and teamwork are of integrated importance in intercompany competition. Starting from the R & D stage to the after-sales services, providing efficiency and productivity at every stage of a product gives the company

DOI: 10.4018/978-1-7998-4814-1.ch010

a competitive advantage. It is not possible to escape from the rapid and continuous change in the competitive environment. In fact, the only condition of being able to get away from the competitors in the intense competition is to adapt to the change. Family businesses have locomotive power in the economic life of countries. While these enterprises struggle to keep up with the changes that are mandatory for each enterprise, on the other hand, they strive to fulfil the requirements of being a "family business". False decisions taken by family members pose an obstacle to the sustainability of family businesses.

As a matter of fact, one of the main problems in family businesses is experienced in the management of human resources. It is frequently encountered in family businesses where the values and beliefs of the family system take precedence over the business values. Prioritization of the emotional dimension can cause a number of problems related to human resources management. However, in today's market conditions where there is an intense competition condition, the value added by the expert employees' presence in the enterprise and the sustainability in this environment is critically important. On the other hand, in line with the technological developments, the rise in the awareness of its internal stakeholders, like other stakeholders, increases by diversifying its expectations from the organization. At the same time, policies carried out within the organization, organizational culture, organizational climate, an institutional structure and etc. factors influence the performance of the internal stakeholder. In contrast to an institutional system in particular, favouritism on issues such as recruitment, promotion, etc. adversely affect the merit, fairness and trust understandings of other professional internal stakeholders other than the favoured employee. This situation has some negative consequences for both the professional employees and for the organization. However, the nepotism understanding and attitudes that have continued throughout the history are fed by the cultural structure of the society. Nepotism is increasingly experienced in today's business life just like in the past (Arasli, Bayik & Ekiz, 2006; Bute, 2011). The most common type of favouritism in organizational life is nepotism (relative favouritism) (Ozler, Ozler & Gumustekin, 2007). In organizations where nepotism practices (especially old nepotism) are exhibited, it is very difficult to perform human resource management (HRM) functions effectively and efficiently (Karacaoglu & Yoruk, 2012; Erdirencelebi & Erturk, 2018; Erdirencelebi, 2020).

In this context, many studies have been conducted in the literature on the effect of nepotism on human resources (Hayajenh et al., 1994; Abdalla et al., 1998; Firfiray et.al, 2018). The main purpose of this study is to determine how nepotism in family businesses affects human resources and how it triggers conflicts. In the study, real events experienced by a family business were analyzed and interpreted using the case study method. When the literature is examined, it has been determined that the effect of nepotism is generally measured by quantitative analysis and between family members and non-family employees. In this study, it is examine that nepotism can also be seen among family members, through the real experiences of the family business and it is aimed to contribute to the literature in this way.

CONCEPTUAL FRAMEWORK

1.Human Resources Management Understanding in Family Businesses

Human Resources Management is a discipline that includes policy making, planning, organizing, directing and supervising activities related to the provision, employment and development of the necessary human resources in order to provide competitive advantages in the enterprise (Saldamli, 2008).

The main purpose of Human Resources Management is to achieve corporate goals in the most efficient way. With the belief that people will play the most important role in achieving this, the human resources management has turned to human relations. Thus, human resources management focuses on business problems and human relations and tries to ensure that the business is prepared for the future and being successful. In this sense, human resources management focuses on people, deals with employee relations within a managerial structure, develops personnel policies suitable for the business culture, and thus functions as a key function in the business management (Akcadag & Ozdemir, 2005).

There is familial management in the ownership of an enterprise, important decision making bodies and the majority of the hierarchical ranks. The main feature of family management is that family members or relatives are in the upper ranks rather than owning the majority share of the business (Kocel, 2010). As a matter of fact, the businesses in which familial management style is applied are called family businesses. In addition, these enterprises have asset ratios that can affect the economies of all countries. For example, 50% of all businesses in the world, 90% of businesses operating in the US, 65-80% of enterprises in European countries and 90% of enterprises in Turkey are composed of family businesses (https://www2.deloitte.com/content/dam/Deloitte/tr/Documents/).

Family businesses can be defined as "Businesses established by one or more members of the same family to ensure economic livelihood, desired to be successfully sustained for generations, where values, beliefs and attitudes of the family are effective on business objectives and where family members are located in a significant part of the ownership and management levels" (Gules, et al., 2013).

As seen in the definition above, family businesses consist of a structure where family and business systems are intertwined. A family system is a structure where emotions and values are inherent in its nature, and the business system is a structure controlled by the logic and rules.

Their superiority that distinguishes them from other businesses is that they have an organizational culture that supports those who work for them, flexible working hours, a structure that promotes organizational work and individual responsibility. However, family businesses also have some weaknesses due to intertwined work-family relationships. Especially the intertwined relationships can lead to some conflicts. For example, saying "no" to the boss can also mean "no" to the husband or father, and this conflict of opinion among members can often be devastating (Lyman et al., 1985; cit. Karpuzoglu, 2002: 19).

There are different periods in family businesses, both in the family life and in the life evolution of the business. While family members grow up, get married, have children and die as a necessity of being human, on the other hand, four life stages can occur in business life (if it can be sustained through generations): Small businesses, Young businesses, Mature businesses and Large businesses. However, the stage of maturation in the life phase of enterprises is the breaking point, because the entrepreneur's life style is the turning point in the sustainability of the business. An entrepreneurial spirit is dominant in small businesses. Production, marketing and finance-accounting functions come into the prominence in the enterprise. The entrepreneur is the sole decision maker. For this reason, the management style, mission, vision, goals, policies, strategic plans, and organizational values in family businesses are put forward by the manager who possesses the organization culture and shapes it as he wants. Therefore, the owner-manager plays an important role in the growth of the business. In family businesses, the way family members choose to participate in the management structure directly indicates their management intent for the company (Nordqvist & Melin, 2002). In this phase where the entrepreneur is partner with his wife, the spouse is expected to be silent but supportive. In other words, the spouse generally has no function in making and implementing decisions. Being a partner at this point does not mean working together in the enterprise. In short, this partnership is mostly only on paper. As a result, even if the spouse makes a comment on issues such as production, etc., the authority and responsibility entirely belongs to the entrepreneur (Longenecker, et al., 2006). On the other hand, the central form of decision making implemented by the founder limits the entrepreneurial ideas that are tried to be put forward by the next generations they work with and consequently reduces the entrepreneurial activities of future generations (Zahra et al. 2005). It is a difficult process for the founder, who has experienced all the stages of the business and raised it as if it was his baby, to transfer his powers to professional managers and accept his changing role. As a result of the growth of the business, its founder becomes unable to respond to the need in communication with its customers, suppliers, etc. In fact, the founder has to make a choice about whether to be rich or a king here. The maturation period of the enterprise generally starts in the second generation period. The maturing enterprise should now switch from an entrepreneurial management system to a professional management. Therefore Institutionalization is of great importance.

2.Nepotism and Its Scope

Nepotism has an important place in human resources practices in many family businesses. High unemployment rates, unsuccessful education systems, distorted political structures and strong family structures cause relatives to be favoured in employment. Therefore, employees and organizations face the problem of nepotism intensely. The increasing and widespread of nepotism creates serious problems for employees and organizations and human resources management activities are mostly affected by this situation. Among human resources practices, nepotism is encountered the most often in recruitment and placement processes (Yazici & Secer, 2018).

"The concept of nepotism, derived from the word nepos (nephew), which means nephew in Latin, is expressed as relatives' favouritism in social sciences" (Ford and McLaughlin, 1986). There are biological/ecological approaches that defend as a rational behaviour, as well as studies describing nepotism, which means "kin selection" or relativity, as an instinct of human and animal nature. According to these approaches, nepotism is a "chosen" behaviour in social ecology for environmental parameters and individual needs (Masters, 1983; Erdirencelebi & Erturk, 2018).

Nepotism is "an individual's work placement of his/her own relatives in the enterprise, institution or organization to which he is affiliated by making special efforts, promoting to a higher authority, making use of certain opportunities (lodging, sending abroad for mission, etc.) or appointing him/her to a better duty (Abdalla, et al., 1998; Ozler, et al., 2007). Briefly, nepotism means "choosing a work for the man rather than choosing a man for the work" (Ozkanan & Erdem, 2014) or moving away from merit in the organization and choosing a job for an unskilled relative.

In the attitude of nepotism, there are individuals (nepos) who are recruited regardless of their ability, based on trust. In other words, nepotism is not an arbitrary and emotional behaviour, but a rational and chosen form of behaviour to survive (Gunduz, 2017). In this form of behaviour, individuals prefer those who are relatives to those who are not relatives and give priority to those with close relatives compared to distant ones. The basis of nepotism, which is the result of the preference of relatives, is the idea that the sacrifices made by people in their life struggle during their lifetime and these sacrifices are wasteful when they are made by mistake. In order to prevent wastage in people's sacrifices, they develop mechanisms that are based on blood tie separation as a source of low-cost and short-term trust (Sagir & Akilli, 2004). Starting from the family, the smallest building block of society, the circle of protection and watchfulness grows increasingly in the direction of relatives, groups, political parties, country, nation, etc. For individuals, relatives are considered to be indispensable after the family and are also important in their socialization. Consequently, due to kinship relationships, individuals communicate with each other, giving the family a social reputation and strengthening the foundation of the family position. It also aims to prevent wastage. In fact, nepotism is an innate "picture in individuals that reflects the favoured side and welfare of kinship ties" (Avci, 2017: 7). The possibility of practising nepotism is more in cultures with strong family ties. In these cultures, individuals prefer their relatives to be in key positions rather than a professional manager. The main reason for this is to prevent the wastage of sacrifice mentioned above (Bertrand & Schoar, 2006).

Abdalla, Maghrabi & Raggad (1998) explain the main social causes of nepotism as follows;

1. *Socio-Cultural Structure*: Small groups that make up the society are families, and family structures shape social values, norms and behaviours of individuals. These values and norms encourage individuals to fulfil their responsibilities towards their families and cause them to resort to nepotism.
2. *Economic Structure*: Economies based on agriculture and limited industry cause high unemployment rate. The high unemployment rate increases the competition for already limited positions. As a result of this, relatives' links play a major role in placing in limited positions.
3. *Educational Structure:* It is the education systems of countries that prepare people for the labour market. Unsuccessful education systems create imbalances in the labour markets and thus nepotism becomes effective in finding a job.
4. *Political Structure:* In general, the largest employer is the state in countries. Therefore, individuals in the state positions can appoint their relatives to key positions. For these social reasons, the tendency to nepotism is increasing and showing its effect intensely. This increased effect and intensity is mostly seen in recruitment and placement practices (Yazici & Secer, 2018).

Bellow (2003), one of the leading researchers on nepotism, deals with nepotism under two subtitles: old and modern nepotism. The main difference between the two concerns the choice of the individual who benefits from nepotism. The work experience and education of the favoured individual is accepted as the main factor that determines the formation of nepotism. In old nepotism, families find jobs for their children or employ them in their own workplaces, ignoring their qualifications. On the contrary, modern nepotism occurs when children choose to follow their parents with their own request. Modern nepotism is considered an opportunity, as children act voluntarily. In old nepotism, as family wishes and desires are at the forefront of merit, family ties are effective rather than gains and experiences of children. In modern nepotism, merit is at the forefront due to the high standards of individuals (Mulder, 2008). Modern nepotism, also called planned nepotism, is often seen in family businesses in many countries including the USA, Japan, Korea, China and Turkey. Stout (2006), on the other hand, divides nepotism practices into three as personal initiative and free will nepotism, compulsive nepotism and opportunistic nepotism. Nepotism based on personal initiative and free will occurs when the individual accepts the job offered in terms of suitability for the individual's own preferences and ideals. Compulsive nepotism, on the other hand, occurs when the beneficiary individual accepts the work as a result of being forced by a family member. So, it has the same meaning as the old concept of nepotism. The third form of nepotism, opportunistic nepotism, is the acceptance of the job offer from the family member only with the perception of obtaining the job easily and the desire to evaluate the opportunity. Opportunistic nepotism should actually be considered somewhere between free will nepotism and compulsive nepotism (Mulder, 2008).

While the norms prepared on the basis of family and kinship relations prior to the industrial revolution added value to the formation of family solidarity in rural life, there was a radical change in this structuring after the industrial revolution and a new merit-based structure has been created over time thanks to newly developed management theories (Kragh, 2012; Ozuren, 2017). However, nepotism still continues to be widely used in collective cultures (Zencirkiran & Keser, 2018).

Many of the studies on nepotism in the literature have discussed it in terms of family businesses. While the most common type of nepotism used in these businesses is family nepotism (favouring the entrepreneur's blood tie individuals) and subsequently organizational nepotism (favouring the individuals who have blood ties with the employee who still works in the organization) and political nepotism (Williams & Laker, 2010) can also be applied.

Due to the nature of family businesses, it is seen that family values take precedence over business rules. It is seen that a senior shareholder executive family member behaves in a nepotistic way on issues such as recruiting, evaluating, defining salary and promoting, etc. other family members or relatives. It is a very common situation to bring family members to key positions that require expertise, without taking merit and justice principles into consideration (Ates, 2003). The main reason for this favouritism is the lack of trust in non-family workers. In addition, employment of relatives is often encountered in the newly established small or medium-sized family businesses. New positions can be created for family members even if there is no need in the enterprise (Ilter, 2001). However, despite the increase in the number of family members, their appointment or promotion to senior management staff without having the necessary expertise brings various problems. In particular, the fact that the next generation to take over management is sure that they will be employed without the necessary knowledge and skills is a threat that will affect the sustainability of enterprises (Grote, 2003; Erdirencelebi & Erturk, 2018).

In family businesses, the entrepreneur-manager often sees one of the family members suitable for key positions, regardless of knowledge, skills and experience. This decision taken and applied negatively affects other employees (Bertrand & Schoar, 2006). Nepotism victimizes expert workers due to subjective decisions. (Arasli et al., 2006; Oren, 2007). Working at the disposal of a non-professional person causes other non-family specialists to experience discomfort. In particular, the fact that these employees have an imbalance between the contributions made to the business and the share received causes them to examine the perception of organizational justice (Bertrand & Schoar, 2006). Organizational injustice causes lack of trust. The lack of trust negatively affects job satisfaction, motivation and employee performance (Vural & Sohodol, 2004). Indeed, after a while, this causes the expert employee to quit the job. However, keeping qualified personnel in the enterprise reduces costs and provides an advantage in competition. If there is nepotism in the enterprise, the jobs are fantastic for the employee/employees who are favoured, while the opposite is for true the other employees and this poses a danger to the sustainability of the business if the problem is not solved. On the other hand, the tendency of the entrepreneur to work with relatives and friends is very common in newly established small-scale enterprises.

The general perception of nepotism in family businesses and as stated in many studies in the literature is the favouritism of family members towards non-family professional workers. However, one issue that has not been emphasized in the literature is that the unqualified family member can also be favoured against another family member with expert knowledge. It is thought that the chapter will contribute to the literature in this regard. How a successful global family business was divided and destroyed as a result of nepotism practices has been dealt with as a case study:

METHODOLOGY

In the study, a case study will be examined in order to better understand the importance of human resources within the company and the negative effects of nepotism. In this context, it is aimed to reveal the importance of human resources and the negative effects of nepotism.

The case study includes the establishment and development story of a company. In this process, the transitions between generations and all the details about the issue experienced in this process are explained in a fictional way. In the process of creating this story, the authors gathered data about the company from both primary and secondary sources. The events experienced within the scope of the case study are real. However, the characters, dates and locations were created imaginatively by the authors, as the company be remained confidential.

CASE STUDY

How Did Nepotism Separate Family Business?

The XXX family business was founded by Hackett X. in the 1900s. The company's field of activity is textiles and today it is a multinational company with an international network.

Hackett has gained a reputation for making cash payments to all the people who made production for it in the first years of its establishment and gained a social reputation in its environment. Meanwhile, he married Felicia and had a son and two daughters from this marriage. Hackett was a tough, disciplined, hard-working and very tradition-bound person. Therefore, it was not customary to include girls in the family business according to the tradition at that time and due to the possibility of including a family of different descendants when they got married, he did not include his daughters in the family business (*Does the inability of girls to be shareholders or employees in the business lead to nepotism within the business?*).

He did all the work with his only son, Arnold X. As a result, along with his father, Arnold started to work from the production section of the business and was involved in all business activities such as sales and distribution. In this context, Hackett raised his son Arnold as he wished. However, unlike his father, Arnold did not only focus on the production, but also looked for ways how to grow the company. He even realized that this small initiative should be incorporated and conveyed this to his father, Hackett. Arnold, who insistently conveyed this idea to his father, had finally what he said done and founded the "XXX Production" business. Some sources even point out Arnold X. as the principal founder of the XXX. family business. After father Hackett X. died and the company was completely under the control of his son Arnold (2nd Generation).

The second generation Arnold had a marriage with Latisha at the time and had four sons and two daughters. First, his daughter Madison, then Arnold Junior, Ramsey, Eva, Harold and Willy were born respectively. Arnold, who passed through training of his father Hackett, and who grew up in his shadow, was hardworking, disciplined, silent, tough, and very devoted to his traditions, just like his father. In this context, he was also against the working of the daughters in the family business like his father, and as a result, he did not give any duties to the girls. Arnold was even so strict and prescriptive to his children that when they wanted to buy something outside of their basic needs, they had to work and earn money. Despite having a very quiet personality, what they said was done both in the family and in the business.

He took the same attitude towards his employees, but because he was a very fair manager, he was loved by everyone. His wife, Latisha, on the contrary, had a very cheerful, talkative and friendly nature. He became the sought-after name of all social responsibility, that is, aid projects in his environment. The eldest of her children, Madison, had a shy and quiet nature. The eldest boys Andrew J. and Ramsey had a hardworking and disciplined character, just like their father, with the influence of their father. Eva number four, unlike his other siblings, took after her mother and became a very cheerful child. The last two brothers Harold and Willy, on the other hand, had a contradictory and rule-free structure that had nothing to do with the family. The fact that the ages of the last two brothers were close together caused them to grow up like twins and resemble each other in all aspects. They went to the same school, they slept in the same bed, often even shared their clothes. In this context, they were regarded as inseparable-two by the family.

Time passed, and the 2nd generation Arnold expanded the company steadily. Meanwhile, his children grew up and got married. In this context, the family business became increasingly crowded. The two oldest boys, Andrew J. and Ramsey, worked in the family business, while the youngest Harold and Willy refused to work with their father on the grounds of their opposite personality and started to work in a different company. These different personalities gave them the ability to think differently from everyone else in the business life and led them to be very successful and be loved in the company they worked for. Girls were also excluded from the enterprise for similar reasons and did not undertake any duties.

Arnold X., the second generation, the legendary founder of the XXX. Company, died in 1940s. While he was alive, he did not conduct any distribution, transfer or inheritance about the company, and thought that the law would give everyone the rightful share, and that early distribution of shares would harm the company and the family. In this context, one third of the inheritance was legally allocated to her wife and the rest to 6 children. Likewise, the company's share distribution was made as 33.33% of it to the spouse and 11.11% to each children.

Therefore, after Arnold died, the company continued its activities under the honorary presidency of his wife Latisha. The eldest sons Andrew J. and Ramsey, who were already working actively in the company, took over the business (with the approval of his wife, Latisha). The younger siblings Harold and Willy were offered to work in the family business after their father died, but the two brothers refused. At that time, they still continue to work in a different company. But instead of serving someone else for the rest of his life, Harold wanted to be the boss of his own business. That's why he is constantly on the lookout for new business ideas. He resigned from his current job to start a new business. In this context, he came to his family business, which he owned, to control the works and focused on new business ideas. The youngest brother, Willy, made it clear that he would support Harold's ideas, even if he did not leave his job.

Their mother (Latiska) is extremely uncomfortable with this situation. Latiska asked to Ramsey to protect them. Then, Ramsey started looking for new business ideas for his younger siblings. One day, while Ramsey was still busy with these thoughts, he saw an advertisement of a business called Major Textile. This business operates in the textile sector just like themselves. However, while their enterprise deals with yarn and fabric business, he learns that Major Textile deals with ready-made garment. This helped Ramsey find the business idea he was looking for. Harold and Willy cut out fort his work. Because they are both knowledgeable about the family business and successful in their commercial lives in the other company. In this way, both their companies will develop and they will fulfil their mother's request with the new brothers starting a new business. He immediately calls Harold and talks about this business idea. Harold accepts it with great enthusiasm and calls Willy. Willy immediately resigns from his job and reports that he will support Harold, whom he sees as his twin brother. With Ramsey's support, they went into ready-made garment business. Thus, the partnership structure of the new company has gradually become evident.

The new company, "XXX Textile", started its commercial life as a subsidiary company of the family-owned XXX Production business. Harold and Willy owned the two largest shares at the establishment of the company. In addition, Andrew, Ramsey and Jamie Winter (Husband of the elder sister Madison) were the financiers of the company. The company was chaired by Harold X. Harold also made strategic investment decisions. Willy, on the other hand, led the finance, human resources and product development departments. The two brothers demonstrated their business intelligence and quickly made a breakthrough in the XXX textile business. The company has invested in many different countries within only 15 years and they had their names listed among the largest businesses soon. Thanks to this success, Harold, who was the president of the company, became the new leader of the family as well.

The rapid growth of the company brought about various challenges for the enterprise which did not have a corporate structure. The first problem arose when the brothers intervened in each other's work. One started to say "no" for the thing the other said "yes" and there was an uncertainty of authority in the company. Since the two brothers grew up like twins, they tolerated everything in the early days, and these problems did not create too much conflict. However, the increase in the activities of the company caused this confusion to increase. To overcome this situation, the two brothers decided to set limits within the company and shared the markets. Although this move resolved the conflicts that emerged in the early times, it did not prevent the emergence of new problems in later times.

The growth of the company with great momentum also strengthened the company managers. However, Harold gained more power and fame than his brother Willy, because he was the president of the company. Harold was then a very successful businessman who had cost the his country and had always been a wanted and desired businessman in different social projects. However, Willy told his brother about his discomfort about this situation. Because, Willy wanted his brother to focus on the family business, he believed he was wasting time with these projects.

In fact, one of the main problems between the two was that these two brothers, who had grown as twins by sharing everything since their childhood, were not been able to get the same share in terms of gained fame and power. From now on, Harold had begun to treat Willy like a boss, rather than his twin brother *(Does unequal power between brothers create nepotism in the selection of human resources?)* On the other hand, Willy did not accept this situation and the two started to argue constantly and clash. The first serious conflict occurred at an executive board meeting on a proposal by Willy and his other brothers about the share distribution of the business. Harold reacted very harshly to this proposal. By returning to his brothers, he stated that the distribution of shares was untimely and that the people in front of him could not be trusted in business life even if he was a member of the family. Willy was shocked by his brother, Harold's words and had difficulty in understanding what he meant. He tried to say that he did not trust anybody, even if he is his brother, where he grew up and shared everything, even if he was a family member. Willy was hurt by these words even if he tried to hide it, and he realized that nothing would be in its former intimacy anymore. This event became a turning point for all the conflicts that will be experienced from then on, and the two brothers started to experience frequent conflicts. Meanwhile, in each conflict of the two, it was their brother Ramsey, who compromised between the brothers. Ramsey was a highly respected figure for both Harold and Willy, since he was the person who created the business idea. For this reason, he easily resolved all the conflicts between the two brothers.

During these developments, two brothers got married and had children. Harold had 3 girls and 2 boys; Willy had two boys and two girls. Another reason for the clashes between the two brothers originated from their children. Willy had an advantage over his brother Harold in terms of children. Willy's first children were boys, and Harold's were girls. It was a great advantage that girls were not able to work in the business, that Willy's boys were older than Harold's boys and that they were involved in the family business before. This is because it is an ideal condition for the future leader of the business to be involved in the family business before the others and to experience more. This was known by both brothers. In addition, Willy's sons, Sanford and Marty's commercial intelligence outperformed Harold's boys Marcus and Philip. Their achievements when they joined in the business already revealed the difference between nephews clearly. Marcus, one of Harold's sons, could not achieve any significant success in the business. Besides, Harold's favourite son for the leadership was his other son, Philip. However, he was also aware that Philip did not have enough talent and expertise. Willy's both two sons achieved great success since the day they had joined the family business. The eldest son, Sanford was well loved and appreciated by all in the company. However, his other son, Marty, was different from everyone else and had incredible business intelligence. Willy was also aware of his son's potential and considered his son, Marty as a new leader of the enterprise. These transfer plans, which the brothers made by themselves, were actually one of the main reasons underlying many conflicts, because both brothers saw their own son as the ideal candidate for the next leader *(In a business with an effective human resources department, is every family member hired? Does taking only gender, age or experience under consideration create nepotism in the transfer of the business to the next generation?)*

While these problems were experienced, his brother Ramsey passed away. This situation was not only a painful loss for the family but also a great loss for the family business. His absence caused conflicts to be unresolved. Now the two brothers have become almost at draggers with each other. These inseparable duos, who were lying in the same bed when they were young, and shared everything by growing up like twins, turned into individuals who do not talk to each other, and who communicate only in a standard way for things to work. Even one day, the business was going to open a new facility in a country that was under Harold's control of line. Harold did not invite his brother Willy to the opening as a result of an intentional or mistake. The brothers, who had every facility opened by the enterprise together, did not open a facility together for the first time. Although Willy was not invited, he attended the opening and watched it from afar. On the evening of that day, there was "Most Successful Businessmen Night", in which both were invited. Harold was going to receive the award as well. Willy came to the night before Harold and sat down at the table shown to him. The same table was reserved for many businessmen and of course, the brother of the award owner, Harold. After attending the night, Harold first went to the stage and received his award and then went to his desk. When he sat at the table, he greeted and chatted to all the businessmen. However, even though he was at the same table, he did not even greet his brother Willy. This was the biggest proof that an irreversible path was entered between the two brothers. The conflict will be tough and harder *(Do lack of communication, nepotism and conflicts affect each other?)*

Willy was more emotional than Harold, and his resentment to his brother made him very upset. Therefore, he has always been in a search to solve about this impasse of the family business and be on the outs with his brother. He asked a eminent Proffessor Watson to prepare a report for professional assistance. Professor Watson's report advised the establishment of an independent board and the management of the works by this board would play a critical role for the future of the enterprise. However, Harold rejected this report, irrespective of whether it was right or not, and presented an opposing view with a new move. According to him, the board of directors should be composed of family members rather than independent members; his own family should be represented by two shares and his older brother, Andrew J. and Ramsey's families by one share. This idea clearly expressed the removal of his brother Willy from the board. In this way, Willy realized that his efforts would be of no use *(Could the views of an effective human resources management and independent board member be more effective than the views of a foreign consultant to the business?)*

As the time went by, work for the future new leader of the business began and the candidates were clearly announced. Willy stated that his son Marty should be the future leader of the company, because of the success he achieved. Marty's success was noticed by his uncle Harold, who saw him as a great danger. Harold stated that his son Philip should be the new leader, but he knew he did not have much luck against Marty. Therefore, he was aware of the need to develop a new strategy. It should be such a strategy that the move should be easily accepted by the whole family, and it should stop the biggest threat, Marty. The new strategy was called Alexander, the son his brother Andrew J's. Harold appointed Alexander, as a head of the department, to the market that his brother Willy controls and his son Marty worked. With this move, Harold blocked Marty's front and also got the approval of the family easily as being the son of his eldest brother. Alexander had worked in companies other than the family business, but was not very talented and successful. His appointment, despite his shortcomings, made both Willy and his son Marty very angry. Willy didn't react even though he was angry with this decision. However, his son Marty could not accept this situation and requested an appointment with his uncle Harold. Uncle-nephew interview went very controversial. Marty made it clear to her uncle what his potential was and how he couldn't get the tasks he deserved. His uncle did not even consider his nephew's reproaches, but he started to think he was even more dangerous than he had hoped. Willy changed Marty's department to protect his son from a further damage. However, in order to make Marty even more unsuccessful, his uncle endeavoured at the expense of damaging the company and he even succeeded in it. In response, n response, Willy transferred his powers to his son, but Harold, the chairman of the board, cancelled this decision the next day. These two game of thrones of the family business began to cause great losses, and therefore business management and family council had to warn these two.

The net decision of the management and the council was that the two should solve these problems within a year or both brothers would be removed from the board of directors.

The first move came from Willy. He presented two ideas. The first one was the geographical division of the company. This idea was immediately rejected by the family business management, because this would cause a great loss of power and prestige. The second idea was the purchase of shares. He contacted other family members with shares in the management and asked them to sell their shares to him. However, this move was prevented by Harold. There was nothing Willy could do anymore. After some time, Harold passed the plan of his choice from the board of directors and formed the family business board of directors as he wished (two shares to his own family and one share to his brothers' families). This meant that Willy and his entire family were to be removed from the board of directors and all positions they held. Harold got what he wanted and got his brother Willy fired from the family business. In the process, Willy never had the feeling that things would go worse, of being upset with his brother Harold or firing him from the business. In fact, he was always the side that wanted to make peace. However, he was not successful in it. Under these circumstances, in order not to further the problem, he transferred all his shares to the enterprise and he had no connection with XXX Textile any longer.

After leaving the family business, Willy founded a new company. He brought his son, Marty, who he trusted with his talents to the head of the company. This trust was not wasted and Marty showed that he was a very successful businessman, placing the family business among the leading his country's business. Both companies still continue their activities successfully.

CONCLUSION AND RECOMMENDATIONS

Family businesses play an important role in the development and prosperity of countries' economies, considering their asset rates. For this reason, the survival of family businesses is critical for both countries' economies and the families that own the business. However, it is also a known fact that these enterprises have a lot of problems when they are handed down from generation to generation and the number of companies that can be transferred falls very low. When the literature is analyzed, many issues related to the problems faced by family businesses and the reasons for the decrease in the ratio has been handled in this process. In this section, the nepotism problem (Abdalla et al, 1998), which has a great importance on human resources and human resources functions and policies in family businesses, is discussed.

Nepotism, according to many studies conducted in the literature, harms the sustainability, performance of family businesses, and sense of trust and justice, mutual harmony of family and business systems. It also leads to competition among family members for the transfer of the management, resulting in conflicts (Ichniowski, T. 1988; Bennedsen et al. 2007; Cucculelli & Micucci, 2008). However, many of these studies express nepotism as a triumph of blood tie against merit, and this situation creates a false perception that the concept takes place only in the process between the family members and non-family members. In fact, nepotism describes the favouritism between the merit and non-merit. In other words, as stated in our case study, nepotism practices can be seen among the people who are connected by blood (members of the same family). In order to better identify the practices of nepotism, readers were asked various questions in the text. Through the answers to these questions, it is aimed to reveal nepotism and the effect of human resources in the case study.

Does the inability of girls to be shareholders or employees in the business lead to nepotism within the business?

Gender-based discrimination is in itself an example of nepotism. In this story, the founder Hackett X did not include girls in their business. This situation has been maintained by the 2nd and 3rd generations as a corporate culture. However, without such a culture, Harold, who is in the 3rd generation, would have been able to put a more talented daughter in charge of the job instead of the incompetent boys, and there would be no separation with these conflicts between siblings. Therefore, the gender-based nepotism in this story was instrumental in the breakup of the company. In this context, it is very important to establish an effective human resources department in a company and to ensure merit-based recruitment and promotion, in order to prevent nepotism.

Does unequal power between brothers create nepotism in the selection of human resources?

Power inequality between siblings had been had an impact on decisions to be made within the business. Harold, who was much stronger within the company, had been started treating his brother and partner Willy like his boss after a while. For example, he had hired Alexander, son of his brother Andrew J. to one of the companies for which Willy was responsible, without consulting him, and had appointed him as a chairman above his son Marty. As mentioned in the story, actually it was Marty's right to be promoted to that position. However, this was a deliberate move by Harold. Because Harold had wanted the company to be headed by either one of his own boys or Alexander, whom he can more easily control. According to him, Marty was dangerous in terms of his and his family's presence in the company. Consequence, Harold's this behaviors, aiming for Marty to fail, are an examples of a nepotism practises.

In a business with an effective human resources department, is every family member hired? Does taking only gender, age or experience under consideration create nepotism in the transfer of the business to the next generation?

Recruitments in a business should be based on merit. Human resources play an important role in this process. In this story, girls had subjected to gender-based nepotism and were not accepted for a job in her family business. Boys, on the other hand, were hired on the basis of blood ties, regardless of merit. In addition, depending on the age and age of the boys, the fact that they worked much more in the business had been determined as the most important criteria for being a leader. Recruitments, promotions and leader elections in businesses should not be selected based on gender, age or experience, and nepotism related to them should be avoided.

Do power, lack of communication, nepotism and conflicts affect each other?

Harold, who is stronger than his brother Willy, had triggered nepotism by trying to put his own children or someone he could more easily control to maintain this power. Willy believed that his own son Marty should get this promotion. For this reason, a conflict started between the two brothers. In this process, the communication between the two brothers had been completely broken and the conflict could not be resolved. In this context, power, lack of communication, nepotism and conflicts are like a spiral. They all trigger each other.

Could the views of an effective human resources management and independent board member be more effective than the views of a foreign consultant to the business?

Proffessor Watson, who had been invited to the business to solve the problems, was disregarded by Harold because of his lack of objective. Because Proffessor Watson had been invited to the business by Willy, and Harold had believed this person would not write a fair report. If this business had created an efficient human resources department and hired an independent board member, their views could have been much more influential in this process.

Consequently, the person who was supposed to be the leader of the XXX family business should had been Willy's son, Marty according to his talents and his success in the business. But Harold wanted one of his own sons to be the leader although he knew that they did not deserve, and made various attempts to prevent his nephew Marty. Moreover, in order to make his nephew unsuccessful and damage his career, he even damaged the business. As a result, the brothers Harold and Willy, who grew up like twin brothers, left in a feuding manner. In addition, the XXX family business lost Marty, who was very talented and perhaps capable of bringing the XXX business to much better places, as a result of nepotism.

In this context, various recommendations can be given to businesses on this issue. Firstly, it is essential to adopt meritocracy management approach and establish a merit-based system for human resources management in family businesses. No privilege should be given to gender, age, seniority or blood ties in recruitment, promotion, reward, penalty and transfer of business management. In addition, instead of "Protective Family" structures where communication is low and nepotism applications can be applied easily, "Plurulastic Family" structures where communication is high and nepotism applications are less common should be created (Rueter & Koerner, 2008:717; Koerner & Fitzpatrick, 2002: 44; Koerner & Schrodt, 2014:8). In general, while family elders want to establish a protective structure in family businesses, they want to establish a sub-generation pluralistic structure. This difference in understanding between the two generations, may lead to loss of motivation, poor performance, differentiation of goals, and family member leaving the business (Çini, 2020:223). As a result, effective management of human resources prevents nepotism. Preventing nepotism eliminates various conflicts within the company. Experiencing fewer conflicts positive affects the sustainability and profitability of businesses.

REFERENCES

Abdalla, H. F., Maghrabi, A. S., & Raggad, B. G. (1998). Assessing the perceptions of human resource managers toward nepotism: A cross-cultural study. *International Journal of Manpower*, *19*(8), 554–570. doi:10.1108/01437729810242235

Akcadag, S. & Özdemir, E. (2005). İnsan kaynakları kapsamında 4 ve 5 yıldızlı otel işletmelerinde iş tatmini: İstanbul'da yapılan ampirik bir çalışma. *Kocaeli Üniversitesi Sosyal Bilimler Dergisi*, (10), 193-167.

Arasli, H., Bavik, A., & Ekiz, E. H. (2006). The effects of nepotism on human resource management, the case of three, four and five star hotels in northern cyprus. *The International Journal of Sociology and Social Policy*, *26*(7/8), 295–308. doi:10.1108/01443330610680399

Ates, Ö. (2003). *Aile Şirketlerinde Değişim ve Süreklilik Anlayışı*. Ankara Üniversitesi, Sosyal Bilimler Enstitüsü, Doktora Tezi.

Avci, A. (2017). *Şirketlerde nepotizm uygulamasının çalışanların iş tatmini ve tükenmişlik düzeylerine etkisi*. İstanbul Sabahattin Zaim Üniversitesi, Sosyal Bilimler Enstitüsü, Yüksek Lisans Tezi.

Bertrand, M., & Schoar, A. (2006). The role of family in family firms. *The Journal of Economic Perspectives*, *20*(2), 73–96. doi:10.1257/jep.20.2.73

Bute, M. (2011). Kayırmacılığın çalışan davranışları ve insan kaynakları yönetimi uygulamaları üzerine etkileri: Türk kamu bankalarına yönelik bir araştırma. *Amme Idaresi Dergisi*, *44*(1), 135–153.

Cini, M. A. (2020). The effects of family communication patterns on family satisfaction in family business. B. Christiansen (Edt.). In *Global Applications of Multigenerational Management and Leadership in the Transcultural Era* (pp. 196–230). IGI Global. doi:10.4018/978-1-5225-9906-7.ch007

Cucculelli, M., & Micucci, G. (2008). Family succession and firm performance: Evidence from Italian family firms. *Journal of Corporate Finance*, *14*(1), 17–31. doi:10.1016/j.jcorpfin.2007.11.001

Erdirencelebi, M. (2020). Nepotism. Farklı Boyutlarıyla Örgütsel Davranış. Üyesi Mehtap Öztürk, 1th baskı Ankara: Gazi Kitapevi.

Erdirencelebi, M., & Erturk, E. (2018). Türkiye'de nepotizm konusunda hazırlanan çalışmalara yönelik bir inceleme. *Osmaniye Korkut Ata Üniversitesi İktisadi ve İdari Bilimler Fakültesi İşletme Bölümü, 18th International Business Congress*, 2344-2359.

Firfiraya, S., Cruz, C., Neacsu, I., & Gomez-Mejia, L. R. (2018). Is nepotism so bad for family firms? A socioemotional wealth approach. *Human Resource Management Review*, *28*(1), 83–97. doi:10.1016/j.hrmr.2017.05.008

Grote, J. (2003). Conflicting generations: A new theory of family business rivalry. *Family Business Review*, *16*(2), 113–124. doi:10.1111/j.1741-6248.2003.00113.x

Gules, H. K., Arıcıoglu, M. A., & Erdirencelebi, M. (2013). *Aile İşletmeleri Kurumsallaşma Sürdürülebilirlik ve Uyum*. Gazi Kitapevi.

Gunduz, S. (2017). *İş Yerinde Yaşanan Sendromlar*. Beta Yayıncılık.

Guney, S. (2004). *Açıklamalı Yönetim-Organizasyon ve Örgütsel Davranış Terimler Sözlüğü*. Siyasal Kitabevi.

Ilter, H. M. (2001). Aile Şirketlerinde Kurumsallaşma ve KOBİ'lerin Yönetim Sorunları. İstanbul Ticaret ve Sanayi Odası Yayın No:2001-19, İstanbul.

Karacaoglu, K., & Yoruk, D. (2012). Çalışanların nepotizm ve örgütsel adalet algılamaları: Orta Anadolu bölgesinde bir aile işletmesi uygulaması. *İş-Güç. Endüstri İlişkileri ve İnsan Kaynakları Dergisi*, *14*(3), 43–64.

Karpuzoglu, E. (2002). İşletmenizi sürekli kılmak için: süreklilik planı ve varis planı. *Peryon Dergisi*, 18-19.

Kocel, T. (2010). *İşletme Yöneticiliği. 12th baskı*. Beta Yayıncılık.

Koerner, A. F., & Schrodt, P. (2014). An introduction to the special issue on family communication patterns theory. *Journal of Family Communication*, *14*(1), 1–15. doi:10.1080/15267431.2013.857328

Korner, A. F., & Fitzpatrick, M. A. (2006). Toward a theory of family communication. *Communication Theory*, *12*(1), 70–91. doi:10.1111/j.1468-2885.2002.tb00260.x

Longenecker, J. G., Moore, C. W., Petty, J. W., & Palich, L. E. (2006). Small Business Management: An Entrepeneurial Emphasis (13th ed.). Academic Press.

Masters, R. D. (1983). The biological nature of the state. *World Politics*, *35*(2), 161–193. doi:10.2307/2010269

Mulder, B. K. (2008). *Risking the business or reaping the benefits: the antecedents and consequences of nepotism*. Ph. D. DePaul University.

Nordqvist, M., & Melin, L. (2002). The dynamics of family firms, an institutional perspective on corporate governance and strategic change. Routledge.

Ören, K. (2007). Sosyal sermayede güven unsuru ve işgücü performansına etkisi. *Kamu-İş*, *9*(1), 71–90.

Ozkanan, A., & Erdem, R. (2014). Yönetimde kayırmacı uygulamalar: Kavramsal bir çerçeve. *Süleyman Demirel Üniversitesi Sosyal Bilimler Enstitüsü Dergisi*, *20*, 179–206.

Ozler, H., Ozler, D. E., & Gumustekin, G. E. (2007). Aile işletmelerinde nepotizmin gelişim evreleri ve kurumsallaşma. *Selçuk Üniversitesi Sosyal Bililer Enstitüsü Dergisi*, *17*, 437–450.

Ozuren, Ü. (2017). *Tekstil işletmelerinde nepotizm uygulamalarına bağlı olarak üretkenlik karşıtı davranışlar ve sonuçları*. İstanbul Kültür Üniversitesi, Sosyal Bilimler Enstitüsü, Yüksek Lisans Tezi.

Rueter, M. A., & Koerner, A. F. (2008). The effect of family communication patterns on adopted adolescent adjustment. *Journal of Marriage and the Family*, *70*(3), 715–727. doi:10.1111/j.1741-3737.2008.00516.x PMID:19649145

Sagır, M. Ö., & Akıllı, H. S. (2004). Etnisite kuramları ve eleştirisi. *C.Ü. Sosyal Bilimler Dergisi. Mayıs*, *28*(1), 1–22.

Vural, B. A., & Sohodol, Ç. (2004), Aile Şirketlerinde Kurumsal Kültür: Avantajlar-Dezavantajlar ve Öneriler Üzerine Bir Çalışma. 1. Aile İşletmeleri Kongresi Bildiri Kitabı. İstanbul Kültür Üniversitesi İktisadi ve İdari Bilimler Fakültesi.

Williams, M. L., & Laker, D. (2010). Nepotism: can it affect the bottom line? *Northeastern Association of Business, Economics, and Technology Proceedings,* 230-236.

Yazici, M. O., & Secer, B. (2018). İşe alma ve yerleştirmede nepotism. *Iş, Güç. Endüstri İlişkileri ve İnsan Kaynakları Dergisi*, *20*(4), 117–134.

Zahra, S. A. (2005). Entrepreneurial risk taking in family firms. *Family Business Review*, *18*(1), 23–40. doi:10.1111/j.1741-6248.2005.00028.x

Zencirkıran, M., & Keser, A. (2018). Örgütsel Davranış. Dora Basım-Yayın.

KEY TERMS AND DEFINITIONS

Conflict: Dispute, disagreement between persons or groups for various reasons.

Conflict Management: Managing the process in order to reconcile existing conflicts and turn negative conflicts into functional conflicts.

Family Businesses: Businesses on which the family values of individuals from the same family have an impact and all or most of the ownership and management are in the family members.

Institutionalization: The unification of the enterprise around the corporate culture shared by everyone and having common rules, principles and standards, and having a corporate identity that distinguishes it from other enterprises.

Nepotism: Employment of individuals in favor of nepotism, regardless of merit, based on kinship.

Professional Manager: Person who has a managerial talent and has acquired a profession by training in this job; who is a salary employee, assumes the management responsibility of the enterprise at the risk of profit and loss for someone else and tries to achieve organizational objectives.

Chapter 11
Entrepreneurial Intention in Family Business

Ivona Mileva
University American College, Skopje, Macedonia

Marjan Bojadjiev
University American College, Skopje, Macedonia

Miodraga Stefanovska-Petkovska
University American College, Skopje, Macedonia

Ana Tomovska Misoska
https://orcid.org/0000-0003-2018-1606
University American College, Skopje, Macedonia

ABSTRACT

The goal of the chapter is to provide a comprehensive understanding of the entrepreneurial intentions in family businesses. Furthermore, the chapter will provide and assess how the role of prior family business background has influence on entrepreneurial intention. The chapter will provide introduction of the term entrepreneurship, entrepreneurial intentions, and the family significant impact on entrepreneurial intentions, and it is important because it studies the effect of the entrepreneurial family background on entrepreneurial intentions in family firms. The chapter will provide the reader with an increased understanding of whether the role of parents has influence over the entrepreneurial intentions of their offspring. The reader will be introduced to the up-to-date scientific research in the area of entrepreneurial intentions in family firms.

1. INTRODUCTION

As a drivers for creating economic growth worldwide, the family business gain significant interest in the last years. They compromise 70%-80% of the economy where 40%-50% of the employment are accounted (Mandl,2008). Since they are an important factor in the economy studying the dynamics of the

DOI: 10.4018/978-1-7998-4814-1.ch011

human relations and the impact this experience has on the individual members and especially on the second generation is of paramount importance. Despite its importance a meta-analysis of literature has shown that studying the link between entrepreneurship and family firms has begun relatively recently (López-Fernández, Serrano-Bedia and Pérez-Pérez, 2015). The family as a social system has an important role on decisions of family individuals and this social environment is a significant factor when a person decides whether to start a business. It is more likely for a person to choose an entrepreneurial career if he/she belongs to entrepreneurial family. Moreover, the family background does not only affect the career decision only, but has role in the early stages of the business (Klyver, 2007). Therefore, the family role is fundamental in creating entrepreneurial intentions through influencing desirability and feasibility of entrepreneurial endeavors (Shapero and Sokol, 1982). The socialization aspect impacts the individual feelings toward an entrepreneurship as well; children develop entrepreneurial perceptions as they are "feeling" the entrepreneurial spirit within the family (Chrisman, Chua and Sterier, 2003). Studies show that having an entrepreneurial parent increases the probability that a child will become entrepreneur for 30%-200% (Andersson and Hammarstedt 2010).

According to Mangundjaya (2012), it is not easy to develop an entrepreneur, and in this regard, the parent's contribution should be boosted. To support this, Ayuni (2018), recommends entrepreneurial families to give unconditional support to their children, since starting a business or deciding to become a successor in a family owned business is something that is planned (Sharma, et al., 2003; Thompson, 2009). Therefore, this paper uses Theory of Planned Behavior to understand the entrepreneurship and succession intentions of students with special accent of students who have self-employed parents or parents involved in a family business.

In addition certain authors have found that preferences to become a successor in the family business, starting an own business as an entrepreneur or becoming an employee varies by country background (Zellweger, et al., 2011). This topic is even more important in countries like the Republic of North Macedonia that are still transitional economies and are still struggling to boost economic activity of the population. Family businesses in such countries are shown to be younger. Therefore, they have not faced generational transition yet. This means that most of the business are still operated by the founder and his/her marriage partner, although his/her offspring are possible business successors (Mandl, 2008). Therefore understanding the impact of living in a family with a family business on the intentions of the students to own their own business of become a successor of a family business is quite important.

Having this in mind, the aim of this paper is to provide an understanding of the entrepreneurial intentions and succession intentions of students in the country. It tries to differentiate between students with and without experience in family business when it comes to entrepreneurial intentions and to see what are the differences in succession intentions of the students with and without personal experience in the family business. The paper will look at different factors related to the entrepreneurial and succession intentions of students to try to offer practical advice on how they can be stimulated and boosted. The paper will start by outlining the concept of family firms and their importance in the country, then move to looking at entrepreneurial intentions and succession intentions and factors that affect them by drawing upon the Theory of Planned Behavior. This will be followed by the explanation of the methodology and the results and the chapter will end with recommendations for the future.

2. THEORETICAL BACKGROUND

2.1. SME's, Family Firms and Transitional Economies

Small and medium sized enterprises (SMEs) are enormously significant to the economy of any country because they play a vital role in the development of one country (Savlovschi and Robu, 2011). SMEs are seen as a major source of employment therefore contributor to economic growth and development (Savlovschi and Robu,2011). For this reason, SMEs in developing countries are described as a center of economic activities (Aga, Francis, and Rodríguez-Meza, 2015). However, Sorasalmi and Tuovinen (2016) state that in comparison with developed countries, developing countries are also facing pool of issues such as financing, fragile structures, low capabilities, lack of know-how from technological aspect and issues with capital.

In Eastern countries, the era of entrepreneurship and family business development started once the private enterprises become banned. However, due to the closed economies that Yugoslavian countries had at that time, the family businesses were mainly based on crafting and agriculture. Later, with the changes in political and social terms, the Yugoslavian countries started to promote open economies, which lead to increased and developed private ownership. This results in increased attractiveness and interest for family businesses in the developing countries (Debarliev and Janeska-Iliev,2015).

As a key driver of the economic growth, there are 54.026 SMEs in the Republic of North Macedonia representing 99.7% where 273.811 or 74.4% of the population is employed, representing nearly three quarters of all jobs. However, in 2015, SME productivity was only around EUR 8.800 per person, or no less than 80% below the EU average. In addition, as a candidate country for EU membership, the country is continuously taking measures, creating policies and strategies for supporting the development of the SMEs. This is due to the requirement of the Small Business Act by European Commission, according which the economic policies of each country should encourage and stimulate entrepreneurship and eliminate the problems in development of SMEs (Commission of the European Communities, 2008).

The performance of the Republic of North Macedonia on entrepreneurship seems to be within the EU average. According to the analysis of the European Commission (2017), this positive trend can be interpreted due to lack of other opportunities, which is supported by the bellow average score on successful entrepreneurship. In other words, people become entrepreneurs due to lack of availability of other career options in the country. The country is trying to stimulate innovation and entrepreneurship within the Program for competitiveness, innovation and entrepreneurship of the Republic of North Macedonia by stimulating innovation from within, supporting investment and supporting professional development of SMEs (Economic Reform Report, 2019).

It has to be noted that the traditional SMEs have fewer propensities to invest in innovation in comparison with the family SMEs and tend to be more risk averse and conservative (DeDee and Vorhies, 1998). In addition, family SMEs have a tendency to outperform traditional SMEs regarding process innovation outcomes while controlling the venture development (Carree, Van Gils and Peters, 2014).

From an academic perspective, there are twenty-one different definitions regarding the concept of family businesses (Sharma et al., 1996). The definitions look at the following concepts: ownership, family involvement, generation transition as well as combination of these dimensions (Handler, 1989). According to Ward (1987), family businesses are considered to be businesses that will be transferred to the next family generation. Intihar and Pollac (2012), define a family business as a business in which the ownership and management is held by the family. They explain family involvement in the business as “a substantial family presence in ownership, governance, management, succession, and/or employment” (p.77). Punder (2015) defines the family firm as firm where the family uses enough capital to be able to control the strategy and engage in top management positions. Nevertheless, the most common understanding for family business is the company where the relations of one family have strong influence over the business operations.

The performance of the family businesses is different in different countries. Transition countries are characterized with weak institutions, friable business environments; complex economic and social issues for instance unemployment, poverty, low income per capital, and unstable economic growth (DeDee and Vorhies, 1998). Trying to escape these issues, the business activities are focused on maximizing opportunities in different locations (Deng, Hofman and Newman, 2013).This is a key point for family businesses in transition countries, where there is a large scale of uncertainty and crisis in social, political and economic perspective. Nevertheless, different studies show that in transition countries, the number of family businesses is promptly increasing (Poutziouris et al. 1996; Duh 2003; Dyer, Panicheva Mortensen, 2005). Therefore it is important to study the influence that such activities have on the offspring and whether this family business experience stimulates their entrepreneurial and succession intentions.

2.2. Theory of Planned Behavior and Intentions

Intentions are known to predict behavior in a long-run, thus cancelling variation in actual behavior over time and they can be seen as better predictors of entrepreneurial or succession plans than attitudes, beliefs, personality or demographics (Linan and Chen, 2009; Tkachev and Kolvereid, 1999). The intentions are especially useful when it comes to predicting the career choices of students (Krueger, et.al., 2000; Veciana, et.al., 2005; Wenjun, et.al., 2011) as they show stability even over a period of time as long as 5 years (Sieger, Fueglistaller and Zellweger, 2011).

In order to enhance the understanding of entrepreneurial intentions most authors use two models: the Model of Entrepreneurial Event (Shapero and Sokol, 1982) and Theory of Planned Behaviour (TBP) (Ajzen, 1991). Shapero’s model is specific to the field of entrepreneurship and is based on the premise that the intentions to become entrepreneur are derived from perceptions of desirability and feasibility and propensity to act upon opportunities. On the other hand the TPB is founded on theoretical developments in psychology and is applied in a number of other fields which makes the theory more robust (Krueger et.al., 2000). The TPB proposes that behavior is based on intentions which are in turn result of three determinants: attitude towards behavior, subjective norm and perceived behavioral control (Ajzen, 1991).

According to the TPB (Ajzen, 1991; 2012) intentions capture the motivational aspect of behaviour and are dependent on three different beliefs: beliefs about the likely consequences of the behavior (behavioral beliefs), beliefs about the normative expectations of other people (normative beliefs) and beliefs about presence of factors that might hinder behavior (control beliefs) (Ajzen, 2012). Behavioral beliefs results in Perceived Behavioral Control (PBC) which means the extent to which people think that they will be successful in performing a certain behavior if they want to do so and this is closely related to self-efficacy and also perceived controllability of behavior (Ajzen, 2012). The normative beliefs result in Subjective Norm (SN) which means the perceived social pressure to perform a particular behavior (Ajzen, 1991). The control beliefs result in Attitude towards Behavior which means the attractiveness of the outcomes of certain behavior (Ajzen, 2012).

2.3. Entrepreneurial Intentions and Experience with Family Business

Entrepreneurship is "enjoying" its momentum that is spreading more and more in this dynamic world. It is an "hot" topic and an attractive concept for the policy practice and development in all domains of politics, education and business (Ball,2005). Entreprenurship can be seen as a process of discovery (Stevenson, 1983) and activity that is vital factor in creating employment, thus increasing the productivity of country's economy (Junaid et al.2015). Additionally, entrepreneurship is playing a vital role not only in production, but also in supporting social capital and technological progress and innovation (Dabic and Pietrzykowski, 2011) thus acting as promoter of economic development (Ćoćkalo,Đorđević, Bogetić, Sajfert and Minovski 2013; Shneor, Jenssen and Vissak, 2016; Singh and Singh, 2014).

Many authors explain that being an entrepreneur is a planned behavior and that the intentions are the best predictors (Mboko, 2011). Therefore, when deciding to start new ventures (Krueger et al. 2000, Linan et al. 2011), entrepreneurial intentions are considered to be drivers of one's behavior towards it (Kautonen et all. 2013, Linan and Chen, 2009). People who show high intentions toward entrepreneurial activity are more likely to start a business, unlike those with lower intentions (Thompson, 2009).

Looking at the ATB aspect of the Theory of Planned Behavior positive attitudes toward entrepreneurship will lead to better entrepreneurial intention. In other words, attitude is a strong predictor of entrepreneurial intention (Almobaireek and Manolova, 2012; Liñán and Chen, 2009).

Subjective norm includes two components: normative beliefs, which are related with the influential others, will approve or not the start-up behavior and motivation to comply, which is related to the individual wish to follow such norms (Ajzen, 1991). Many studies show that subjective norms are the least or even insignificant predictor of entrepreneurial intention (Almobaireek and Manolova, 2012; Krueger et al., 2000; Liñán and Chen, 2009). However, according to Zellweger et al. (2011), the family has a central role regarding the career intentions of the offspring. Therefore, the experiences which are related with the family are main factor in "creating" intentions (Chua, Chrisman and Sharma,1999).

In addition, the PBC, which controls beliefs that are linked with the presence or absence of the resources and opportunities, is considered to be influential determinant of entrepreneurial intention (Veciana et al., 2005, Almobaireek and Manolova, 2012).

IN the factors being studied, one of the most prominent predictor is the family environment. Whether a person will choose to follow a career as an entrepreneur seems to affect the formation of entrepreneurial intention (Ajzen, 2001; Solesvik et al., 2012; Liñán and Chen, 2006). The transmission of entrepreneurship from parents to children was a subject of interest for centuries. It is believed that the entrepreneurial career intentions and behaviors are transmitted across generations (Laspita, Breugst, Heblich and Patzelt 2012). A recent study found that students with self-employed parents, especially if both parents are self-employed have higher entrepreneurial intentions (Sieger, et al., 2019). Other studies show that having an experience in a family-owned business is beneficial for success in a start-up company (Fairlie and Robb, 2004).Some authors explained the transmission of entrepreneurial behavior from parents to offspring through genetic inheritance (Uitterlinden and Hofman 2010). There is a possibility that the parents boost their offspring's entrepreneurial intentions by providing human, social, and financial capital (Edelman, et al., 2016; Dunn and Holtz-Eakin 2000). On the other hand, parents are considered to be role models of their children whose knowledge, values and entrepreneurial skills is acquired by them (Wyrwich 2015; Junge and Malchow-Møller 2015; Sahinidis et al., 2019). Positive role models have been found to influence the entrepreneurial intentions when combined with positive attitude (ATB) and perceived self-efficacy (PBC) (Nowinski and Haddoud, 2019). Certain authors emphasize that parents who have experience in family business provide more supportive environment for the children to start their own ventures and trust them more when it comes to running a business (Jiang et al., 2017). Certain studies have shown that experience in family firms is positively connected to entrepreneurial intentions where and that the relationship is mediated by perception of increased self-efficacy (which is PBC in TPB), perceived feasibility of starting a business, desirability for starting a business and attitude towards starting a business (another element of TPB) (Oluwafunmilayo et al., 2018). Testing the TPB, Carr and Sequeira (2007) found a direct link between the exposure to family business and entrepreneurial intentions that was also partially mediated by perceived self-efficacy (PBC), perceived family support (SN) and attitudes towards starting a business. This research points to the value of socialization and development of the self of the offspring done in the family business. The parental role through giving rewards and support to their offspring has been positively linked to entrepreneurial intentions and mediated by the perceived self-efficacy (PBC from TPB) of the offspring (Wang, Wang and Chen, 2018). It has to be noted that the authors (Wang, Wang and Chen, 2018) accentuate that involvement in the family business strengthens the perceived self-efficacy possibly due to the learning experiences and positive role models and weakens the effect of rewards on the entrepreneurial intentions. In addition, the family support and family cohesion was found to motivate entrepreneurs to stay with their venture even in hard times (Edelman et al., 2016; Zhu, Burmeister-Lamp and Hsu, 2017). A recent meta-analysis of literature accentuated that research so far has concentrated much more on the effects of education and society on entrepreneurial intentions of students rather than family experiences so a precise link between the role of the family firms and entrepreneurial intentions cannot be established (Cardella, Hernandez-Sanchez and Sanchez, 2020).

However, there are opposite findings stating that there is no influence of entrepreneurial parents over the offspring's career (Kuckertz and Wagner, 2010). A research conducted in North Macedonia shows that the social norms indirectly influence entrepreneurial intentions, where the family influence does not reveal any significant connection to entrepreneurial intentions (Egger et al., 2019). Zellweger, Sieger and Halte (2010), also show that children often do not follow their parent's steps and that there is a negative relationship between entrepreneurial parents and offspring's entrepreneurial intentions. Whether the entrepreneurial parents affect the intentions of their children mainly depends on parental failure in self-employment (Mungai and Velemuri, 2011). The children whose parents faced failure are less likely to become entrepreneurs than those children whose parents achieved success.

Although, according to some author's findings, there is no relationship between entrepreneurial intentions and family businesses or there is even negative relationship between entrepreneurial intentions and family businesses (Zellweger et al.,2011; Zhang et al. 2014), the major part of literature review suggests that the entrepreneurial intention among children who belong to entrepreneurial families is higher in comparison with children who do not have any entrepreneurial family background. In other words, children who have entrepreneurial parents are more likely to start a business (Georgescu and Herman,2020).

Therefore the current study expects to find differences in the entrepreneurial intentions between students with and without family business experience. The study also expects to find differences in the perceived social norm, attitude towards entrepreneurship and perceived behavioral control between students with and without family business experience.

2.4. Succession Intentions

Company succession can be referred as the transfer of the property and/or management of a firm from one individual to another (Ip and Jacobs, 2006). Additionally, Olbrich (2005) gives an additional part of the definition by stating that the succession is a transfer of the management to an individual who does or does not have connection with the family, but also can be employed there or even be employed elsewhere. Since the company succession can be seen as business start-up with all accompanying opportunities and difficulties within, company succession is interpreted as resembling entrepreneurship (Szyperski and Nathusius, 1999).

Due to rare succession situations in SMEs, the practical implications is fairly low in comparison with large companies (Kesner and Sebora, 1994). As a result, there is a small pool of potential successors for SMEs, comparable with for larger public firms. (Le Breton-Miller, Miller and Steier, 2004). According to the studies, 30% of family firms endure the change in first generation, while only 15% of such firms complete the transition further, from the second to the third generation (Aronoff, 1998; Lambrecht, 2005). Usually, these organizations' life is approximately 24 years and the end is linked mainly with the first generational change (Lambrecht, 2005).

Due to the low rate of successfully completed successions, this issues should be studies in depth (Sund et al.,2015). When assessing the success within the process, there are two main factors that have to be taken into consideration: family member's satisfaction and process efficiency based on the objective data of the company (Pyromalis and Vozikis, 2009; Sharma et al., 2003). In other words, the business viability, family integrity and the individual interests as well as the satisfaction degree of the stakeholders are main factors whether the succession will be successful or not (Cabrera-Suárez et al., 2001; Venter et al., 2005; Cabrera-Suárez and Martín-Santana, 2010).

The successor is desirable when the individual knowledge is relevant to successful business functioning (Bjuggren and Sund,2001). In addition, successors must be willing and interested in taking over the family business and this plays a key role in the successful business transition from one generation to another (Sharma, 2004, Sharma, Chrisman and Chua, 1997). Moreover, this interest in taking over the business is main factor for the successful succession process. In other words, if the successor is not willing or reluctant to the business takeover, the succession is likely to be not successful. Therefore the Theory of Planned Behavior is important in Succession Intentions. For succession intentions to be effectuated the successor has to perceive that the succession of the family business is a desirable option and this is the ATB aspect of the theory of Planned Behavior; it then has to perceive that succeeding the family firm is a feasible option for career advancement and this constitutes the PBC aspect of Theory of Planned Behavior; and the it needs to perceive the commitment of the family towards the business and this constitutes the SN aspect of Theory of Planned Behavior (Sharma et al, 2003b). As such certain studies have found that the social norm and feasibility (PBC) are important determinants of succession intentions among family firms offspring (Sharma, et al., 2003b) and other have found the issue to be complex and connected to a number of variables that are individual or situational and their relative interactions (De Massis, et al., 2016). According to Handler (1989) and later supported by Sharma (1997), the family members will experience positive succession if the career needs, psychosocial needs and life-stage needs are fulfilled.

Another succession factor is the enjoyment; financial security and satisfaction make the business more attractive to the potential successors (Fox et al., 1996, p. 19; Stavrou, 1995, p. 173). According to Dumas et al. (1995,) the financial opportunities can be motivators for succession intentions of offspring. However, there are other authors (Sharma,1997) who do not see a link between business rewards and succession intentions and connect succession intentions to the match of the career interests and business opportunities available. Positive association is found between succession intentions and the size of the business (Stavrou,1999), which means that succession intentions are higher for the larger business.

The relationship between the owner and the successor is crucial factor for the process of succession (Dickinson, 2000, p. 70). Quality relationship is consisted of high level of trust, communication, mutual support and recognitions of other's achievements (Harvey and Evans, 1995, p. 10; Neubauer and Lank, 1998, p. 142). Besides these, the mutual respect, feedback and mutual learning, as well as the quality of a successor's experience with process of succession are of crucial importance for the quality relationship (Handler,1989). Some authors believe that there is a better relationship between the effective successor and his/her father which is considered as the business owner, in comparison with the relationship between less effective successor and the business owner (Goldberg and Wooldbridge,1993).

The succession can occur outside the family as a result of unwillingness of the offspring to take over the family business. This is mainly ascribed to the desire of the offspring to start their own business (Bjuggren and Sund, 2001, 13). Besides the various number of advantages of taking over a business such as existing network, structure and brand image, the studies show that 65% of the Europeans prefer to start their own business (Eurobarometer, 2003, as cited in Transfer of Businesses, 2003). The reason for this is that the entrepreneurs has an opportunity to shape the business the way he/she wants and it requires less financing than a takeover i.e. the takeover requires 60% more investment comparable with a start-up (Marketplaces, 2006, 14).

Looking at the various characteristics of the family firms and their intertwined nature it becomes even more important to study the impact and effects of family business experience to the succession intentions of the offspring. The characteristics of the family firms provide both advantages and disadvantages to their functioning. Family firms have family members taking on simultaneous roles as owners, managers and family members; there is emotional involvement in the firm by the family members and a lifelong common history; there is shared identity and private language; there is mutual awareness of each other and shared meaning of the family company. Depending on how these roles are enacted and managed by the family members can either stimulate or hinder the succession intentions of the offspring (Tagiuri and Davis, 1996).

The succession intentions within a family are linked with a number of offspring in a family and parental support of the offspring (De Massis, et al., 2016). In a competitive environment, the managerial and entrepreneurial skills are of pivotal importance for the successor. Therefore, the succession transfer should depend on the preparation, which should start adequately early (Sharma et al., 2003b). The link between the level of parental support, perception of such parental support and succession intentions has been shown in a meta-analysis (Cardella, Hernandez-Sanchez and Sanchez, 2020). As such having experience within the family business seems important for succession intentions.

Therefore this study expects to find differences in opinions of those students that regard their parent's business as a family one and those that do not. In addition we expect to find differences in the succession intentions, attitude towards behavior, perceived behavioral control, perception of social norm and commitment to the business between students with work experience within the family business and those that do not have such experience.

3. METHODOLODY

The chapter uses data from the Global University Entrepreneurial Spirit Survey (GUESSS) from 2018. The survey is one of the largest student entrepreneurship surveys in the world and the Republic of North Macedonia has been involved in the latest one in 2018. The survey itself contains a range of questions about career intentions, entrepreneurial intentions, succession intentions and a range of different other variables connected to starting and leading an own business or becoming a successor of family business. The questions are based on the Theory of Planned Behavior. The questions use Likert type items with 7 point scale. There are 6 questions for Entrepreneurial intentions (EI) and 6 questions for Succession intentions (SI) adapted from Linan and Chen (2009); there are five questions for Attitude Towards Behavior (ATB) for Entrepreneurship and Succession which are adapted from Linan and Chen (2009); there are 7 questions for Self-Efficacy for Entrepreneurship and adapted from Chen et.al. (1998) and Zhao et.al. (2005) and 8 items for Self-Efficacy for Succession and self-efficacy is used in this research as it is regarded as part of Perceived Behavioral Control; there are three items measuring Subjective Norm for Entrepreneurship (SNE) and 4 measuring Subjective Norm for Succession (SNS) adapted from Linan and Chen (2009); there are 3 items for measuring Affective Commitment (AC) to family business and 3 measuring Normative Commitment (NC) to family business adapted from Dawson et.al. (2014). The internal consistency of the scales has been tested again and as can be seen in Table 1 all scale show good reliability (internal consistency) as the values are above 0.7. In order to test the links between different variables the current research transformed the items in the appropriate scales by creating collated variables for each scale based on the mean value of each item in the scale.

Table 1. Cronbach Alpha values for all scales

Scale	Cronbach Alpha
Entrepreneurial Intentions	.941
Attitude towards behaviour entrepreneurship	.926
Perceived behavioural control entrepreneurship (Self-efficacy)	.922
Social norm entrepreneurship	.721
Succession intentions	.974
Attitude towards behaviour succession	.911
Perceived behavioural control succession (Self-efficacy)	.903
Social norm succession	.887
Affective commitment succession	.906
Normative commitment succession	.911

The data collection was done using convenient sampling in the spring semester of 2018. A total of 398 students filled the questionnaire. Most of the students in the sample were in undergraduate programs (74.4%), followed by master level students (20.1%) and the rest of the sample was composed from students in other programs (like MBA or PhD students). The majority of the students came from Business/Management programs (48.3%), followed by Economics (30%) and the rest were a mixture of students from Social Sciences (5.9%), Computer Sciences (4.8%), and others. Most of the sample were full-time students (77.4%) and about a fifth (22.6%) declared that they work alongside their studies.

Around half of the students stated that their parents are self-employed (20.9 stated that their father is self-employed, 4.8% that their mother is self-employed and 21.9% that both their parents are self-employed) and the rest stated that neither parent is self-employed (52.5%). This breakdown of the sample with student that have experience with parent's self-employment and those that do not have that experience allows for comparison between the two groups. The comparisons for entrepreneurial intentions will be done between those students without self-employed parents and those with self-employed parents. In addition majority of the students with self-employed parents regard that business as a family business (77.2%). For succession intentions the data analysis will be done only on the students that have self-employed parents (189 students). The next section of the paper will present the findings regarding entrepreneurial and succession intentions of the students.

4. RESULTS

The preferences of the students for various employment options provide initial insight into their preferences for starting their own business or becoming a successor in a family business. The students were asked about their career preferences after finishing their studies and 5 years onwards. The data presented in Table 2 shows that the students pick becoming Entrepreneurs as most attractive option 5 years after their graduation or after they get some work experience. About 1 in 10 students see themselves as successor in family business immediately after and 5 years after finishing their current degree. However, if the family background is taken into consideration than the most attractive career option for students with both self-employed parents is successor in family business immediately after their degree (31% of those that have said that their parents are self-employed) and the second most attractive option for them is to become entrepreneurs (19.5%). The situation changes in favor of entrepreneurship after 5 years and 42.5% of those with both parents in family business would like to start their own business, with succession of a family business being the second most preferred career option (28.7%). In general students that have self-employed parents show slightly higher preference towards entrepreneurship as career option than those without such experience. The next analyses will delve deeper into the aspects connected to entrepreneurial intentions.

To test the differences in opinions and expectation of students regarding entrepreneurial intentions, a comparison was made based on whether the students reported that their parents are self-employed or not. The ANOVA test was used where the self-employment status of the parents was a grouping variable and Entrepreneurial intentions, Attitude towards behavior, Self-efficacy and Social norm were used as criterion variables as they are pointed as important aspects of Entrepreneurial intentions in the Theory of Planned Behavior. Table 3 provides the results of the ANOVA for the above mentioned variables. As it can be seen statistically significant differences have been found between the students with self-employed parents and those without self-employed parents in regards to Entrepreneurial Intentions, Self-Efficacy and Social Norm. In addition there are no differences between students in their attitudes towards entrepreneurship based on whether their parents are self-employed or not. For the other variables of interest to investigate the issue further and explore differences between different groups of students a series of post-hoc tests were done (Tuckey). The results reveal that when it comes to Entrepreneurial intentions there are statistically significant differences (p=.006) between the students that report to have self-employed father (M=5.33) and those without self-employed parents (M=4.39), as well as statistically significant differences (p=.00) between those with both self-employed parents (5.66) and those without self-employed parents (M=4.39). There were no statistically significant differences (p=.97) between those with self-employed mothers (M=4.57) and those without self-employed parents (M=4.39). When it comes to the perceived Self-Efficacy there are statistically significant differences (p=.022) between

Table 2. Employment preferences of students

	Immediately after degree				5 years after degree			
	No self-employed parent	**Father self-employed**	**Mother self-employed**	**Both self-employed**	**No self-employed parent**	**Father self-employed**	**Mother self-employed**	**Both self-employed**
Employee in a small business (1-49 people)	23%	24.1%	21.1%	18,4%	4.3%	3.6%	0	2.3%
Employee in a medium business (50-249 people)	18.7%	16.9%	10.5%	14.9%	5.3%	7.2%	10.5%	6.9%
Employee in a large business (250+ people)	18.2%	8.4%	21.1%	5.7%	14.8%	7.2%	0	9.2%
Employee in NGO sector	3.8%	2.4%	10.5%	0	1.9%	2.4%	5.3%	0
Academic career	2.9%	0	0	3.4%	6.7%	2.4%	10.5%	2.3%
Employee in public service	3.3%	0	5.3%	3.4%	3.8%	3.6%	5.3%	0
Founder of own business (Entrepreneur)	19.6%	16.9%	15.8%	19.5%	50.7%	53%	52.6%	42.5%
Successor in family business	1.4%	25.3%	5.3%	31%	1%	8.4%	5.3%	28.7%
Other/Do not know	8.1%	6%	10.5%	3.4%	10%	9.6%	10.5%	4.6%

those with self-employed father (M=5.51) and those without self-employed parents (M=4.87), as well as those having both parents self-employed (M=5.46) and those without self-employed parents (M=4.87). Again there were no statistically significant differences (p=.215) between having a self-employed mother (M=5.1) and those without self-employed parents (M=4.87). When it comes to the perception of Social Norm regarding entrepreneurship similar pattern is noticeable. Namely, there are statistically significant differences (p=.043) between those with self-employed father (M=5.83) and those without self-employed parents (M=5.45) and there are statistically significant differences (p=.018) between those with both self-employed parents (M=5.87) and those without self-employed parents (M=5.45). There are no statistically significant differences (p=.707) between those with self-employed mothers (M=5.74) and those without self-employed parents (M=5.45).

Table 3. ANOVA results for Entrepreneurial intentions and related variables

		Sum of Squares	df	Mean Square	F	Sig.
Entrepreneurial Intentions	Between Groups	70,488	3	23,496	**9,506**	**,000**
	Within Groups	593,233	240	2,472		
	Total	663,721	243			
Attitude Towards Behavior	Between Groups	13,802	3	4,601	2,392	,069
	Within Groups	463,570	241	1,924		
	Total	477,372	244			
Self-Efficacy (PBC)	Between Groups	22,209	3	7,403	**5,178**	**,002**
	Within Groups	343,157	240	1,430		
	Total	365,366	243			
Social Norm	Between Groups	15,613	3	5,204	**4,093**	**,007**
	Within Groups	501,018	394	1,272		
	Total	516,631	397			

Another important aspect of the study is to provide understanding into the succession intentions of those students from the sample that declared to have self-employed parents. To test the similarities and differences in opinions and perspectives of students when it comes to succession intentions an analysis was performed for the succession intentions of those students that reported to have one or both self-employed parents. The analysis here was made based on whether the students perceive the business where their self-employed parents work to be a family business and whether they have worked in the business or not. The analysis was done using t-tests.

The results in Table 4 show differences between those that perceive the business to be a family business and those that do not think that the business where their self-employed parents work is a family one. As can be seen from the results those students that perceived their parent's business to be a family business have higher Succession Intentions, more positive Attitude Towards Succession, perceive more positive Social Norm when it comes to business succession, perceive higher Self-Efficacy in being able to run the business after succession, and have higher levels of commitment to the business (both affective and normative) and those perceived differences are statistically significant.

Table 4. Comparison between those that regard their parent's business a family one or not

	Do you regard this business as a "family business"?	N	Mean	df	Sig (2-tailed)
Succession Intentions	No	28	3,1810	124	**.012**
	Yes	98	4,3092		
Attitude Towards Behavior	No	29	3,8034	125	.025
	Yes	98	4,6184		
Social Norm	No	28	5,0000	123	**.046**
	Yes	97	5,7964		
Self-Efficacy	No	29	4,4957	123	**.000**
	Yes	96	5,4911		
Affective Commitment	No	28	4,0179	123	**.010**
	Yes	97	5,1680		
Normative Commitment	No	27	3,3519	121	**.002**
	Yes	96	4,6936		

The results in Table 5 present the findings regarding opinions of the students with work experience in the parents' business and those without such experience. As it can be seen there are statistically significant differences when it comes to the Succession Intentions, perceived self-efficacy and affective and normative commitment. That means that those with work experience in the parents' business are more prepared to become successors of the business, think that they will be successful in running the business and show higher levels of commitment to the business in comparison to those without work experience in the parents' business.

Table 5. Comparison between those with work experience in the family business and those without work experience in the family business

	Have you been working for your parents' business?	N	Mean	df	Sig (2-tailed)
Succession Intentions	No	38	3,3088	126	**.006**
	Yes	90	4,4089		
Attitude Towards Behavior	No	41	4,0951	129	.110
	Yes	90	4,6089		
Social Norm	No	40	5,4375	127	.275
	Yes	89	5,7388		
Self-Efficacy (PBC)	No	41	4,9294	127	**.050**
	Yes	88	5,4308		
Affective Commitment	No	38	4,2921	125	**.018**
	Yes	89	5,1831		
Normative Commitment	No	37	3,7568	123	**.029**
	Yes	88	4,6884		

5. CONCLUSION

In this study, our aim was to provide understanding of the entrepreneurial intentions and succession intentions of students. In order to achieve this the study utilized the Theory of Planned Behavior and looked at entrepreneurial intentions and succession intentions as well as the components that lead to higher intentions such as attitude towards behavior, perceived behavioral control and social norm for both entrepreneurial intentions and succession intentions. In addition we looked at affective and normative commitment to the family business. In order to gain an insight into the experiences and opinions of students we conducted analyses of differences between students with and without self-employed parents. For succession intentions we deepened the analysis looking at differences between those that regard the business as family business and those that do not, as well as differences between students that have working experience in the family business and those that do not have such experience. In order to meet our goal, we used data from the Global University Entrepreneurial Spirit Survey (GUESSS) from 2018, the largest student entrepreneurship survey in the world.

The results of the study are in line with the suggestions derived from literature and other empirical studies (Sieger et al., 2019) in which entrepreneurship is one the most preferable career choice among the students, especially five years after graduation. The results of this study showed that the entrepreneurship is the most attractive career choice for students regardless of whether their parents are self-employed or not. However, if the family background is taken into consideration, the parent's professional career has and influence on the preferred career choice. Those students whose parents are self-employed prefer to be business successors rather than entrepreneurs immediately after graduation. However after five years those students prefer to become entrepreneurs or start their own business and list being successors of their parents family business as their second preferred option.

In testing the differences in student's opinions and expectations, ANOVA test was used to understand whether parent's professional career has impact over the career choice of their offspring. There are statistically significant differences between the students with self-employed parents and those without in regards to entrepreneurial intentions, self-efficiency and social norm. These findings are in line with findings from previous studies as well (Carr and Sequeira, 2007; Laspita, Breugst, Heblich and Patzelt 2012; Oluwafunmilayo et al., 2018). There is no difference between students in their attitudes towards entrepreneurship which is not in line with some previous studies (Carr and Sequeira, 2007; Oluwafunmilayo et al., 2018), but is in line with other studies that have also found no differences (Zellweger, Sieger and Halte, 2010). The findings generally provide support to the expectations of the study and are in line with the Theory of Planned Behavior.

Concerning the succession intentions, differences in opinion among the students was studied based on t-tests, according to which the students who perceived their parent's business to be a family business show higher succession intentions, more positive attitude towards succession and social norm, as well as higher self-efficiency and commitment. This is line with some previous studies (Sharma, 2004, Sharma, Chrisman and Chua, 1997).

In testing the difference in students' opinions, based on the work experience in the family business, additional test were used, according to which there is statistically difference between those who have experience and those who do not, in terms of succession intentions, self-efficiency and both affective and normative commitment. This is an important finding which is line with other studies on the topic (De Massis, et al., 2016; Sharma et al, 2003b) and shows the importance of the dynamics within the family business (Tagiuri and Davis, 1996) as well as immersion of the offspring in family business where they see the business from the inside and have an opportunity to experience the positive role model of their parents to be important for their succession intentions (Cardella, Hernandez-Sanchez and Sanchez, 2020; Sharma et al., 2003b)

This study is focuses on investigation in how students in the Republic of North Macedonia perceive themselves in terms of entrepreneurship and succession intentions. In view of the above research, it can be indicate that, the entrepreneurial intentions are linked to the parents' professional career, while the succession intentions are linked to work experience of the students within the family firms. Therefore, the findings of this study could be useful for both theory and practice in understanding factors on one's choice of entrepreneurial career path or choosing to become a successor of the family business. The research is also enhancing existing research linked to a deeper understanding of entrepreneurial and succession intentions among the students in the country.

5.1. Practical Implications

Following the survey and the analysis of the results, having in mind all limitations of the survey in terms of the small sample which is not representative of the overall student population in the country we can still offer several conclusions regarding the practical implications of the entrepreneurial and succession intentions among students.

The main purpose of this research was to investigate intentions that the students in the Republic of North Macedonia, have toward becoming an entrepreneurs and succeeding a family business. This had not been previously done in the Macedonian context and family focus and would therefore be a new contribution to the understanding of the concepts: entrepreneurial intentions and succession intentions in family businesses. Moreover, we believe that this research will provide prospective benefits of this knowledge for family business owners and managers. Having an understanding of how students perceive the entrepreneurship and their potential professional career is the first step in creating better prepared people in the field of entrepreneurial business.

Therefore, this study proposes to the academia to focus their attention on providing students with knowledge and skills linked to entrepreneurship, stimulating positive attitudes towards star-ups, providing climate conducive for supporting students that want to become entrepreneurs. Moreover, as a credible career option, entrepreneurship can be promoted through entrepreneurial role models in order to stimulate and encourage the students to chase their own ideas and projects. From here, the interaction between experienced entrepreneurs and the students should be facilitated and emphasized. Academia should thus partner with the family firms to provide students with support in gaining valuable skills and experience necessary for starting their own business.

In light of the findings of the study regarding the succession intentions the study proposes that parents offer their offspring a chance to work in the family firm. This will provide the offspring with and inside view of the company and enhance their succession intentions, make them more likely to believe they can be successful in running the family business and feel more committed towards the business. This will also enable the offspring to see their parents as role models and gain valuable managerial skills in the process of working. As such family firms should be given support in educating the next generation by building a quality relationship between the parents as owners and the offspring as successors (Dickinson, 2000) as well as providing clarification of the often dual roles of the family members and the dual characteristics of the family firms (Tagiuri and Davis, 1996).

5.2 . Research Limitations

This study has potential limitations which should be noted. Those appeared as a result of:

- the limited sample size,
- the student's education i.e. GUESSS research was done mostly by business school students
- the non-representative sample

However, all of these limitations can face a comprehensive extension in a future research. Future studies can utilize larger samples and possibly even representative samples to further enhance the knowledge about entrepreneurial and succession intentions of the students in the country and their linkage with experience in family businesses.

What is also important to be stated is the fact that the family businesses in the Republic of North Macedonia are facing the transition stage in terms of business and leadership. This means that companies would definitely need an additional support while facing takeovers from one generation to another.

Entrepreneurial intentions, succession and family businesses are fascinating topics for research and therefore we propose future research in the direction of entrepreneurship and family business. In addition, as an already proved and recognized survey, GUESSS has to be put in practice to explore the issues further. The findings of the study point to exploring how to provide better support to students in realizing their entrepreneurial intentions in the future and also exploring how best to support family business in ensuring smooth generational transitions.

REFERENCES

Aga, G. A., Francis, D., & Rodríguez-Meza, J. (2015). *SMEs, age, and jobs: A review of the literature, metrics, and evidence.* World Bank policy research working paper.

Ajzen, I. (1991). The theory of planned behavior. *Organizational Behavior and Human Decision Processes, 50*(2), 179–211. doi:10.1016/0749-5978(91)90020-T

Ajzen, I. (2012). Theory of Planned Behavior. In P. A. M. Lange, A. W. Kruglanski, & E. T. Higgins (Eds.), *Handbook of Theories of Social Psychology* (pp. 439–459). Sage. doi:10.4135/9781446249215.n22

Almobaireek, W. N., & Manolova, T. S. (2012). Who wants to be an entrepreneur? Entrepreneurial intentions among Saudi university students. *African Journal of Business Management, 6*(11), 4029–4040. doi:10.5897/AJBM11.1521

Andersson, L., & Hammarstedt, M. (2010). Intergenerational transmissions in immigrant self-employment: Evidence from three generations. *Small Business Economics, 34*(3), 261–276. doi:10.100711187-008-9117-y

Aronoff, C. E. (1998). Megatrends in family business. *Family Business Review, 11*(3), 181–185. doi:10.1111/j.1741-6248.1998.00181.x

Ball, S. (2005). The importance of entrepreneurship to hospitality, leisure, sport and tourism. Hospitality, Leisure. *Sport and Tourism Network, 1*(1), 1–14.

Bjuggren, P., & Sund, L. A. (2002). Transition Cost Rationale for Transition of the Firm within the Family. *Small Business Economics*, *19*(2), 123–133. doi:10.1023/A:1016289106477

Cabrera-Suárez, K., De Saá-Pérez, P., & García-Almeida, D. (2001). The succession process from a resource and knowledge-based view of the family firm. *Family Business Review*, *14*(1), 37–46. doi:10.1111/j.1741-6248.2001.00037.x

Cabrera-Suárez, M. K., & Martín-Santana, J. D. (2010). La influencia de las relaciones intergeneracionales en la formación y el compromiso del sucesor: Efectos sobre el proceso de sucesión en la empresa familiar. *Revista Europea de Dirección y Economía de la Empresa*, *19*(2), 111–128.

Cardella, G. M., Hernandez-Sanchez, B. R., & Garcia, J. C. S. (2020). Entrepreneurship and Family-Role: A Systematic Review of a Growing Research. *Frontiers in Psychology*, *10*, 2939. Advance online publication. doi:10.3389/fpsyg.2019.02939 PMID:31998192

Carr, J. C., & Sequeira, J. M. (2007). Prior family business exposure as intergenerational influence and entrepreneurial intent: A Theory of Planned Behavior approach. *Journal of Business Research*, *60*(10), 1090–1098. doi:10.1016/j.jbusres.2006.12.016

Carree, M., Van Gils, A., & Peters, B. (2014). Innovation in family and non-family SMEs: An exploratory analysis. *Small Business Economics*, *42*(3), 595–609. doi:10.100711187-013-9490-z

Chen, C. C., Greene, P. G., & Crick, A. (1998). Does entrepreneurial self-efficacy distinguish entrepreneurs from managers? *Journal of Business Venturing*, *13*(4), 295–316. doi:10.1016/S0883-9026(97)00029-3

Chua, J. H., Chrisman, J. J., & Sharma, P. (1999). Defining the family business by behavior. *Entrepreneurship Theory and Practice*, *29*(4), 19–39. doi:10.1177/104225879902300402

Ćoćkalo, D., Đorđević, D., Bogetić, S., Sajfert, D., & Minovski, R. (2013). Quality of business, entrepreneurship education and business startup intentions among students in Serbia: Research results. *Industrija*, *41*(3), 125–145. doi:10.5937/industrija41-3889

Commission of the European Communities. (2008). *Think Small First - A Small Business Act for Europe*. Author.

Dawson, A., Irving, G. P., Sharma, P., Chirico, F., & Marcus, J. (2014). Behavioural outcomes of next-generation family members' commitment to their firm. *European Journal of Work and Organizational Psychology*, *23*(4), 570–581. doi:10.1080/1359432X.2013.781155

De Massis, A., Sieger, P., Chua, J. H., & Vismara, S. (2016). Incumbent's Attitudes Towards Intra-family Succession: An Investigation of its Antecendents. *Family Business Review*, *29*(3), 278–300. doi:10.1177/0894486516656276

Debarliev, S., & Janeska-Iliev, A. (2015). Challenges for the family business in transition economics: with an emphasis on the Republic of Macedonia economic recovery in the post-crisis period. *Proceedings from the International Conference held at the Faculty of Economics*.

DeDee, J. K., & Vorhies, D. W. (1998). Retrenchment activities of small firms during economic downturn: An empirical investigation. *Journal of Small Business Management*, *36*(3), 46–62.

Deng, Z., Hofman, P. S., & Newman, A. (2013). Ownership concentration and product innovation in Chinese private SMEs. *Asia Pacific Journal of Management*, *30*(3), 717–734. doi:10.100710490-012-9301-0

Dickinson, T. M. (2000). *Critical success factors for succession planning in family businesses.* Unpublished research report in partial fulfillment of Master in Business Administration degree, Faculty of Business Administration, University of the Witwatersrand, Johannesburg.

Dumas, C., Dupuis, J. P., Richer, F., & St.-Cyr, L. (1995). Factors that influence the next generation's decision to take over the family farm. *Family Business Review*, *8*(2), 99–120. doi:10.1111/j.1741-6248.1995.00099.x

Dunn, T., & Holtz-Eakin, D. (2000). Financial capital, human capital, and the transition to self-employment: Evidence from intergenerational links. *Journal of Labor Economics*, *18*(2), 287–305. doi:10.1086/209959

Edelman, L. F., Manolova, T., Shirokova, G., & Tsukanova, T. (2016). The impact of family support on young entrepreneurs' start-up activities. *Journal of Business Venturing*, *31*(4), 428–448. doi:10.1016/j.jbusvent.2016.04.003

Egger, E., Misoska Tomovska, A., & Dimitrova, M. (2019). Entrepreneurial intentions among students in SEEC's factors related to education and family. *From Transition to development: Emerging challenges and perspectives: Conference Proceedings of 3rd International Scientific Conference on Business and Economics.*

European Commission. (2017). *SBA Fact Sheet.* European Neighbourhood Policy and Enlargement Negotiations.

FairlieR. W.RobbA. (2004). *Families, Human Capital and Small Business: Evidence from the Characteristics of Business Owners Survey.* IZA Discussion Paper No. 1296. http://ssrn.com/abstract=464243

Fox, M., Nilakant, V., & Hamilton, R. T. (1996). Managing succession in family-owned businesses. *International Small Business Journal*, *15*(1), 15–25.

Georgescu, M. A., & Herman, E. (2020). The impact of the Family Background on Students' Entrepreneurial Intentions: AN empirical analysis. *Sustainability*, *12*, 4775.

Gephard, R. P. (1978). Status degradation and organizational succession: An ethno methodological approach. *Administrative Science Quarterly*, *23*(4), 553–581.

Goldberg, S. D., & Wooldridge, B. (1993). Self-confidence and managerial autonomy: Successor characteristics critical to succession in family firms. *Family Business Review*, *6*(1), 55–73.

Handler, W. C. (1989). *Managing the family firm succession process: The next-generation family member's experience* (Unpublished doctoral thesis). Boston University, Boston, MA.

Harvey, M., & Evans, R. E. (1995). Life after succession in the family business: Is it really the end of problems? *Family Business Review*, *8*(1), 3–16.

Hoffmann, A., Junge, M., & Malchow-Møller, N. (2015). Running in the family: Parental role models in entrepreneurship. *Small Business Economics*, *44*(1), 79–104.

Hofman, A., Uitterlinden, A. G., & Rooij, F. J. A. (2010). *Genome-wide association studies in economics and entrepreneurship research: promises and limitations. In Small Business Economics*. Springer. doi:10.100711187-010-9286-3

Intihar, A., & Pollack, J. M. (2012). Exploring small family-owned firms' competitive ability: Differentiation through trust, value -orientation, and market specialization. *Journal of Family Business Management*, *2*(1), 76–86.

Ip, B., & Jacobs, G. (2006). Business succession planning: A review of the evidence. *Journal of Small Business and Enterprise Development*, *13*(3), 326–350. Advance online publication. doi:10.1108/14626000610680235

Jiang, D. S., Hayward, S. D., & Morris, M. L. (2017). Raising entrepreneurs: Can parenting style amplify entrepreneurial intentions and behaviours? *International Journal of Management and Enterprise Development*, *16*(1/2), 13–33. doi:10.1504/IJMED.2017.082544

Junaid, M., Mehboob-ur-Rashid, M., & Shaheen, N. (2015). Entrepreneurship as a Socially Constructed Phenomenon: Importance of Alternate Paradigms Research. *Journal ofManagerial Sciences*, *9*(1), 35–48.

Kautonen, T., van Gelderen, M., & Tornikoski, E. T. (2013). Predicting entrepreneurial behavior: A test of the theory of planned behavior. *Applied Economics*, *45*(6), 697–707. doi:10.1080/00036846.2011.610750

Kesner, I. F., & Sebora, T. C. (1994). Executive Succession: Past, Present & Future. *Journal of Management*, *20*(2), 327–372. doi:10.1177/014920639402000204

Klyver, K. (2007). Shifting family involvement during the entrepreneurial process.". *International Journal of Entrepreneurial Behaviour & Research*, *13*(5), 258–277. doi:10.1108/13552550710780867

Krueger, N. F. Jr, Reilly, M. D., & Carsrud, A. (2000). Competing models of entrepreneurial intentions. *Journal of Business Venturing*, *15*(5-6), 411–432. doi:10.1016/S0883-9026(98)00033-0

Kuckertz, A., & Wagner, M. (2010). The influence of sustainability orientation on entrepreneurial intentions—Investigating the role of business experience. *Journal of Business Venturing*, *25*(5), 524–539. doi:10.1016/j.jbusvent.2009.09.001

LambrechtJ. (2005). Multigenerational Transition in Family Businesses: A New Explanatory Model. *Family Business Review*, *18*(4), 267-282. https://ssrn.com/abstract=1501523

Laspita, S., Breugst, N., Heblich, S., & Patzelt, H. (2012). Intergenerational transmission of entrepreneurial intentions. *Journal of Business Venturing*, *27*(4), 414–435. doi:10.1016/j.jbusvent.2011.11.006

Le Breton-Miller, I., Miller, D., & Steier, L. (2004). Toward an Integrative Model of Effective FOB Succession. *Entrepreneurship Theory and Practice*, *28*(4), 305–328. doi:10.1111/j.1540-6520.2004.00047.x

Liñán, F., & Chen, Y. (2009). Development and cross cultural application of a specific instrument to measure entrepreneurial intentions. *Entrepreneurship Theory and Practice*, *33*(3), 593–617. doi:10.1111/j.1540-6520.2009.00318.x

Linan, F., Rodríguez-Cohard, J. C., & Guzman, J. (2011). Temporal stability of entrepreneurial intentions: A longitudinal study. Entrepreneurial Research in Europe: Evolving Concepts and Processes, 34-55.

Ljunggren, E. (2011). *Entrepreneurship research in Europe: Evolving concepts and processes*. Edward Elgar.

López-Fernández, M. C., Serrano-Bedia, A. M., & Pérez-Pérez, M. (2015). Entrepreneurship and family firm research: A bibliometric analysis of an emerging field. *Journal of Small Business Management, 54*(2), 622–639. doi:10.1111/jsbm.12161

Mandl, I. (2008). *Overview of Family Business Relevant Issues*. Austrian Institute for SME Research.

Mangundjaya, W. (2012). Challenges in Developing Young Entrepreneurs (A Study at Unemployed Youth in Jakarta). *Conference Proceedings of International Conference on Entrepreneurship Forum (IEF).*

Mboko, S. (2011). Towards and explanation of the growth in young entrepreneurship activities: A cross country survey of work values of college students. *Journal of Marketing Development and Competitiveness, 5*, 108–118.

Mungai, E., & Velamuri, S. R. (2011). Parental entrepreneurial role model influence on male offspring: Is it always positive and when does it occur? *Entrepreneurship Theory and Practice, 35*(2), 337–357. doi:10.1111/j.1540-6520.2009.00363.x

Neubauer, F., & Lank, A. G. (1998). *The family business— Its governance for sustainability*. Routledge.

Nowinski, W., & Haddoud, M. Y. (2019). The role of inspiring role models in enhancing entrepreneurial intention. *Journal of Business Research, 96*, 183–193. doi:10.1016/j.jbusres.2018.11.005

Oluwafunmilayo, A. M., Olokundun, M. A., Moses, C. L., & Grace, A. C. (2018). The Role of Prior Family Business Background on Entrepreneurial Intentions. *Covenant Journal of Entrepreneurship, 2*(1), 1–14.

Pounder, P. (2015). Family business insights: An overview of the literature. *Journal of Family Business Management., 5*(1), 116–127. doi:10.1108/JFBM-10-2014-0023

Poutziouris, P., & Chittenden, F. (1996). Family businesses or business families? Leeds: Institute for Small Business Affairs.

Pyromalis, V. D., & Vozikis, G. S. (2009). Mapping the successful succession process in family firms: Evidence from Greece. *The International Entrepreneurship and Management Journal, 5*(4), 439–460. doi:10.100711365-009-0118-3

Economic Reform Report. (2019). *Structural Reforms*. Republic of North Macedonia.

Risca, F. A. (2018). The Role of Family Business and Education in Forming Actual Entrepreneurs. *The 2018 International Conference of Organizational Innovation. KnE Social Sciences*, 329–340. 10.18502/kss.v3i10.3384

Sahinidis, A., Stavroulakis, D., Kossieri, E., & Varelas, S. (2019). Entrepreneurial intention determinants among female students. The influence of role models, parents' occupation and perceived behavioral control on forming the desire to become a business owner. In Strategic Innovative Marketing and Tourism. Springer Proceedings in Business and Economics. Springer. DOI.1007/978-3-030-12453-3_20.

Savlovschi, L.I., & Robu, N.R. (2011). The Role of SMEs in Modern Economy. *Economia Seria Management, 14*(1).

Shapero, A., & Sokol, L. (1982). The social dimensions of entrepreneurship. In C. A. Kent, D. L. Sexton, & K. E. Vesper (Eds.), *The encyclopedia of entrepreneurship*. Prentice-Hall.

Sharma, P. (1997). *Determinants of the satisfaction of the primary stakeholders with the succession process in family firms* (Unpublished doctoral thesis). University of Calgary, Canada.

Sharma, P. (2004). An overview of the field of family business studies: Current status and directions for the future. *Family Business Review*, *17*(1), 1–36. doi:10.1111/j.1741-6248.2004.00001.x

Sharma, P., Chrisman, J. J., & Chua, J. (2003a). Predictors of Satisfaction with the Succession Process in Family Firms. *Journal of Business Venturing*, *18*(5), 667–687. doi:10.1016/S0883-9026(03)00015-6

Sharma, P., Chrisman, J. J., & Chua, J. (2003b). Succession Planning as Planned Behavior: Some Empirical Results. *Family Business Review*, *16*(1), 1–16. doi:10.1111/j.1741-6248.2003.00001.x

Sharma, P., Chrisman, J. J., & Chua, J. H. (1997). Strategic management of the family business: Past research and future challenges. *Family Business Review*, *10*(1), 1–35. doi:10.1111/j.1741-6248.1997.00001.x

Shneor, R., Jenssen, J. I., & Vissak, T. (2016). Introduction to the special issue: Current challenges and future prospects of entrepreneurship in Nordic and Baltic Europe. *Baltic Journal of Management*, *11*(2), 134–141. doi:10.1108/BJM-01-2016-0013

Sieger, P., Fueglistaller, U., & Zellweger, T. (2011). Entrepreneurial Intentions and Activities of Students across the World. International Report of the GUESSS Project 2011. St. Gallen: Swiss Research Institute of Small Business and Entrepreneurship at the University of St.Gallen (KMU-HSG).

Sieger, P., Fueglistaller, U., Zellweger, T., & Braun, I. (2019). *Global Student Entrepreneurship 2018: Insights From 54 Countries*. KMU-HSG/IMU.

Singh, T., & Singh, S. (2014). Entrepreneurial intentions among university students in Manipur. *International Journal of Management and Social Science Research Review*, *1*(7), 55–64.

Siu, W., & Lo, E. S. (2011). Cultural contingency in the cognitive model of entrepreneurial intention. *Entrepreneurship Theory and Practice*, *37*(2), 147–173. doi:10.1111/j.1540-6520.2011.00462.x

Solesvik, M., Westhead, P., Kolvereid, L., & Matlay, H. (2012). Student intentions to become self-employed: The Ukrainian context. *Journal of Small Business and Enterprise Development*, *19*(3), 441–460. doi:10.1108/14626001211250153

Sorasalmi, T., & Tuovinen, J. (2016). *Entering emerging markets: A dynamic framework dynamics in logistics*. Springer.

Stavrou, E. (1995). The next generation's dilemma: To join or not to join the family business. *Family Firm Institute Conference Proceedings*.

Stavrou, E. (1999). Succession in family businesses: Exploring the effects of demographic factors on offspring intentions to join and take over the business. *Journal of Small Business Management*, *37*(3), 43–62.

Stevenson, H. H. (1983). A perspective on entrepreneurship. *Harvard Business School Working Paper*, *9*, 384-131.

Sund, L. G., Melin, L., & Haag, K. (2015). Intergenerational ownership succession. Shifting the focus from outcome measurement to preparatory requirements. *Journal of Family Business Strategy*, *6*(3), 166–177. doi:10.1016/j.jfbs.2015.07.001

Szyperski, N., & Nathusius, K. (1999). *Probleme der Unternehmensgründung: Eine betriebswirtschaftliche Analyse unternehmerischer Startbedingungen*. Josef Eul Verlag.

Tagiuri, R., & Davis, J. (2016). „Bivalent Attributes of Family Firms". *Family Business Review*, *9*(2), 199–208. doi:10.1111/j.1741-6248.1996.00199.x

Thompson, E. R. (2009). Individual entrepreneurial intent: Construct clarification and development of an internationally reliable metric. *Entrepreneurship Theory and Practice*, *33*(3), 669–694. doi:10.1111/j.1540-6520.2009.00321.x

Tkachev, A., & Kolvereid, L. (1999). Self-employment intentions among Russian students. *Entrepreneurship and Regional Development*, *11*(3), 269–280. doi:10.1080/089856299283209

Transfer of Businesses. (2003). Transfer of bsuiensses- continuity through a new beginning. Final report of the MAP 2002 project, European Commission, 23(9).

Transfer of SMEs. (2002). Final report of the expert group on the transfer of SMEs. European Commission, 23(9).

Veciana, J. M., Aponte, M., & Urbano, D. (2005). University students' attitudes towards entrepreneurship: A two countries comparison. *The International Entrepreneurship and Management Journal*, *1*(2), 165–182. doi:10.100711365-005-1127-5

Venter, E., Boshoff, C., & Mass, G. (2005). The influence of successor-related factors on the succession process in small and medium-sized family businesses. *Family Business Review*, *18*(4), 283–303. doi:10.1111/j.1741-6248.2005.00049.x

Wang, D., Wang, L., & Chen, L. (2018). Unlocking the influence of family business exposure on entrepreneurial intentions. *The International Entrepreneurship and Management Journal*, *14*(4), 951–974. doi:10.100711365-017-0475-2

Ward, L. J. (1987). *Keeping the Family Business Healthy: How to plan for continuing Growth, Profitability and Family Leadership*. Jossey-Bass.

Wenjun, W., Wei, L., & Millington, J. K. (2011). Determinants of Entrepreneurial Intention among College Students in China and USA. *Journal of Global Entrepreneurship Research*, *1*(1), 35–44.

Wyrwich, M. (2015). Entrepreneurship and the intergenerational transmission of values. *Small Business Economics*, *45*(1), 191–213. doi:10.100711187-015-9649-x

Zellweger, T., Sieger, P., & Halter, F. (2011). Should I stay or should I go? Career choice intentions of students with family business background. *Journal of Business Venturing*, *26*(5), 521–536. doi:10.1016/j.jbusvent.2010.04.001

Zhang, Y., Duysters, G., & Cloodt, M. (2014). The role of entrepreneurship education as a predictor ofuniversity students' entrepreneurial intention. *The International Entrepreneurship and Management Journal*, *10*(3), 623–641. doi:10.100711365-012-0246-z

Zhao, H., Hills, G. E., & Siebert, S. E. (2005). The mediating role of self-efficacy in the development of entrepreneurial intentions. *The Journal of Applied Psychology*, *90*(6), 1265–1272. doi:10.1037/0021-9010.90.6.1265 PMID:16316279

Zhu, F., Burmeister-Lamp, K., & Hsu, D. K. (2017). To leave or not? The impact of family support and cognitive appraisals on venture exit intention. *International Journal of Entrepreneurial Behaviour & Research*, *23*(3), 566–590. doi:10.1108/IJEBR-04-2016-0110

Chapter 12
The Enhancement of HR Systems Through Entrepreneurial Succession in Family SMEs

Enrico Cori
Polytechnic University of Marche, Italy

Mariacristina Bonti
PIsa University, Italy

ABSTRACT

This chapter aims at shedding light on the "hidden relationship" between the process of entrepreneurial succession in family SMEs and the development of the HR management system in such firms. Starting from a literature review, the authors develop a reflection based on evidence from a sample of Italian family SMEs, collected through a longitudinal qualitative inquiry. They question if and how the change at the helm of the family firm may constitute an opportunity to develop or strengthen the HR management system. The ultimate goal of the chapter is to lay the foundation for building a conceptual framework in which some possible relationships between the variables involved are outlined.

INTRODUCTION

The aim of this chapter is to shed light on the impacts that the processes of entrepreneurial succession within family SMEs may have on the development of human resources (from now on HR) culture, practices, and skills. This study is part of a broader research project, that we launched in 2009 and that have been conducted on a sample of family SMEs. The aim of this project was to investigate how the generational shift impacts on the transfer of knowledge and skills, on governance structures, on the orientation towards innovation, and on the HR management.

DOI: 10.4018/978-1-7998-4814-1.ch012

We question if and how the change at the top of the family firm, from the preparatory phase until its completion, may constitute an opportunity to develop or strengthen the HR management system of a family SME. In light of the literature on the succession process and the evidence gathered in the field, we propose to lay the foundation for building a conceptual model in which a set of items are included and some links between them are outlined.

We start from an awareness that the extant literature on generational transition and that on the HR management in family firms has generally proceeded along parallel tracks that have crossed only on rare occasions. In other words, the literature review highlights the strong shortage, if not the absolute lack, of studies on the possible impact of the "passage of the baton" at the helm of the family firm on the HR management systems. On the contrary, the evidences that emerged during our research project have progressively confirmed the existence of hidden relationships between the two phenomena: that of entrepreneurial succession, extensively studied in managerial and organizational literature, and that of the development of the HR system in family businesses, object of this volume precisely because of the need to strengthen the theoretical basis. Hence the evidence of a gap in the literature, which our study aims first of all to highlight, and secondly to help fill, by proposing a conceptual model.

Our intention is twofold: on a theoretical level we believe that our research may contribute to bridging the abovementioned gap in the literature; on an operational level, we argue that our research can improve entrepreneurs' and managers' awareness of the opportunities the entrepreneurial succession process might present, in terms of the evolution and consolidation of the HR management systems. For the purpose of this work, we define 'entrepreneurial succession' as a process that opens up opportunities for a firm's development, innovation, and change (Bonti & Cori, 2011; Dyck et al., 2002).

In this perspective, we are interested in exploring how the management of people in a family business can be developed, innovated, and changed as a result of the entrepreneurial succession process. In this regard, it seems noteworthy that some peculiar features of the generational transition may facilitate or hinder the pursuit of a mature vision of HR management, through some specific outcome(s) of the succession itself. Among these outcomes, we refer, in particular, to a re-balancing of entrepreneurial and managerial skills, in favor of the latter; a more pronounced propensity to develop a wider variety of skills , not confined to the production and commercial areas, that are traditionally overseen by the entrepreneur; a higher propensity for inter-organizational collaboration, both through the intertwining of interpersonal relationships and through the establishment of formalized networks; and finally, a deeper awareness of the role of organizational and personnel management choices in pursuing the firm's objectives effectively.

The chapter is structured as follows. The next section proposes a literature review concerning the outcomes of the entrepreneurial succession process and the scarce conceptual links between research on HR management systems and studies dealing with the succession process within family firms. In the third paragraph, based on evidence gathered through multi-case, qualitative research, we suggest how the entrepreneurial succession processes can enhance the HR system in SMEs. In the fourth section we identify some key-factors which, in our opinion, can facilitate the development of the HR management system in family SMEs. The paragraph ends with a proposal to incorporate these factors in a possible conceptual model. Finally, in the fifth paragraph, after highlighting some limitations of the study, we point out the importance of this area of research for practical and theoretical development and suggest some further research questions on this topic.

BACKGROUND

The Outcomes of the Entrepreneurial Succession Process in Family Firms

Entrepreneurial succession is one of the most relevant topics in family business studies. The main reason for this is that a very small number of family firms survive the first generation hand-off and an even smaller number make it to the second and subsequent ones. Consequently, entrepreneurial succession can be considered one of the major challenges facing family firms.

In line with De Massis et al. (2008), the mainstream literature considers the issue of succession as an intra-family phenomenon, i.e. the transfer of ownership and management from one family member to another (Sharma et al., 2001). The family is sometimes considered in the narrow sense (the founder's immediate family), sometimes in a more comprehensive sense (the families of the early heirs of the founder). The attention paid by scholars in studies on intra-family succession plausibly allows one to assume that this could mean that the goals of succession would be unattainable for members outside of the immediate family.

From a "procedural" point of view (Bonti & Cori, 2013), entrepreneurial succession is described as a process that develops over time. It is articulated in a series of phases and activities, observable contextually or in sequence (Cabrera-Suarez et al., 2001). It involves a number of roles and pursues some specific goals. From a "substantive" point of view, succession at the helm of the family firm can be regarded as process of organizational change that can take alternative paths and directions, leading towards outcomes that cannot be known *a priori*. As with any change, it entails opportunities to be seized, as well as threats to be tackled, or possible "new" problems to be faced (Del Bene, 2005), thus determining the future paths of the firm (Dyck et al., 2002).

Like every process, succession has to be designed and managed: for this reason, numerous scholars (Murray, 2003; Sharma et al., 2003; Le Breton-Miller et al., 2004; Lambrecht, 2005; Cadieux, 2005, 2007) have addressed this issue. They have identified different transition phases and highlighted key roles and tasks in each phase to be taken into consideration in order to carefully plan the succession. The most relevant and recurring issues concerning succession planning and management are outlined below:

- the agreement of the family regarding the continuation of the company activity;
- the evaluation and choice of the successor, according with his/her aptitudes and skills;
- the relationship between founder and successor, with particular reference to the propensity of the founder to take a step back and relinquish the "reins of the command" and the propensity of the successor to take over and wait;
- the extension of the overall succession period;
- the planning of the formative/educational path, aimed at defining the time needed to train and develop of the heir, with regard to the skills and competences needed;
- the evaluation of the whole process, in order to improve future entrepreneurial successions.

Central to the topic of succession planning is the supposed relationship between "effective" planning and "effective" succession, leading to a satisfactory entrepreneurial succession. However, the meaning attributed to the expression "success of the generational shift" is not well defined. Simply considering the formal transfer of ownership appears to be a contradiction of the very concept of succession as a process of change. The post-succession phase may prove to abound in unforeseen phenomena and situations; this means that, while the succession process can be said to be "technically successful" (as regards the transfer of ownership/leadership), the family firm may not be able to survive (Dyck et al., 2002). From this point of view, even stakeholders' satisfaction (Le Breton-Miller et al., 2004) or the absence of conflicts among family members cannot be considered valid indicators of the success of a single inter-generational transition.

In other terms, by analyzing the post-succession phase and the related changes, it is possible to obtain a more complete, accurate, and faithful view of the entrepreneurial succession and its outcomes, which may be more or less satisfactory. From such a perspective, it seems appropriate to add to mainstream literature's interpretations of what "a good output" of the entrepreneurial succession would look like.

From a different perspective, Cabrera-Suarez et al. (2001) suggest interpreting entrepreneurial success with reference to the continuity of the family firms, taking into consideration the degree of a family's integrity, as well as with the satisfaction of the actors involved in the process, while Sharma et al. (2003) propose looking at the ability of the family firm to preserve its idiosyncratic knowledge and original characteristics over time. In line with this perspective, the success of the generational transition processes can be evaluated in terms of the balance between the transfer of the existing stock of knowledge/skills and the aware development of innovative competences, i.e. by the ability to pursue "innovation around tradition" (Bonti & Cori, 2013).

The Professionalization of the Family SMEs

Mainstream literature has provided some different explanatory answers relating to how family firms can continue to survive across generations. Among these, we underscore the importance of professionalization followed by development of HR practices, as well as the ability to nurture innovative spirit, orientation, and behavior over time and along internationalization paths (Nordqvist & Melin, 2010; Bonti & Cori, 2018). Professionalization seems to be, in any case, the key to survival.

According to the studies that consider professionalization in a broad sense, it often takes on the characteristics of a complex and multidimensional phenomenon (Gomez-Mejia et al., 2001; Schulze et al., 2003; Songini & Gnan, 2014) that revolves around the acquisition of a differentiated set of knowledge and skills, as well as the development of cultural orientations (Hall & Nordqvist, 2008). Those competences constitute the basis for the introduction of structured and formalized "managerial" practices, tools, and logics for running the family firm. Thus, family managers and professionalization are not contradictory terms (Hall & Nordqvist, 2008). The aim of professionalizing the family business may be achieved through the hiring of outside managers, or through the education and training of family managers (Kotey & Folker, 2007; Sardeshmukh & Corbett, 2011; Stewart & Hitt, 2012), as well as by developing operating systems.

In the effort to understand how a family business can develop and maintain managerial skills over time and, in particular, seize the opportunities for change offered by generational shift, developing HR practices that are usable in managing generational transitions seem to be something of a privileged pathway. Many authors (Kellermanns & Eddleston, 2004; de Kok et al., 2006; Kopriva & Bernik, 2009, Kotey & Folker, 2007; Dekker et al., 2013, 2015) have dwelled on the importance of putting personnel practices in place, within the family firm's context, in order to face some common problems related to altruism and nepotism. Such phenomena may lead the firm to apply potentially ineffective selection and performance evaluation criteria, especially when family members are involved. That reinforces the need for the development and use formalized practices and tools concerning recruitment, training, evaluation, and reward systems.

The development of cultural orientations and managerial skills must be related to the evolutionary path of each firm, in order to progressively provide the firm with a suitable set of tools. This process often fails, due to an exclusive focus on hiring non-family managers, as if the key problem was the manager's familiar or non-familiar nature, not his/her actual professionalism. Even if a family firm chooses to remain small-sized, the complexity of the tasks performed, along with the environmental "turbulence" that may be present, give rise to the need for a high level of competences and for more formalized management and organizational practices.

Professionalization of family firms may also enhance conditions that strongly encourage entrepreneurship over generations (Miller & Le Breton-Miller, 2005; Nordqvist et al., 2008). According with Cherchem (2017), the strengthen of a "hierarchical culture" can impact positively on the family firm's entrepreneurial orientation, when multiple generations are involved. This appear to be an important issue in family SMEs where less informal mechanisms are often seen as a source of problems. As Salvato (2004) pointed out, to accept and develop innovative ideas may become difficult when the founder is so closely focused on himself, whereas the freshness of ideas brought by the successors may revitalize innovation. Indeed, the new generations involved in the family firm may nurture a strong orientation to long-term entrepreneurial behavior (Miller & Le Breton-Miller, 2005) and exhibit a set of values and beliefs inclined to reinvent the business and fuel innovation.

As far as the governance structure is concerned, the professionalization of family firms, generally encourages the involvement of external directors (Johannisson & Huse, 2000; Gabrielsson & Huse, 2005; Voordeckers et al., 2007). It is frequently underlined that outside managers can promote a better awareness of managerial issues and provide information, experience, as well as different perspectives, thereby increasing the firm's ability to interpret and face environmental changes (Schulze et al., 2003; Bammens et al., 2011). When the firm's level of professionalization is low, external directors may play a key advisory and support role, besides than a control role. The effectiveness of the outside managers depends on contingent factors (Corbetta & Salvato, 2012); so, it is difficult to say which managerial orientation will prevail, due to the heterogeneity of family firms. In their advisory role, they can also contribute to promoting the idea of networking, thus stimulating a different approach to innovation as a result of the joint efforts of a number of organizations; moreover networking would also increase the firm's ability to access to knowledge and skills held by networked firms. This may be the case for HR management skills, for instance.

At the Crossroads Between Research on HR Management and on Entrepreneurial Succession Processes

If the literature on the business succession process offers a fairly generic and fragmented picture of the possible changes that the process itself may induce, evidence relating to a specific area such as that of personnel management is even sparser. In particular, it is extremely difficult to follow studies that focus on the possible effects of change at the helm of the family firm on the development or strengthening of the HR management system, in terms of structures, roles, skills, and practices in use.

However, many authors start from the assumption that the succession process itself can be classified as an HR management activity (Astrachan & Kolenko, 1994; Cabrera Suárez et al., 2001; Sambrook, 2005; Daspit et al., 2018), addressed to nurture and develop the skills and capabilities of the family firm's most important human resource: the next generation leaders (Mustafa & Elliott, 2019). Sharing this perspective, however, would mean moving away from the meaning traditionally attributed to the expression "human resources", with which it is customary to indicate people linked to the company by a formalized, subordinated employment relationship.

Closer to our perspective are studies that observe how some organizational choices can have a cascading effect on the dynamics of the succession process and the subsequent outcomes. For example, Bracci & Vagnoni (2011: 21) view succession as a process capable of impacting the firm on the intellectual capital level; thus, they affirm the importance of HR management on the development of human capital, considered one of the three pillars of intellectual capital. According to these authors, some choices, primarily related to the organization of work, such as "the delegation of responsibility towards some key employees (…) might reduce the risk of loss of knowledge and failure due to the succession".

More recently, the research conducted by Blanco-Mazagatos et al. (2018: 344), provides evidence supporting that "generational stage affects the intensity of the influence of family employee HR practices on organizational human capital". In this case, not the succession process itself, but its outcome, that is the generational change at the helm of the company, seems to represent an important factor in favoring the quality of the human capital available to the family firm.

Yedder (2018: 401), for his part, observes how "HRM can help to diminish the risk of family business succession by reducing the dependence to family management through personnel empowerment and improvement of organizational environment". In his analysis, aimed at observing the role of HR management respectively in the antecedent, concomitant and subsequent phases of passing the baton in the family business, the author underlines how HR management can become either "victim" or "savior" of the succession. It is a "victim" in the sense of being negatively influenced by it, and a "savior" if it is able to mitigate the critical issues concerning the management of non-family personnel. As for the post-succession phase in particular, according to Yedder (2018: 417) "HRM can have a role to play, especially to prepare a favorable ground to dialogue between family management and employees", provided that the action of the staff managers is legitimized by the members of the owner family.

Mustafa & Elliott (2019: 284), aware of the paucity of studies on the subject, affirm "the process of succession offers scholars ample opportunities to examine HRD in a unique organizational context, and from a long-term perspective". Based on this belief, they outline the possible relationships between the entrepreneurial succession process on the one hand, and HR development, in terms of informal and formal learning, on the other. Organizational learning opportunities are also recalled by Flamini et al. (2020), according to which "the interplay between the incumbent and the next generation, along with the family's involvement, can affect the provision of new knowledge".

From a different perspective Steijvers et al. (2017), while not directly addressing the issue of business succession, find evidence regarding the relationship between the CEO's skills and the level of implementation of formal HR management practices. They claim that "family CEOs that have a university degree and thus have sufficient knowledge on the types and advantages of formal HR practices seem to implement more formal HR systems" (2017: 161). Indirectly, the result of their research recalls the choices related to the successor's training and professional development path, both in terms of school-university career, and in terms of work experience outside the family business (Bonti & Cori, 2011).

From these few fragments in the literature we can discern a hinted-at relationship between the features of the entrepreneurial succession process, visible since its preparatory stages, and the subsequent evolution of the HR management system. However, there are no direct references to the possible impacts of changes at the helm of the family firm on the diffusion of HR management skills and practices. This, in our opinion, represents a not-secondary theoretical gap in family business studies. In the following paragraphs we will endeavor to pave the way for the gradual filling of this gap, by first proposing some reflections on previously carried out research; we then follow by broadly outlining a possible conceptual model, which can serve as a reference for subsequent studies aimed at directly addressing the question of the relationship between entrepreneurial succession and HR management in family SMEs.

HOW THE ENTREPRENEURIAL SUCCESSION PROCESSES CAN ENHANCE THE HR SYSTEM IN SMEs

Research Purposes and Methodological Choices

In this paragraph we propose to carry out an analysis of the opportunities that entrepreneurial succession in family SMEs can open to the development of the HR management system. To do this, we rely on the evidence that emerged from a 2009 research program that we launched and conducted on a sample of family SMEs.

The aim of this long-term project was to investigate the dynamics of the generational shift in terms of its effects on the transfer of skills, on governance structures, on the orientation towards innovation, and on the HR management. To date, this research project has given rise to various publications, including those on the factors supporting the longevity of family SMEs, on the dynamics of entrepreneurial knowledge and skills along the succession processes, and on the relationship between governance choices and innovation orientation (Bonti & Cori, 2011, 2018; Cori & Bonti, 2014).

Six firms joined the research project; of these, four expressed a particular interest in the potential impact of succession on HRM system. Hence, for the purpose of this work, we focused our attention on: Lanificio Cangioli, Giusto Manetti Battiloro, Distilleria Varnelli, and Confetti Pelino (Table 1). The interviewees previously shared the general lines of the research project and agreed to disseminate the results among the scientific community. For the purposes of this publication, the same protocol used in previous steps of the research was followed: the excerpts from the interviews that have been included in this chapter were sent to the interviewees, requesting confirmation of the correspondence of the content, and authorization for publication.

The firms were selected mainly according to the following criteria:

- homogeneity in terms of firm size (consistent with the EU definition of SMEs: having between 11 and 250 employees and a turnover between 5 and 50 million Euros)
- homogeneity as regards the business culture, the path of industrial development, and the geographical location (central Italy);
- belongingness to the traditional industries of the Italian economy.

These four companies are still owned by the founder's family and have maintained their own product specialization to date. These features provided an opportunity for the researchers and authors of this chapter to analyze the various and specific evolutionary paths and dynamics of companies that have remained faithful to their original industry sector.

Table 1. Participants in the survey

Company	Industry	Region	Year of establish-ment	Interviewed people	Role of interviewed people	Entrepre-neurial generation
Lanificio Cangioli	clothing-textile	Tuscany	1859	Vincenzo Cangioli	Chair	5th
Giusto Manetti Battiloro	gold-beating	Tuscany	1820	Niccolò Manetti	Marketing Director	6th
Distilleria Varnelli	alcoholic beverages	Marche	1868	Orietta Maria Varnelli	CEO	4th
Confetti Pelino	confectionery	Abruzzo	1783	Antonio Pelino	former CEO	7th

Source: our elaboration

We adopted a qualitative research design, carried out through the multi-case study approach, in order to collect thick insights about issues that require observation in a meaningful time horizon. Indeed, the multi-case approach makes it possible to highlight a variety of situations, even divergent ones, in the ultimate aim of contributing to the elaboration of an explanatory theory (Eisenhardt & Graebner, 2007; Yin, 2009). The construction of the sample took place according to the "convenience sampling" approach (Mayan, 2016), based on the current entrepreneurs' willingness to be interviewed and to comply with the research protocol (i.e., recording of the interviews, authorization to publish excerpts).

Among the evidence collected, the cases studied allowed us to shed light on some relevant changes that have taken place in the HR management practices of the firms as a result of the entrepreneurial succession processes.

Two sources of data have been used to collet relevant insights from the four firms:

- semi-structured, in-depth, face-to-face interviews with the latest generation entrepreneurs;
- company website, internal documents, press releases and journal articles, and historical-celebratory publications.

In the period from 2009 to 2016 the authors conjointly carried out at least two interviews at each company. The interviews, lasting from one to two hours, were recorded and transcribed and their content was shared with the respondents. In accordance with the qualitative approach (Yin, 2009), prolonged interaction with respondents at the company headquarters has allowed us to become familiar with the history of the firms themselves, to better understand the firm's context, and to get a sense of the organizational/managerial choices as seen through the "eyes" of the respondents.

The first interview was conducted using a narrative approach. The entrepreneurs were left free to tell, in their own words, of the family firm's history, in such a way as to highlight the paths followed in its productive and commercial development, the current strategic positioning, the forms of competence developed over time, the evolution of organizational models, the eventual discontinuity and radical changes introduced either coincidentally or with no connection whatsoever to the shift of entrepreneurial succession.

For the second interview, we prepared a semi-structured questionnaire in order to collect qualitative open-ended data and achieve some specific outcomes. The goals was to avoid answer that were excessively schematized and laconic, to leave respondents free to express their view regarding some features of the phenomena investigated, and to construct a "chain of evidence" comparable among the diverse cases (Yin, 2009).

The set of sources used has allowed us to gather rich evidence regarding the dynamics of the business succession processes, the modes of transmitting skills from one generation to another, and the most significant impacts of the succession on the management and organization of firms. For the purposes of this work, we have mainly taken into consideration the last generational change, the one that has affected current entrepreneurs, so as to have more varied and in-depth information available in order to hypothesize a pattern of relationships between variables.

In these companies, the repeated "passages of the baton" at the top were studied. We observed the processes of succession in their complete extension: from the preparatory phase, to the actual transition phase, often characterized by a period of cohabitation, and, finally, to the phase following the formal closure of the succession process, in which the outgoing entrepreneur tends to gradually reduce his/her involvement, while the first impacts on management and organization begin to emerge and the innovative scope of the entrepreneurial transition is revealed.

Two aspects seemed particularly relevant to us, in terms of impact on the HR management system. The first refers to the preparatory phase of the succession, and concerns the educational paths and any outside work experience of the members of the incoming generation. The second aspect, which mainly affects the transition phase and the intergenerational cohabitation period, concerns the modes of transferring skills associated with the entrepreneurial role from one generation to another.

Educational Paths and Outside Work Experience of the Heirs: Why They Count

The concept of "familiness" (Habbershon et al. 2003) sums up well the idea that certain idiosyncratic forms of competence are developed over time; these are linked to the firm's proprietorial structure and represent a sort of "secret recipe" for its longevity. Due to the mainly tacit nature of such competence, Cabrera-Suàrez et al. (2001) suggest a period of "intergenerational cohabitation" as a prerequisite for its effective transfer to the incoming entrepreneurial generation. To this aim many authors stress the importance of an "early exposure" to the working environment of the family firm (Steier, 2001; Schröder et al. 2011). Consequently, the designed heir's choice of particular courses of study as well as work experience outside the company is of secondary importance.

In our view, if on the one hand the internal development of the designated successor is important for the transfer of idiosyncratic knowledge and skills to the incoming generation, on the other hand the external development of a successor may reinforce his/her propensity to innovate the management of the family firm. This perspective is shared by Goto (2010: 3), according to whom "professional work experiences outside of the family provides opportunities", and Sardeshmukh & Corbett (2011: 115) who point out how training paths outside the company may provide the successor with a "greater exposure to newer ideas" and pursuits of "more novel initiatives".

In the story of current entrepreneurs, the analysis of the "passing of the baton" by the previous generation starts from the antecedents, which can be identified primarily in the choices concerning the educational paths and in the youthful ambitions of the designated heirs. In this work, we are not interested in exploring how autonomous or imposed the choices relating to study paths have been, nor whether any work experiences outside the family business have been suggested, shared or opposed by the previous generation. Instead, we are interested in understanding whether and to what extent training and work experiences has contributed to developing a particular orientation or certain skills regarding the HR management. We are also interested in observing whether and to what extent this orientation and these skills were then translated, once the reins of the company were assumed, into new working practices, in the formalization of those in use and, more generally, in a different "personnel idea".

In the companies studied, some work experiences outside the family business take on particular significance. For example, Orietta Maria Varnelli, the current CEO of the distillery founded four generations ago in Pievebovigliana, in the Marche region, summarized the value of her work experience at a tourism service company in these words:

Having experienced working in the position of employee was useful to me when I started dealing with HR management; I could count on greater credibility among employees as I had been "one of them" and at the same time I had gained more awareness about what it means to be an employee.

In this case, beyond any specific management skills that may have matured during that experience, the most important aspect consists in the development of an awareness hitherto absent in the family firm, as well as an attitude of listening to employees and knowing how to play their role. These are skills which, as a whole, are recognized as greatly significant for someone in a managerial role and that, in this specific case, may have stimulated innovation-oriented behaviors by the distillery's employees.

A different experience, in both context (an American company) and duration, was had by Niccolò Manetti, member of the board of Giusto Manetti Battiloro, a historic Florentine company, and Vice-President of the Chamber of Commerce of Florence.

What I experienced in the United States was a particularly significant period for me; I had the opportunity to enter a very different context from that of the family business; in particular (the) internship in the company has left its mark: it taught me the value of planning one's career, but also the importance of formalizing roles and responsibilities (...), as well as the opportunities of teamwork.

The exposure, albeit short, to a culture the is decidedly distant from that "breathed" in the family allows one of the members of the incoming generation to develop not only a different orientation with respect to the dominant one in the family business, but also to mature fairly precise ideas about the opportunities associated with some choices of work organization. In the preparatory phase of the succession, the foundations are laid for the changes that will be made, not always in harmony with the other members of the new generation, once the generational change is over. The exposure to a more "evolved" organizational culture also impact on how one understands the contribution made by human resources:

Since my entry into a managerial role, in the late 90s, the contribution of ideas by the workers is considered a normal occurrence and not limited to foremen; it can be said that it is only from those years on that there has been a full recognition of the professionalism of the employees and the possibility for each of them to fully express themselves (interview to Niccolò Manetti)

In the case of Mario Pelino, the current President of the famous confectionery (specialized in Jordan almonds) in Sulmona, in the Abruzzo region, the experience away from the family business is linked to his choice to undertake a university career. This opportunity led him to work for a few years in the United States, and to indirectly enter into contact with a profoundly different managerial culture, thanks to contacts with numerous companies for research reasons.

As regards personnel management, the paternalist style typical of the previous entrepreneurial generations has been replaced by Mario's harder and more formal one. Over time, his managerial style, combined with the introduction of the Total Quality System, has stimulated widespread proactive behavior, capable of generating some significant incremental innovations. (interview to Antonio Pelino)

The educational and research path undertaken allows one of the members of the new generation to expand the knowledge base of the historic family firm; it also allowed him to assimilate the typical logics of the American managerial culture. These include the approach to personnel management, which underwent a radical change once the transition process from one generation to another was completed. In this case, the impact on the HR system is more evident, also because it translates into a progressive formalization of management practices.

The experiences mentioned above present some commonalities: on the one hand, consistent with Sardeshmukh & Corbett (2011), they bring to light the younger heirs' ability to grasp different concepts, models, practices and the opportunity to be open to new ideas and trends, thanks to their times lived away from the family firm; on the other hand, these experiences are also the source of innovation-oriented behaviors among employees (Janssen, 2005; De Jong & Den Hartog, 2007), and they show the relevance of some incremental innovations as a result of a "bottom-up" approach, as well.

Selecting and Integrating Entrepreneurial Competences Along the Succession Process

As mentioned above, the idea embraced in this work is that the outcome of the succession must be evaluated in relation to the ability of the family firm to pursue "innovation around tradition" (Bonti & Cori, 2013). In our view, the possibility of integrating tradition and innovation depends primarily on how the inter-generational transition is managed, with particular reference to the ways in which the idiosyncratic knowledge of the firm is handled and transferred during the period of cohabitation between the entrepreneur and successor.

In line with mainstream literature, along the entrepreneurial succession process it is important to ensure the full transfer of this heritage, a sort of necessary condition for the continuity of the family business. Yet, the full transfer of knowledge may prove to be a less-than-optimal choice, as stated before: it seems preferable to move forward and seize new opportunity, while looking back to not forget the origins.

Four different modes of transferring competences can thus be identified (Bonti & Cori, 2011, 2013): integral, incomplete, selective, and lacking. When the stock of knowledge and skills that have been accumulated over time and embedded in the *familiness* of the firm remains fully usable, an integral mode of transfer is identified. An integral transfer becomes possible when the successor recognizes the full usefulness of such knowledge and skills, which are shared during the cohabitation with the predecessor. An incomplete mode of transfer occurs when the stock of knowledge and skills, although considered effective and useful, remains only partially available after the succession process, in an unintentional manner. On the contrary, if either the founder or the successor intentionally filter the stock of knowledge and skills, choosing not to share the outdate ones, a selective mode of transfer takes place. Finally, the case in which the direct or indirect transfer of *familiness* becomes impossible, and is therefore lacking due to, for example, the premature death of the father, an abrupt interruption in the evolutionary path of the firm could occur.

In light of these considerations, the selective mode of transfer seems to offer the greater opportunities to give new vitality to the family business. The cases examined provided some evidence in this regard, albeit in different ways. So Vincenzo Cangioli, chair of the wool mill bearing the same name and located in Prato:

In the period of cohabitation between the outgoing and the incoming generation, the latter thinks of the necessary changes, clashing with the crystallized culture of the former, which did not want to know how to detach itself from the choices of the past. (...) They realize that some people working in the company are absolutely inadequate ("you didn't know what they were doing there"); so, they engage in developing people's assessment skills.

The situation described above is evidence of the awareness that new generation entrepreneurs have, as regards the need to overcome some old management logic that is believed to be the origin of wrong choices. In this case, the cohabitation period gives the heirs, above all, time to reflect on the adequacy of the management practices followed by the previous generation and to identify the areas of competence to be developed. Among these, HR management skills are considered a priority, as the consequences of past choices, not supported by adequate knowledge and skills, are evident.

The process of selecting and integrating skills along the generational shift is substantiated not only in the acquisition of "missing" knowledge and skills, but also in the development of particular attitudes. Among these, the propensity to networking, in the form of both interpersonal relationships and inter-organizational networks, is the one that most often marks a discontinuity between the current generation and previous one. The experiences of two members of the new generation currently leading the firms studied offer significant evidence of this. In one case, Vincenzo Cangioli told us:

The new technical designer brought a network of relationships that he had previously developed in the area. This model is replicated at a higher level, through the personal choice to participate in the activity of the local employers' association.

In this case the awareness that fostering inter-organizational relationships can help to enhance learning processes and provide access to useful knowledge for the company was developed thanks to the new entry in one of the critical technical roles.

In other case, Vincenzo Manetti, on his part, also stated:

I decided to invest in ideas, skills, creativity ... I became a member of more than a dozen Boards of industrial and financial companies... I take care of relationships.

Young entrepreneurs perceive the importance of joining interpersonal networks, in the first case by assiduously participating in the association activity, in the other by being co-opted into a large number of boards. The common goal is to open new channels of access to knowledge and skills not held by the respective firms, to voluntarily and consciously expose themselves to different organizational cultures, and "to keep one's finger on the pulse". Although the literature identifies a rather weak relationship between participation in advisory networks and the adoption of HRM practices, whereas joining coercive networks would produce more significant effects (Bacon & Hoque, 2005), we can still assume that the inclusion in networks of relations that are similar to advisory ones gives rise to phenomena of mimetic isomorphism. In other words, the introduction of innovative HR practices or the formalization of those already in use could represent the result of imitative choices, dictated by the comparison with other entrepreneurs, or by the observation of the results obtained by them.

By and large, the excerpts from the interviews conducted with the latest generation of entrepreneurs offer a significant insight into the possible links between the business succession process and HR management systems. The variety of evidence collected does not allow, at the moment, to identify specific dynamics and recurring options, but it does shed light on a, underexplored phenomenon and could serve to reach a synthesis.

The dynamics associated with the shift at the top of family SMEs show that the succession process, in itself, hardly produces 360° changes in HR management. Although many entrepreneurs of the new generation show a tendency to somehow rethink the employer-employees relationship, also following a critical reflection on the choices made by their predecessors, their orientation towards innovation and their desire for change will not always, and not immediately, translate into choices concerning structures and roles, as well as in the identification of a system of "advanced" management practices. More often, the new generation entrepreneurs proceed step by step, by introducing a tool that they believe can impact almost immediately on performance (for example a new selection or evaluation criteria), or by formalizing and giving new and stronger legitimacy to a practice already in use.

However, it would be premature to draw conclusions relating to the low impact of the succession process on the evolution of attitude towards the HR management system. Indeed, some considerations lead us to the withhold judgment. The first, of a methodological nature, concerns the fact that the evidence collected refers to time periods that are not too distant from the conclusion of the succession process, if not even to situations in which the process itself is still open, in which the "veto power" of the older generation can still be felt, in the form of overt resistance or underground inertia. A second regards the educational and professional path taken by many of the future entrepreneurs: they become aware of the need to renew the approach to HR management in the family's firm, but it may not yet be clear which choices are most consistent with their orientation, which practices should be introduced, or which conditions determine the effectiveness of each practice, in terms of underlying competences and pursuing synergy between one practice and another. A third consideration regards the context in which the new "personnel idea" should apply. It may be that entrepreneurs belonging to the new generation are aware not only of the obsolescence of the management logic of the previous generation, but also of the choices that should be made in terms of introducing new practices or even just formalizing those in use. Nevertheless, they hesitate to proceed too quickly in this renewal process because they believe that the size of the company does not justify the use of some practices, their formalization, much less of the hiring of a HR manager. Another underlying reason for the hesitance is the fear that a radical change is not compatible with the dominant culture, in which not only the outgoing entrepreneur, but perhaps also the older employees can recognize themselves. Lastly, there is also the awareness that the effectiveness of the changes could be conditioned by the firm's *imprinting*, an expression of the "genes" that are written in the company's DNA and which are at the origin of behaviors of acceptance or rejection of organizational changes.

TOWARDS A CONCEPTUAL FRAMEWORK

The previous steps of our research project offer wide evidence to support the existence of a series of impacts exerted by the entrepreneurial succession process on the development and strengthening of the HR management system in the family SMEs. In particular, the analysis of the long-lived firms we investigated highlights a significant impact on the HR culture and on the diffusion of practices, which mostly remain non-formalized.

So, despite having investigated only a small number of companies, the depth of the analysis carried out and the observation of the dynamics related to business succession in a sufficiently long time lapse allowed us to identify a set of factors that come into play in orienting the relationship between the entrepreneurial succession process and the HR management systems in a family SME.

The two main factors that emerge from the analysis of the literature coupled with the evidence of empirical research are, on the one hand, the choices related to the *educational and professional paths* of the designated heirs; on the other, the *ways of transferring entrepreneurial knowledge and skills* during the period of transition. Choices relating to training courses and professional experiences are not necessarily connected in an intentional way to the prospect of succession. In any case, they are able to influence, even in the medium-long term, behaviors and orientations assumed by the heirs both during the succession process and when performing the entrepreneurial role.

In line with the analysis carried out, in identifying the training path for the designated successor, a trade off occurs between internal and external training of the future entrepreneur. Calling back Sardeshmukh & Corbett (2011), the intensity of experience within the family firms is considered more important than the years of experience spent developing the successor's ability to become a leader and his perception of entrepreneurial self-efficacy. At the same time, training paths outside the company, i.e. an external development of a successor, may positively influence his ability to lead the firm in a new direction.

In this regard, we recall here the distinction, proposed previously (Bonti & Cori, 2013), between the "procedural" and the "substantive" dimensions of the succession process. The first dimension concerns some formal stages and activities of the succession process: planning degree, length of the whole process, length of cohabitation. The second one regards some key decisions that can generate more or less intense and pervasive organizational changes, and that are related to the educational path (external or internal / external, firm-oriented or differentiated) and the work experience (cohabitation or outside experience).

As regards the impact of substantive dimensions, what emerges is that external or balanced educational paths, combined with work experiences outside the family firm, are likely to lead to adoption of a "selective mode", concerning the intergenerational transfer of knowledge (Bonti & Cori, 2011, 2013). In this mode, an aware and intentional process in which prior knowledge and capabilities are filtered by the entrepreneur in charge or/and the incumbent occurs. Therefore, the educational path and the work experiences away from the family firm seem to affect, first of all, how the knowledge and skills of the outgoing entrepreneur are transferred to the successor and subsequently, affect the outcome of the succession process itself, in terms of competences acquired or consolidated. More specifically, we can assume that the choices regarding the educational-professional path of the designated successor impact directly on the development of a cultural orientation that differs in a more or less significant way from the dominant one in the family business. Moreover, as noted in the literature, a direct impact on the degree of formalization of HR practices can be traced to the professional qualifications possessed by the successor (Steijvers et al., 2017). In addition, an indirect impact can be seen in the mode in which entrepreneurial knowledge and skills are transferred during the crucial phase of the succession. In particular, a selective mode of transferring entrepreneurial competences may bring about either an extension of the firm's knowledge base or an increased propensity to activate inter-organizational relationships.

A third factor, referred to in the literature, can have an effect on the implementation of innovations in the level of HR management in family SMEs. These are the choices relating to the *organization of work* made *prior the succession process* starts. To the extent they are geared to practicing delegation and favoring the empowerment of employees, some of the attitudes adopted by the new entrepreneurial generation will translate into work practices and into individual and group behaviors such as, for example, the propensity to favor widespread innovation or to stimulate proactive behaviors in problematic situations. Moreover, it has also been observed that the organizational choices made prior to the succession may also indirectly impact the development of the HR system. In sum, these choices can alternatively inhibit or strengthen the orientations developed by the entrepreneurs of the new generation; in fact, these require the preparation of fertile ground in order to find full realization.

Finally, a fourth factor capable of exerting an impact on the relationship between succession and development of the HR system can be identified in the *length of the intergenerational cohabitation*, that is, the period in which the incoming generation shares the responsibilities of managing the family business with the outgoing generation. An excessively long period of cohabitation can be considered an obstacle and, in the long term, likely to weaken the ability of the incoming generation to translate their innovative orientations into management practices and tools; this might be the case when the outgoing generation tries to resist to the innovation of HR management practices. In other words, the duration of cohabitation can also be seen as an element capable of affecting, either positively or negatively, the likelihood that a more marked managerial culture introduced by the new entrepreneurial generation is followed by a real ability to innovate management logics and tools, including the HR-related ones.

Based on the previous considerations regarding the relevance of certain factors and some possible relationships between them, we propose a possible conceptual model, outlined below. We firmly believe that the progressive narrowing of the theoretical gap mentioned above can usefully benefit from such a starting point, built on modest, but significant, empirical evidence. The conceptual framework, illustrated in Figure 1, represents a first, raw attempt to systematize the analyzed phenomena. The intention is primarily to provide a reference, certainly partial and incomplete, for subsequent research aimed at investigating in depth the relationship between business succession processes in family SMEs and the evolution of HR management systems.

A reading of the model, in terms of the nature of the variables, leads us to consider the heirs' choices of educational and professional paths as a key variable. This key variable is capable of orienting, both directly and indirectly, the evolution of the HR management system in family-owned SMEs, in terms of the introduction of new practices, the formalization of the existing ones, the diffusion of innovative ways of organizing work, etc. As regards the other variables included in the framework, the way of transferring entrepreneurial knowledge and skills takes on the role of a mediation variable, able to condition the dynamics of the knowledge usable by the company and to strengthen (or inhibit) the propensity to activate relationships. The organizational choices prior to the start of the succession process, and the length of the intergenerational coexistence period, seem to rise to the role of moderating variables, able, depending on the case, to facilitate or make it more difficult the translation into operational terms of values and principles that guide the entrepreneurs belonging to the new generation when managing the relationship with employees.

Figure 1. Succession process and HR system development: a conceptual framework
Source: our elaboration

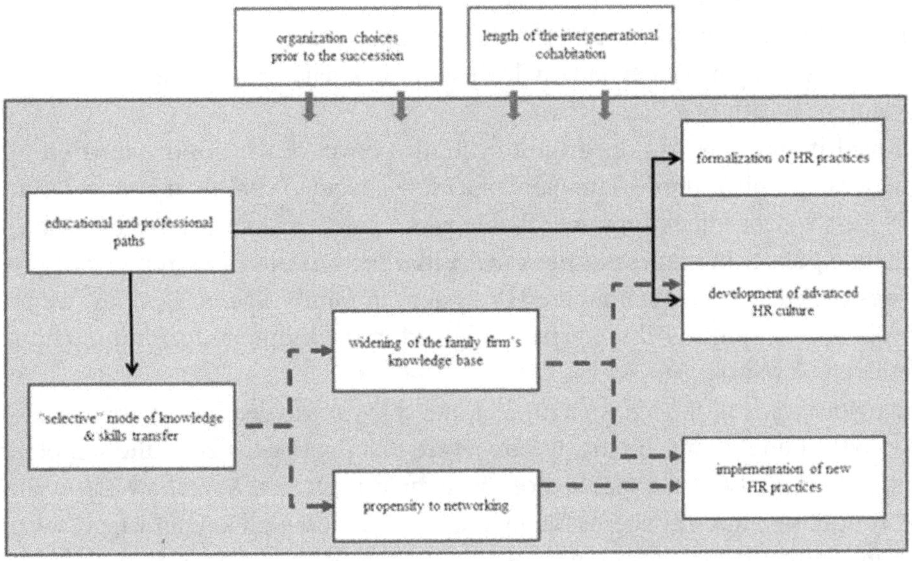

FUTURE RESEARCH DIRECTIONS

In light of the scarcity of previous research on the subject, as well as the evidence that emerged in this study, we believe we can suggest some possible lines of research on the subject of the relationship between entrepreneurial succession and development of the HR management system in family SMEs. Firstly, future research will be able to test the validity of the proposed framework, by confirming or not the relevance of the hypothesized relationships, or adding further variables. Secondly, we believe that the nebulous but indubitable relationship between the entrepreneurial succession processes and HR management systems can be better understood by attempting to answer the following research questions:

- does the generational stage reached by the family firm represent a significant variable in determining a greater or lesser intensity of the link between the entrepreneurial succession process (including the preparatory phase) and the dynamics of the HR management system?
- can differences in size, geographical location, or sector to which firms belong represent, and if so, to what extent, as many variables capable of amplifying (or attenuating) the impact of entrepreneurial succession on the development of the HR system?

In a nutshell, we believe that there is an urgent need to further explore the relationship that was investigated in this study. Future efforts in this direction may strengthen the idea that the changeover at the top of the family business is really an opportunity to be seized, even before being a delicate phase to manage.

CONCLUSION

In this work, we have endeavored to contribute to the understanding of how the entrepreneurial succession process within family SMEs can contribute to strengthening the culture and practices of human resource management, without necessarily leading to the formal establishment of an HR function. The assumption from which the analysis and reflection carried out are based is that the business succession process represents not only a critical and difficult step to manage, but also an opportunity to be seized along the development path of a family firm.

We questioned if and how this opportunity can also concern the implementation of HR policies, tools, and practices, as well as the development of a more adequate culture of human resources. Far from indicating any best way or attempting improbable generalizations, we believe that the findings of our study can generate greater awareness of the impact that the process of entrepreneurial succession can exert on choices aimed at strengthening the HR system in family SMEs. Besides, we believe that our conceptual proposal, helping to fill the gap highlighted in the literature, can represent a starting point for further research on the same topic.

Like the previous steps of the research project, the study presented in this chapter also suffers from some methodological limitations. Firstly, we are aware that the small size of the sample and the choice to seek a high homogeneity of the features of the sample itself, can somehow affect the reliability of the results. A further limitation concerns the fact that not all potential key informants were interviewed (only some of the entrepreneurs currently leading their respective companies), with the consequence of possible biases due to the perceptions of the interviewed entrepreneurs. Such biases might relate to the description of the succession process in which they have been involved, as well as possible conflicts with other family members or branches. Finally, one limitation that is unlikely to be easily surmountable refers to the undetermined reliability of some information concerning the early transitions from one generation to another.

The limitations related to the small sample size can be overcome by an extension of the sample itself or by resorting to a quantitative survey. The long-term project within which this study was developed will provide us with further opportunities to deepen the issues dealt with here. Indeed, the main objectives will be to pursue greater reliability of the results obtained so far, and to test the validity of the proposed framework.

Finally, it seems appropriate to recall some possible theoretical and managerial implications of the research. In the first realm, the study has contributed, on the one hand, to shedding light on how the issue concerning the impact of the entrepreneurial succession process on the development of the HR system in family SMEs is still largely unexplored and, on the other hand, to proposing a hypothetical conceptual model that can be completed and improved in many ways through future research. Regarding the managerial implications, any evidence that can highlight the opportunity aimed at underlining the opportunities that the succession process offers in terms of developing the HR management system can only enhance the awareness on the part of both the outgoing and the incoming entrepreneurial generation. In sum, these reflections serve to reinforce the conviction that the preparation of the succession process represents a critical phase, not only for what the literature indicates as the "success" of the process itself, but also to indirectly favor an evolution and strengthening of the HR system in family SMEs.

REFERENCES

Astrachan, J. H., & Kolenko, T. A. (1994). A neglected factor explaining family business success: Human resource practices. *Family Business Review*, *7*(3), 251–262. doi:10.1111/j.1741-6248.1994.00251.x

Bacon, N., & Hoque, K. (2005). HRM in the SME sector: Valuable employees and coercive networks. *International Journal of Human Resource Management*, *16*(11), 1976–1999. doi:10.1080/09585190500314706

Bammens, Y., Voordeckers, W., & Van Gils, A. (2011). Boards of directors in family businesses: A literature review and research agenda. *International Journal of Management Reviews*, *13*(2), 134–152. doi:10.1111/j.1468-2370.2010.00289.x

Blanco-Mazagatos, V., de Quevedo-Puente, E., & Delgado-García, J. B. (2018). Human resource practices and organizational human capital in the family firm: The effect of generational stage. *Journal of Business Research*, *84*, 337–348. doi:10.1016/j.jbusres.2017.09.017

Bonti, M., & Cori, E. (2011). La longevità delle PMI familiari: riflessioni teoriche ed evidenze empiriche. *Impresa Progetto-Electronic Journal of Management*, (2).

Bonti, M., & Cori, E. (2013). Intergenerational passages and firm longevity: evidence from Italian family SMEs. In *Proceedings of Annual AIDEA Conference, The firm's role in the economy. Does a growth-oriented model exist?* Bari: Cacucci Editore.

Bonti, M., & Cori, E. (2018). Traditional Governance and Innovative Strategies in Italian Family SMEs: Evidence from Tuscany. *International Business Research*, *11*(2), 103–115. doi:10.5539/ibr.v11n2p103

Bracci, E., & Vagnoni, E. (2011). Understanding Small Family Business Succession in a Knowledge Management Perspective. *IUP Journal of Knowledge Management*, *9*(1).

Cabrera Suárez, K., De Saá Pérez, P., & García Almeida, D. (2001). The succession process from a resource and knowledge-based view of the family firm. *Family Business Review*, *14*(1), 37–48. doi:10.1111/j.1741-6248.2001.00037.x

Cadieux, L. (2005). La succession dans les PME familiales: Proposition d'un modèle de réussite du processus de disengagement du prédécesseur. *Revue Internationale du PME*, *18*(3-4).

Cadieux, L. (2007). Succession in Small and Medium-Sized Family Businesses: Towards a Tipology of Predecessor Roles During and After Instatement of the Successor. *Family Business Review*, *20*(2), 95–109. doi:10.1111/j.1741-6248.2007.00089.x

Cherchem, N. (2017). The relationship between organizational culture and entrepreneurial orientation in family firms: Does generational involvement matter? *Journal of Family Business Strategy*, *8*(2), 87–98. doi:10.1016/j.jfbs.2017.04.001

Corbetta, G., & Salvato, C. (2012). *Strategies for Longevity in Family Firms. A European perspective.* Palgrave-MacMillan. doi:10.1057/9781137024589

Cori, E., & Bonti, M. (2014). Handling knowledge through entrepreneurial generations: lessons from long-lived family SMES. *Piccola Impresa/Small Business*, (3), 17-38.

Daspit, J. J., Madison, K., Barnett, T., & Long, R. G. (2018). The emergence of bifurcation bias from unbalanced families: Examining HR practices in the family firm using circumplex theory. *Human Resource Management Review*, *28*(1), 18–32. doi:10.1016/j.hrmr.2017.05.003

De Kok, J. M. P., Uhlaner, L. M., & Thurik, A. R. (2006). Professional HRM practices in family owned-managed enterprises. *Journal of Small Business Management*, *44*(3), 441–460. doi:10.1111/j.1540-627X.2006.00181.x

De Massis, A., Chua, J. H., & Chrisman, J. J. (2008). Factors preventing intra-family succession. *Family Business Review*, *21*(2), 183–199. doi:10.1111/j.1741-6248.2008.00118.x

Dekker, J., Lybaert, N., Steijvers, T., & Depaire, B. (2015). The effect of family business professionalization as a multidimensional construct on firm performance. *Journal of Small Business Management*, *53*(2), 516–538. doi:10.1111/jsbm.12082

Dekker, J. C., Lybaert, N., Steijvers, T., Depaire, B., & Mercken, R. (2013). Family firm types based on the professionalization construct: Exploratory research. *Family Business Review*, *26*(1), 81–99. doi:10.1177/0894486512445614

Del Bene, L. (2005). *Aziende familiari tra imprenditorialità e managerialità*. Giappichelli.

Dyck, B., Mauws, M., Starke, F. A., & Mischke, G. A. (2002). Passing the baton: The importance of sequence, timing, technique and communication in executive succession. *Journal of Business Venturing*, *17*(2), 143–162. doi:10.1016/S0883-9026(00)00056-2

Eisenhardt, K. M., & Graebner, M. E. (2007). Theory Building from Cases: Opportunities and Challenges. *Academy of Management Journal*, *50*(1), 25–32. doi:10.5465/amj.2007.24160888

Flamini, G., Gnan, L., & Pellegrini, M. M. (2020). Forty years of research on human resource management in family firms: analyzing the past; preparing for the future. *Journal of Family Business Management*. . doi:10.1108/JFBM-05-2020-0040

Gabrielsson, J., & Huse, M. (2005). Outside directors in SME boards: a call for theoretical reflections. *Corporate Board: Role, Duties and Composition, 1*(1), 28-37.

Gomez-Mejia, L. R., Nunez-Nickel, M., & Gutierrez, I. (2001). The role of family ties in agency contracts. *Academy of Management Journal*, *44*(1), 81–95.

Goto, T. (2010). Secrets of family business longevity in Japan from the social capital perspective. In *Handbook of Research on Family Business*. Edward Elgar Publishing.

Habbershon, T. G., Williams, M., & MacMillan, I. C. (2003). A unified systems perspective of family firm performance. *Journal of Business Venturing*, *18*(4), 451–465. doi:10.1016/S0883-9026(03)00053-3

Hall, A., & Nordqvist, M. (2008). Professional management in family businesses: Toward an extended understanding. *Family Business Review*, *21*(1), 51–69. doi:10.1111/j.1741-6248.2007.00109.x

Johannisson, B., & Huse, M. (2000). Recruiting outside board members in the small family business: An ideological challenge. *Entrepreneurship and Regional Development*, *12*(4), 353–378. doi:10.1080/08985620050177958

Kellermanns, F. W., & Eddleston, K. A. (2004). Feuding families: When conflict does a family firm good. *Entrepreneurship Theory and Practice*, *28*(3), 209–228. doi:10.1111/j.1540-6520.2004.00040.x

Kopriva, I., & Bernik, M. (2009). Comparison of human resource management in Slovenian family and non-family businesses. *Organizacija*, *42*(6), 246–254. doi:10.2478/v10051-009-0021-2

Kotey, B., & Folker, C. (2007). Employee training in SMEs: Effect of size and firm type - Family and non-family. *Journal of Small Business Management*, *45*(2), 214–238. doi:10.1111/j.1540-627X.2007.00210.x

Lambrecht, J. (2005). Multigenerational transition in family businesses: A new explanatory model. *Family Business Review*, *18*(4), 267–282. doi:10.1111/j.1741-6248.2005.00048.x

Le Breton-Miller, I. L., Miller, D., & Steier, L. P. (2004). Toward an integrative model of effective FOB succession. *Entrepreneurship Theory and Practice*, *28*(4), 305–328. doi:10.1111/j.1540-6520.2004.00047.x

Mayan, M. J. (2016). *Essentials of qualitative inquiry*. Routledge. doi:10.4324/9781315429250

Miller, D., & Le Breton-Miller, I. (2005). *Managing for the long run: Lessons in competitive advantage from great family businesses*. Harvard Business Press.

Murray, B. (2003). The succession transition process: A longitudinal perspective. *Family Business Review*, *16*(1), 17–33. doi:10.1111/j.1741-6248.2003.00017.x

Mustafa, M. J., & Elliott, C. (2019). The curious case of human resource development in family-small-to-medium sized enterprises. *Human Resource Development Quarterly*, *30*(3), 281–290. doi:10.1002/hrdq.21370

Nordqvist, M., Habbershon, T. G., & Melin, L. (2008). Transgenerational entrepreneurship: Exploring entrepreneurial orientation in family firms. *Frontiers in European Entrepreneurship Research*, 93-116.

Nordqvist, M., & Melin, L. (2010). Entrepreneurial families and family firms. *Entrepreneurship and Regional Development*, *22*(3-4), 211–239. doi:10.1080/08985621003726119

Salvato, C. (2004). Predictors of entrepreneurship in family firms. *Journal of Private Equity*, *7*(3), 68–76. doi:10.3905/jpe.2004.412339

Sambrook, S. (2005). Exploring succession planning in small, growing firms. *Journal of Small Business and Enterprise Development*, *12*(4), 579–594. doi:10.1108/14626000510628243

Sardeshmukh, S. R., & Corbett, A. C. (2011). The duality of internal and external development of successors: Opportunity recognition in family firms. *Family Business Review*, *24*(2), 111–125. doi:10.1177/0894486510391783

Schröder, E., Schmitt-Rodermund, E., & Arnaud, N. (2011). Career choice intentions of adolescents with a family business background. *Family Business Review*, *24*(4), 305–321. doi:10.1177/0894486511416977

Schulze, W. S., Lubatkin, M. H., & Dino, R. N. (2003). Toward a theory of agency and altruism in family firms. *Journal of Business Venturing*, *18*(4), 473–490. doi:10.1016/S0883-9026(03)00054-5

Sharma, P., Chrisman, J. J., & Chua, J. H. (2003). Succession planning as planned behavior: Some empirical results. *Family Business Review*, *16*(1), 1–15. doi:10.1111/j.1741-6248.2003.00001.x

Sharma, P., Chrisman, J. J., Pablo, A. L., & Chua, J. H. (2001). Determinants of initial satisfaction with the succession process in family firms: A conceptual model. *Entrepreneurship Theory and Practice*, *25*(3), 17–36. doi:10.1177/104225870102500302

Songini, L., & Gnan, L. (2014). The glass ceiling in SMEs and its impact on firm managerialisation: A comparison between family and non-family SMEs. *International Journal of Business Governance and Ethics*, *9*(2), 170–196. doi:10.1504/IJBGE.2014.063278

Steier, L. (2001). Next-generation entrepreneurs and succession: An exploratory study of modes and means of managing social capital. *Family Business Review*, *14*(3), 259–276. doi:10.1111/j.1741-6248.2001.00259.x

Steijvers, T., Lybaert, N., & Dekker, J. (2017). Formal human resource practices in family firms. *Journal of Family Business Management.*, *7*(2), 151–165. doi:10.1108/JFBM-07-2016-0016

Stewart, A., & Hitt, M. A. (2012). Why can't a family business be more like a nonfamily business? Modes of professionalization in family firms. *Family Business Review*, *25*(1), 58–86. doi:10.1177/0894486511421665

Voordeckers, W., Van Gils, A., & Van den Heuvel, J. (2007). Board composition in small and medium-sized family firms. *Journal of Small Business Management*, *45*(1), 137–156. doi:10.1111/j.1540-627X.2007.00204.x

Yedder, M. B. (2018). Human resource management in family business succession: Victim or saviour? *Journal of Enterprising Culture*, *26*(4), 401–421. doi:10.1142/S0218495818500152

Yin, R. K. (2009). *Case study research: Design and methods* (4th ed.). Sage.

ADDITIONAL READING

Boyd, B., Royer, S., Pei, R., & Zhang, X. (2015). Knowledge transfer in family business successions. *Journal of Family Business Management.*, *5*(1), 17–37. doi:10.1108/JFBM-05-2014-0009

Dyer, W. G. (1989). Integrating professional management into a family owned business. *Family Business Review*, *2*(3), 221–235. doi:10.1111/j.1741-6248.1989.00221.x

Flamholtz, E. (1986). *Managing the Transition from an entrepreneurship to a professionally managed firm*. JosseyBass.

Flamini, G., & Gnan, L. (2019). Family Firms' HRM Practices Configurations: An empirical analysis. *Proceedings of the 14th International Conference on European Integration–Innovating Europe* (pp. 27-81). Skopje: University American College.

Gersick, K. E., Lansberg, I., Desjardins, M., & Dunn, B. (1999). Stages and transitions: Managing change in the family business. *Family Business Review*, *12*(4), 287–297. doi:10.1111/j.1741-6248.1999.00287.x

Habbershon, T. G., & Williams, M. L. (1999). A resource-based framework for assessing the strategic advantages of family firms. *Family Business Review*, *12*(1), 1–25. doi:10.1111/j.1741-6248.1999.00001.x

Handler, W. C. (1990). Succession in Family Firms: A Mutual Role Adjustment between Entrepreneur & Next-Generation Family Members. *Entrepreneurship Theory and Practice*, *15*(1), 37–52. doi:10.1177/104225879001500105

Tagiuri, R., & Davis, J. (1996). Bivalent attributes of the family firm. *Family Business Review*, *9*(2), 199–208. doi:10.1111/j.1741-6248.1996.00199.x

Ward, J. L. (1988). The special role of strategic planning for family businesses. *Family Business Review*, *1*(2), 105–117. doi:10.1111/j.1741-6248.1988.00105.x

KEY TERMS AND DEFINITIONS

Entrepreneurial Succession: Process aimed at transferring ownership and management from one family member to another, generally belonging to two different generations. It develops over time, is articulated in a series of steps, and involves a number of roles. Its actual outcomes cannot always be known a priori.

Familiness: Concept used with reference to family businesses, to indicate a mix of tangible and intangible resources, explicit and tacit knowledge, technical and behavioral skills, which each firm combines in an absolutely unique way.

HR Management System: Set of values, structures, roles, practices, tools, and skills supporting people management in a firm.

Intergenerational Cohabitation: In a family business, the stage of the entrepreneurial succession process in which the outgoing and the incoming generation share management responsibilities.

Professionalization: Organizational transformation process, referring primarily to family businesses, aimed at integrating entrepreneurial skills with managerial skills, as well as the formalization of structures, roles and work practices and tools.

Propensity to Networking: Propensity to establish cooperative relationships, both through the intertwining of interpersonal and informal relationships and through the establishment of formalized inter-firm networks.

Selective Mode of Knowledge and Skills Transfer: In a family firm, the mode of intergenerational shift in which the outgoing entrepreneur or his heir intentionally filter the stock of knowledge and skills, choosing not to share the outdate ones.

Chapter 13
Managing Generational Handover in Family Business:
A Multistakeholders' Perspective Focusing on HR Role

Barbara Barabaschi
Università Cattolica del Sacro Cuore, Italy

Franca Cantoni
Università Cattolica del Sacro Cuore, Italy

Roberta Virtuani
Università Cattolica del Sacro Cuore, Italy

ABSTRACT

The aim of this chapter is to highlight the peculiarities of the succession in family-owned businesses and to discuss the main difficulties encountered by second and third-generation entrepreneurs during the succession process. By the use of direct interviews, the authors collected information about the specific role played by the multiplicity of stakeholders involved, first of all the HR function and the relationship with non family employees. The case studies analysed consider family firms that are managing their succession process. Two generations coexist in two cases with family members belonging to different branches of the same family. Non-family managers and employees represents a fundamental stakeholder that influence the success and sustainability of the succession process. One aim of the chapter is to analyse how the HR practices have changed during the succession process considering how the successors entered and integrated with non-family managers and employees according to the management for stakeholders approach.

DOI: 10.4018/978-1-7998-4814-1.ch013

INTRODUCTION

It is soon after the 1990s that family studies have been academically recognized as a separate field of research (Bird, Welsch, Astrachan Pisturi, 2002; Porfírio, Felício, Carrilho, 2019). A specific body of knowledge of family business have been requested by the peculiarity of family business and by its importance for economic progress (Nordqvist & Melin, 2010). In fact, the family involvement and the aptitude and vision of family members support the family business development in a unique and specific way (Chua, Chrisman, Sharma, 1999).

Demographic trends indicate an inversion of the age pyramid with individuals 65 years and over constituting the fastest growing sector of the population (22.8% in 2019 and is projected to rise 51.2% in 2070, European Commission, 2017). With this greying of the population, the number of family business leaders confronting succession and retirement will accelerate in the coming decades. A large majority of these family firm leaders (70% in Italy) wish to have their businesses controlled by their families in the future. Evidence indicates, however, that probability of fulfilling the wish is reducing overtime; most family businesses barely outlive the tenure of their founders (Stamm, Lubinski, 2011) Estimates show that only 25% of Italian family firms survive the transition to the second generation and only 15% make it to the third generation (Barbaresco, 2019). Only about 3% of family businesses survive to the fourth generation and beyond (Mokhber, Rasid, Vakilbashi, Zamil & Seng, 2017). For these factors and results succession appears as one of the biggest challenges faced by family businesses (Le Breton-Miller, Miller & Steier, 2004; Bocatto, Gispert, & Rialp, 2010).

THE PECULIARITIES OF SUCCESSION IN FAMILY-OWNED BUSINESSES

Succession planning in family-owned businesses is defined as '*the explicit process by which the management control is transferred from one family member to another*' (Sharma et al., 2000, pg. 233). As stated by Porfírio, Felício, Carrilho (2019) "*we are interested in considering that succession is not a moment but rather a process*". To understand this process Nordqvist, Wennberg, Bau, & Hellerstedt, 2013 underly the demand for a closer integration of entrepreneurship theories and family business theories. "*Succession can be understood if considered from an entrepreneurial process perspective* (Habbershon & Pistrui, 2002; Nordqvist & Melin, 2010) *where both the entry of new owners and exit of old owners are associated with the pursuit of new business opportunities*" (Nordqvist, Wennberg, Bau, & Hellerstedt, 2013, p.1087; Porfírio, Carrilho, & Mónico, 2016). Succession is either the entry and exit of the entrepreneurial process. Moreover, the literature on family firm research views succession as a complex process, due to the personal goals of the owners, family structure, ability and ambitions of potential successors and legal and financial issues (De Massis et al. 2008; Le Breton-Miller et al., 2004; Sharma et al., 2003). In fact, one of the main characteristics of family business succession is that the process is not primarily governed by market values but by the relationships within the business and the family (Churchill & Hatten, 1997).

Dealing with relational factors in the succession process is crucial, since it involves different groups of stakeholders inside and outside the family. In this context, the management for stakeholders approach could represent a useful option enabling the course of the process minimizing the risk of conflicts. This approach requires to govern and shape relationships among the various actors involved, directly and indirectly (successor, family members having or not an active role within the firm, management, employees, HR, customers, financiers) and not only to arrange a series of exchanges of material resources to maximize the interest of a particular stakeholder. The purpose to act a sustainable development of the succession process calls for paying attention to specific values typical of management-for-stakeholders, such as transparency, fairness, trust. The main challenge in this case is to combine the specific goals of the succession process with others expression of the firm common good, for example, along with the firm survival and development, the new corporate structure perceived as fair by employees and other stakeholders, so more general goals, but still crucial to assure succession success (Di Maddaloni & Devis, 2017).

Managing for stakeholder requires that the interest of all groups of stakeholders need to go together over time. This is obviously more difficult than focusing on the priorities of a specific group. The managing for stakeholder mindset tries to find how it is possible to create and share the value of succession process during each different phase with all the stakeholders, because this is the best way to reach long-term goals (Freeman, Harrison, Wicks 2007). Managerial practice, in particular, has demonstrated that, in the long-term, it is no possible to obtain benefits for a stakeholder without caring for those of others.

Furthermore, in case of conflicts, it is necessary to reframe the main succession propositions so that more stakeholders perceive their interests as guaranteed over time. Stakeholders that are difficult to please or are in dissonance with the process guidelines can be in any case source of value creation, if approached with the ''win-win'' mindset of managing-for-stakeholders.

Within stakeholder management theory (see Clarkson, 1995 and Freeman, 1984), another probably useful suggestion comes from distinguishing the succession stakeholders between primary and secondary stakeholders. The first refers to those having the more direct impact on the succession process, often their collaboration is essential to obtain the succession success (i.e. family members working into the firm, employees, management, HR), consequently managers have to assign great attention to their needs. Moreover, stakeholder theory also stresses the importance of secondary stakeholders (Clarkson, 1995), which are not directly involved into the company's succession process and have no formal contractual relationships, such as, family members not directly engaged in business, financers, clients. Clarkson underlines the interdependence between the two groups of stakeholders. Indeed, some scholars (see Turner & Zolin 2012; Di Maddaloni & Devis, 2017) underline the beneficial effect on succession deriving from managing secondary, but legitimate, stakeholders, by considering them as a part of a wider (although complex) succession project. In particular, actions addressed to this group will help the owner to reduce planning misjudgment and to increase transparency and collaboration to the succession process.

In fact, many of what are considered family firm benefits can quickly turn into obstacles to the business and can create irreversible conflict within the family if not promptly resolved.

In order to pass from theory to practice Freeman (2010) (the most convinced scholar of the management-for-stakeholder approach) suggests analysing the stakeholders behavior and possible coalitions among groups by investigating in their past actions. In particular, from a practical point of view it is required to study the actual behavior of stakeholders, their cooperative potential and competitive threats. Savage et al. (1991) gave guidance on how to measure these variables. The possibility of each group of stakeholder to influence succession process is determined by the type and the entity of resources that stakeholders have, their ability to build coalitions and relevance of the threat for the process. The potential to cooperate depends on how the stakeholder interest is taken into count into the succession: the closer is the link, the higher is the interest to cooperate. As a result of these two variables combination, it is possible to identify four types of stakeholders and the relative strategy that founder and managers could adopt to optimize the relations with each group. Supportive stakeholders require an offensive strategy, that implies actions to reinforce stakeholders view or perception of the process to maximize their convergence on it (examples of this kind of stakeholders are the owner and the family members actively engaged in the firm, or the managers). Non supportive stakeholders are addressed a defensive strategy in order to prevent potential threats by reinforcing beliefs and values of the succession process, in order to favor stakeholders integration (examples are the family members do not involved in the firm activities and potentially, or a specific group of employees). When owner deals with mixed-blessing stakeholders a swing strategy is functional to adapt rules or transaction process to the stakeholders current needs and features (in this case examples could be particular types of clients of financers having historical and personal relation with the owner and not completely convinced by the new generation guiding the firm). Marginal stakeholders require a hold strategy and so managers continue their succession program (providers may represent an example).

Bozer, Levin and Santora (2017) propose a multi-stakeholder model to define succession process in family business drawing attention to the perspectives and interests of both the family and nonfamily members. Consequently, a multi-perspective investigation of the key factors associated with effective family business succession across four key stakeholders: incumbent, successor, family, and nonfamily members. The model requires to identify personal and professional variables and associated components related to FBS as perceived by each of the four protagonists, focusing especially on the role played by nonfamily employees in the family-business sustainability (e.g. Santarelli and Lotti, 2005), revealing how overt acts of nepotistic behavior can have a detrimental effect on nonfamily employees' commitment and performance (Barnett and Kellermanns, 2006) reducing outcomes for the family business (Lee, 2008)

The firm dimension is a relevant factor having an impact on the definition and the deployment of the succession process. Governance of small family business is typically consolidated in the figure of the founder who often acts as the sole arbiter and may be the only one taking decisions concerning succession. As the business dimension grows, preparing for transition to the next generation becomes more complex. In this case a consolidated corporate governance could play an important role in supporting the founder to define the succession plan, especially to select the best candidate for succession.

An adequate HR strategy is essential to the success of the handover from a generation to another. Despite of the existence of a formally structured HR function, an inclusive HRM addressed to sustain employees engagement and motivation at all stages of the firm lifecycle is a key factor. In synthesis, that of sustainable HRM is an umbrella concept aimed at reconciling competitiveness and responsibility towards oneself and society as a whole (Botella-Carrubi and González-Cruz, 2019). HRM practices are usually monitored in terms of organizational practices, paying little attention to employees, both family and non family members These latter, in a family business need to be considered to avoid the risk of conflict, jealousy and sibling rivalries that could worsen such relationships and affect business stability levels (Savolainen and Kansikas 2013). In this sense, relationships between family and non family business members are affected by factors such as communication, trust, commitment, loyalty, family turmoil, sibling rivalries, resentment, conflicts, shared values and traditions. That is why HR practices in order to develop employees motivation, skills and potential, increasing clarity and parity have demonstrated having beneficial effects on succession process and on performances, assuring firm survival in the long run. However, Kumar (2014) noted that almost 71% of all family firms have not adopted any procedures for resolving family conflicts and the most common reason behind this is that in such firms, HRM system is not in place or else not give proper weightage.

In this chapter, the Authors analyzed the case studies from the environmental, organizational, interpersonal and individual perspective having in mind the entrepreneurial role of the incumbent, the successor and the family and the role played by other stakeholders in particular non family managers and employees. At this stage of the research they mainly consider the critical points emerged from the interviews paying attention to the results that family firms have achieved in managing the succession process with a specific focus on how HR practices have changed during the ongoing process

Just like the previous stages, this one in particular requires a lot of attention in stakeholders' management involved in the succession process. As expected, it involves overcoming a multiplicity of difficulties largely associated with the heterogeneity of stakeholders involved, mainly:

- HR function
- Non family Employees
- Providers
- Predecessor(s)
- Successor(s)
- Other family members
- Management.

Besides ownership succession, there are many other aspects that a firm succession plan needs to give attention to, including management succession, exit strategy planning, strategic planning and leadership development planning. Management succession planning and related issues are key elements of a complete business succession plan. Management succession can be even more important than ownership succession, because if the owner appoints the wrong person as CEO, or there is a controversial CEO transition, it can have a profoundly negative impact on the firm and its employees (Wilson, 2016).

THE RESEARCH METHODOLOGY

Our research adopts a qualitative method of investigation, in particular, structured interviews. The intention is to derive some preliminary information which will be tested with a further investigation phase with an expansion of the sample investigated. Therefore, this research intends to lay the foundations for further and subsequent investigation and does not provide answers to questions already asked, but rather to understand directly from the actors involved the critical issues experienced first hand and the role played by the main stakeholders involved.

For the preliminary study, five companies operating in different fields (agriculture and milling, industrial and zootechnical prefabricated buildings and urban furniture, mechanical) where initially engaged and both the first and second generation interviewed but separately. The text of the interview as well as the objective were anticipated so that the interviewees could adequately prepare. Aim of the interviews - lasting in average 1 our - was to understand the main difficulties encountered in the succession process, the role played by the main stakeholders involved, mainly the other family members, employees and specifically the HR function.

This methodology has been chosen basically for two reasons: the first aspect is that such practice will progress the knowledge and understanding of specific situations; secondly, because of its duality of being both situationally grounded and generalizable. Moreover, the case study method facilitates the collection of more extensive amounts of information than other methodologies: this provides for more comprehensive data and a greater understanding of the phenomenon. The value of interviewing is explained by Seidman (2006): "*interviewing provides access to the context of people's behavior and thereby provides a way for researchers to understand the meaning of the behavior*" (p. 4). Due to the nature of the investigation, most of the questions were open questions.

EMERGING ISSUES

Some recurring and shared critical points emerged from the interviews conducted. The latter are described in the following paragraphs.

HR Role

A recursive element that we found in several interviews concerned how families influenced HR practices. In the majority of the family owned companies interviewed decisions related to HRs were centralized and taken behind closed doors. Lack of transparency and communication seemed to be fairly frequent traits of all decisions on HRs. Some examples may relate to selection and promotion or rewards criteria.

One of the main concerns that emerged from the interviews carried out on the second generations was related to the fact that in the past, the first generation has often made selection, favoring local resources even at the expense of actual qualification or guaranteed career improvements based on completely subjective and personalistic criteria. One of the biggest challenges that the second-generation businesses has to face is the effective management of non-family employees (Chua, Chrisman, & Sharma, 2003). Although family members hold key executive positions in family businesses, many family firms employ non-family managers, and most employ a larger number of non-family employees than family members (Deloitte & Touche Study, 1999). Thus, attracting qualified non-family employees and fostering value-creating attitudes and behaviors among these employees can be major factors in the success or failure of family firms (Chrisman, Chua, & Litz, 2003; Chua et al., 2003).

For these reasons, leaving a margin of discretion and subjectivity to selective processes - just as the first generation has always done - could damage the organization's image and performance.

Same criteria/non-criteria for the recognition of increases on the remuneration packages and career paths that were often recognized simply on the basis of the requests made by those directly involved.

The generations following the first realized these critical issues and strengthened the role of the HR functions or – in case of absence - were promoters of their establishment. In any case, the HR function - if any - seemed not to have played any active or supportive role in managing the succession being mostly engaged in administrative rather than strategic matters.

Relations Predecessor-successor and Employees

Our case studies have revealed that within the succession process relations of the successor with employees could represent a critical aspect, since the differences between the founder leadership style and that of the successor. In particular, in some cases the passage from one generation to another could correspond to an increase in the firm dimension and this requires shifting from an informal management style to a more formalized one. Concerning the human resources management, we have observed that establishing the HR function signify to increase the "distance" between the owner and the employee, since communication will be written and mediated by employee representatives. This is the case of a daughter representative of the second generation that explained:

"When I became director instead of my dad, my way of managing human resources was different, more formal. I think it is important to define rules and enforce them. My father negotiated directly with employees, he had a paternalistic relationship with them, while I believe that relationships must be regulated by written procedures and codes of conduct, so that hierarchical relationships are clear. Last year, for the first time, we involved trade union organizations". (Second generation, 4)

In some cases, this has increased conflicts and employee contestations, at least in the first phase of the succession process.

Establishing and maintaining strong trust relationships will feed the link between the different generations and employees. The introduction of a second generation changes the dynamics of these relationships, so care is critical because employees could become anxious with change and the loyal relationships need to be tested. It is up to the successor to assure all stakeholders, included employees, that they are a valued part of the succession process. Ongoing care toward trusted human resources contributes to develop fair relations. Inability to do this will likely lead to an erosion of the business' loyal base and may end in failure of the whole succession process. In addition, the damaged relationships with employee could reflect on firm results, in particular, in terms of higher turnover, loss in customers and negative firm reputation (Walsh, 2011). In this context, it is important to identify and understand the developmental needs of employees. Successor has to ensure that all key employees understand their career paths and the roles they are expected to fill. Probably it is convenient to invest time on key employee retention, so managers are aware of the employees more qualified for a certain position (especially strategic positions). Finally, it is useful to formalize every phase and action of the succession planning, since this gives more visibility to all actors involved in each of them and reinforce their sense of belonging to the company. This would not be possible in an informal system though.

Another finding of our interviews concerns the consistent benefit potential of the two generations sharing and integrating each other's skill sets and views of the world to make better strategic decisions for the firm, but the necessary condition is that the role of each generation and rules of the decision-making process are clear. In this case, the quality of relations with all the stakeholders could significantly improve and the succession process could be deployed in the name of a higher perceived equality.

The new HR Vision Supported by the Second and Third Generation

Our analysis shows in all cases considered that the new generations tend to be more educated than the first. This gives them to be more sensitive with respect to employees training and the advantages coming from investment in human capital. This is supported also by the desire to select and hire employees with higher quality despite the resistance of the first generation. All the cases analysed plan to formally introduce a HRM function with responsibility and decision-making autonomy. In all the cases analyzed, we note the existence of plans and projects for the introduction of greater formalization with written and shared rules. The first generation managed his employees with oral agreement establishing a kind of complicity.

"We are not convinced that this approach is helpful and productive. It doesn't allow clear and equal behaviour. It could be un-heathy when the company is growing. Our behaviour is less friendly and more detached. We prefer to resort to other methods, like training or smart working, to transmit to our employees that we value them and support their development" (Third generation, 3)

as stated by a third generation successor. In one case the successor involved the trade unions to manage a conflict. It was the first time in his company

New generations strongly believe in education and training of all employees, family and non family members. Their plan is to raise the level of employees training to strengthen the quality of human capital with benefits for the climate and organizational culture. In one case the incumbent hasn't retired yet. His successor is a daughter that can decide almost freely even if the father doesn't always agree.

"We are working to the internationalization of our company. I participate in many fairs abroad. I'm used to being accompanied by some employees. This is a strong form of field training that can strengthen commitment and engagement because employees feel valued". (Second generation, 7)

the dauther affirmed.

Other aspects that have emerged from the interviews are the strong commitment of the new generations towards innovation and internationalization. They are available and looking for stable relationships with the University both for technical and managerial aspects. The new culture has led to the inclusion of young employees who have begun to support the historical figures of the company. In one case this has produced on one hand a form of mentoring for a passing of the baton in the near future on the other a form of reverse mentoring with young employees supporting the older ones especially for the use of the new technologies that the companies are adopting. There have been major benefits for the companies adopting these new policies especially from the engagement and commitment point of view.

Smart Working as a new HR Practice

The emergency of COVID-19 has allowed the experimentation of smart working as a new way of organizing work with decidedly positive results thanks to the preparation in terms of technology (networks, portals and software) taken care of by the new generations.

The new generations have also shown that they have begun to introduce performance evaluation systems also for workers and not just for managers. Work by objectives has been easily integrated into their companies and this made performance management system compatible with smart working. In one case the successor explained his idea of creating a manual of procedures to manage smart working, with indications relating not only to internal but also to external stakeholders, that is not only to employees and managers, but also to customers, suppliers, financers. Smart working has revealed a useful solution especially for employees, in particular non family members, helping them to gain a good level of work-life balance. This has also proven having beneficial effect on employees motivation and productivity as well. Finally, if added to increasing investment in workers training, they represent a set of services consistent with sustainable human resources management.

Baines and Gelder (2003) have focused on the family issues when examining telework. Increasingly a work-life balance discourse is being put forward in relation to telework (see for example, Baines, 2002;

Demerouti et al., 2004). Clearly the adoption and practice of telework in the companies covered by our analysis has shown a shift towards improving the work-life balance for both workers and managers.

The ability to work remotely has had a great impact on the motivation of both managers and workers with a consequent positive result on productivity. Our analysis also revealed that the greater the importance recognized to the relationship of trust with one's manager, the greater is the increase in productivity perceived by employees and the importance of receiving regular feedback from the leader.

Lack of Codified Procedures and Adequate Formal Preparation

From the interviews it appeared that the generational shift is in all the cases still in progress and it is performed without following codified procedures or specific knowledge. In none of the cases analyzed the preparation for succession took place through specific academic or similar courses. But in all the cases successors have a degree in Economics, type of degree that allows to have an overall view of the corporate system.

In only one case, the company turned to external consultants, coaches and advisers to facilitate the difficult phases of the transition. In all the cases the preparation took place through the support and the gradual delegation of responsibility from predecessor to successor. Janjuha-Jivraj and Woods (2002) found that only with the transition from second to third generation firms began to work on a formalized succession plan involving both generations.

Family business succession planning must take account of countless unknown future circumstances and current facts that are continuously changing and interacting. Business factors (like the economy, the regulatory environment and the state of the market in which the business operates) and family factors (like family dynamics) are elements of not negligible complexity, especially as they are equally important.

Under these circumstances of pervasive uncertainty and complexity, it is understandably difficult for family business owners to comprehend how they could construct a proper business succession plan. Moreover, it is understandable that there is no formalized plan as the formalization of family-run companies is reduced if compared to other companies.

If, on the one hand, the lack of formalization of the process can make it more flexible and open to collecting a multiplicity of suggestions, on the other, it can represent a difficulty for both internal and external stakeholders as regards understanding the responsibilities and communication mechanisms. In fact, during the succession period employees may encounter difficulties in understanding the reporting mechanisms while external stakeholders may be confused in identifying the reference interlocutor.

Successor-predecessor Relationships

In their studies Venter et al. (2005) noted that satisfaction with the succession process is strongly influenced by the willingness to take over the business and the positive relationship between the owner and successor. A recurring problem we encountered in our interviews was the difficulty in the overall transfer of proxies as often predecessors do not wish to contemplate the total succession. Handler (1990) asserts that the succession process involves a mutual role adjustment between predecessor and successor. Within this process, the predecessor adopts sequentially the roles of sole operator, monarch, delegator and finally consultant. On the other hand, the successor moves from a no role position to the positions of helper, manager and finally leader/chief decision-maker. The last two stages of this role transition appear to be the most critical to effective successions (Handler, 1990) and it is during these pivotal phases that the preparation of the next generation becomes most apparent. It is often not until the predecessor has progressed into the role of delegator that the level of challenge, responsibility, and task complexity for the successor can increase. This is seemingly a very sensitive transition, which depends on the owner's capacity to trust, share and delegate.

The progressive delegation of authority to the successor is fundamental if the successor is to assume full control. We all agree that:

- the succession process is considered complete when the successor has gained legitimacy and is widely accepted by the stakeholders (both internal and external);
- completion of the process is contingent on the successor's ability to exercise appropriate leadership in the business (Fox et al., 1996).

In all the cases examined, there was a strong willingness on the part of the second generation to take responsibility but gradually and always monitored by the first generation. Indeed, the lack of delegation not only frustrates the learning process of the successor but, perhaps more importantly, it serves to reduce their credibility in the eyes of employees and other key stakeholders (Fox et al., 1996). This situation did not occur in any of the cases analyzed and interviews carried out. The succession processes are not yet fully completed but the first generation is gradually giving way to the second which is well accepted - albeit initially with a thread of mistrust - by all stakeholders.

The initial and somewhat temporary resistance to the transition was essentially connected to the innovations that the second generation intend to implement which are quite often considered with distrust by older workers who have consolidated some organizational routines over time.

One of the recurring elements in our preliminary interview was precisely the fact that the successors aim to introduce operational and managerial innovations demarcating a point of discontinuity with the predecessors. One of the companies interviewed has promoted, followed and analyzed an automation project for the entire administrative part, from logistics to purchases and budgeting for cost control. It is also preparing to automate all the part of sales currently entirely managed by the predecessor. The aim is to make processes and procedures transparent and independent by the knowledge of administrative managers, especially when they are close to retirement.

Successor and Family Member/Stakeholder Relationships

Relations between family members may be crucial in maintaining business harmony as well as achieving successful transition (Bachkaniwala, 2001). As noted by Martin (2001: 223), the need to '*keep the business in the family*' has been identified as a key motivator for family-run firms globally. Janjuha-Jivraj and Woods (2002) found that family members who were not active in the business had considerable influence during succession, in particular the mother of the successor who acted as a 'silent buffer' between the generations. Janjuha-Jivraj and Woods (2002) also found that greater communication across the generations resulted in goal congruence between the predecessor and the successor and a commitment to the long-term strategy by the successor.

Handler (1991) found that a key factor to succession was the level of mutual respect and understanding between current and next-generation family members. This was defined as the degree to which these individuals had a good working relationship that included trust, support, communication, feedback and mutual learning. Mutual respect between the next-generation family member and the founder or owner can build over time as the working relationship progresses. An essential characteristic of this relationship is that the respect should be mutual. For this to happen, the next-generation family members must have sufficient confidence in themselves, which enables others to gain trust in their ability. To earn respect, the next-generation family members are expected to prove themselves to other family members, particularly those that are the founders or owners.

"My father belongs to a different generation, but he is a far-sighted person and he shows me a lot of confidence. For example, I strongly believe in the internationalization of the company, I invest a lot to find new customers abroad and to train employees. My father, with whom I continue to consult, because I know he suffers from being away from the company, supports me". (Second generation, 2)

Distrust of External Consultants

Our interviews have revealed a certain distrust of external consultants. Owners having assumed a consultant to be supported during the most critical passages of succession process have expressed dissatisfaction. In particular, when succession is guided with the support of external consultant, too much attention tends to be reserved to the technical component of succession (e.g., family trusts, buy-sell agreements, management development plans, etc.) with too little attention being paid to the people or non-technical components (such as communication among family members, or family members expectations, values, skills, etc.) of the succession process. For professional advisers focusing on the technical components rather than the family components, usually reveals to be easier. Nevertheless in family business people constitute the most important component since are the family members who will ultimately decide if the succession succeeds or not. It is the inability to effectively manage the family component that has proven to be the major stumbling block for family businesses in the succession process (Walsh, 2011). The existing literature and ongoing research on family business recommends that a significant or major portion of the succession activities focus on managing the family expectations and the family dynamics. This is achieved by actively integrating the family into the process. The ability of a multigenerational family business to effectively deal with these unique management challenges and opportunities will play a pivotal role in its short and long-term success. In particular, professional advisers should have a multidimensional approach, not only economic or financial or legal, but also social and psychological in order to give support to all the stakeholders to manage relationships. Handler (1992) identified the following factors as impacting on the next generation: personal need satisfaction, career ambitions, personal identity and charisma, individual power on other family members, mutual respect and understanding between generations, family members not actively involved in business accommodation, commitment to family business perpetuation, conflicts among family members. The mix of management, financial, familiar and psychological factors affecting the relations between different generation defines the need for specific expertise beyond that occurring in other types of firms. In this sense, the new generation may be helped by an external advisory committee as well as individual consultants, but a crucial prerequisite is a sentiment of confidence at the basis of the advisory contract. Our cases, in fact, have demonstrated that top-down solutions proposed by external consultants usually fails, while customized support tends producing more durable and successful relations.

Lack of Communication

From our case studies is also emerged that the lack of effective communication among family members is the root cause of most family business failures. It could be convenient establishing a family council and organizing constantly meetings, sometimes open to family members not directly engaged in the firm since they provide one of the most important communication channels through which the family is effectively managed during succession. Family characteristics also influence whether management succession will be a success or a failure. Tightly knit families with strong desire to honouring their parents' wishes about business continuity should face fewer problems than fragmented families. As the number of adult children in the business expands (also considering members not working in the firm, but, expecting cash from their parents' estates) the complexity of management succession increases. When there are more than one owner (for example, three owners, as one of our most interesting cases of a family business at the fourth generation), the number of family members aspiring to obtain an important role within the governance board of the firm increases and conflictual relations could develop among a so high number of persons. In this case, a successful succession process has benefitted of a constant and transparent communication, along with the convergence of all stakeholders toward the same goal, that is the firm survival in the best conditions. Features of the communication implemented tend to the model of the communities of practice. Communities of practices can be seen as social entities, a set of relationships among multiple interrelated stakeholder networks constantly crossed by information flows, essential to maintain vital the networks themselves and to create value for the succession process. This value is not merely instrumental for work, but it helps to share a body of common knowledge, practices and approaches, it increases the sense of belonging, finally developing a common identity (Wenger, McDermott, Snyder, 2002). As a result, communication should be based on trust-facilitating behaviours to promote stakeholders' confidence during all phases of the succession process. This model emerges from a voluntary basis and can be seen as a way to enhance individual competencies through the sharing of common information. It is from this shared practice that a community's member relies on the knowledge commonly produced in order to enhance further activities. The principles of inclusiveness, trust and social cohesion at the basis of communities of practices are in line with the ones sustained in management-for-stakeholders approach to govern succession process (cited in the first part). They then need to keep this knowledge up to date, deploy it and spread it across the entire firm. Potential disagreement has to be considered as a natural part of a process of communal involvement, anyway useful to assure the process equilibrium and its development. The involvement of different views, in this case is considered as an enriching factor that complement owner and managers knowledge. This collective characteristic of knowledge does not mean that individuals don't count. In fact, the most inclusive and cohesive communities welcome strong personalities and encourage disagreements and debates. These factors are well synthetised in the narrative of a second generation owners having realized the succession to the third generations:

"When my brother and I decided how to divide the tasks between our children, it was difficult for me to accept to give the most prestigious position of CEO to my niece instead of my daughter, but in the end I recognized that my niece was more fit for that role. However, we agreed that everyone on the board of directors had the same ownership stakes […]. It wasn't easy, it took a few years in which we had discussions with not just my brother and I, but with all the grandchildren concerned. We involved external parties, a university professor and a coach, but it didn't help, because they didn't consider the emotional

aspect that emerges in this delicate phase of the life of a company and a family. In the end we decided on the basis of common sense and the will to keep the family-owned company and we made arrangements that made all family members feel valued, but also the closest collaborators". (Second generation, 1)

SOLUTIONS AND RECOMMENDATIONS

Our analysis evidences some common points in all the cases considered. Among criticalities we can consider these points as solutions and attention aspects, if not recommendations, toward a successful succession process. The successor entry in the family company corresponded in fact with its growth and with a stronger market position especially in the last years.

From the interviews it appeared that the generational shift is in all the cases still in progress and it is performed without following codified procedures or specific knowledge. In all the cases the preparation took place through the support and the gradual delegation of responsibility from predecessor to successor. If, on the one hand, the lack of formalization of the process can make it more flexible and open to collecting a multiplicity of suggestions, on the other, it can represent a difficulty for both internal and external stakeholders as regards understanding the responsibilities and communication mechanisms. In fact, during the succession period employees may encounter difficulties in understanding the reporting mechanisms while external stakeholders may be confused in identifying the reference interlocutor.

The success of the transition depends on the owner's capacity to trust, share and delegate. The succession processes are not yet fully completed but the first generation is gradually giving way to the second which is well accepted - albeit initially with a thread of mistrust - by all stakeholders.

The initial and somewhat temporary resistance to the transition was essentially connected to the innovations that the second generation intend to implement which are quite often considered with distrust by older workers who have consolidated some organizational routines over time. One of the recurring elements in our preliminary interview was precisely the fact that the successors aim to introduce operational and managerial innovations demarcating a point of discontinuity with the predecessors. The new wave of managerial innovation includes the HR role. For example the generations following the first realized some critical issues in the discretion and subjectivity in the selective processes. To avoid a damage for the organization's image and performance the successors started to strengthen the role of the HR functions or – in case of absence - were promoters of their establishment. In any case, the HR function - if any - seemed not to have played any active or supportive role in managing the succession being mostly engaged in administrative rather than strategic matters.

From the interviews emerged that relations between family members were crucial in maintaining business harmony as well as achieving successful transition. To gain mutual respect the next-generation family members must have sufficient confidence in themselves, which enables others to gain trust in their ability.

Our interviews have revealed a certain distrust of external consultants. Owners having assumed a consultant to be supported during the most critical passages of succession process have expressed dissatisfaction. In particular, when succession is guided thanks external consultant, too much attention continues to be paid to the technical component of succession (e.g., family trusts, buy-sell agreements, wealth management, etc.) with far too little attention being paid to the people or non-technical component (family communication, family expectations, family values, family competencies, family dynamics, etc.) of the succession process.

In one case the involvement of advisors was a very positive experience. It is still continuing starting from the first insertion of the successor. The resulting benefits are numerous and have manifested themselves at all levels, in the context of family relationships, of the relationships between incumbent and successor and at the level of difficult balances within the company, in particular for the relationships between the successor, employees and management.

Our case studies have revealed that within the succession process relations of the successor with employees could represent a critical aspect, since the differences between the founder leadership style and that of the successor. In particular, in some cases the passage from one generation to another could correspond to an increase in the firm dimension and this requires shifting from an informal management style to a more formalized one. Concerning the human resources management, we have observed that establishing the HR function signify to increase the "distance" between the owner and the employee, since communication will be written and mediated by employee representatives. In some cases, this has increased conflicts and employee contestations, at least in the first phase of the succession process. Another finding of our case studies/interviews concerns the profound benefit potential of the two generations leveraging each other's skill sets and views of the world to make better strategic decisions for the company, as long as each individual's roles and decision-making allocation are clear.

A successful succession process has benefitted of a constant and transparent communication, along with the convergence of all stakeholders toward the same goal, that is the firm survival in the best conditions. The involvement of different views, in this case is considered as an enriching factor that complement managers knowledge. This collective characteristic of knowledge does not mean that individuals don't count. In fact, the most inclusive and cohesive communities welcome strong personalities and encourage disagreements and debates.

FUTURE RESEARCH DIRECTIONS

The successors showed that they know how to acquire and develop a strong entrepreneurial attitude oriented towards growth and innovation by taking on the risks that this entails. Even if the successions are not yet completed, the family firms have continued to grow after their entry, strengthening their position in the sector and in the market. This confirms that succession can be a process in support of the long-term sustainability and development of the family business (Botella-Carrubi, González-Cruz, 2019). The entrepreneurial orientation has also been accompanied by a progressive development of the leadership skills of the successors who have gradually been able to establish themselves as capable of credibility, trust and authority.

However, the critical points that emerged induce the Authors to deepen their investigation. The preliminary survey on the themes handover in family business suggest some hypotheses to be tested such as:

H_1: the **HR function** became necessary for the second generation to avoid excess discretion and autonomy in the management of HRs

H_2: **employees** are reluctant to change and continue to refer to the first generation (still present in the company) and tend to behave according to the organizational culture they set

H_3: the **family members involved in the succession** suffer a strong influence in the decision-making processes still largely guided by the first generation

H_4: the **family members not active in the succession** are in any case committed with different roles in the succession process.

During the research, some others will be certainly added. This list is not exhaustive but only representative of the survey that will follow the conclusion of this qualitative part.

Our work is original in that it is practitioner-oriented and proposes useful tips for the family business owner.

CONCLUSION

From the interviews it has clearly emerged that all the founders of the family business view ownership succession as dynastic but management succession as meritocratic. In case of dispute among different family members aspiring to become the successor, especially in the case of shared ownership between two or more persons, they finally sustain the most capable and charismatic family member. This type of behaviour reveals that the owner is moved both by emotional feelings (guiding him to support one the members of his own family as candidate to the succession), but also by rationality, because the final aim of succession process is to guarantee firm survival and development. Another common scenario is to bring in outside management to bridge a gap between when the current generation will cease being a part of the management team (for example, they will still be owners and sit on the board of directors but will not be involved in day-to-day management) and when the next generation has the skills and experience to assume the reins of management. Sometimes management succession may skip one or two generations, and management may be transitioned to non-family professional managers from either inside or outside the business. These examples seem revealing a mixed approach to stakeholder relationships, joining the features of the management for stakeholder and of the management of stakeholder.

To conclude, the interviews revealed a very interesting reality of second and third generation small and medium-sized family businesses with a solid market position and constantly growing. From the experiences analysed it emerged that although the succession process from the first to the second generation is not completed, many changes have emerged with the advent of successors who are bearers of new ideas and clear managerial practices recognized in the field of incumbents. The succession process did not manifest itself as planned through a succession plan but was however carried out with progressive adjustments benefiting from the preparation with degrees in economics of all the successors interviewed and thanks to a careful management of stakeholders starting from the family of the incumbent. The driver that guided the succession process and that allowed to find solutions to the obstacles that arose and the challenges that emerged is the search for sustainability of the company's development in the long term with a wide profusion of efforts and commitment on the part of all those involved. At the company organization level, a progressive formalization and definition of the procedures emerged which resulted in greater transparency and greater control. This is also associated with the creation of HR management offices, even if only at the administrative management level. The transition is however important because it is part of the new managerial practices introduced by the successor and accepted by the predecessor. The new generations are bearers of new ideas and support plans and projects for the internationalization and innovation of the company. They are careful to involve their employees with HR practices that can motivate and engage them making them feeling valued. In all the companies analysed the successors are investing in the education and training of their employees, family and non family members. They believe that only a growing quality of the human and social capital of the company can support their plans of growth. The graduality with which the succession process is taking place with a careful and progressive delegation by the incumbent to the successor both present and active in the management of the company seems to be the critical factor in the success of the succession processes analysed. The small size of the companies favours constant communication flows between all stakeholders fueled by shared values of respect and trust and by the common goal of the good of the company and the family, both strongly characterized by a strong entrepreneurial spirit oriented towards growth, careful and accurate management of risks and innovation.

REFERENCES

Bachkaniwala, D., Wright, M., & Ram, M. (2001). Succession in South Asian Family Businesses in the UK. *International Small Business Journal, 19*(4), 15–27. doi:10.1177/0266242601194001

Baines, S. (2002). New Technologies and Old Ways of Working in the Home of the Self-Employed Teleworker. *New Technology, Work and Employment, 17*(2), 89–101. doi:10.1111/1468-005X.00096

Baines, S., & Gelder, U. (2003). What Is Family Friendly about the Workplace in the Home? The Case of Self-Employed Parents and Their Children. *New Technology, Work and Employment, 3*(18), 223–234. doi:10.1111/1468-005X.00123

Barbaresco, G. (2019). *Medie imprese italiane, squadra che vince non si cambia, oppure sì? In Cineas-Mediobanca, Osservatorio sul risk management nelle medie imprese manifatturiere*. Ufficio Studi Mediobanca.

Barnett, T., & Kellermanns, F. W. (2006). Are we family and are we treated as family? Non-family employ*ees' perceptions of justice in the family firm. Entrepreneurship Theory and Practice, 30*(6), 837–854. doi:10.1111/j.1540-6520.2006.00155.x

Bertschi-Michel, A., Kammerlander, N., & Strike, V. M. (2020). Unearthing and Alleviating Emotions in Family Business Successions. *Entrepreneurship Theory and Practice, 44*(1), 81–108. doi:10.1177/1042258719834016

Bird, B., Welsch, H., Astrachan, J., & Pistrui, D. (2002). Family business research: The evolution of an academic field. *Family Business Review, 15*(4), 337–350. doi:10.1111/j.1741-6248.2002.00337.x

Bocatto, E., Gispert, C., & Rialp, J. (2010). Family-Owned business succession: The influence of pre-performance in the nomination of family and nonfamily members: Evidence from Spanish firms. *Journal of Small Business Management, 48*(4), 497–523. doi:10.1111/j.1540-627X.2010.00306.x

Botella-Carrubi, M. D., & González-Cruz, T. F. (2019). Context as a Provider of Key Resources for Succession: A Case Study of Sustainable Family Firms. *Sustainability, 11*(7), 1–18. doi:10.3390u11071873

Bozer, G., Levin, L., & Santora, J. C. (2017). Succession in family business: A multi-sourced perspective. *Journal of Small Business and Enterprise Development, 24*(4), 753–774. doi:10.1108/JSBED-10-2016-0163

Chrisman, J., Chua, J., & Litz, R. (2003). A unified systems perspective of family firm performance: An extension and integration. *Journal of Business Venturing*, *18*(4), 467–472. doi:10.1016/S0883-9026(03)00055-7

Chua, J., Chrisman, J., & Sharma, P. (1999). Defining the family business by behavior. *Entrepreneurship and Practice*, *23*(4), 19–39. doi:10.1177/104225879902300402

Chua, J., Chrisman, J., & Sharma, P. (2003). Succession and Nonsuccession Concerns of Family Firms and Agency Relationship with Nonfamily Managers. *Family Business Review*, *16*(2), 89–107. doi:10.1111/j.1741-6248.2003.00089.x

Churchill, N., & Hatten, K. (1997). Non-market-based transfers of wealth and power: A research framework for family business. *Family Business Review*, *10*(1), 53–67. doi:10.1111/j.1741-6248.1997.00053.x

Clarkson, M. B. E. (1995). A Stakeholder Framework for Analyzing and Evaluating Corporate Social Performance. *Academy of Management Journal*, *20*(1), 92–118.

Deloitte & Touche Study. (1999). *Are Canadian Family Businesses An Endangered Species? The First Success Readiness Survey of Canadian Family-Owned Business*. Deloitte & Touche Centre for Tax Education and Research, University of Waterloo.

Demerouti, E., Geurts, S., & Kompier, M. (2004). Positive and Negative Work–Home Inter- action: Prevalence and Correlates. *Equal Opportunities International*, *1*(23), 6–35. doi:10.1108/02610150410787837

Di Maddaloni, F., & Davis, E. (2017). The influence of local community stakeholders in megaprojects: Rethinking their inclusiveness to improve project performance. *International Journal of Project Management*, *35*(8), 1537–1556. doi:10.1016/j.ijproman.2017.08.011

European Commission. (2017). *The Ageing Report 2018. Underlying Assumptions & Projection Methodologies*. Institutional paper 65. Retrieved March 6, 2020 from https://ec.europa.eu/info/sites/info/files/economy-finance/ip065_en.pdf

Fox, M., Nilakant, V., & Hamilton, R. T. (1996). Managing Succession in Family-Owned Businesses. *International Small Business Journal*, *15*(1), 15–25. doi:10.1177/0266242696151001

Freeman, R. E. (1984). *Stakeholder Management: a Stakeholder Approach*. Cambridge University Press.

Freeman, R. E. (2010). Managing for Stakeholders: Trade-offs or Value Creation. *Journal of Business Ethics*, *96*(S1, Suppl. 1), 7–9. doi:10.100710551-011-0935-5

Freeman, R. E., Harrison, J. S., & Wicks, A. C. (2007). *Managing for Stakeholders: Survival, Reputation, and Success*. Yale University Press.

Gaumer, C. J., & Shaffer, K. (2018). Family business succession: Impact on supplier relations and customer management. *Human Resource Management International Digest*, *26*(6), 1–4. Retrieved March 6, 2020, from. doi:10.1108/HRMID-05-2018-0104

Habbershon, T., & Pistrui, J. (2002). Enterprising families domain: Family-influenced ownership groups in pursuit of transgenerational wealth. *Family Business Review*, *15*(3), 223–237. doi:10.1111/j.1741-6248.2002.00223.x

Handler, W. C. (1990). Succession in Family Firms: A Mutual Role Adjustment between Entrepreneur and Next-generation Family Members. *Entrepreneurship Theory and Practice*, *15*(1), 37–52. doi:10.1177/104225879001500105

Handler, W. C. (1991). Key interpersonal relationships of next-generation family members in family firms. *Journal of Small Business Management*, *29*(3), 21–32.

Handler, W. C. (1992). The Succession Experience of the Next Generation. *Family Business Review*, *3*(5), 283–307. doi:10.1111/j.1741-6248.1992.00283.x

Irava, W. J., & Moores, K. (2010). Clarifying the strategic advantage of familiness: Unbundling its dimensions and highlighting its paradoxes. *Journal of Family Business Strategy*, *1*(3), 131–144. doi:10.1016/j.jfbs.2010.08.002

Janjuha-Jivraj, S., & Woods, A. (2002). Successional Issues within Asian Family Firms: Learning from the Kenyan Experience. *International Small Business Journal*, *20*(1), 77–94. doi:10.1177/0266242602201006

Kim, Y., & Gaob, F. Y. (2013). Does family involvement increase business performance? Family-longevity goals' moderating role in Chinese family firms. *Journal of Business Research*, *66*(2), 265–274. doi:10.1016/j.jbusres.2012.08.018

Kumar, R. (2014). Beyond strategic human resource management: Is sustainable human resource management the next approach? *International Journal of Human Resource Management*, *25*(8), 1069–1089. doi:10.1080/09585192.2013.816863

Le Breton-Miller, I., Miller, D., & Steier, L. (2004). Toward an integrative model of effective FOB succession. *Entrepreneurship Theory and Practice*, *28*(4), 305–328. doi:10.1111/j.1540-6520.2004.00047.x

Lee, S. H. (2008). A theoretical framework on the role of HRM practices in Family business succession. In *Theoretical Developments and Future Research in Family Business* (pp. 261–286). Information Age Publishing.

Litz, R. A. (2010). Jamming across the generations: Creative intergenerational collaboration in the Marsalis family. *Journal of Family Business Strategy*, *1*(4), 185–199. doi:10.1016/j.jfbs.2010.10.002

Martin, H. F. (2001). Is Family Governance an Oxymoron? *Family Business Review*, *14*(2), 91–96. doi:10.1111/j.1741-6248.2001.00091.x

Mokhber, M., Gi, T. G., Rasid, S. Z. A., Vakilbashi, A., Zamil, N. M., & Seng, Y. W. (2017). Succession planning and family business performance in SMEs. *Journal of Management Development*, *36*(3), 330–347. doi:10.1108/JMD-12-2015-0171

Nordqvist, M., & Melin, L. (2010). Entrepreneurial families and family firms. *Entrepreneurship and Regional Development*, *22*(3), 211–239. doi:10.1080/08985621003726119

Nordqvist, M., Wennberg, K., Bau, M., & Hellerstedt, K. (2013). An entrepreneurial process perspective on succession in family firms. *Small Business Economics*, *40*(4), 1087–1122. doi:10.100711187-012-9466-4

Porfírio, J. A., Carrilho, T., & Mónico, L. (2016). Entrepreneurship in different contexts in cultural and creative industries. *Journal of Business Research*, *69*(11), 5117–5123. doi:10.1016/j.jbusres.2016.04.090

Porfírio, J. A., Felício, J. A., & Carrilho, T. (2020, July). Family business succession: Analysis of the drivers of success based on entrepreneurship theory. *Journal of Business Research, 115*, 250–257. doi:10.1016/j.jbusres.2019.11.054

Santarelli, E., & Lotti, F. (2005). The survival of family firms: The importance of control and family ties. *International Journal of the Economics of Business, 12*(2), 183–192. doi:10.1080/13571510500127246

Savolainen, S., & Kansikas, J. (2013). Non-family employees in small family business succession: The case of psychological ownership. *World Review of Entrepreneurship, Management and Sustainable Development, 1*(9), 64–81. doi:10.1504/WREMSD.2013.050936

Seidman, I. (2006). *Interviewing as Qualitative Research: A Guide for Researchers in Education and the Social Sciences* (3rd ed.). Tearchers College Press.

Sharma, P., Chrisman, J., & Chua, J. (2000). Perceptions About the Extent of Succession Planning in Canadian Family Firms. *Canadian Journal of Administrative Sciences, 17*(3), 233–244. doi:10.1111/j.1936-4490.2000.tb00223.x

Sharma, P., Chrisman, J., & Chua, J. (2003). Predictors of satisfaction with the succession process in family firms. *Journal of Business Venturing, 18*(5), 667–687. doi:10.1016/S0883-9026(03)00015-6

Stamm, I., & Lubinski, C. (2011). Crossroads of family business research and firm demography - A critical assessment of family business survival rates. *Journal of Family Business Strategy, 2*(3), 117–127. doi:10.1016/j.jfbs.2011.07.002

Turner, R., & Zolin, R. (2012). Forecasting success on large projects: Developing reliable scales to predict multiple perspectives by multiple stakeholders over multiple time frames. *Project Management Journal, 45*(5), 87–99. doi:10.1002/pmj.21289

Uhlaner, L. M., Kellermanns, F. W., Eddleston, K. A., & Hoy, F. (2012). The entrepreneuring family: A new paradigm for family business research. *Small Business Economics, 38*(1), 1–11. doi:10.100711187-010-9263-x

Umans, I., Lybaert, N., Steijvers, T., & Voordeckers, W. (2019, January). The influence of transgenerational succession intentions on the succession planning process: The moderating role of high-quality relationships. *Journal of Family Business Strategy.*, 100269. doi:10.1016/j.jfbs.2018.12.002

Venter, E., Boshoff, C., & Maas, G. (2005). The Influence of Successor-Related Factors on the Succession Process in Small and Medium Sized Family Businesses. *Family Business Review, 18*(4), 283–303. doi:10.1111/j.1741-6248.2005.00049.x

Webba, J. W., Ketchen, D. J. Jr, & Ireland, D. (2010). Strategic entrepreneurship within family-controlled firms: Opportunities and challenges. *Journal of Family Business Strategy, 1*(2), 67–77. doi:10.1016/j.jfbs.2010.04.002

Wenger, E. C., McDermott, R., & Snyder, W. C. (2002). *Cultivating Communities of Practice: A Guide to Managing Knowledge*. Harvard Business School Press.

Wilson, M. J. (2016). *Management Succession in Family Businesses*. Requisite Series, Williams Parker Edition. Retrieved March 6, 2020, from https://williamsparker.com/DigitalPublications/requisiteissue6/index.html

KEY TERMS AND DEFINITIONS

Entrepreneurial Process Perspective: The analysis of succession as a beneficial exchange of resources between two different generations aiming to improve the firm position in the market.

Family-Owned Business: A firm owned and/or managed by the members of the same family.

HR Role in Succession: The position assigned to Human Resources function within the firm succession process.

Intergenerational Management: The process seeing more than one generation representatives in the same firm, sharing responsibilities in the firm governance.

Management for Stakeholders: A socially inclusive managerial approach to deal with all the firm stakeholders, primary and secondary stakeholders.

Non-Family Members: Employees who worked in the business – independent professionals who bring skills into the business other protagonists may not possess.

Succession Plan: A process describing a series of steps useful to pass the firm ownership and/or management from one generation to another.

Successor-Predecessor Relationships: Interpersonal exchanges, through communication, between the firm owner and the candidate to substitute him.

Chapter 14
Organizing Human Resources in Family Firms During Generational Succession

Anna Maria Melina
University Magna Graecia di Catanzaro, Italy

Concetta Lucia Cristofaro
University Magna Graecia di Catanzaro, Italy

Marzia Ventura
https://orcid.org/0000-0001-6339-7103
University Magna Graecia di Catanzaro, Italy

Rocco Reina
https://orcid.org/0000-0002-0788-2996
University Magna Graecia di Catanzaro, Italy

ABSTRACT

HRM in family firm (FF) research has moved from its narrow focus on selection and succession planning towards studying the broader antecedents, content and outcomes of HRM. Today, HRM is acknowledged as a crucial factor for attracting new talent, improving employee attitude and behavior, enhancing performance, and fostering the long-term competitive advantages. The aim of this study is to identify which tools and practices FFs adopt with HR during succession planning. For example, do they use the replacement table with the aim of providing the firm and its management with a map that allows them to make the most appropriate decisions to replace a person who is no longer available to fill a certain position? Or is it possible to identify other tools? Similar questions help the authors to investigate around the importance regarding people in firms during generational succession.

DOI: 10.4018/978-1-7998-4814-1.ch014

INTRODUCTION

The uniqueness of a family firm is the overlaps between the two different social institutions: family and business. Opinions vary on the impact of such overlap on HRM in family firms. Some researchers are concerned about the contradictions between the norms and principles that operate in the family and those in the business, and worried that such contradictions may interfere with and compromise effective HRM (Lansberg, 1983). Human resource management (HRM) research in the context of family firms is still relatively scarce (Combs et al, 2018; Flamini et al, 2017; Reid et al., 2002) in fact how families' diverse structures, family member relationships, family goals and emotions affect HR practices remains a black box (Hoon et al, 2019). Researchers have commonly assumed that family firms are less sophisticated in the use of HR practices compared to their corporate counterparts (Hornsby et al, 1990). Astrachan and Kolenko (1994) have pointed out that the proper implementation and use of human resources practices can have a positive impact on the performance of family firms; in fact they found in their studies significant positive relationships between HRM practices and family firms and CEO revenues personal income levels. The few existing studies claim that family firms differ substantially from non-family firms, as well as from each other, in their human capital management, compensation systems, performance evaluation, knowledge transfer (Combs et al, 2018). Therefore it is not known how relationships with family members influence the management of human resources practices (Jam et al, 2012). The family firms literature on HRM mainly focuses on the formality and informality of specific practices, exploring the potential benefit of implementing different practices (Reid et al, 2002; Delaney et al, 1996). Family firms share common characteristics and face common problems, including generational change, understood as the transfer of leadership from one generation to the next, that is a critical process in family firms (Ibrahim et al, 2001). To successfully conclude the succession process, family firms need to plan this process. Although there are clear advantages to succession planning, family firms frequently postpone the succession planning and this may be harmful for the survival of the firm (Breton - Mille et al, 2004; Sharm et al, 2003). The planning for succession is a "deliberate and systematic effort by an organization to ensure leadership continuity in key positions, retain and develop intellectual and knowledge capital for the future and encourage individual advancement" (Phikiso et al, 2017). In addition to succession planning, the most commonly used HRM practices are formal employee reviews, compensation plans, written employee handbooks and the use of written job descriptions (Cater et al, 2019). Succession planning is an essential component of any strategy to ensure the survival of family-owned businesses. Planning for succession entails a process in which firms plan the transferring of their ownership. It is embarked upon in instances in which although the owner of a firm wishes to terminate own involvement in it, nevertheless desires the firm to continue operating. According to Le Breton-Miller, Miller and Steier (2004), maintaining leadership from one generation to the next is one of the greatest challenges to the longevity of family firms. A succession plan for a family-owned firm entails the transferring of both ownership and control of management from one generation to the other (Sonfield et al, 2004). Although succession planning is one of the success factors of the generational change, many companies arrive unprepared for that moment. This happens both because of the reticence of the founder to give way to his heirs and because of objective difficulties in managing the context in which the passage can take place. It is necessary to plan generational succession in the appropriate times and ways. First and foremost, planning must precede the time of the predecessor's withdrawal and start before the potential heir enters the firm and is integrated into strategic and operational planning (Davis 1986; Chiesa et al, 2007). Planning is considered by most literature to be one of the most significant tools available to the family firm for managing inheritance risks. It is believed, in fact, that to anticipate its effects by artificially recreating the scenarios following the departure of the current generation, allows to channel the course of events into a river of greater rationality and awareness, allowing to harmonize, in a unitary vision, the needs of the family, business and heritage (Montanari, 2003). Although the possibility of degenerations and conflicts cannot be excluded, the only process of defining and implementing the objectives can represent for the family firms the decisive passage from the condition of randomness, in which most of them are, to that of intentionality, in which the will is of the parts, it is not the case to determine the course of events (Tomaselli, 1996). Planning must be seen as a mental approach to strategic thinking and should help predict, in a particular way, the areas of conflict and the difficulties that arise during generational succession (Vallone, 2009). On these premises, in this study, the authors focus on generational succession, from the incumbent / family CEO to a next-generation family member trying to identify actually have planned or are planning their succession process. Using data from some family firms located in South Italy, organizations in which family members dominate the ownership and/or management of a firm and that perceive themselves as a family business (Sonfield et al,2004), the aim is to identify which tools and practices they adopt to proceed with succession planning. Do they for example use the replacement table with the aim of providing the firm and its management with a map that allows them to make the most appropriate decisions to replace a person who is no longer available to fill a certain position? Is it a good practice to have tools and methodologies for planning succession? Since the literature on the use of the replacement table in family firms is rather sparse if not non-existent, the objective of the work is precisely to explore a new theme concerning the use of this formal practice of human resource management in an environment in which very often less sophisticated and informal human resource management practices are used, such as are family firms (De Kok et al., 2006, Pellegrini et al, 2019). Through this practice it will be possible to identify the family resources with the highest potential for development which, adequately prepared and accompanied, could make the greatest contribution to the firm.

Succession, in terms of passing the business down to the next generation, has a strong influence on HR decisions (Chrisman et al., 1998; Hoon et al, 2019). Therefore planning it through the replacement table could open new avenues of research in such scope. The present work helps to identify the gaps still existing in the HR literature in family businesses and to suggest some possible future research directions. The contribution consists of three sections, the first relating to the review of the literature on HRM in family firms and succession planning. The second section refers to the methodology used, while the third shows the results of the analysis and their comments. The final section concludes the work and proposes future research indications.

HRM IN FAMILY FIRMS

Over recent years, research on human resource management (HRM) in the context of family firms has gained increasing momentum and has received increasing attention in family firms scholarship (Reid et al, 2002; Thach et al, 2009; Kim et al, 2010; Flamini et al, 2017). The family firm have become an important part of the Italian economy. Family firm HRM research has moved from its narrow focus on selection and succession planning (Astrachan et al, 1994; Dailey et al, 1980; Welsch, 1993) towards studying the broader antecedents, content and outcomes of HRM. Today, HRM is acknowledged as a crucial success factor for attracting new talent (Botero, 2014), improving employee attitude and behaviour, enhancing performance and fostering the long term competitive advantages of family firms (Chrisman et al., 2003; Cruz et al., 2011; Le Breton-Miller et al, 2006; Madison et al., 2018). However, works on human resource management in the context of family firms remain relatively low as compared to the more general body of studies on human resource management. HRM practices include techniques in recruiting, hiring, job design, training, compensation, performance evaluation, and leadership (Mathis et al, 2014). While succession research has been a dominant focus, only a minority of the over-all workforce in family firms are actual family members (Tabor et al., 2018; Xi et al., 2015). This is particularly salient for family firms, where the impact of ownership and management intersects with practices such as succession planning and the education and training of family managers (Cruz et al., 2011; Ibrahim et al., 2004). Non-family employees and managers constitute the vast majority of recipients of HRM (Tabor et al., 2018; Xi et al., 2015). Accordingly, family business research needs to emphasize non-family employees as HR recipients, as they are at the centre of the owning family's HR values, policies and practices. Consequently, individual employees and managers (both family and non-family) constitute the entity that needs to be acknowledged when defining a family firm HRM framework. Success of every organization depends today more and more from is not necessarily physical or even financial capital, but human capital. When we consider human capital as a combination of qualification, skills, abilities and intelligence of people, that means as a factor, that gives special, original and extraordinary character to every business or not business organization, then we know that namely employees are source that is able to learn, able to make changes, innovation and possibility to have creative effort, that means source, that is properly motivated, and by this way they will secure long – term prosperity of its organization. Gutiérrez-Broncano et al. (2014), who reviewed the HRM literature to identify positive and negative aspects of family firm–specific phenomena, show that research on HRM has utilized only a limited number of theoretical perspectives and has insufficiently accounted for family business heterogeneity. Similarly, Combs et al. (2018) demonstrate how families influence HRM and how HRM impacts family firms' outcomes. Although there appears to be significant progress in family firms' HRM, researchers are still searching for answers. Only by demonstrating its impact can HRM be taken seriously. There is still work to be done before human resource management can find its 'place in the sun' in the Family Firm community (Hoon et al, 2019). Researchers have commonly assumed that family firms are less sophisticated in the use of human resource practices than their larger corporate counterparts (Hornsby et al, 1990). Early studies have shown that the implementation and proper use of human resource practices may have a positive impact on the performance of family businesses (Astrachan et al, 1994: Hornsby et al, 1990). In their study, Astrachan and Kolenko (1994) found significant positive relationships between HR practices and income levels. Beyond succession planning, the most commonly used HR practices were formal employee reviews, set compensation plans, written employee manuals, and the use of written job descriptions. Family tradition (Ward, 1997), family members' intentions, interests and experiences (Baron, 2008; Zellweger et al., 2010) and attitudes towards protecting socio-emotional wealth (SEW) (Gómez-Mejía et al., 2007) are likely to affect family firms' HRM. Hall and Nordqvist (2008, p. 63), argued that professional management in family firms is constituted by "*an in-depth enough understanding of the owner-family's dominant goals and meanings of being in business (i.e., cultural competence) to be able to make effective use of relevant education and experience (i.e., formal competence) in a particular family firm*". Hornsby and Kuratko (2003) listed childcare, retention, and flexible scheduling as critical elements in HRM practices. The survey De Kok, Uhlaner, and Thurik (2006) confirmed that family firms were less likely to use professional HRM practices. Consequently, more professional HRM is assumed to be positively related to performance (Dekker et al., 2015; Gimeno et al, 2013). Kotey and Slade (2005) found that HRM practices change as firms grow in size, becoming more formal, and that changes for workers come sooner in the process than more formal practices at the managerial level. Kidwell and Fish (2006) observed that formalizing HR systems was largely a function of company size in the industry; also, found that establishing formal HR systems was positively associated with HR effectiveness, alignment with strategy, and firm profitability relative to the industry. Then, in a comparison of HR practices in U.S. and Australian family wineries, Thach and Kidwell (2009) found that U.S. family firms were more likely to formalize their HR practices than their Australian counterparts. Kim and Gao's (2010) study of 205 family firms in China found that firm size was a key factor in HRM practices; However, lack of formal HRM in smaller firms allowed them flexibility to cope with the country's turbulent business environment. In a study of Vietnamese family firms located in London, Hitchcock and Wesner (2009) they found support for the idea that Vietnamese cultural values provided a competitive advantage in business to the firm. These studies provide evidence that professional HR practices can transcend cultures and benefit family firms.

THE IMPORTANCE OF PLANNING FOR GENERATIONAL SUCCESSION IN FAMILY FIRMS

According Alayo et al (2016), family firms represent the engine of the most important economies worldwide given their contributions to generating wealth and creating employment. Family firms are unique institutions; they represent a context in which two seemingly separated social units (families and businesses) are highly integrated (Harveston et al, 2009) In the family firm, "*. . . the intimate connection between family and business is considered natural and compatible*" (Davis, 1968).

A company is considered a family firm when most of its property is owned by a family, family members are actively involved in the management of the company, and there exists the desire for continuity by transferring the business to the next generation (Alayo et al, 2016; Venter et al., 2005; Astrachan et al. 2002). According to researchers in this area, succession is one of the most important challenges that family firms face (Alayo et al, 2016; Mussolino and Calabrò, 2014; Handler, 1994; Venter et al., 2005; Daspit et al., 2016).

Sharma et al (2001) defined succession *as the actions and events that lead to the transition of leadership from one family member to another in family firms. The two family members may be part of the nuclear or extended family, and may or may not belong to the same generation. For succession in the family firm to occur there must be three components: a leader who hands over the leadership role, a successor who takes over the role, and a mechanism by which the transition takes place* (Sharma et al, 2001, p.7). It is also necessary that family members are willing to continue the business and that there is an acceptance among them of their relative roles in the firm (Handler, 1992).

Johnson et al. (2019) argued that the challenge for family firms is to survive more than one generation, to achieve this, family members must plan the succession. The high grade of mortality that exists among family firms indicates that the planning of the succession process is carried out late and incorrectly, or that no planning occurs. An incorrectly planned succession, apart from causing the end of the firm, can also destroy the family. Therefore, planning and managing the succession is vital to the continuity of family firms and all groups involved in this issue should participate in the succession planning process (Cabrera-Suárez et al., 2001).

The planning for succession is a "deliberate and systematic effort by an organization to ensure leadership continuity in key positions, retain and develop intellectual and knowledge capital for the future and encourage individual advancement" (Phikiso et al, 2017). It is an essential component of any strategy to ensure the survival of family-owned businesses Planning for succession entails a process in which firms plan the transferring of their ownership. It is embarked upon in instances in which although the owner of a firm wishes to terminate own involvement in it, nevertheless desires the firm to continue operating. According to Le Breton-Miller, Miller and Steier (2004), maintaining leadership from one generation to the next is one of the greatest challenges to the longevity of family firms. A succession plan for a family-owned firm entails the transferring of both ownership and control of management from one generation to the other (Sonfield et al, 2004). Although succession planning is one of the success factors of the generational change, many companies arrive unprepared for that moment. This happens both because of the reticence of the founder to give way to his heirs and because of objective difficulties in managing the context in which the passage can take place. It is possible to identify some of the possible causes of this reticence and that lead to a sort of "conspiracy of silence" (De Vries, 1993). De Vecchi (2007) underlines how, with regard to the founder, the refusal to deal with succession planning may depend on:

- from the fear of death: talking about one's own death is a taboo as if the event interested everyone except the founder;
- from personal identification with the company: for many founders the firm becomes a part and symbol of its own identity, as well as a measure of consideration and self-esteem;
- from the dilemma of choosing the successor;
- from generational envy: a phenomenon not to be underestimated is, in fact, the father's fear of confronting himself with the skills and managerial abilities emerging in his son/heir. Awareness of the qualities of the heir can delay the decision to abandon his office for fear of losing the power, the role and the esteem derived from it.

On the family front, among the other elements that can help fuel the conspiracy of silence, we recall:

- death as a taboo: we try to exorcise death for fear of not being able to continue the work of the father without his guidance;
- the fear of rivalry: there is concern about conflicts that could arise or become aggravated in the absence of the figure of the founder in the role of arbitrator and mediator.

As regards, instead, the objective difficulties in managing the context within which the generational change takes place are:

- the cohabitation within the family nucleus of strongly motivated and prepared potential heirs to take over the family firms, intending to benefit from a position income through the mere possession of a part of the capital and heirs with projects completely unrelated to the company of family intending to sell their shares;
- situations in which all the heirs have the will to continue the entrepreneurial activity;
- cases in which no heir intends to continue in the family firms or cases in which there are no heirs.

The joint action of some of these phenomena can delay the awareness of how it is necessary to plan the generational succession in the appropriate times and ways. First and foremost, planning must precede the time of the predecessor's withdrawal and start before the potential heir enters the firm and is integrated into strategic and operational planning (Davis 1986; Chiesa et al, 2007). Planning is considered by most literature to be one of the most significant tools available to the family firm for managing inheritance risks. It is believed, in fact, that to anticipate its effects by artificially recreating the scenarios following the departure of the current generation, allows to channel the course of events into a river of greater rationality and awareness, allowing to harmonize, in a unitary vision, the needs of the family, business and heritage (Montanari, 2003). Although the possibility of degenerations and conflicts cannot be excluded, the only process of defining and implementing the objectives can represent for the family firms the decisive passage from the condition of randomness, in which most of them are, to that of intentionality, in which the will is of the parts, it is not the case to determine the course of events (Tomaselli, 1996). The themes generally present within the succession planning project can be included in the definition of the following points:

- the training and selection process for candidates,
- the path of progressive handover between the outgoing and the incoming leadership,
- the development of the withdrawal plan for the outgoing entrepreneur,
- the definition of the times and ways in which to control the implementation of the plan and the identification of the ways in which to bring it to the attention of the interested parties.

It is natural that the elaboration of a plan can bring about hidden needs, or elements of bad temper; however this allows for an awareness and a subsequent attempt to reorganize and resolve issues that, in other cases, could emerge in much more delicate situations than business life.

Therefore, planning should:

- increase the ability to react to changes in the environment,
- make new information available,
- reduce uncertainties,
- increase awareness of one's potential and limits,
- increase the ability to achieve goals,
- allow the entrepreneur to anticipate the identification of harmful events,
- favor the comparison and the preparation of a common action line.

This sharing, which emerges from the sense of planning, should allow for a greater sense of belonging and favor the involvement and union of family members, orienting them towards the achievement of common results. Planning is seen as a mental approach to strategic thinking and should help to foresee, in a particular way, the areas of conflict and the difficulties that arise during the generational succession (Vallone, 2009).

REPLACEMENT TABLE: A POSSIBLE SUCCESSION PLANNING TOOL IN FAMILY FIRM

Some research has shown that organizations that can identify a successor to the CEO have a higher profitability, probably because the ability to select a successor is considered as an indicator of the presence of adequate management development policies (Zajac, 1990). In addition, succession planning represents a fundamental support for the company's strategy and allows identifying the leaders capable of leading the organization at times when a change in business strategy is required (Rothwell, 2010). The planning activity generally makes use of a tool called replacement table, which has the aim of providing the company and its management with a map that allows them to make the most appropriate decisions to replace a person who is not more willing to hold a certain position.

In family firms where executive turnover is limited to family management, the replacement table is a tool that is not used, in fact the literature on the matter is scarce. In this way, human capital accumulated over the generations is maintained in the company. Furthermore, family members develop a strong knowledge of the sector in which the company operates and this means that every opportunity for meeting and debate creates new opportunities for knowledge and mutual exchange of opinions, ideas and solutions to better manage the business. business activity. However, planning the succession in family businesses with the replacement table could be a good human resource management practice in choosing the most suitable family member to fill a given position.

In fact the replacement Planning features replacement tables--periodically updated lists of viable candidates for the targeted positions. Replacement tables focus on specific job positions rather than on job profiles or job analyses that identify the critical competencies for effective performance. Most replacement-table approaches to succession let job incumbents identify their potential replacements. The tables don't include subjective assessments completed by the candidate's supervisor and peers on such areas as his or her readiness (the time required before a candidate could perform effectively in a job position), performance (current strengths and weaknesses), and potential (highest achievable performance level). Replacement-table succession systems are confidential. Most replacement candidates never hear about the succession system or their inclusion in the tables. Only top-level managers have access to the tables. Replacement-table planning is designed to remain separate from other HRD systems such as performance appraisal and management development.

Using the results of the assessment process, senior-level managers meet to finalize replacement tables-a feature retained from the more traditional approaches. But in the new system, the managers discuss each high-potential replacement candidate with respect to strategic competencies that have been identified. The competencies provide an objective basis for a fair discussion.

In agreement with Gabrielli (2010), the construction of the replacement tables is achieved through a methodology which involves the following phases:

1. choose the people and roles that will enter the substitution plan;
2. decide which involvement system to activate in the company;
3. define the standards with which to help identify the successor candidate (work experience, potential, performance ...);
4. decide the time horizon of the suitability for succession and any management and development actions and tools to support them;
5. establish what type of feedback to give and to whom in the organization.

Although this tool is widespread in managerial practice, it has however been criticized by many for the risk that it generates promotional expectations that cannot always be met by the company, remaining an exclusively theoretical exercise as well as very expensive. However, this process represents, in the perspective of development, the advantage of forcing the organization to reflect on managerial assets and available skills, thus urging a different commitment from top management in enhancing the adoption of all those management, training and organizational necessary to support the choices indicated in the planning and to enhance the internal labor market. Research conducted on hundreds of Italian companies confirms the diffusion of this tool among large companies and multinationals, even if it is not known among medium-large ones. This practice does not seem to be reserved exclusively for top management roles but is widely used for all those managerial roles considered key for the company, as well as for middle management and professionals who hold strategic skills. In small and medium-sized enterprises, especially family-owned, the presence of good practice in this sense is more easily traced to manage the succession in the leadership of the company, generational succession, with structured programs (Gabrielli et al 2012).

In order to identify the human resources that can be included in a succession table, the organization must choose what are the key dimensions on the basis of which to segment the corporate population. An activity, defined as people value mapping, which is generally accomplished by crossing two dimensions: The assessment levels achieved by the individual in terms of potential and performance. In this way it will be possible to segment the company population into different clusters, each of which characterized by different levels of performance and potential and therefore susceptible to different management and development levels as well as rewarding.

METHODOLOGY

According to AIDF Italian Family Business Association in the Italian economy, family businesses represent 65% of the total of Italian businesses. Family-owned businesses create jobs, grow more than other types of businesses and record higher profitability. In terms of the incidence of family firms, the Italian context is in line with that of the main European economies such as France (80%), Germany (90%), Spain (83%) and UK (80%), while the differentiating element with respect to these countries is represented by the lesser recourse to external managers by entrepreneurial families: 66% of Italian family firms have all management made up of family members. In this research the authors take Calabria as a benchmarking region because it reflects national photography. The weak Calabrian industrial fabric is made up mainly of small family firms, where the transfer of management from father to son is a consolidated phenomenon. Considering the different sectors in which family firms are rooted, the private health sector seemed to us little explored, therefore the aim of this research is to identify which tools and practices some family firm operating in private health sector adopt to proceed with succession planning. Do they for example use the replacement table with the aim of providing the firm and its management with a map that allows them to make the most appropriate decisions to replace a person who is no longer available to fill a certain position? Through this practice it will be possible to identify the resources with the highest potential for development which, adequately prepared and accompanied, could make the greatest contribution to the firm. In this case the literature does not offer adequate analysis, by bringing out and examining with a qualitative analysis the problems existing in those who are currently living or have experienced this particular moment of business life. Following our aim, the approach adopted is similar to the studies with same aim to analyze the conceptual aspect of the phenomenon (Dooley, 2002; Cassell & Symon, 2004); so according to these authors, we have thus developed an overview of the existing academic literature related to HRM and succession planning in family firm. We examined databases like Wiley-Blackwell- Elsevier, All Springer Lik 2018, Emerald Insight and ProQuest Social Science Journals in order to find and analyze specific academic literature about the phenomenon. So, we created a search string related to the phenomenon under investigation using keywords as "HRM", "family firms", "succession planning ", and "Generational succession". The research approach has an exploratory nature, since the intention is to become familiar with a phenomenon that is a little known in healthcare. In detail, the work was developed in three phases described as follows:

- a first phase of the work was characterized by theoretical and conceptual reflections through the study of literature (monographs, articles, research on sites, etc.) as well as by the analysis of the documents relating to the issue of generational succession in family firms, planning succession and HRM.
- The second phase of analysis provided for an empirical verification that resulted in the examination of the four accredited private health organizations. The data collection took place through a composite research, that is, referring both to the elaboration of the interviews administered and through the analysis of the institutional documents.
- The last part of the work consists in the feedback, aimed at the critical analysis of the evidences found, that will find a synthesis in the conclusions of the work.

Furthermore, considering that the purpose of the research work is to provide possible representations of reality, the study, as described, has allowed us to investigate the phenomena in depth, allowing us to grasp different related aspects.

Sample

The selection of organizations within our case study was based on analyzing the private health organizations that experienced the generational succession and the impact on corporate strategies. On this basis, a mapping was made of the private accredited health and social-health organizations within the existing database on the site of the Department of Health Protection and Health Policies of Calabria Region. This identification followed a process of systematic selection and subsequent steps, which identified a sample of analysis based on the following characteristics:

- The Health Organizations involved are all private accredited structures;
- All organizations belong to the "Care Homes" type;
- Organizations are all Family Firms;
- All involved organizations have experienced the moment of generational succession.

Taking into consideration the characteristics indicated above, 4 home cares have been identified (for privacy reasons they will be indicated with the letters: A B C D).

Method

The research developed has proposed an exploratory approach through the "case study" method. This is a widespread study in organizational and management research, which is adapted to all those circumstances in which the verification of phenomena is particularly linked to the organizational conditions of the context. The case study stems from the desire to analyze and understand the Calabrian territorial reality based on the choice of some accredited private health organizations that have experienced or are experiencing the phase of generational succession. Through this method it was possible to "learn lessons" from phenomena described in a systematic and comparative way in one particular context represented by accredited private health organizations. After identifying the accredited private health organizations of the province of Catanzaro, the survey method used are qualitative interview. Specifically, in this study, the tool for collecting the necessary information is represented by the semi-structured interview, this use has been prepared in order to propose a framework of common reference to all the subjects interviewed in order to read in a comparative manner the perception of the phenomenon and to reduce and concentrate the variability of the answers.

Respondents of 4 home care were contacted by telephone to make an appointment and start face-to-face interviews. The "face to face" interview was used to give more freedom to the interlocutor, which lasted about 60 minutes. So, in our analysis, there were two figures of interlocution subject to interview in two different moments: outgoing generation, that is, father; incoming generation, son.

The interview presented to the outgoing generation - father - it was structured as follows:

- A first part called "Register" section was intended to identify the history of the company from its origins.
- The second and last part identified as "family firms and generational succession" was aimed at understanding the succession planning process and its tools.

The interview submitted to the incoming generation son, was concentrated in a single section relating to understanding the methods and tools needed to manage the family business.Through this tool we study the impact and ways in which private family health organizations manage their succession process, collecting suggestions or strategies put into practice by entrepreneurs to better manage the phenomenon of succession in their organizations and the impact that this phenomenon has on HRM business strategies.

RESULTS AND DISCUSSION

The empirical analysis conducted through the semi-structured interview focuses on the Private Accredited Homes Care of the Province of Catanzaro.

Care Homes A, B, C, D have had a face-to-face interview. The structured interviews have interpreted all the top functions involved in the management and governance of health organizations. So, in two of the Home Care, it was possible to submit the interview only to the incoming generation as the only figure present within the organization, in the others, there was the opportunity to meet the incoming generation and outgoing generation because the latter is still in office.

The table below shows the first results, it reports the characteristics of the family firms on which the survey was conducted.

Table 1. First results

Home Care	Years in business (approx.)	Ownership/Management	Numbers of family members in the business
A	55	3° Generation	Three
B	53	2° Generation	Two
C	60	2° Generation	Two
D	58	2° Generation	Three

As you can see, all the companies interviewed have been in business for more than fifty years, three are in the second generation while one is in the third.

The family at the head of a company plays an economic and social role. At the time of the generational transfer, as well as the company, the credibility, capacity and name of the family pass from one generation to the other; successors must live up to the responsibilities.

From the interviews it was possible to understand how the greatest challenge for the company was the succession.

The importance of succession for the survival of family firms (Poza, 2004; Steier et al., 2004) justifies the centrality of the theme in literature (Handler, 1992; Montemerlo, 2000; Sharma, 2004). The various authors who have studied succession in family businesses have focused on different areas of interest over the years (Brockhause, 2004; Sharma, 2004), but among all the issue of succession planning is relevant, namely the study of the importance of plan the succession process and the reduced diffusion of this planning among family businesses.

So during the interview we focused precisely on this issue and the question "*have you already planned or are you planning a path for generational succession*?" two out of three gave positive answers.

This means that they become aware of the fact that the generational succession constitutes a moment to be programmed and not left to chance.

The tools they will use for succession planning are still unclear, also because the company will move to the new generation, which already operates within the company itself.

Planning means discussing the various issues of corporate life and allows you to question the strategies, objectives and methods of behavior. Planning becomes one of the most significant tools that the family business has available for managing successor risks. In fact, anticipating the effects by artificially recreating the scenarios subsequent to the departure of the current generation, it allows to channel the course of events in a bed of greater rationality and awareness, allowing to harmonize, in a unitary vision, the needs of the family, of the business and heritage.

CONCLUSION AND FINAL REMARKS

The aim of this work was to deepen the knowledge on the relationships between HRM and family firm, trying to understand if even in a family context it is possible to take advantage of the introduction of formal human resource management practices and systems, in order to provide useful information to managers operating in these realities.

Despite the importance assumed in Europe and especially in Italy by this type of company, both at an economic and occupational level, there is still little empirical evidence on these links. One of the most interesting aspects of the research was to analyze the effect of sets of formalized HR practices in environments traditionally devoted to informality.

From this research the authors believe that the generational succession can represent an HRMP since planning the succession by choosing the human resources of the family suitable for covering the key positions within a company guarantees the same survival and continuity.

The replacement table is a completely rationale tool for planning a succession and, for this, is rare for the family firms where everything happens between the family members.

Several studies have shown that in family firms, in fact, where the owners / managers have full control and are often the focus of all decision-making processes, human resource management practices are affected particularly of the tendency towards informality.

Consequently, the most recurrent behaviors are assumed as practice, influenced by the personality and leadership style of the owner, whose figure plays a fundamental role in daily management and employment relationships (Songini et al, 2017).

Succession planning forms an integral part of any corporate structure especially when it comes to family businesses, the succession event planning is the vital gear in the wheel of business continuity. From this study, it was observed that in all four cases, family members grabbed the meaning of succession planning, which was evident from the fact that all the families clearly understood the importance of succession planning, guaranteeing the continuity of the company even after the outgoing generation, but had not prepared the individual succession plan, as well as the replacement table. The families they proactively answered the question: who will be after me? This shows that the the leaders of the companies studied are different from the typical owners who do not want to lose control and power (Ballal et al, 2019).

The process of succession planning can be steady and systematic when there is good planning with respect to transferring the baton from one generation to the other (Wolfe, 1996; Rothwell, 2010). This can be accomplished when there is maturity, financial stability, and close ties between family members (Beckhard et al, 1983). It is essential to understand that ensuring a proper flow of family values from generation to generation is challenging, but once this is mastered then there is no stopping the entrepreneurial activities in the family (Singh, 2016).

The research carried out wants to be a starting point for reflection and a stimulus for future insights on the topic, focusing in particular on the analysis of further fundamental elements for the success and survival of Private Healthcare Organizations in the regional context. The results obtained may be used for future cross-country comparisons with respect to the analysis of other Regional, or Extranational, Healthcare Systems, with the aim of verifying starting positions and organizational methods.

Research limitations are, in fact, that the data has been collected in a few organizations. Future studies should consider longitudinal projects between multiple organizations.

REFERENCES

Alayo, M., Iturralde, T., Maseda, A., & Arzubiaga, U. (2016). Critical factors for successful succession of family firms. European Journal of Economics. *Finance and Administrative Sciences*, *85*, 89–103.

Astrachan, J. H., Klein, S. B., & Smyrnios, K. X. (2002). The F-PEC scale of family influence: A proposal for solving the family business definition problem. *Family Business Review*, *15*(1), 45–58. doi:10.1111/j.1741-6248.2002.00045.x

Astrachan, J. H., & Kolenko, T. A. (1994). A neglected factor explaining family business success: Human resource practices. *Family Business Review*, *7*(3), 251–262. doi:10.1111/j.1741-6248.1994.00251.x

Ballal, J. M., & Bapat, V. (2019). In che modo la successione familiare influisce sull'innovazione delle imprese familiari? *Asian Journal of Innovation & Policy*, *8*(2).

Beckhard, R., & Dyer, W. (1983). Managing continuity in the family-owned business. *Organizational Dynamics*, *12*(1), 5–12. doi:10.1016/0090-2616(83)90022-0

Botero, I. C. (2014). Effects of communicating family ownership and organizational size on applicant's attraction to a firm: An empirical examination in the USA and China. *Journal of Family Business Strategy*, *5*(2), 184–196. doi:10.1016/j.jfbs.2014.01.004

Breton-Miller, I. L., Miller, D., & Steier, L. P. (2004). Toward an integrative model of effective FOB succession. *Entrepreneurship Theory and Practice*, *28*(4), 305–328. doi:10.1111/j.1540-6520.2004.00047.x

Brockhaus, R. H. (2004). Family Business Succession: Suggestions for Future Research. *Family Business Review*, *17*(2), 165–177. doi:10.1111/j.1741-6248.2004.00011.x

Cabrera-Suárez, K., De Saá-Pérez, P., & García-Almeida, D. (2001). The succession process from a resource and knowledge based view of the family firm. *Family Business Review*, *14*(1), 37–47. doi:10.1111/j.1741-6248.2001.00037.x

Carlson, D. S., Upton, N., & Seaman, S. (2006). The Impact of Human Resource Practices and Compensation Design on Performance: An Analysis of Family-Owned SMEs. *Journal of Small Business Management*, *44*(4), 531–543. doi:10.1111/j.1540-627X.2006.00188.x

Cater, J., James, K., Kidwell, R., Camp, K., & Young, M. (2019). HRM practices and effectiveness: A comparison of US Hispanic and non-Hispanic family firms. *Journal of Small Business and Enterprise Development*, *26*(5), 726–746. doi:10.1108/JSBED-12-2018-0364

Chiesa, V., De Massis, A., & Pasi, M. L. (2007). Gestire la successione nei Family Business. *Piccola impresa/Small business*, (1).

Chrisman, J. J., Chua, J. H., & Litz, R. (2003). A unified systems perspective of family firm performance: An extension and integration. *Journal of Business Venturing*, *18*(4), 467–472. doi:10.1016/S0883-9026(03)00055-7

Chrisman, J. J., Chua, J. H., & Sharma, P. (1998). Important attributes of successor in family businesses: An exploratory study. *Family Business Review*, *11*(1), 19–34. doi:10.1111/j.1741-6248.1998.00019.x

Chua, J. H., Chrisman, J. J., & Sharma, P. (1999). Defining the family business by behavior. *Entrepreneurship Theory and Practice*, *23*(4), 19–39. doi:10.1177/104225879902300402

Coggiola, D., Morelli, C., & Songini, L. (2017). *Gestione delle risorse umane e performance nelle piccole e medie imprese familiari italiane*. Academic Press.

Combs, J. G., Jaskiewicz, P., Shanine, K. K., & Balkin, D. B. (2018). Making sense of HR in family firms: Antecedents, moderators, and outcomes. *Human Resource Management Review, 28*(1), 1–4. doi:10.1016/j.hrmr.2017.05.001

Cruz, C., Firfiray, S., & Gómez-Mejía, L. R. (2011). Socioemotional wealth and human resource management (HRM) in family-controlled firms. In A. Joshi, H. Liao, & J. J. Martocchio (Eds.), *Research in Personnel and Human Resources Management* (pp. 159–217). Elsevier. doi:10.1108/S0742-7301(2011)0000030006

Daspit, J. J., Holt, D. T., Chrisman, J. J., & Long, R. G. (2016). Examining family firm succession from a social exchange perspective: A multiphase, multistakeholder review. *Family Business Review, 29*(1), 44–64. doi:10.1177/0894486515599688

Davis, P. (1986). Family business: Perspectives on change. *Agency Sales Magazine, 6*, 9–16.

De Kok, J. M. P., Uhlander, L. M., & Thurik, A. R. (2006). Professional HRM practices in family owned-managed enterprises. *Journal of Small Business Management, 44*(3), 441–460. doi:10.1111/j.1540-627X.2006.00181.x

De Vries, M. F. K. (1993). The dynamics of family controlled firms: The good and the bad news. *Organizational Dynamics, 21*(3), 59–71. doi:10.1016/0090-2616(93)90071-8

Dekker, J., Lybaert, N., Steijvers, T., & Depaire, B. (2015). The effect of family business professionalization as a multidimensional construct on firm performance. *Journal of Small Business Management, 53*(2), 516–538. doi:10.1111/jsbm.12082

Delaney, J. T., & Huselid, M. A. (1996). The impact of human resource management practices on perceptions of organizational performance. *Academy of Management Journal, 39*(4), 949–969.

Deng, X. (2018). Embedding 'familiness' in HRM practices to retain a new generation of migrant workers in China. *Asia Pacific Business Review, 24*(4), 561–577. doi:10.1080/13602381.2018.1451124

Devecchi, C. (2007). *Problemi, criticità e prospettive dell'impresa di famiglia* (Vol. 1). Vita e pensiero.

Flamini, G., & Gnan, L. (2017). A forty years' Literature Review on HRM in Family Businesses: Reshaping the Research Agenda. In Academy of Management Proceedings (Vol. 2017, No. 1, p. 13851). Briarcliff Manor, NY: Academy of Management.

Gabrielli, G. (2010). *People management: teorie e pratiche per una gestione sostenibile delle persone.* F. Angeli.

Gabrielli, G., & Profili, S. (2012). *Organizzazione e gestione delle risorse umane*. Isedi.

Gimeno, A., & Parada, M. J. (2013). Professionalization of the family business: decision making domains. In *Exploring Transgenerational Entrepreneurship. The Role of Resources and Capabilities* (pp. 42–61). Camberley. doi:10.4337/9781781003626.00009

Gómez-Mejía, L. R., Haynes, K. T., Núñez-Nickel, M., Jacobson, K. J. L., & Moyano-Fuentes, J. (2007). Socioemotional wealth and business risk in family-controlled firms: Evidence from Spanish olive oil mills. *Administrative Science Quarterly, 52*(1), 106–137. doi:10.2189/asqu.52.1.106

Gutiérrez-Broncano, S., Rubio-Andrés, M., & Jimenez Esterez, P. (2014). Managing human resources in family businesses: a review on the current state of research and new proposals for the future. In C. F. Machado & P. M. R. N. de Melo (Eds.), *Effective Human Resources Management in Small and Medium Enterprises* (pp. 96–112). Business Science Reference. doi:10.4018/978-1-4666-4731-2.ch005

Handler, W. C. (1992). Succession in Family Business: A review of the research. *Family Business Review*, *2*(2), 133–157. doi:10.1111/j.1741-6248.1994.00133.x

Handler, W. C. (1992, Fall). The Succession experience of the next generation. *Family Business Review*, *5*(3), 283–307. doi:10.1111/j.1741-6248.1992.00283.x

Handler, W. C. (1994). Succession in family business: A review of the research. *Family Business Review*, *7*(2), 133–157. doi:10.1111/j.1741-6248.1994.00133.x

Harveston, P. D., Davis, P. S., & Lyden, J. A. (1997). Succession planning in family business: The impact of owner gender. *Family Business Review*, *10*(4), 373–396. doi:10.1111/j.1741-6248.1997.00373.x

Hitchcock, M., & Wesner, S. (2009). Vietnamese values, networks and family businesses in London. *Asia Pacific Business Review*, *15*(2), 265–282. doi:10.1080/10438590701719032

Hoon, C., & Bövers, J. (2019). Unpacking socioemotional wealth: Exploring the origins of affective endowment in founder firms. *International Journal of Entrepreneurship and Small Business*.

Hoon, C., Hack, A., & Kellermanns, F. W. (2019). Advancing knowledge on human resource management in family firms: An introduction and integrative framework. *German Journal of Human Resource Management*, *33*(3), 147–166. doi:10.1177/2397002219847883

Hornsby, J., & Kuratko, D. (1990). Human resource management in small firms: Critical issues for the 1990. *Journal of Small Business Management*, *28*, 9–18.

Hornsby, J., & Kuratko, D. (2003). Human resource management in U.S. small business: A replication and extension. *Journal of Developmental Entrepreneurship*, *8*(1), 73–92.

Huselid, M. A. (1995). The impact of human resource management practices on turnover, productivity, and corporate financial performance. *Academy of Management Journal*, *38*, 635–672.

Ibrahim, A. B., Soufani, K., & Lam, J. (2001). A study of succession in a family firm. *Family Business Review*, *14*(3), 245–258. doi:10.1111/j.1741-6248.2001.00245.x

Ibrahim, A. B., Soufani, K., Poutziouris, P., & Lam, J. (2004). Qualities of an effective successor: The role of education and training. *Education + Training*, *46*(8–9), 474–480. doi:10.1108/00400910410569597

James, A. E., Jennings, J. E., & Breitkreuz, R. S. (2012). Worlds apart? Rebridging the distance between family science and family business research. *Family Business Review*, *25*(1), 87–108. doi:10.1177/0894486511414271

Johnson, F. W., Pelayo Maciel, J., & Valenzo Jiménez, M. A. (2019). L'importanza di pianificare la successione nell'azienda di famiglia prima che sia troppo tardi: Un caso di studio di una piccola azienda manifatturiera. *Review of Business & Finance Studies*, *10*(1), 25–32.

Julien, P. A. (2018). *The state of the art in small business and entrepreneurship.* Routledge. doi:10.4324/9780429429545

Kidwell, R. E., & Fish, A. (2007). High-performance human resource practices in Australian family businesses: Preliminary evidence from the wine industry. *The International Entrepreneurship and Management Journal, 3*(1), 1–14. doi:10.100711365-006-0020-1

Kim, Y., & Gao, F. Y. (2010). An empirical study of human resource management practices in family firms in China. *International Journal of Human Resource Management, 21*(12), 2095–2119. doi:10.1080/09585192.2010.509619

Kotey, B., & Slade, P. (2005). Formal human resource management practices in small, growing firms. *Journal of Small Business Management, 43*(1), 16–40. doi:10.1111/j.1540-627X.2004.00123.x

Lansberg, I. S. (1983). Managing Human Resources in Family Firms: The Problem of Institutional Overlap. *Organizational Dynamics, 12*(1), 39–46. doi:10.1016/0090-2616(83)90025-6

Le Breton-Miller, I., & Miller, D. (2006). Why do some family businesses out-compete? Governance, long-term orientation, and sustainable capability. *Entrepreneurship Theory and Practice, 30*(6), 731–746. doi:10.1111/j.1540-6520.2006.00147.x

MacDuffie, J. P. (1995). Human Resource Bundles and Manufacturing Performance. Organizational Logic and Flexible Production Systems in the World Auto Industry. *Industrial & Labor Relations Review, 48*(2), 197–221. doi:10.1177/001979399504800201

Madison, K., Daspit, J. J., Turner, K., & Kellermanns, F. W. (2018). Family firm human resource practices: Investigating the effects of professionalization and bifurcation bias on performance. *Journal of Business Research, 84*(5), 327–336. doi:10.1016/j.jbusres.2017.06.021

Mathis, R. L., Jackson, J. H., & Valentine, S. R. (2014). *Human Resource Management* (14th ed.). Cengage Learning.

Montanari, S. (2003). *Le aziende familiari. Continuità e successione* (Vol. 1). Cedam.

Mussolino, D., & Calabrò, A. (2014). Paternalistic leadership in family firms: Types and implications for intergenerational succession? *Journal of Family Business Strategy, 5*(2), 197–210. doi:10.1016/j.jfbs.2013.09.003

Pellegrini, M., & Flamini, G. (2019). *Gestione delle risorse umane nelle imprese familiari: Analisi della letteratura attraverso il text mining*. Prospettive in Organizzazione.

Pfeffer, J. (1994). *Competitive advantage through people*. Harvard Business School. doi:10.2307/41165742

Phikiso, Z., & Tengeh, R. (2017). Challenges to intra-family succession in South African townships. *Academy of Entrepreneurship Journal.*

Reid, R. S., & Adams, J. S. (2001). Human resource management – a survey of practices within family and non-family firms. *Journal of European Industrial Training, 35*(6), 310–320. doi:10.1108/03090590110401782

Reid, R. S., & Harris, R. I. (2002). The determinants of training in SMEs in Northern Ireland. *Education + Training, 44*(8/9), 443–450. doi:10.1108/00400910210449286

Reid, R. S., Morrow, T., Kelly, B., & McCartan, P. (2002). People management in SMEs: An analysis of human resource strategies in family and non-family businesses. *Journal of Small Business and Enterprise Development, 9*(3), 245–259. doi:10.1108/14626000210438571

Rothwell, W. (2010). *Effective succession planning: Ensuring leadership continuity and building talent from within*. Amacom.

Rothwell, W. J., & Kazanas, H. C. (2003). *The strategic development of talent*. Human Resource Development.

Schmid, A., & Sender, A. (2019). How social capital influences performance in family firms: The moderating role of nepotism. *International Journal of Human Resource Management*, 1–21. doi:10.1080/09585192.2019.1674355

Sharma, P. (2004). An overview of the field of family business studies: Current status and directions for the future. *Family Business Review, 17*(1), 1–36. doi:10.1111/j.1741-6248.2004.00001.x

Sharma, P., Chrisman, J. J., & Chua, J. H. (2003). Succession planning as planned behavior: Some empirical results. *Family Business Review, 16*(1), 1–15. doi:10.1111/j.1741-6248.2003.00001.x

Singh, R. (2016). Kavil Ramachandran, The 10 Commandments for Family Business. Sage Publications.

Sonfield, M. C., & Lussier, R. N. (2004). First-, second-, and third-generation family firms: A comparison. *Family Business Review, 17*(3), 189–201. doi:10.1111/j.1741-6248.2004.00013.x

Tabor, W., Chrisman, J. J., Madison, K., & Vardaman, J. M. (2018). Nonfamily members in family firms: A review and future research agenda. *Family Business Review, 31*(1), 54–79. doi:10.1177/0894486517734683

Thach, L., & Kidwell, R. E. (2009). HR practices in United States and Australian family wineries: Cultural contrasts and performance impact. *The International Entrepreneurship and Management Journal, 5*(2), 219–240. doi:10.100711365-008-0099-7

Tommaselli, S. (1996). *Longevità e sviluppo delle imprese familiari: problemi, strategie e strutture di governo*. Giuffrè.

Vallone, C. (2009). *Il passaggio generazionale nel family business ei fattori strategici di successo per continuità aziendale. Analisi comparata tra Italia e Gran Bretagna*. Giuffrè Editore.

Venter, E., Boshoff, C., & Mass, G. (2005). The influence of successor-related factors on the succession process in small and medium-sized family businesses. *Family Business Review, 18*(4), 283–303. doi:10.1111/j.1741-6248.2005.00049.x

Wolfe, R. (1996). *Systematic Succession Planning: Building Leadership from Within*. Crisp Publications.

Xi, J., Filser, M., & Kellermanns, F. W. (2015). Mapping the field of family business research: Past trends and future directions. *The International Entrepreneurship and Management Journal, 11*(1), 113–132. doi:10.100711365-013-0286-z

Zajac, E. J. (1990). CEO selection, succession, compensation and firm performance: A theoretical integration and empirical analysis. *Strategic Management Journal, 11*(3), 217–230. doi:10.1002mj.4250110304

Chapter 15
Law and HRM Challenges in Generational Transition of Family Firms

Emiliano Marchisio
"Giustino Fortunato" University of Benevento, Italy

ABSTRACT

This chapter examines some of the most relevant HRM problems in generational transition of family firms and proposes a number of legal instruments capable of resolving them. Use of corporations as vehicles to run the family business is examined, also with respect to consequences of this choice in business transition. Definition and "protection" of family roles within the firm are observed. Patrimonial issues are compared to personal issues and their interplay is explained by reference to five different scenarios. Last, the possibility to "select", so to say, the law applicable to one's succession under Regulation (EU) no 650/2012 of the European Parliament and of the Council of 4 July 2012 is explored. At the end, it is concluded that even if HRM in family business shows informality along with formality in designing business practices, generational transition of family firms requires structuring and needs be planned, appropriately and in detail, in advance.

INTRODUCTION

There is much literature on family firms and related HRM (Human Resource Management) issues (e.g.: Combs, Jaskiewicz, Shanine & Balkin, 2018; Astrachan Binz & al., 2017; Bammens et al., 2015; Botero & Litchfield, 2013; Barnett, and Kellermanns, 2006; Astrachan, and Kolenko, 1994). Inheritance law is widely studied as well, also with reference to family firms (e.g.: Gallanis, 2019; Fusaro, 2013; Anderson, Arroyo & Amayuelas, 2011; La Porta, 2010; Kerridge & Parry, 2009; De Waal, 2008; Cretney, 1995). However, it is definitely uncommon to find works putting these two areas together. Such a lack prevents scholars from having a wider view of how succession of family firms need take into consideration HRM features and, more in general, the interplay between business needs and strategies, on the one hand, and the law and legal profession, on the other.

DOI: 10.4018/978-1-7998-4814-1.ch015

This chapter is aimed at filling the gap recalled above, adopting the jurist's perspective. To this end, it is built on practical HRM problems emerging within succession of family firms and focuses on presenting legal techniques and strategies capable of facing and solving them. To be explicit, in this chapter HRM aspects will not be dealt with as such; instead, emphasis will be put on legal precautions capable of meeting HRM needs (which are dealt with in much greater detail elsewhere in this book). There appears to be no relevant previous research on the issue carried out following this path of reasoning (problem-based legal analysis appears confined only to works addressed to practitioners, while research tend to be carried out in accordance with systematic reasoning) so that the approach adopted in this chapter appears innovative.

The paper is structured in five sections. In the first part ("background"), family firms and their special features, including their "emotional dimension", are shortly addressed. In the second part, it is highlighted that inheritance default rules applicable to successions are mostly not appropriate to govern family succession of businesses and in particular to address HRM issues, so that planning is always recommended in succession of family firms. In the third part, it is examined how use of a corporation may contribute to ease succession of family firms. In the fourth part, which is the most relevant and original contribution provided by this work, I propose to classify the different HRM exigencies that may arise within succession of family firms into five different scenarios. Each scenario presents a peculiar arrangement of features relevant to HRM (e.g.: how many heirs are in place, their mutual relations, their interest and capability in carrying on management of the family firm etc.) and is examined with reference to its specific problems and opportunities, providing a picture of the main legal techniques available in order to resolve the former and take advantage of the latter. In particular, it is clarified how legislation in different jurisdictions may allow decedents to predetermine roles within the family firm after succession takes place and to reduce conflicts between heirs. Occasionally, personal suggestions and professional hints are also presented. In the fifth part short reference is made to "private international law" and, more in particular, to the possibility to "select" the law applicable to one's succession. At the end of this chapter, a brief set of conclusions is provided.

BACKGROUND

For the purposes of this chapter, family firms are defined as firms owned and run, to a relevant extent, by members of the same family, so that they range from small "mom and pop" businesses to much bigger organizations – such as the U.S. Walmart and Tyson Foods. Even if such a variability may bring about completely different issues and problems, they are all organizations where ownership and business roles overlap with family relations. Such element, which allows to consider all of them as sharing common characteristics, is capable of enriching family firms with peculiar features as concerns many aspects of their activity. In particular, their management may be fostered and enhanced by reason of the relationship existing between members of the same family as regards, among others, vision of the business, definition of goals and loyalty (De Massis, Kotlar, Chua & Chrisman, 2014; De Massis, Sharma, Chua & Chrisman 2012).

The above said peculiar features make family firms unique and characteristic model of business, intrinsically not comparable to other firms (Carlock, de Vries & Florent-Treacy, 2007). In fact, the above recalled "familiar inspiration" may lead to organizational choices and managerial strategies not necessarily consistent with organization and management of other, "common" (to be understood, here, as referring to non-family based), firms (Kidwell & Fish, 2007; Barnett & Kellermanns, 2006; Moshavi & Koch, 2005; Cascio, 1991; Combs, Jaskiewicz, Shanine & Balkin, 2018; Astrachan & Kolenko, 1994).

The "emotional dimension" of family firms, which is part of their competitive advantage (Carlock, de Vries & Florent-Treacy, 2007), at the same time is the origin of their peculiar (sometimes *unique*) challenges and problems. A successful business may be destroyed if the family who runs it fails to address the psychological and "familiar" issues involved in it, thus unbalancing family and business dynamics. Such an "emotional dimension" is particularly relevant within successions, insofar as it may determine decisions that may challenge (if not contrast *tout court*) inheritance law and (or) economic efficiency.

Under the first perspective, one may think to cases where the decedent leaves ownership of the family firm to only one or some of his or her heirs but does not transfer to the others assets sufficient to equal their "reserved portion", which is a minimum share of the estate reserved to certain heirs within certain jurisdictions (Anderson, Arroyo & Amayuelas, 2011; Ruggeri, Kunda & Winkler, 2019)[1] such as, e.g., Italy, Belgium, Germany, Spain, France *but not*, e.g., Poland and, at least as a general rule, in England and Wales[2]. In these cases, any violation of the reserved portion would entitle the relevant heir to legal claims that could eventually lead to impairment of the inherited firm (e.g.: in case compensation paid to the heir to reach his or her reserved portion is financed through sale of business assets).

As regards economic efficiency, one may think to cases where heirs sue one another notwithstanding each of them received a sufficient portion of the estate under governing inheritance law, because only some heirs were appointed to managerial roles and the others do not accept to be excluded from the running of the business in the future. Such a scenario, which is rather frequent, shows a serious misunderstanding of the difference between inheritance of a piece of estate (that may be required by the law in favor of *each* heir, if legislation on "reserved portions" is in place) and appointment to managerial roles (which should happen only if transferees are interested in, and adequate to, the role and may not be claimed under inheritance law). Of course, heirs are not entitled to sue on the basis of their exclusion from management; however, it would be easy to find instrumental (even ill-founded) grounds for action in order to *induce* co-heirs to share business roles. This leads invariably to costs and inefficiencies.

Every business succession has its own features and peculiarities. HRM risks and threats that may arise during a succession depend on several factors. First of all, one should consider the environment external to the firm and, in particular, the latter's competitive positioning, along with country and industry perspectives.

Internal characteristics of the firm should also be considered. Succession differs radically if the firm is owned only by members of the same family (a situation that connotes a family business in its infant stage) or not. The size of the firm should also be considered, since this may require specific managerial ability, technical expertise and commitment (Arieu, 2010). Among other characteristics one may also mention actual organizational variables (e.g.: whether management lies only in the hands of one or a few family members or external professionals and advisor are involved as well: Hause & Tutelman, 2008), professionalization, firm life cycle, past performances, presence of knowledge and skills.

Along with external environment and internal characteristics of the firm, one should also consider the particular features of the family the business belongs to. In this sense, it is necessary to assess the family involvement in the business, culture and family values, family ties, family embeddedness and resources, family leadership styles, emotional attachment, entrepreneurial orientation and goals.

Planning of Succession

In this context, planning of succession of family firms involves many aspects and requires awareness on a rather high number of issues. HRM, in particular, is an area particularly relevant and sensitive in this respect. Many HRM strategic variables, in fact, need be taken in adequate account when planning succession of family businesses, as regards, e.g.: appointment and stability of management, recruitment and selection, compensation, workforce planning and career planning management (Combs, Liu, Hall & Ketchen, 2006; Boselie, Dietz & Boon, 2005).

Apart from all aspects relating to non-legal issues (e.g. the needs to plan with adequate advance education and skilling of successors: Pittino, Visintin & Lauto, 2018; to entrust external professionals with specific roles within transition; to allow a certain flexibility in planning; along with other HRM variables not relevant to this chapter, which may be better handled with managerial instruments instead of legal ones, such as performance appraisal, training and development, job design and internal communication: Combs, Liu, Hall & Ketchen, 2006; Boselie, Dietz & Boon, 2005; *etc.*), many HRM concerns and difficulties involved in family succession may well be handled, if not solved at all, with a wise recourse to available and appropriate legal means.

What is most relevant to note from the very beginning is that all jurisdictions provide rules applicable to successions in case the decedent have neither planned any transition nor written any will. It is not relevant, here, to spend much words on the rules in force within different jurisdictions. What is important to note is that these rules are mostly not appropriate to govern succession of family businesses and, in particular, HRM issues. Inheritance default rules, in fact, take into account mainly (if not only) "patrimonial" aspects (i.e.: define *values*, calculated on the whole estate, different heirs are entitled to) but ignore all other factors which are of paramount importance for family succession.

What makes the difference, in succession of family firms, is maintaining and enhancing their "emotional dimension" preventing the risk that the latter degenerates and prevails over business needs. In fact, an efficient succession need taking into account the familiar features of each business, providing HRM systems capable of preserving and developing them. This would constitute a key factor to enhancing performance (Batt, 2002; Guthrie, 2001; Wood, 1999; Ichniowski & Shaw, 1999; Becker, 1996; Huselid, 1995; MacDuffie, 1995; Arthur, 1992) and maintaining competitive advantage (Zakaria, 2011; Othman, 2009; Karami, Jones & Kakabadse, 2008; Gooderham, Nordhaug & Ringdal, 2006; Hiltrop, 2005; Wright, Gardner, Moynihan & Allen, 2005; Collins, 2003; Guest, Michie, Conway & Sheehan, 2003; Panayotopoulou, Bourantas & Papalexandris, 2003; Bjorkman, 2002; Ferris, Hochwarter, Buckley, Harrell-Cook & Frink, 1999; Huselid, 1995; Jackson, 1995; Wright & McMahan, 1992; Ulrich, 1991; Schuler & MacMillan, 1984).

Succession of family firms involves inheritance law under numerous points of view. Many of them, however, fall outside the matter of HRM (as it is the case of agreements on future successions, conjunct wills, reciprocal wills *etc.*) and would not be appropriate with the context of this book. My interest, therefore, will be limited to legal remarks on succession of family businesses relating to HRM variables. In this perspective, most part of the analysis concerns two main problems: misalignment of interests and needs between family members and the business, on the one hand, and conflicts between different family members, on the other.

Conflicts of interests may derive from people's expectations, departure from the "*unique cultures and procedures*" developed within the firm over time (Pittino, Visintin & Lauto, 2017), conflicts between family and external shareholders (emotional capital *v* performance) and managers (emotional capital *v* strategy and social capital) (Carlock, de Vries & Florent-Treacy, 2007) *etc.*. Different needs, on the other hand, may emerge as regards funds' distribution or investment (Loewen, 2008), confusion between family and business assets (Walczak & Voss, 2013) *etc.*. Whatever their origins, they are key points to be addressed in succession planning.

Title to the Assets *v* Title to a Vehicle

Succession of family firms may be appropriately planned, first of all, by vesting the business with a "company" and, in particular, with a "corporation", instead of leaving ownership and title to the firm directly to physical persons. Such a solution determines many advantages.

First of all, co-ownership of a firm by more persons is disciplined, in principle, pursuant to legislation on shared ownership, which mainly focus on "static" aspects and requires, in many instances, unanimity of co-owners for several decisions. Ownership of the business by a corporation between the same persons, on the other hand, allows successors availability of an organization designed for "dynamic" running of businesses and makes virtually all decisions subject to majority rules.

Second of all, participation of successors to a corporation makes it much easier to dispose of their quotas (which is disciplined by rules on circulation of company shares or quotas) when compared to disposing of an ideal quota of ownership in a business – especially when the business includes assets whose sale or disposition requires special formalities, as it happens typically for real estate. This is particularly true if a corporation is adopted (where transfer of shares or quotas is, in principle, free even if almost invariably subject, in family firms, to contractual right of first refusal or approval clause). Use of partnerships may make it more complicated transfer of participations, especially in favor of heirs[3].

Thirdly, corporate organization allows formation of sophisticated group schemes, that can be used to pursue many different organizational goals. E.g.: if successors belong to different family logs, they could be grouped within different companies all participating into a single corporation running the family business, in order to make sure that decisions taken in the latter represent the position of the majority of the members of each family log and not a one, single, majority regardless of the family logs expressing it.

In some instances it could be advisable the use, as parent company (i.e.: company that has a controlling interest in one or more other companies, giving the former control of operations of the latter), of an entity organised as the Italian *società in accomandita* or the French, Belgian and Luxembourgish *société en commandite*; the German, Belgian, Austrian or the Dutch *Kommandgesellschaft*; the Spanish *sociedad comanditaria*). Such companies, which may be established either in the form of a partnership or of a corporation, share the common feature of being participated by two types of partners/shareholders: managing partners/shareholders, entrusted with managing powers and unlimited liable for the company's obligations, and limited partners/shareholders, foreclosed by any managing power and liable for the companies' obligations only limitedly to their contributions to the partnership/corporation. Adoption of such type of companies makes directors more stable than in any other type of company, since substitution of any director requires, as a general rule, *not only* a decision taken by the majority of partners/shareholders *but also* consent by the other directors[4]. Such a special feature makes it more difficult for hypothetical partners/shareholders not belonging to the family to take management of the company over. It is true that the "managing" partners/shareholders, in these kind of companies, are liable for social debts without limits. Commercial practice found a remedy to this problem, however, by use, e.g. in Germany, of a *Kommandgesellschaft* where the managing partner (*Komplementär*) is a *Gesellschaft mit beschränkter Haftung* (GmbH: company with limited liability): the so-called *GmbH*

& Co. KG (Arnold, 2001). Similar solutions are available also in other jurisdictions, as far as a limited liability company is allowed to participate in such companies as managing partner.

In some jurisdictions other legal entities are sometimes used for succession of family firms because of different benefits recognised to them by legislation. E.g., under German law use of a *Familienstiftung* (family foundation: §§ 80 ss. BGB) prevents legitimate heirs from any claim with respect to company shares after ten years from contribution to the foundation (Fusaro, 2013); in England and Wales, charitable trusts are exempted from most forms of tax (Hudson, 2009) *etc.*.

Legal Instruments to Prevent Dissention, Deadlocks and Litigation Within Corporations

Even if family succession is sometimes pursued carrying out the family business through different legal entities (such as foundations or trusts, as noted above), use of a corporation is capable of producing several remarkable advantages. In particular, it helps preventing dissention, deadlocks and litigation among successors, which represents a much relevant goal within planning of any family succession. However, pursue of such scope requires competence: poor drafting of a company's bylaws and shareholders' agreements may lead rather easily to conflict. In some jurisdictions, if any conflict produces a deadlock, this could determine dissolution of the company under the law[5]; such event, in any way, would almost invariably cause inefficiencies to the firm.

The problem of dissention, deadlocks and litigation among successors is particularly felt when the company running the family business was originally held by a single founder or if the participation was divided among founders in equal shares. In all these cases, unless differently provided, (groups of) successors hold equivalent participations and could easily find themselves stuck in a deadlock.

The first strategy to avoid such problems is that of avoiding, as much as possible, the attribution of equal voting position within any relevant corporate organ. As regards shareholder meetings, 50-50% shareholdings are never a good idea. Of course, the issue, here, is not the amount of shareholding in itself but the weight of voting powers; therefore, 50-50% shareholding-like solutions could be acceptable as far as they attribute to their holders *different* voting powers (non-voting, ordinary voting, super-voting shares) (Milman, 2018).

In all cases where such different conformation of voting powers is not possible (e.g. in companies where voting powers are attributed to members "one head-one vote" or, typically, when dealing with voting powers within the board of directors), mechanisms of casting vote should always be provided.

Of course, ease of reaching a majority may be desirable with respect to some decisions (especially those necessary for the very "survival" of the company, i.e.: appointment of directors and approval of annual accounts) but could be too rough in other cases. Other decisions (e.g.: transfer of business of relevant part thereof, enter into loan agreements of relevant amounts, constitution of guarantees on company's assets *etc*), in fact, may require the opposite solution of providing *higher* majorities, instead, in order to allow to relevant groups of shareholders veto or other bargaining powers.

Shareholders may even bind themselves to exercise their voting powers in a given manner or to a pre-determined end through shareholders' agreements, as it happens when they want to guarantee that specific persons are appointed as directors or member of the supervisory board of the company and that such appointment is preserved for a certain span of time – as it is noted below.

Legal Instruments to React to Deadlocks and Litigation After They Show Out

As noted above, company's bylaws and shareholders' agreements should be drafted in such a way as to prevent, as much as possible, dissention, deadlocks and litigation. However, troubles happen and may show even if drafting was impeccable. In case conflicts arise and show impossible to be settled, bylaws (and, if the case, shareholders' agreements) should provide mechanisms and procedures capable of allowing the interest of the firm to prevail over the desires of its shareholders.

There could be many different strategies to this end and, of course, each of them may fit differently to each different situation. An effective strategy for handling conflicts, if some heirs are interested in running the family business in the future and other ones are not, is commonly that of allowing only part of the successors to remain owners of the firm, providing others with cash consideration (or other estates) for their exit. Of course parties could negotiate a sale and purchase agreement after the conflict has shown, but this strategy may be pursued only very seldom. Once the relationship is deteriorated, cognitive biases would play an important role in negotiation (Priest, 2019) so that perspective seller(s) would invariably require an higher price that that perspective purchaser(s) would be willing to pay.

A less draconian, and equally effective, strategy would be that of providing, in well drafted clauses within the corporate bylaws or shareholders' agreements, exit strategies that activate and work by default as soon as given triggering events are in place. One may think, for example, to withdrawal clauses or "put" options in shareholders' agreements, which allow dissenting shareholders to exit the corporation in given hypotheses or even whenever they want.

Another strategy is that of providing shares redeemable by the corporation or "call" options, which allow the company or its stable shareholders to exclude the dissenting shareholders in given hypotheses or even after a certain period of time.

One may even think of providing exclusion clauses, which allow the company to exclude shareholders in some given cases, even if such clauses, if allowed, have usually a rather narrow scope of application: in fact, they may be commonly triggered only by serious violation of company rules by the members to be excluded.

Transfer of Shareholding to Third Parties and "Going Public"

The adoption of corporate structures for vesting businesses would also allow reaching further goals. Family firms, even when run through corporate structures, are rather likely to be held, especially in the first generation, by members of the founding family. Family ownership may well last for future generations. It is likely, however, that over the time a progressively larger shareholding is transferred to third parties and even to the public.

Of course, the nature, structure and duration of any such transfer depends on the needs aimed at. If the *manoeuvre* is aimed at raising cash to buy-out other shareholders, in case of conflict (this hypothesis was mentioned above), the financing is substantially in favour of the remaining shareholders, who will be likely to ask an investor to purchase the participation of the shareholders bought-out and enter an obligation to repurchase it within a limited span of time at a predetermined price, which includes both restitution of the anticipated sum and interests and fees for the service provided.

If, on the other hand, further financing is required by the firm's needs (because of the plan of expanding, growing up, restructuring *etc.*), it is more likely that the company increases its share capital and issues new shares, to be sold to third parties willing to contribute cash to the business (and not to its shareholders, as in the previous case). These third parties could agree to become shareholders without any predetermined time-limit or could agree to resell their participation to original shareholders after a certain span of time – in this latter case, at a price which will be likely to incorporate restitution of the sums plus interests and a fee for the finance provided. Another version of this operation could be that of allowing the investor to resell the shareholding purchased onto the market.

Shareholders may also be interested simply to leave the business and convert their participation in the company with cash, either in part or even selling the whole 100% of the company. This would be a strategy to be pursued in case none of the successors is willing or capable to run the business inherited by the decedent – a situation examined below.

All the above mentioned paths of action may provide or be coupled with listing of the company into regulated markets such as the stock exchange; if the corporation has all the characteristics to do so and meets the legal and economic conditions required therefor, listing would certainly provide a much larger base of potential purchasers of the company's shares.

One further remark. Except for the case where shareholders want to sell the whole business, in all other instances it is possible that "family" shareholders want to maintain some form of control over the company even if their shareholding is reduced. This "control" could be aimed at rather different scopes but, substantially, may be designed in two main alternative forms. If after the sale conditions are such as original shareholders are allowed to maintain the power to run the business, it is likely that they will design their "control" in such a way as to keep a voting majority in strategic decisions such as appointment and removal of directors, approval of the annual accounts *etc.*.

If on the other hand, the purchasing third party (or parties) requires to take over management of the company or anyway the original shareholders cannot maintain the power to run the company, the latter may want to reserve control over the way the business is managed by others. This could imply, e.g., reservation to appoint members of the supervisory board *etc.*.

Both the above mentioned goals could be pursued following different strategies. In closely held corporations (such as Italian *società a responsabilità limitata*, the German and Austrian *Gesellschaft mit beschränkter Haftung*, the French *Société à responsabilité limité*, the Spanish *sociedad de responsabilidad limitada etc.*) different jurisdictions allow to empower one or more partners with appointment of either one or more directors or one or more members of the supervisory board regardless of their actual participation to the company's capital (Gerner-Beuerle & Schillig, 2019; Cahn & Donald, 2018; Siems & Cabrelli, 2018; Cahn & Donald, 2010; Andenas & Wooldridge, 2009; Balouziyeh, 2010).

In public corporations (such as Italian *società per azioni*, the German and Austrian *Aktiengesellschaft*, the French *Société par actions*, the Spanish *sociedad anónima etc.*) the above mentioned reallocation of powers need be pursued through differentiation of shares into different types, attributing to their holders different rights and powers (Gerner-Beuerle & Schillig, 2019; Cahn & Donald, 2018; Siems & Cabrelli, 2018; Cahn & Donald, 2010; Andenas & Wooldridge, 2009; Balouziyeh, 2010). In either case, of course, the said results could be reached through appropriate provisions in shareholders' agreements.

HRM-Specific Issues: Definition and "Protection" of Family Roles Within the Firm

It is likely that within successions of family businesses some family members are entrusted with specific roles within the firm and that the decedent wanted such roles to be permanent – or, at least, long lasting.

This may be the case, e.g., when the decedent plans to leave the role of managing director to one specific successor, who was specifically trained to that end and showed specific competence and attitude over time.

Even if such allocation of roles shows useful also when the company is owned only by family members, it is of paramount importance when ownership or anyway control of the company is transferred to third parties (a scenario which is referred to above). Third parties, in fact, may want to remove all people currently holding company roles to substitute them with others of their own trust, thus determining changes in management of the business.

It is clear that any allocation of roles by the decedent needs adoption of some legal technique in order to make it stable or, at least, difficult or burdensome to modify.

Pursue of the above stability goal depends on several factors. First of all, if the role to be entrusted relates to a employee or employee-like position, labour law usually provide the relevant successor (in hypothesis family member) with an higher stability. It is acknowledged that such stability may vary very much between different jurisdictions and, within the same jurisdiction, between the status and level of each single employee (Finkin & Mundlak, 2015; Blanpain, 2014; Blanplain, Bisom-Rapp, Corbett, Josephs & Zimmer, 2012; Pennings & Bosse, 2011). However, given the higher protection provided by labour law with respect to company law, it is usually appropriate that successors are employed within the family business in transition notwithstanding they also have company roles (as far as these roles are compatible with employment). Even if the successor is revoked as director, e.g., he or she would maintain the role (and salary) as director general or similar.

If the position relates to participation to corporate organs (member of the board of directors, typically), the situation becomes certainly less stable. In principle, all directors are appointed for a pre-determined period of time and may be revoked, as a general principle, even without any just cause. Revocation without just cause, in fact, gives rise, in principle, only to the directors' right to compensation (Gerner-Beuerle & Schillig, 2019; Cahn & Donald, 2018; Siems & Cabrelli, 2018; Cahn & Donald, 2010; Andenas & Wooldridge, 2009; Balouziyeh,2010).

It is true that in closely held corporations bylaws may provide, in some jurisdictions and in some cases, longer appointments, even for the whole life of the director, but this would never prevent members from revoking directors, at least if a just cause is in place (Gerner-Beuerle & Schillig, 2019; Cahn & Donald, 2018; Siems & Cabrelli, 2018; Cahn & Donald, 2010; Andenas & Wooldridge, 2009; Balouziyeh, 2010).

In public corporations, on the other hand, it is not possible, in principle, to provide any appointment longer than the span of time provided by law - but this is not a problem impossible to bypass. In fact, if it is not possible to guarantee a long duration in the role within the company bylaws, such goal may be pursued through shareholders' agreements, which could also provide waivers to fire or revoke the person appointed at the relevant role. Of course, such agreements could never prevent a different decision from being adopted within the company (e.g.: parties to the shareholders' agreement voting on revocation of a director even if the agreement prohibited such a decision for a certain period of time) but could provide a penalty clause on the members whose vote was expressed in contrast with the stability clause provided in the agreement.

Another technique rather used to the same end consists in entering clauses that impose disincentives on the company for the case of removal from the role of specified persons. This is the case, e.g., with respect to the so-called "golden parachutes" clauses. They consists in clauses, to be provided within employment or other engagement contracts (even within the appointment as director), under which the company commits to pay a much relevant *exit bonus* in case such person is removed from a specific role. This corresponds to implicitly binding the company to maintain that person in charge with that role (Kasper, 2014).

Patrimonial *v* Personal Issues

As noted above, one of the most relevant (and, incidentally, most frequent) problems within successions of family businesses is that of failing to differentiate between inheritance of a given estate, which may be required by the law in some jurisdictions if legislation on "reserved portions" is in place, and appointment to managerial roles, which should happen only if transferees are interested in, and adequate to, the transferred role. The latter may never be claimed as a inheritance right.

Of course, emergence and magnitude of such a problem depends on the situation at stake and may vary depending on many factors. I propose to examine the different hypotheses following a taxonomy made of five scenarios (which are, of course, hyper-simplified and do not take into account many relevant variables such as, e.g., the number of successors).

Each of these scenarios relate to a specific HRM need within the family business and presents specific problems and opportunities. In some cases, e.g., all heirs are interested in, and adequate to, taking over the family firm and are in good relationship to one another, so the "HRM challenge" relates to allocating roles and fostering coordination. In other cases some heirs want to carry on managing the firm while others do not, so that attribution of managing roles to the former requires an appropriate patrimonial compensation to the latter and a clear distinction of their respective roles within the firm. In the following pages, each scenario is matched with a brief overview of the legal techniques capable of solving (or, at least, reducing) problems and take advantage of the opportunities which characterise it.

First Scenario: All Successors are Interested in, and Adequate to, Taking Over the Family Firm and They are in Good Relationship to one Another

The first scenario one may think of is that where all successors are interested in, and adequate to, taking over the family firm and they are in good relationship to one another (or there is only one successor who happen to be interested and adequate for running the business). In this case it may make sense to leave ownership of the whole firm to all successors or, even more, to the sole successor, providing, in case successors are more than one, that dissention, deadlocks and litigation are prevented through appropriate regulatory mechanisms.

It should be noted, however, that if any of these conditions (interest in the firm, adequacy to run it and good relationship among successors) lacks, there is no sense to leave the whole firm to all successors *pro quota*. This would invariably bring to misunderstandings, litigation and eventually to the destruction of the business.

If successors are more than one, there arise the issue of allocating among them the different management roles: president, managing director, CFO *etc.*. Such an allocation could be made more complicated in case the business is articulated in a group of companies, as briefly noted above. Allocation of roles would depend on the number of successors and their specific competences: if there is only a limited number of heirs and they are specialised in different areas of the business, their presence within the firm would be an asset, insofar as each of them could be assigned the role he or she belongs to on the basis of his or her skills and attitudes.

On the other hand, if successors are many and/or their competences overlap (or, even worse: correspond), the risk on conflict is more likely to arise. In this case one may think of several solutions. One may be that of creating different roles (e.g.: with respect to different companies within the group or to different markets, geographic areas *etc.*) in order not to have overlapping between different successors, even splitting the business and allocate different companies to different successors if the risk of conflict is high (as noted below). Another solution could be that of providing collegial organs where successors could co-operate (e.g.: within a board of directors). Allowing alternation over time within the same role could be a further solution but would require a very good cooperative attitude by the successors called to interchange.

Second Scenario: One or More Successors are Interested in, and Adequate to, Taking Over the Family Firm and Others are Not

The second scenario is that where one or more successors are interested in, and adequate to, taking over the family business but other ones are not. Of course, if the legal system does not impose any "reserved portion" in favor of heirs, the problem may be easily solved out: the family firm might be attributed only to skilled and enthusiastic successors without any need to compensate adequately the others. However, if the legal system imposes such "reserved portions", it is not possible to reserve the whole patrimony only to *some* of those identified by the law as legitimate heirs.

With respect to the latter hypothesis there may be rather different scenarios. If the value of the family firm represent a similar proportion to the *personal* patrimony of the decedent than the interested and adequate heirs to the others, then the issue may be dealt with by allocating personal assets to the latter and the family business to the former. The family firm, e.g., could be left to the skilled and enthusiastic daughter, leaving to the son, dedicated to painting or playing violin, apartments, other investments and cash. In fact, legislation on "reserved portions" reserves in favour of successors proportional values, not specific assets.

What happens if such favourable, and rather uncommon, situation does not exist? In this case, it is necessary to see whether the legal system allows derogation to "reserved portions" as long as family firms are concerned. This may be the case in some jurisdictions, as some commentators believe it happens, e.g., with respect to the Italian *patto di famiglia*, disciplined by artt. 768 *bis* ff. c.c., introduced by art. 2 of the Italian law 14 February 2006, n. 55 (Busani, 2019; Caliendo, 2018; La Porta, 2010).

Otherwise, it could be attributed to disinterested or inadequate successors only the minimum value of ownership of the family business required by the law ("reserved portion"), leaving to interested and adequate ones majority shareholdings. Management roles in the future should be vested only with the appropriate heirs and no derogation to such principle should be provided. Disinterested or inadequate successors could be benefited through agreements allowing them minimum dividends or other remuneration and could be granted other advantages, but should be put in such a position as not to interfere to management of the firm.

Another legal instrument which may be used in this hypothesis is a trust, which implies that the trustee is the *legal owner* of the property in trust but is called to exercise such title for the beneficiaries, who are the equitable owners of the trust property. Therefore, the trustee owes to the beneficiaries a number of fiduciary duties (including the duties of loyalty, of prudence, of impartiality) and ancillary duties in support of the primary duties (including duties of openness, transparency, recordkeeping, accounting, disclosure *etc.*) (Gallanis, 2019; Sterk & Leslie, 2019; Panico, 2017; Sitkoff & Dukeminier, 2017; Gleason Bogert, Oaks, Hansen & Neeleman, 2012).

The decedent may transfer all his or her title to and in the family firm to a trustee, requiring the trustee to pursue the best interest of the family. Use of the trust in inheritance strategies requires all people concerned to be aware that such instrument requires property to be effectively transferred upon a trustee and settlor (and beneficiaries) to lose control over it. The trust deed, however, could well provide that management of the firm is attributed, as much as reasonable, to successors of the settlor. Of course, use of a trust instrument is viable only insofar as, among others, the law governing succession recognizes validity and effectiveness of trusts and does not allow trust deeds to be disregarded if they relate to inheritance issues (Panico, 2017).

Third Scenario: More Successors are Interested in, and Adequate to, Taking Over the Family Firm but are not in Good Relationship to one Another

Maturity of the business is a crucial variable in both its running and its succession. In fact, one may expect that, during the first generation of the family firm, the founders maintain rather good relationships among them and with their partners, if any. During the second generation their sons and daughters may be more likely to enter into disagreement on the way the firm should be run and develop over time, on the investments required in one or another area, on the dividends that should be paid out *etc.*. If every person involved in the family firm generates at least one child, it is invariable that during the third generation disagreement will emerge. This is almost unavoidable.

The mere hope that this will not happen or the decision to leave litigation to courts are not good strategies in planning succession of family businesses. It is much better to (try to) defuse future litigation. This is possible following different paths of action. The most effective solution to this end is that of splitting the family firm into different companies, run by different groups of heirs. Of course, such strategy may be adopted only if the family firm may be divided (e.g. if it includes different sectors of activity, geographical areas of operation *etc.*) and if such division is appropriate under a managerial point of view (which may be if there is no economy of scale, scope or integration in the common running of the different sectors *etc.*).

If division is not possible or efficient, one may think of opening participation to the corporation running the family firm to third parties and even to the general public. It is true that such a strategy would reduce the power of the family on management of the business but it would bring an important consequence: shareholders external to the family could represent the "deciding vote" which would discipline successors to pursue the interest of the business and refrain from indulging in mere familiar quarrels. This reasoning is carried out on the hypothesis that unreasonable attitudes of "family" shareholders would lead external shareholders to distance and uphold sound alternatives. Of course, the higher the shareholding transferred to third parties or the public, the lower the probabilities that successors maintain (or, at least, *exclusively* maintain) management of the business.

One may imagine different scenarios where division of the firm is not possible and the decedent and his or her descendants do not want to sell out shareholdings in their family business. The latter attitude may depend on several variables, e.g.: wish to maintain control of the firm, dissatisfaction with the conditions others may want to buy shareholdings, desire to keep the firm as "familiar" as possible *etc.*. In this case, which certainly increases risks, the ideal strategy is that of providing at least legal means aimed at preventing conflicts as much as possible and, in case of disagreement, defining settlement strategies or, for the worst cases, exit strategies. Such strategies were referred to above.

Fourth Scenario: No Successor is Interested in, or Adequate to, Taking Over the Family Firm

When succession of family business is planned, it is rarely considered that one or more successors, and even *all* successors, may be either not interested or not adequate to taking over the firm. The founders may hold the emotional, and rather irrational, desire that their sons and daughters carry on for their whole life running the firm they built from scratch. However, sons and daughters may want to become musicians, travel-agents, teachers, scientists or whatever else.

In this scenario, the worse idea is that of exercising parental authority to force successors to change the projects they made for their lives and dedicate their future to the family business, instead. This would lead to unsatisfactory lives and, probably, to destruction of the firm. If they want to do something else in their lives, they should be able to do that.

The most appropriate strategy, here, is that of insulating the estate from business roles and transferring to successors the benefits of the former without the burden of the latter. This strategy may be pursued with different degrees of intensity. The first solution is that of leaving to successors participation in the company running the business, providing that at the moment of family succession the corporation is already run by skilled managers adequate to run the firm and devoted to it (Stewart & Hitt, 2012). Pursuant to this strategy, successors would maintain both patrimonial benefits deriving from the firm (dividends, possibility to sell out shareholdings *etc.*) and powers to govern it or, at least, have a voice in the way it is governed (by exercising powers and other prerogatives deriving from their shareholdings, such as appointment, revocation and substitution of company's directors: Gerner-Beuerle & Schillig, 2019; Cahn & Donald, 2018; Siems & Cabrelli, 2018; Cahn & Donald, 2010; Andenas & Wooldridge, 2009; Balouziyeh, 2010).

A second solution is that of transferring all participations to a trustee in charge of managing them for the benefit of the family. As noted above, use of the trust in inheritance strategies involves some specific problems as to recognition of validity and effectiveness of trusts under the law governing succession and the risk, in some jurisdictions, that trust deeds are disregarded if they relate to inheritance. Such strategy would leave to successors all patrimonial benefits deriving from the firm but would deprive them of all powers to influence the way it is run, with the sole, marginal and legally not binding exception of their "letter of wishes" they may be entitled to address to the trustee, being it clear that letter of wishes are non-binding on the trustee. All binding instruction, in fact, must be contained in the trust instrument itself (Gallanis, 2019; Sterk & Leslie, 2019; Sitkoff & Dukeminier, 2017; Gleason Bogert, Oaks, Hansen & Neeleman, 2012).

A third solution is that of transferring to third parties, and even to the general public, participations in the corporation running the family firm. Such a strategy would allow successors to convert shareholding in cash and bring the effects and consequences already noted above.

Fifth Scenario: Protecting Weak Members of the Family

There may be also the case, at the end, that among successors there are family members which are particularly *frail* – either because of physical or intellectual illness or because of other weaknesses (e.g.:

inability, addictions to gaming or similar). Also in this case successors would not be adequate to taking over the family firm, so that should not be allowed to run the family business, as it happens in the fourth scenario examined above. Moreover, they would not be adequate to manage their own patrimony, either. Even if in this case there is no specific connection of succession with HRM needs, protection of weak members of the family may be appropriately dealt with here since such activity represents precisely one of the areas where the "family nature" of family firms may show its potential.

It is clear that illness or weaknesses should not deprive heirs of economic benefits deriving from succession. In fact, such benefits could be of fundamental importance for their lives, if they are not able to support themselves financially. The problem, therefore, is that of allowing them all benefits deriving from succession depriving them any power to influence business (management aspects) or dispose of assets (patrimonial aspects). Their illness or weakness, in fact, would be most likely to induce irrational decisions and, therefore, lost of economic means.

Family members could be of great relevance in supporting fragile persons. In case they cannot, do not want or are not in such a position to do it appropriately, legislations provide specific pieces of regulation designed to assist weak persons, differently designed depending on the relevant jurisdiction examined (e.g.: guardianship in England and Wales and the USA and, in particular in the USA, conservatorship; in Germany *Vormundschaft* with respect to minors and *Betreuung* for people of majority age; *tutelle* and *curatelle* in France; *tutela* and *curatela* in Spain; *tutela* and *curatela* in Italy *etc.*) (National Guardianship Association, 2016; Dayton, 2014; Arai, Becker & Lipp, 2013). Such remedies should be appropriately taken into account while planning transition of family businesses and other inheritance issues.

Similar goals could be reached also through adoption of a trust scheme or setting up of a foundation (more precisely designed, in common law, as charitable trust; *fundación* in Spain, *fondazione* in Italy, *fondation* in France; *Familienstiftung* would be a foundation specifically constituted for family needs in Germany *etc.*), which are structures that may well be used to assist people in need of support.

SELECTION OF THE LAW GOVERNING FAMILY SUCCESSION

It was occasionally observed that inheritance law may vary rather relevantly between different jurisdictions and that such dissimilarities may relate to most important variables of family succession: definition of heirs, existence and definition of reserved portions *etc.*. The possibility to "select", so to say, the law applicable to one's succession may represent a convenient strategy to plan succession of one's family business.

The issue falls within the so-called "private international law" (in anglo-american tradition also referred to as "conflict of laws"), i.e.: pieces of legislation concerning relations across different legal jurisdictions between legal subject, their legal obligations and the appropriate forum and procedure for resolving disputes between them (Muir, Bíziková, Brandão De Oliveira & Fernández Arroyo, 2019; Grušic', Heinze, Merrett, Mills, García-Castrill6n, Tang, Trimmings, Walker, Torremans & Fawcett, 2017; Hay, Borchers & Freer, 2017; Symeonides, 2008).

It ought to be noted that, within the European Union, the rules of international private law with respect to successions are defined by Regulation (EU) no 650/2012 of the European Parliament and of the Council of 4 July 2012 "*on jurisdiction, applicable law, recognition and enforcement of decisions and acceptance and enforcement of authentic instruments in matters of succession and on the creation of a European Certificate of Succession*"[6].

In extreme synthesis, the Regulation is relevant, here, with respect to both choice of law and jurisdiction. As regards the "applicable law" (which may or may not be a law of a Member State: art. 20), which is called to "*govern the succession as a whole*" (art. 23.1), the Regulation provides, as a general rule, that, unless otherwise provided, "*the law applicable to the succession as a whole shall be the law of the State in which the deceased had his habitual residence at the time of death*" (art. 21.1). This means that, unless circumstances of the case lead to believe differently[7], a "strategic" transfer of residence may influence "applicable law" and, therefore, allow a wider choice as to the definition of the discipline of succession of family businesses[8].

Such instrument of generational planning would be rather reliable but would not allow disapplication of *every* succession rule: in fact, the application of a provision of the law of any State specified by the Regulation may be refused (only) "*if such application is manifestly incompatible with the public policy (ordre public) of the forum*" (art. 35).

As regards "jurisdiction", the Regulation provides that the courts of the Member State in which the deceased had his or her habitual residence at the time of death "*shall have jurisdiction to rule on the succession as a whole*" (art. 4). It is allowed, however, that the parties concerned agree to choice courts of a Member State to have exclusive jurisdiction to rule on any succession matter provided that "*the law chosen by the deceased to govern his succession pursuant to Article 22 is the law of a Member State*" (art. 5.1). Of course, "*a decision given in a Member State shall be recognised in the other Member States without any special procedure being required*" (art. 39.1), unless any of the grounds for non-recognition spelled in art. 40 is in place.

CONCLUSION

At the end of this research, some conclusions may be drawn:

a. family firms have special features, including a specific "emotional dimension", which strongly interfere on the way they are managed, so that they need be considered in family succession;
b. default inheritance rules are mostly not appropriate to govern family succession of businesses and in particular to address HRM issues, since they mostly deal with *patrimonial aspects* and do not consider *personal engagement* in the family firm. Therefore, planning of succession is always recommended in succession of family firms;
c. vesting the family firm with a corporation may contribute to ease succession. An appropriate drafting of the by-laws may help preventing dissention, deadlocks and litigation within corporations and reacting to deadlocks and litigation after they show out. Use of a corporation would allow transfer of shareholding to third parties while maintaining control or, at least, a somehow qualified "voice" in managing the firm;
d. many variables influence the way the succession of a family firm need be planned. They relate to how many heirs are in place, their mutual relations, their interest and capability in carrying on management of the family firm *etc.*. Different combinations of these variables require appropriate solutions in order to allow willing and capable heirs to manage the firm, recognize the others appropriate compensation, set up assistance for the weak members of the family and prevent litigation among all of them;

e. whenever possible, the possibility to "select" the law applicable to one's succession should be considered as a strategy to plan family succession of one's family business, since different jurisdictions may provide different rules with respect to most important variables thereof.

Of course, the need to confine the length of this article within practicable boundaries imposed two main limitations. On the one hand, presentation of HRM challenges in succession of family firms was rather simplified and general, as it was specifically noted with respect to the five scenarios examined above. On the other hand, legal techniques and strategies were only shortly referred to and many practical problems were disregarded. This has not prevented the achievement of the scope of this chapter that, as noted above, was that of providing a general and case-based overview of how legal techniques and strategies may be relied on in order to face and solve HRM problems in succession of family firms. Future directions of research could reduce the above recalled gaps either identifying more accurately specific scenarios and describing different legal techniques capable of meeting their HRM features or, on the other hand, deepening specific legal techniques and providing articulated sets of applications with respect to HRM within succession of family firms.

If one wanted to sum up all the above reasoning in a nutshell, one may observe that, even if HRM in family business shows informality along with formality in designing business practices (Reid, Morrow, Kelly & McCartan, 2002; Becker & Huselid, 1998; Delaney & Huselid, 1996), succession of family firms (but not only succession; in general, on designing HRM systems: Ferraro & Marrone, 2016; Gersick, 2015; Le Breton-Miller & Miller, 2014; Botero & Litchfield, 2013; Berrone, Cruz & Gomez-Mejia, 2012; Stewart & Hitt, 2012) requires structuring and needs be planned, appropriately and in detail, in advance (Sharma, Chrisman & Chua, 2003; Handler, 1990). This brings about relevant implication for practice and professional advice, which need take all of this into appropriate consideration, insofar as inappropriate planning may easily bring a family firm to wreck within relatively few years.

Otherwise, as Kin Hubbard once noted, one will have, as the sole consolation for the negative outcome of bad management, to call it just "destiny".

REFERENCES

Andenas, M., & Wooldridge, F. (2009). *European Comparative Company Law*. Cambridge University Press. doi:10.1017/CBO9780511770494

Anderson, M., Arroyo, E., & Amayuelas, I. (Eds.). (2011). *The Law of Succession: Testamentary Freedom*. Europa Law Publishing.

Arai, M., Becker, U., & Lipp, V. (Eds.). (2013). *Adult Guardianship Law for the 21st Century: Proceedings of the First World Congress on Adult Guardianship Law 2010 (Schriften zum Familien- und Erbrecht)*. Baden-Baden, Deutschland: Nomos Verlagsgesellschaft.

Arieu, A. (2010). The legacy of family firms. *Management Herald*, 88.

Arnold, A. (2001). *Die GmbH & Co. KGaA*. Verlag Dr. Otto Schmidt.

Arthur, J. (1992). The Link between Business Strategy and Industrial Relations Systems in American Steel Minimills. *Industrial & Labor Relations Review*, *45*(3), 488–506. doi:10.1177/001979399204500306

Astrachan, J. H., & Kolenko, T. A. (1994). A Neglected Factor Explaining Family Business Success: Human Resource Practices. *Family Business Review*, *7*(3), 251–262. doi:10.1111/j.1741-6248.1994.00251.x

Astrachan Binz, C., Ferguson, K. E., Pieper, T. M., & Astrachan, J. H. (2017). Family business goals, corporate citizenship behaviour and firm performance: Disentangling the connections. *International Journal of Management and Enterprise Development*, *16*(1/2), 34–56. doi:10.1504/IJMED.2017.082549

Balouziyeh, J.M.B. (2010). *Business Organizations: The Law of Partnerships, Corporations, and Limited Liability Companies* (2nd ed.). Teller Law.

Bammens, Y., Notelaers, G., & Van Gils, A. (2015). Implications of family business employment for employees' innovative work involvement. *Family Business Review*, *28*(2), 123–144. doi:10.1177/0894486513520615

Barnett, T., & Kellermanns, F. W. (2006). Are We Family and Are We Treated as Family? Nonfamily Employees' Perceptions of Justice in the Family Firm. *Entrepreneurship Theory and Practice*, *30*(6), 837–854. doi:10.1111/j.1540-6520.2006.00155.x

Batt, R. (2002). Managing Customer Services: Human Resource Practices, Quit Rates, and Sales Growth. *Academy of Management Journal*, *45*(3), 587–597.

Becker, B., & Gerhart, B. (1996). The impact of human resource management on organizational performance: Progress and prospects. *Academy of Management Journal*, *39*(4), 779–801.

Becker, B. A., & Huselid, M. A. (1998). High Performance Work Systems and Firm Performance: A Synthesis of Research and Managerial Applications. *Research in Personnel and Human Resources Management*, *16*, 53–101.

Berrone, P., Cruz, C., & Gomez-Mejia, L. R. (2012). Socioemotional wealth in family firms: Theoretical dimensions, assessment approaches, and agenda for future research. *Family Business Review*, *25*(3), 258–279. doi:10.1177/0894486511435355

Bjorkman, I., & Fan, X. (2002). Human Resource Management and the Performance of Western Firms in China. *International Journal of Human Resource Management*, *13*(6), 853–864. doi:10.1080/09585190210134246

Blanpain, R. (2014). Comparative Labour Law and Industrial Relations in Industrialized Market Economies (11th ed.). The Hague, The Netherlands: Wolters Kluwer Law & Business.

Blanplain, R., Bisom-Rapp, S., Corbett, W. R., Josephs, H. K., & Zimmer, M. (2012). The Global Workplace: International and Comparative Employment Law: Cases and Materials (2nd ed.). New York: Aspen Publishers.

Boselie, P., Dietz, G., & Boon, C. (2005). Commonalities and contradictions in HRM and performance research. *Human Resource Management Journal*, *15*(4), 67–94. doi:10.1111/j.1748-8583.2005.tb00154.x

Botero, I. C., & Litchfield, S. R. (2013). Exploring human resource management in family firms: a summary of what we know and ideas for future development. In K. X. Smymios, P. Z. Poutziouris, & S. Goel (Eds.), *Handbook of Research on Family Business* (2nd ed., pp. 371–405). Edward Elgar.

Busani, A. (2019). *Il patto di famiglia*. Cedam.

Cahn, A., & Donald, D. C. (2010). *Comparative Company Law*. Cambridge University Press. doi:10.1017/CBO9780511779909

Cahn, A., & Donald, D. C. (2018). Comparative Company Law: Text and Cases on the Laws Governing Corporations in Germany, the UK and the USA (2nd ed.). Cambridge, UK: Cambridge University Press. doi:10.1017/9781316888971

Caliendo, B. (2018). Patto di famiglia e tutela dei legittimari. Bologna, Italia: In Riga Edizioni.

Carlock, R. S., Kets de Vries, M., & Florent-Treacy, E. (2007). Family Business. In S. r. Clegg & J. R. Bailey (Eds.), *International Encyclopedia of Organizational Studies*. Sage Publication, Inc.

Cascio, W. F. (1991). *Costing human resources: The financial impact of behavior in organizations*. PWS-Kent.

Collins, C. J., & Clark, K. D. (2003). Strategic Human Resource Practices, Top Management Team Social Networks, and Firm Performance: The Role of Human Resource Practices in Creating Organizational Competitive Advantage. *Academy of Management Journal*, *46*(6), 740–751.

Combs, J., Liu, Y. M., Hall, A., & Ketchen, D. (2006). How much do high-performance work practices matter? A meta-analysis of their effects on organizational performance. *Personnel Psychology*, *59*(3), 501–528. doi:10.1111/j.1744-6570.2006.00045.x

Combs, J. G., Jaskiewicz, P., Shanine, K. K., & Balkin, D. B. (2018). Making sense of HR in family firms: Antecedents, moderators, and outcomes. *Human Resource Management Review*, *20*(1), 1–4. doi:10.1016/j.hrmr.2017.05.001

Cretney, S. (1995). Reform of intestacy: The best we can do? *The Law Quarterly Review*, *111*, 77–84.

Dayton, A. K. (2014). *Comparative Perspectives on Adult Guardianship*. Carolina Academic Press.

De Massis, A., Kotlar, J., Chua, J. H., & Chrisman, J. J. (2014). Ability and Willingness as Sufficiency Conditions for Family-Oriented Particularistic Behavior: Implications for Theory and Empirical Studies. *Journal of Small Business Management*, *52*(2), 344–364. doi:10.1111/jsbm.12102

De Massis, A., Sharma, P., Chua, J. H., & Chrisman, J. J. (2012). *Family Business Studies: An Annotated Bibliography*. Edward Elgar Pub. doi:10.4337/9781781002988

De Waal, M. J. (2008). Comparative Succession Law. In M. Reimann & R. Zimmermann (Eds.), *The Oxford Handbook of Comparative law (pp* (pp. 1071–1098). Oxford University Press.

Delaney, J. T., & Huselid, M. A. (1996). The Impact of Human Resource Management Practices on Perceptions of Organizational Performance. *Academy of Management Journal*, *39*(4), 949–969.

Ferraro, H., & Marrone, J. (2016). Examining employment relationship activities in family business research. *Journal of Family Business Management*, *6*(3), 210–224. doi:10.1108/JFBM-01-2016-0001

Ferris, G., Hochwarter, W., Buckley, M., Harrell-Cook, G., & Frink, D. (1999). Human resources management: Some new directions. *Journal of Management*, *25*(3), 385–415. doi:10.1177/014920639902500306

Finkin, M. W., & Mundlak, G. (2015). *Comparative Labor Law*. Edward Elgar Pub. doi:10.4337/9781781000137

Fusaro, A. (2013). Uno sguardo comparatistico sui patti successori e sulla distribuzione negoziata della ricchezza d'impresa. *Ricerche giuridiche*, *2*(1), 353-376.

Gallanis, T. (2019). *Family Property Law, Cases and Materials on Wills, Trusts, and Estates* (7th ed.). Foundation Press.

Gerner-Beuerle, C., & Schillig, M. A. (2019). *Comparative Company Law*. Oxford University Press. doi:10.1093/oso/9780199572205.001.0001

Gersick, K. (2015). Essay on Practice: Advising Family Enterprise in the Fourth Decade. *Entrepreneurship Theory and Practice*, *39*(6), 1433–1450. doi:10.1111/etap.12176

Gleason Bogert, G., Oaks, D. H., Hansen, H. R., & Neeleman, S. D. (2012). *The Law of Trusts* (9th ed.). Foundation Press.

Gooderham, P., Nordhaug, O., & Ringdal, K. (2006). National Embeddedness and Calculative Human Resource Management in US Subsidiaries in Europe and Australia. *Human Relations*, *59*(11), 1491–1513. doi:10.1177/0018726706072843

Grušic', U., Heinze, C., Merrett, L., Mills, A., García-Castrillón, C. O., Tang, Z. S., Trimmings, K., Walker, L., Torremans, P., & Fawcett, J. J. (2017). Cheshire, North & Fawcett: Private International Law (15th ed.). Oxford University Press.

Guest, D., Michie, J., Conway, N., & Sheehan, M. (2003). Human Resource Management and Corporate Performance in the UK. *British Journal of Industrial Relations*, *41*(2), 291–314.

Guthrie, J. P. (2001). High-Involvement Work Practices, Turnover, and Productivity: Evidence From New Zealand. *Academy of Management Journal*, *44*(1), 180–190.

Handler, W. C. (1990). Succession in Family Firms: A Mutual Role Adjustment Between Entrepreneur and Next-Generation Family Members. *Entrepreneurship Theory and Practice*, *15*(1), 37–51.

Hay, P., Borchers, P., & Freer, R. (2017). Conflict of Laws, Private International Law, Cases and Materials (15th ed.). Foundation Press.

Hiltrop, J. M. (2005). Creating HR capability in high performance organizations. *Strategic Change*, *14*(3), 121–131.

Hudson, A. (2009). Equity and Trusts (6th ed.). Routledge-Cavendish.

Huselid, M. A. (1995). The impact of human resource management practices on turnover, productivity, and corporate financial performance. *Academy of Management Journal*, *38*(3), 635–672.

Ichniowski, C., & Shaw, K. (1999). The Effects of Human Resource Management Systems on Economic Performance: An International Comparison of U.S. and Japanese Plants. *Management Science*, *45*(5), 704–721.

Jackson, S. E., & Schuler, R. S. (1995). Understanding Human Resource Management in the Context of Organizations and Their Environments. *Annual Review of Psychology*, *46*(1), 237–264.

Karami, A., Jones, B. M., & Kakabadse, N. K. (2008). Does strategic human resource management matter in high-tech sector? Some learning points for SME managers. *Corporate Governance International Journal of Business in Society*, *8*(1), 7–17.

Kasper, J. (2014). *Golden Parachutes. Pros, Cons and a Problem-solving Approach*. Műnchen, Deutscheland: GRIN Verlag GmbH.

Kerridge, R., & Parry, D. (2009). The Law of Succession (12th ed.). Sweet & Maxwell.

Kets de Vries, M. F. R., Carlock, R. S., & Florent-Treacy, E. (2007). *Family Business on the Couch: A Psychological Perspective*. John Wiley & Sons.

Kidwell, R. E., & Fish, A. J. (2007). Article. *The International Entrepreneurship and Management Journal*, *3*(1), 1–14.

La Porta, U. (2010). *Il patto di famiglia*. Utet.

Le Breton-Miller, I., & Miller, D. (2014). Temporal considerations in the study of family firms: Reflections on "the study of organizational behaviour in family business". *European Journal of Work and Organizational Psychology*, *23*(5), 669–673.

Loewen, J. (2008). *Money Magnet: Attract Investors to Your Business*. John Wiley & Sons.

MacDuffie, J. P. (1995). Human Resource Bundles and Manufacturing Performance: Organizational Logic and Flexible Production Systems in the World Auto Industry. *Industrial & Labor Relations Review*, *48*(2), 197–221.

Milman, D. (2018). *The Company Share: Legal Regulation and Public Policy*. Edward Elgar Pub.

Moshavi, D., & Koch, M. J. (2005). The adoption of family-friendly practices in family-owned firms: Paragon or paradox? *Community Work & Family*, *8*(3), 237–249.

Muir, W. H., Bíziková, L., Brandão De Oliveira, A., & Fernández Arroyo, D. P. (2019). *Global Private International Law: Adjudication Without Frontiers*. Edward Elgar Pub.

National Guardianship Association. (2016). *The Fundamentals of Guardianship: What Every Guardian Should Know*. American Bar Association Pub.

Othman, A. (2009). Strategic integration of human resource management practices: Perspectives of two major Japanese electrical and electronics companies in Malaysia. *Cross Cultural Management*, *16*(2), 197–214.

Panayotopoulou, L., Bourantas, D., & Papalexandris, N. (2003). Strategic human resource management and its effects on firm performance: An implementation of the competing values framework. *International Journal of Human Resource Management*, *14*(4), 680–699.

Panico, P. (2017). International Trust Laws (2nd ed.). Oxford University Press.

Pennings, F., & Bosse, C. (2011). *Extension Protection By Labour Law: Comparative Study*. Kluwer Law International.

Pirro D. (2016). La morte del socio e la clausola di continuazione automatica. *Rivista del diritto commerciale e del diritto generale delle obbligazioni, 2016*(2), 303-331.

Pittino, D., Visintin, F., & Lauto, G. (2017). A configurational analysis of the antecedents of entrepreneurial orientation. *European Management Journal, 35*(2), 224–237.

Pittino, D., Visintin, F., & Lauto, G. (2018). Fly Away From the Nest? A Configurational Analysis of Family Embeddedness and Individual Attributes in the Entrepreneurial Entry Decision by Next-Generation Members. *Family Business Journal, 31*(3), 271–294.

Priest, H. (2019). *BIASES and HEURISTICS: The Complete Collection of Cognitive Biases and Heuristics That Impair Decisions in Banking, Finance and Everything Else*. Cognitt Consulting.

Reece Thomas, K., & Ryan, C. (2014). The Law and Practice of Shareholders' Agreements (4th ed.). Lexis Nexis UK.

Reid, R., Morrow, T., Kelly, B., & McCartan, P. (2002). People Management in SMEs: An Analysis of Human Resource Strategies in Family and Non-Family Businesses. *Journal of Small Business and Enterprise Development, 9*(3), 245–259.

Ruggeri, L., Kunda, I., & Winkler, S. (Eds.). (2019). Family Property and Succession in EU Member States National Reports on the Collected Data. Rijeka, Croatia: Sveučilište u Rijeci, Pravni fakultet/ University of Rijeka, Faculty of Law.

Schuler, R. S., & MacMillan, I. C. (1984). Gaining competitive advantage through human resource management practices. *Human Resource Management, 23*(3), 241–255.

Sharma, P., Chrisman, J., & Chua, J. (2003). Predictors of satisfaction with the succession process in family firms. *Journal of Business Venturing, 18*(5), 667–687.

Siems, M., & Cabrelli, D. (2018). Comparative Company Law: A Case-Based Approach (2nd ed.). Hart Publishing.

Sitkoff, R. H., & Dukeminier, J. (2017). Wills Trusts & Estates (10th ed.). Aspen Publishers.

Sterk, S. E., & Melanie, B.L. (2019). Estates and Trusts, Cases and Materials (6th ed.). Foundation Press.

Stewart, A., & Hitt, M. (2012). Why can't a family business be more like a non-family business: Modes of professionalization in family firms. *Family Business Review, 25*(1), 58–86.

Symeonides, S. (2008). *American Private International Law*. Kluwer Law International.

Tutelman, C. J., & Hause, L. D. (2008). *The Balance Point: New Ways Business Owners Can Use Boards*. Famille Press.

Ulrich, D. (1991). Using human resources for competitive advantage. In R. Kilmann, I. Kilmann, & ... (Eds.), *Making Organizations Competitive*. Jossey-Bass.

Walczak, D., & Voss, G. (2013). New Possibilities of Supporting Polish SMEs within the Jeremie Initiative Managed by BGK. *Mediterranean Journal of Social Sciences*, *4*(9), 759–765.

Wood, S. (1999). Human resource management and performance. *International Journal of Management Reviews*, *1*(4), 367–413.

Wright, P., & McMahan, G. (1992). Theoretical Perspective for Strategic Human Resource Management. *Journal of Management*, *18*(2), 295–320.

Wright, P. M., Gardner, T. M., Moynihan, L. M., & Allen, M. R. (2005). The relationship between hr practices and firm performance: Examining causal order. *Personnel Psychology*, *58*(2), 409–446.

Zakaria, S. (2011). Transforming Human Resources into Human Capital. *Information Management and Business Review*, *2*(2), 48–54.

Zoppini, A. (2002). *Le successioni in diritto comparato*. Utet.

ENDNOTES

1 This pieces of information, among others, are available for all EU member States, in https://e-justice.europa.eu/content_succession-538-en.do.

2 This issue deserves some further remarks. In England freedom of the decedent to dispose of assets is a non contested principle, so that there is no provision on "reserved portions": Cretney, 1995. However, a mechanism similar to "reserved portions" was enacted with the *Inheritance (Provision for Family and Dependants) Act 1975*, so-called "Family Provisions", under which specified family members and persons maintained by the deceased may apply to the court for an award of financial provision from the estate: Zoppini, 2002.

3 The contractual and personalistic nature of partnerships, in fact, determines as a consequence, in some jurisdictions, that after the death of a partner his or her heirs are not allowed to became partners unless other partners expressly consent: see, e.g., art. 2284 of the Italian *codice civile*. See, on this issue in Italian law: Pirro, 2016.

4 See, e.g., under Italian law, art. 2319 of the *codice civile* as regards the "società in accomandita semplice" and art. 2457 of the *codice civile* as regards the "società in accomandita per azioni".

5 E.g. the New York Business Corporation Law provides, at § 1104, that deadlock occurs, at the shareholder level, either when the shareholders are so divided that the votes required for the election of directors cannot be obtained or there is internal dissension and two or more shareholder factions are so divided that dissolution would be beneficial to the shareholders. In these cases dissolution may be sought in court: *Matter of Hussein*, [2019 WL 2407257 (Kings Cnty Sup Ct June 3, 2019)]; *Matter of DeAngelis* [2019 WL 3400946 (Kings Cnty Sup Ct July 19, 2019)].

6 It may be read at https://eur-lex.europa.eu/legal-content/EN/TXT/PDF/?uri=CELEX:32012R0650&from=EN.

7 In fact, the rule mentioned above does not apply if it is clear from all the circumstances of the case that, at the time of death, the deceased was manifestly more closely connected with a State other than the said State, in which case "*the law applicable to the succession shall be the law of that other State*" (art. 21.2). It is, anyway, allowed to choose as the law to govern one's succession as

a whole the law of the State whose nationality one possesses "*at the time of making the choice or at the time of death*" (art. 22.1).

8 Some further remarks on this issue may be read at https://europa.eu/youreurope/citizens/family/inheritances/planning-inheritance/index_en.htm.

Compilation of References

Abdalla, H. F., Maghrabi, A. S., & Raggad, B. G. (1998). Assessing the perceptions of human resource managers toward nepotism: A cross-cultural study. *International Journal of Manpower*, *19*(8), 554–570. doi:10.1108/01437729810242235

Acikgoz, Y., & Bergman, S. (2016). Social media and employee recruitment: Chasing the run away bandwagon. In R. Landers & G. Schmidt (Eds.), *Social media in employee selection and recruitment* (pp. 175–195). Springer. doi:10.1007/978-3-319-29989-1_9

Acquah, I.S.K., Agyabeng-Mensah, Y. & Afum, E. (2020). Examining the link among green human resource management practices, green supply chain management practices and performance. *Benchmarking: An International Journal*, ahead-of-print.

Adams, J. S., Taschian, A., & Shore, T. H. (1996). Ethics in Family and Non-Family Owned Firms: An Exploratory Study. *Family Business Review*, *9*(2), 157–170. doi:10.1111/j.1741-6248.1996.00157.x

Aga, G. A., Francis, D., & Rodríguez-Meza, J. (2015). *SMEs, age, and jobs: A review of the literature, metrics, and evidence*. World Bank policy research working paper.

Aga, G. A., Francis. D. and Rodríguez-Meza. J. (2015). *SMEs, age, and jobs: A review of the literature, metrics, and evidence*. World Bank policy research working paper. https://openknowledge.worldbank.org/handle/10986/23455

Agbim, K. C. (2018). *Social networking and the family business performance: A conceptual consideration. Journal of Entrepreneurship, Management, and Innovation*. doi:10.7341/20191514

Aguado, D., Rico, R., Rubio, V., & Fernández, L. (2016). Applicant reasons to social network web use in personnel section and assessment. *Revista de Psicología del Trabajo y de las Organizaciones*, *32*(3), 183–190. doi:10.1016/j.rpto.2016.09.001

Aguado, J. (2002). *Dirigir y motivar equipos, claves para un buen gobierno*. Madrid: Ariel.

Ahmad, S. (2015). Green Human Resource Management: Policies and Practices. *Cogent Business & Management*, (2), 1–13. Retrieved from https://www.cogentoa.com/article/10.1080/23311975.2015.1030817

Ainsworth, S., & Cox, J. W. (2003). Families divided: Culture and control in family business. Organization Studies, 24, 1463-1485. http://dx/doi.org/ doi:10.1177/0170840603249004

Ajzen, I. (1991). The theory of planned behavior. *Organizational Behavior and Human Decision Processes*, *50*(2), 179–211. doi:10.1016/0749-5978(91)90020-T

Ajzen, I. (2012). Theory of Planned Behavior. In P. A. M. Lange, A. W. Kruglanski, & E. T. Higgins (Eds.), *Handbook of Theories of Social Psychology* (pp. 439–459). Sage. doi:10.4135/9781446249215.n22

Akcadag, S. & Özdemir, E. (2005). İnsan kaynakları kapsamında 4 ve 5 yıldızlı otel işletmelerinde iş tatmini: İstanbul'da yapılan ampirik bir çalışma. *Kocaeli Üniversitesi Sosyal Bilimler Dergisi*, (10), 193-167.

Aktar, A., & Islam, Y. (2019). *Green Human Resource Management Practices and Employee Engagement: Empirical Evidence from RMG sector in Bangladesh*. Academic Press.

Alami, R., Gorji, O. H., Asrami, M. S., Saravi, H. R., Soteh, M. J., & Ahangari, F. R. (2016). The role of information technology (IT) in development and increase of the efficiency of human resources. *Journal of Social Science Studies*, *3*(2), 188–197. doi:10.5296/jsss.v3i2.8602

Alawani, A. S., & Singh, A. D. (2017). A smart mobile learning conceptual framework for professional development of UAE in-service teachers. *International Journal of Management and Applied Research*, *4*(3), 146–165. doi:10.18646/2056.43.17-012

Alayo, M., Iturralde, T., Maseda, A., & Arzubiaga, U. (2016). Critical factors for successful succession of family firms. European Journal of Economics. *Finance and Administrative Sciences*, *85*, 89–103.

Aldrich, H. E., & Langton, N. (1998). Human resource management and organizational life cycles. In P. D. Reynolds, W. Bygrave, N. M. Carter, P. Davidsson, W. B. Gartner, C. M. Mason, & P. P. McDougall (Eds.), *Frontiers of Entrepreneurship Research* (pp. 349–357). Babson College, Center for Entrepreneurial Studies.

Alewell, D., & Hansen, N. K. (2012). Human Resource Management Systems – A Structured Review of Research Contributions and Open Questions. *The German Journal of Industrial Relations*, *19*, 90–123.

Alexander, P. (2015). *Corporate Social Irresponsibility*. Routledge. doi:10.4324/9781315863108

Almada, L., & Borges, R. (2018). Sustainable Competitive Advantage Needs Green Human Resource Practices: A Framework for Environmental Management. *Revista de Administração Contemporânea*, *22*(3), 424–442. doi:10.1590/1982-7849rac2018170345

Almobaireek, W. N., & Manolova, T. S. (2012). Who wants to be an entrepreneur? Entrepreneurial intentions among Saudi university students. *African Journal of Business Management*, *6*(11), 4029–4040. doi:10.5897/AJBM11.1521

Alvesson, M. (2003). Beyond Neopositivists, Romantics, and Localists: A Reflexive Approach to Interviews in Organisational Research. *Academy of Management Review*, *28*(1), 13–33. doi:10.5465/amr.2003.8925191

Amar, A. D., Hentrich, C., & Hlupic, V. (2009). To Be a Better Leader, Give up Authority. *Harvard Business Review*, *87*(12), 22–24. PMID:19968054

Andenas, M., & Wooldridge, F. (2009). *European Comparative Company Law*. Cambridge University Press. doi:10.1017/CBO9780511770494

Anderson, M., Arroyo, E., & Amayuelas, I. (Eds.). (2011). *The Law of Succession: Testamentary Freedom*. Europa Law Publishing.

Anderson, R. C., & Reeb, D. M. (2003). Founding-Family Ownership and Firm Performance: Evidence from the S&P 500. *The Journal of Finance*, *58*(3), 1301–1328. doi:10.1111/1540-6261.00567

Andersson, L., & Hammarstedt, M. (2010). Intergenerational transmissions in immigrant self-employment: Evidence from three generations. *Small Business Economics*, *34*(3), 261–276. doi:10.100711187-008-9117-y

Andrews, R., & Beynon, M. J. (2011). Organizational form and strategic alignment in a local authority: A preliminary exploration using fuzzy clustering. *Public Organization Review*, *11*(3), 201–218. doi:10.100711115-010-0117-4

Antonakis, J., Avolio, B., & Sivasubramaniam, N. (2003). Context and leadership: An examination of the nine-factor full-range leadership theory using the Multifactor leadership Questionnaire. *The Leadership Quarterly*, *14*(3), 261–295. doi:10.1016/S1048-9843(03)00030-4

Arai, M., Becker, U., & Lipp, V. (Eds.). (2013). *Adult Guardianship Law for the 21st Century: Proceedings of the First World Congress on Adult Guardianship Law 2010 (Schriften zum Familien- und Erbrecht)*. Baden-Baden, Deutschland: Nomos Verlagsgesellschaft.

Arasli, H., Bavik, A., & Ekiz, E. H. (2006). The effects of nepotism on human resource management, the case of three, four and five star hotels in northern cyprus. *The International Journal of Sociology and Social Policy*, *26*(7/8), 295–308. doi:10.1108/01443330610680399

Ardichvili, A., Jondle, D., & Kowske, B. (2012). Minding the gap: Exploring differences in perceptions of ethical business cultures among executives, mid-level managers and non-managers. *Human Resource Development International. Routledge*, *15*(3), 337–352. doi:10.1080/13678868.2012.687625

Arieu, A. (2010). The legacy of family firms. *Management Herald*, 88.

Arijs, D., Botero, I. C., Michiels, A., & Molly, V. (2018). Family business employer brand: Understanding applicants' perceptions and their job pursuit intentions with samples from the US and Belgium. *Journal of Family Business Strategy*, *9*(3), 180–191. doi:10.1016/j.jfbs.2018.08.005

Arino, A., De LaTorre, J., & Smith Ring, P. (2005). Relational quality and inter-personal trust in strategic alliances. *European Management Review*, *2*(1), 15–27. doi:10.1057/palgrave.emr.1500026

Armstrong, M. B., Ferrell, J., Collmus, A., & Landers, R. (2016a). Correcting misconceptions about gamification of assessment: More than SJTs and badges. *Industrial and Organizational Psychology: Perspectives on Science and Practice*, *9*(3), 671–677. doi:10.1017/iop.2016.69

Arnold, A. (2001). *Die GmbH & Co. KGaA*. Verlag Dr. Otto Schmidt.

Aronoff, C. E. (1998). Megatrends in family business. *Family Business Review*, *11*(3), 181–185. doi:10.1111/j.1741-6248.1998.00181.x

Arregle, J. L., Hitt, M. A., Sirmon, D. S., & Very, P. (2007). The Development of Organizational Social Capital: Attributes of Family Firms. *Journal of Management Studies*, *44*(1), 73–95. doi:10.1111/j.1467-6486.2007.00665.x

Arrow, K. J. (1969). *The organization of economic activity: Issues pertinent to the choice of the market versus non-market allocations*. Joint Economic Committee of Congress.

Arthur, J. (1992). The Link between Business Strategy and Industrial Relations Systems in American Steel Minimills. *Industrial & Labor Relations Review*, *45*(3), 488–506. doi:10.1177/001979399204500306

Astrachan Binz, C., Ferguson, K. E., Pieper, T. M., & Astrachan, J. H. (2017). Family business goals, corporate citizenship behaviour and firm performance: Disentangling the connections. *International Journal of Management and Enterprise Development*, *16*(1/2), 34–56. doi:10.1504/IJMED.2017.082549

Astrachan, J. H. (2010). Strategy in Family Business: Toward a Multidimensional Research Agenda. *Journal of Family Business Strategy*, *1*(1), 6–14. doi:10.1016/j.jfbs.2010.02.001

Astrachan, J. H., Klein, S. B., & Smyrnios, K. X. (2002). The F-PEC scale of family influence: A proposal for solving the family business definition problem. *Family Business Review*, *15*(1), 45–58. doi:10.1111/j.1741-6248.2002.00045.x

Astrachan, J. H., & Kolenko, T. A. (1994). A neglected factor explaining family business success: Human resource practices. *Family Business Review*, *7*(3), 251–262. doi:10.1111/j.1741-6248.1994.00251.x

Astrachan, J. H., & Shanker, M. C. S. (2003). Family Businesses' Contribution to the U.S. Economy: A Closer Look. *Family Business Review*, *16*(3), 211–219. doi:10.1177/08944865030160030601

Ates, Ö. (2003). *Aile Şirketlerinde Değişim ve Süreklilik Anlayışı.* Ankara Üniversitesi, Sosyal Bilimler Enstitüsü, Doktora Tezi.

Aust, I., Matthews, B. & Muller-Camen, M. (2020). Common Good HRM: A paradigm shift in Sustainable HRM?', *Human Resource Management Review*, *30*(3), 1-11. doi:10.1016/j.hrmr.2019.100705

Avci, A. (2017). *Şirketlerde nepotizm uygulamasının çalışanların iş tatmini ve tükenmişlik düzeylerine etkisi.* İstanbul Sabahattin Zaim Üniversitesi, Sosyal Bilimler Enstitüsü, Yüksek Lisans Tezi.

Avolio, B. J., & Gardner, W. L. (2005, June). Authentic leadership development: Getting to the root of positive forms of leadership. *The Leadership Quarterly*, *16*(3), 315–338. doi:10.1016/j.leaqua.2005.03.001

Avolio, B. J., & Walumbwa, F. O. (2014). Authentic leadership theory, research and practice: Steps taken and steps that remain. In D. V. Day (Ed.), *Oxford library of psychology. The Oxford handbook of leadership and organizations* (pp. 331–356). Oxford University Press.

Bac, D. P. (2008). A history of the concept of sustainable development: Literaturt review. *The Annals of the University of Oradea, Economic Sciences Series, 17*(2), 576–580. Retrieved from http://steconomice.uoradea.ro/anale/volume/2008/v2-economy-and-business-administration/101.pdf

Bachkaniwala, D., Wright, M., & Ram, M. (2001). Succession in South Asian Family Businesses in the UK. *International Small Business Journal*, *19*(4), 15–27. doi:10.1177/0266242601194001

Bacon, N., Ackers, P., Storey, J., & Coates, D. (1996). It's a Small World: Managing Human Resources in Small Businesses. *International Journal of Human Resource Management*, *7*(1), 82–100. doi:10.1080/09585199600000119

Bacon, N., & Hoque, K. (2005). HRM in the SME Sector: Valuable Employees and Coercive Networks. *International Journal of Human Resource Management*, *16*(11), 1976–1999. doi:10.1080/09585190500314706

Baines, S. (2002). New Technologies and Old Ways of Working in the Home of the Self-Employed Teleworker. *New Technology, Work and Employment*, *17*(2), 89–101. doi:10.1111/1468-005X.00096

Baines, S., & Gelder, U. (2003). What Is Family Friendly about the Workplace in the Home? The Case of Self-Employed Parents and Their Children. *New Technology, Work and Employment*, *3*(18), 223–234. doi:10.1111/1468-005X.00123

Ballal, J. M., & Bapat, V. (2019). In che modo la successione familiare influisce sull'innovazione delle imprese familiari? *Asian Journal of Innovation & Policy*, *8*(2).

Ball, S. (2005). The importance of entrepreneurship to hospitality, leisure, sport and tourism. Hospitality, Leisure. *Sport and Tourism Network*, *1*(1), 1–14.

Balouziyeh, J.M.B. (2010). *Business Organizations: The Law of Partnerships, Corporations, and Limited Liability Companies* (2nd ed.). Teller Law.

Bammens, Y., Notelaers, G., & Van Gils, A. (2015). Implications of family business employment for employees' innovative work involvement. *Family Business Review*, *28*(2), 123–144. doi:10.1177/0894486513520615

Bammens, Y., Voordeckers, W., & Van Gils, A. (2011). Boards of directors in family businesses: A literature review and research agenda. *International Journal of Management Reviews*, *13*(2), 134–152. doi:10.1111/j.1468-2370.2010.00289.x

Banasiak, A. (2012). Bariera finansowa w rozwoju firm rodzinnych sektora MSP. *Przedsiębiorczość i Zarządzanie*, *13*(8), 137–155.

Bang, H., Fuglesang, S. L., Ovesen, M. R., & Eilertsen, D. E. (2010). Effectiveness in top management group meetings: The role of goal clarity, focused communication, and learning behavior. *Scandinavian Journal of Psychology*, *51*(3), 253–261. doi:10.1111/j.1467-9450.2009.00769.x PMID:20132458

Bangwal, D., & Tiwari, P. (2015). Green HRM –A way to greening the environment. *Journal of Business and Management*, *17*(12), 45–53. doi:10.9790/487X-171214553

Barbaresco, G. (2019). *Medie imprese italiane, squadra che vince non si cambia, oppure sì? In Cineas-Mediobanca, Osservatorio sul risk management nelle medie imprese manifatturiere*. Ufficio Studi Mediobanca.

Barnett, T., & Kellermanns, F. W. (2006). 'Are We Family and Are We Treated as Family? Nonfamily Employees' Perceptions of Justice in the Family Firm', Entrepreneurship Theory and Practice. *SAGE PublicationsSage CA: Los Angeles, CA*, *30*(6), 837–854. doi:10.1111/j.1540-6520.2006.00155.x

Barney, J. (1991). Firm resources and sustained competitive advantage. *Journal of Management*, *17*(1), 99–120. doi:10.1177/014920639101700108

Barney, J. B., & Wright, P. M. (1998). On becoming a strategic partner: The role of human resources in gaining competitive advantage. *Human Resource Management*, *37*(1), 31–46. doi:10.1002/(SICI)1099-050X(199821)37:1<31::AID-HRM4>3.0.CO;2-W

Barret, R. (2017). *The Values-Driven Organization. Cultural health and Employee Well-Being as a Pathway to Sustainable Performance*. Routledge. doi:10.9774/gleaf.9781315558530

Barrett, R. (2016). *La Organización impulsada por valores: Liderando el potencial humano para maximizar rendimiento y beneficios*. Editorial Lulucom.

Bart, C. K., Bontis, N., & Taggar, S. (2001). A model of the impact of mission statements on firm performance. *Management Decision*, *39*(1), 19–35. doi:10.1108/EUM0000000005404

Bartkus, B., Glassman, M., & McAfee, R. B. (2006). Mission statement quality and financial performance. *European Management Journal*, *24*(1), 86–94. doi:10.1016/j.emj.2005.12.010

Basco, R., & Rodriguez, M. J. P. (2011). The Cognitive Legitimacy of the Family Business Field. *Family Business Review*, *24*(4), 322–342. doi:10.1177/0894486511416356

Başkurt, G., & Altindağ, E. (2017). The impact of institutionalization of family business on strategic human resources management and company performance. *Business Management Dynamics*, *7*(3), 10–25.

Başkurt, G., & Altindağ, E. (2017). The Impact of Institutionalization of Family Business on Strategic Human Resources Management and Company Performance. *Business Management Dynamics*, *7*, 10–25.

Bassanini, A., Breda, T., Caroli, E., & Rebérioux, A. (2013). Working in family firms: Paid less but more secure? Evidence from French matched employer-employee data. *Industrial & Labor Relations Review*, *66*(2), 433–466. doi:10.1177/001979391306600206

Bass, B. (1985). *Transformational Leadership*. Taylor & Francis.

Bassi, L. (2011). Raging debates in HR analytics. *People & Strategy*, *34*, 14–18.

Batt, R. (2002). Managing Customer Services: Human Resource Practices, Quit Rates, and Sales Growth. *Academy of Management Journal*, *45*(3), 587–597.

Becker, B. A., & Huselid, M. A. (1998). High Performance Work Systems and Firm Performance: A Synthesis of Research and Managerial Applications. *Research in Personnel and Human Resources Management*, *16*, 53–101.

Becker, B. E., & Huselid, M. A. (1998). High performance work systems and firm performance: A synthesis of research and managerial implications. In G. E. Ferris (Ed.), *Research in Personnel and Human Resources Management* (Vol. 16, pp. 53–102). JAI Press, Inc.

Becker, B., & Gerhart, B. (1996). The impact of human resource management on organizational performance: Progress and prospects. *Academy of Management Journal*, *39*(4), 779–801.

Beckhard, R., & Dyer, W. (1983). Managing continuity in the family-owned business. *Organizational Dynamics*, *12*(1), 5–12. doi:10.1016/0090-2616(83)90022-0

Beck-Krala, E. (2017). *Badanie efektywności wynagrodzeń: od kontroli kosztów do aktywizowania pracowników*. Wydawnictwo AGH.

Beck-Krala, E., & Klimkiewicz, K. (2016). Occupational Safety and Health as an Element of a Complex Compensation System Evaluation within an Organization. *International Journal of Occupational Safety and Ergonomics*, *22*(4), 523–531. doi:10.1080/10803548.2016.1183338 PMID:27191788

Bedell, M., Canniff, M., & Wyrick, C. (2018). Systems considerations in the design of an HRIS: Planning for implementations. *Human resource information systems: Basics, applications, and future directions*. In M. J. Kavanagh & R. D. Johnson (Eds.), *Human resource information systems: Basics, applications, and future directions* (pp. 45–66). Sage.

Bello-Pintado, A., & Garcés-Galdeano, L. (2017). Bundles of HRM Practices in Family and Non- Family Firms: The Impact on Enhancing Performance. *International Journal of Human Resource Management*, 1–22.

Benavides-Velasco, C. A., Quintana-García, C., & Guzmán-Parra, V. F. (2013). Trends in family business research. *Small Business Economics*, *40*(1), 41–57. doi:10.100711187-011-9362-3

Bennet, N., & Lemoine, G. J. (2014). What VUCA Really Means for You. *Harvard Business Review*, *92*(1-2), 27.

Bernhard, F., & O'Driscoll, M. P. (2011). Psychological Ownership in Small Family-Owned Businesses: Leadership Style and Nonfamily-Employees' Work Attitudes and Behaviors. *Group & Organization Management*, *36*(3), 643–665. doi:10.1177/1059601111402684

Berrone, P., Cruz, C., & Gomez-Mejia, L. R. (2012). Socioemotional Wealth in Family Firms: Theoretical Dimensions, Assessment Approaches, and Agenda for Future Research. *Family Business Review*, *25*(3), 258–279. doi:10.1177/0894486511435355

Berry, L. L. (1995). Relationship marketing of services growing interest, emerging perspectives. *Journal of the Academy of Marketing Science*, *23*(4), 236–245. doi:10.1177/009207039502300402

Bertrand, M., & Schoar, A. (2006). The role of family in family firms. *The Journal of Economic Perspectives*, *2*, 73–96.

Bertrand, M., & Schoar, A. (2006). The Role of Family in Family Firms. *The Journal of Economic Perspectives*, *20*(2), 73–96. doi:10.1257/jep.20.2.73

Bertschi-Michel, A., Kammerlander, N., & Strike, V. M. (2020). Unearthing and Alleviating Emotions in Family Business Successions. *Entrepreneurship Theory and Practice*, *44*(1), 81–108. doi:10.1177/1042258719834016

Bhargava, A. (2018). A study of the role of mobile technology on organizational effectiveness. *International Journal of Pure and Applied Mathematics*, *118*(15), 97–102.

Biggs, A., Brough, P., & Barbour, J. P. (2014). Strategic alignment with organizational priorities and work engagement: A multi-wave analysis. *Journal of Organizational Behavior*, *35*(3), 301–317. doi:10.1002/job.1866

Bird, B., Welsch, H., Astrachan, J., & Pistrui, D. (2002). Family business research: The evolution of an academic field. *Family Business Review*, *15*(4), 337–350. doi:10.1111/j.1741-6248.2002.00337.x

Birje, M. N., Challagidad, P. S., Goudar, R. H., & Tapale, M. T. (2017). Cloud computing Review: Concepts, technology, challenges, and security. *International Journal of Cloud Computing*, *6*(1), 32–57. doi:10.1504/IJCC.2017.083905

Birkinshaw, J. (2010). The critical need to reinvent management. *Business Strategy Review*, *21*(1), 4–11. doi:10.1111/j.1467-8616.2010.00636.x

Birkinshaw, J. (2013). *Becoming a better boss*. Jossey-Bass.

Bjorkman, I., & Fan, X. (2002). Human Resource Management and the Performance of Western Firms in China. *International Journal of Human Resource Management*, *13*(6), 853–864. doi:10.1080/09585190210134246

Bjuggren, P., & Sund, L. A. (2002). Transition Cost Rationale for Transition of the Firm within the Family. *Small Business Economics*, *19*(2), 123–133. doi:10.1023/A:1016289106477

Blanchard, K., & Stoner, J. (2004). The Vision Thing: Without It You'll Never Be a World-Class Organization. *Leader to Leader*, *31*(31), 1–8. doi:10.1002/ltl.59

Blanco-Mazagatos, V., de Quevedo-Puente, E., & Delgado-García, J. B. (2018). Human resource practices and organizational human capital in the family firm: The effect of generational stage. *Journal of Business Research, 84*(July), 337–348.

Blanco-Mazagatos, V., de Quevedo-Puente, E., & Delgado-García, J. B. (2018). Human resource practices and organizational human capital in the family firm: The effect of generational stage. *Journal of Business Research*, *84*, 337–348. doi:10.1016/j.jbusres.2017.09.017

Blanpain, R. (2014). Comparative Labour Law and Industrial Relations in Industrialized Market Economies (11th ed.). The Hague, The Netherlands: Wolters Kluwer Law & Business.

Blanplain, R., Bisom-Rapp, S., Corbett, W. R., Josephs, H. K., & Zimmer, M. (2012). The Global Workplace: International and Comparative Employment Law: Cases and Materials (2nd ed.). New York: Aspen Publishers.

Bocatto, E., Gispert, C., & Rialp, J. (2010). Family-Owned business succession: The influence of pre-performance in the nomination of family and nonfamily members: Evidence from Spanish firms. *Journal of Small Business Management*, *48*(4), 497–523. doi:10.1111/j.1540-627X.2010.00306.x

Bojadjiev, M. (2019). Development of Instrument for Measurement of the Organizational Alignment - from Vox Organizationis to "Four Organizational Culture Types and Four Leadership Styles". *Universal Journal of Management.*, *7*(5), 186–199. doi:10.13189/ujm.2019.070504

Bojadjiev, M., Tomovska Misoska, A., Mirocevic, B., & Stefanovska-Petkovska, M. (2018). Organizational culture and the "voice" of Small Entreprises in the electrical engineering service sector in the Republic of Macedonia, Universal. *Journal of Management*, *6*(8), 263–272. doi:10.13189/ujm.2018.060801

Bojadziev, M., Tomovska Misoska, A., Pesev, A., & Stefanoska Petkovska, M. (2016). Organizational alignment in the ICT company in the Republic of Macedonia. *Business and Economic Review*, *6*(2), 424–438. doi:10.5296/ber.v6i2.10258

Bondarouk, T., Trullén, J., & Valverde, M. (2016). Conceptual and empirical discoveries in successful HRM implementation. *International Journal of Human Resource Management*, *27*(8), 906-909.

Bonti, M., & Cori, E. (2011). La longevità delle PMI familiari: riflessioni teoriche ed evidenze empiriche. *Impresa Progetto-Electronic Journal of Management*, (2).

Bonti, M., & Cori, E. (2013). Intergenerational passages and firm longevity: evidence from Italian family SMEs. In *Proceedings of Annual AIDEA Conference, The firm's role in the economy. Does a growth-oriented model exist?* Bari: Cacucci Editore.

Bonti, M., & Cori, E. (2018). Traditional Governance and Innovative Strategies in Italian Family SMEs: Evidence from Tuscany. *International Business Research*, *11*(2), 103–115. doi:10.5539/ibr.v11n2p103

Boonstra, J. (2017). Aptitudes para aconseguir un impacto en el cambio estratégico y cultural. *Harvard Deusto Business Review*, *6*(267), 78–83.

Borda, D. G., Hansen, N., & Gore, J. (2019). *Control and Commitment HRM Systems in SME Family Firms: A Qualitative Study of Hybrid Forms. In Understanding the inclusive organisation.* Academy of Management Conference.

Borim-de-Souza, R., Balbinot, Z., Travis, E. F., Munck, L., & Takahashi, A. R. W. (2015). Sustainable development and sustainability as study objects for comparative management theory. *Cross Cultural Management*, *22*(2), 201–235. doi:10.1108/CCM-02-2013-0027

Boselie, P., Dietz, G., & Boon, C. (2005). Commonalities and contradictions in HRM and performance research. *Human Resource Management Journal*, *15*(4), 67–94. doi:10.1111/j.1748-8583.2005.tb00154.x

Botella-Carrubi, M. D., & González-Cruz, T. F. (2019). Context as a Provider of Key Resources for Succession: A Case Study of Sustainable Family Firms. *Sustainability*, *11*(7), 1–18. doi:10.3390u11071873

Botero, I. C. (2014). Effects of communicating family ownership and organisational size on an applicant's attraction to a firm: An empirical examination in the USA and China. *Journal of Family Business Strategy*, *5*(2), 184–196. doi:10.1016/j.jfbs.2014.01.004

Botero, I. C., Astrachan, C. B., & Calabrò, A. (2018). A receiver's approach to family business brands: Exploring individual associations with the term "family firm.". *Journal of Family Business Management*, *8*(2), 94–112. doi:10.1108/JFBM-03-2017-0010

Botero, I. C., & Litchfield, S. R. (2013). Exploring human resource management in family firms: a summary of what we know and ideas for future development. In *Handbook of Research on Family Business* (2nd ed.). Edward Elgar Publishing.

Bowen, H. R. (1953). Social Responsibilities of the Businessman. Academic Press.

Boyatzis, R. (2008). Competencies in the 21st century. *Journal of Management Development*, *27*(1), 5–12. doi:10.1108/02621710810840730

Boyatzis, R. E. (1998). *Transforming Qualitative Information: Thematic Analysis and Code Development.* SAGE Publications.

Bozer, G., Levin, L., & Santora, J. C. (2017). Succession in family business: A multi-sourced perspective. *Journal of Small Business and Enterprise Development*, *24*(4), 753–774. doi:10.1108/JSBED-10-2016-0163

Bracci, E., & Vagnoni, E. (2011). Understanding Small Family Business Succession in a Knowledge Management Perspective. *IUP Journal of Knowledge Management, 9*(1).

Bradford, M. & Leberman, S. (2017). *Bewedo: a dynamic approach to leadership development for co-creation.* Sage.

Brătianu, C., & Bălănescu, G. V. (2008). Vision, mission and corporate values. A comparative analysis of the top 50 U.S. companies. *Management & Marketing, 3*(3), 19–39.

Braun, V., & Clarke, V. (2006). Using Thematic Analysis in Psychology. *Qualitative Research in Psychology, 3*(2), 77–101. doi:10.1191/1478088706qp063oa

Brewis, J., & Way-Bliss, E. (2008). Re-searching Ethics: Towards a More Reflexive Critical Management Studies. *Organization Studies, 29*(12), 1521–1540. doi:10.1177/0170840607096385

Briz-Ponce, L., Pereira, A., Carvallho, L., Juanes-Méndez, J. A., & García-Peñalvo, F. J. (2017). Learning with mobile technologies – Students' behavior. *Computers in Human Behavior, 72*, 612–620. doi:10.1016/j.chb.2016.05.027

Broccardo, L., Truant, E., & Zicari, A. (2019). Internal corporate sustainability drivers: What evidence from family firms? A literature review and research agenda. *Corporate Social Responsibility and Environmental Management, 26*(1), 1–18. doi:10.1002/csr.1672

Brockhaus, R. H. (2004). Family Business Succession: Suggestions for Future Research. *Family Business Review, 17*(2), 165–177. doi:10.1111/j.1741-6248.2004.00011.x

Bryde, D. (2008). Perceptions of the impact of project sponsorship practices on project success. *International Journal of Project Management, 26*(8), 800–809. doi:10.1016/j.ijproman.2007.12.001

Bryman, A., & Bell, E. (2015). *Business Research Methods* (4th ed.). Oxford University Press.

Brzeziński, A. (2016). Społeczna odpowiedzialność firm rodzinnych. *Przedsiębiorczość i Zarządzanie, 17*(6), 147–158.

Buckley, M. R., Beu, D. S., Frink, D. D., Howard, J. L., Berkson, H., Mobbs, T. A., & Ferris, G. R. (2001). Ethical issues in human resources systems. *Human Resource Management Review, 11*(1/2), 11–29. doi:10.1016/S1053-4822(00)00038-3

Burke, B. (2014). *Gamify: How gamification motivates people to do extraordinary things.* Bibliomotion, Inc.

Busani, A. (2019). *Il patto di famiglia.* Cedam.

Bute, M. (2011). Kayırmacılığın çalışan davranışları ve insan kaynakları yönetimi uygulamaları üzerine etkileri: Türk kamu bankalarına yönelik bir araştırma. *Amme Idaresi Dergisi, 44*(1), 135–153.

Cabrera-Suárez, K., De Saá-Pérez, P., & García-Almeida, D. (2001). The succession process from a resource and knowledge-based view of the family firm. *Family Business Review, 14*(1), 37–46. doi:10.1111/j.1741-6248.2001.00037.x

Cabrera-Suárez, M. K., & Martín-Santana, J. D. (2010). La influencia de las relaciones intergeneracionales en la formación y el compromiso del sucesor: Efectos sobre el proceso de sucesión en la empresa familiar. *Revista Europea de Dirección y Economía de la Empresa, 19*(2), 111–128.

Cadieux, L. (2005). La succession dans les PME familiales: Proposition d'un modèle de réussite du processus de disengagement du prédécesseur. *Revue Internationale du PME, 18*(3-4).

Cadieux, L. (2007). Succession in Small and Medium-Sized Family Businesses: Towards a Tipology of Predecessor Roles During and After Instatement of the Successor. *Family Business Review, 20*(2), 95–109. doi:10.1111/j.1741-6248.2007.00089.x

Cahn, A., & Donald, D. C. (2018). Comparative Company Law: Text and Cases on the Laws Governing Corporations in Germany, the UK and the USA (2nd ed.). Cambridge, UK: Cambridge University Press. doi:10.1017/9781316888971

Cahn, A., & Donald, D. C. (2010). *Comparative Company Law*. Cambridge University Press. doi:10.1017/CBO9780511779909

Caliendo, B. (2018). Patto di famiglia e tutela dei legittimari. Bologna, Italia: In Riga Edizioni.

Camacho, I., Fernández, J. L., González, R., & Miralles, J. (2013). *Ética y Responsabilidad Empresarial*. Desclée De Brouwer.

Cameron, K. S., & Quinn, R. E. (2011). *Diagnosing and Changing Organizational Culture: Based on the Competing Values Framework*. John Wiley & Sons Ltd. Available at: https://books.google.co.uk/bookshl=en&lr=&id=EgADAwAAQBAJ&oi=fnd&pg=PR9&ots=o_tE2JRg-R&sig=_igxZgoJ8ik-Z4TNLeUSzUlp9Sg&redir_esc=y#v=onepage&q&f=false

Camfield, C., & Franco, M. (2019). Theoretical framework for family firm management: Relationship between personal values and professionalization and succession. *Journal of Family Business Management*, *9*(2), 201–227. doi:10.1108/JFBM-06-2018-0020

Campopiano, G., De Massis, A., & Kotlar, J. (2019). Environmental Jolts, Family-Centered Non-Economic Goals, and Innovation: A Framework of Family Firm Resilience. In E. Memili & C. Dibrell (Eds.), *The Palgrave Handbook of Heterogeneity among Family Firms* (pp. 773–789). Palgrave-Macmillan. doi:10.1007/978-3-319-77676-7_28

Cardella, G. M., Hernandez-Sanchez, B. R., & Garcia, J. C. S. (2020). Entrepreneurship and Family-Role: A Systematic Review of a Growing Research. *Frontiers in Psychology*, *10*, 2939. Advance online publication. doi:10.3389/fpsyg.2019.02939 PMID:31998192

Carlock, R. S., Kets de Vries, M., & Florent-Treacy, E. (2007). Family Business. In S. r. Clegg & J. R. Bailey (Eds.), *International Encyclopedia of Organizational Studies*. Sage Publication, Inc.

Carlson, D. S., Upton, N., & Seaman, S. (2006). The Impact of Human Resource Practices and Compensation Design on Performance: An Analysis of Family Owned SMEs. *Journal of Small Business Management*, *44*(4), 531–543. doi:10.1111/j.1540-627X.2006.00188.x

Carlson, J. R., Carlson, D. S., Zivnuska, S., Harris, R. B., & Harris, K. J. (2017). Applying the job demands resources model to understand technology as a predictor of turnover intentions. *Computers in Human Behavior*, *77*, 317–325. doi:10.1016/j.chb.2017.09.009

Carney, M., Van Essen, M., Gedajlovic, E. R., & Heugens, P. P. M. A. R. (2015). What Do We Know About Private Family Firms? A Meta-Analytical Review. *Entrepreneurship Theory and Practice*, *39*(3), 513–544. doi:10.1111/etap.12054

Caron, F., Vanthienen, J., & Baesens, B. (2013, February). Comprehensive rule-based compliance checking and risk management with process mining. *Decision Support Systems*, *54*(3), 1357–1369. doi:10.1016/j.dss.2012.12.012

Carrasco-Hernandez, A., & Sánchez-Marín, G. (2007). The determinants of employee compensation in family firms: Empirical evidence. *Family Business Review*, *20*(3), 215–228. doi:10.1111/j.1741-6248.2007.00096.x

Carree, M., Van Gils, A., & Peters, B. (2014). Innovation in family and non-family SMEs: An exploratory analysis. *Small Business Economics*, *42*(3), 595–609. doi:10.100711187-013-9490-z

Carrington, D. J., Combe, I.A., & Mumford, M.D. (2018). Cognitive shifts within leader and follower teams: Where consensus develops in mental models during an organizational crisis. *The Leadership Quarterly*, *30*(3), 335-350.

Carr, J. C., & Sequeira, J. M. (2007). Prior family business exposure as intergenerational influence and entrepreneurial intent: A Theory of Planned Behavior approach. *Journal of Business Research*, *60*(10), 1090–1098. doi:10.1016/j.jbusres.2006.12.016

Carroll, A. B. (1979). A Three-Dimensional Conceptual Model of Corporate Performance. *Academy of Management Review*, *4*(4), 497–505. doi:10.5465/amr.1979.4498296

Cascio, F. F. (1992). *Managing Human Resources: Productivitiy of Life Profits*. Mc Grill-Hill Company.

Cascio, W. F. (1991). *Costing human resources: The financial impact of behavior in organizations*. PWS-Kent.

Casillas, J. C., Díaz, C., Rus, S., & Vázquez, A. (2014). *La gestión de la empresa familiar. Conceptos, casos y soluciones*. Paraninfo.

Cassell, C., Nadin, S., Gray, M., & Clegg, C. (2002). Exploring Human Resource Management Practices in Small and Medium Sized Enterprises. *Personnel Review*, *31*(6), 671–692. doi:10.1108/00483480210445962

Cater, J., James, K., Kidwell, R., Camp, K., & Young, M. (2019). HRM practices and effectiveness: A comparison of US Hispanic and non-Hispanic family firms. *Journal of Small Business and Enterprise Development*, *26*(5), 726–746. doi:10.1108/JSBED-12-2018-0364

Chami, R. (1999). *What's different about family businesses?* University of Notre Dame Working Paper. University of Notre Dame.

Chan, R. Y. K. (2005). Does the Natural-Resource-Based View of the Firm Apply in an Emerging Economy? A Survey of Foreign Invested Enterprises in China. *Journal of Management Studies*, *42*(3), 625–672. doi:10.1111/j.1467-6486.2005.00511.x

Chen, C. C., Fosh, P., & Foster, D. J. (2007). Gender Differences in Perceptions of Organizational Cultures in the Banking Industry in Taiwan. *The Journal of Industrial Relations*, *50*(1), 139–156. doi:10.1177/0022185607085698

Chen, C. C., Greene, P. G., & Crick, A. (1998). Does entrepreneurial self-efficacy distinguish entrepreneurs from managers? *Journal of Business Venturing*, *13*(4), 295–316. doi:10.1016/S0883-9026(97)00029-3

Cheong, M., Yammarino, F. J., Dionne, S. D., Spain, S. M., & Chou-Yu, T. (2019, February). A review of the effectiveness of empowering leadership. *The Leadership Quarterly*, *30*(1), 34–58. doi:10.1016/j.leaqua.2018.08.005

Cherchem, N. (2017). The relationship between organizational culture and entrepreneurial orientation in family firms: Does generational involvement matter? *Journal of Family Business Strategy*, *8*(2), 87–98. doi:10.1016/j.jfbs.2017.04.001

Chiang, F. K., Zhu, G., Wang, Q., Cui, Z., Cai, S., & Yu, S. (2015). Research and trends in mobile learning from 1976 to 2013: A content analysis of patents in selected databases. *British Journal of Educational Technology*, *47*(6), 1006–1019. doi:10.1111/bjet.12311

Chiavenato, I. (2011). *Administración de recursos humanos: el capital humano de las organizaciones*. McGraw Hill.

Chiesa, V., De Massis, A., & Pasi, M. L. (2007). Gestire la successione nei Family Business. *Piccola impresa/Small business*, (1).

Chirico, F., Ireland, R. D., & Sirmon, D. G. (2011). Franchising and the family firm: Creating unique sources of advantage through familiness. *Entrepreneurship Theory and Practice*, *35*(3), 483–501. doi:10.1111/j.1540-6520.2011.00441.x

Choi, Y. S., Seo, M., Scott, D., & Martin, J. (2010). Validation of the OrganizationalCultureAssessment Instrument: An application of the Korean version. *Journal of Sport Management*, *24*(2), 169–189. http://digitalcommons.wayne.edu/cgi/viewcontent.cgi?article=1002&context=coe_khs. doi:10.1123/jsm.24.2.169

Chrisman, J. J., Chua, J. H., & Kellermanns, F. (2009). Priorities, Resource Stocks, and Performance in Family and Nonfamily Firms. *Entrepreneurship Theory and Practice, 33*(3), 739–760. doi:10.1111/j.1540-6520.2009.00324.x

Chrisman, J. J., Chua, J. H., Pearson, A. W., & Barnett, T. (2012). Family Involvement, Family Influence, and Family-Centered Non-Economic Goals in Small Firms. *Entrepreneurship Theory and Practice, 36*(2), 267–293. doi:10.1111/j.1540-6520.2010.00407.x

Chrisman, J. J., Chua, J. H., & Sharma, P. (1998). Important attributes of successor in family businesses: An exploratory study. *Family Business Review, 11*(1), 19–34. doi:10.1111/j.1741-6248.1998.00019.x

Chrisman, J. J., Kellermanns, F. W., Chan, K. C., & Liano, K. (2010). Intellectual foundations of current research in family business: An identification and review of 25 influential articles. *Family Business Review, 23*(1), 9–26. doi:10.1177/0894486509357920

Chrisman, J. J., Memili, E., & Misra, K. (2014). Nonfamily managers, family firms, and the winner's curse: The influence of noneconomic goals and bounded rationality. *Entrepreneurship Theory and Practice, 38*(5), 1103–1127. doi:10.1111/etap.12014

Chrisman, J., Chua, J., & Litz, R. (2003). A unified systems perspective of family firm performance: An extension and integration. *Journal of Business Venturing, 18*(4), 467–472. doi:10.1016/S0883-9026(03)00055-7

Chua, J. H., Chrisman, J. J., & Bergiel, E. B. (2009). An Agency Theoretic Analysis of the Professionalized Family Firm. *Entrepreneurship Theory and Practice, 33*(2), 355–372. doi:10.1111/j.1540-6520.2009.00294.x

Chua, J. H., Chrisman, J. J., & Sharma, P. (1999). Defining the Family Business by Behavior. *Entrepreneurship Theory and Practice, 23*(4), 19–39. doi:10.1177/104225879902300402

Chua, J., Chrisman, J., & Sharma, P. (2003). Succession and Nonsuccession Concerns of Family Firms and Agency Relationship with Nonfamily Managers. *Family Business Review, 16*(2), 89–107. doi:10.1111/j.1741-6248.2003.00089.x

Churchill, N., & Hatten, K. (1997). Non-market-based transfers of wealth and power: A research framework for family business. *Family Business Review, 10*(1), 53–67. doi:10.1111/j.1741-6248.1997.00053.x

Ciasullo, M., Cosimato, S., Gaeta, M., & Palumbo, R. (2017). Comparing two approaches to team building: A performance measurement evaluation. *Team Performance Management, 23*(7/8), 333–351. doi:10.1108/TPM-01-2017-0002

Ciasullo, M., Cosimato, S., & Palumbo, R. (2017). Improving health care quality: The implementation of whistleblowing. *The TQM Journal, 29*(1), 167–183. doi:10.1108/TQM-06-2016-0051

Cini, M. A. (2020). The effects of family communication patterns on family satisfaction in family business. B. Christiansen (Edt.). In *Global Applications of Multigenerational Management and Leadership in the Transcultural Era* (pp. 196–230). IGI Global. doi:10.4018/978-1-5225-9906-7.ch007

CIPD. (2013). Talent analytics and big data: The challenge for HR. *Chartered Institute for Personnel and Development.* https://www.cipd.co.uk/Images/talent-analytics-and-big-data_2013-challenge-for-hr_tcm18-9289.pdf

Clarke, M. (2011). Sustainable HRM: A new approach to people management. In M. Clarke (Ed.), *Readings in HRM and sustainability* (pp. 1–7). Tilde University Press.

Clarkson, M. B. E. (1995). A Stakeholder Framework for Analyzing and Evaluating Corporate Social Performance. *Academy of Management Journal, 20*(1), 92–118.

Cleveland, J. N., Byrne, Z. S., & Cavanagh, T. M. (2015). The future of HR is RH: Respect for humanity at work. *Human Resource Management Review, 25*(2), 146–161. doi:10.1016/j.hrmr.2015.01.005

Clinton, E. (2016). Human resources in the family business-maximsing the power of your people. *Irish Journal of Management, 35*(2), 176–178. Advance online publication. doi:10.1515/ijm-2016-0014

Ćoćkalo, D., Đorđević, D., Bogetić, S., Sajfert, D., & Minovski, R. (2013). Quality of business, entrepreneurship education and business startup intentions among students in Serbia: Research results. *Industrija, 41*(3), 125–145. doi:10.5937/industrija41-3889

Coggiola, D., Morelli, C., & Songini, L. (2017). *Gestione delle risorse umane e performance nelle piccole e medie imprese familiari italiane*. Academic Press.

Cohen, E., Taylor, S., & Muller-Camen, M. (2012). *HR's role in corporate social responsibility and sustainability.* SHRM Foundation Executive Briefing. Retrieved from https://www.shrm.org/foundation/ourwork/initiatives/building-an-inclusive-culture/Documents/HR%27s%20Role%20in%20Corporate%20Social%20Responsibility.pdf

Collins, C. J., & Clark, K. D. (2003). Strategic Human Resource Practices, Top Management Team Social Networks, and Firm Performance: The Role of Human Resource Practices in Creating Organizational Competitive Advantage. *Academy of Management Journal, 46*(6), 740–751.

Collmus, A. B., Armstrong, M. B., & Landers, R. N. (2016). Game thinking within social media to recruit and select job candidates. In R. Landers & G. Schmidt (Eds.), *Social media in employee selection and recruitment* (pp. 103–124). Springer. doi:10.1007/978-3-319-29989-1_6

COM. (2010). *Europe 2020: A strategy for smart, sustainable and inclusive growth.* Retrieved from https://ec.europa.eu/eu2020/pdf/COMPLET%20EN%20BARROSO%20%20%20007%20-%20Europe%202020%20-%20EN%20version.pdf

Combs, J. G., Jaskiewicz, P., Shanine, K. K., & Balkin, D. B. (2018). Making Sense of HR in Family Firms: Antecedents, Moderators, and Outcomes. *Human Resource Management Review, 28*(1), 1–4. doi:10.1016/j.hrmr.2017.05.001

Combs, J., Liu, Y. M., Hall, A., & Ketchen, D. (2006). How much do high-performance work practices matter? A meta-analysis of their effects on organizational performance. *Personnel Psychology, 59*(3), 501–528. doi:10.1111/j.1744-6570.2006.00045.x

Commission of the European Communities. (2008). *Think Small First - A Small Business Act for Europe*. Author.

Corbetta, G., & Salvato, C. (2012). *Strategies for Longevity in Family Firms. A European perspective*. Palgrave-MacMillan. doi:10.1057/9781137024589

Corbin, J., & Strauss, A. (2015). *Basics of Qualitative Research: Techniques and Procedures for Developing Grounded Theory* (4th ed.). SAGE Publications, Inc.

Cori, E., & Bonti, M. (2014). Handling knowledge through entrepreneurial generations: lessons from long-lived family SMES. *Piccola Impresa/Small Business*, (3), 17-38.

Cormier, D., & Magnan, M. (2017). Does a firm's exposure to ethical failures matter to financial markets? A governance perspective. *The Journal of Management and Governance, 21*(2), 267–289. doi:10.100710997-016-9341-9

Corona, J. F. (Coord.). (2017). Empresa familiar: análisis estratégico. Barcelona: Ed. Deusto.

Cortés, C., & Carreras, I. (2019). *La influencia de la RSE en la gestión de personas: buenas prácticas*. ESADE.

Coury, C., & Pecanha, D. L. (2016). Leadership and organizational culture in family businesses: Systemic and psychodynamic case study. *Boletim Academia Paulista de Psicologia, 36*(91), 465–488. Retrieved March 6, 2020, from http://pepsic.bvsalud.org/scielo.php?pid=S1415-711X2016000200014&script=sci_abstract&tlng=en

Craig, J. B., Dibrell, C., & Davis, P. S. (2008). Leveraging family-based brand identity to enhance firm competitiveness and performance in family businesses. *Journal of Small Business Management*, *46*(3), 351–371. doi:10.1111/j.1540-627X.2008.00248.x

Crane, A., Matten, D., Glozer, S., & Spence, L. J. (2016). *Business Ethics: Managing Corporate Citizenship and Sustainability in the Age of Globalization*. Oxford University Press.

Cretney, S. (1995). Reform of intestacy: The best we can do? *The Law Quarterly Review*, *111*, 77–84.

Crifo, P., Durand, R., & Gond, J. P. (2019). Encouraging Investors to Enable Corporate Sustainability Transitions: The Case of Responsible Investment in France. *Organization & Environment*, *32*(2), 125–144. doi:10.1177/1086026619848145

Crompton, H., Burke, D., Gregory, K., & Cräbe, C. (2016). The use of mobile learning in science: A systematic review. *Journal of Science Education and Technology*, *25*(2), 149–160. doi:10.100710956-015-9597-x

Crots, J. C., & Ford, R. C. (2008). Achieving service excellence by design: The organizational alignment audit. *Business Communication Quarterly*, *71*(2), 233–240. doi:10.1177/1080569908317319

Cruz, C., Firfiray, S., & Gómez-Mejía, L. R. (2011). Socioemotional wealth and human resource management (HRM) in family-controlled firms. In A. Joshi, H. Liao, & J. J. Martocchio (Eds.), *Research in Personnel and Human Resources Management* (pp. 159–217). Elsevier. doi:10.1108/S0742-7301(2011)0000030006

Cucculelli, M., & Micucci, G. (2008). Family succession and firm performance: Evidence from Italian family firms. *Journal of Corporate Finance*, *14*(1), 17–31. doi:10.1016/j.jcorpfin.2007.11.001

Cummings, T. G., & Worley, C. G. (2009). *Organizational development and change* (9th ed.). Cengage.

D'Amato, V. (2015). Management Innovation Road Map. Milano: Egea.

Dachler, H. P., & Enderle, G. (1989). Epistemological and ethical considerations in conceptualizing and implementing human resource management. *Journal of Business Ethics*, *8*(8), 597–606. doi:10.1007/BF00383028

Daily, CM & Dollinger, M.J. (1993). Alternative methodologies for identifying family vs. non- family managed businesses. *Journal of Small Business Management, 31*(2).

Damian, I., Baur, T., Lugrin, B., Gebhard, P., Mehlmann, G., & André, E. (2015). Games are better than books: In-situ comparison of an interactive job interview game with conventional training. In N C. Conati, N. Heffernan, A. Mitrovic, & F. M. Vergejo (Eds.), Artificial intelligence in education (pp. 84-94). Springer.

Daniels, A. C., & Whitener, B. (2000). *Bringing out the best in people: How to apply the astonishing power of positive reinforcement*. McGraw-Hill.

Daspit, J. J., Holt, D. T., Chrisman, J. J., & Long, R. G. (2016). Examining family firm succession from a social exchange perspective: A multiphase, multistakeholder review. *Family Business Review*, *29*(1), 44–64. doi:10.1177/0894486515599688

Daspit, J. J., Madison, K., Barnett, T., & Long, R. G. (2018). The Emergence of Bifurcation Bias from Unbalanced Families: Examining HR Practices in the Family Firm Using Circumplex Theory. *Human Resource Management Review*, *28*(1), 18–32. doi:10.1016/j.hrmr.2017.05.003

Das, T. K., & Teng, B. (1996). Risk types and inter-firm alliance structures. *Journal of Management Studies*, *33*(6), 827–843. doi:10.1111/j.1467-6486.1996.tb00174.x

Dastmalchian, A., Lee, S., & Ng, I. (2000). The interplay between organizational and national cultures: A comparison of organizational practices in Canada and South Korea using the Competing Values Framework. *International Journal of Human Resource Management*, *11*(2), 388–412.

Davenport, T., & Ronanki, R. (2018). Artificial intelligence for the real world. *Harvard Business Review*. https://www.kungfu.ai/wp-content/uploads/2019/01/R1801H-PDF-ENG.pdf

Davis, P. S., & Harveston, P. D. (2001). *The Family Firm: A Cross-Generational Study*. Academic Press.

Davis, P. (1986). Family business: Perspectives on change. *Agency Sales Magazine*, *6*, 9–16.

Dawson, A., Irving, G. P., Sharma, P., Chirico, F., & Marcus, J. (2014). Behavioural outcomes of next-generation family members' commitment to their firm. *European Journal of Work and Organizational Psychology*, *23*(4), 570–581. doi:10.1080/1359432X.2013.781155

Dayton, A. K. (2014). *Comparative Perspectives on Adult Guardianship*. Carolina Academic Press.

de Kok, J. M. P., Uhlaner, L. M., & Thurik, A. R. (2006). Professional HRM Practices in Family Owned Managed Enterprises. *Journal of Small Business Management*, *44*(3), 441–460. doi:10.1111/j.1540-627X.2006.00181.x

De Massis, A., Chua, J. H., & Chrisman, J. J. (2008). Factors preventing intra-family succession. *Family Business Review*, *21*(2), 183–199. doi:10.1111/j.1741-6248.2008.00118.x

De Massis, A., Kotlar, J., Chua, J. H., & Chrisman, J. J. (2014). Ability and Willingness as Sufficiency Conditions for Family-Oriented Particularistic Behavior: Implications for Theory and Empirical Studies. *Journal of Small Business Management*, *52*(2), 344–364. doi:10.1111/jsbm.12102

De Massis, A., Sharma, P., Chua, J. H., & Chrisman, J. J. (2012). *Family Business Studies: An Annotated Bibliography*. Edward Elgar Pub. doi:10.4337/9781781002988

De Massis, A., Sieger, P., Chua, J. H., & Vismara, S. (2016). Incumbent's Attitudes Towards Intrafamily Succession: An Investigation of its Antecendents. *Family Business Review*, *29*(3), 278–300. doi:10.1177/0894486516656276

De Prins, P. (2011), Duurzaam HRM: Synthetische academische introductie. In I. Rompa (Ed.), *Explorative research on Sustainable Human Resource Management*. Retrieved from https://www.innovatiefinwerk.nl/sites/innovatiefinwerk.nl/files/field/bijlage/sustainable_hrm.pdf

De Vries, M. F. K. (1993). The dynamics of family controlled firms: The good and the bad news. *Organizational Dynamics*, *21*(3), 59–71. doi:10.1016/0090-2616(93)90071-8

De Waal, M. J. (2008). Comparative Succession Law. In M. Reimann & R. Zimmermann (Eds.), *The Oxford Handbook of Comparative law (pp* (pp. 1071–1098). Oxford University Press.

Dearborn, J., & Swanson, D. (2018). *The data driven leader: A powerful approach to delivering measurable business impact through people analytics*. Wiley.

Debarliev, S., & Janeska-Iliev, A. (2015). Challenges for the family business in transition economics: with an emphasis on the Republic of Macedonia economic recovery in the post-crisis period. *Proceedings from the International Conference held at the Faculty of Economics.*

Debarliev, S., & Janeska-Iliev, A. (2015).Challenges for the family business in transition economics: with an emphasis on the Republic of Macedonia economic recovery in the post-crisis period. *Proceedings from the International Conference held at the Faculty of Economics*, Skopje, Macedonia.

DeCenzo, D., Robbins, S. P., & Verhulst, S. L. (2016). *Fundamentals of human resource management*. Wiley.

Deckop, J. R. (2006). *Human Resource Management Ethics*. Information Age Publishing.

DeDee, J. K., & Vorhies, D. W. (1998). Retrenchment activities of small firms during economic downturn: An empirical investigation. *Journal of Small Business Management, 36*(3), 46–62.

Deephouse, D. L., & Jaskiewicz, P. (2013). Do Family Firms Have Better Reputations Than Non-Family Firms? An Integration of Socioemotional Wealth and Social Identity Theories. *Journal of Management Studies, 50*(3), 337–360. doi:10.1111/joms.12015

Dekker, J. C., Lybaert, N., Steijvers, T., Depaire, B., & Mercken, R. (2013). Family firm types based on the professionalization construct: Exploratory research. *Family Business Review, 26*(1), 81–99. doi:10.1177/0894486512445614

Dekker, J., Lybaert, N., Steijvers, T., & Depaire, B. (2015). The effect of family business professionalization as a multidimensional construct on firm performance. *Journal of Small Business Management, 53*(2), 516–538. doi:10.1111/jsbm.12082

Del Baldo, M. (2013). CSR-Oriented SMEs: A Question of Entrepreneurial Virtues in Action? Reflections in Theory and Practice. In J. Okpara & S. Idowu (Eds.), *Corporate Social Responsibility. CSR, Sustainability, Ethics & Governance* (pp. 145–170). Springer. doi:10.1007/978-3-642-40975-2_9

Del Bene, L. (2005). *Aziende familiari tra imprenditorialità e managerialità*. Giappichelli.

Delaney, J. T., & Huselid, M. A. (1996). The impact of human resource management practices on perceptions of organizational performance. *Academy of Management Journal, 39*(4), 949–969.

Delaney, J. T., & Huselid, M. A. (1996). The Impact of Human Resource Management Practices on Perceptions of Organizational Performance. *Academy of Management Journal, 39*(4), 949–969.

Delery, J. E. (1998). Issues of Fit in Strategic Human Resource Management: Implications for Research. *Human Resource Management Review, 8*(3), 289–309. doi:10.1016/S1053-4822(98)90006-7

Delery, J. E., & Doty, D. H. (1996). Modes of Theorizing in Strategic Human Resource Management: Tests of Universalistic, Contingency, and Configurational Performance Predictions. *Academy of Management Journal, 39*(4), 802–835. doi:10.5465/256713

Delery, J., & Gupta, N. (2016). Human resource management practices and organizational effectiveness: Internal fit matters. *Journal of Organizational Effectiveness: People and Performance, 3*(2), 139–163. doi:10.1108/JOEPP-03-2016-0028

Deloitte & Touche Study. (1999). *Are Canadian Family Businesses An Endangered Species? The First Success Readiness Survey of Canadian Family-Owned Business*. Deloitte & Touche Centre for Tax Education and Research, University of Waterloo.

Deloitte. (2013). *Understanding the bring-your-own device landscape*. https://www2.deloitte.com/content/dam/Deloitte/uk/Documents/about-deloitte/deloitte-uk-understanding-the-bring-your-own-device%20landscape.pdf

Demerouti, E., Geurts, S., & Kompier, M. (2004). Positive and Negative Work–Home Inter- action: Prevalence and Correlates. *Equal Opportunities International, 1*(23), 6–35. doi:10.1108/02610150410787837

Deng, X. (2018). Embedding 'familiness' in HRM practices to retain a new generation of migrant workers in China. *Asia Pacific Business Review, 24*(4), 561–577. doi:10.1080/13602381.2018.1451124

Deng, Z., Hofman, P. S., & Newman, A. (2013). Ownership concentration and product innovation in Chinese private SMEs. *Asia Pacific Journal of Management, 30*(3), 717–734. doi:10.100710490-012-9301-0

DeNisi, A., Hitt, M. A., & Jackson, S. E. (2003). The knowledge-based approach to sustained competitive advantage. In Managing knowledge for sustained competitive advantage: Designing strategies for effective human resource management. San Francisco: Jossey Bass.

DeNisi, A. S., & Murphy, K. R. (2017). Performance Appraisal and Performance Management: 100 Years of Progress. *The Journal of Applied Psychology*, *102*(3), 421–433. doi:10.1037/apl0000085 PMID:28125265

Denison, D. R., & Mishra, A. K. (1989). Organizational culture and organizational effectiveness:A theory and some preliminary empirical evidence. *Academy of Management Proceedings*, *1*(1), 168–172. doi:10.5465/ambpp.1989.4980714

Denison, D. R., & Spreitzer, G. M. (1991). Organizational Culture and Organizational Development: A Competing Values Approach. *Research in Organizational Change and Development*, *5*, 1–21.

Dessler, G. (2010). *Human Resources Management*. Prentice Hall-Pearson.

Devecchi, C. (2007). *Problemi, criticità e prospettive dell'impresa di famiglia* (Vol. 1). Vita e pensiero.

Dhaenens, A., Marler, L., Vardaman, J., & Chrisman, J. (2018). Mentoring in family businesses: Toward an understanding of commitment outcomes. *Human Resource Management Review*, *28*(1), 46–55. doi:10.1016/j.hrmr.2017.05.005

Di Maddaloni, F., & Davis, K. (2017). The influence of local community stakeholders in megaprojects: Rethinking their inclusiveness to improve project performance. *International Journal of Project Management*, *35*(8), 1537–1556. doi:10.1016/j.ijproman.2017.08.011

Dickinson, T. M. (2000). *Critical success factors for succession planning in family businesses.* Unpublished research report in partial fulfillment of Master in Business Administration degree, Faculty of Business Administration, University of the Witwatersrand, Johannesburg.

Dickson, M. W., Aditya, R. N., & Chhokar, J. S. (2000). Definition and interpretation in crosscultural organizational culture research. In N. M. Ashkanasy, C. P. M. Wilderom, & M. F. Peterson (Eds.), *Handbook of organizational culture and climate* (pp. 447–464). Sage.

Dinc, L., & Gastmans, C. (2011). Trust and trustworthiness in nursing: An argument-based literature review. *Nursing Inquiry*, *19*(3), 223–237. doi:10.1111/j.1440-1800.2011.00582.x PMID:22050646

Ding, S., & Wu, Z. (2014). Family Ownership and Corporate Misconduct in U.S. Small Firms. *Journal of Business Ethics*, *123*(2), 183–195. doi:10.100710551-013-1812-1

Docherty, P., Forslin, J., & Shani, A. B. (2002). *Creating Sustainable Work Systems: Emerging Perspectives and Practice*. Psychology Press.

Dolan, S. (2012). *Coaching por valores*. Madrid: LID Editorial empresarial, colecciõn Acciõn Empresarial.

Dolan, S. (2014). *Gestión de personas y del talento*. McGraw Hill.

Dolan, S. (2016). Reflections on leadership, coaching and values: a framework for understanding the consequences of value congruence and incongruence in organizations and a call to enhance value alignment. *The Study of Organizations and Human Resource Management Quarterly*, *1*(2), 56-74.

Donaldson, L. (2008). Ethics Problems and Problems with Ethics: Toward a Pro-Management Theory. *Journal of Business Ethics*, *78*(3), 299–311. doi:10.100710551-006-9336-6

Drucker, P. F. (1981). What is Business Ethics? *The Public Interest*, *63*, 19–36.

Drucker, P. F. (1984). The new meaning of corporate social responsibility. *California Management Review*, *26*(2), 53–63. doi:10.2307/41165066

Dubkevics, L. and Barbars, A. (2010). The role of organizational culture in human resource management. *Human Resource Management and ergonomics*, 4 (1), 1-10.

Dubois, C. L. Z., & Dubois, D. A. (2012). Strategic HRM as social design for environmental sustainability in organization. *Human Resource Management*, *51*(6), 799–826. doi:10.1002/hrm.21504

Dulebohn, J. H., & Hoch, J. E. (2017). Virtual teams in organizations. *Human Resource Management Review*, *27*(4), 569–574. doi:10.1016/j.hrmr.2016.12.004

Dull, M. (2010). Leadership and organizational culture: Sustaining dialogue between practitioners and scholars. *Public Administration Review*, *17*(6), 857–866. doi:10.1111/j.1540-6210.2010.02217.x

Dumas, C., Dupuis, J. P., Richer, F., & St.-Cyr, L. (1995). Factors that influence the next generation's decision to take over the family farm. *Family Business Review*, *8*(2), 99–120. doi:10.1111/j.1741-6248.1995.00099.x

Dunn, T., & Holtz-Eakin, D. (2000). Financial capital, human capital, and the transition to self-employment: Evidence from intergenerational links. *Journal of Labor Economics*, *18*(2), 287–305. doi:10.1086/209959

Dunphy, D., Benveniste, J., Griffiths, A., & Sutton, P. (2000). *Sustainability; the Corporate Challenge of the 21st Century*. Allen & Unwin.

Dyck, B., Mauws, M., Starke, F. A., & Mischke, G. A. (2002). Passing the baton: The importance of sequence, timing, technique and communication in executive succession. *Journal of Business Venturing*, *17*(2), 143–162. doi:10.1016/S0883-9026(00)00056-2

Dyer, J., & Nobeoka, K. (2000). Creating and managing a high-performance knowledge-sharing network: The Toyota case. *Strategic Management Journal*, *21*(3), 345–367. doi:10.1002/(SICI)1097-0266(200003)21:3<345::AID-SMJ96>3.0.CO;2-N

Dyer, W. G. (1988). Culture and Continuity in Family Firms. *Family Business Review*, *1*(1), 37–50. doi:10.1111/j.1741-6248.1988.00037.x

Dyer, W. G. Jr. (2006). Examining the "family effect" on firm performance. *Family Business Review*, *19*(4), 253–273. doi:10.1111/j.1741-6248.2006.00074.x

Dyer, W. G., & Mortensen, S. P. (2005). Entrepreneurship and family business in a hostile environment: The case of Lithuania. *Family Business Review*, *18*(3), 247–258. doi:10.1111/j.1741-6248.2005.00045.x

Dyllick, T., & Muff, K. (2016). Clarifying the Meaning of Sustainable Business. *Organization & Environment*, *29*(2), 156–174. doi:10.1177/1086026615575176

Economic Reform Report. (2019). *Structural Reforms*. Republic of North Macedonia.

Edelman, L. F., Manolova, T., Shirokova, G., & Tsukanova, T. (2016). The impact of family support on young entrepreneurs' start-up activities. *Journal of Business Venturing*, *31*(4), 428–448. doi:10.1016/j.jbusvent.2016.04.003

Edersheim, E. H. (2007). *Przesłanie Druckera. Zarządzanie oparte na wiedzy*. Warszawa: MTBiznes.

Egger, E., Misoska Tomovska, A., & Dimitrova, M. (2019). Entrepreneurial intentions among students in SEEC's factors related to education and family. *From Transition to development: Emerging challenges and perspectives: Conference Proceedings of 3rd International Scientific Conference on Business and Economics*.

Ehnert, I. (2009). *Sustainable Human Resource Management. A conceptual and exploratory analysis from a paradox perspective*. Physica-Verlag.

Ehnert, I., Harry, W., & Zink, K. J. (2014). Sustainability and HRM. In I. Ehnert, W. Harry, & K. J. Zink (Eds.), *Sustainability and human resource management developing sustainable business organizations* (pp. 3–32). Springer.

Ehnert, I., Parsa, S., Roper, I., Wagner, M., & Muller-Camen, M. (2016). Reporting on sustainability and HRM: A comparative study of sustainability reporting practices by the world's largest companies. *International Journal of Human Resource Management*, *27*(1), 88–108. doi:10.1080/09585192.2015.1024157

Eisenhardt, K. M. (1989). Building theories from case study research. *Academy of Management Review*, *14*(4), 532–550. doi:10.5465/amr.1989.4308385

Eisenhardt, K. M., & Graebner, M. E. (2007). Theory Building from Cases: Opportunities and Challenges. *Academy of Management Journal*, *50*(1), 25–32. doi:10.5465/amj.2007.24160888

El Ouird, A., El Quird, M., Segers, J., & Henderickx, E. (2015). Employees' use of social media technologies: A methodological and thematic Review. *Behaviour & Information Technology*, *34*(5), 454–464. doi:10.1080/0144929X.2015.1004647

Elicegui-Reyes, J. I., Barrena-Martínez, J., & Romero-Fernández, P. M. (2017). Emotional Capital and Sustainability in Family Businesses: Human Resource Management Perspective and Sustainability. In M. A. Camilleri (Ed.), *CSR 2.0 and the New Era of Corporate Citizenship* (pp. 231–250). IGI Global. doi:10.4018/978-1-5225-1842-6.ch012

Elkhair, Z., & Mutalib, A. A. (2019). Mobile learning applications: Characteristics, perspectives, and future trends. *International Journal of Interactive Digital Media*, *5*(1), 18–21.

Elkington, J. (1997). *Cannibals with forks: the triple bottom line of 21st century business*. Captone.

Erdirencelebi, M. (2020). Nepotism. Farklı Boyutlarıyla Örgütsel Davranış. Üyesi Mehtap Öztürk, 1th baskı Ankara: Gazi Kitapevi.

Erdirencelebi, M., & Erturk, E. (2018). Türkiye'de nepotizm konusunda hazırlanan çalışmalara yönelik bir inceleme. *Osmaniye Korkut Ata Üniversitesi İktisadi ve İdari Bilimler Fakültesi İşletme Bölümü, 18th International Business Congress*, 2344-2359.

Erdoğmuş, N., Olcay, G. A., & Erdemir, E. (2017). Building Innovative Strategies for the Competitiveness of Family Firms in Emerging Markets. In Ü. Hacioğlu, H. Dinçer, & N. Alayoğlu (Eds.), *Global Business Strategies in Crisis. Contributions to Management Science*. Springer. doi:10.1007/978-3-319-44591-5_14

European Commission. (2011), *Communication from the Commission to the European Parliament, the Council, the European Economic and Social Committee and the Committee of the Regions, A Renewed EU Strategy for Corporate Social Responsibility*. Retrieved from https://op.europa.eu/en/publication-detail/-/publication/ae5ada03-0dc3- 48f8-9a32-0460e65ba7ed/language-en

European Commission. (2017). *SBA Fact Sheet*. European Neighbourhood Policy and Enlargement Negotiations.

European Commission. (2017). *The Ageing Report 2018. Underlying Assumptions & Projection Methodologies*. Institutional paper 65. Retrieved March 6, 2020 from https://ec.europa.eu/info/sites/info/files/economy-finance/ip065_en.pdf

European Commission. (2018). *What is an SME?* Retrieved June 23, 2018, from https://ec.europa.eu/growth/smes/business-friendly-environment/sme-definition_en

Fabi, B., Raymond, L., & Lacoursière, R. (2007). HRM Practice Clusters in Relation to Size and Performance: An Empirical Investigation in Canadian Manufacturing SMEs. *Journal of Small Business and Entrepreneurship, 20*(1), 25–40. doi:10.1080/08276331.2007.10593384

Fabi, B., Raymond, L., & Lacoursière, R. (2009). Strategic Alignment of HRM Practices in Manufacturing SMEs: A Gestalts Perspective. *Journal of Small Business and Enterprise Development, 16*(1), 7–25. doi:10.1108/14626000910932854

FairlieR. W.RobbA. (2004). *Families, Human Capital and Small Business: Evidence from the Characteristics of Business Owners Survey.* IZA Discussion Paper No. 1296. http://ssrn.com/abstract=464243

Fakomogbon, M. A., & Bolaji, H. O. (2017). Effects of collaborative Learning styles on performance of students in a ubiquitous collaborative mobile Learning environment. *Contemporary Educational Technology, 8*(3), 268–279.

Falkenberg, L., & Herremans, I. (1995). Ethical Behaviours in Organizations: Directed by the Formal or Informal Systems? *Journal of Business Ethics, 14*(2), 133–144. doi:10.1007/BF00872018

Farrell, W. A. (2018). Learning becomes doing: Applying augmented and virtual reality to improve performance. *Performance Improvement, 57*(4), 19–28. doi:10.1002/pfi.21775

Fassin, Y., Van Rossem, A., & Buelens, M. (2011). Small-Business Owner-Managers' Perceptions of Business Ethics and CSR-Related Concepts. *Journal of Business Ethics, 98*(3), 425–453. doi:10.100710551-010-0586-y

Fawad Latif, K. (2020). Revisiting the relationship between corporate social responsibility and organizational performance: The mediating role of team outcomes. *Corporate Social Responsibility and Environmental Management, 27*(1).

Feng, Z., Gonzálex, V. A., Amor, R., Lovreglio, R., & Cabrera-Guerrero, G. (2018). Immersive virtual reality serious games for evacuation training and Research: A systemic literature review. *Computers & Education, 127*, 252–266. doi:10.1016/j.compedu.2018.09.002

Ferraro, H., & Marrone, J. (2016). Examining employment relationship activities in family business research. *Journal of Family Business Management, 6*(3), 210–224. doi:10.1108/JFBM-01-2016-0001

Ferris, G., Hochwarter, W., Buckley, M., Harrell-Cook, G., & Frink, D. (1999). Human resources management: Some new directions. *Journal of Management, 25*(3), 385–415. doi:10.1177/014920639902500306

Fink, L. (2018). *BlackRock CEO Annual Letter to CEOS 2018.* Academic Press.

Finkin, M. W., & Mundlak, G. (2015). *Comparative Labor Law.* Edward Elgar Pub. doi:10.4337/9781781000137

Firfiray, S., Cruz, C., Neacsu, I., & Gomez-Mejiad, L. R. (2018). Is nepotism so bad for family firms? A socioemotional wealth approach. *Human Resource Management Review, 28*(1), 83–97. doi:10.1016/j.hrmr.2017.05.008

Fisher, C.D. (2010). Happiness at work. *International Journal of Management Reviews, 12*, 384-412.

Flamini, G., & Gnan, L. (2017). A forty years' Literature Review on HRM in Family Businesses: Re-shaping the Research Agenda. In Academy of Management Proceedings (Vol. 2017, No. 1, p. 13851). Briarcliff Manor, NY: Academy of Management.

Flamini, G., Gnan, L., & Pellegrini, M. M. (2020). Forty years of research on human resource management in family firms: analyzing the past; preparing for the future. *Journal of Family Business Management*. . doi:10.1108/JFBM-05-2020-0040

Flamini, G., & Gnan, L. (2019). Family Firms' HrM Practices Configurations: an empirical analysis. In L. Gnan & M. Stefanovska–Petkovska (Eds.), *Innovating Europe* (pp. 29–84). University American College Skopje. doi:10.5281/zenodo.3533762

Flint, D. J., Blocker, C. P., & Boutin, P. J. Jr. (2011). Customer value anticipation, customer satisfaction, and loyalty: An empirical examination. *Industrial Marketing Management, 40*(2), 2019–2230. doi:10.1016/j.indmarman.2010.06.034

Fox, M., Nilakant, V., & Hamilton, R. T. (1996). Managing succession in family-owned businesses. *International Small Business Journal, 15*(1), 15–25.

Fox, M., Nilakant, V., & Hamilton, R. T. (1996). Managing Succession in Family-Owned Businesses. *International Small Business Journal, 15*(1), 15–25. doi:10.1177/0266242696151001

Freeman, R. E. (1984). Strategic management: A stakeholder approach. Academic Press.

Freeman, R. E. (1984). *Stakeholder Management: a Stakeholder Approach*. Cambridge University Press.

Freeman, R. E. (2010). Managing for Stakeholders: Trade-offs or Value Creation. *Journal of Business Ethics, 96*(S1, Suppl. 1), 7–9. doi:10.100710551-011-0935-5

Freeman, R. E., & Greenwood, M. (2020). Deepening Methods in Business Ethics. *Journal of Business Ethics, 161*(1), 1–3. doi:10.100710551-019-04374-7

Freeman, R. E., Harrison, J. S., & Wicks, A. C. (2007). *Managing for Stakeholders: Survival, Reputation, and Success*. Yale University Press.

Freiling, J., & Fichtner, H. (2010). Organizational culture as the glue between people and organization: A competence-based view on learning and competence building. *German Journal of Research in Human Resource Management, 24*(2), 152–172. doi:10.1177/239700221002400204

Fusaro, A. (2013). Uno sguardo comparatistico sui patti successori e sulla distribuzione negoziata della ricchezza d'impresa. *Ricerche giuridiche, 2*(1), 353-376.

Gabrielli, G. (2010). *People management: teorie e pratiche per una gestione sostenibile delle persone*. F. Angeli.

Gabrielli, G., & Profili, S. (2012). *Organizzazione e gestione delle risorse umane*. Isedi.

Gabrielsson, J., & Huse, M. (2005). Outside directors in SME boards: a call for theoretical reflections. *Corporate Board: Role, Duties and Composition, 1*(1), 28-37.

Gallanis, T. (2019). *Family Property Law, Cases and Materials on Wills, Trusts, and Estates* (7th ed.). Foundation Press.

Gallo, A. (2014). The value of keeping the right customers. *Harvard Business Review*.

Gallo, M. A. (1998). Ethics in Personal Behavior in Family Business. *Family Business Review, 11*(4), 325–335. doi:10.1111/j.1741-6248.1998.00325.x

Gallo, M. A. (2004). The family business and its social responsibilities. *Family Business Review, 17*(2), 135–149. doi:10.1111/j.1741-6248.2004.00009.x

GalloM. A.CappuynsK. (2004). *Effort, Loyalty and Idealism*. IESE Business School Working Paper No. 571. https://ssrn.com/abstract=619321 doi:10.2139srn.619321

Galpin, T. J. (2018). Realizing your strategy's potential: A seven-step model for its effective execution. *Strategy and Leadership, 46*(6), 35–43. doi:10.1108/SL-09-2018-0088

Garba, A. B., Armarego, J., Murray, D., & Kenworthy, W. (2015). Review of the information security and privacy challenges in bring your own device (BYOD) environments. *Journal of Information Privacy and Security, 11*(1), 38–54. doi:10.1080/15536548.2015.1010985

García-Sánchez, I. M., Martínez-Ferrero, J., Cuadrado-Ballesteros, B., & Rodríguez-Ariza, L. (2015). Ethics and corporate performance in family firms. In K. Nelson (Ed.), *Business Intelligence, Strategies and Ethics* (pp. 127–148). Nova Science Publishers.

Gaumer, C. J., & Shaffer, K. J. (2018). Family business succession: Impact on supplier relations and customer management. *Human Resource Management International Digest*, *26*(6), 1–4. doi:10.1108/HRMID-05-2018-0104

Georgescu, M. A., & Herman, E. (2020). The impact of the Family Background on Students' Entrepreneurial Intentions: AN empirical analysis. *Sustainability*, *12*, 4775.

Gephard, R. P. (1978). Status degradation and organizational succession: An ethno methodological approach. *Administrative Science Quarterly*, *23*(4), 553–581.

Gersick, K. (2015). Essay on Practice: Advising Family Enterprise in the Fourth Decade. *Entrepreneurship Theory and Practice*, *39*(6), 1433–1450. doi:10.1111/etap.12176

Ghudayyer, M. B., Javed, Y., & Alenezi, M. (2017). A security perspective on adoption and migration to mobile cloud technology. *International Journal of Informatics Visualization*, *1*(4), 143–149. doi:10.30630/joiv.1.4.54

Giberson, T. R., Resick, C. J., Dickson, M. W., Mitchelson, J. K., Randall, K. R., & Clark, M. A. (2009). Leadership and Organizational Culture: Linking CEO Characteristics to Cultural Values. *Journal of Business and Psychology*, *24*(2), 123–137. doi:10.100710869-009-9109-1

Gimeno, A., & Parada, M. J. (2013). Professionalization of the family business: decision making domains. In *Exploring Transgenerational Entrepreneurship. The Role of Resources and Capabilities* (pp. 42–61). Camberley. doi:10.4337/9781781003626.00009

Gleason Bogert, G., Oaks, D. H., Hansen, H. R., & Neeleman, S. D. (2012). *The Law of Trusts* (9th ed.). Foundation Press.

Gokce, K. G., & Dogerlioglu, O. (2019). "Bring your own device" policies: Perspectives of both employees and organizations. *Knowledge Management & E-Learning*, *11*(2), 233–246.

Goldberg, S. D., & Wooldridge, B. (1993). Self-confidence and managerial autonomy: Successor characteristics critical to succession in family firms. *Family Business Review*, *6*(1), 55–73.

Gomez-Mejia, L. R., Cruz, C., Berrone, P., & De Castro, J. (2001). The Bind that Ties: Socioemotional Wealth Preservation in Family Firms. *The Academy of Management Annals*, *5*(1), 653–707. doi:10.5465/19416520.2011.593320

Gomez-Mejia, L. R., Larraza-Kintana, M., & Makri, M. (2003). The Determinants of Executive Compensation in Family-Controlled Public Corporations. *Academy of Management Journal*, *46*(2), 226–237.

Gomez-Mejia, L. R., Nunez-Nickel, M., & Gutierrez, I. (2001). The role of family ties in agency contracts. *Academy of Management Journal*, *44*(1), 81–95.

Gomez-Mejia, L. R., Takacs Haynes, K., Nunez-Nickel, M., Jocobson, K. J. L., & Moyano-Fuentes, J. (2007). Socioemotional Wealth and Business Risks in Family- Controlled Firms Evidence from Spanish Olive Oil Mills. *Administrative Science Quarterly*, *52*(1), 106–137. doi:10.2189/asqu.52.1.106

Gooderham, P., Nordhaug, O., & Ringdal, K. (2006). National Embeddedness and Calculative Human Resource Management in US Subsidiaries in Europe and Australia. *Human Relations*, *59*(11), 1491–1513. doi:10.1177/0018726706072843

Goto, T. (2013). Secrets of family business longevity in Japan from the social capital perspective. In K. X. Smyrnios, P. Z. Poutziouris, & S. Goel (Eds.), *Handbook of Research on Family Business* (2nd ed., pp. 554–587). Edward Elgar Publishing.

Gratton, L. (2011). Workplace 2025: What will it look like? *Organizational Dynamics*, *40*(4), 246–254. doi:10.1016/j.orgdyn.2011.07.002

Greene, P. G., & Brown, T. E. (1997). Resource needs and the dynamic capitalism typology. *Journal of Business Venturing*, *12*(3), 161–173. doi:10.1016/S0883-9026(96)00060-2

Greenwood, M. R. (2002). Ethics and HRM: A Review and Conceptual Analysis. *Journal of Business Ethics*, *36*(3), 261–278. doi:10.1023/A:1014090411946

Greve, H. R., Palmer, D., & Pozner, J. E. (2010). Organizations gone wild: The causes, processes, and consequences of organizational misconduct. *The Academy of Management Annals*, *4*(1), 53–107. doi:10.5465/19416521003654186

Grote, J. (2003). Conflicting generations: A new theory of family business rivalry. *Family Business Review*, *16*(2), 113–124. doi:10.1111/j.1741-6248.2003.00113.x

Grudzewski, W., & Hejduk, I. (2000). Kierowanie mała firmą – wyzwania przyszłości. *Ekonomika i Organizacja Przedsiębiorstw*, *1*, 3–5.

Gruman, J. A., & Saks, A. M. (2011). Performance management and employee engagement. *Human Resource Management Review*, *21*(2), 123–136. doi:10.1016/j.hrmr.2010.09.004

Grušic', U., Heinze, C., Merrett, L., Mills, A., García-Castrillón, C. O., Tang, Z. S., Trimmings, K., Walker, L., Torremans, P., & Fawcett, J. J. (2017). Cheshire, North & Fawcett: Private International Law (15th ed.). Oxford University Press.

Grześ, A. (2012). Specyfika pozyskiwania zasobów ludzkich w firmach rodzinnych. *Przedsiębiorczość i Zarządzanie*, *13*(7), 157–176.

Guba, E. G., & Lincoln, Y. S. (1982). Epistemological and methodological bases of naturalistic inquiry. *Educational Communication and Technology*, *30*(4), 233–252.

Guerci, M., & Carollo, L. (2016). A paradox view on green human resource management: Insights from the Italian context. *International Journal of Human Resource Management*, *27*(2), 212–238. doi:10.1080/09585192.2015.1033641

Guerci, M., & Pedrini, M. (2014). The consensus between Italian HR and sustainability managers on HR management for sustainability-driven change – towards a 'strong' HR management system. *International Journal of Human Resource Management*, *25*(13), 1787–1814. doi:10.1080/09585192.2013.860388

Guerci, M., Radaelli, G., Siletti, E., Cirella, S., & Rami Shani, A. B. (2015). The Impact of Human Resource Management Practices and Corporate Sustainability on Organizational Ethical Climates: An Employee Perspective. *Journal of Business Ethics*, *126*(2), 325–342. doi:10.100710551-013-1946-1

Guest, D. (2011). Human Resource Management and Performance: Still Searching for Some Answers. *Human Resource Management Journal*, *21*(1), 3–13. doi:10.1111/j.1748-8583.2010.00164.x

Guest, D., Michie, J., Conway, N., & Sheehan, M. (2003). Human Resource Management and Corporate Performance in the UK. *British Journal of Industrial Relations*, *41*(2), 291–314.

Guest, G., Bunce, A., & Johnson, L. (2006). How Many Interviews Are Enough? An Experiment with Data Saturation and Variability. *Field Methods*, *18*(1), 59–82. doi:10.1177/1525822X05279903

Gules, H. K., Arıcıoglu, M. A., & Erdirencelebi, M. (2013). *Aile İşletmeleri Kurumsallaşma Sürdürülebilirlik ve Uyum*. Gazi Kitapevi.

Gunduz, S. (2017). *İş Yerinde Yaşanan Sendromlar*. Beta Yayıncılık.

Guney, S. (2004). *Açıklamalı Yönetim-Organizasyon ve Örgütsel Davranış Terimler Sözlüğü*. Siyasal Kitabevi.

Gupta, N., & Sharma, V. (2016). Exploring Employee Engagement – A Way to Better Business Performance. *Global Business Review*, *17*(3), 45–63. doi:10.1177/0972150916631082

Gupta, P., Fernandes, S., & Manish, J. (2018). Automation in recruitment: A new frontier. *Journal of Information Teaching Cases*, *8*(2), 118–125. doi:10.105741266-018-0042-x

Gupta, V., & Levenburg, N. (2012). Cultures, ideologies and family business. *Journal of Family Business Management*, *2*(1), 57–75. doi:10.1108/20436231211216420

Gupta, V., Levenburg, N., Moore, L., Motani, J., & Schwarz, T. (2008). Exploring the Construct of Family Business in the Emerging Markets. *International Journal of Business and Emerging Markets*, *1*(2), 189–208. doi:10.1504/IJBEM.2008.020869

Gustafson, P. (2013). Control and Commitment in Corporate Travel Management. *Research in Transportation Business & Management*, *9*, 21–28. doi:10.1016/j.rtbm.2013.03.002

Gustafsson, S., Gillespie, N., Hope Hailey, V., Ros, S., & Dietz, G. (2020). Preserving organizational trust during disruption. *Organization Studies*. Advance online publication. doi:10.1177/0170840620912705

Guthrie, J. P. (2001). High-Involvement Work Practices, Turnover, and Productivity: Evidence From New Zealand. *Academy of Management Journal*, *44*(1), 180–190.

Gutiérrez-Broncano, S., Rubio-Andrés, M., & Jimenez Esterez, P. (2014). Managing human resources in family businesses: a review on the current state of research and new proposals for the future. In C. F. Machado & P. M. R. N. de Melo (Eds.), *Effective Human Resources Management in Small and Medium Enterprises* (pp. 96–112). Business Science Reference. doi:10.4018/978-1-4666-4731-2.ch005

Habbershon, T. G., Williams, M. L., & MacMillan, I. C. (2003). A unified systems perspective of family firm performance. *Journal of Business Venturing*, *18*(4), 451–465. doi:10.1016/S0883-9026(03)00053-3

Habbershon, T., & Pistrui, J. (2002). Enterprising families domain: Family-influenced ownership groups in pursuit of transgenerational wealth. *Family Business Review*, *15*(3), 223–237. doi:10.1111/j.1741-6248.2002.00223.x

Habbershon, T., Williams, M., & Kaye, K. (1999). A resource-based framework for assessing the strategic advantages of family firms. *Family Business Review*, *12*(1), 2. doi:10.1111/j.1741-6248.1999.00001.x

Hall, A., & Nordqvist, M. (2008). Professional management in family businesses: Toward an extended understanding. *Family Business Review*, *21*(1), 51–69. doi:10.1111/j.1741-6248.2007.00109.x

Hamel, G. (2009). Moon Shots for Management. *Harvard Business Review*, *87*(2), 91–98. PMID:19266704

Hamel, G. (2012). *What Matters Now. How to Win in a World of Reletless Change. Ferocious Competition, and Unstoppable Innovation*. Jossey-Bass.

Handler, W. C. (1989). *Managing the family firm succession process: The next-generation family member's experience* (Unpublished doctoral thesis). Boston University, Boston, MA.

Handler, W. C. (1990). Succession in Family Firms: A Mutual Role Adjustment Between Entrepreneur and Next-Generation Family Members. *Entrepreneurship Theory and Practice*, *15*(1), 37–51.

Handler, W. C. (1990). Succession in Family Firms: A Mutual Role Adjustment between Entrepreneur and Next-generation Family Members. *Entrepreneurship Theory and Practice*, *15*(1), 37–52. doi:10.1177/104225879001500105

Handler, W. C. (1991). Key interpersonal relationships of next-generation family members in family firms. *Journal of Small Business Management*, *29*(3), 21–32.

Handler, W. C. (1992). Succession in Family Business: A review of the research. *Family Business Review*, *2*(2), 133–157. doi:10.1111/j.1741-6248.1994.00133.x

Handler, W. C. (1992). The Succession Experience of the Next Generation. *Family Business Review*, *3*(5), 283–307. doi:10.1111/j.1741-6248.1992.00283.x

Hansen, N. K., & Alewell, D. (2013). Employment Systems as Governance Mechanisms of Human Capital and Capability Development. *International Journal of Human Resource Management*, *24*(11), 2131–2153. doi:10.1080/09585192.2012.725071

Hao, Y., & Helo, P. (2017). The role of wearable devices in meeting the needs of cloud manufacturing: A case study. *Robotics and Computer-integrated Manufacturing*, *45*, 168–179. doi:10.1016/j.rcim.2015.10.001

Harmon, P. (2019). *Business Process Change*. Morgan Kaufmann Publ. Imprint Elsevier. doi:10.1016/B978-0-12-815847-0.00001-7

Harris, R. I., Reid, R. S., & McAdam, R. (2004). Employee involvement in family and non-family-owned businesses in Great Britain. *International Journal of Entrepreneurial Behaviour & Research*, *10*(1/2), 49–58. doi:10.1108/13552550410521371

Harris, S. R., Kemmerling, R. L., & North, M. N. (2004). Brief virtual reality therapy for public speaking anxiety. *Cyberpsychology & Behavior*, *5*(6), 543–550. doi:10.1089/109493102321018187 PMID:12556117

Hart, S. L., & Sharma, S. (2004). Engaging fringe stakeholders for competitive imagination. *The Academy of Management Perspectives*, *18*(1), 7–18. doi:10.5465/ame.2004.12691227

Harveston, P. D., Davis, P. S., & Lyden, J. A. (1997). 'Succession planning in family business: The impact of owner gender', Family Business Review. John Wiley & Sons. *Ltd*, *10*(4), 373–396. doi:10.1111/j.1741-6248.1997.00373.x

Harvey, G., Williams, K., & Probert, J. (2013). Greening the airline pilot: HRM and the green performance of airlines in the UK. *International Journal of Human Resource Management*, *24*(1), 152–166. doi:10.1080/09585192.2012.669783

Harvey, M., & Evans, R. E. (1995). Life after succession in the family business: Is it really the end of problems? *Family Business Review*, *8*(1), 3–16.

Hauff, S., Alewell, D., & Hansen, N. K. (2014). HRM Systems Between Control and Commitment: Occurrence, Characteristics and Effects on HRM Outcomes and Firm Performance. *Human Resource Management Journal*, *24*(4), 424–441. doi:10.1111/1748-8583.12054

Hay, P., Borchers, P., & Freer, R. (2017). Conflict of Laws, Private International Law, Cases and Materials (15th ed.). Foundation Press.

Hayes, B., & Kotwica, K. (2013). *Bring your own device (BYOD) to work*. Elsevier.

Hecklau, F., Galeitzke, M., Flachs, S., & Kohl, H. (2016). Holistic approach for human resource management in industry 4.0. *Procedia CIRP*, *54*, 1–6. doi:10.1016/j.procir.2016.05.102

Hedberg, L. M., & Luchak, A. A. (2018). Founder Attachment Style and its Effects on Socioemotional Wealth Objectives and HR System Design. *Human Resource Management Review*, *28*(1), 33–45. doi:10.1016/j.hrmr.2017.05.004

Heller, N. A., & Heller, V. L. (2011). Business Ethics Education: Are Business Schools Teaching to the AACSB Ethics Education Task Force Recommendations? *International Journal of Business and Social Science*, *2*(20), 30–38.

Heyden, L. V. D., Blondel, C., & Carlock, R. S. (2005). Fair process: Striving for justice in family businesses. *Family Business Review*, *18*(1), 1–21. doi:10.1111/j.1741-6248.2005.00027.x

Higgins, V. (2017). Augmented & virtual reality: The future of work, not just play. *Vantage Point*, *62*(6), 86–87.

Hilarowicz, A. (2015). Koncepcja pracownika we współczesnych modelach zarządzania zasobami ludzkimi. *Zeszyty Naukowe Politechniki Śląskiej. Seria Organizacja i Zarządzanie*, *79*, 77–85.

Hill, R., & Stewart, J. (2000). Human Resource Development in Small Organizations. *Journal of European Industrial Training, 24*(2/3/4), 105-117.

Hill, R., & Stewart, J. (2000). Human resource development in small organizations. *Journal of European Industrial Training*, *24*(January), 105–117. doi:10.1108/03090590010321070

Hiltrop, J. M. (2005). Creating HR capability in high performance organizations. *Strategic Change*, *14*(3), 121–131.

Hirsig, N., Rogovski, N., & Elkin, M. (2014). Enterprise sustainability and HRM in Small and Medium-Sized Enterprises, a Decent Work Perspectives. In K. J. Z. Ehnert & W. Harry (Eds.), *Sustainability and Human Resource Management: Developing sustainable business organizations*. Springer. doi:10.1007/978-3-642-37524-8_6

Hitchcock, M., & Wesner, S. (2009). Vietnamese values, networks and family businesses in London. *Asia Pacific Business Review*, *15*(2), 265–282. doi:10.1080/10438590701719032

Hoffman, L., Marquis, J., Poston, D., Summers, J. A., & Turnbull, A. (2006). Assessing family outcomes: Psychometric evaluation of beach center family quality of life scale. *Journal of Marriage and the Family*, *68*(4), 1069–1083. doi:10.1111/j.1741-3737.2006.00314.x

Hoffmann, A., Junge, M., & Malchow-Møller, N. (2015). Running in the family: Parental role models in entrepreneurship. *Small Business Economics*, *44*(1), 79–104.

Hofman, A., Uitterlinden, A. G., & Rooij, F. J. A. (2010). *Genome-wide association studies in economics and entrepreneurship research: promises and limitations. In Small Business Economics*. Springer. doi:10.100711187-010-9286-3

Hofstede, G. (1997). *Cultures and Organizations: Software of the mind*. McGraw-Hill.

Hofstede, G., Neuijen, B., Ohayv, D. D., & Sanders, G. (1990). Measuring organizational cultures: A qualitative and quantitative study across twenty cases. *Administrative Science Quarterly*, *35*(2), 286–318. doi:10.2307/2393392

Holm, A., & Haahr, L. (2018). e-Recruitment and selection. In M. Thite (Ed.), e-HRM digital approaches, directions, & applications (pp. 374-398). Routledge.

Hoon, C., & Bövers, J. (2019). Unpacking socioemotional wealth: Exploring the origins of affective endowment in founder firms. *International Journal of Entrepreneurship and Small Business*.

Hoon, C., Hack, A., & Kellermanns, F. W. (2019). Advancing knowledge on human resource management in family firms: An introduction and integrative framework. *German Journal of Human Resource Management*, *33*(3), 147–166. doi:10.1177/2397002219847883

Hornsby, J., & Kuratko, D. (1990). Human resource management in small firms: Critical issues for the 1990. *Journal of Small Business Management*, *28*, 9–18.

Hornsby, J., & Kuratko, D. (2003). Human resource management in U.S. small business: A replication and extension. *Journal of Developmental Entrepreneurship*, *8*(1), 73–92.

Hornsby, J., & Kuratko, D. (2003). Human Resource Management in U.S. Small Businesses: A Replication and Extension. *Journal of Developmental Entrepreneurship*, *8*, 73–92.

Ho, S. M., Ocasio-Valázquez, M., & Booth, C. (2017). Trust or consequences? Causal effects of perceived risk and subjective norms on cloud technology adoption. *Computers & Security*, *70*, 581–595. doi:10.1016/j.cose.2017.08.004

Hudson, A. (2009). Equity and Trusts (6th ed.). Routledge-Cavendish.

Huselid, M. A. (1995). The impact of human resource management practices on turnover, productivity, and corporate financial performance. *Academy of Management Journal*, *38*, 635–672.

Huselid, M. A. (1995). The Impact of Human Resource Management Practices on Turnover, Productivity, and Corporate Financial Performance. *Academy of Management Journal*, *38*, 635–672.

Ibrahim, A. B., Soufani, K., & Lam, J. (2001). A study of succession in a family firm. *Family Business Review*, *14*(3), 245–258. doi:10.1111/j.1741-6248.2001.00245.x

Ibrahim, A. B., Soufani, K., Poutziouris, P., & Lam, J. (2004). Qualities of an effective successor: The role of education and training. *Education + Training*, *46*(8–9), 474–480. doi:10.1108/00400910410569597

Ichniowski, C., & Shaw, K. (1999). The Effects of Human Resource Management Systems on Economic Performance: An International Comparison of U.S. and Japanese Plants. *Management Science*, *45*(5), 704–721.

Ilter, H. M. (2001). Aile Şirketlerinde Kurumsallaşma ve KOBİ'lerin Yönetim Sorunları. İstanbul Ticaret ve Sanayi Odası Yayın No:2001-19, İstanbul.

Intihar, A., & Pollack, J. M. (2012). Exploring small family-owned firms' competitive ability: Differentiation through trust, value -orientation, and market specialization. *Journal of Family Business Management*, *2*(1), 76–86.

Ip, B., & Jacobs, G. (2006). Business succession planning: A review of the evidence. *Journal of Small Business and Enterprise Development*, *13*(3), 326–350. Advance online publication. doi:10.1108/14626000610680235

Irava, W. J., & Moores, K. (2010). Clarifying the strategic advantage of familiness: Unbundling its dimensions and highlighting its paradoxes. *Journal of Family Business Strategy*, *1*(3), 131–144. doi:10.1016/j.jfbs.2010.08.002

Jabbour, C. J. C., & Santos, F. C. A. (2008). The central role of human resource management in the search for sustainable organizations. *International Journal of Human Resource Management*, *19*(12), 2133–2154. doi:10.1080/09585190802479389

Jackson, S. E., & Schuler, R. S. (1995). Understanding Human Resource Management in the Context of Organizations and Their Environments. *Annual Review of Psychology*, *46*(1), 237–264. doi:10.1146/annurev.ps.46.020195.001321 PMID:19245335

Jackson, S. E., Schuler, R. S., & Jiang, K. (2014). An Aspirational Framework for Strategic Human Resource Management. *The Academy of Management Annals*, *8*(1), 1–56. doi:10.5465/19416520.2014.872335

Jacobs, J. V., Hettinger, L., Huang, Y. H., Jeffries, S., Lesch, M. F., Simmons, L. A., Verma, S. K., & Willetts, J. (2019). Employee acceptance of wearable technology in the workplace. *Applied Ergonomics*, *78*, 148–156. doi:10.1016/j.apergo.2019.03.003 PMID:31046946

Jamali, D., El Dirani, A., & Harwood, I. A. (2015). Exploring human resource management roles in corporate social responsibility: The CSR–HRM co-creation model. *Business Ethics (Oxford, England)*, *2*(2), 125–143. doi:10.1111/beer.12085

Jamali, D., Safieddine, A., & Rabbath, M. (2008). Corporate governance and corporate social responsibility: Synergies and inter-relationships. *Corporate Governance*, *16*(5), 443–459. doi:10.1111/j.1467-8683.2008.00702.x

James, A. E., Jennings, J. E., & Breitkreuz, R. S. (2012). Worlds apart? Rebridging the distance between family science and family business research. *Family Business Review*, *25*(1), 87–108. doi:10.1177/0894486511414271

James, H. (1999). Owner as manager, extended horizons and the family firm. *International Journal of the Economics of Business*, *6*(1), 41–56. doi:10.1080/13571519984304

Janjuha-Jivraj, S., & Woods, A. (2002). Successional Issues within Asian Family Firms: Learning from the Kenyan Experience. *International Small Business Journal*, *20*(1), 77–94. doi:10.1177/0266242602201006

Janssens, M., & Steyaert, C. (2009). HRM and performance: A plea for reflexivity in HRM studies. *Journal of Management Studies*, *46*(1), 143–155. doi:10.1111/j.1467-6486.2008.00812.x

Jayakumar, T. (2020). Professionalising Indian Family Firms: An Analysis of the Role of HR—Current Reality and Future Perspectives. *NHRD Network Journal*, 25-37.

Jeżak, J., Popczyk, W., & Winnicka-Popczyk, A. (2004). *Przedsiębiorstwo rodzinne: funkcjonowanie i rozwój*. Difin.

Jiang, D. S., Hayward, S. D., & Morris, M. L. (2017). Raising entrepreneurs: Can parenting style amplify entrepreneurial intentions and behaviours? *International Journal of Management and Enterprise Development*, *16*(1/2), 13–33. doi:10.1504/IJMED.2017.082544

Jiang, K., Lepak, D. P., Han, K., Hong, Y., Kim, A., & Winkler, A. L. (2012). Clarifying the Construct of Human Resource Systems: Relating Human Resource Management to Employee Performance. *Human Resource Management Review*, *22*(2), 73–85. doi:10.1016/j.hrmr.2011.11.005

Johannisson, B., & Huse, M. (2000). Recruiting outside board members in the small family business: An ideological challenge. *Entrepreneurship and Regional Development*, *12*(4), 353–378. doi:10.1080/08985620050177958

Johnson, F. W., Pelayo Maciel, J., & Valenzo Jiménez, M. A. (2019). L'importanza di pianificare la successione nell'azienda di famiglia prima che sia troppo tardi: Un caso di studio di una piccola azienda manifatturiera. *Review of Business & Finance Studies*, *10*(1), 25–32.

Jones, C., Parker, M., & ten Bos, R. (2005). *For Business Ethics. A critical approach*. Routledge.

Julien, P. A. (2018). *The state of the art in small business and entrepreneurship*. Routledge. doi:10.4324/9780429429545

Junaid, M., Mehboob-ur-Rashid, M., & Shaheen, N. (2015). Entrepreneurship as a Socially Constructed Phenomenon: Importance of Alternate Paradigms Research. *Journal of Managerial Sciences*, *9*(1), 35–48.

Kachaner, N., Stalk, G., & Bloch, A. (2012). What You Can Learn from Family Business. *Harvard Business Review*, *90*, 102–106.

Kaczmarska-Krawczak, J. (2012). Specyfika działalności firm rodzinnych. *Przedsiębiorczość i Zarządzanie*, *13*(7), 177–190.

Kahneman, D., & Tversky, A. (1979). Prospect theory an analysis of decisions under risk. *Journal of the Econometric Society*, *47*(2), 263–291. doi:10.2307/1914185

Kail, E. G. (2011). *Leading Effectively in a VUCA Environment: A is for Ambiguity*. Retrieved from https://hbr.org/2011/01/leading-effectively-in-a-vuca-1

Kalm, M., & Gomez-Mejia, L. R. (2016). Socioemotional wealth preservation in family firms. *Revista de Administração*, *51*(4), 409–411. . doi:10.1016/j.rausp.2016.08.002

Kang, S. C., Morris, S. S., & Snell, S. A. (2007). Relational archetypes, organizational learning, and value creation: Extending the human resource architecture. *Academy of Management Review*, *32*(1), 236–256. doi:10.5465/amr.2007.23464060

Karacaoglu, K., & Yoruk, D. (2012). Çalışanların nepotizm ve örgütsel adalet algılamaları: Orta Anadolu bölgesinde bir aile işletmesi uygulaması. *İş-Güç. Endüstri İlişkileri ve İnsan Kaynakları Dergisi, 14*(3), 43–64.

Karami, A., Jones, B. M., & Kakabadse, N. K. (2008). Does strategic human resource management matter in high-tech sector? Some learning points for SME managers. *Corporate Governance International Journal of Business in Society, 8*(1), 7–17.

Karpuzoglu, E. (2002). İşletmenizi sürekli kılmak için: süreklilik planı ve varis planı. *Peryon Dergisi*, 18-19.

Kasper, J. (2014). *Golden Parachutes. Pros, Cons and a Problem-solving Approach.* Műnchen, Deutscheland: GRIN Verlag GmbH.

Kassenberg, A. (2007). Zrównoważony rozwój a koncepcja przestrzennego zagospodarowania kraju. In G. Gorzelak & A. Tucholska (Eds.), *Rozwój, region, przestrzeń* (pp. 53–90). MRR, Euroreg.

Kaufman, B. E. (2015). Evolution of Strategic HRM as Seen Through Two Founding Books: A 30th Anniversary Perspective on Development of the Field. *Human Resource Management, 54*(3), 389–407. doi:10.1002/hrm.21720

Kautonen, T., van Gelderen, M., & Tornikoski, E. T. (2013). Predicting entrepreneurial behavior: A test of the theory of planned behavior. *Applied Economics, 45*(6), 697–707. doi:10.1080/00036846.2011.610750

Kavanagh, M. J., & Johnson, R. D. (2018). A brief history and overview of technology in HR. In M. J. Kavanagh & R. D. Johnson (Eds.), *Human resource information systems: Basics, applications, and future directions* (pp. 2–23). Sage.

Kellermanns, F. W., & Eddleston, K. A. (2004). Feuding families: When conflict does a family firm good. *Entrepreneurship Theory and Practice, 28*(3), 209–228. doi:10.1111/j.1540-6520.2004.00040.x

Kelly, L., Athanassiou, N., & Crittenden, W. F. (2000). Founder Centrality and Strategic Behavior in the Family Owned Firm. *Entrepreneurship Theory and Practice, 25*(2), 27–42. doi:10.1177/104225870002500202

Kennedy, H., & Lakshmi, V. R. (2017). The role of business sustainability in Human Resource Management: A study on Indian manufacturing companies. *The South East Asian Journal of Management, 11*(1), 70–85.

Kerridge, R., & Parry, D. (2009). The Law of Succession (12th ed.). Sweet & Maxwell.

Kesner, I. F., & Sebora, T. C. (1994). Executive Succession: Past, Present & Future. *Journal of Management, 20*(2), 327–372. doi:10.1177/014920639402000204

Kets de Vries, M. F. R. (1996). The anatomy of the entrepreneur: Clinical observations. *Human Relations, 49*(7), 853–883. doi:10.1177/001872679604900701

Kets de Vries, M. F. R., Carlock, R. S., & Florent-Treacy, E. (2007). *Family Business on the Couch: A Psychological Perspective*. John Wiley & Sons.

Khaddage, F., Müller, W., & Flintoff, K. (2016). Advancing mobile learning in formal and informal settings via mobile app technology: Where to from here, and how? *Journal of Educational Technology & Society, 19*(3), 16–26.

Khadelwal, K., & Upadhyay, A. K. (2019). Virtual reality interventions in developing and managing *human resources. Human Resource Development International*, 1–15. doi:10.1080/13678868.2019.1569920

Kidwell, R. E., Eddleston, K. A., Cater, J. J. III, & Kellermanns, F. W. (2013). Harmony, Justice, Confusion, and Conflict in Family Firms: Implications for Ethical Climate and the "Fredo Effect". *Business Horizons, 56*(1), 5–12. doi:10.1016/j.bushor.2012.08.004

Kidwell, R. E., Eddleston, K. A., & Kellermanns, F. W. (2018). Learning bad habits across generations: How negative imprints affect human resource management in the family firm. *Human Resource Management Review*, *28*(1), 5–17. doi:10.1016/j.hrmr.2017.05.002

Kidwell, R. E., & Fish, A. (2007). High-performance human resource practices in Australian family businesses: Preliminary evidence from the wine industry. *The International Entrepreneurship and Management Journal*, *3*(1), 1–14. doi:10.100711365-006-0020-1

Kidwell, R. E., & Fish, A. J. (2007). Article. *The International Entrepreneurship and Management Journal*, *3*(1), 1–14.

Kim, K., Haider, Z. A., Wu, Z., & Dou, J. (2019). Corporate Social Performance of Family Firms: A Place-Based Perspective in the Context of Layoffs. *Journal of Business Ethics*, ahead of print. Doi:10.100710551-019-04152-5

Kim, K., Eltarabishy, A., & Bae, Z. (2018). Humane Entrepreneurship: How Focusing on People Can Drive a New Era of Wealth and Quality Job Creation in a Sustainable World. *Journal of Small Business Management*, *56*(1), 10–29. doi:10.1111/jsbm.12431

Kim, Y., & Gaob, F. Y. (2013). Does family involvement increase business performance? Family-longevity goals' moderating role in Chinese family firms. *Journal of Business Research*, *66*(2), 265–274. doi:10.1016/j.jbusres.2012.08.018

Kim, Y., & Gao, F. Y. (2010). An Empirical Study of Human Resource Management Practices in Family Firms in China. *International Journal of Human Resource Management*, *21*(12), 2095–2119. doi:10.1080/09585192.2010.509619

King, S. W., Solomon, G. T., & Fernald, L. W. Jr. (2001). Issues in growing a family business: A strategic human resource model. *Journal of Small Business Management*, *39*(1), 3–13. doi:10.1111/0447-2778.00002

Klyver, K. (2007). Shifting family involvement during the entrepreneurial process.". *International Journal of Entrepreneurial Behaviour & Research*, *13*(5), 258–277. doi:10.1108/13552550710780867

Kocel, T. (2010). *İşletme Yöneticiliği. 12th baskı*. Beta Yayıncılık.

Koch, T., Gerber, C., & de Klerk, J. J. (2018). The impact of social media on recruitment: Are you LinkedIn? *SA Journal of Human Resource Management*, *16*(1), 1–14. doi:10.4102ajhrm.v16i0.861

Koerner, A. F., & Schrodt, P. (2014). An introduction to the special issue on family communication patterns theory. *Journal of Family Communication*, *14*(1), 1–15. doi:10.1080/15267431.2013.857328

Koh, D. (2017). *The future of VR/AR tech in the public safety domain*. www.opengovasia.com/blogs/5-opengov-expert-opinion/post/7321-the-future-of-vrar-tech-in-the-public-safety-domain

Kontinen, T., & Ojala, A. (2011). *Network ties in the international opportunity recognition of family SMEs. In International Business Review* (Vol. 20). Elsevier.

Koopman, P. L. (1991). Between Control and Commitment: Management and Change as the Art of Balancing. *Leadership and Organization Development Journal*, *12*(5), 3–7. doi:10.1108/01437739110004947

Kopriva, I., & Bernik, M. (2009). Comparison of human resource management in Slovenian family and non-family businesses. *Organizacija*, *42*(6), 246–254. doi:10.2478/v10051-009-0021-2

Korner, A. F., & Fitzpatrick, M. A. (2006). Toward a theory of family communication. *Communication Theory*, *12*(1), 70–91. doi:10.1111/j.1468-2885.2002.tb00260.x

Korn, O., Brenner, F., Börsig, J., Lalli, F., Mattmüller, M., & Müller, A. (2017). Defining recruitment: A model and a survey on the gamification of recruiting and human resources. In L. E. Freund & W. Cellary (Eds.), *Human side of service engineering* (pp. 37–49). Springer.

Korucu, T., & Alkan, A. (2011). Differences between m-learning (mobile learning) and e-learning, basic terminology and usage of m-learning in education. *Social and Behavioral Science*, *15*, 1925–193. doi:10.1016/j.sbspro.2011.04.029

Kotey, B., & Folker, C. (2007). Employee training in SMEs: Effect of size and firm type - Family and nonfamily. *Journal of Small Business Management*, *45*(2), 214–238. doi:10.1111/j.1540-627X.2007.00210.x

Kotey, B., & Sheridan, A. (2004). Changing HRM Practices with Firm Growth. *Journal of Small Business and Enterprise Development*, *11*(4), 474–485. doi:10.1108/14626000410567125

Kotey, B., & Slade, P. (2005). Formal human resource management practices in small, growing firms. *Journal of Small Business Management*, *43*(1), 16–40. doi:10.1111/j.1540-627X.2004.00123.x

Kotlar, J., & De Massis, A. (2013). Goal setting in family firms: Goal diversity, social interactions, and collective commitment to family-centered goals. *Entrepreneurship Theory and Practice*, *37*(6), 1263–1288. doi:10.1111/etap.12065

Kramar, R. (2014). Beyond Strategic Human Resource Management: Is Sustainable Human Resource Management the Next Approach? *International Journal of Human Resource Management*, *25*(8), 1069–1089. doi:10.1080/09585192.2013.816863

Krishnan, G., & Peytcheva, M. (2019). The Risk of Fraud in Family Firms: Assessments of External Auditors. *Journal of Business Ethics*, *157*(1), 261–278. doi:10.100710551-017-3687-z

Krueger, N. F. Jr, Reilly, M. D., & Carsrud, A. (2000). Competing models of entrepreneurial intentions. *Journal of Business Venturing*, *15*(5-6), 411–432. doi:10.1016/S0883-9026(98)00033-0

Kuckertz, A., & Wagner, M. (2010). The influence of sustainability orientation on entrepreneurial intentions—Investigating the role of business experience. *Journal of Business Venturing*, *25*(5), 524–539. doi:10.1016/j.jbusvent.2009.09.001

Kukulu, K., & Öncel, S. (2009). Factors influencing women's decision to have a home birth in rural Turkey. *Midwifery*, *25*(1), 32–38. doi:10.1016/j.midw.2006.12.009 PMID:17368665

Kumar, R. (2017). Cloud technology and human resource management. *Research Journal of SCMS*, *5*, 82–91.

Kuźniarska, A. (2018a). Controlling personalny jako narzędzie wspomagające tworzenie zrównoważonego personelu w organizacji. *Humanizacja Pracy*, *4*(294), 31–45.

Kuźniarska, A. (2018b). Pillars of Creating Sustainable Personnel in an Organization. *Entrepreneurship and Management*, *19*(6), 159–172.

Labelle, R., Hafsi, T., Francoeur, C., & Amar, W. B. (2018). Family Firms' Corporate Social Performance: A Calculated Quest for Socioemotional Wealth. *Journal of Business Ethics*, *148*(3), 511–525. doi:10.100710551-015-2982-9

Labovitz, G.H. (2004). The power of alignment: How the right tools enhance organizational focus. *Business Performance Management*, 30-34.

Lafforet, S. (2016). Effects of organizational culture on organizational innovation performance in family firms. *Journal of Small Business and Enterprise Development*, *23*(2), 379–407. doi:10.1108/JSBED-02-2015-0020

Lambrecht, J. (2005). Multigenerational transition in family businesses: A new explanatory model. *Family Business Review*, *18*(4), 267–282. doi:10.1111/j.1741-6248.2005.00048.x

LambrechtJ. (2005). Multigenerational Transition in Family Businesses: A New Explanatory Model. *Family Business Review*, *18*(4), 267-282. https://ssrn.com/abstract=1501523

Landers, R. N., & Schmidt, G. B. (2016). Social media in employee selection and recruitment: An overview. In R. N. Landers & G. B. Schmidt (Eds.), *Social media employee selection and recruitment* (pp. 3–14). Springer. doi:10.1007/978-3-319-29989-1_1

Langley, A. (1999). Strategies for theorizing from process data. *Academy of Management Review*, *24*(4), 691–710. doi:10.5465/amr.1999.2553248

Langley, A. N. N., Smallman, C., Tsoukas, H., & Van de Ven, A. H. (2013). Process studies of change in organization and management: Unveiling temporality, activity, and flow. *Academy of Management Journal*, *56*(1), 1–13. doi:10.5465/amj.2013.4001

Lansberg, I. S. (1983). Managing Human Resources in Family Firms: The Problem of Institutional Overlap. *Organizational Dynamics*, *12*(1), 39–46. doi:10.1016/0090-2616(83)90025-6

Laplume, A. O., Sonpar, K., & Litz, R. (2008). Stakeholder theory: Reviewing a theory that moves us. *Journal of Management*, *34*(6), 1152–1189. doi:10.1177/0149206308324322

Laspita, S., Breugst, N., Heblich, S., & Patzelt, H. (2012). Intergenerational transmission of entrepreneurial intentions. *Journal of Business Venturing*, *27*(4), 414–435. doi:10.1016/j.jbusvent.2011.11.006

Lawler, E. E., & Mohrman, S. A. (2003). HR, as a strategic partner, what does it take to make it happen. *Human Resource Planning*, *26*, 15–29.

Le Breton-Miller, I., & Miller, D. (2006). Why do some family businesses out-compete? Governance, long-term orientation, and sustainable capability. *Entrepreneurship Theory and Practice*, *30*(6), 731–746. doi:10.1111/j.1540-6520.2006.00147.x

Le Breton-Miller, I., & Miller, D. (2014). Temporal considerations in the study of family firms: Reflections on "the study of organizational behaviour in family business". *European Journal of Work and Organizational Psychology*, *23*(5), 669–673.

Le Breton-Miller, I., Miller, D., & Steier, L. (2004). Toward an Integrative Model of Effective FOB Succession. *Entrepreneurship Theory and Practice*, *28*(4), 305–328. doi:10.1111/j.1540-6520.2004.00047.x

LeBreton-Miller, I., & Miller, D. (2016). Family firms and practices of sustainability: A contingency view. *Journal of Family Business Strategy*, *7*(1), 26–33. doi:10.1016/j.jfbs.2015.09.001

Lee, J., Warkentin, M., Crossler, R., & Ontondo, R. F. (2016). Implications of monitoring mechanisms of bring your own device adoption. *Journal of Computer Information Systems*, *57*(4), 309–318. doi:10.1080/08874417.2016.1184032

Lee, S. H. (2008). A theoretical framework on the role of HRM practices in Family business succession. In *Theoretical Developments and Future Research in Family Business* (pp. 261–286). Information Age Publishing.

Lemańska-Majdzik, A., & Sipa, M. (2015). *Selected Aspects of Family Company Management in Employees View in Poland, Aktualne problemy podnikovej sfery 2015. Zbornik vedeckych prac.* Vydavatel'stvo EKONOM.

Lengnick-Hall, M. L., & Lengnick-Hall, C. A. (1999). Expanding customer orientation in the HR function. *Human Resource Management Journal*, *38*(3), 201–214. doi:10.1002/(SICI)1099-050X(199923)38:3<201::AID-HRM3>3.0.CO;2-B

Lengnick-Hall, M. L., & Lengnick-Hall, C. A. (2003). *Human resource management in the knowledge economy: New challenges, new roles, new capabilities.* Berrett- Koehler.

Leonardi, P., & Contractor, N. (2018). Analytics: Better people analytics. *Harvard Business Review.* https://empowerment.ee/wp-content/uploads/2018/11/Better-People-Analytics-Measure-Who-They-Know-Not-Just-Who-They-Are.pdf

Leon-Guerrero, A. Y., McCann, J. E. III, & Haley, J. D. Jr. (1998). A study of practice utilization in family businesses. *Family Business Review*, *11*(2), 107–120. doi:10.1111/j.1741-6248.1998.00107.x

Lepak, D. P., Liao, H., Chung, Y., & Harden, E. E. (2006). A Conceptual Review Of Human Resource Management Systems In Strategic Human Resource Management Research. *Research in Personnel and Human Resources Management, 25*, 217–271. doi:10.1016/S0742-7301(06)25006-0

Lepak, D. P., & Shaw, J. D. (2008). Strategic HRM in North America: Looking to the Future. *International Journal of Human Resource Management, 19*(8), 1486–1499. doi:10.1080/09585190802200272

Lepak, D. P., & Snell, S. A. (1999). The Human Resource Architecture: Toward a Theory of Human Capital Allocation and Development. *Academy of Management Review, 24*(1), 31–48. doi:10.5465/amr.1999.1580439

Lepak, D., & Gowan, M. (2019). *Human resources management*. Pearson Prentice Hall.

Lester, R. H., & Cannella, A. A. (2006). Interorganizational familiness: How family firms use interlocking directorates to build community-level social capital. *Entrepreneurship Theory and Practice, 30*(6), 755–775. doi:10.1111/j.1540-6520.2006.00149.x

Levin, I. M. (2000). Vision revisited. *The Journal of Applied Behavioral Science, 36*(1), 91–107. doi:10.1177/0021886300361005

Lewis, P. W. (1985). Defining 'business ethics': Like nailing jello to a wall. *Journal of Business Ethics, 4*(5), 377–383. doi:10.1007/BF02388590

Li, J. (2016). Technology advancement and the future of HRD research. *Human Resource Development Journal, 19*(3), 189–191. doi:10.1080/13678868.2016.1181846

Limani, A., Tomovska-Misoska, A., & Bojadjiev, M. (2015). Organizational alignment as a model of sustainable development in the public sector in the Republic of Macedonia. *Journal of Sustainable Development, 5*(12), 51–68.

Linan, F., Rodríguez-Cohard, J. C., & Guzman, J. (2011). Temporal stability of entrepreneurial intentions: A longitudinal study. Entrepreneurial Research in Europe: Evolving Concepts and Processes, 34-55.

Liñán, F., & Chen, Y. (2009). Development and cross cultural application of a specific instrument to measure entrepreneurial intentions. *Entrepreneurship Theory and Practice, 33*(3), 593–617. doi:10.1111/j.1540-6520.2009.00318.x

Lindner, P., Miloff, A., Fagernas, S., Anderson, J., Sigeman, M., Andersson, G., Furmark, T., & Carlbring, P. (2019). Therapist-led and self-led one session virtual reality exposure therapy for public speaking anxiety with consumer hardware and software: A randomized controlled trail. *Journal of Anxiety Disorders, 61*, 45–54. doi:10.1016/j.janxdis.2018.07.003 PMID:30054173

Lin, N., Vaughn, J. C., & Ensel, W. M. (1981). Social resources and occupational status attainment'. *Social Forces, 59*(4), 1163–1181. doi:10.2307/2577987

Litz, R. A. (2010). Jamming across the generations: Creative intergenerational collaboration in the Marsalis family. *Journal of Family Business Strategy, 1*(4), 185–199. doi:10.1016/j.jfbs.2010.10.002

Litz, R. A., & Turner, N. (2013). Sins of the Father's Firm: Exploring Responses to Inherited Ethical Dilemmas in Family Business. *Journal of Business Ethics, 113*(2), 297–315. doi:10.100710551-012-1305-7

Ljunggren, E. (2011). *Entrepreneurship research in Europe: Evolving concepts and processes*. Edward Elgar.

Loan Clarke, J., Boocock, G., Smith, A., & Whittaker, J. (1999). Investment in management training and development by small businesses. *Employee Relations, 21*(3), 296–311. doi:10.1108/01425459910273134

Loewen, J. (2008). *Money Magnet: Attract Investors to Your Business*. John Wiley & Sons.

Longenecker, J. G., Moore, C. W., Petty, J. W., & Palich, L. E. (2006). Small Business Management: An Entrepeneurial Emphasis (13th ed.). Academic Press.

Long, R. G., & Mathews, K. M. (2011). Ethics in the Family Firm: Cohesion through Reciprocity and Exchange. *Business Ethics Quarterly*, *21*(2), 287–308. doi:10.5840/beq201121217

López-Cózar, C., Priede, T., & Hilliard, I. (2014). Family and Non-Family Business Differences in Corporate Social Responsibility Approaches. *Asean Journal of Management & Innovation*, *1*(2), 74–85.

López-Fernández, M. C., Serrano-Bedia, A. M., & Pérez-Pérez, M. (2015). Entrepreneurship and family firm research: A bibliometric analysis of an emerging field. *Journal of Small Business Management*, *54*(2), 622–639. doi:10.1111/jsbm.12161

López-Pérez, M. E., Melero-Polo, I., Vázquez-Carrasco, R., & Cambra-Fierro, J. (2018). Sustainability and Business Outcomes in the Context of SMEs: Comparing Family Firms vs. Non-Family Firms. *Sustainability*, *10*(11), 4080. doi:10.3390u10114080

Lovas, B., & Ghoshal, S. (2000). Strategy as guided evolution. *Strategic Management Journal*, *21*(9), 875–896. doi:10.1002/1097-0266(200009)21:9<875::AID-SMJ126>3.0.CO;2-P

Lubatkin, M. H., Durand, R., & Ling, Y. (2007). The missing lens in family firm governance theory: A self-other typology of parental altruism. *Journal of Business Research*, *60*(10), 1022–1029. doi:10.1016/j.jbusres.2006.12.019

Lune, H., & Berg, B. L. (2017). *Methods for the Social Sciences* (Global Edition).

Lyman, A. R. (1991). Customer service: Does family ownership make a difference? *Family Business Review*, *4*(3), 303–324. doi:10.1111/j.1741-6248.1991.00303.x

MacDuffie, J. P. (1995). Human Resource Bundles and Manufacturing Performance: Organizational Logic and Flexible Production Systems in the World Auto Industry. *Industrial & Labor Relations Review*, *48*(2), 197–221. doi:10.1177/001979399504800201

Maclagan, P. (1998). *Management and Morality: A Developmental Perspective*. Sage Publication.

Madison, K., Daspit, J. J., Turner, K., & Kellermanns, F. W. (2018). Family firm human resource practices: Investigating the effects of professionalization and bifurcation bias on performance. *Journal of Business Research*, *84*(3), 327–336. doi:10.1016/j.jbusres.2017.06.021

Maditheti, N. N. (2017). A comprehensive literature review of the digital HR research field. *Information and Knowledge Management*, *7*(4), 15–20.

Mandip, G. (2012). Green HRM: People Management Commitment to Environmental Sustainability. *Research Journal of Recent Sciences*, *1*, 244–252.

Mandl, I. (2008). *Overview of Family Business Relevant Issues*. Austrian Institute for SME Research.

Mangundjaya, W. (2012). Challenges in Developing Young Entrepreneurs (A Study at Unemployed Youth in Jakarta). *Conference Proceedings of International Conference on Entrepreneurship Forum (IEF)*.

Marchington, M., Cooke, F. L., & Hebson, G. (2010). Human resource management across organizational boundaries. In The SAGE Handbook of Human Resource Management (pp. 460-474). SAGE Publication. doi:10.4135/9780857021496.n27

Marchington, M., Grimshaw, D., Rubery, J., & Willmott, H. (Eds.). (2005). *Fragmenting Work: Blurring Organisational Boundaries and Disordering Hierarchies*. Oxford University Press.

Marchington, M., Wilkinson, A., Donnelly, P., & Kynighou, A. (2016). *Human Resource Management at Work* (6th ed.). Chartered Institute of Personnel and Development.

Mariappanadar, S. (2020). Characteristics of Sustainable HRM System and Practices for Implementing Corporate Sustainability. In *Sustainable Human Resource Management* (pp. 9–35). Springer Singapore., doi:10.1007/978-981-15-5656-2_2

Marler, J. H., & Boudreau, J. W. (2017). An evidence-based review of HR analytics. *International Journal of Human Resource Management*, *28*(1), 3–26. doi:10.1080/09585192.2016.1244699

Marler, J. H., & Fisher, S. L. (2017). *Making HR technology decisions: A strategic perspective*. Business Expert Press.

Martin, H. F. (2001). Is Family Governance an Oxymoron? *Family Business Review*, *14*(2), 91–96. doi:10.1111/j.1741-6248.2001.00091.x

Masters, R. D. (1983). The biological nature of the state. *World Politics*, *35*(2), 161–193. doi:10.2307/2010269

Matass, E., & Vosniakos, G. C. (2017). Design of a virtual reality training System for human-robot collaboration in manufacturing tasks. *International Journal of Interactive Design and Manufacturing*, *11*(2), 139–153. doi:10.100712008-015-0259-2

Mathew, T. P., & Kannan, R. (2019). Effect of Human Resource Management Practice on Jov Performance of Employees in Luxury Hotels in Cochin. *Global Journal for Research Analysis*, *8*(3), 16–19.

Mathis, R. L., Jackson, J. H., & Valentine, S. R. (2014). *Human Resource Management* (14th ed.). Cengage Learning.

Matlay, H. (2002). Training and HRD strategies in Family and Non- Family Owned Small Businesses: A Comparative Approach. *Education + Training*, *44*(8/9), 357–369. doi:10.1108/00400910210449196

Mayan, M. J. (2016). *Essentials of qualitative inquiry*. Routledge. doi:10.4324/9781315429250

Mayer, R. C., Davis, J. H., & Schoorman, F. D. (1995). An integrative model of organizational trust. *Academy of Management Review*, *20*(3), 709–734. doi:10.5465/amr.1995.9508080335

Mazur–Wierzbicka, E. (2016). Odpowiedzialność wobec środowiska naturalnego w biznesie rodzinnym. *Przedsiębiorczość i Zarzadzanie*, *17*(6), 229–238.

Mboko, S. (2011). Towards and explanation of the growth in young entrepreneurship activities: A cross country survey of work values of college students. *Journal of Marketing Development and Competitiveness*, *5*, 108–118.

McAfee, R. B., Glassman, M., & Honeycutt, E. D. Jr. (2002). The effects of culture and human resource management policies on supply chain management strategy. *Journal of Business Logistics*, *23*(1), 1–18. doi:10.1002/j.2158-1592.2002.tb00013.x

McCathy, I., Plangger, K., Robson, K., Kietzmann, J., & Pitt, L. (2019). Dynamic game plans: Using gamification to entrain strategic renewal with environmental velocity. In A. Tunchdogan, A. Lindgreen, van den Bocsh, & Volberda, H. (Eds), Handbook of strategic renewal (pp. 391-405). Elsevier.

McConaughy, D. L., Matthews, C. H., & Fialko, A. S. (2001). Founding family-controlled firms: Efficiency, risk, and value. *Journal of Small Business Management*, *39*(1), 31–49. doi:10.1111/0447-2778.00004

McKinsey & Company. (2017). *Smartening up with artificial intelligence*. https://www.mckinsey.com/industries/semiconductors/ourinsights/smartening-up-with-artificial-intelligence

Melanthiou, Y., Pavlou, F., & Constantinou, E. (2015). The use of social network sites as an e-recruitment tool. *Journal of Transnational Management*, *20*(1), 31–49. doi:10.1080/15475778.2015.998141

Memili, E., Chang, E. P., Kellermanns, F. W., & Welsh, D. H. (2015). Role conflicts of family members in family firms. *European Journal of Work and Organizational Psychology*, *24*(1), 143–151. doi:10.1080/1359432X.2013.839549

Memili, E., Chrisman, J. J., Chua, J. A., Chang, E. P., & Kellermanns, K. W. (2011). The determinants of family firms' subcontracting: A transaction cost perspective. *Journal of Family Business Strategy*, *2*(1), 26–33. doi:10.1016/j.jfbs.2011.01.003

Men, L. R. (2017). Strategic Internal Communication: Transformational Leadership, Communication Channels, and Employee Satisfaction. *Management Communication Quarterly*, *28*(2), 264–284. doi:10.1177/0893318914524536

Merino, F., Monreal-Pérez, J., & Sánchez-Marín, G. (2015). 'Family SMEs' Internationalization: Disentangling the Influence of Familiness on Spanish Firms' Export Activity', Journal of Small Business Management. *Blackwell Publishing Ltd*, *53*(4), 1164–1184. doi:10.1111/jsbm.12111

Meroño-Cerdán, A. L., López-Nicolás, C., & Molina-Castillo, F. J. (2018). Risk aversion, innovation and performance in family firms. *Economics of Innovation and New Technology*, *27*(2), 189–203. doi:10.1080/10438599.2017.1325569

Merron, K. A. (1994). Creating TQM organizations. *Quality Progress*, *27*(1), 51–54.

Metzger, E. C., Lubin, L., Patten, R. T., & Whyte, J. (2016). Applied gamification: Creating reward systems for organizational professional development. In D. Ifenthaler, N. Bellin-Mularski, & D. K. Mah (Eds.), *Foundation of digital badges and micro-credentials*. Springer. doi:10.1007/978-3-319-15425-1_25

Michiels, A., Voordeckers, W., Lybaert, N., & Steijvers, T. (2013). CEO compensation in private family firms: Pay-for-performance and the moderating role of ownership and management. *Family Business Review*, *26*(2), 140–160. doi:10.1177/0894486512454731

Mikušová, M., Friedrich, V., & Horváthová, P. (2020). Who is More Sustainable? Family Business or Non-Family Business? Czech Evidence. *Sustainability*, *12*(14), 5540. doi:10.3390u12145540

Millar, C. C. J. M., Groth, O., & Mahon, J. F. (2018). Management Innovation in a VUCA World: Challenges and Recommendations. *California Management Review*, *61*(1), 5–14. doi:10.1177/0008125618805111

Miller, D., & Le Breton-Miller, I. (2003). Challenge versus advantage in the family business. *Strategic Organization*, *1*(1), 127–134. doi:10.1177/1476127003001001222

Miller, D., & Le Breton-Miller, I. (2005). *Managing for the long run: Lessons in competitive advantage from great family businesses*. Harvard Business Press.

Miller, D., & Le Breton-Miller, I. (2016). *Managing for the Long Run: Lessons in Competitive Advantage from Great Family Businesses*. Harvard Business School Press.

Miller, D., Minichilly, A., & Corbetta, G. (2013). Is Family Leadership always benefitial? *Strategic Management Journal*, *34*(5), 553–571. doi:10.1002mj.2024

Milman, D. (2018). *The Company Share: Legal Regulation and Public Policy*. Edward Elgar Pub.

Miniaoui, Z. (2020). The impact of country-level institutional differences on corporate social responsibility disclosure engagement. *Corporate Social Responsibility and Environmental Management*, *26*(6), 1307-1320.

Mintzberg, H. (2013). Simply Managing: What Managers Do – and Can Do Better. Oakland, CA: Berrett-KIoehler.

Miotti, L., & Sachwald, F. (2003). Cooperative R&D: Why and with whom? An integrated framework of analysis. *Research Policy*, *32*, 1481–1499. doi:10.1016/S0048-7333(02)00159-2

Mishra, R. K., & Sarkar, S. (2020). Sustainable HRM Practices - A Drive Towards Sustainability (The case of NLCIL). In Sustainable Human Resource Management. Singapore: Springer Singapore. doi:10.1007/978-981-15-5656-2_11

Mohan, R. (2019). The chatbot revolution and the Indian HR professional. *International Journal of Information and Computing Science*, *6*(3), 489–499.

Mokhber, M., Gi, T. G., Rasid, S. Z. A., Vakilbashi, A., Zamil, N. M., & Seng, Y. W. (2017). Succession planning and family business performance in SMEs. *Journal of Management Development*, *36*(3), 330–347. doi:10.1108/JMD-12-2015-0171

Montanari, S. (2003). *Le aziende familiari. Continuità e successione* (Vol. 1). Cedam.

Morgeson, F. P., Aguinis, H., Waldman, D. A., & Siegel, D. S. (2013). Extending corporate social responsibility research to the human resource management and organizational behavior domains: A look to the future. *Personnel Psychology*, *66*(4), 805–824. doi:10.1111/peps.12055

Morris, M., & Revels, M. A. (2012). Technology impacts in organizational recruitment and retention. *Franklin Business & Law Journal*, *1*, 61–69.

Moshavi, D., & Koch, M. J. (2005). The adoption of family-friendly practices in family-owned firms: Paragon or paradox? *Community Work & Family*, *8*(3), 237–249.

Mozaffari, F. A. (2008). A study of relationship between organizational culture and leadership. *International Conference on Applied Economics*, 679-688. Retrieved from: https://faculty.mu.edu.sa/public/uploads/1360858719.3627organizational%20cult180.pdf

Muir, W. H., Bíziková, L., Brandão De Oliveira, A., & Fernández Arroyo, D. P. (2019). *Global Private International Law: Adjudication Without Frontiers*. Edward Elgar Pub.

Mulder, B. K. (2008). *Risking the business or reaping the benefits: the antecedents and consequences of nepotism*. Ph. D. DePaul University.

Mullane, J. V. (2014). Reinvigorating the mission statement through top management commitment. *Management Decision*, *52*(3), 446–459. doi:10.1108/MD-10-2012-0736

Mungai, E., & Velamuri, S. R. (2011). Parental entrepreneurial role model influence on male offspring: Is it always positive and when does it occur? *Entrepreneurship Theory and Practice*, *35*(2), 337–357. doi:10.1111/j.1540-6520.2009.00363.x

Muñoz-Bullon, F., Maria, J., Sanchez-Bueno, M. J., & Suárez-González, I. (2018). Diversification decisions among family firms: The role of family involvement and generational stage. *Business Research Quarterly*, *2018*(21), 39–52. doi:10.1016/j.brq.2017.11.001

Murray, B. (2003). The succession transition process: A longitudinal perspective. *Family Business Review*, *16*(1), 17–33. doi:10.1111/j.1741-6248.2003.00017.x

Muskin, J. B. (2000). Interorganizational Ethics: Standards of Behavior. *Journal of Business Ethics*, *24*(4), 283–297. doi:10.1023/A:1006008506543

Mussolino, D., & Calabrò, A. (2014). Paternalistic leadership in family firms: Types and implications for intergenerational succession? *Journal of Family Business Strategy*, *5*(2), 197–210. doi:10.1016/j.jfbs.2013.09.003

Mustafa, M. J., Caspersz, D., Ramos, H. M. L., & Siew, C. M. M. (2018). The Satisfaction of Non-Family Employees with High Involvement HR Practices: Evidence from Family SMEs. *Human Resource Development International*, *21*(3), 163–185. doi:10.1080/13678868.2017.1410005

Mustafa, M. J., & Elliott, C. (2019). The curious case of human resource development in family-small-to-medium sized enterprises. *Human Resource Development Quarterly, 30*(3), 281–290. doi:10.1002/hrdq.21370

Nakayama, M., Chen, C., & Taylor, C. W. (2017). The effects of perceived functionality and usability on privacy and security concerns about cloud application adoptions. *Journal of Information Systems Applied Research, 10*(2), 4–11.

Nascimento, B., Oliveira, T., & Tam, C. (2018). Wearable technology: What explains continuance intention in smartwatches? *Journal of Retailing and Consumer Services, 43*, 157–169. doi:10.1016/j.jretconser.2018.03.017

National Guardianship Association. (2016). *The Fundamentals of Guardianship: What Every Guardian Should Know*. American Bar Association Pub.

Naumovski, S., Bojadjiev, M., Tomovska-Misoska, A., & Stefanovska-Petkovska, M. (2017). Organizational alignment in the food industry: Case study of a company in the Republic of Macedonia. *Economic Development, 18*(3), 267–280.

Navarro, M. S., & Ansón, S. G. (2009). Do families shape corporate governance structures? *Journal of Management & Organization, 15*(3), 327–345. doi:10.5172/jmo.2009.15.3.327

Navimipour, N. J., Rahmani, A. M., Navin, A. H., & Hosseinzadeh, M. (2015). Expert cloud: A cloud-based framework to share the knowledge and skills of human resources. *Computers in Human Behavior, 46*, 57–74. doi:10.1016/j.chb.2015.01.001

Nawaz, N., & Gomes, A. M. (2019). Artificial intelligence chatbots are new recruiters. *International Journal of Advanced Computer Science and Applications, 10*(9), 1–5. doi:10.14569/IJACSA.2019.0100901

Nayak, B., Bhattacharyya, S. S., & Krishnamoorthy, B. (2019). Integrating wearable technology products and big data analytics in business strategy: A study of health insurance firms. *Journal of Systems and Information Technology, 21*(2), 255–275. doi:10.1108/JSIT-08-2018-0109

Neckebrouck, J., Schulze, W., & Zellweger, T. (2018). Are Family Firms Good Employers? *Academy of Management Journal, 61*(2), 553–585. doi:10.5465/amj.2016.0765

Neubauer, F., & Lank, A. G. (1998). *The family business— Its governance for sustainability*. Routledge.

Neubaum, D. O. (2018). Family business research: Roads traveled and the search for unworn paths. *Family Business Review, 31*(3), 259–270. doi:10.1177/0894486518792948

Ngai, E. W., Moon, K. K., Lam, S. S., Chin, E. S., & Tao, S. S. (2015). Social media models, technologies, and applications: An academic review and case study. *Industrial Management & Data Systems, 115*(5), 769–802. doi:10.1108/IMDS-03-2015-0075

Nguyen, B., & Mutum, D. S. (2012). A review of customer relationship management: Successes, advances, pitfalls, and futures. *Business Process Management Journal, 18*(3), 400–419. doi:10.1108/14637151211232614

Nguyen, T. V., & Bryant, S. E. (2004). A Study of the Formality of Human Resource Management Practices in Small and Medium-Size Enterprises in Vietnam. *International Small Business Journal, 22*(6), 595–618. doi:10.1177/0266242604047412

Nicholson, L. A., & Lashley, J. (2016). *Understanding the Caribbean Enterprise Insights from MSMEs and Family-Owned Businesses*. Palgrave Macmillan. doi:10.1057/978-1-349-94879-6

Nordqvist, M., Habbershon, T. G., & Melin, L. (2008). Transgenerational entrepreneurship: Exploring entrepreneurial orientation in family firms. *Frontiers in European Entrepreneurship Research*, 93-116.

Nordqvist, M., & Melin, L. (2002). The dynamics of family firms, an institutional perspective on corporate governance and strategic change. Routledge.

Nordqvist, M., & Melin, L. (2010). Entrepreneurial families and family firms. *Entrepreneurship and Regional Development, 22*(3-4), 211–239. doi:10.1080/08985621003726119

Nordqvist, M., Wennberg, K., Bau, M., & Hellerstedt, K. (2013). An entrepreneurial process perspective on succession in family firms. *Small Business Economics, 40*(4), 1087–1122. doi:10.100711187-012-9466-4

Norlin, L-M. (2020). *The Courage to Lead through Values: How Management by Values Supports Transformational Leadership, Culture and Success*. London: Routledge.

Nowinski, W., & Haddoud, M. Y. (2019). The role of inspiring role models in enhancing entrepreneurial intention. *Journal of Business Research, 96*, 183–193. doi:10.1016/j.jbusres.2018.11.005

O'Boyle, E. H. Jr, Rutherford, M. W., & Pollack, J. M. (2010). Examining the Relation Between Ethical Focus and Financial Performance in Family Firms: An Exploratory Study. *Family Business Review, 23*(4), 310–326. doi:10.1177/0894486510375412

Oczkowska, R. (2014). *Rozwój zasobów ludzkich organizacji*. Difin.

Odun-Ayo, I., Misra, S., Omoregbe, N., Onibere, E., Bulama, Y., & Damasevicius, R. (2017). Cloud-based security driven human resource management system. In J. Mizera-Pietraszko, R. Rodriguez, & A. Pérez (Eds.), *Advances in digital technology* (pp. 96–106). IOS Press.

Oliveira, N., & Lumineau, F. (2019). The Dark Side of Interorganizational Relationships: An Integrative Review and Research Agenda. *Journal of Management, 45*(1), 231–261. doi:10.1177/0149206318804027

Oliveira, T., Thomas, M., & Espadanal, M. (2014). Assessing the determinants of cloud computing adoption: An analysis of the manufacturing and service sectors. *Information & Management, 51*(5), 497–510. doi:10.1016/j.im.2014.03.006

Oluwafunmilayo, A. M., Olokundun, M. A., Moses, C. L., & Grace, A. C. (2018). The Role of Prior Family Business Background on Entrepreneurial Intentions. *Covenant Journal of Entrepreneurship, 2*(1), 1–14.

Ören, K. (2007). Sosyal sermayede güven unsuru ve işgücü performansına etkisi. *Kamu-İş, 9*(1), 71–90.

Orth, U. R., & Green, M. T. (2009). Consumer loyalty to family versus non-family business: The roles of store image, trust, and satisfaction. *Journal of Retailing and Consumer Services, 16*(4), 248–259. doi:10.1016/j.jretconser.2008.12.002

Osterwalder, A., & Pigneur, Y. (2010). *Business Model Generation, A Handbook for Visionaries, Game Changers, and Challengers*. John Wiley & Sons, Inc.

Othman, A. (2009). Strategic integration of human resource management practices: Perspectives of two major Japanese electrical and electronics companies in Malaysia. *Cross Cultural Management, 16*(2), 197–214.

Özcan, G. B. (1995). *Small firms and local economic development: entrepreneurship in Southern Europe and Turkey*. Avebury.

Ozkanan, A., & Erdem, R. (2014). Yönetimde kayırmacı uygulamalar: Kavramsal bir çerçeve. *Süleyman Demirel Üniversitesi Sosyal Bilimler Enstitüsü Dergisi, 20*, 179–206.

Ozler, H., Ozler, D. E., & Gumustekin, G. E. (2007). Aile işletmelerinde nepotizmin gelişim evreleri ve kurumsallaşma. *Selçuk Üniversitesi Sosyal Bililer Enstitüsü Dergisi, 17*, 437–450.

Ozuren, Ü. (2017). *Tekstil işletmelerinde nepotizm uygulamalarına bağlı olarak üretkenlik karşıtı davranışlar ve sonuçları*. İstanbul Kültür Üniversitesi, Sosyal Bilimler Enstitüsü, Yüksek Lisans Tezi.

Pabian, A. (2011). Sustainable personnel – pracownicy przedsiębiorstwa przyszłości. *Zarządzanie Zasobami Ludzkimi, 5*, 9–27.

Pabian, A. (2015). Zrównoważone zarządzania zasobami ludzkimi – zarys problematyki. *Zeszyty Naukowe Politechniki Częstochowskiej, 17*, 7–16.

Pabian, A. (2016). Pozyskiwanie pracowników w koncepcji zrównoważonego zarządzania zasobami ludzkimi. *Marketing i Rynek*, (3), 671–680.

Pabian, A. (2017). Planowanie strategiczne z perspektywy sustainability. *Handel Wewnętrzny, 3*(368), 341–350.

Palanski, M., Newman, A., Leroy, H., Moore, C., Hannah, S., & Den Hartog, D. (2019). Quantitative Research on Leadership and Business Ethics: Examining the State of the Field and an Agenda for Future Research. *Journal of Business Ethics*, ahead of print. doi:10.100710551-019-04267-9

Palumbo, R. (2016). Challenging Servant Leadership In The Nonprofit Sector: The Side Effects Of Servant Leadership. *Journal of Nonprofit Education and Leadership, 6*(2), 81–98. doi:10.18666/JNEL-2016-V6-I2-6824

Palumbo, R., & Manna, R. (2019). Una ricetta per rendere un'organizzazione. *Impresa progetto – Electronic Journal of Management, 2019*(2), 1–22.

Panayides, P. M., & So, M. (2005). Logistics service providers-client relationships, relationships. *Transportation Research Part E, Logistics and Transportation Review, 41*(3), 79–200. doi:10.1016/j.tre.2004.05.001

Panayotopoulou, L., Bourantas, D., & Papalexandris, N. (2003). Strategic human resource management and its effects on firm performance: An implementation of the competing values framework. *International Journal of Human Resource Management, 14*(4), 680–699.

Panico, P. (2017). International Trust Laws (2nd ed.). Oxford University Press.

Pan, Y., Weng, R., Xu, N., & Chan, K. C. (2018). The role of corporate philanthropy in family firm succession: A social outreach perspective. *Journal of Banking & Finance, 88*, 423–441. doi:10.1016/j.jbankfin.2018.01.011

Parente, R., Eltarabishy, A., Vesci, M., & Botti, A. (2018). The Epistemology of Humane Entrepreneurship: Theory and Proposal for Future Research Agenda. *Journal of Small Business Management, 56*(1), 30–52. doi:10.1111/jsbm.12432

Parkes, C., & Borland, H. (2012). Strategic HRM: Transforming Its Responsibilities Toward Ecological Sustainability-The Greatest Global Challenge Facing Organizations. *Thunderbird International Business Review, 54*(6), 811–824. doi:10.1002/tie.21505

Parry, E., & Tyson, S. (2013). *Managing people in a contemporary context*. Routledge. doi:10.4324/9781315885872

Patanakul, P., & Shenhar, A. J. (2012). What Project Strategy Really Is: The Fundamental Building Block in Strategic Project Management. *Project Management Journal, 43*(1), 4–20. doi:10.1002/pmj.20282

Payne, G. T., Brigham, K. H., Broberg, J. C., Moss, T. W., & Short, J. C. (2011). Organizational Virtue Orientation and Family Firms. *Business Ethics Quarterly, 21*(2), 257–285. doi:10.5840/beq201121216

Pellegrini, C., Rizzi, F., & Frey, M. (2018). The role of sustainable human resource practices in influencing employee behavior for corporate sustainability. *Business Strategy and the Environment, 27*(8), 1221–1232. doi:10.1002/bse.2064

Pellegrini, M., & Flamini, G. (2019). *Gestione delle risorse umane nelle imprese familiari: Analisi della letteratura attraverso il text mining*. Prospettive in Organizzazione.

Pennings, F., & Bosse, C. (2011). *Extension Protection By Labour Law: Comparative Study*. Kluwer Law International.

Perrini, F., & Minoja, M. (2008). Strategizing corporate social responsibility: Evidence from an Italian medium-sized, family-owned company. *Business Ethics (Oxford, England)*, *17*(1), 47–63. doi:10.1111/j.1467-8608.2008.00519.x

Perry, J., Ring, J. K., Matherne, C. F., & Markova, G. (2013). Ethical Human Resource Practices from the Perspective of Family Ownership. *Academy of Management Proceedings, 2013*(1). . doi:10.5465/ambpp.2013.172

Peters, T. & Waterman R.H. Jr (1982). *En busca de la excelencia*. Madrid: Harper bolsillo.

Petruškevičius, D. (2016). A consideration of sustainable HR management implementation in a SME context: The T optimus case. *Humanities and Social Sciences:Latvia*, *24*(2), 84–109.

Pfeffer, J. (1994). *Competitive advantage through people*. Harvard Business School. doi:10.2307/41165742

Phikiso, Z., & Tengeh, R. (2017). Challenges to intra-family succession in South African townships. *Academy of Entrepreneurship Journal*.

Pieper, T. M. (2019). Editor's note. *Journal of Family Business Strategy*, *10*(1), 1–2. doi:10.1016/j.jfbs.2019.04.001

Pirro D. (2016). La morte del socio e la clausola di continuazione automatica. *Rivista del diritto commerciale e del diritto generale delle obbligazioni, 2016*(2), 303-331.

Pittino, D., & Visintin, F. (2011). The propensity toward inter-organizational cooperation in small- and medium-sized family businesses. *Journal of Family Business Strategy*, *2*(2), 57–68. doi:10.1016/j.jfbs.2011.03.005

Pittino, D., Visintin, F., & Lauto, G. (2017). A configurational analysis of the antecedents of entrepreneurial orientation. *European Management Journal*, *35*(2), 224–237.

Pittino, D., Visintin, F., & Lauto, G. (2018). Fly Away From the Nest? A Configurational Analysis of Family Embeddedness and Individual Attributes in the Entrepreneurial Entry Decision by Next-Generation Members. *Family Business Journal*, *31*(3), 271–294.

Pittino, D., Visintin, F., Lenger, T., & Sternad, D. (2016). Are high performance work practices really necessary in family SMEs? An analysis of the impact on employee retention. *Journal of Family Business Strategy*, *7*(2), 75–89. doi:10.1016/j.jfbs.2016.04.002

Pocztowski, A. (2016). Zrównoważone zarządzania zasobami ludzkimi w teorii i praktyce. *Journal of Management and Finance*, *14*(2), 303–314.

Porfírio, J. A., Carrilho, T., & Mónico, L. (2016). Entrepreneurship in different contexts in cultural and creative industries. *Journal of Business Research*, *69*(11), 5117–5123. doi:10.1016/j.jbusres.2016.04.090

Porfírio, J. A., Felício, J. A., & Carrilho, T. (2020, July). Family business succession: Analysis of the drivers of success based on entrepreneurship theory. *Journal of Business Research*, *115*, 250–257. doi:10.1016/j.jbusres.2019.11.054

Posso, M.L. (2003). *A expansão das empresas familiares através de alianças est*. Academic Press.

Pounder, P. (2015). Family business insights: An overview of the literature. *Journal of Family Business Management.*, *5*(1), 116–127. doi:10.1108/JFBM-10-2014-0023

Poutziouris, P., & Chittenden, F. (1996). Family businesses or business families? Leeds: Institute for Small Business Affairs.

Powell, T. C. (1992). Organizational alignment as competitive advantage. *Strategic Management Journal*, *13*(2), 119–134. doi:10.1002mj.4250130204

Poza, E. J. (2013). *Family Business*. South-Western Cengage Learning.

Poza, E. J., Alfred, T., & Maheshwari, A. (1997). Stakeholder perceptions of culture and management practices in family and family firms - A preliminary report. *Family Business Review*, *10*(2), 135–155. doi:10.1111/j.1741-6248.1997.00135.x

Priest, H. (2019). *BIASES and HEURISTICS: The Complete Collection of Cognitive Biases and Heuristics That Impair Decisions in Banking, Finance and Everything Else*. Cognitt Consulting.

Pyromalis, V. D., & Vozikis, G. S. (2009). Mapping the successful succession process in family firms: Evidence from Greece. *The International Entrepreneurship and Management Journal*, *5*(4), 439–460. doi:10.100711365-009-0118-3

Ramírez-Solís, E., & Baños-Monroy, V. I. (2019). Dangerous Liaisons? Ethical Challenges on Entrepreneurship in Family Business. In S. R. Nair & J. M. Saiz-Álvarez (Eds.), *Handbook of Research on Ethics, Entrepreneurship, and Governance in Higher Education* (pp. 263–282). IGI Global. doi:10.4018/978-1-5225-5837-8.ch012

Randall, D. M., & Gibson, A. M. (1990). Methodology in business ethics research: A review and critical assessment. *Journal of Business Ethics*, *9*(6), 457–471. doi:10.1007/BF00382838

Rauch, A., & Hatak, I. (2016). A Meta- Analysis of Different HR- Enhancing Practices and Performance of Small and Medium Sized Firms. *Journal of Business Venturing*, *31*(5), 485–504. doi:10.1016/j.jbusvent.2016.05.005

Razaq, R., Beck, V., & Soliman, A. (2017). Utilization of Value-based Management in the Strategic Management of German Automotive Industry. *Global Business Review*, *20*(4), 871–886.

Reece Thomas, K., & Ryan, C. (2014). The Law and Practice of Shareholders' Agreements (4th ed.). Lexis Nexis UK.

Reid, R. S., & Adams, J. S. (2001). Human resource management-a survey of practices within family and non-family firms. *Journal of European Industrial Training*, *25*(6), 310–320. doi:10.1108/03090590110401782

Reid, R. S., & Harris, R. I. (2002). The determinants of training in SMEs in Northern Ireland. *Education + Training*, *44*(8/9), 443–450. doi:10.1108/00400910210449286

Reid, R., Morrow, T., Kelly, B., & McCartan, P. (2002). People Management in SMEs: An Analysis of Human Resource Strategies in Family and Non-Family Businesses. *Journal of Small Business and Enterprise Development*, *9*(3), 245–259. doi:10.1108/14626000210438571

Renwick, D. W. S., Redman, T., & Maguire, S. (2013). Green Human Resource Management: A Review and Research Agenda. *International Journal of Management Reviews*, *15*(1), 1–14. doi:10.1111/j.1468-2370.2011.00328.x

Report of the World Commission on Environment and Development. (1987). *Our Common Future*. Retrieved from http://www.un-documents.net/ocf-02.htm#I

Report, F., & the European Commission. DG Employment. (2011). *Studies on sustainability issues — Green jobs; trade and labour*, Cambridge Econometrics. Retrieved from https://www.google.com/url?sa=t&rct=j&q=&esrc=s&source=web&cd=1&ved=2ahU

Report, F., & the European Commission. DG Employment. (2012). *The jobs potential of a shift towards a low carbon economy; OECD Employment Outlook 2012*. Retrieved from https://www.oecd.org/els/emp/50503551.pdf

Research, I. F. F. (2015). *Fairness, Dignity and Respect in Small- and Medium-Sized Enterprise Workplaces*. UK Data Archive.

Richards, M., & Schembera, S. (2019). Managing Legitimacy Through Conventionality Rather Than Alignment: Anti-Corruption at Family Versus Non-Family Firms. ahead of print. doi:10.2139srn.3484973

Richmond, B. (1997). The Strategic Forum: Aligning objectives, strategy and process. *System Dynamics Review*, *13*(2), 131–148. doi:10.1002/(SICI)1099-1727(199722)13:2<131::AID-SDR121>3.0.CO;2-J

Risca, F. A. (2018). The Role of Family Business and Education in Forming Actual Entrepreneurs. *The 2018 International Conference of Organizational Innovation. KnE Social Sciences*, 329–340. 10.18502/kss.v3i10.3384

Roessl, D. (2005). Family businesses and interfirm cooperation. *Family Business Review*, *18*(3), 203–214. doi:10.1111/j.1741-6248.2005.00042.x

Rondi, E., De Massis, A., & Kotlar, J. (2019). Unlocking innovation potential: A typology of family business innovation postures and the critical role of the family system. *Journal of Family Business Strategy*, *10*(4), 100236. Advance online publication. doi:10.1016/j.jfbs.2017.12.001

Rothenberg, S., Hull, C. E., & Tang, Z. (2017). The Impact of Human Resource Management on Corporate Social Performance Strengths and Concerns. *Business & Society*, *56*(3), 391–418. doi:10.1177/0007650315586594

Roth, P. L., Bobko, P., Van Iddekinge, C. H., & Thatcher, J. B. (2013). Social media in employee-selection-related decisions: A research agenda for uncharted territory. *Journal of Management*, *42*(1), 269–298. doi:10.1177/0149206313503018

Rothwell, W. (2010). *Effective succession planning: Ensuring leadership continuity and building talent from within*. Amacom.

Rothwell, W. J., & Kazanas, H. C. (2003). *The strategic development of talent*. Human Resource Development.

Rubery, J., Carroll, M., Cooke, F. L., Grugulis, I., & Earnshaw, J. (2004). Human resource management and the permeable organization: The case of the multi-client call-centre. *Journal of Management Studies*, *41*(7), 22–2380. doi:10.1111/j.1467-6486.2004.00472.x

Rubery, J., Cooke, F. L., Earnshaw, J., & Marchington, M. (2003). Inter-Organizational Relations and Employment in a Multi-employer Environment. *British Journal of Industrial Relations*, *41*(2), 265–289. doi:10.1111/1467-8543.00272

Rueter, M. A., & Koerner, A. F. (2008). The effect of family communication patterns on adopted adolescent adjustment. *Journal of Marriage and the Family*, *70*(3), 715–727. doi:10.1111/j.1741-3737.2008.00516.x PMID:19649145

Ruggeri, L., Kunda, I., & Winkler, S. (Eds.). (2019). Family Property and Succession in EU Member States National Reports on the Collected Data. Rijeka, Croatia: Sveučilište u Rijeci, Pravni fakultet/University of Rijeka, Faculty of Law.

Ruiz, C. (2016). Responsabilidad empresarial y Recursos Humanos: gestión responsable de las personas. In C. Ruiz & F. Álvarez (Eds.), *Empresa Familiar Responsable*. Huygens.

Ruiz, C., & Parra, C. (Eds.). (2013). *New Forms of Organisation in Knowledge-Based Societies*. Routledge. doi:10.4324/9780203082874

Ruiz-Viñals, C., & Álvarez-Gómez, F. (2018, August). Ownership and the Desire for Continuity Over Time, the Principal "Drivers" of the Family Business Culture en China-USA. *Business Review*, *17*(8), 419–437.

Rus, S., & Trevinyo-Rodríguez, R. N. (2011). *Redefiniendo la empresa familiar. In Empresa familiar: aspectos jurídicos y económicos*. Centro Libros PAPF.

Rusydan, W. M., Ibrahim, W., & Hassan, R. (2019). Recruitment trends in the era of industry 4.0 using artificial intelligence: Pro and cons. *Asian Journal of Research in Business and Management*, *1*(1), 16–21.

Sadler-Smith, E., Gardiner, P., Badger, B., Chaston, I., & Stubberfield, J. (2000). Using Collaborative Learning to Develop Small Firms. *Human Resource Development International*, *3*(3), 285–306. doi:10.1080/13678860050128483

Sadler-Smith, E., & Lean, J. (2004). The Practice of HRD in Smaller Firms. In J. Stewart & G. Beaver (Eds.), *HRD in Small Organizations. Research and Practice* (pp. 124–148). Routlege.

Sadun, R., Bloom, N., & Van Reenen, J. (2017). Why Do We Undervalue Competent Management? *Harvard Business Review*.

Safin, K. (2007). *Przedsiębiorstwa rodzinne, istota i zachowania strategiczne*. Wydawnictwo Akademii Ekonomicznej.

Sagır, M. Ö., & Akıllı, H. S. (2004). Etnisite kuramları ve eleştirisi. *C.Ü. Sosyal Bilimler Dergisi. Mayıs*, *28*(1), 1–22.

Sahinidis, A., Stavroulakis, D., Kossieri, E., & Varelas, S. (2019). Entrepreneurial intention determinants among female students. The influence of role models, parents' occupation and perceived behavioral control on forming the desire to become a business owner. In Strategic Innovative Marketing and Tourism. Springer Proceedings in Business and Economics. Springer. DOI.1007/978-3-030-12453-3_20.

Salvato, C. (2004). Predictors of entrepreneurship in family firms. *Journal of Private Equity*, *7*(3), 68–76. doi:10.3905/jpe.2004.412339

Samara, G., & Arenas, D. (2017). Practicing fairness in the family business workplace. *Business Horizons*, *60*(5), 647–655. doi:10.1016/j.bushor.2017.05.008

Samara, G., & Paul, K. (2019). Justice versus fairness in the family business workplace: A socioemotional wealth approach. *Business Ethics (Oxford, England)*, *28*(2), 175–184. doi:10.1111/beer.12209

Sambrook, S. (2005). Exploring succession planning in small, growing firms. *Journal of Small Business and Enterprise Development*, *12*(4), 579–594. doi:10.1108/14626000510628243

Samnani, A. K., & Singh, P. (2013). Exploring the Fit Perspective: An Ethnographic Approach. *Human Resource Management*, *52*(1), 123–144. doi:10.1002/hrm.21516

Sánchez Marín, G., Carrasco Hernández, A. J., Danvila del Valle, I., & Sastre Castillo, M. Á. (2016). 'Organizational culture and family business: A configurational approach', European Journal of Family Business. *Malaga University*, *6*(2), 99–107. doi:10.1016/j.ejfb.2017.05.002

Sanchez-Bueno, M. J., Muñoz-Bullón, F., & Galan, J. I. (2020). Socially responsible downsizing: Comparing family and non-family firms. *Business Ethics (Oxford, England)*, *29*(1), 35–55. doi:10.1111/beer.12244

Sánchez-Marín, G., Meroño-Cerdán, Á. L., & Carrasco-Hernández, A. J. (2019). Formalized HR practices and firm performance: An empirical comparison of family and non-family firms. *International Journal of Human Resource Management*, *30*(7), 1084–1110. doi:10.1080/09585192.2017.1289547

Santarelli, E., & Lotti, F. (2005). The survival of family firms: The importance of control and family ties. *International Journal of the Economics of Business*, *12*(2), 183–192. doi:10.1080/13571510500127246

Santoro, G., Messeni-Petruzzelli, A., & Del Giudice, M. (2020). Searching for resilience: the impact of employee-level and entrepreneur-level resilience on firm performance in small family firms. *Small Business Economics*, ahead of print. . doi:10.100711187-020-00319-x

Sardeshmukh, S. R., & Corbett, A. C. (2011). The duality of internal and external development of successors: Opportunity recognition in family firms. *Family Business Review*, *24*(2), 111–125. doi:10.1177/0894486510391783

Saunders, M. N. K., & Bezzina, F. (2015). Reflections on Conceptions of Research Methodology Among Management Academics. *European Management Journal*, *33*(5), 297–304. doi:10.1016/j.emj.2015.06.002

Savlovschi, L.I., & Robu, N.R. (2011). The Role of SMEs in Modern Economy. *Economia Seria Management, 14*(1).

Savolainen, S., & Kansikas, J. (2013). Non-family employees in small family business succession: The case of psychological ownership. *World Review of Entrepreneurship, Management and Sustainable Development*, *1*(9), 64–81. doi:10.1504/WREMSD.2013.050936

Scarfo, A. (2012). New security perspectives around BYOD. *Seventh International Conference on Broadband, Wireless Computing, Communication and Applications*.

Schein, E. (1999). *The Corporate Culture: Survival Guide*. Jossey Bass Publishers.

Schein, E. H. (1992). *Organizational culture and leadership* (2nd ed.). Jossey-Bass.

Scherer, R. F., Adams, J. S., Carley, S. F., & Wiebe, F. A. (1989). Role model performance effects on the development of entrepreneurial career preferences. *Entrepreneurship Theory and Practice*, *13*(3), 53–71. doi:10.1177/104225878901300306

Schmid, A., & Sender, A. (2019). How social capital influences performance in family firms: The moderating role of nepotism. *International Journal of Human Resource Management*, 1–21. doi:10.1080/09585192.2019.1674355

Schomaker, M. S., & Zaheer, S. (2014). The role of language in knowledge transfer to geographically dispersed manufacturing operations. *Journal of International Management*, *20*(1), 55–72. doi:10.1016/j.intman.2013.10.004

Schröder, E., Schmitt-Rodermund, E., & Arnaud, N. (2011). Career choice intentions of adolescents with a family business background. *Family Business Review*, *24*(4), 305–321. doi:10.1177/0894486511416977

Schuler, R. S., & MacMillan, I. C. (1984). Gaining competitive advantage through human resource management practices. *Human Resource Management*, *23*(3), 241–255. doi:10.1002/hrm.3930230304

Schuler, R., & Jackson, S. (2014). Human resource management and organizational effectiveness: Yesterday and today. *Journal of Organizational Effectiveness: People and Performance*, *1*(1), 35–55. doi:10.1108/JOEPP-01-2014-0003

Schulze, W. S., Lubatkin, M. H., & Dino, R. N. (2003). Toward a Theory of Altruism in Family Firms. *Journal of Business Venturing*, *18*(4), 473–490. doi:10.1016/S0883-9026(03)00054-5

Schuman, A. M., Sage-Hayward, W., & Ransburg, D. (2016). *Human resources in the family business: maximizing the power of your people*. Palgrave Macmillan.

Schumann, P. L. (2001). A moral principles framework for human resource management ethics. *Human Resource Management Review*, *11*(1/2), 93–111. doi:10.1016/S1053-4822(00)00042-5

Scott, R. (2019). Explaining how group model building supports enduring agreement. *Journal of Management & Organization*, *25*(6), 783–806. doi:10.1017/jmo.2017.12

Seidman, I. (2006). *Interviewing as Qualitative Research: A Guide for Researchers in Education and the Social Sciences* (3rd ed.). Tearchers College Press.

Sels, L., Winne, S., Delmotte, J., Maes, J., Faems, D., & Forrier, A. (2006). Linking HRM and Small Business Performance: An Examination of the Impact of HRM Intensity on the Productivity and Financial Performance of Small Businesses. *Small Business Economics*, *26*(1), 83–101. doi:10.100711187-004-6488-6

Semler, S. W. (1997). Systematic agreement: A theory of organizational alignment. *Human Resource Development Quarterly*, *8*(1), 23–40. doi:10.1002/hrdq.3920080105

Serrat, O. (2017). *Tools, methods, and approaches to drive organizational performance*. Springer.

Shaozhuang, M., Silva, M. G., Callan, V. J., & Trigo, V. (2016). Control and Commitment HR Practices, Job Satisfaction and Turnover Intentions: A Comparison Between Local and Multinational Firms in China. *International Journal of Human Resource Management*, *27*(9), 974–990. doi:10.1080/09585192.2015.1052535

Shapero, A., & Sokol, L. (1982). The social dimensions of entrepreneurship. In C. A. Kent, D. L. Sexton, & K. E. Vesper (Eds.), *The encyclopedia of entrepreneurship*. Prentice-Hall.

Sharma, P. (1997). *Determinants of the satisfaction of the primary stakeholders with the succession process in family firms* (Unpublished doctoral thesis). University of Calgary, Canada.

Sharma, E. (2012). HR issues and intervention model for family business. *International Journal of Business Economics & Management Research*, *2*(12), 288–297.

Sharma, P. (2004). An Overview of the Field of Family Business Studies: Current Status and Directions for the Future. *Family Business Review*, *17*(1), 1–34. doi:10.1111/j.1741-6248.2004.00001.x

Sharma, P., Chrisman, J. J., & Chua, J. (2003a). Predictors of Satisfaction with the Succession Process in Family Firms. *Journal of Business Venturing*, *18*(5), 667–687. doi:10.1016/S0883-9026(03)00015-6

Sharma, P., Chrisman, J. J., & Chua, J. (2003b). Succession Planning as Planned Behavior: Some Empirical Results. *Family Business Review*, *16*(1), 1–16. doi:10.1111/j.1741-6248.2003.00001.x

Sharma, P., Chrisman, J. J., & Chua, J. H. (1997). Strategic management of the family business: Past research and future challenges. *Family Business Review*, *10*(1), 1–35. doi:10.1111/j.1741-6248.1997.00001.x

Sharma, P., Chrisman, J. J., Pablo, A. L., & Chua, J. H. (2001). Determinants of initial satisfaction with the succession process in family firms: A conceptual model. *Entrepreneurship Theory and Practice*, *25*(3), 17–36. doi:10.1177/104225870102500302

Sharma, P., Chrisman, J., & Chua, J. (2000). Perceptions About the Extent of Succession Planning in Canadian Family Firms. *Canadian Journal of Administrative Sciences*, *17*(3), 233–244. doi:10.1111/j.1936-4490.2000.tb00223.x

Sharma, P., Chrisman, J., & Chua, J. (2003). Predictors of satisfaction with the succession process in family firms. *Journal of Business Venturing*, *18*(5), 667–687.

Sharma, P., & Sharma, S. (2011). Drivers of Proactive Environmental Strategy in Family Firms. *Business Ethics Quarterly*, *21*(2), 309–334. doi:10.5840/beq201121218

Sherman, W., & Craig, A. (2019). *Understanding virtual reality: Interface, application, and design*. Morgan Kaufman Publishers.

Shneor, R., Jenssen, J. I., & Vissak, T. (2016). Introduction to the special issue: Current challenges and future prospects of entrepreneurship in Nordic and Baltic Europe. *Baltic Journal of Management*, *11*(2), 134–141. doi:10.1108/BJM-01-2016-0013

Shuck, S., Kearney, M., & Burden, K. (2017). Exploring mobile learning in the third space. *Technology, Pedagogy and Education*, *26*(2), 121–137. doi:10.1080/1475939X.2016.1230555

Sieger, P., Fueglistaller, U., & Zellweger, T. (2011). Entrepreneurial Intentions and Activities of Students across the World. International Report of the GUESSS Project 2011. St. Gallen: Swiss Research Institute of Small Business and Entrepreneurship at the University of St.Gallen (KMU-HSG).

Sieger, P., Fueglistaller, U., Zellweger, T., & Braun, I. (2019). *Global Student Entrepreneurship 2018: Insights From 54 Countries*. KMU-HSG/IMU.

Sieger, P., Zellweger, T., Nason, R. S., & Clinton, E. (2011). Portfolio entrepreneurship in family firms: A resource-based perspective. *Strategic Entrepreneurship Journal*, *5*(4), 327–351. doi:10.1002ej.120

Siems, M., & Cabrelli, D. (2018). Comparative Company Law: A Case-Based Approach (2nd ed.). Hart Publishing.

Singh, R. (2016). Kavil Ramachandran, The 10 Commandments for Family Business. Sage Publications.

Singh, T., & Singh, S. (2014). Entrepreneurial intentions among university students in Manipur. *International Journal of Management and Social Science Research Review*, *1*(7), 55–64.

Singh, T., & Srivastav, S. K. (2012). QWL and Organization efficiency: A proposed framework. *Journal of Strategic Human Resource Management*, *1*(1), 1–13.

Sirmon, D. G., & Hitt, M. A. (2003). Managing Resources: Linking Unique Resources, Management, and Wealth Creation in Family Firms. *Entrepreneurship Theory and Practice*, *27*(4), 339–358. doi:10.1111/1540-8520.t01-1-00013

Sitkoff, R. H., & Dukeminier, J. (2017). Wills Trusts & Estates (10th ed.). Aspen Publishers.

Siu, W., & Lo, E. S. (2011). Cultural contingency in the cognitive model of entrepreneurial intention. *Entrepreneurship Theory and Practice*, *37*(2), 147–173. doi:10.1111/j.1540-6520.2011.00462.x

Sloof, R. & Von Siemens. (2019). Effective leadership and the allocation and exercise of power in organizations. *The Leadership Quarterl, 29*. Available at doi:10.1016/j.leaqua.2018.12.001

Snell, S. A., Shadur, M. A., & Wright, P. M. (2000). *Human resources strategy: The era of our ways* (CAHRS Working Paper #00-17). Ithaca, NY: Cornell University, School of Industrial and Labor Relations, Center for Advanced Human Resource Studies.

Solesvik, M., Westhead, P., Kolvereid, L., & Matlay, H. (2012). Student intentions to become self-employed: The Ukrainian context. *Journal of Small Business and Enterprise Development*, *19*(3), 441–460. doi:10.1108/14626001211250153

Sonfield, M. C., & Lussier, R. N. (2004). First-, second-, and third-generation family firms: A comparison. *Family Business Review*, *17*(3), 189–201. doi:10.1111/j.1741-6248.2004.00013.x

Songini, L., & Gnan, L. (2014). The glass ceiling in SMEs and its impact on firm managerialisation: A comparison between family and non-family SMEs. *International Journal of Business Governance and Ethics*, *9*(2), 170–196. doi:10.1504/IJBGE.2014.063278

Sorasalmi, T., & Tuovinen, J. (2016). Entering emerging markets: A dynamic frame-work dynamics in logistics. 675–683. Berlin: Springer

Sorasalmi, T., & Tuovinen, J. (2016). *Entering emerging markets: A dynamic framework dynamics in logistics*. Springer.

Sorenson, R. L. (2011). *Family business and social capital*. Edward Elgar Publishing. doi:10.4337/9781849807388

Stalk, G. Jr, & Foley, H. (2012, January-February). Avoiding Traps That Can Destroy Family Businesses. *Harvard Business Review*, •••, 25–27.

Stamm, I., & Lubinski, C. (2011). Crossroads of family business research and firm demography - A critical assessment of family business survival rates. *Journal of Family Business Strategy*, *2*(3), 117–127. doi:10.1016/j.jfbs.2011.07.002

Stankeviciute, Z., & Savaneviciene, A. (2013). Sustainability as a concept for human resource management. *Economics and Management*, *18*(4), 837-846. doi:10.5755/j01.em.18.4.5631

Stankevičiūtė, Ž., & Savanevičienė, A. (2018). Designing Sustainable HRM: The Core Characteristics of Emerging Field. *Sustainability*, *10*(12), 4798. doi:10.3390u10124798

Statistica. (2019). *Number of social network users worldwide from 2010 to 2021*. https://www.statista.com/statistics/278414/number-of-worldwide-social-network-users/

Stavrou, E. (1995). The next generation's dilemma: To join or not to join the family business. *Family Firm Institute Conference Proceedings*.

Stavrou, E. (1999). Succession in family businesses: Exploring the effects of demographic factors on offspring intentions to join and take over the business. *Journal of Small Business Management*, *37*(3), 43–62.

Steier, L. (2001). Family firms, plural forms of governance and the evolving role of trust. *Family Business Review*, *14*(4), 353–367. doi:10.1111/j.1741-6248.2001.00353.x

Steier, L. (2001). Next-generation entrepreneurs and succession: An exploratory study of modes and means of managing social capital. *Family Business Review*, *14*(3), 259–276. doi:10.1111/j.1741-6248.2001.00259.x

Steijvers, T., Lybaert, N., & Dekker, J. (2017). Formal human resource practices in family firms. *Journal of Family Business Management*, *7*(2), 151–165. doi:10.1108/JFBM-07-2016-0016

Steijvers, T., & Niskanen, M. (2013). The determinants of cash holdings in private family firms. *Accounting and Finance*, *53*(2), 537–560. doi:10.1111/j.1467-629X.2012.00467.x

Sterk, S. E., & Melanie, B.L. (2019). Estates and Trusts, Cases and Materials (6th ed.). Foundation Press.

Sternberg, E. (2000). *Just Business: Business Ethics in Action*. Oxford University Press.

Stevenson, H. H. (1983). A perspective on entrepreneurship. *Harvard Business School Working Paper*, *9*, 384-131.

Stewart, A., & Hitt, M. (2012). Why can't a family business be more like a non-family business: Modes of professionalization in family firms. *Family Business Review*, *25*(1), 58–86.

Stewart, A., & Hitt, M. A. (2012). Why Can't a Family Business Be More Like a Nonfamily Business? *Family Business Review*, *25*(1), 58–86. doi:10.1177/0894486511421665

Stewart, G. L., & Brown, K. G. (2020). *Human resource management*. Wiley.

Stone, D. L., Deadrick, D. L., Lukaszewski, K. M., & Johnson, R. (2015). The influence on technology on the future of human resource management. *Human Resource Management Review*, *25*(2), 216–231. doi:10.1016/j.hrmr.2015.01.002

Storey, D. J., Saridakis, G., Sen-Gupta, S., Edwards, P. K., & Blackburn, R. A. (2010). Linking HR Formality with Employee Job Quality: The Role of Firm and Workplace Size. *Human Resource Management*, *49*(2), 305–329. doi:10.1002/hrm.20347

Stor, M. (2010). Międzynarodowe zarządzanie kadrami. In T. Listwan (Ed.), *Zarządzanie kadrami*. C.H. Beck.

Stradomski, M. (2010). *Finansowanie obce firm rodzinnych na rynku niedoskonałym*. PWE.

Strohmeier, S., & Piazza, F. (2015). Artificial intelligence techniques in human resources management: A conceptual exploration. In C. Kahraman & O. S. Çevik (Eds.), *Intelligent techniques in engineering management: Intelligent systems reference library* (pp. 149–172). Springer. doi:10.1007/978-3-319-17906-3_7

Suh, A., Cheung, C. M., Ahuja, M., & Wagner, C. (2017). Gamification in the workplace: The central role of the aesthetic experience. *Journal of Management Information Systems*, *34*(1), 268–305. doi:10.1080/07421222.2017.1297642

Sułkowski, Ł. (2003). Bariery rozwoju przedsiębiorstw rodzinnych. In H. Bieniok (Ed.), *Przedsiębiorczość, konkurencyjność oraz kondycja małych i średnich przedsiębiorstw w obliczu integracji z Unią Europejską* (pp. 444–445). Wydawnictwo Akademii Ekonomicznej.

Sułkowski, Ł., & Marjański, A. (2009). *Firmy rodzinne. Jak osiągnąć sukces w sztafecie*. Poltext.

Sund, L. G., Melin, L., & Haag, K. (2015). Intergenerational ownership succession. Shifting the focus from outcome measurement to preparatory requirements. *Journal of Family Business Strategy*, *6*(3), 166–177. doi:10.1016/j.jfbs.2015.07.001

Suyono, A. A., Radianto, D. O., & Elisabeth, D. R. (2019). Antecedents of job satisfaction of production employees: Leadership, compensation and organizational culture. *International Journal of Entrepreneurship and Business Development*, *3*(1), 96–110. doi:10.29138/ijebd.v3i1.955

Su, Z. X., & Wright, P. M. (2012). The Effective Human Resource Management System in Transitional China: A Hybrid of Commitment and Control Practices. *International Journal of Human Resource Management*, *23*(10), 2065–2086. doi:10.1080/09585192.2011.610335

Sweeney, E. (2013). The people dimension in logistics and supply chain management – its role and importance. In R. Passaro & A. Thomas (Eds.), *Supply Chain Management: Perspectives, Issues, and Cases* (pp. 73–82). McGraw-Hill.

Swinth, R., & Vinton, K. (1993). Do family-owned businesses have a strategic advantage in international joint ventures? *Family Business Review*, *6*(1), 19–30. doi:10.1111/j.1741-6248.1993.00019.x

Symeonides, S. (2008). *American Private International Law*. Kluwer Law International.

Szyperski, N., & Nathusius, K. (1999). *Probleme der Unternehmensgründung: Eine betriebswirtschaftliche Analyse unternehmerischer Startbedingungen*. Josef Eul Verlag.

Tabor, W., Chrisman, J. J., Madison, K., & Vardaman, J. M. (2018). Nonfamily members in family firms: A review and future research agenda. *Family Business Review*, *31*(1), 54–79. doi:10.1177/0894486517734683

Tabor, W., Madison, K., Daspit, J. J., & Holt, D. T. (2019). The Heterogeneity of Family Firm Ethical Cultures: Current Insights and Future Directions. In *The Palgrave Handbook of Heterogeneity among Family Firms* (pp. 615–642). Palgrave MacMillan. doi:10.1007/978-3-319-77676-7_23

Tagiuri, R., & Davis, J. (2016). „Bivalent Attributes of Family Firms". *Family Business Review*, *9*(2), 199–208. doi:10.1111/j.1741-6248.1996.00199.x

Taperesu, B. A., & Van Belle, J. P. (2017). Organisational capabilities required for embracing Employee mobility through bring-your-own-device concept. *Business Systems Research*, *8*(1), 17–29. doi:10.1515/bsrj-2017-0002

Tapies, J. (2018). *Empresa Familiar: 30 años de preguntas con respuesta*. Editorial Cátedra de Empresa Familiar.

Tàpies, J., & Ward, J. L. (Eds.). (2008). *Family Values and Value Creation: The Fostering of Enduring Values Within Family-Owned Businesses*. Palgrave Macmillan. doi:10.1057/9780230594227

Taylor, F. W. T. (1997). *Principles of Scientific Management*. Dover Publications Inc.

Taylor, S., Osland, J., & Egri, C. P. (2012). Guest Editors' Introduction: Introduction to HRM's Role in Sustainability: Systems, Strategies, and Practices. *Human Resource Management*, *51*(6), 789–798. doi:10.1002/hrm.21509

Thach, L., & Kidwell, R. E. (2009). HR practices in United States and Australian family wineries: Cultural contrasts and performance impact. *The International Entrepreneurship and Management Journal*, *5*(2), 219–240. doi:10.100711365-008-0099-7

Thom, N., & Zaugg, R. (2004). Das prinzip nachhaltigkeit im personal management. *Personal Führung*, *7*, 52–55.

Thompson, E. R. (2009). Individual entrepreneurial intent: Construct clarification and development of an internationally reliable metric. *Entrepreneurship Theory and Practice*, *33*(3), 669–694. doi:10.1111/j.1540-6520.2009.00321.x

Tipu, S. A. A. (2018). *What have we learned? Themes from the literature on organizational culture in family firms. European Business Review*. doi:10.1108/EBR-02-2017-0042

Tkachev, A., & Kolvereid, L. (1999). Self-employment intentions among Russian students. *Entrepreneurship and Regional Development, 11*(3), 269–280. doi:10.1080/089856299283209

Tokarczyk, J., Hansen, E., Green, M., & Down, J. (2007). A resource-based view and market orientation theory examination of the role of "familiness" in family business success. *Family Business Review, 20*(1), 17–31. doi:10.1111/j.1741-6248.2007.00081.x

Tommaselli, S. (1996). *Longevità e sviluppo delle imprese familiari: problemi, strategie e strutture di governo*. Giuffrè.

Tomovska-Misoska, A., Bojadizev, M., Stefanoska, M., & Nikolovska, Z. (2011). *Vox-Organizationis – theoretical basis and methodological considerations in the development of an instrument for organizational culture*. MPRA Paper No. 42571. http://mpra.ub.uni-muenchen.de/42571/

Torres, I. B., Riba, A., & Freeman, J. (2015). Influence of personal values and the adoption of analytical tools using laddering methodology. *International Journal of Information Management, 5*(1), 37–56.

Tosti, D. T. (2007). Aligning the culture and strategy for success. *Performance Improvement, 46*(1), 21–25. doi:10.1002/pfi.035

Towards a sustainable Europe by 2030, COM. (2019). Retrieved from https://ec.europa.eu/commission/sites/beta-political/files/rp_sustainable_europe_30-01_en_web.pdf

Transfer of Businesses. (2003). Transfer of bsuiensses- continuity through a new beginning. Final report of the MAP 2002 project, European Commission, 23(9).

Transfer of SMEs. (2002). Final report of the expert group on the transfer of SMEs. European Commission, 23(9).

Traxler, J. (2009). Defining, discussing, and evaluating mobile learning: The moving finger writes and having writ…. *The International Review in Open and Distance Learning, 8*, 1–13.

Trojanowski, T. (2017). Innovations in Human Resource Management through the Creation of Sustainable Staff Members. *Handel Wewnętrzny, 1*(366), 119–128.

Tufts, S. H., Jacobson, W. S., & Stevens, M. S. (2014). Status update: Social media and local government human resource practices. *Review of Public Personnel Administration, 35*(2), 193–207. doi:10.1177/0734371X14558066

Turner, V., Gantz, J. F., Reinsel, D., & Minton, S. (2014). The digital universe of opportunities: Rich data and the increasing value of the internet of things. *IDC Corporate*. http://www.idcdocserv.com/expired.asp?1678

Turner, D. W. (2010). Qualitative Interview Design: A Practical Guide for Novice Investigators. *Qualitative Report, 15*(3), 754–760.

Turner, R., & Zolin, R. (2012). Forecasting success on large projects: Developing reliable scales to predict multiple perspectives by multiple stakeholders over multiple time frames. *Project Management Journal, 45*(5), 87–99. doi:10.1002/pmj.21289

Turulja, L., & Bajgorić, N. (2016). Human resources or information technology: What is more important for companies in the digital era? *The Journal of Society for Advancing Innovation and Research in Economy, 7*(1), 35–45. doi:10.1515/bsrj-2016-0003

Tushman, M. (1977). Special Boundary Roles in the Innovation Process. *Administrative Science Quarterly, 22*(4), 587–605. doi:10.2307/2392402

Tutelman, C. J., & Hause, L. D. (2008). *The Balance Point: New Ways Business Owners Can Use Boards*. Famille Press.

U.S. Bureau of Labor Statistics. (2019). *Current employment statistics highlights*. https://www.bls.gov/web/empsit/ceshighlights.pdf

Uhlaner, L. M., Goor-Balk, H. J. M. V., & Masurel, E. (2004). Family business and corporate social responsibility in a sample of Dutch firms. *Journal of Small Business and Enterprise Development*, *11*(2), 186–194. doi:10.1108/14626000410537128

Uhlaner, L. M., Kellermanns, F. W., Eddleston, K. A., & Hoy, F. (2012). The entrepreneuring family: A new paradigm for family business research. *Small Business Economics*, *38*(1), 1–11. doi:10.100711187-010-9263-x

Ulrich, D. (1998). Os campeões de recursos humanos (7th ed.). São Paulo: Futura.

Ulrich, D., & Beatty, D. (2001). From partners to players: Extending the HR playing field. *Human Resource Management, 40*(4), 293-307.

Ulrich, D. (1991). Using human resources for competitive advantage. In R. Kilmann, I. Kilmann, & ... (Eds.), *Making Organizations Competitive*. Jossey-Bass.

Ulrich, D., & Lake, D. G. (1990). *Organizational capability: Competing from the inside out*. John Wiley & Sons.

Umans, I., Lybaert, N., Steijvers, T., & Voordeckers, W. (2019, January). The influence of transgenerational succession intentions on the succession planning process: The moderating role of high-quality relationships. *Journal of Family Business Strategy.*, 100269. doi:10.1016/j.jfbs.2018.12.002

United Nations. (2002). *World Summit on Sustainable Development*. Retrieved from https://www.un.org/ga/search/view_doc.asp?symbol=A/CONF.199/20&Lang=E

United Nations. (2005). *Principles of Responsible Investment (PRI- 2005)*. Author.

Urban, S., Bobek, S., & Tomin, P. (2017). TAM based research of CRM analytical tools acceptance. *SIES Journal of Management*, *17*(13), 3–17.

Urlich, D., & Lake, D. (1990). *Organizational Capability*. John Wiley & Sons.

Vallejo, M. C. (2008). Is the Culture of Family Firms Really Different? A Value-based Model for Its Survival through Generations. *Journal of Business Ethics*, *81*(2), 261–279. doi:10.100710551-007-9493-2

Vallejo-Martos, M. C., Antequera-Solis, J. M., & Ruiz-Jiménez, M. C. (2013). *Are Family Firms More Harmonious Organisations? An Analysis of the Effects of Organisational Harmony on Their Performance*. International Conference on Business Strategy and Organizational Behaviour (BizStrategy), Global Science and Technology Forum, Singapore.

Vallone, C. (2009). *Il passaggio generazionale nel family business ei fattori strategici di successo per continuità aziendale. Analisi comparata tra Italia e Gran Bretagna*. Giuffrè Editore.

Vázquez, A. (2001). *Retando al Futuro*. Editorial Díaz de Santos.

Vazquez, P. (2018). Family Business Ethics: At the Crossroads of Business Ethics and Family Business. *Journal of Business Ethics*, *150*(3), 691–709. doi:10.100710551-016-3171-1

Veciana, J. M., Aponte, M., & Urbano, D. (2005). University students' attitudes towards entrepreneurship: A two countries comparison. *The International Entrepreneurship and Management Journal*, *1*(2), 165–182. doi:10.100711365-005-1127-5

Velasquez, M. G. (2002). *Business Ethics: Concepts and Cases*. Prentice Hall.

Velilla, R., & Valduérteles, J. (2016). *Claves para la comunicación interna de las empresas*. Madrid: Almon.

Veljkovic, I., & Budree, A. (2019). Development of bring-your-own device risk management model: Case study from a South African organization. *The Electric Journal of Information Systems Evaluation, 22*(1), 1–14.

Venter, E., Boshoff, C., & Mass, G. (2005). The influence of successor-related factors on the succession process in small and medium-sized family businesses. *Family Business Review, 18*(4), 283–303. doi:10.1111/j.1741-6248.2005.00049.x

Vermeulen, F. (2010). *Business exposed: The naked truth about what really goes on in the world of business.* Prentice Hall.

Vickers, M. R. (2005). Business ethics and the HR role: Past, present, and future. *Human Resource Planning, 28*(1), 26–32.

Vieira, W., & Dixit, M. (2019). *The 5 Gs of Family Business.* SAGE.

Vlatka, H. (2014). *The Management Shift. How to Harness the Power of People and Trasform Your Organization for Sustainable Success.* Palgrave Macmillan.

Voordeckers, W., Van Gils, A., & Van den Heuvel, J. (2007). Board composition in small and medium-sized family firms. *Journal of Small Business Management, 45*(1), 137–156. doi:10.1111/j.1540-627X.2007.00204.x

Vural, B. A., & Sohodol, Ç. (2004), Aile Şirketlerinde Kurumsal Kültür: Avantajlar-Dezavantajlar ve Öneriler Üzerine Bir Çalışma. 1. Aile İşletmeleri Kongresi Bildiri Kitabı. İstanbul Kültür Üniversitesi İktisadi ve İdari Bilimler Fakültesi.

Wach, K. (2008). *Regionalne otoczenie małych i średnich przedsiębiorstw.* Wydawnictwo Uniwersytetu Ekonomicznego.

Walczak, D., & Voss, G. (2013). New Possibilities of Supporting Polish SMEs within the Jeremie Initiative Managed by BGK. *Mediterranean Journal of Social Sciences, 4*(9), 759–765.

Walls, J. L., Phan, P. H., & Berrone, P. (2011). Measuring Environmental Strategy: Construct Development, Reliability, and Validity. *Business & Society, 50*(1), 71–115. doi:10.1177/0007650310394427

Wang, D., Wang, L., & Chen, L. (2018). Unlocking the influence of family business exposure on entrepreneurial intentions. *The International Entrepreneurship and Management Journal, 14*(4), 951–974. doi:10.100711365-017-0475-2

Ward, J. (1997). Growing the family business: Special challenges and best practices. *Family Business Review, 10*(4), 323–337. doi:10.1111/j.1741-6248.1997.00323.x

Ward, J., Dogan, H., Apeh, E., Mylonas, A., & Kators, V. (2017). Using human factor approaches to an organisation's bring your own device scheme. In T. Tryfonas (Ed.), *Human aspects of information security, privacy and trust* (pp. 396–413). Springer.

Ward, L. J. (1987). *Keeping the Family Business Healthy: How to plan for continuing Growth, Profitability and Family Leadership.* Jossey-Bass.

Waterman, R. H. Jr, Peters, T., & Phillips, J. R. (1980). Structure is not organization. *Business Horizons, 23*(3), 14–26. doi:10.1016/0007-6813(80)90027-0

Weaver, G. R., & Trevino, L. K. (2001). The role of human resources in ethics/compliance management: A fairness perspective. *Human Resource Management Review, 11*(1/2), 113–134. doi:10.1016/S1053-4822(00)00043-7

Webba, J. W., Ketchen, D. J. Jr, & Ireland, D. (2010). Strategic entrepreneurship within family-controlled firms: Opportunities and challenges. *Journal of Family Business Strategy, 1*(2), 67–77. doi:10.1016/j.jfbs.2010.04.002

Weissenrieder, J., & Kosel, M. (2010). *Nachhaltiges Personalmanagement in der Praxis: mit Erfolgsbeispielen mittelstandischer Unternehmen.* Gabler Verlag. doi:10.1007/978-3-8349-8588-0

Wenger, E. C., McDermott, R., & Snyder, W. C. (2002). *Cultivating Communities of Practice: A Guide to Managing Knowledge.* Harvard Business School Press.

Wenjun, W., Wei, L., & Millington, J. K. (2011). Determinants of Entrepreneurial Intention among College Students in China and USA. *Journal of Global Entrepreneurship Research, 1*(1), 35–44.

Więcek-Janka, E. (2013). *Wiodące wartości w zarządzaniu przedsiębiorstwami rodzinnymi.* Wydawnictwo Politechniki Poznańskiej.

Wilkinson, A., Hill, M., & Gollan, P. (2001). The sustainability debate. *International Journal of Operations & Production Management, 21*(12), 1492–1502. doi:10.1108/01443570110410865

Williams, M. L., & Laker, D. (2010). Nepotism: can it affect the bottom line? *Northeastern Association of Business, Economics, and Technology Proceedings,* 230-236.

Wilson, M. J. (2016). *Management Succession in Family Businesses.* Requisite Series, Williams Parker Edition. Retrieved March 6, 2020, from https://williamsparker.com/DigitalPublications/requisiteissue6/index.html

Wilton, N. (2016). An introduction to human management. *Sage (Atlanta, Ga.).*

Winstanley, D., & Woodall, J. (2000). The ethical dimension of human resource management. *Human Resource Management Journal, 10*(2), 5–20. doi:10.1111/j.1748-8583.2000.tb00017.x

Winstanley, D., Woodall, J., & Heery, E. (1996). Business ethics and human resource management: Themes and issues. *Personnel Review, 25*(6), 5–12. doi:10.1108/00483489610148491

Winterbotham, M., Oldfield, K., Stewart, G., Rossiter, H., & Research, I. F. F. (2015). *Fairness, dignity and respect in SME workplaces.* Equality and Human Rights Commission.

Wolf, M. V., Sims, J., & Yang, H. (2014). Social media utilization in human resource management. In Web based communities and social media 2014 conference, Lisbon, Portugal.

Wolfe, R. (1996). *Systematic Succession Planning: Building Leadership from Within.* Crisp Publications.

Wood, D. J. (1991). Corporate Social Performance Revisited. *Academy of Management Review, 16*(4), 691–718. doi:10.5465/amr.1991.4279616

Wood, S. (1999). Human resource management and performance. *International Journal of Management Reviews, 1*(4), 367–413.

Wood, S., & de Menezes, L. (1998). High Commitment Management in the U.K.: Evidence from the Workplace Industrial Relations Survey, and Employers' Manpower and Skills Practices Survey. *Human Relations, 51*(4), 485–515. doi:10.1177/001872679805100403

Wright, P. M., & Boswell, W. R. (2002). Desegregating HRM: A Review and Synthesis of Micro and Macro Human Resource Management Research. *Journal of Management, 28*(3), 247–276. doi:10.1177/014920630202800302

Wright, P. M., Gardner, T. M., Moynihan, L. M., & Allen, M. R. (2005). The relationship between hr practices and firm performance: Examining causal order. *Personnel Psychology, 58*(2), 409–446.

Wright, P., & McMahan, G. (1992). Theoretical Perspective for Strategic Human Resource Management. *Journal of Management, 18*(2), 295–320.

Wright, P., McMahan, G., & McWilliams, A. (1994). Human resources and sustained competitive advantage: A resource based perspective. *International Journal of Human Resource Management, 5*(2), 301–326. doi:10.1080/09585199400000020

Wyrwich, M. (2015). Entrepreneurship and the intergenerational transmission of values. *Small Business Economics, 45*(1), 191–213. doi:10.100711187-015-9649-x

Xi, J., Filser, M., & Kellermanns, F. W. (2015). Mapping the field of family business research: Past trends and future directions. *The International Entrepreneurship and Management Journal*, *11*(1), 113–132. doi:10.100711365-013-0286-z

Yalçınkaya, T., & Durcan, N. M. (2011). The Institutional Basis of the Socioeconomic Situation of Turkey in The Context Of Globalization. *Uludağ Üniversitesi İİBF Dergisi*, *30*(1), 95–112.

Yamagishi, T., Jin, N., & Miller, A. S. (1998). In-group bias and culture of collectivism. *Asian Journal of Social Psychology*, *1*(3), 315–328. doi:10.1111/1467-839X.00020

Yang, Y., Hu, T., Ye, Y., Gao, W., & Zhang, C. (2018). A knowledge generation mechanism of machining process planning using cloud technology. *Journal of Ambient Intelligence and Humanized Computing*, 1–12.

Yazici, M. O., & Secer, B. (2018). İşe alma ve yerleştirmede nepotism. *Iş, Güç. Endüstri İlişkileri ve İnsan Kaynakları Dergisi*, *20*(4), 117–134.

Yedder, M. B. (2018). Human resource management in family business succession: Victim or saviour? *Journal of Enterprising Culture*, *26*(4), 401–421. doi:10.1142/S0218495818500152

Yildirim, H., & Ali-Eldin, A. (2019). A model for predicting user intention to use wearable IoT devices at the workplace. *Journal of King Saud University – Computer and Information Sciences, 31*(4), 497-505.

Yin, R. K. (2009). *Case study research: Design and methods* (4th ed.). Sage.

Zahra, S. A. (2005). Entrepreneurial risk taking in family firms. *Family Business Review*, *18*(1), 23–40. doi:10.1111/j.1741-6248.2005.00028.x

Zahra, S. A. (2010). Harvesting family firm's organizational social capital: A relational perspective. *Journal of Management Studies*, *47*(2), 345–366.

Zajac, E. J. (1990). CEO selection, succession, compensation and firm performance: A theoretical integration and empirical analysis. *Strategic Management Journal*, *11*(3), 217–230. doi:10.1002mj.4250110304

Zakaria, S. (2011). Transforming Human Resources into Human Capital. *Information Management and Business Review*, *2*(2), 48–54.

Zaugg, R., Blum, A., & Thom, N. (2001). *Sustainability in Human Resource Management. Evaluation Report*. Retrieved from https://www.researchgate.net/publication/276906300_Sustainability_in_Human_Resource_Management

Zayed, K. (2016). Information security awareness: Managing web, mobile, and endpoint security; overcoming the challenges of bring your own device. *International Journal of Teaching and Case Studies*, *7*(3-4), 271–288.

Zellweger, T. (2007). Time horizon, costs of equity capital, and generic investment strategies of ðrms. *Family Business Review*, *20*(1), 1–15. doi:10.1111/j.1741-6248.2007.00080.x

Zellweger, T. M., Kellermanns, F. W., Eddleston, K. A., & Memili, E. (2012). Building a family firm image: How family firms capitalize on their family ties. *Journal of Family Business Strategy*, *3*(4), 239–250. doi:10.1016/j.jfbs.2012.10.001

Zellweger, T., Sieger, P., & Halter, F. (2011). Should I stay or should I go? Career choice intentions of students with family business background. *Journal of Business Venturing*, *26*(5), 521–536. doi:10.1016/j.jbusvent.2010.04.001

Zencirkıran, M., & Keser, A. (2018). Örgütsel Davranış. Dora Basım-Yayın.

Zhang, Y., Duysters, G., & Cloodt, M. (2014). The role of entrepreneurship education as a predictor ofuniversity students' entrepreneurial intention. *The International Entrepreneurship and Management Journal*, *10*(3), 623–641. doi:10.100711365-012-0246-z

Zhao, H., Hills, G. E., & Siebert, S. E. (2005). The mediating role of self-efficacy in the development of entrepreneurial intentions. *The Journal of Applied Psychology*, *90*(6), 1265–1272. doi:10.1037/0021-9010.90.6.1265 PMID:16316279

Zheng, C., Morrison, M., & O'Neill, G. (2006). An Empirical Study of High Performance HRM Practices in Chinese SMEs. *International Journal of Human Resource Management*, *17*, 1772–1803. doi:10.1080/09585190600965282

Zhu, F., Burmeister-Lamp, K., & Hsu, D. K. (2017). To leave or not? The impact of family support and cognitive appraisals on venture exit intention. *International Journal of Entrepreneurial Behaviour & Research*, *23*(3), 566–590. doi:10.1108/IJEBR-04-2016-0110

Zide, J., Elman, B., & Shahani-Denning, C. (2014). LinkedIn and recruitment: How profiles differ across occupations. *Employee Relations*, *36*(5), 583–604.

Zoppini, A. (2002). *Le successioni in diritto comparato*. Utet.

About the Contributors

Luca Gnan is Full Professor of Organizational Behavior at Tor Vergata University, where also he is the Director of the Bachelor in Business Administration and Economics. He is the past-president of the European Academy of Management. He is and has been involved in various academic and public associations, including membership of the Education Ethics Executive Committee of AOM, AOM BPS Division representative for Europe, AOM OMT Division Research Committee, Review Board member of FERC, Sub-theme Convenor of EGOS, and Stream Chair of CMS. Luca Gnan is Editor in chief of the International Journal of transition and Innovation and he has been and is guest editor of various journals, and he has published on topics related to family businesses.

* * *

Barbara Barabaschi is Lecturer and Research fellow in Economic Sociology at Università Cattolica del Sacro Cuore, Piacenza. She received her Ph.D. in Sociology and Social Research Methods from Università Cattolica del Sacro Cuore, Milano. The main research topics concern welfare and labour policies, intergenerational relations in the workplaces and stakeholder management. She has been a visiting scholar at OECD – ELSA (Employment, Labour and Social Affairs) and at the Université Lyon III.

Marjan I. Bojadjiev, PhD, is a Provost and a full professor at University American Collage Skopje since the year of 2010. Previously, he has worked as CEO of the Macedonian Savings House from 1996 to 1999 and as CEO of the third largest bank in Macedonia from 1999 to 2004. Prof. Bojadjiev has served as manager of several companies in Macedonia, as a board member in professional organizations and as a moderator in conferences on national Macedonian energy and investment policies. He has completed his doctoral studies at the Ss. Cyril and Methodius University – Skopje. He earned his Specialization degree in International Business Management at the University of Trieste. He has a Master of Science degree in Banking Marketing. Prof. Bojadjiev has completed executive education courses at Harvard Business School in 2008 and 2009.

Mariacristina Bonti, PhD in Business Administration, is Full Professor of Organization Studies and Human Resource Management at the Department of Economics and Management, University of Pisa. Her main research interests are family SMEs, with a focus on entrepreneurial succession, competences transfer across generations, human resource practices. Other research interests: new ventures, small business growth, and corporate museum.

Franca Cantoni is Associate Professor in Business Organization. Following her degree in Economics from Università Cattolica, she obtained her PhD in Business Information Systems from LUISS Guido Carli. The main research topics concern the micro and macro organizational impacts of change, outsourcing and organizational boundary choices. Author of several volumes, national and international publications, she has been a visiting researcher at the Department of Information Systems of the Siegen Universität and the Institut for Informatik of the Copenhagen Business School.

Mehmet Çini received and his Ph.D. in 2017 in the Department of Business Administration. He has been working as an academician since 2008. Currently, he is an academician at Selcuk University in Cihanbeyli Vocational School Department of Accountant and Task Program of Accounting and Taxation.

Enrico Cori, PhD in Business Management, Full Professor of Business Organization at the Department of Management of the Polytechnic University of the Marche (Ancona, Italy). He is currently involved in the following research fields: organization and HR management in family SMEs, strategic and organizational issues of digitization processes of the cultural heritage.

Concetta Lucia Cristofaro is PhD in Economics and Management in Health at the University of Catanzaro. She is currently lecturer in Business Organization, Conflict Management and Human Resource Management at University of Catanzaro "Magna Graecia". Her research is focused on the fields of: intellectual capital, small and medium business, ITC, digitalization, family business, performance, gender diversity and knowledge management. Her publications appeared in academic journals and presented her research at several international conferences.

Vittorio D'Amato is Associate Professor of Leadership & Management at LIUC-Università Cattaneo. Director of the Research Centre on Change, Leadership and People Management and Director of the Master Division at LIUC-Business School. He is the author of 14 books and of several publications on International Scientific Journals including the prestigious MIT Sloan Management Review.

Meral Erdirencelebi received and her Ph.D. in 2012 in the Department of Business Administration. She has been working as an academician since 2013. Currently, she is an academician at Necmettin Erbakan University in Applied Sciences Faculty at Banking Department. She specialized in organizational behavior. She studies entrepreneurship, woman entrepreneurship, family business, and current issues at organizational behavior (presenteeism, burnout, intention to leave, nepotism, organizational loneliness, workaholism, work-life balance, emotional labor, etc.). She has married and has two daughters.

Daniela Gauci Borda received her MSc in Human Resource Management & Consulting from the University of Bath, United Kingdom. She was awarded the University of Bath School of Management MSc Scholarship on the basis of academic excellence and went on to graduate with a Distinction. Daniela also holds a first class Bachelor of Commerce (Hons) degree in Banking & Finance from the University of Malta. Daniela is a People & Organisation Consultant and has been involved in various advisory projects in the field of human resource management.

Julie Gore received her PhD in Applied Psychology from Oxford Brookes Univeristy, UK in 1997. Dr Gore is a Reader in Organizational Psychology, Chartered Psychologist and Fellow of the British

Psychological Society at the University of Bath, UK. Julie is a Director of the Centre for Qualitative Research and Associate Editor for the Journal of Occupational & Organizational Psychology. She writes and presents widely on Naturalistic Decision Making and expertise (see Ward, Schraagen, Gore & Roth, 2020 – The Oxford Handbook of Expertise).

Nina Katrin Hansen is a Full Professor of Human Resource Management & Leadership Studies at the Faculty of Economics and Business Administration, Chemnitz University of Technology, Germany. Nina's main areas of research lie at the intersection of Human Resource Management, Organization Studies and Strategic Management. Based on a multi-level approach, her research focuses on the question of how human resource management systems influence intellectual capital architectures, organizational capabilities and firm performance especially in the field of Professional Service Firms (PSFs). She is furthermore interested in topics such as the Micro-Foundations of Strategic Management or Strategy-as-Practice. She thereby applies quantitative methods such as structural equation modelling as well as qualitative methods such as expert interviews. Her research results have been published in leading international journals such as 'Human Resource Management', 'Human Resource Management Journal' or the 'International Journal of Human Resource Management' as well as in relevant academic text books such as the 'Oxford Handbook of Professional Service Firms'.

Séverine Le Loarne-Lemaire is full professor at Grenoble Ecole de Management, specialized in Women Entrepreneurship and women in family businesses. She created and holds the Research Chair "Women and Economic Renewal". She published a various number of articles in peer review ranked journals and manuals on the topic.

Stephanie Lezama-Rogers is also a Doctoral graduate (Business Administration) at the Grenoble Ecole de Management, France where her research focused on family business in inter-firm relationships. She holds an MSc. in Development Statistics (specialized in the areas of Policy Development and Survey Research) and a BSc degree in Sociology (Major) and Economics (Minor) Social Policy (Minor) from the University of the West Indies, Trinidad and Tobago.

Rosalba Manna, PhD, is a Research Fellow in Statistics at the Department of Business Studies and Quantitative Methods, University "Parthenope", Naples, Italy. Moreover, she is national evaluator of mandatory schools' performances at MIUR, fellow statistician at the ISTAT and, currently, data analyst at INDIRE. Her main research interests include, but are not limited to: income inequality, educational organizations' performances, school and workplace bullying.

Emiliano Marchisio is an Associate Professor (qualified in the first bracket since 2018) of Commercial Law at the Giustino Fortunato University of Benevento. He graduated in law with full marks, cum laude, at the "La Sapienza" University of Rome (1999), he was Researcher of Commercial Law at the Tor Vergata University of Rome (2008-2014), holds a Ph.D. in Public Economic Law (Rome, 2005) and a Master of Laws (LL.M.) in International Business Law (London, 2001). Among other positions, since 2013 he has been a Fellow of the Center for Economic and International Studies (CEIS), "Tor Vergata" University of Rome, he is a member of numerous associations and research institutions. Over the years he has taught, at public and private universities, as well as institutes and training centers, Commercial Law, Industrial Law, Competition Law, Market Law and Protection of Innovation, Bankruptcy

Law, Antitrust Law, Law of Extraordinary Transactions, International Business Law, Corporate Law. Active, as manager or participant, in numerous research activities, he has participated, as organizer and speaker, in numerous conferences on matters relating to commercial law and civil law. He is the author of four monographs and over seventy articles, book chapters and sentence notes

Anna Maria Melina is PhD in Economics and Management in Health at the University of Catanzaro. She is teaching assistant in organizational behavior. Her research focuses on small and medium business, knowledge management and family firms. She is member of ASSIOA. Her publications appeared in academic journals and presented her research at several international conferences.

Ivona Mileva is teaching assistant and Head of Business Administration and Economics department at University American College Skopje. She is currently enrolled in DBA program at the same university. She has earned her MS degree in the field of luxury management from International University of Monaco. She has been involved in a number of research projects and conferences. Her research interests include organizational culture, entrepreneurship and leadership.

Büşra Müceldili is an Assistant Professor in Business Administration at Yıldız Technical University, Turkey. Her research interests include positive organizational scholarship, organizational behavior and human resource management.

Rocco Palumbo, PhD, is a Research Fellow in Organization Studies at the Department of Management & Innovation Systems, University of Salerno, Italy. His main research interests include, but are not limited to human resource management, team performance management and workplace discrimination.

Massimiliano M. Pellegrini is an Associate Professor of Organizational Studies and Entrepreneurship Behaviour at University of Rome "Tor Vergata". From the same university he also received his Ph.D. 2011. Previously, he was a Senior lecturer in Entrepreneurship at Roehampton University Business School. During his career he covered several roles as permanent staff e.g. at Princess Sumaya University for Technology (Jordan) and University of West-London (UK) as lecturer. His research interests and publications are focused on entrepreneurial and organizational behaviours; he published more than 60 contributions focused on entrepreneurial, ethical, and organizational behaviours in high-ranked journals e.g., Small Business Economics, Journal of Business Ethics, Journal of Managerial Psychology, IEEE Transactions on Engineering Management, International Journal of Entrepreneurial Behaviours & Research, International Journal of Entrepreneurship & Small Business, and Business Process Management Journal.

Rocco Reina is a Full Professor in Organization Studies & HRM at the University of Catanzaro "Magna Graecia", Department of Law Economics and Sociology. The research interest focus on intellectual capital, small & medium enterprises, knowledge and change management, public performance. He is speaker in national and international conferences and authored and co-authored more publications, including book, articles, research reports, working papers.

Carmen Ruiz-Viñals is Director, Chair of Family Business and Entrepreneurship at University Abat Oliba CEU. Associate Professor at UAO CEU. Ph D. in Public Administration and Management by Pompeu Fabra University (UPF, 1998); Senior Fellow in Urban Studies by the Institute for Policy Studies

(IPS) The Johns Hopkins University (JHU, 1992-1993); Master in Public Management by Autonomous University of Barcelona (UAB, 1990-1992). Degree in Economics by the University of Barcelona (UB, 1985-1990) and Degree in Law by University Abat Oliba CEU (UAO; 2010-2015). Active participant in different research groups (national and international), author of several publications in the fields of Family Business, Decision Making processes, Management by Values and Entrepreneurship. European research project evaluator in the V; VI and VII EU Framework Programmes (Brussels, 1999-2008).

Aubrey Statti, Ed.D., earned a Bachelor of Arts in Political Science and Spanish from the University of Florida and a Master's of Professional Counseling and a Doctorate of Education from Liberty University. She has worked in higher education for 13 years and has taught at the undergraduate, graduate, and post-graduate levels in areas of psychology, counseling, education, and research. Additionally, she has worked in the Florida public schools as both a high school teacher and a school counselor. Dr. Statti is currently a professor for The Chicago School of Professional Psychology's (TCSPP) Educational Psychology and Technology program, primarily teaching research and ethics courses. She also serves as a Dissertation Chair and reader on doctoral student's dissertations. Her research interests in the areas of educational technology include K-12 education, online education, early childhood education, digital storytelling, mentorship, and rural education.

Miodraga Stefanovska-Petkovska, MBA, PhD, is an Associate Professor at the School of Political Sciences and Psychology and the School of Business Administration and Management, University American College Skopje. She graduated on the topic of individual and economic determinants of retirement and was awarded an honorary Masters in business administration on her research on well-being among ageing workforce. Part of her doctoral studies was at Staffordshire University, United Kingdom as a scholar of the Open Society Institute on the topic of economic trust and cooperation among religious and ethnic minorities. She obtained a doctoral degree in social sciences and gender issues at the on the topic of discrimination and disparities in health care. Dr. Stefanovska-Petkovska has been awarded a certificate in Statistics for health research from Oxford University. Her academic research is focused on the area of medical sociology and sociology of health, with special emphasis on the intersection of employment and health, health literacy and self-efficacy. She has co-authored books and academic articles domestically and internationally and has been a mentor/co-mentor of over 20 master theses. She is has also been an NGO activist for more than 15 years on the field of health promotion and education with special focus on vulnerable group and she has participated, designed and coordinated numerous national and international projects on this issue.

Berivan Tatar is a Research Assistant and PhD student in the School of Business Administration at Gebze Technical University, Turkey. Her research interests include management and organization, organizational behavior, and human resource management.

Ana Tomovska Misoska, PhD, is a Professor at the UACS, School of Business Economics and Management. She obtained her PhD from the School of Education, Queen's University Belfast. Her professional engagements involve a number of research projects in Northern Ireland and the Republic of North Macedonia. Her work has been concentrated on educational reforms, exploring identity building as well as entrepreneurial intentions, organizational culture, human resource management and consumer behavior. She has attended a number of national and international conferences and published in renowned academic journals.

Kelly Torres is the Department Chair of the Educational Psychology and Technology program at The Chicago School of Professional Psychology. She has taught numerous university-level courses in both online and face-to-face settings in content areas such as educational psychology, foundations of education, assessment, curriculum development, linguistics, and culture. Dr. Torres's research interests are focused on the implementation of technology into educational settings in order to enhance student academic outcomes and on various aspects of the motivational influences that may impact second language learning and culture.

Elena Tosca is a Professor of Organizational Behavior at LIUC-Università Cattaneo. Researcher of the Research Centre on Change, Leadership and People Management and Director of the Master in Meccatronica & Management at LIUC-Business School. She is the author of several publications on International Scientific Journals including the prestigious MIT Sloan Management Review.

Alberto Trallero-Fort is a Member Chair of Family Business and Entrepreneurship at University Abat Oliba CEU; PDD General Management IESE University of Navarra (2001); DAF Marketing Manager ESADE Barcelona (1994-1995); Diplomated in Business Science University of Barcelona (1990-1995); Manager in several companies as CaixaBank, Deutsche Bank, Axa Winterthur, Aegon and Optima Management, with diferent roles as General Manager, RRHH Manager, Sales Manager and Consultant; Founder of a Start-up in Consulting Services; Co-Founder of the Social Project "Apadrina un Amigo"; Business Mentor at IESE University of Navarra.

Marzia Ventura is PhD in Economics and Management in Health and Post doctor in Social Capital at the University of Catanzaro "Magna Graecia"- Department of Law History Economics and Social Science -. His activities are oriented towards the field of Intellectual and Social capital, Small and Medium Business and Knowledge Management. His publications appeared in academic journals and presented her research at several international conferences.

Roberta Virtuani is Lecturer and Senior Research fellow at the Faculty of Economics and Law at the Università Cattolica del Sacro Cuore in Piacenza, She teaches the course of "Personal Development ". Her main interest areas are Organization Theory and Human Resources Management with a special focus on the development of soft and digital skills. She has been a visiting scholar at the University of Amsterdam. She published on the topic of Outsourcing of Information Systems and of Individual Creativity Management to foster the innovation process.

Index

Q

R

S

T

V

W

www.ingramcontent.com/pod-product-compliance
Lightning Source LLC
LaVergne TN
LVHW060405300926
849162LV00006B/1354